The Recorded History Of The Grateful Dead

John Kilbride

sonicbondpublishing.com

Sonicbond Publishing Limited
www.sonicbondpublishing.co.uk
Email: info@sonicbondpublishing.co.uk

First Published in the United Kingdom 2022
First Published in the United States 2022

British Library Cataloguing in Publication Data:
A Catalogue record for this book is available from the British Library

Copyright John Kilbride 2022

ISBN 978-1-78952-156-6

Typeset in ITC Garamond & ITC Avant Garde
Printed and bound in England

Graphic design and typesetting: Full Moon Media

The Golden Road

The Recorded History Of The Grateful Dead

John Kilbride

sonicbondpublishing.com

Magic is what we do. Music is how we do it.
Jerry Garcia

This book is dedicated to Susan and Louis

Without love in the dream it'll never come true

Grateful thanks

There are many people to thank for their inspiration and encouragement in writing this book. Firstly, and above all, Susan and Louis. Without them, none of this would have been possible.

Thanks to Tommy and Margaret McManus, Pete and Cherry Beaney, Jeanette and Alan Castle for their support, also Robbie, Andrew, Emily, Victoria and Laura. Thanks to Thomas and William Kilbride for putting up with my taste in music. Thanks to Gregor Peat, even though he thinks the Jefferson Airplane are better. Mark McLellan and Andy Todd for ongoing music discussions, beer and escapades since the 1980s.

With appreciation to all the team at Glasgow Caledonian University for their encouragement and enthusiasm, especially Therese Hooper, Gill Woodlock, Mick McGlinchy and Julie Adair and all in team digital engagement. With appreciation to those involved in Spiral Light, Eurotraders and Worldwide Deadheads for all they've done for the Grateful Dead community in this part of the world over the years.

Grateful to the good people of the Grateful Dead Forever Facebook community, and the Hawkwind Fans Worldwide Facebook group, even the ones that don't get The Dead.

Thanks to Stephen Lambe for his patience and for his support.

The Golden Road
The Recorded History Of The Grateful Dead

Contents

Introduction

Perhaps unsurprisingly for a band from the West Coast of the USA, The Grateful Dead were pioneers. You don't have to be a tie-dyed-in-the-wool Deadhead to appreciate some of their innovations – from selling band-related T-shirts at gigs to sound systems designed for arenas and stadiums, The Dead were the first with much that's now taken for granted. But one of their innovations was perhaps more significant than others: their practice of recording their shows.

The Grateful Dead were active from 1965 to 1995, but over their 30-year career, managed to release only thirteen studio albums. Some were great, others less so. The recording studio was perhaps not their natural environment. They did, however, release a number of live albums documenting the concert experience, where they excelled. While their studio output was patchy – only a handful of their albums coming close to capturing the band's magic – several of their live albums are cited as the band's finest releases. Whether it be *Live/Dead*, *Europe '72* or *Reckoning*, The Grateful Dead's reputation was built on their live performances and the recordings that captured their unique genius.

From early in their career they routinely recorded their performances, a practice their sound engineer Owsley 'Bear' Stanley introduced, to check after the show that they'd been operating with the optimal sound quality, and so the band could listen back to how they'd played. This was important for the musicians, as they worked more like an exploratory jazz act than a regular rock band. Instead of simply performing a static repertoire of the same songs, their live set varied from night to night – the songs themselves often used as platforms for extended improvisation and jamming, taking the song's original ideas into new unexplored areas; the musicians inspiring each other to spontaneously create new music every time they played. While these 'sonic journals' gave the technical staff an indication of how their work was being received by audiences, they also gave the band a chance to look back on what had been created in the moment, so they could consider what and how they played and continue to develop it.

The band knew their live performances were their strength, and so did their fans: The Deadheads. In another pioneering move, The Dead encouraged them to record the shows from the audience, and circulate the recordings, trade them, compare them and listen to them, building a community of devotees with a loyalty unique amongst music fans. While other acts strongly discouraged the practice for fear of losing money, The Dead realised the live performance could be the end in itself, rather than just an opportunity to sell their latest studio album. And what better way to encourage an audience than to give them a taste of what they might expect to see for themselves? While the band enjoyed increasing commercial success in the 1980s, they didn't even release an album between 1981 and 1987. As 21st-century musicians struggled to adjust to an environment where album sales had collapsed and they had to focus on their live experience, The Grateful Dead were decades ahead of the curve.

The band's lineup changed over the years, but centred on guitarists Jerry Garcia and Bob Weir, bassist Phil Lesh and drummers Mickey Hart and Bill Kreutzmann. Other musicians played their parts – whether Ron 'Pigpen' McKernan or Keith and Donna Jean Godchaux, Brent Mydland and Vince Welnick – all bringing their contributions to the band's development.

The recordings from the sound desk – along with those made as the band experimented with the use of professional recording equipment on the road – created a unique archive of a constantly-developing act that was always in the process of creating new art. These live recordings – snapshots of an entity in perpetual motion – would come into their own towards the end of the band's career and in the years following the death of Garcia.

The live recordings would be the band's true legacy. There have been around 70 retrospective live releases so far – most of them multiple-disc sets, and some of them extraordinary collections like the 80-disc *30 Trips Around The Sun* or the 73-disc *Europe '72: The Complete Recordings*. There have also been 36 volumes of the *Dick's Picks* series curated by late Dead archivist Dick Latvala, and its successor *Dave's Picks* – overseen by Dave Lemieux – is currently at over 40 volumes. There has also been a series of fifteen official downloads and seventeen volumes of the *Road Trips* series. While focussing on the live experience, they created an incredible body of work almost by accident. These live releases are no mere posthumous cash-in or pension pot for former members. Instead, they reveal the band in their true colours, and their colours are tie-dye bright. Many of The Dead's live releases surpass their *official* output.

This book looks at the band's career through these live releases, putting the live albums that have emerged from the archive in their historical context – showing them to be as legitimate a representation of their work as their studio output or the live albums released at the time. Key solo albums also add to the band's story, at times being essentially Grateful Dead albums in all but name, others being showcases for songs that would go on to be central to the band's live shows. Others would be experiments that provided new elements that would be incorporated into the band's identity. Elsewhere, band members would collaborate with other musicians, weaving contemporaries like Janis Joplin, Bob Dylan or Crosby, Stills, Nash & Young into The Dead's history.

They began recording their shows on the advice of legendary soundman Augustus Owsley Stanley III, known as Owsley – later, following time in jail, going by the name Bear. His habit of creating what he called 'sonic journals', allowed the band to review their performances. Where Owsley trod, others followed in his tracks after he left The Grateful Dead organisation. The sound desk would remain in the hands of innovators, with Dan Healey responsible for the policy of allowing fans to record the shows, and Betty Cantor-Jackson recording shows from the sound desk with such high sound quality that the 'Betty Boards' became a measure of quality in The Grateful Dead tape-trading community, with her recording of the Cornell University 1977 show released as the *Cornell 5/8/77* album and included in the National Recording Registry of the Library of Congress.

It was this willingness to get the band on tape – whether from the sound desk, the mobile recording studio or the taping section of the audience – that led to The Grateful Dead being one of the most thoroughly documented live acts ever. The fans were encouraged to trade the tapes, as long as they didn't make a profit from the deal, meaning tapes were usually traded one for another like baseball cards or football stickers or as 'blanks and postage' deals, where someone would offer copies in return for being sent blank tapes (later CDRs) and either enough stamps or currency to cover the return postage. While some tapes did get pressed as bootleg vinyl albums or later CDs, these never had the same kind of market that bootlegs of the likes of Led Zeppelin or Bob Dylan had, in that they rarely presented a full concert, which was what the dedicated Deadhead was after. Better-sounding tapes or CDs were available without the eye-watering cost, and overall, most respected the band's position on not making a profit out of the recordings that were circulating.

This social network for music was crucial for the fan, like me: in the UK or elsewhere outside North America. For those fortunate enough to be close enough, The Dead were about the experience of the shows: the travel, the friendships, and of course, the music. For those of us who would need an expensive plane ticket to even reach the same continent, the music was what sustained us – small bundles of used C-90 tapes (TDK of course) in the post with handwritten labels bearing cryptic names like 'Greek Theatre', 'Winterland' or 'MSG'; copying them and trading with friends, spending hours at a time listening and hours debating which were best and why. The Dead were rarely on the radio or TV in the UK, or in the press until the late-1980s, and in the pre-internet age, information spread slowly.

I'd first heard of The Dead through friends and the *Glastonbury Fayre* album. At first, I couldn't name the members of the band, and there were few places to turn to for information. I came across a box of live tapes for sale cheaply at a local market – the Barras in Glasgow: the kind of low-budget bazaar where traders buy junk and sell antiques, other stalls sell odd shoes, and shady characters hawk Polish cigarettes. The stall obviously wanted rid of these obscure tapes, selling them cheaper than blank tapes, so I picked them up on the strength of what I'd heard and the fact there were some Dylan covers. This was – to paraphrase the lyric – being shown the light in the strangest of places.

From then, it became a task to acquire whatever information came up about the band and that circulated among friends with shared left-field tastes in music. Fanzines like *The Music Never Stopped* and *Spiral Light* revealed there were more of us on this side of the Atlantic – these inky fanzines printing setlists for gigs we never attended, and we'd imagine the shows, eventually listening to some of them. We were distant cousins, keeping in touch by long-distance calls.

With music available digitally in the 21st century, the audience recordings that The Grateful Dead made available are now more accessible than ever before. At the time of writing, archive.org offers over 15,000 Grateful Dead recordings, as well as recordings of shows by successor acts – whether Bob Weir and Wolf Brothers, Dead & Company or Phil and Friends – and hundreds of artists inspired by their policy of making the recordings available. Often the recordings are available within hours of the shows. Meanwhile, the underground bootlegging industry continues to make Grateful Dead product available, exploiting legal loopholes surrounding radio broadcast recordings, at times producing lavish CD box sets and expensive vinyl releases for those who covet a physical product or who don't realise there's an entire mountain of recordings available for free. These days you don't even need a shady record shop with an under-the-counter section – just Wi-Fi or broadband and an online retailer that doesn't know the difference.

However, the most significant way The Dead's music has been made available, is via the official archive releases. These began in 1991 with *One From The Vault* – a two-CD set of The Dead's 1975 show at the Great American Music Hall in San Francisco – and have continued over the subsequent 30 years with key shows on CD, multi-disc box sets of complete tours, special vinyl releases and downloads. There have been several curated collections, including 36 volumes of the previously-mentioned *Dick's Picks* and *Dave's Picks* (over 40 volumes) series, the latter selected by David Lemieux, who took over after Latvala passed away in 1999. Additionally, there was the *Road Trips* series – 17 volumes, and 15 in the official download series. While these collections mostly focussed on two-track recordings, other releases have featured professional multitrack recordings from the 1960s to the 1990s, documenting the band's career as it progressed from dance halls and theatres to stadiums across the USA. Some of these – like *One From The Vault* – feature particular shows; others compile performances from a series of concerts, and others are massive box sets including every concert in a particular tour such as *Europe '72* and *Spring 1990*. There's even one 80-disc box set that features a live show from each of the 30 years the band was in existence.

It's these archive recordings released officially by the band – both professional recordings and soundboard tapes – that this book looks at. The band chose and approved these releases, each representing a particular point in the band's career. The Grateful Dead's success came from their live performances, their willingness to experiment on stage and leave themselves open to the possibilities of improvisation, and the opportunities of a flexible setlist with a wealth of material to choose from. They pretty much never played the same set twice, with some of their most famous numbers extended and performed with a spontaneity that defied any easy categorisation, but with underpinning elements of jazz, rock, soul, blues, gospel, country, world music, electronics and the avant-garde. And they made it fun too.

The band changed over the years. Some members left, and new ones came on board. They were at the heart of the San Francisco counterculture in 1967 and established that it was possible for a band to be commercially viable but remain outside the mainstream. They performed with Bob Dylan, Janis Joplin, Santana, Jefferson Airplane and Crosby, Stills, Nash & Young. New music was created while old songs were dropped or adapted. They experienced triumph and tragedy, highs and lows. They were at Monterey Pop, Woodstock and Altamont. They played the pyramids in Egypt, the Olympia in Paris, Wembley Arena in London, Winterland, the Fillmore West and East, and stadiums and arenas across the USA and beyond. The venues they played changed; the locations they toured changed, and the band members themselves changed, becoming with age, more experienced as musicians and more mature as songwriters. They were inevitably also subject to the problems associated with unwise lifestyle choices that eventually took their toll. But through it all, the music never stopped, and they made sure that it was captured and shared.

It's through looking at these live releases that the band's story emerges. From the dance halls of the Bay Area to the stadiums of North America via the pyramids of Egypt and the theatres of Europe; from bluegrass and folk beginnings to MTV via country, blues and rock. Through lineup changes, tragedy and triumph, The Grateful Dead danced to no rhythm but their own.

1965 – The First Days

Jerry Garcia wasn't cut out to be in the army. After his father (a former professional musician and bar co-owner) died when he was young, Garcia was brought up by his mother and his grandparents, living at various locations in and around San Francisco. A fan of country and bluegrass music from an early age, he took up playing the banjo, before listening to rock 'n' roll and rhythm and blues artists inspired him to move on to guitar. While far from a model school pupil (he changed schools frequently), he was inspired by the work of Jack Kerouac, and was encouraged to develop his talent as an artist. Like many youngsters, he regularly found himself in trouble, and faced with the possibility of prison at an early age, he was given the option to join the army instead. Following basic training, he was stationed at a fort in San Francisco's Presidio, where he clocked up a number of reprimands for his poor attitude and behaviour: his commanding officer noting Garcia was 'unreliable, irresponsible, immature, unwilling to accept authority, and completely lacking in soldierly qualities'. His proximity to the city and his friends, along with his disinterest in the military life, meant frequent absences and led to a general discharge in December 1960: just nine months after his military career began. Garcia's life would instead go down a very different path.

Hanging out in San Francisco a few months later, Garcia met Robert Hunter while living a hand-to-mouth existence as part of the local beatnik scene of art galleries, coffee houses and book shops close to Stanford University – particularly Kepler's Books: a vibrant independent store that attracted young people with new ideas about culture, art, literature, politics and philosophy. Hunter would go on to be Garcia's primary songwriting collaborator for the rest of his life. But in the early years, the pair formed an acoustic folk duo, playing at Kepler's and other university and college venues around the San Francisco Bay area. This collaboration produced one of the earliest Grateful-Dead-related performances to be released, in the form of a set performed by the act then known as Bob And Jerry, in May 1961. Released in 2018, *Before The Dead* – a four-CD collection – compiles Garcia's musical development from the early set with Hunter, through to 1964, with Garcia playing in a variety of acts with other musicians and as a solo artist. Bob and Jerry play eight numbers – most of them traditional folk songs – recorded at the sixteenth birthday party of Garcia's then-girlfriend Barbara Meier. The performance is basic, and gives little indication of Garcia or Hunter's later art. It's an informal run-through of songs at a party in front of friends who probably already knew all the songs and would join in occasionally.

Garcia's art benefitted from the environment he was a part of. While he personally experienced hardship at the time (both he and Hunter living in their cars for a while and surviving off tinned army-surplus food), it was a supportive, well-educated, tolerant and well-resourced community, where appearances on radio shows were possible and recording equipment was accessible. That recordings were not only made at these early stages in Garcia's career, but were stored and were good enough for release decades later on a format that couldn't even have been imagined at the time, is an achievement in itself and a reflection of the forward-looking, open-minded attitudes that prevailed at the time. Not only was there the creativity of the artists, but there was also money available to make recordings and a network that was able to preserve them.

The release shows Garcia in a number of other musical settings, presenting bands whose names had previously only been footnotes in the many books about The Dead – The Sleepy Hollow Hog Stompers from 1962, The Hart Valley Drifters from the same year, The Wildwood Boys from 1963, Garcia performing with his then-wife Sara Ruppenthal Garcia as Jerry and Sara from 1963, The Black Mountain Boys from 1963 and 1964, and the Asphalt Jungle Mountain Boys from 1964. There's a rotating cast of musicians, and while Hunter played alongside Garcia in a number of the bands included in the set, other musicians that would figure later in the history of The Grateful Dead were also involved. Among them was David Nelson, who would later guest on a number of key early Grateful Dead recordings, and perform alongside Garcia in the New Riders Of The Purple Sage in the late-1960s, and as part of the Jerry Garcia Acoustic band in the late-1980s. Sandy Rothman – another Black Mountain Boy – would also be part of this band.

In keeping with the folk-music revival at the time, many of the songs are traditional folk songs, including 'All My Trials', 'Man Of Constant Sorrow' and 'We Shall Not Be Moved'. Others were by bluegrass artists like Earl Scruggs, Bill Monroe or Ralph Stanley, others by country performers like Merle Travis or Jimmie Rodgers. There is one self-penned song – 'Jerry's Breakdown' – performed by the Wildwood Boys. Some – like 'Sitting On Top Of The World' and 'Deep Elem Blues' – continued to inform Garcia's music for the rest of his career, and reappeared in The Grateful Dead's repertoire and in the sets by his own acts. Some songs echo in The Dead's later work in other ways – the song 'Little Birdie' by the Sleepy Hollow Hog Stompers containing lyrical seeds that would later take root in the songs 'Dark Hollow' and 'Box Of Rain'. These performances showed the young Garcia as a musically voracious artist, unafraid to adapt, take on new musical styles and explore new avenues as far as he possibly could. Much of his later musical restlessness and curiosity could be seen emerging in these early shows, as well as a familiarity with a rich bedrock of work that would continue to inform his art for the rest of his life. While *Before The Dead* presents Garcia in what is to many listeners an unfamiliar context, threads that would run through his entire career were already there – except when he said at the end of his 1961 set with Hunter: 'Me play rock 'n' roll? No. Never going to happen'. The Hart Valley Drifters section of the *Before The Dead* collection (recorded in 1962 at a local radio station at Stamford University) was originally released on its own in 2016 under the title *Folk Time*.

By 1964 there had been a change in musical direction, with Garcia moving from acoustic folk and bluegrass to a different genre of music, and this time playing as a member of a band. Mother McCree's Uptown Jug Champions were a jug band – a knowingly rough-hewn folk genre popular in the 1920s and 1930s, where the musicians played banjo, guitar and mandolin along with more basic instruments like kazoo and washboard, along with a jug that was blown into to act as a primitive tuba, delivering a rough bass line. Like skiffle – its UK equivalent – jug band became popular as a genre again in the early-1960s. Bands would play songs from the original jug-band era, along with modern songs that lent themselves to the style. Mother McCree's Uptown Jug Champions was a six-piece band, bringing together three future Grateful Dead members; Garcia, Bob Weir – then on guitar, washtub bass, jug, kazoo and vocals – and Ron 'Pigpen' McKernan on harmonica and vocals.

Weir – then sixteen years old – had first met Garcia in a Palo Alto music shop on New Year's Eve 1963. Weir heard Garcia playing banjo in the shop while waiting for his students. As it was unlikely they'd come due to it being New Year's Eve, he invited Weir to play along with him. They went on to play together for several hours, and realised they had the combined talent to put together a jug band. Garcia – having explored bluegrass in depth by not only playing, but learning from other more experienced musicians – had concluded that he'd have to move on if he was to further his musical ambitions, as there just weren't enough people in the area that shared his enthusiasm for the genre. A jug band would give him a vehicle for his talents and experience, as well as the opportunity to pick up new skills. The band also featured Ron 'Pigpen' McKernan on harmonica and vocals. A blues fanatic (His father had been a leading DJ in the late-1950s, with a blues show broadcast across the San Francisco Bay area), Pigpen had lived alongside Garcia in Palo Alto, and with Garcia more than capable of playing some blues guitar, Pigpen would accompany him.

A recording of the band from July 1964 was released in 1999 on CD. Entitled *Mother McCree's Uptown Jug Champions,* the collection features the band performing for folk music show *Live From The Top Of The Tangent* on Stanford University's FM radio station. Two brothers who were students at the university had recorded it, and they discovered the tapes again in 1997 in their family home after their mother died. The tapes were then mastered by Jeffrey Norman, who'd worked with The Dead since working on their *Dead Set* album in 1980, and a variety of other projects, including mixing many of the band's multitrack recordings for archival releases. It gives a unique insight (with characteristically high-quality sound) into the early development of the musicians who would go on to be at the centre of The Grateful Dead.

The album's seventeen tracks include several covers that would go on to feature in The Dead's set – 'Overseas Stomp' and the Lightnin' Hopkins' song 'Ain't It Crazy' would be favourites of Pigpen, 'The Monkey And The Engineer' would be an occasional number and feature extensively in acoustic sets in 1980, 'On The Road Again' would also reappear for these shows, while 'Beat It On Down The Line' would not only appear on their debut album but in their live sets almost every year until 1994. Among the other numbers, is a cover of Chuck Berry's 'Memphis Tennessee' (originally released in 1959). Berry's song (which The Beatles also performed around the same time) gives a clear indication that rock 'n' roll was on their radar, and that it was something they were confident performing, even in a slightly different style. The Grateful Dead would go on to perform Chuck Berry songs throughout their career. The number 'Cocaine Habit Blues' perhaps also gave another indication of where the band might go in the future, although perhaps not in a musical sense.

A contemporary interview with Garcia, Weir and the others in the band included on the disc, reveals the band as a relaxed, down-to-earth and good-humoured bunch, with Pigpen credited with 'playing the harmonica and singing the blues quite well': an understatement. There's also some background on the music they play – a mix of jug band (described as 'early blues band music' from the start of the 20th century), early Dixieland jazz from New Orleans, some 1920s and 1930s popular music, and some more recent blues. Having this variety in their sources, they say, doesn't restrict them to any particular idea or style. Asked about the future, a young Garcia notes that they'll play the music as long as they're together, as it's fun and rewarding, even if they don't expect to make a fortune or be popular or be worshipped for it, and that they'll continue to play regardless of what or who it's for, because it's fun for them. While young musicians have probably always said similar things in similar circumstances, it's fascinating to hear voices that would go on to be so familiar and have the opportunity to live the lives they could only have dreamed of, speak like this at the dawn of their careers.

The Beatles changed things for young musicians everywhere, and reverberations of the new electric sound meant a change in direction for the Jug Champions. New questions had arisen, and the answers were to be found in new musical inspiration. What would it be like if you took traditional folk music and played it in an electric rock 'n' roll band? Could songs from the pre-rock'n' roll era be reinvented for the new sound? Does blues, bluegrass, country and folk have a place in this electric environment? It was around this time, that Dylan – one of the prime influences on Garcia – was asking similar questions and coming up with his own theories. Garcia, Weir and Pigpen wanted to find their own answers too.

To be a rock band, they needed a new lineup with a drummer and a bass player. Bill Kreutzmann was already a friend of the three musicians, so he was quickly enlisted, and Dana Morgan – the son of the owner of the Palo Alto music shop where Garcia hung out and met Weir – was drafted in on bass. Kreutzmann played in a number of local acts, and first met Garcia in 1962 when he sold him a banjo. While their paths crossed frequently, they became close when they both worked in Dana Morgan's music shop. With a slight but significant adjustment to their sound, the new band – now named The Warlocks – were formed. The first Warlocks gig took place on 5 May at Magoo's Pizza Parlor in Menlo Park, California.

The band had not long been playing when there was a change, with Dana Morgan replaced by an acquaintance of Garcia's named Phil Lesh. Lesh wasn't a bass player, but had a serious musical background. He'd been into classical music and learned the violin before moving on to trumpet, going on to study music. He'd gotten heavily into jazz and modern composing, and while living in the San Francisco area, came into contact with Garcia, inviting him to appear on a radio show he was involved in. He'd already told Garcia he wanted to take up an electric instrument – perhaps the bass – and seeing The Warlocks one night convinced him this was the way to go. When Garcia asked him if he wanted to join – despite not having previously played the bass – he didn't need to be asked twice.

It was a humble beginning, going on from there to play numerous sets a night, six nights a week at local bars, where they'd develop their craft – craft in their case being to play longer, louder and weirder than anyone else. Their sets consisted predominantly of cover versions, but they soon put on some songs of their own. They found a couple of local bars where their style fitted in – The In Room and The Fireside – with a crowd and staff that not only tolerated their foibles, but actively encouraged them.

It was during this time that they crossed paths with writer Ken Kesey – author of *One Flew Over The Cuckoo's Nest* – and his entourage. These included Beat-Generation-icon Neal Cassady (upon whom Jack Kerouac had based his Dean Moriarty character in *On The Road*), and dozens of others, including Garcia's long-term partner Mountain Girl, and Ken Babbs, who would become close friends of the band for years. They were dubbed The Merry Pranksters, and were evangelists for the then-legal LSD. The drug – first synthesized in Switzerland in 1938 by chemist Albert Hoffman at Sandoz Pharmaceuticals – had been found to have a powerful mind-altering effect, inducing visual hallucinations and intensified senses, with no risk of addiction; any side effects including paranoia, anxiety and delusions generally being temporary. Research had been done into it being used to treat mental health conditions, and the US army and CIA had been investigating its potential uses. Kesey was one of the subjects of these experiments, as was Robert Hunter.

With funding from Kesey's earnings from his bestseller, they were also experimenting with audio and video equipment to create environments to reflect and heighten the LSD effects. In The Warlocks, they found natural allies, and they were soon providing a live soundtrack to what these days would probably be described as multimedia real-time immersive installations. In those days, it was just the band playing for hours amidst an arsenal of light, sound and film equipment: events that soon were named Acid Tests. At times, the band would play songs, and other times they'd create lengthy periods of feedback and drones. Sometimes they'd be accompanying spoken-word sessions from Kesey, Babbs, Cassady or anyone else at the mic. These unpredictable, open-ended and essentially spontaneous events would be held at different locations, attracting hundreds of curious and open-minded young people, all prepared to engage with the experience – usually including the LSD – rather than just be a passive audience. The Acid Tests were essentially the fuse that set the West Coast counterculture ablaze and brought it to world attention just a few months later.

Early in autumn 1965, the band abandoned their Warlocks name after they discovered another band apparently using the same name. In need of a new name, it would take a month or two until they'd finally settle on something. In November, the band – under their briefly-adopted name The Emergency Crew – made their first studio recordings, at Golden Gate Recorders in San Francisco. The six tracks appear on the 2001 *Birth Of The Dead* album – 'Early Morning Rain', 'I Know You Rider', 'Mindbender (Confusion's Prince)', 'The Only Time Is Now', 'Caution (Do Not Stop On Tracks)' and 'Can't Come Down' revealing an act moving from covers and traditional numbers, to confidently recording their own work. While they'd quickly outgrow the majority of the numbers on the demo – sounding very much of their era, and much more dated compared to the material they would produce just a short time later – 'Caution (Do Not Stop On Tracks)' would go on to be a classic Pigpen live number, while their take on the traditional song 'I Know You Rider' would become one of the band's most loved standards, remaining in their set throughout, and even featuring in their penultimate concert in 1995.

A new name presented itself to the band later that month, and this time it would stick: The Grateful Dead. In suitably legendary style, the name chose them. Garcia – while at Lesh's home and predictably as high as a kite – opened a dictionary at a page where the term was defined; all the other words on the page, falling away to reveal the unusual phrase: a recurring motif from folk tales where a hero comes across a group of people refusing to bury a man who had died with debts. He pays the debts so a burial can happen, and then meets another man who accompanies him and helps him out in some manner. The stories end with the revelation that this other man is in fact, The Dead man whose burial he'd paid for. It was mysterious, unusual, a bit creepy, and above all: weird. It was perfect. They'd play their first gig under their new name on 4 December at the San Jose Acid Test and the first show under their new name at the Fillmore in San Francisco on 10 December.

One person the band met during the Acid Tests era who would figure large in their mythology – as well as in their recordings – went by the name of Augustus Owsley Stanley III, though was known to most as Owsley, and later by the nickname Bear. Owsley would become a pioneering sound engineer working for The Grateful Dead. He'd develop their Wall Of Sound PA, inspire their skull and lightning-bolt 'Steal Your Face' logo, and enthusiastically record the band's rehearsals and live performances – initially to check the shows' sound quality – establishing along the way an archive of recordings that would for decades make the music of the era accessible to an audience far beyond the ones that filled the dance halls, theatres and arenas in the late-1960s and early-

1970s. But Owsley's business at the time he first met The Grateful Dead, was manufacturing LSD, and business was good.

Owsley had an immense and unique mind. He'd initially studied engineering and worked for the US Air Force, specialising in electronics, and working as an actual rocket scientist. He then studied ballet in Los Angeles, working as a professional dancer before enrolling at the University of California's Berkeley campus, where he became interested in LSD, creating his own laboratory to produce the drug. Despite police intervention – but no charges, as LSD was legal at the time – he went on to produce LSD of a quality comparable to that made by Sandoz, which was becoming increasingly difficult to acquire in California. He also made it in industrial quantities, having by mid-1965 produced around 300,000 doses. While he regularly circulated his product without charge – particularly to those who would in the 21st century be described as *influencers* – he also made a considerable amount of money, which he spent on his other interests (electronics and The Grateful Dead), funding much of the band's equipment and rehearsal time, and recording much of what they produced.

1966 – The Acid Test

The Acid Tests experience made it onto vinyl – to some extent – in early-1966, with the release of *The Acid Test*: essentially a spoken-word album with the various pranksters being interviewed, performing rambling routines or ad-lib *poetry*, with occasional added electronic effects, tape loops and noises. The Grateful Dead make some of that background racket. As a memento of such a strange and influential scene, it's a pretty poor document, and for something considered at the time avant-garde and threatening to societal norms, it's remarkably pedestrian. Perhaps you had to be there to appreciate it; perhaps it's not really possible to capture the spirit of a spontaneous event. Either way, it certainly doesn't lend itself to repeated listening. The album was an obscure relic for decades, before various reissues made it more accessible to those who could then find out for themselves that there was actually a pretty good reason why it had languished in obscurity for so long. If the album had focused more on the band in the background, and less on the voices on the mics, it could've been something quite groundbreaking – genuine Beat-era spoken-word *raps* interplaying with a fiery-edged young rock act; a countercultural and intergenerational passing-of-the-torch. But as time would tell, The Grateful Dead all too often took to the stage and stepped up to the mic at the historic moment, only to fall through an artistic trapdoor in front of the audience.

A more interesting document of the time comes in a tape of the earliest recording of a gig by The Grateful Dead, from 8 January 1966, at the Acid Test at the Fillmore Auditorium in San Francisco. The Dead hitting their peak just off the target, would again be a recurring experience. The Fillmore Acid Test displayed how far they'd developed during their time as the Acid Tests' house band, having learned how improvisation and experimentation could benefit both audience and performer, making each performance unique and essential, and how source material could be reshaped into something distinctive and new every night. These were lessons that would serve them well for the rest of their career.

The five-piece Grateful Dead played live extensively in 1966, their set leaning heavily on cover versions that showed where they were coming from – folk numbers performed with an electric edge, blues numbers where Pigpen rapidly established himself as the band's frontman, and their own songs with a psychedelic garage-rock edge, brimming with youthful energy. Shows in 1966 moved from Acid Tests to comparatively conventional dance halls; Kesey fleeing to Mexico following a drugs bust. Although, in the wake of the Acid Test shows, these venues themselves became homes to the counterculture and its associated music, fashion, lights, artists, and above all, people.

They may not have discovered their own unique sound yet, but they were working on it every night, and rapidly establishing a reputation as a live act that were at the forefront of the new sound that was emerging from the West Coast. Perhaps The Dead had simply outgrown the Acid Tests, and needed a bigger stage. Perhaps they wanted to at least appear to have some of the trappings of a conventional music act, so they could secure a record deal. Or perhaps what had been an underground phenomenon that The Dead were actually only a part of, had begun its gradual move into the mainstream.

The earliest live show to be released by the band so far was recorded at the Fillmore Auditorium in San Francisco on 3 July 1966. The two-disc set – part of the *30 Trips Around The Sun* collection – was recorded by Owsley on an evening where they played two separate sets: the L.A. folk-rock band Love playing a set between The Dead's performances. Opening with a brief take of 'Nobody's Fault But Mine' – the Blind Willie Johnson blues song later made famous by Led Zeppelin – the first set features a collection of covers, including 'Dancing In The Street', 'I Know You Rider', 'Viola Lee Blues' and 'Big Boss Man': songs they'd go on to make their own. Others like 'He Was A Friend Of Mine' and 'Sitting On Top Of The World' would be performed frequently in their early years. 'Keep Rolling By' – the final song of the set – remains something of a rarity. The second disc – documenting the second set – features a handful of Dead originals among the covers, including Pigpen's 'Tastebud', Garcia's 'Cream Puff War', Lesh's 'Cardboard Cowboy', and a collective 'You Don't Have To Ask'. While being interesting pieces, they fail to match other numbers in the set like 'New, New Minglewood Blues', 'Cold Rain And Snow' or 'Beat It On Down The Line', which, though covers, would remain integral to The Dead's shows for decades. Their self-written early material would be quietly dropped from their repertoire. A couple of rare covers – 'Don't Mess Up A Good Thing' by R&B artist Oliver Sain, and Johnny 'Guitar' Watson's 'Gangster Of Love' – make appearances in this recording.

In 2017, a concert from 1966 appeared as the double-vinyl release *July 29 1966. P.N.E Garden Aud., Vancouver Canada.* Despite the unimaginative title, the release shows the early Dead as a band with potential they were beginning to realise on their first official shows outside California, as part of the Vancouver Trips Festival. They were pushing beyond the self-imposed stylistic boundaries of garage rock and finding in themselves the ability to push their playing that little bit further than they did before. Garage rock was a genre famous for celebrating the short-lived one-hit acts that made an intense proto-punk sound inspired by R&B and then-recent British-invasion bands. These bands normally burned brightly but quickly, leaving at best a legacy of a handful of rare 45s. The Dead from this era could easily have been one of many vaguely-remembered names on an obscure garage-rock rarities compilation, but their creativity and ability were able to sustain them much, much longer. Their musical confidence was growing, even then; their quirky uniqueness was already visible, their songwriting would mature, and their live performances would quickly establish their reputation as a formidable act.

The set is heavy with cover versions, their roots in folk and blues clearly visible. But with versions of 'I Know You Rider', 'Beat It On Down the Line' and Dylan's 'It's All Over Now, Baby Blue', the band would be recognised by anyone whose experience of them was limited to their mid-1980s/1990s repertoire.

Other early favourites are here – 'Sitting On Top Of The World', 'Big Boss Man', 'Viola Lee Blues' and 'Good Morning Little Schoolgirl', Garcia's 'Cream Puff War', a rare release of Lesh's 'Cardboard Cowboy', and the band's jointly-written 'Standing On The Corner', 'New, New Minglewood Blues' and 'You Don't Have To Ask'. 'Standing On The Corner' was only ever played a few times, this being its final performance, and 'You Don't Have To Ask' and 'Cardboard Cowboy' would also not make the setlist again. The songs were shorter than the usual extravagant length associated with The Grateful Dead, and were shot-through with a youthful energy. The fireworks they'd soon be blazing, might not all be present yet, but there's a smell of gunpowder, and something's beginning to catch alight. This collection is a witness to that moment.

Four tracks on the release – 'Cold Rain And Snow', 'One Kind Favor', 'Hey Little One' and 'New, New Minglewood Blues' – were actually from the show on 30 July, and all seventeen tracks from the two shows also appeared as a bonus disc on the 50th-anniversary double-CD deluxe edition of the band's debut album when it was released in 2017.

Two other releases that captured The Dead's early live sound were the albums *Historic Dead* and *Vintage Dead*. These two unauthorised releases emerged as a consequence of a contract they signed to have live material recorded for inclusion on a compilation album of San Francisco Bay bands. The recordings were made at the Avalon Ballroom in autumn 1966, probably on 16 September. The label behind the collection – Together Records – went under before the project was completed, and the tapes were bought by MGM Records, who released two volumes of the recordings: *Vintage Dead* in 1970 and *Historic Dead* in 1971. While The Dead had no involvement in the releases, the two albums do present a solid picture of the band in this period. Both collections only feature covers, as possibly a release including any of The Dead's original material could have been prevented, but there are versions here of 'Dancing In The Street', a side-long version of 'In The Midnight Hour', 'Good Morning Little Schoolgirl', and Dylan's 'It's All Over Now, Baby Blue'. The two albums were combined – *Vintage Dead* in full and two tracks from *Historic Dead* as the release *The History Of The Grateful Dead* in 1972. Neither album has been released on CD, but one track from *Vintage Dead* – their version of 'I Know You Rider' – appeared as part of the *So Many Roads (1965-1995)* box set. By the time the two albums were released, The Dead had long moved on from their 1966 incarnation, but the two volumes, unauthorised as they were, established that there was an appetite for archive Grateful Dead releases: an appetite that decades later has not abated.

However, the most detailed release of material from 1966, comes in the form of the *Rare cuts And Oddities 1966* collection: a CD released in 2005. Consisting of recordings made by Owsley to assess how his experiments with developing the band's PA were progressing, Archivist David Lemieux was in The Dead's vault with Owsley in around 2002 when Owsley suggested he investigate an unlabelled box of recordings. The reel-to-reel tapes contained a variety of valuable recordings, including early studio sessions and live material. Some were rough versions, others more carefully recorded. Some songs would find a place in The Dead's repertoire for decades, while others would remain obscurities. Seven tracks were recorded in the studio in early 1966, including Chuck Berry's 'The Promised Land' with Garcia on lead vocals, 'Walking The Dog' with Weir on vocals, and the first known versions of 'Good Lovin'' and 'Not Fade Away'. There are also originals, including Garcia's 'Cream Puff War', the band's 'Standing On The Corner', and the Pigpen rarity 'You See A Broken Heart'. A studio session from March 1966 delivers the tracks 'Stealin'' – which would be their first single – and a cover of 'Betty And Dupree': a traditional song they would later adapt to become 'Dupree's Diamond Blues'. A studio session also produced a cover of 'Silver Threads And Golden Needles'. Live material from early-1966 includes the earliest version of 'Big Railroad Blues', and a rare cover of The Rolling Stones' 'Empty Heart' (from their second US album *12x5*). There are two tracks from the 3 July Fillmore Auditorium show that features on *30 Trips Around The Sun*, and three from a show at the Danish Centre in L.A. on 12 March, including covers of 'Hey Little One', 'I'm A King Bee' and an early version of 'Caution (Do Not Stop On Tracks)'. The collection gives an in-depth picture of the band's artistic development across 1966, from their mastery of well-chosen covers to their early steps into writing their own material.

More of the early Dead's studio output is present on *The Birth Of The Dead*. Following on from their Emergency Crew session, The Dead entered San Francisco's Buena Vista studio in June to record what became known as the Scorpio Sessions, to capture the tracks for a single to be released locally by the label of the same name. The CD includes both instrumental and vocal takes of the single's A-side 'Don't Ease Me In' and its B-side 'Stealin''. Both songs were traditional numbers, The Dead giving them an electric arrangement. Other tracks recorded at the session included two versions of 'Cold Rain And Snow', a second studio version of 'I Know You Rider', and two originals: 'You Don't Have To Ask' and 'Tastebud', the latter in both instrumental and vocal form.

The Birth Of The Dead also includes a disc of live material from various sources. The only original included is a version of 'Standing On The Corner', but among the covers are numbers they would closely be associated with, including 'Viola Lee Blues', 'Big Boss Man' and Dylan's 'It's All Over Now, Baby Blue'. Blues legends Blind Willie Johnson and Lightnin' Hopkins are represented by the songs 'Nobody's Fault But Mine' and 'One Kind Favor', and the song 'In The Pines' – popularised by two significant Dead influences: Lead Belly and Bill Munro – makes a rare appearance. It's perhaps a credit to The Dead's taste that the song would go on to a whole new audience almost three decades later after Nirvana released it on their *Unplugged In New York* album.

1967 – Love and Haight

If 1967 was the point when the countercultural seed that had been planted in the San Francisco Area came to fruition, the event that heralded it was held on 14 January at the Polo Fields at San Francisco's Golden Gate Park. Between 20,000 and 30,000 people attended the Human Be-In event intended to memorialise the Californian authorities' October-1966 decision to ban the use of LSD. Speakers included psychedelic psychologist Timothy Leary, Beat-Generation poets Allen Ginsberg and Michael McClure, and social activist Jerry Rubin. The Dead played at the event alongside Big Brother And The Holding Company, Jefferson Airplane and Blue Cheer. Owsley distributed large quantities of newly-produced White Lightning LSD. The Dead opened their set with a cover of 'Morning Dew': their first performance of the song also known as '(Walk Me Out In The) Morning Dew', originally by Canadian folk artist Bonnie Dobson. It would become a classic of The Dead's repertoire, and go on to be covered by artists as diverse as Lulu, Robert Plant and Einstürzende Neubauten. It was a considered and thoughtful start for The Dead's involvement at the epicentre of what later became known as the Summer Of Love, and a suggestion that there was more depth to what they wanted to express: it wasn't just opportunistic hedonism or appropriation of the circumstances that put them in the right place at the right time. While the countercultural environment of San Francisco in the late-1960s provided fertile ground, The Dead's roots ran deeper than most.

At the beginning of 1967, The Dead moved to L.A. to record their self-titled debut album. Grammy-award-winning sound engineer David Hassinger was chosen to produce, primarily because of his work on Jefferson Airplane's *Surrealistic Pillow* album that Garcia had contributed to the previous year. The recording of The Dead album took four days, and of the nine tracks, only two were original compositions: the opening number 'The Golden Road (To Unlimited Devotion)' – credited to the band under the pseudonym McGannahan Skjellyfetti – and 'Cream Puff War'. Pigpen – then very much the band's frontman – only took lead vocals on one track: their cover of 'Good Morning Little Schoolgirl'.

The album was a serviceable introduction to the band for a wider audience beyond their regular west-coast haunts, but only gave hints of the band's full potential. Compared to other debut albums released that year – from acts like Velvet Underground, The Doors or Pink Floyd – it was more a road sign pointing to where the band was going, rather than a statement that they had arrived. The Grateful Dead still felt like a band that were developing and hadn't fully materialised yet. There's no denying the songs were great, from the punchy 'The Golden Road (To Unlimited Devotion)' to 'Viola Lee Blues', and many would go on to be band standards – 'Cold Rain And Snow' and 'Morning Dew' would still be part of their set in their final tour in June 1995 (19 June at Giants Stadium, East Rutherford, New Jersey, and 21 June at the Knickerbocker Arena, Albany, New York, respectively), just weeks before their final gig with

Jerry Garcia the following month. But given the intensity of their early live performances, there's a feeling that things aren't maybe as good as they could have been on vinyl.

Perhaps it was their unfamiliarity with being in a studio – they were recording in L.A. and were far removed from the positive feedback of an audience and the more-relaxed natural environment of the live show. Maybe there was the added pressure of a clock, a budget and deadlines. But maybe there should just have been more room for the songs to breath – It's hard to imagine given The Dead's reputation for extended jamming, that of the nine tracks committed to vinyl, six clock in at around two and a half minutes each. Four of the tracks – 'New, New Minglewood Blues', 'Sitting On Top Of The World', 'Cream Puff War' and 'Good Morning Little School Girl' – were edited to keep their running time down. The latter, usually being a platform for a lengthy Pigpen-centred workout, is held to just under six minutes on the release. 'Morning Dew' – later to be one of the jewels of their *Europe '72* album – comes in at five minutes. Even the early-2000s reissue with full-length versions of the four tracks, only added an extra couple of minutes to the total playing time.

Had they had the opportunity to show what they really could do with the material, it may have been a very different album. The bonus material added to the 2001 CD reissue (originally issued as part of the *The Golden Road (1965-1973)* box set), gives a flavour of what might have been, with a live version of 'Viola Lee Blues' from September 1967 that's over 23 minutes long, even with the opening verse and part of the second verse missing from the original recording, while the version of 'In the Midnight Hour' from the same gig (at the Dance Hall, Rio Nido, California) – clocking in at almost 32 minutes – is the centrepiece of the *Fallout from the Phil Zone* collection released in 1997. There was no doubt that in the live environment, the band could take a song – whether a traditional number, a blues or even a contemporary soul song – and reshape it into something uniquely their own. An album with a couple of lengthy pieces combined with a couple of their shorter early gems would've been a bold opening statement for a band indeed, even in 1967.

The reissue also includes four studio outtakes recorded in Los Angeles in February. These consist of covers of Rev. Gary Davis' 'Death Don't Have No Mercy', 'Overseas Stomp' (a tune performed in their Mother McCree's Uptown Jug Champions days), and two originals – 'Alice D. Millionaire' (a group composition inspired by a headline about Owsley and his LSD enterprise) and Pigpen's 'Tastebud'. The 50th-anniversary deluxe edition features a second disc recorded on 29 and 30 July 1966 at the Garden Auditorium, Vancouver, Canada.

If there are few full-length live releases of The Dead performing in 1967, there are a number of fascinating snippets that have emerged. As well as 'Viola Lee Blues' and 'In The Midnight Hour' from September, there's a cover of Willie Dixon's 'The Same Thing' recorded at Winterland that's included on the *So Many Roads (1965-1995)* box set. One interesting if brief sonic document from 1967, is a recording of The Dead backing Neal Cassady at the Straight Theatre, which was released in 1973 as a flexi disc with the first edition of the book *The Dead* by the band's former manager Hank Harrison. Titled 'Neal Cassady Raps', The Dead improvise in the background, while Cassady unleashes a mumbled and at times incoherent stream-of-consciousness. At times, The Dead's noodling is close to *Turn On Your Lovelight*, while other times, it's far more abstract. The document runs for ten minutes, and while interesting, you probably had to be there. Cassady may have been one of the inspirations for the Beat Generation, but he was associated more with his life than his actual literary output. When he died aged 41 – less than a year after his appearance on stage with The Dead – he left little more than an unfinished manuscript of his own work but had made an unforgettable impact as a character in the work of others.

The official start of the Summer Of Love was reckoned to be the Monterey Pop Festival – a genuinely iconic three-day event held on 16, 17 and 18 June at the county's fairground, just over 100 miles south of San Francisco. The Dead played as part of an era-defining bill: including Jimi Hendrix, The Who, Jefferson Airplane, and Big Brother And The Holding Company featuring Janis Joplin. It featured a roll call of artists that decades later would be close to answering the 'Who would you put on at your ideal festival?' question. Simon and Garfunkel, The Byrds, The Mamas & The Papas, Otis Redding, Buffalo Springfield, Moby Grape and Laura Nyro all performed, along with many, many more. The event would not just establish the careers of those who played, but in the cases of Hendrix, The Who and Janis Joplin, their performances that weekend alone are cited to this day as justification for the legendary status they would go on to achieve. While Monterey attracted a huge audience at the actual event, a film of it made by D. A. Pennebaker – who in 1965 had made the *Dont Look Back* documentary about Bob Dylan's 1965 tour of England – brought it to a receptive international audience, inspiring countless multi-day music festivals, ensuring the West Coast was the epicentre of the new cultural movement, and giving a raft of artists the biggest possible platform. The Grateful Dead, as had seemingly become their habit when the spotlight beckoned, basically blew it.

To be fair, it wasn't really their fault. An unfortunate position in the running order put The Dead on stage on the Sunday evening between The Who and Jimi Hendrix: two artists whose performances literally wrecked the joint or were literally incendiary. The Who and Jimi Hendrix would've been unfamiliar to many in the crowd, being acts that had built their reputation in the UK. They both had the element of surprise and used this unfamiliarity to its full extent. They may not have been well known to an American audience before Monterey, but The Who and Hendrix played genuinely unforgettable sets. The Dead, however, were essentially playing to a home crowd who'd probably seen them many times before, and it was a shorter set than they'd usually play, with little time to get into overdrive. Lesh was playing on a borrowed bass, which didn't help. After the spectacle of The Who and before the intensity of Hendrix, The Dead were a brief, familiar reprieve: not a situation they'd normally be associated with. They didn't make the cut for the movie.

A DVD box set released in 2002 included the original movie along with two bonus discs. One features two stand-alone films of the Hendrix and Otis Redding performances – *Jimi Plays Monterey* and *Shake! Otis At Monterey* – but another disc features a selection of outtakes, including The Dead's performance of 'Viola Lee Blues'. At just under nine minutes long, it's a muscular version of the song, with some intense soloing from Garcia. It's a great piece of video of the young band at a historic event, and while not capturing the subtlety and depth they were capable of, it gives a brief snapshot of what they could do. It also makes you wish there was more footage of this quality and vintage that captured better and more complete performances.

If The Dead had missed a career opportunity at Monterey, the same cannot be said for Owsley, who in the run-up to the event had been working in his underground lab to ensure a plentiful supply of his LSD was available. With the audience and the festival performers being the main customers, he seized the opportunity to acquaint the stars with his product. Among them was Hendrix, who – although a keen consumer – wasn't keen on the results of Owsley recording him under the influence. He'd arranged to privately record Hendrix on the guitar, but following the session, Hendrix threw the resulting tape on a fire. Owsley would, however, get a name-check from Hendrix later that year in a version of The Beatles' 'Day Tripper' recorded for the BBC in London. And it was The Beatles who would be among the most influenced by Owsley. John Lennon had (apparently) despatched a camera operator to Monterey to capture the event for himself, though it was in fact, a cover for a courier importing an industrial quantity of Owsley's product for The Beatles. The *Magical Mystery Tour* film and double EP released at the end of 1967, were the direct result.

A different movie would record The Grateful Dead as part of the backdrop of 1967 San Francisco. *Petulia* – directed by Richard Lester, who'd directed the Beatles' movies *A Hard Day's Night* and *Help!,* and would go on to make *Superman II* and Superman *III* – starred Julie Christie, George C. Scott and Richard Chamberlain, and is the tale of a troubled relationship. Shot in San Francisco, there are appearances from various local figures, including Janis Joplin and The Dead. The Dead are seen performing 'Viola Lee Blues' in a nightclub scene, and members of the band make appearances as onlookers in street scenes. While not quite as memorable as Guns N' Roses' cameo appearance in the San-Francisco-set 1988 Dirty Harry movie *The Dead Pool,* it's an interesting addition to an otherwise little-remembered film.

Broadcast in August 1967, The Dead featured more prominently in TV documentary *The Hippie Temptation* – a mainstream-media attempt to explain what was going on in San Francisco: 'The hippie capital of the world'. Presented by Harry Reasoner, the show – made by CBS News as part of a short-lived series that was a predecessor to *60 Minutes* – is a heavy-handed attempt to scare middle-class white America with what was going on. It makes the case repeatedly that the hippie movement is completely entwined with LSD use, leading to all manner of 'horrors behind the scenes at the hospitals'. While there are mentions of the *San Francisco Oracle*, The Diggers and the Haight-Ashbury Free Clinic, more screen time is given to numerous sombre psychologists and doctors warning of dire consequences and brain damage, including the soon-discredited claim of LSD being linked to chromosome damage. The filmmakers inevitably link every aspect of the 1960s counterculture, to LSD.

The Dead, described as a 'popular local band who plays hard rock music', feature in a lengthy sequence in their Haight-Ashbury home. Garcia, Lesh and Weir are questioned about what the hippie movement is trying to accomplish, Garcia saying that they are focusing on people, not revolution of war or struggle, and they just want to live a simple, good life. Lesh adds that many came into the hippie movement through drugs. A highlight, though, is the footage of The Dead playing 'Dancing In The Street' at Golden Gate Park. They'd regularly play free, spontaneous shows in the neighbourhood throughout their time living there, with little objection from the authorities as they'd perform without notice or advertising, the performance normally being over before they attracted the attention of those who would've objected.

The hippies are ultimately described as childish, unruly youngsters who act up in a way that attracts adult intervention and then complain about it; their philosophy based on hallucinations, a style without content. It's an unsubtle piece of pro-establishment propaganda designed to leave the viewer concerned that a movement entwined with drug use is spreading, and young Americans are somehow reneging on their responsibilities at a time when American society is more at risk than ever. Ironically, the show was broadcast in August, by which time the Summer of Love was over, and before too long, the Haight-Ashbury area was attracting crowds of youngsters who had no interest in hippie ideals but were simply in search of a good time, having heard about it from... TV news reports.

A show from 22 October at the Winterland in San Francisco would later be released as a bonus disc on the 50th-anniversary issue of the *Anthem Of The Sun* album, and while some of the songs celebrate where the band have been – with versions of 'Morning Dew', a lengthy 'Turn On Your Love Light' and a punchy 'Beat It On Down The Line' – others, like 'New Potato Caboose' and 'That's It For The Other One', show where they were going with the recording of their forthcoming *Anthem Of The Sun* album.

Elsewhere, 1967 is represented on the *30 Trips Around the Sun* box set by a 10 November show at the Shrine Exposition Hall in Los Angeles. The show was also released as a limited triple-vinyl set in 2016. It was one of the few 1967 shows that was a multitrack recording, and was one of the live recordings used in the making of the *Anthem Of The Sun* album; parts of 'Alligator' and 'Caution (Do Not Step On Tracks)' forming segments of The Dead's second album. The

Dead were supported at the Shrine Exposition on 10 and 11 November by Blue Cheer and Buffalo Springfield. Both nights would've been quite an experience.

The gig at the Shrine Exposition reveals some of the changes the band had been going through since their debut. New drummer Mickey Hart was on board, while Robert Hunter – Garcia's partner from their folk duo days – had co-written the lyrics of 'Alligator': a new song that would feature on their forthcoming album. While there are still many covers in the set – the first disc consisting entirely of covers, from 'Viola Lee Blues' to 'Good Morning Little School Girl' via 'It Hurts Me Too', 'Beat It On Down The Line' and 'Morning Dew' – discs two and three feature entirely new material written by members of the band. The jump in the quality of the compositions from their debut album – released just a few short months previously – is massive. The two band-written songs on their debut – 'The Golden Road (To Unlimited Devotion)' and 'Cream Puff War' – have their charms as gems of garage psych, but the new material moves far beyond any genre, into a field that is entirely their own.

With 'That's It For The Other One', 'New Potato Caboose', 'Alligator' and 'Caution (Do Not Stop On Tracks)', they demonstrate a real confidence, their cover-version improvising skills now being applied to their own material, where they show they're capable of handling complexity with both finesse and strength. 'That's It For The Other One' would go on to become one of their key live pieces for much of their career, while 'Alligator' and 'Caution (Do Not Step On Tracks)' are absolute highlights of the set they'd perform in the late-1960s. The fiery playing on this version shows what can happen when an energetic, imaginative and supremely capable band are given a piece that lends itself to musical exploration. The band skips through musical hoops with the skills and grace of an Olympic acrobat. The presence of Hart, and Kreutzmann on drums, gives extra drive and a solid percussive foundation for the rest of the band to build on.

Hart had joined the band after being introduced to Kreutzmann at a Count Basie Orchestra concert at the Fillmore. Hart – whose parents had both been drummers – had served a spell in the Air Force, and was working in his father's drum shop. After the Count Basie show, Kreutzmann took Hart to see Big Brother at the Matrix, and invited him to sit in with The Dead. Hart played alongside Kreutzmann for the first time, on 29 September in the band's second set of their second night at the Straight Theater: the set consisting of 'Alligator' and 'Caution (Do Not Step On Tracks)'. Without even an audition, Hart became a member of The Grateful Dead.

Robert Hunter re-entered Garcia's orbit around the time of The Dead's Rio Nido gig in September. He'd spent time in New Mexico overcoming a drug dependency, and hitchhiked back to San Francisco, where Lesh took him to Rio Nido. The band had been playing 'Alligator' – which featured Hunter's lyrics – as a staple of their set, and he'd been writing poetry ever since, passing some on to Garcia for consideration. While listening to Garcia playing a new guitar piece he was working on, Hunter was himself inspired to create the first verse of a new piece. While only a short collection of lines – with a nod to T. S. Eliot – it was itself an extraordinary poetic work. He passed it on to Garcia, who quickly brought the words and music together. It took Hunter a few days to finish the song, but a piece called 'Dark Star' was born that would go on to be one of the central pillars of The Dead's art.

Since September, The Dead had been working on their second album, but the process would be a difficult one. While their debut had been recorded in a matter of days, their second would be considerably more complicated and take much longer. Work began at the RCA Victor studio in Hollywood in September, before moving to the American Recording Company studios in L.A. with David Hassinger again as producer. It would prove to be a frustrating experience – the band keen to push the limits of the available recording technology, with a suite of complex pieces that were themselves challenging to record. The resulting album would go way over the time allocated for its recording – the team relocating to different studios repeatedly during the process – and well over the record company's allocated budget.

After a month in an L.A. studio, they relocated to San Francisco, then in November, they were back in the L.A. studio again. In December, the recording work moved to New York. Frustrated with the band's lack of progress and their methods (Weir apparently wanting to use a recording of 'thick air', being one memorable incident), Hassinger quit as producer, leaving the band with their album only about a third completed. Much of the studio experimentation and misadventure would be recalled in the 1997 documentary *Anthem To Beauty*, with archive footage of the band combined with interviews, and recent interviews with Lesh, Weir, Hart and Hunter, among others.

Other complications would try them while they were working on the album, including a high-profile drugs bust at the band's Haight-Ashbury headquarters at the beginning of October, and an event held just days later in the local community, to mark the 'Death of hippie'. For many in the original Haight-Ashbury community, the scene was over. Owsley getting busted towards the end of the year was just another nail in the psychedelic coffin. The Dead may be readily associated with events of 1967 and the Haight-Ashbury hippie scene, but before the year was over, they were already looking beyond that horizon.

1968 – Cryptical Envelopment

Faced with a second album that was far from complete and expensive studio bills mounting, The Dead came up with an innovative solution based on their strengths as a live act. The studio recordings would be blended with live recordings to create an amalgam that was something entirely new. Using the studio capabilities to their fullest extent, different live versions of songs would be edited together, studio-recorded elements added, the mixing process adding new layers. Their studio creativity was unleashed, with everything from kazoos to prepared piano augmenting the recordings; Garcia and Lesh fully enjoying the opportunity to incorporate their admiration of modern composer Karlheinz Stockhausen into their work. Keyboard player Tom 'TC' Constanten – a friend of Lesh – took part in the recordings, adding instruments like spinet, and piano-based effects.

Live recordings from the Shrine Exposition in November 1967 were among those used, as were recordings of shows from early-1968 (20 January at Eureka Municipal Auditorium, Eureka, California; 26/27 January at Eagles Auditorium, Seattle, Washington; 2/3 February at Crystal Ballroom, Portland, Oregon; 14 February at Carousel Ballroom, San Francisco, California; 22-24 February at Kings Beach Bowl, Lake Tahoe, California). Shows from March at the Carousel in San Francisco, also featured. The Dead had by now a considerable reputation as a live act, and incorporating performances from concerts seemed a solution to their apparent studio claustrophobia, and using the technology at their disposal allowed them to create a very different work combining the best of both live and studio environments. While being an innovative move, the final result wasn't perhaps all it could've been.

Anthem Of The Sun remains a dense and demanding work. While The Dead meet the opportunities and drawbacks of the studio, it's easier to respect the album's experimentation than it is to love it. Perhaps it lacks the immediacy of the live recording: the studio elements stifling its spontaneity and obscuring it under layers of psychedelic fog. The album's best tracks – 'That's It For The Other One' and 'Alligator'/'Caution (Do Not Step On Tracks)' – would go on to be breakthrough live numbers, and while the others are not without their charms, their presence in the set would not outlast this period of The Dead's career. Lesh remixed *Anthem Of The Sun* in 1972, with some differences in vocals and editing. However, the original version was used for CD issues. The CD issued as part of the *Golden Road 1965-1973* box set, included three bonus tracks – 'Alligator', 'Caution (Do Not Stop On Tracks)' and 'Feedback' – from their 23 August 1968 Shrine Auditorium gig, and also the studio version of 'Born Cross-Eyed'. The 50th-anniversary edition included a second disc with performances from their 22 October show at the Winterland Ballroom in San Francisco.

A show from February would feature on the 2009 *Road Trips Volume 2 Number 2* release. The two-disc collection features the 14 February show at the Carousel Ballroom in San Francisco: one of the shows recorded as part of the material used in *Anthem Of The Sun*. In January, The Dead had played the Carousel – a venue operated jointly by the management of The Dead, Jefferson Airplane and Quicksilver Messenger Service, in competition with other venues in the city, such as The Avalon and Bill Graham's Fillmore Auditorium. The 14 February gig was, however, its official opening. The artist-led consortium would run the venue – not entirely successfully – for six months before Bill Graham took it over and renamed it the Fillmore West. The first disc includes a sequence of 'Dark Star' into 'China Cat Sunflower', then 'The Eleven' and 'Turn On Your Love Light' – the band's set already starting to take the shape that would become widely known in *Live/Dead*, and there are four bonus tracks from January and early-February, including a six-minute 'Dark Star' from Portland, Oregon on 2 February. Disc two continues the 14 February 14 show – the set dedicated to Neal Cassady who had died just ten days earlier – beginning with an appropriate and lengthy 'That's It For The Other One', rare appearances of 'New Potato Caboose' and 'Born Cross-Eyed', with 'Alligator'/'Caution (Do Not Step On Tracks)' and 'In The Midnight Hour' rounding it up. A bonus disc features material recorded on dates in the Pacific Northwest in January 1968, including the earliest-released live version of 'Dark Star', from Seattle, Washington on 23 January.

Two shows from 23/24 February at Kings Beach Bowl, Kings Beach, California, were released in 2001 in the form of the two-disc set *Dick's Pick's Vol 22*: one on each disc. These recordings, too, were among those made for *Anthem Of The Sun*. While disc one opens with an engaging 'Viola Lee Blues', it's the sequence of four numbers – 'Dark Star', 'China Cat Sunflower', 'The Eleven' and 'Turn On Your Love Light' – that give the clearest indication of The Dead's development into the act that would lay down *Live/Dead* in 1969. The blues songs (there's a version of 'It Hurts Me Too') and covers they made their own, like 'Viola Lee Blues', might be there too, but there are clear signs here of a band that are taking a new and interesting shape. 'Born Cross-Eyed' also features on this disc, blending in to their 'Spanish Jam' piece: The Dead's nod to the track 'Solea' from Miles Davis' *Sketches Of Spain*. Disc two sees 'Alligator' consume 'China Cat Sunflower' and 'The Eleven', before 'Alligator' returns and moves on to 'Caution (Do Not Stop On Tracks)'. The Dead have quickly digested the new material that Hunter has put on the menu.

The Dead would be back at the Carousel on 17 March for a show released as volume six in their *Download Series* in 2005. It's perhaps unsurprising that they'd be regulars at a venue they were invested in. The release again comes from tapes used in the creation of *Anthem Of The Sun*, and features 'Turn On Your Love Light' from the end of their first set, and the complete second set performed that night. 'New Potato Caboose' gets an outing, as does Hunter's recent contribution 'China Cat Sunflower', but the set is easily dominated by a version of 'The Eleven' – again a recent addition to their set involving Hunter – and a version of 'Caution (Do Not Stop On Tracks)' that clocks in at over 20 minutes. If having two drummers in a band at the time seemed unusual,

Hart was certainly no passenger, and he brought a considerable momentum to performances of numbers like this.

The Dead released a single in April 1968. Like their previous singles, it wouldn't trouble the *Billboard* charts. Their record company no doubt hoped that the release – a new track that hadn't featured on their debut album and wasn't scheduled for their forthcoming album – might generate some airplay and some publicity. But the track chosen for the single – 'Dark Star' – would go down in legend as The Dead's most significant work of their entire career. While the studio version of 'Dark Star' was just 2:44 in length, it quickly became the cornerstone of The Dead's lengthy improvised live performances. The original structure would be extended, new passages added, other songs incorporated into it, drum solos added, and other instrumental pieces slotted into it. 'Dark Star' gave the band an open-ended and malleable piece that lent itself to live experimentation. It wasn't the only piece that The Dead extended in live performances – 'Turn On Your Love Light' and 'Dancing In The Street' had been in their setlist for a few years, and then-recent numbers like 'That's It For The Other One' and 'Alligator'/'Caution (Do Not Step On Tracks)' were developing in similar ways, but *Dark Star* gave them a vessel that would both contain and showcase what they could do best, like no other.

Live versions of the track would be key performances on albums like *Live/ Dead* and *Europe '72*. And among collectors of Dead tapes, the inclusion of a version of 'Dark Star' would be seen as an indicator of a likely high-quality performance that night. Live performances would see the track extended, with versions between 20 and 30 minutes long, not uncommon. With many live recordings circulating, fans to this day debate best versions, and discuss and analyse the structure and quality of versions played. Perhaps it was Hunter's zen poetry in the lyrics, perhaps it's even the mysteries and paradoxes implied by the title, or maybe it's the fact that the most circulated versions of the piece were live ones from early in the band's career – the studio version essentially overlooked or at best seen as a demo version – but 'Dark Star' seemed to bring out the best in The Grateful Dead. It would feature regularly in their set up until 1973, occasionally for the rest of the decade, then rarely until the end of the 1980s, then again making occasional appearances until 1994. The single version of 'Dark Star' – along with the single version of 'Born Cross-Eyed' on the B side – appeared on 1977's *What A Long Strange Trip It's Been* compilation of the band's Warner Bros. output.

The band would be back in L.A. for a gig at the Shrine Auditorium: released in 1992 as *Two From The Vault*, the band's second archive release in the early-1990s. Warner Bros. recorded the show on eight-track, but it wasn't able to be used at the time due to recording problems. The record company – wary of letting the band using their then state-of-the-art equipment – sent their own crew to take care of the recording: their inexperience in setting up the microphones for a rock band (especially one with two drummers) soon becoming apparent. However, the problem would be solved decades later using 1990s digital equipment that wasn't available at the time of recording. The release captures The Dead in their prime psychedelic acid-rock glory – the first release that captures them at what would be their late-1960s peak. The first disc's sequence of 'Dark Star' into 'St. Stephen', 'The Eleven' and 'Death Don't Have No Mercy' is absolutely crucial, covering the ground The Dead make their own. The collection is also one for fans of Pigpen, with a lengthy 'Good Morning Little School Girl' and 'Turn On Your Love Light' both represented. But Garcia's tone on 'Death Don't Have No Mercy' and 'Morning Dew' is absolutely perfect, although 'Morning Dew' comes to an abrupt end when the power is cut off due to a curfew.

An expanded 2007 reissue of *Two From The Vault* included the three tracks from the 23 August show at the Shrine, that had been included on the extended CD version of *Anthem Of The Sun*; 'Alligator'/'Caution' (Do Not Step On Tracks)' giving Pigpen fans even more reason to love this release.

The *30 Trips Around The Sun* collection includes the 20 October show from the Greek Theatre in Berkeley, California. It was the second time they'd played a venue that would go on to be one of the band's and their fan's favourites. After lengthy 'Good Morning Little School Girl' and 'Turn On Your Love Light' workouts, a meditative 'Dark Star' leads into a rousing 'St. Stephen' and a raw 'The Eleven'. 'Caution (Do Not Stop On Tracks)' and 'Feedback' close the set.

The band were going through a transition at the time, with Garcia and Lesh expressing frustration with the musical ability of other band members: Pigpen and Weir in particular. The new music demanded more creative playing, and there was a feeling that some members just weren't up to it. Hart and Garcia – at times accompanied by Lesh or Jack Casady from Jefferson Airplane – were playing instrumental sets at the Matrix in San Francisco under the name Mickey And The Hartbeats from October to December, possibly taking exploratory steps in what a Dead without Weir or Pigpen might sound like. Despite this, The Dead continued to play with all members in place throughout, Garcia playing down any possible stripped-down version of The Dead. In fact, rather than jettisoning members, before the year was out, The Dead recruited a new member – Tom Constanten taking up a full-time position from 23 November: the day after his honourable discharge from the Air Force.

1969 – Live and Dead

With *Anthem of the Sun* having cost the record company a considerable amount of time, money and patience, and current work on what would become *Aoxomoxoa* apparently heading the same way, a live album seemed an obvious move for both commercial and artistic reasons. The studio adventures with *Aoxomoxoa* eventually cost the record company in the region of $180,000, so it was agreed that a live album would be recorded to balance the costs while the band were still working in the studio. If *Aoxomoxoa* cost a fortune and lost money, a quickly released live album as a follow up might recoup the balance while capitalising in the band's growing reputation as a live act.

The challenge was to capture the magic of the live shows in full flight, rather than the hints of it they'd given in their last two albums. While the band's playing had evolved – even in recent months with the addition of TC on keyboards – live recording technology was still a new proposition, and The Grateful Dead would have to innovate.

Loading the dice in their favour as much as they could, over the first three months of 1969 they recorded seven nights of home-territory gigs in San Francisco – at the Avalon and the Fillmore West – moving a recording desk into the venues to create the first live rock album recorded on 16-track. The resulting hours of tapes were then edited and produced by the band with Bob Matthews and Betty Cantor, employing skills like those of Teo Macero when compiling a Miles Davis album from hours of session tapes. 'Dark Star' and 'St. Stephen' would come from the show at the Fillmore West on 27 February 1969, 'The Eleven' and 'Turn On Your Love Light' from 26 January 26 at the Avalon, and the final tracks from the Fillmore West on 2 March 1969.

If there's a pinnacle of The Grateful Dead's art, it has to be *Live/Dead*. Emerging from a formless void, 'Dark Star' takes shape like clouds gathering, the elements moving together in a strange synchronisation, to build a structure that seemingly defies mathematics. Each member brings their own distinct contribution. Removed from the whole, each musician could at times be playing different pieces from each other, yet at times they're tighter than any of James Brown's backing bands. As a whole, it shouldn't work, but it does. Effortlessly. It's so beyond the ordinary that other than the instruments being played, at times it's barely recognisable as rock music: closer to the exploratory work of John Coltrane or Miles Davis than it is to Chuck Berry.

They maintain this breathless intensity across the album, the tracks flowing seamlessly to the point that the album itself becomes one complete work. If the 'Dark Star'>'St. Stephen'>'The Eleven' jam is the centrepiece, 'Turn On Your Love Light', 'Death Don't Have No Mercy', 'Feedback' and 'And We Bid You Goodnight' are a perfect continuation. They move the album through different moods, showing the band could effortlessly incorporate not only experimental improvised soundscapes but also R&B, blues and gospel – each with their own specific rigorous discipline – into their work without either diminishing the authenticity of the source material or compromising their unique musical vision. It's hard to believe there are only seven tracks on the album: the music does strange things to the listener's sense of time.

Live/Dead not only set a high watermark for The Dead, it established the live double album as the artistic showcase for any serious band. If the live album had previously been the cheap contractual-obligation album or the quick release between albums to maintain an act's career momentum, *Live/Dead* showed its potential as an artistic vehicle. Where *Live/Dead* led, others followed throughout the 1970s and 1980s, with greater or lesser success. Free from the studio and in an environment of their choosing, bands could express themselves on their own terms. If that meant long jams, so be it. If the singer wanted to unleash his poetry, this was the place. Few managed it as well or as apparently effortlessly as The Grateful Dead did with *Live/Dead*.

With so much live material recorded on 16-track, it was perhaps inevitable that more of it would be released. *Fillmore West 1969: The Complete Recordings* would eventually come out in 2005, featuring most of the original recordings made for *Live/Dead*. There are many highlights, not least the *Live/Dead* version of 'Dark Star' in its original context coming out of 'Mountains Of The Moon'; 'St. Stephen' running into a different version of 'The Eleven', and on to 'Turn On Your Love Light'. And if you like that, there are another three 'Dark Stars' in the set making similar journeys. There are many extraordinary performances, including recent material from *Aoxomoxoa*, some of which wouldn't remain in the set much beyond this era. The ten-disc set was released in a limited edition of 10,000 copies, and needless to say, such a sought-after item now commands a high price. A reissue of these crucial recordings is long overdue.

Some of the *Live/Dead* bonus recordings feature elsewhere in The Dead's discography. The three-CD collection *Fillmore West 1969* collects material that didn't make it onto *Live/Dead*, along with extended versions of 'Feedback' and 'And We Bid You Goodnight'. Unlike the box set, it's more widely available, and it's a fascinating addition to *Live/Dead*. A version of 'That's It For The Other One' featured on the 1999 *So Many Roads (1965-1995)* box set, and material from the January Avalon gigs that produced the *Live/Dead* versions of 'The Eleven' and 'Turn On Your Love Light', can be found on the second disc of the 50th-anniversary edition of *Aoxomoxoa*. Two rehearsal tracks for the 23 January Avalon gig appear on the *Download Series Volume 12* collection as bonus tracks. Meanwhile, the 27 February gig emerged as a four-disc vinyl box set for Record Store Day in 2018, in a limited edition of 9,000 copies. This collection included the *So Many Roads (1965-1995)* version of 'That's It For The Other One', the *Live/Dead* versions of 'Dark Star' and 'St. Stephen', and the *Fillmore West 1969* version of 'Cosmic Charlie'.

Between the *Live/Dead* recordings at the Avalon in January, and the Fillmore West at the end of February and the beginning of March, the band's live activities continued, including two high-profile dates in New York at the Fillmore East on 11/12 February. They'd play two sets each night – early and late – supporting Janis Joplin with her new band on their first East Coast excursion. The first day's two Dead sets were released as the double-CD *Live at the Fillmore East 2-11-69* in 1997: one show on each disc. They were unusual shows in that – despite featuring their usually-lengthy numbers like 'That's It For The Other One', 'Turn On Your Love Light' and 'Dark Star' – they played shorter versions: the band packing as much as they could into the shorter running times due to their support slot. The early show ended with a Pigpen-fronted triple bill of 'I'm A King Bee', 'Turn On Your Love Light' and a version of The Beatles' 'Hey Jude'.

Another February gig emerged as part of the *30 Trips Around The Sun* collection – the show from 22 February at Dream Bowl Vallejo, California: their second of two nights at the venue, over two discs. A fluid first set featured 'Dark Star' (with a slight vocal goof from Garcia) coming out of a crystaline 'Mountains Of The Moon' into 'Cryptical Envelopment/The Other One'; the second set featuring 'St. Stephen' into 'The Eleven', and a rousing 22 minutes of 'Turn On Your Love Light' to close.

Three more 1969 shows recorded between the end of the *Live/Dead* Fillmore West dates and the release of *Aoxomoxoa*, would be issued: two from April and one from May. The first date was from 17 April at Washington University, St. Louis, Missouri, released in 2006 as Volume 12 of the *Download Series*. Opening with 'Hard To Handle', it's again heavy on the *Live/Dead* set, this time featuring the rare Jimmy Reed number 'I Know It's A Sin' in the middle of a two-part 'St. Stephen'. The opening ten minutes of the release weren't recorded on reel-to-reel, and were remastered from a cassette recording. The gig ends abruptly just a couple of minutes into 'Caution (Do Not Stop On Tracks)', as the police ordered the plug to be pulled, as the *St. Louis Post-Dispatch* reported:

> Police in St. Louis County got several calls about midnight, complaining that the amplified beat of the acid-rock group from San Francisco was audible a mile away. About 300 young persons – many in hippie attire – were found grouped around a band shell on the quadrangle, listening to music played to the flashing of psychedelic lights. Police suggested The Grateful Dead stop living it up, and the concert ended.

Perhaps the forces of law and order had picked up the line 'The heat came by and busted me for smiling on a cloudy day' from 'That's It For The Other One'. By way of compensation, two tracks supplement the release: 'The Eleven' and 'Dupree's Diamond Blues', from a rehearsal at the Avalon on 23 January 1969.

The double-disc *Dick's Picks Volume 26* would pick up The Dead's 1969 live adventures by presenting the 26 April Electric Theater, Chicago, Illinois gig – where they shared the bill with Velvet Underground – and the following night's show at Labor Temple, Minneapolis, Minnesota. The 26 April material isn't the complete gig, which is a pity, as the set that night included a cover of Dylan's 'It's All Over Now, Baby Blue', and the astonishing encore of 'Viola Lee Blues' > 'Feedback' > 'What's Become Of The Baby' > 'And We Bid You Goodnight. It was to be a unique performance of 'What's Become Of The Baby', involving the recorded (and not-yet-released) version of the song played through the PA, the band accompanying it with feedback. Whether it was the first time a band would be accompanied by a DJ, is open to debate. What's certain is that as pop-art pioneers, The Dead could match the Velvets: both bands coincidentally originally going by the name The Warlocks. 'Viola Lee Blues' would appear on the *Fallout From The Phil Zone* collection. While a good quality recording of the complete show is easy to source, this show merits an official release in full. The 27 April show is represented completely – 'Turn On Your Love Light' both opening the evening and being the penultimate number before 'Morning Dew' brings the show to a close. The set also included 'Me And My Uncle' and 'Sitting On Top Of The World': an indication of the more country direction the band would move in before the end of the year.

The three-disc set *Road Trips Volume 4 Number 1* chronicled two gigs at the Hollywood Seminole Indian reservation in West Hollywood, Florida, on 23/24 May. The Dead were playing two nights of the three-day Big Rock Pow-Wow festival – one of the many festivals that had started to emerge – alongside other acts, including Johnny Winter and Muddy Waters. Both full shows are included in the release, and while each was perhaps shorter than their regular length, there was still time on the first night to close the show with a version of 'Turn On Your Love Light' that clocked in at over half an hour. They would start the show the following night with a version of the same song that was just a little shorter, almost as if they wanted to continue where they left off. While the first night featured 'Dark Star' > 'St. Stephen' > 'The Eleven', the second night's improvisational centrepiece was 'Alligator' > 'Drums' > 'St. Stephen' > 'Feedback'. Despite facing sound and tuning issues during the shows, the band's playing throughout maintains the high standards of their 1969 performances.

June 1969 would finally see the release of The Grateful Dead's third studio album *Aoxomoxa* – a collection they'd been working on since autumn 1968. Like its predecessor, it had a lengthy gestation; the introduction of 16-track recording ensuring the band felt the need to take full advantage of the then-cutting-edge technology. Early eight-track recordings were scrapped, the band starting again from scratch while investigating possibilities of the new technology; the final collection showing them as comfortable with experimental sounds as with acoustic interpretation of traditional songs. The collection can be seen as a snapshot of the band on the cusp of moving from their experimental phase to the more structured songs they would adopt for *Workingman's Dead* and *American Beauty*.

All eight songs were co-written with Garcia's longtime collaborator Robert Hunter, who would deliver some of the band's most memorable lyrics for decades to come. The only other member to get a writing credit was Phil Lesh, who co-wrote 'St. Stephen'. *Aoxomoxoa* would also be the only studio album

41

to feature Tom Constanten as a full band member following his involvement in *Anthem Of The Sun*, adding distinctive keyboard textures. *Aoxomoxoa* was also one of the first rock albums to feature a Moog synthesizer, it being used to treat Garcia's vocals on 'What's Become Of The Baby' and 'Rosemary'.

Several of the *Aoxomoxoa* tracks would go on to be setlist favourites. 'St. Stephen''s legendary status would be assured by its inclusion on *Live/Dead*. 'China Cat Sunflower' paired with 'I Know You Rider' would be a show staple throughout their career, even featuring in their second last show in 1995. 'Dupree's Diamond Blues' would be a feature of their 1980s shows, while 'Cosmic Charlie' would be played until the mid-1970s. The other tracks wouldn't last long in the setlists – no surprise perhaps for the lengthy electronic escapade that is 'What's Become Of The Baby', but 'Mountains Of The Moon' remains a gem that deserved more of a chance to shine.

In a contemporary review, *Rolling Stone* described *Aoxomoxoa* as 'The work of a magical band'. The reaction of the *New York Times* was mixed, saying: 'One experimental cut which hasn't made it for me yet, otherwise fantastic'. Garcia apparently had reservations about the songs: quoted in manager Rock Scully's book *Living With The Dead* as saying, 'God, we make shitty records'. He and Lesh remixed the album in 1971, stripping it of some of the sonic clutter. The original mix wouldn't get reissued until 2010 due to the master tapes apparently being misplaced.

Some of the pieces abandoned when the band moved to 16-track – 'Clementine Jam', 'Nobody's Spoonful Jam' and 'The Eleven Jam' – would feature on a 2001 CD reissue of the album. Their jazz-informed instrumental styles were closer to their live output, but with the band – in the studio at least – moving in a different direction, there was perhaps a feeling that studio time should be used to create something new rather than just replicate their live sound. While it's a pity they didn't record a live-in-the-studio type album – which may have resulted in a less overproduced album – perhaps it gave them greater incentive to get a definitive recording of their live output.

The CD reissue also included a live take of 'Cosmic Charlie' from the show at the Avalon Ballroom on 25 January 1969 – one of the shows recorded for *Live/Dead* – while the 50th-anniversary deluxe edition featured a second disc of nine tracks recorded live at the January 1969 Avalon shows. It's a strong live collection, featuring some of the lesser-known tracks of this era, such as 'New Potato Caboose' and 'Clementine'.

Following the release of *Aoxomoxoa*, the live schedule continued through the summer, with dates in California and New York. One particularly strange appearance was on the *Playboy After Dark* TV show: hosted by Hugh Hefner in a set echoing the late-1960s aspirational consumerist square male lifestyle his magazine sold. Jerry – bearded and in a poncho – looks a little out of place in a room full of men in polo necks, cravats or bow ties milling around with models. But the version of 'Mountains Of The Moon' performed on an acoustic guitar with TC and Weir, sparkles, and the full-band version of 'St. Stephen' shows how far from the mainstream the band were at the time.

That August, The Dead played Woodstock: one of the genuinely iconic events of the 1960s. With a crowd of 400,000 and a subsequent film and album that made artists like Santana and Joe Cocker stars, it was the moment America's counterculture rose into full view, grasped the moment and gained international visibility. Whether you were part of the counterculture, wanted to be part of it, or completely opposed it, Woodstock was the turning point where it could no longer be ignored, and the artists who took to the stage were at the centre of it. Except for The Grateful Dead, who again stepped up at the key moment and blew it.

The band's set was held back until Owsley had the electrics set up to his satisfaction, and they eventually took to the stage at 10.30 p.m. The waiting, the muddy conditions, the lack of food and facilities, and the rain put the band – already high as kites – in a bad place, especially when they realised the wet stage and Owsley's tinkering with the electrics left them at serious risk of electrocution. Garcia told *Jazz & Pop* magazine:

We played such a bad set at Woodstock. The weekend was great, but our set was terrible. We were all pretty smashed, and it was at night. Like, we knew there were a half million people out there, but we couldn't see one of them. There were about a hundred people on stage with us, and everyone was scared that it was gonna collapse. On top of that, it was raining or wet, so that every time we touched our guitars, we'd get these electrical shocks. Blue sparks were flying out of our guitars.

After an introduction of 'One of the best fuckin' rock groups in the world, The Grateful Dead!', it was downhill all the way. A ragged and hesitant 'St. Stephen' opened the set and was abandoned before it was completed, the band quickly moving on to 'Mama Tried'. They could probably play the punchy Merle Haggard western number in their sleep, but even here, the vocals wandered off track.

There's an attempt at 'High Times', but the gremlins resume their work and a ten-minute pause follows. Band members speak aimlessly: Ken Babbs rambles into a mic, and Country Joe makes a public service announcement about dubious drugs. The massive audience gets to experience the joy of a lengthy mid-set soundcheck and technical intervention in an attempt to salvage the stage setup before it either collapses entirely or one of the band gets fried. When the band resume playing, 'Dark Star' gives the audience some idea of just how good The Dead can be. It's by no means exceptional, but it does move in the right direction, and is probably the highlight of the 90-minute set before resolving into 'High Times': this time without a pause.

With their collective backs to the wall, Pigpen is called upon to end the set on a high with 'Turn On Your Love Light', but as the song begins, another voice intervenes: a powerfully-stoned audience member babbling incoherently into a stage mic, about the Atlantic Ocean, and the Pacific ocean at the 'third coast'. It's a strange spontaneous moment of weirdness, and he has his moment in the spotlight before being led off. '...Love Light' goes on for almost 40 minutes, and it's more a well-drilled performance than a groundbreaking one, although it does have some quality moments.

They managed just five songs before the amps finally gave up the ghost. For one of the greatest live bands of their generation, Woodstock was a disaster, as Bob Weir told *Rolling Stone*: 'Some people made their careers at Woodstock, but we've spent about 20 years making up for it. It was probably the worst set we've ever performed. And to have performed it in front of a crowd that size, was not an altogether fulfilling experience'.

Needless to say, The Grateful Dead would not feature in the era-defining film or soundtrack album. Jerry does make a brief blink-and-you'll-miss-him cameo, but while Woodstock may have been the epicentre of the late-1960s hippie culture, it was to be a gig The Dead would rather have forgotten. Decades later, the Woodstock version of 'Dark Star' would surface on the *Woodstock 50th Anniversary Collection* three-CD set; the band's complete set on two discs of the *Woodstock Definitive 50th Anniversary Archive* 38-CD set.

Garcia had been inspired to learn to play the pedal steel guitar in 1969, and despite initial difficulties, he quickly rose to the challenge and mastered it. Wanting to take his playing further, he formed a band with David Nelson (who'd played with Garcia in his bluegrass days) and John 'Marmaduke' Dawson. The band – New Riders Of The Purple Sage (NRPS) – explored a more country-rock field than The Dead, becoming a regular opening act on Dead shows, often including other members of the band as well as Garcia.

Live August 1969 NRPS performances that Owsley captured on tape, were released in 2020 as the box set *Dawn Of The New Riders Of The Purple Sage*: part of the *Bear's Sonic Journals* series produced by the Owsley Stanley Foundation. Two discs capture a show from 1 August 1969 at Bear's Lair in Berkeley; the band featuring Dawson, Nelson, Garcia, Mickey Hart and Dead sound engineer Bob Matthews on bass. The third disc – from 28 August at the Family Dog at the Great Highway in San Francisco – features an appearance by Bobby 'Ace' Weir, as he's credited, on guitar and vocals on a number of songs, including 'Me And My Uncle' and 'Mama Tried'.

In October, Garcia's pedal-steel-playing got its most recognised outing when he helped out fellow Woodstock veterans Crosby, Stills, Nash & Young by playing on the Graham-Nash-written track 'Teach Your Children'. Returning the favour, CSNY helped The Dead develop their vocal harmonies, which would have a significant impact on their studio recordings the next year.

A far stronger performance than The Dead mustered at Woodstock, was released in 2000, with *Dick's Picks Volume 16* presenting the 8 November Fillmore Auditorium show. The complete show is over three discs, the second a highlight with a sublime 'Dark Star' in three parts, interspersed with 'The Other One' and an instrumental 'Uncle John's Band' jam, the final part moving into 'St. Stephen' and 'The Eleven'. As well as 'Uncle John's Band', the set features a total of six songs of the eight on their forthcoming *Workingman's Dead* album: only 'New Speedway Boogie' and 'Black Peter' are absent. There's also a cover of Merle Haggard's 'Mama Tried', and an early version of 'Playing In The Band' under its original title 'The Main Ten'. *Dick's Picks Volume 16* adds a 25-minute version of 'Turn On Your Love Light' from the previous night's show at the venue. With the show taking place the week *Live/ Dead* was released, it gives a clear indication of not only how far the band has come in the space of a few months but of the more country-orientated direction they'd shortly be pursuing.

The year, and the decade, would end on a troubled note, with the notorious Altamont Free Festival on 6 December 1969. A crowd of 300,000, attended an event originally intended to be a West Coast Woodstock-style event marking the conclusion of The Rolling Stones' US tour and including the cream of local bands. It would ultimately be remembered for violence, disorder, and the killing of an audience member. The 1970 documentary *Gimme Shelter* covered the buildup, the event and its aftermath. Scheduled to play after Crosby, Stills, Nash & Young and before the Stones, The Grateful Dead pulled out. Garcia and Lesh are featured briefly in the film, arriving at the scene by helicopter to be told by Santana drummer Michael Shrieve that a Hells Angel had knocked Jefferson Airplane's Marty Balin unconscious on stage. Blame would be shared between The Rolling Stones for blowing the opportunity for it to be held at Golden Gate Park; Hells Angels for responding with brutality to their bikes being threatened, and The Dead's management for settling on an inappropriate venue at short notice without the facilities or security for a massive crowd. Altamont would go down in history as the event that finally marked the dark and bloody end of the optimistic spirit of the 1960s.

Dave's Picks Volume 10 was recorded on 12 December – a matter of days after Altamont – at the Thelma in Los Angeles. Again, it captures the band in the days between *Live/Dead* and *Workingman's Dead*, the first set seeing 'Cumberland Blues' and 'Black Peter' rubbing shoulders with a 30-minute plus version of 'Love Light'. 'Casey Jones', 'High Time' and 'Dire Wolf' appear in the second set, along with a version of 'Uncle John's Band' that moves into 'He Was A Friend Of Mine'. 'Alligator', 'Caution (Do Not Stop On Tracks)', 'Feedback' and the closing 'And We Bid You Goodnight' present primal Dead material that featured on *Live/Dead*. It's a fascinating document of a band in transition, moving from folk and blues covers to psychedelic rock to a more country-flavoured output, all in the course of one show. A fourth bonus disc covers much of the show from the previous night at the same venue, with a sequence of 'Dark Star', 'St. Stephen', 'The Eleven' and 'Cumberland Blues' from the first set, and a lengthy 'That's It For The Other One' and 'Cosmic Charlie' from the second. The Dead were growing at speed into something unique.

1970 – High Time

The Dead had much to draw on following the highs and lows of 1969. They were older and wiser, they'd worked on their craft, and releasing *Live/Dead* had played to their strengths as a live band. Outside their touring and recording, the members had all moved from San Francisco and communal living, to separate homes in more rural areas. It may have felt like they were personally maturing and settling down, starting afresh. Their music was changing too, with the new Garcia/Hunter songs entering the set, settling on a country-rock sound that was a natural fit. The songs were more crafted and polished and less about being open-ended platforms for musical exploration. They already looked like cowboys, so they might as well sound like them too. Garcia's background in bluegrass and folk would feed into the new sound, and Weir was a natural for these songs and the cover versions they were now featuring regularly.

The fans held their 1970 shows in high regard, with many circulating on tape before their eventual release as high-quality recordings. Their many dates at friendly venues like the Fillmores and a number of radio broadcasts of performances, helped ensure there was a supply of performances on tape to meet the demand from The Deadheads. Some would appear as bootlegs, and even at this point in the 21st century, the market for these seems to remain, with a huge number of unauthorised and lesser-quality CDs available.

In 1970, the band released two studio albums – that many would regard as the band's finest studio work – and perform over 140 live shows. They'd often play two shows on the same day, each show featuring different material. With their live performances being of such a high standard, it's little surprise that so many of them have been released. Owsley's decision to record the band live as often as he could, continues to pay dividends decades later, by casting light on a band at the peak of their game.

Following a New Year's Eve show in Boston – the final time they'd play a show bringing in the new year away from home – in January, they played in New York, followed by dates around the West Coast and Hawaii, before returning for a notorious engagement in New Orleans.

In February, the film *Zabriskie Point* was released; The Dead's involvement in film soundtrack being another development for the band. It wasn't the first time they'd been involved in cinema (they made a brief appearance in 1968's San-Francisco-set *Petulia*), but this time, rather than just adding a bit of local colour, they'd be providing some of the soundtrack of *Zabriskie Point*: a million-dollar meditation on the US counterculture by auteur Michelangelo Antonioni. Alongside Pink Floyd, The Rolling Stones and John Fahey, an excerpt from The Dead's 'Dark Star' was used in a memorable scene, while Garcia provided a guitar piece called 'Love Theme'. Garcia, a major cinephile, was contacted by the director and jumped at the chance to get involved. He travelled to L.A., and sitting in the MGM studio with the section of the film he was soundtracking playing on a loop, recorded an improvised piece. Over the space of a couple of hours, he recorded a few takes, two of which were edited together for inclusion in the movie. An extended version of the soundtrack released as a two-CD set features extra takes of Garcia's piece. Despite winning credit for its cinematography, the film proved to be a critical and commercial failure, but it did at least have an excellent soundtrack.

Released in 2019, their early-January shows at the Fillmore East in New York appear on *Dave's Picks Volume 30*. Over four discs (including a bonus disc), the release covers the two 2 January performances, with bonus tracks from the following night at the venue. The 2 January gig clearly shows the band in transition from their late-1960s psychedelic rock to more structured songwriting. Over the course of both shows, they present a mix of their more exploratory work – the late show includes a full 'Dark Star'>'St. Stephen'>'The Eleven'>'Love Light' sequence that clocks in at over an hour and a quarter – as well as their more recent acoustic Americana-flavoured work. Many of the *Workingman's Dead* tracks feature, as well as a cover of 'Me And My Uncle', and the rarely-played 'Mason's Children'. The version of 'Mason's Children' recorded here would also appear on the *Fallout From The Phil Zone* compilation.

They were soon back on the West Coast for a series of shows, including one at Springer's Inn, Portland, Oregon, on 18 January, released as *Volume 2* of the *Download Series*. This release is an interesting one, as it only features 'Love Light' from their *Live/Dead* era, and 'Black Peter' from their forthcoming *Workingman's Dead*. The once-elusive 'Mason's Children' gets an airing, as does 'China Cat Sunflower'. But the highlights on this collection are the cover versions, particularly the fourteen-minute take of 'Dancing In The Street'. There's also 'Big Boss Man', 'Cold Rain And Snow' and 'I Know You Rider', which, along with 'Dancing In The Street', are flashbacks to their earlier years in the ballrooms and bars of the Bay Area. These, along with Pigpen-favourite 'Good Lovin'', are played here with the confidence of a band with a few more years under their belt, but with no less enthusiasm.

Two shows from Hawaii on 23/24 January feature on *Dave's Picks Volume 19*, recorded at the Honolulu Civic Arena. Disc one and two feature the first night, with predominantly shorter numbers until they move into 'Good Lovin'' and 'The Other One'. Disc Two features the subsequent 'Dark Star'>'St. Stephen', and an almost forty-minute run-through of 'Love Light'. The band play a fine balancing act between their more exploratory work and the more-direct newer work. While the two versions of 'Black Peter' on this collection are over eight minutes long, it's a very different creature from the lengthy beasts they conjure elsewhere in the set. That the band are able to handle the storming and the extravagant, as well as the reflective and the understated, is a measure of their strength. The version of 'Mason's Children' played on the second night also appears as a bonus track on the reissue of *Workingman's Dead*. This show would be the final release to feature TC on keyboards.

On 30 and 31 January, they were scheduled to play two nights in New Orleans with Fleetwood Mac. It marked the end of TC's time with The Dead, but more significantly, it marked a high-profile drugs bust that would be remembered in the lyrics of 'Truckin'' – a song that would appear on their second 1970 studio release *American Beauty*, and go on to be something of an anthem for the band. Although eventually, no charges were forthcoming, the band quickly added a benefit gig to their schedule to help cover their bail.

A gig from 4 February, back in California a couple of days later, would be released in 2005 as *Download Series: Family Dog at the Great Highway*; three tracks – 'Hard To Handle', 'China Cat Sunflower' and 'I Know You Rider' – having been broadcast on a PBS TV special and broadcast around the country later in the year. The gig itself was arranged specially for the broadcast with an invited audience, and also featured performances from Jefferson Airplane and Santana. Members of the three bands, including Garcia, jammed together at the end of the show.

The Dead's set was roughly an hour long, each act playing a similar time for the benefit of broadcast. There's little space for any extended jamming in the performance, but the version of 'St. Stephen'>'Not Fade Away'>'St. Stephen'>'The Midnight Hour' gives more than a flavour of what they could do. The relatively-short running time is boosted with three bonus tracks – 'In The Midnight Hour' recorded at San Francisco's Winterland Ballroom on 5 October 1970, and 'Monkey And The Engineer' and 'Good Lovin'' from the New Year's Eve show, also at Winterland. The TV show, featuring the three Grateful Dead numbers and the closing jam, was released commercially as *A Night At The Family Dog*, and it's a real treat to see such sharp footage of the band from this era, with Pigpen at the mic and Garcia in a plaid shirt playing a Stratocaster.

On 11, 13 and 14 February, they were back in New York for a series of shows at the Fillmore East that would become legendary. The Dead were on a bill that included Love and the Allman Brothers, playing two sets a night. With high-quality recordings available, the shows were among those that were circulated widely on tape among fans in the 1970s and beyond as evidence of the band's genius. Two releases document these shows – the *Bear's Choice* album released in 1973 and the *Dick's Picks Volume 4* collection. A 14-minute section of the 'Dark Star' from the 13 February performance is incorporated into the *Grayfolded* collaboration the band did with John Oswald using his Plunderphonics process.

With *Bear's Choice* – or to use its official name: *History Of The Grateful Dead Volume One (Bear's Choice)* – producer Owsley (by the time the album was compiled, using the nickname Bear to distance himself from his LSD-manufacturing notoriety that resulted in a prison sentence following the New Orleans bust) selected his favourites, putting the spotlight on Pigpen, who died while the album was in production. With an acoustic side and an electric side, *Bear's Choice* takes a more song-based approach to the material, an 18-minute

'Smokestack Lightning' being the only extended piece. On *Bear's Choice*, 'Katie Mae', 'Wake Up Little Susie', 'Black Peter' and 'Smokestack Lightning' came from the 13 February show, while 'Dark Hollow', 'I've Been All Around This World' and 'Hard To Handle' came from the following day. A version of 'Good Lovin'' from the 13 February show was added to the album's 2001 CD reissue. Pigpen's solo acoustic performance of 'Katie Mae' is exceptional, and you can't help but wish he'd recorded more like that. While a change of record company in the 1970s meant there was no Volume Two of *The History Of The Grateful Dead*, a few decades later, things would be very different.

The 1996 release *Dick's Picks Volume 4* features most of the show from 14 February, excluding any tracks that appear on *Bear's Choice*. Disc one begins with the show opener 'Casey Jones', followed by the first half of the final set, before the almost 30-minute 'Dark Star' from the previous night. This sequence continues over the entire second disc with 'The Other One'>'Love Light' clocking in at around 30 minutes each, while disc three returns to the 14th for the remainder of the final set and the encore. In the sleeve notes for *Dick's Picks Volume 4*, Owsley comments: 'The suits have their rules about copyright and such. I would like to be able to present these shows the way they were, but I guess we must make do with what we have'. *Dick's Picks Volume 4* marked the first time the track 'Mason's Children' got an official release. Debuted in mid-December 1969, it was only played live just over a dozen times in total. The song – which according to Hunter was an oblique reference to Altamont – also features on *Dave's Picks Volume 19*, *Dave's Picks Volume 30*, *Fallout From The Phil Zone* and *Download Series Volume 2*.

Hopefully, at some point, a fuller document of the February Fillmore East shows will emerge. It's ripe for a multidisc box set. A high-quality recording of 11 February does circulate, where The Dead are joined by Duane and Gregg Allman, Butch Trucks from the Allmans, and Mick Fleetwood, Danny Kirwin and Peter Green from Fleetwood Mac, in a lengthy 'Dark Star'>'Spanish Jam'>'Love Light'.

The Fillmore East concerts established a link between The Dead and the Allman's, both working in similar ways albeit in different styles. Owsley recorded the Allman's performances at the Fillmore, and these were later released in 1996 as a single disc, before being reissued in 2018 as a more complete set under the title *Bear's Sonic Journals: Fillmore East, February 1970*. The Allman Brothers Band recorded the live album *At Fillmore East* the following year: a collection that established their reputation in a similar way to how *Live/Dead* did for The Grateful Dead.

Later in February, they returned to the Pacific High studio where they'd spent so much time and money working on *Aoxomoxoa*. This time, however, the recording process would be a quick one, with *Workingman's Dead* being recorded in a matter of days rather than months. The band had been playing the songs live for several of months, and the quality of the material needed no discussion. With its emphasis on songwriting rather than instrumentation or production, getting the new songs on tape was – for once – straightforward. The work they'd done on their vocals was immediately evident, and while the quality of their musicianship remained present, their newfound maturity and confidence meant there was no need for novelty or showboating. Where studio experimentation might've previously been the order of the day, the only new sound being brought in was Garcia's pedal steel guitar, which he'd only been playing for just over a year and had already mastered. The album was released in June, reached the *Billboard* top-30, and was named the *Rolling Stone* Album of the Year. *Workingman's Dead* and the thematically-similar *American Beauty* are probably The Dead's most enduring studio releases, and arguably their best. The song quality is exceptional, reflecting a change of tone from the heady optimism of the preceding decade – 'New Speedway Boogie' in particular expressing Hunter's reflection on events at Altamont.

Workingman's Dead got a deluxe CD reissue in 2001, with eight bonus tracks including an alternate mix of 'New Speedway Boogie'. There are also live versions of 'Dire Wolf' from 1969, and versions of 'Black Peter', 'Easy Wind', 'Cumberland Blues', 'Mason's Children' and 'Uncle John's Band' from 1970 concerts. The version of 'Mason's Children' here also appears on *Dave's Pick's Volume 19*. A 2020 50th-anniversary edition of the album includes a live show from 21 February 1971 recorded at the Capitol Theatre, Port Chester, New York, over two discs. A studio outtake of 'Mason's Children' from the recordings, appeared on the *So Many Roads (1965-1995)* box set.

Crosby, Stills, Nash & Young's *Déjà Vu* album was released in March, and the collection became one of the defining albums of that era. *Teach Your Children* – featuring Garcia's pedal-steel-playing at its heart – became a top-20 single in the USA: one of the most significant commercially successful songs to feature a Grateful Dead member.

A four-night run at the Fillmore West from 9-12 April produced a significant release, albeit one by the unusual support act. Promoter Bill Graham enjoyed bringing interesting support acts to his shows, and for these shows, Miles Davis was The Dead's support. Davis had just released *Bitches Brew* – one of the cornerstones of his career and a powerful, inspired work that redefined both the limits of jazz and the potential of rock. It was one of his earliest performances at a rock venue, but the lengthy set – largely improvised and moving between pieces without break – was something The Dead's audience could understand. Davis commented in his autobiography: 'I played a little something like *Sketches of Spain* and then went into the *Bitches Brew* shit, and that really blew them out'. The Dead were fans of Davis: their 'Spanish Jam' borrowed from the Miles Davis and Gil Evans *Sketches of* Spain album. In his autobiography, Lesh remembered, 'Leaning over the amps with my jaw hanging agape, thinking 'How can we possibly play after this?'. We should just go home and try to digest this unbelievable shit ... In some ways, it was similar to what we were trying to do in our free jamming, but ever so much more dense with ideas'.

Davis' 10 April performance was released in 1973 as the double album *Black Beauty: Miles Davis At Fillmore West*. One track by The Dead – recorded on 12 April – eventually appeared on their *Fallout From The Phil Zone* collection.

The *30 Trips Around The Sun collection* features a show from 15 April at the Winterland, where The Dead performed with Jefferson Airplane and Quicksilver Messenger Service. The show opens with 'Cold Rain And Snow' and an early 'China Cat Sunflower'>'I Know You Rider' sequence, before some technical difficulties derail a cover of 'Mama Tried'. The interesting piece comes on the second disc, where, following 'Cryptical Envelopment' and 'Drums', there's a five-minute jam before 'The Other One' featuring a guest guitarist and keyboard player. There's a lot of speculation about who's playing, but it's an incredible high-energy piece – perhaps not a million miles from Santana's *Soul Sacrifice* – where everything falls together perfectly, even if it's being composed on the spot. 'Candyman' from this release featured as a bonus track on the 2001 re-issue *American Beauty*.

An unusual set from 18 April emerged in 2013: a CD and double vinyl release titled *Family Dog at the Great Highway, San Francisco, CA 4/18/70*. The tape was one that hadn't previously circulated among fans, having belonged to Garcia's ex-wife Carolyn 'Mountain Girl' Garcia, who passed them on to the band's management. It had been a stealth gig – the show billed as 'Mickey Hart And His Heartbeats' and 'Bobby Ace And His Cards From The Bottom Of The Deck' rather than The Dead. They performed acoustic and electric numbers; members of the New Riders Of The Purple Sage joining them on some tracks. The highlight, though, are six tracks performed by Pigpen solo on acoustic guitar, including four Lightnin' Hopkins numbers.

Released in 1997, *Dick's Picks Volume 8* records the band's 2 May outing at Harpur College, Binghampton, New York. It was the second of a series of shows they'd play in a new format, under the title *An Evening With The Grateful Dead*, featuring The New Riders Of The Purple Sage and three sets by The Dead: one acoustic and two electric. These shows – apart from showing the band could easily play for over three hours – showcased the variety of the material they had at their command and their expertise in presenting it. The band could swing sweetly in acoustic mode and blaze through new dimensions in their electric sets, all in the space of one night.

For this show, the acoustic set included several traditional numbers – opening with 'Don't Ease Me In' and 'I Know You Rider', and playing 'Deep Elem Blues' and 'Cold Jordan' – and material from *Workingman's Dead* like 'Uncle John's Band', 'Cumberland Blues' and 'Dire Wolf', along with 'Black Peter', 'Friend Of The Devil' and 'Candyman' from the soon-to-be-recorded *American Beauty*. They could play the traditional numbers with the authority of a band who had made them their own, and their own songs could stand shoulder-to-shoulder with them as equals in their timeless appeal.

The second set absolutely takes no prisoners. While the start of 'St. Stephen' is missing, it moves via 'Cryptical Envelopment' and 'Drums' to an absolutely monster version of 'The Other One', into a joyful 'Cosmic Charlie'. 'Good Lovin'' is an intense rendition, with members seemingly trying to outdo each other while maintaining the high-energy groove. Their heavy soul comes to the foreground with covers of James Brown's 'It's A Man's Man's Man's World' and Martha And The Vandellas' 'Dancing In The Street'. The Dead's take on these numbers here is a lesson in performing a cover version – taking the well-known songs and reinventing them for their own purpose, while respecting the original material, developing the song and making it into something new that remains recognisable as the classic it is.

After a break, there's an appropriately apocalyptic 'Morning Dew' to open the third set, into a 'Viola Lee Blues' that builds to an electric 'Feedback' jam, finishing on a heartfelt 'And We Bid You Goodnight' rising from the ashes. It's quite a show, and it was a personal favourite in the days of tape trading, and remains, to these ears at least, one of their absolute best. Missing from the release – presumably to fit on a three-disc set – is a version of 'Cold Rain And Snow' from the second set, which circulates on tape, as does the New Riders Of The Purple Sage set, which features Weir and Garcia on five numbers including Dead favourites 'Mama Tried', 'Me And My Uncle', and The Band's 'The Weight'. Not that it in any way diminishes the power of this release.

Continuing their East Coast dates, *Road Trips Volume 3 Number 3* features their early and late 15 May shows at the Fillmore East, New York. Released in 2010, the set was intended to mark the 40th anniversary of *Workingman's Dead*, and features that album's songs with the exception of 'High Time'. Like *Dick's Picks Volume 8*, there are acoustic and electric sets from both shows. Disc one covers (most of) the first show – acoustic and electric – ranging from covers of 'Ain't It Crazy' and 'Long Black Limousine', to the electric 'St. Stephen'>'The Other One'. Disc two and three cover the late show – its acoustic set including covers of the traditional 'Ballad Of Casey Jones', 'Silver Threads And Golden Needles', two Lightnin' Hopkins numbers, and their own 'Friend Of The Devil' and 'Uncle John's Band'.

The electric set showed the range of material they could offer, with 'Morning Dew', 'Good Lovin'' and a sequence of 'Dark Star'>'St. Stephen'>'Not Fade Away'>'Love Light'. If you'd gone to both shows, you'd have had more than your money's worth. A bonus fourth disc collects the missing early show acoustic-set numbers, some cut from the early and late electric sets, and four bonus tracks from the previous night's show in Missouri.

Later in May, The Dead made their first trip to Europe. Unlike later tours, this was more a one-off guerrilla raid rather than an organised tour, headlining the Hollywood Festival in Newcastle-Under-Lyme in Staffordshire. Other acts on the bill over the rainy English weekend, included Black Sabbath, Free and Ginger Baker's Air Force. But the appearance by The Dead in full 1970 mode – presenting the full range of more accessible songs along with a full serving of 'Dark Star'>'St. Stephen'>'Not Fade Away'>'Love Light' – gave notice that they lived up to their mythic reputation, and they were greeted favourably by both music press and audience when they returned. Footage of the band in England and performing at the festival, can be seen on 2017's *Long Strange Trip* documentary.

In June and July, the band undertook one of their stranger adventures, touring Canada by train alongside The Band, Janis Joplin and others. Billed as The Transcontinental Pop Festival, dates were planned in Montreal, Toronto, Winnipeg, Calgary and Vancouver. By the time they set out, Montreal and Vancouver were cancelled, and there would only be three dates. Travelling between the shows by train, the musicians indulged in lengthy spontaneous jam sessions, also drinking so much that the train had to stop on its way to Winnipeg so the entire stock of a local store could be purchased. Billy Kreutzmann recalled: 'With a train full of musicians, everyone threw in some money and had the managers lead an expedition to go into the store and clean it out. We bought every last bottle in the store'.

A planned film was shot during the tour, but with the promoters losing so much money on the venture, it was cancelled; the footage eventually released as *Festival Express* in 2003. Ironically, the film made more money than the promoters had lost putting on the shows. There's some wonderful footage of The Dead, both performing on stage – songs including 'Don't Ease Me In', 'Hard To Handle' and 'New Speedway Boogie' – and in more informal footage on the train.

The tour included some of the final performance's of Janis Joplin: a long-time associate of the band (and one-time lover of Pigpen) who died on 4 October from a drugs overdose. Robert Hunter wrote *Bird Song* inspired by her, the song eventually appearing on Garcia's 1972 solo album.

October 1970 saw the appearance of the *Vintage Dead* album, recorded at the Avalon in 1966 and discussed earlier. The album wasn't approved by The Dead, but the collection of cover versions could be released legally by an L.A. label. For anyone listening to it in 1970, it must've indicated how far the band had come over the four-year period between its recording and its release.

That autumn, the band were back in the studio, this time at Wally Heider's, and if *Workingman's Dead* showed The Dead could excel in the studio, *American Beauty* showed it wasn't a one-off. Like its predecessor, the focus was on the songwriting, with many of the album's songs amongst their best-known and most-loved compositions. Like *Workingman's Dead*, there's not a substandard song anywhere, and there are so many strong numbers that it's really not possible to select which is the best. 'Ripple', with its lyrics close to zen poetry? 'Brokedown Palace' or 'Attics Of My Life': both reflective and powerful? Or 'Operator'?: Pigpen's only solo writing credit, and the only song on the album not involving Robert Hunter. Hunter was by now at the top of his game, later recalling how during the band's time in London earlier that year, he wrote 'Ripple', 'Brokedown Palace', and 'To Lay Me Down' (which would feature on Garcia's 1972 solo album) all on the same day. 'Box Of Rain' – not only the album's opening number, but also the first song to feature Phil Lesh on vocals – carried more emotional baggage than most, Lesh having co-written it with Hunter, about his then-terminally-ill father. It would also be the final song the band performed live before the death of Jerry Garcia. Elsewhere on the album, 'Truckin'' – with its mention of their New Orleans bust – would become one of their live anthems for the rest of their career.

The band's crew were mostly working on tour with other acts at the time, allowing band members space to concentrate on the recording without the usual distractions. The album was again recorded without complications; the basic tracks laid down in a matter of days.

Like *Workingman's Dead*, *American Beauty* reached the *Billboard* top-30. The album was reissued on CD in 2001 with bonus tracks, including single edits of 'Truckin'' and 'Ripple', a live version of 'Friend Of The Devil' from the May 1970 show that appears on *Road Trips Volume 3 Number 3*, 'Candyman' from the 1970 *30 Trips Around The Sun* release, 'Till The Morning Comes' from Winterland on 4 October, 'Attics Of My Life' from 6 June at the Fillmore, and 'Truckin'' from 26 December at Legion Stadium, El Monte, California. A studio outtake of 'To Lay Me Down' recorded in summer 1970, was released on the *So Many Roads (1965-1995)* box set in 1999.

Though more folky and less of a country-themed work, Garcia's pedal-steel-playing again gave the album much of its flavour. The album featured appearances from a number of Dead associates, including Dave Torbert and David Nelson from New Riders Of The Purple Sage: Nelson playing the only guitar solo on the album, in 'Box Of Rain'. Torbert played bass on this track, freeing Lesh to play acoustic guitar. Also present are Howard Wales, who added organ and piano, keyboard player Ned Lagin who played piano on 'Candyman', and mandolin player David Grisman who would go on to be a close musical associate of Garcia.

This spirit of collaboration was widespread at Wally Heider's studio in late-1970, where many of the Bay Area's musicians were working at the same time as The Dead. David Crosby was recording his solo album *If Only I Could Remember My Name*, while members of Jefferson Airplane were working on Paul Kantner's *Blows Against The Empire* album: the first album to use the Jefferson Starship credit. Members of Santana, CSNY and others were all part of the scene: a constantly-changing multi-membered loose musical conglomerate dubbed The Planet Earth Rock 'n' Roll Orchestra. Members would hang out together and play, the sessions all being recorded. Crosby's album featured significant contributions from Garcia, Lesh, Kreutzmann, Hart and many others. Garcia helped arrange and produce the album, playing guitar, pedal steel, contributing vocals, and also earning a writing credit on the song 'What Are Their Names'. This and other albums with their roots in these sessions would be released in 1971; *Blows Against The Empire* being released in November 1970.

The Dead closed 1970 on home soil at Winterland in San Francisco. Three tracks from this show have been released, two – 'Monkey And The Engineer' and a 15-minute 'Good Lovin'' – are bonus tracks on The Grateful Dead *Download Series: Family Dog At The Great Highway* set, while 'Easy Wind' appears on the bonus disc *New Year's Eves At Winterland* included with the 2003 *The Closing Of Winterland* collection.

1971 – Skulls 'n' Roses

The start of 1971 saw Garcia in the studio, adding finishing touches to the NRPS debut album. They'd been working on it since December, and it would be the only studio album they'd record with Garcia as a member. Mickey Hart played drums and percussion on two tracks, while Lesh was credited with 'executive production'. The ten songs were all Dawson originals. His work with the NRPS would set the tone for the musical restlessness that Garcia displayed for the rest of his career – While The Grateful Dead would always be his main gig, he'd constantly be working on side projects to try out new ideas, performing in different styles from jazz to bluegrass ,and working on new techniques. He was a regular at weekly jam sessions at the Matrix Club in San Francisco, playing with musicians including keyboard player Howard Wales, with whom he would record an album that was released later in 1971. *Hooteroll?* was an instrumental jazz-rock work that flowed from the musical rapport they'd developed in their jamming, Garcia collaborators Bill Vitt and John Kahn on drums and bass. Wales had appeared on *American Beauty,* but the work on *Hooteroll?* was far removed from those laid-back country-rock-influenced tracks.

A run of six February shows at the Capitol Theater, Port Chester, New York, were recorded on multitrack with the possibility of making a new live album from the tapes. A number of new Garcia/Hunter songs made their debut over these gigs, including 'Bertha', 'Loser', 'Wharf Rat', 'Greatest Story Ever Told' and 'Playing In The Band'. Some of these new songs would appear on the *Skull And Roses* double album, recorded at West Coast venues in March and April, and released in October. The shows at Port Chester had another strange feature, as the nearby university were using them as the basis for psychological experiments into extrasensory perception. The audience would be shown a selection of shapes on a screen behind the band and told to focus on them, while a subject in a laboratory was monitored to see if they received the message. The 18 February 1971 show was released as a bonus with the 50th-anniversary edition of *American Beauty* in October 2020. It would be the last gig Mickey Hart would play with the band for a number of years.

The following night's show of 19 February was the first to be released, coming out as *Three From The Vault* in 2007. That night, they played without Mickey Hart for the first time. He decided to leave, after his father Lenny Hart – who'd been hired to manage the band and guide them out of the financial difficulties they'd found themselves in following the cost of *Anthem Of The Sun, Aoxomoxoa* and an ill-fated concert venue investment – embezzled around $150,000 from the band over his time in charge of their affairs. Hart would return some years later, but in the meantime, the band would have Kreutzmann on his own behind the drum kit. That Kreutzmann was able to play the set without any obvious elements missing, is a credit to his ability.

'Deal' and 'Bird Song' made their debut at this show, 'Bird Song' being a tribute to Janis Joplin by Hunter and Garcia. A longtime band associate and key figure of the San Francisco music scene, Joplin died of a drug overdose in October 1970, just months after the Festival Express tour with The Dead, which would be among her final performances. The show concentrated on their more song-based output, and while 'Smokestack Lightning' in the first set and the second-set closer 'Good Lovin'' were certainly lengthy, their main vehicle for extended improvisation was 'The Other One' moving into 'Wharf Rat'. Their show – with two sets, and the main improvisation section in the middle of the second – was taking the shape that it would have for the rest of their career. 'Wharf Rat' would often find its place, bringing some mellow reflection after a lively exploration of the outer limits.

The release of *Three From The Vault* had originally been scheduled for 1993, but it was cancelled, finally emerging 14 years later. The 21 February show at the Capitol Theatre in Port Chester, New York, was released as a bonus show with the 50th-anniversary edition of *Workingman's Dead*. The NRPS opened for The Dead during this run of shows, and the 1986-released album *Vintage NRPS* consisted of tracks featuring Garcia on pedal steel, recorded on 21 and 23 February.

A show from 18 March appeared on the *30 Trips Around The Sun* box set, recorded at the Fox Theatre, St, Louis, Missouri. With new songs settling in to the set, and the previous year's material beginning to take on a new status, the music was subtly changing. The songs from the last year were becoming less rigid and less conforming to their country or folk origins. While they were extending into more improvised territory, it was different to their earlier electric jams, in that their approach was more relaxed, fluid and more natural. This year marked the beginning of what would be regarded as the classic Grateful Dead sound, where they moved from genre restrictions – even ones as open-ended as psychedelia or country rock, to something uniquely their own. The set featured a lengthy Truckin''>'Drums'>'The Other One'>'Wharf Rat' on disc two; the show ending with a lengthy 'Not Fade Away'>'Going Down The Road Feeling Bad'>'Caution (Do Not Stop On Tracks)'>'Feedback', with 'Uncle John's Band', now sitting comfortably in the encore slot.

If the February Port Chester recordings didn't make it as a new live album, a run of shows at New York's Fillmore East in April, would. The first release from these shows was the band's second double live album. Released under the official title *The Grateful Dead* – after their record company (perhaps wisely) turned down their initial suggestion of *Skullfuck* as perhaps being not exactly commercially friendly – the album is also widely known as *Skull And Roses*, on account of its iconic cover art. The bulk of this release came from these shows – 'Johnny B. Goode' was recorded at Winterland on 24 March; 'Big Railroad Blues', 'Playin' In The Band' and 'Not Fade Away'>'Going Down The Road Feeling Bad' recorded at the Manhattan Center on 5 and 6 April. Merl Saunders provided some keyboard overdubs, Pigpen's playing not featuring prominently in the eventual release.

If the five-piece Dead staring from the inner sleeve was in any way diminished by the loss of Hart and TC since their last live album, it's not evident in the new album. Kreutzmann's drum solo at the beginning of 'The Other One' remains convincing, and the rest of the track shows them still mastering long jams. The choice of tracks helps, the focus being on less complex numbers. Shorter rockier numbers feature: 'Bertha' is a punchy opening number, and 'Mama Tried' and 'Big Railroad Blues' keep up the pace. It's The Dead at their most accessible, and while it features several songs that hadn't yet been released ('Bertha', 'Wharf Rat' and 'Playing In The Band'), there were many cover versions that would be widely familiar ('Mama Tried', 'Me And Bobby McGee', 'Johnny B. Goode', 'Not Fade Away'). Perhaps the song selection helped it commercially, too, the album quickly becoming their best-selling release at the time.

The 2001 CD issue of the album featured two bonus tracks – 'Oh Boy' and 'I'm A Hog For You' – appropriately both covers, from the 6 April Manhattan Center show that provided the version of 'Playing In The Band'. The version of 'Bertha' on the CD is slightly longer than the vinyl version, as the original version faded in, giving the listener the impression of joining The Dead mid-set, reminiscent of the start of 'Dark Star' on *Live/Dead*. An expanded 50th-anniversary edition of the album runs over two discs, the second disc featuring ten tracks from their 2 July 1971 performance at the Fillmore West. While some of the tracks echo those on *Skull And Roses* ('Mama Tried', 'The Other One', 'Big Boss Man' and 'Not Fade Away'>'Going Down The Road Feeling Bad'), it also includes a lengthy 'Good Lovin'' and 'Sing Me Back Home'.

The April shows at the Fillmore East would later be released in a fuller form as *Ladies And Gentlemen... The Grateful Dead*: a four-CD set that came out in 2000. Featuring more of the cover versions that peppered the shows ('El Paso', 'I'm A King Bee', 'It Hurts Me Too', 'I Second That Emotion' and 'Sing Me Back Home'), there's more room for their own recent material ('Ripple', 'Casey Jones', 'Truckin'', 'Uncle John's Band') as well as extended numbers from earlier years ('Love Light', 'Good Loving', 'Alligator'). There's even room for 'Dark Star'>'St. Stephen'>'Not Fade Away'>'Going Down The Road Feeling Bad' that features a guest appearance from TC. The collection gives a more complete picture of that band's capabilities, taking in material from early in their career, Pigpen-based blues, *Live/Dead*-era numbers, and their more recent country-rock influenced work. The April 1971 shows at the Fillmore East would be the last time they played there, the venue closing that year along with its West Coast namesake.

A show from San Fransisco's Winterland on 30 May was the source of another double live album released in 2012. A vinyl-only release for Record Store Day, *Winterland: May 30th 1971* is a West Coast companion to *Skull And Roses*, with only 'Big Boss Man' and 'Johnny B. Goode' appearing on both releases. The Winterland album has more of their own songs than covers, and, other than a side-long version of 'Love Light', the songs are (relatively) short and sharp.

There was another look-back release out in June, with the unauthorized *Historic Dead* collection in the shops. Like its predecessor – 1970's *Vintage Dead* – it was a release based on tapes recorded at the Avalon in 1966. Again, The Dead had no involvement in the release. It's an incomplete timepiece featuring four tracks: most notably, versions of 'Good Morning Little School Girl' and 'The Same Thing'.

Although they were by now capable of playing larger venues like Winterland, on 2 July 1971, The Dead played the closing of the Fillmore West: the venue that had acted like a home to them in San Francisco. A series of final shows, including Santana, Quicksilver Messenger Service, NRPS and The Flaming Groovies, were documented in a film and triple live album. Released in 1972, the film *Fillmore* includes footage of The Dead performing 'Casey Jones' and 'Johnny B. Goode', both tracks also appearing on the *Fillmore: The Last Days* album. Ten other tracks from the show would feature as the bonus disc released with the 50th-anniversary edition of *Skull And Roses*.

Two shows from the end of July and the beginning of August featured on the *Road Trips Volume 1 Number 3* collection: one from 31 July at Yale Bowl, New Haven, Connecticut, and the other from 23 August at the Auditorium Theatre, Chicago, Illinois. The first disc features the Yale show in condensed form, skipping the first set's opening numbers, but including the 'Dark Star'>'Bird Song' sequence; the second half of the second set with its 'Not Fade Away'>'Going Down The Road Feeling Bad'>'Not Fade Away' jam and the 'Uncle John's Band'>'Johnny B. Goode' encore. The Second disc covers the 23 August show, again in a condensed form, but with its impressive centrepiece of 'Cryptical Envelopment'>'Drums'>'The Other One'>'Me And My Uncle'>'The Other One'>'Cryptical Envelopment'>'Wharf Rat, intact.

A third bonus disc issued with this album featured two more tracks from the Yale Bowl gig, five from a show at the Hollywood Palladium on 6 August, and three from a 4 August performance at the Terminal Island Correctional Facility in San Pedro, where The Dead played a daytime show in the prison library. While prison performances were at the time not uncommon – following Johnny Cash's San Quentin show in 1969 – The Dead had their own reasons to play there, as the low-security jail was then home to Dead sound engineer Owsley, who'd been serving time there since the New Orleans bust in 1970.

With five tracks from early in their set at the Hollywood Palladium gig on 6 August on *Road Trips Volume 1 Number 3*, highlights of the latter part of the show had already emerged on *Dick's Picks Volume 35*. The end of the show – from 'The Other One' to a rousing 25-minute 'Love Light' – made up the bulk of the collection's fourth disc. Two other August 1971 shows make up the preceding three discs – Golden Hall, San Diego from 7 August, and The Auditorium Theatre in Chicago from 24 August. Both shows feature crisp 1971 Dead performances, the only longer explorations being 'Not Fade Away'>'Going Down The Road Feeling Bad'>'Johnny B. Goode' from San Diego, and a similar sequence from Chicago but with an appearance of 'St.

'Stephen' at the start instead of 'Johnny B. Goode' at the end. However, the absolute highlight of *Dick's Picks Volume 35* has to be from the Chicago set, which features the only released version of Pigpen's song 'Empty Pages'. Apparently, it was only performed twice: at this gig and at one a few days later, which would mark Pigpen's temporary departure from the band for health reasons. He would return in December, but The Dead wouldn't perform the song again.

By 22 October (the show that's featured on *Dave's Picks Volume 3*), there had been a significant change in the band's lineup. With Pigpen ill at home, keyboard player Keith Godchaux was recruited to fill the gap. Others who'd played with The Dead and their associates – such as Merl Saunders, Ned Lagin and Howard Wales – were considered, but the former lounge pianist Godhaux – who was introduvced to the band by his wife Donna Jean – impressed them with his skills and ability to fit in with their style of music. Later, Donna Jean would herself join the band as vocalist. Godchaux made his live debut with The Dead on 19 October, following rehearsals earlier that month. Playing organ and piano, he'd make a noticeable impact on the band's live sound, Pigpen's playing having been more in the background. The Godchauxs remained in the band until 1979.

From the 'Bertha' opening on *Dave's Picks Volume 3*, Godchaux can be heard adding a new element to The Dead's sound, that would be part of their blend through what many regard as their best years. The show was at the Auditorium Theatre in Chicago, where they'd played only a few months earlier (released on *Road Trips Volume 1 Number 3*), and shows a band that have made a considerable transition. While the set remains similar to other 1971 shows – with its western numbers, early rock 'n' roll and improvised numbers – the difference in performance is huge. Godchaux's playing both compliments the other members and brings new elements to songs. The western songs like 'Me And My Uncle', 'Tennessee Jed' and 'Mexicali Blues', had a convincing new barroom swing; the rock 'n'roll tracks like 'Bertha' or 'Johnny B. Goode' benefitting from added boogie-woogie, and the longer improvised numbers like 'The Other One' gave him a platform for improvised jazz that he took to instantly. *Dave's Picks Volume 3* shows a band invigorated, and while perhaps not yet reaching their full potential (that would take until 1972), it gives a clear indication of where they're heading. It's a real pleasure to listen to this show, and you can almost hear the band members smiling throughout.

Disc three of *Dave's Picks Volume 3* features the bulk of the previous night's show, including 'Dark Star'>'Sittin' On Top Of The World'>'Dark Star'>'Me And Bobby McGee'. That Godchaux was able to not only confidently handle this kind of varied set – moving effortlessly from lengthy improvised pieces to contemporary western standards – but also add his own musical voice to the group's sound is a credit to his abilities.

A show from Halloween 1971 was released in 1995 as *Dick's Picks Volume 2*. The only single-disc release in the *Dick's Picks* series, it captures the band's second set at the Ohio Theater in Columbus, Ohio. It's a remarkable release, featuring a 'Dark Star'>'Jam'>'Sugar Magnolia' sequence that shows Godchaux's place in the band was well deserved – the jam here often referred to as 'Tighten Up Jam' due to the similarity in theme to the 1968 R&B track of the same title by Archie Bell & the Drells.

November 1971 would be chronicled with two releases: *Road Trips Volume 3 Number 2* and *Dave's Picks Volume 26*. The former featured a show from 15 November at the Austin Memorial Auditorium in Austin, Texas, over two discs. A bonus third disc includes material from the previous night in Fort Worth, Texas. Disc One features the first set, with an unusual early 'Dark Star': a full twelve minutes of intricate improvisation with Godchaux contributing and pushing forward with the confidence and ease that defies his short time in the bad. Weir brings the band into 'El Paso', and they move back into 'Dark Star' territory after this brief diversion. The second set features another jam section, this time coming during the 'Not Fade Away'>'Going Down The Road Feeling Bad' transition towards the end of the show. It's almost like they've got so many musical ideas that they need to squeeze a few more in before the show comes to a close.

Dave's Picks Volume 26 picks up the late-1971 Dead's live adventures just two days after the show on *Road Trips Volume 3 Number 2*. The three CDs feature the complete concert from 17 November at the Albuquerque Civic Auditorium in New Mexico, as well as some tracks from their 14 December 1970 show at the Hill Auditorium in Ann Arbor, Michigan. A bonus fourth disc features most of the rest of the 14 December show. They hit the ground running in the first set, with the opening 'Truckin'' featuring some strong extended interplay, and while the other fourteen numbers are generally their shorter material, 'Playing In The Band' begins to show its potential as the basis for an extended jam number. Disc Two's centrepiece is 'The Other One'>'Me And My Uncle'>'The Other One'>'Wharf Rat'. The 14 December show on disc three features Pigpen back in the band, singing on 'Next Time You See Me' and 'Big Boss Man', although it's a more laid-back Pigpen, perhaps lacking some of his earlier swagger. There's also a seasonal 'Run Rudolph Run' in the set, and a brief 'Stars And Stripes Forever', suggesting the band were certainly enjoying the show.

The Dead were back in New York in December, and with the closing of the Fillmore East, a new venue was required. A run of shows were held from 4 to 7 December at the Felt Forum, below the main arena of Madison Square Garden. While it was the only time they'd play the Felt Forum, from the late-1970s, they'd be one of the acts that played Madison Square Garden the most. The run at the Felt Forum was released on *Dave's Picks Volume 22*, with the complete set from 7 December over two discs, and the second set from 6 December on the third disc. A bonus fourth disc featured more from the 6 December show.

Opening with 'Cold Rain And Snow' – appropriate for New York in December – the first disc of *Dave's Picks 22* dives into the band's country and folk-rock repertoire, with Pigpen back on vocals for 'Mr Charlie'. While there's a festive 'Run Rudolph Run', it comes after a gem of a 'Brokedown Palace', suggesting the band – though capable of delivering moments of beauty live on stage – don't take it too seriously. The second set features Pigpen at the mic again for 'Big Boss Man' and 'Smokestack Lightning', though the longer number slot is reserved for 'Truckin'' and the 'Not Fade Away'>'Going Down The Road '>'Not Fade Away' set closer. The third disc from the 6 December show includes a 'Playing In The Band' before 'Cryptical Envelopment'>'Drums'>'The Other One'>'Me And Bobby McGee'. It sums up perfectly the depth of the band's playing and the breadth of their repertoire.

Immediately after their New York shows, The Dead played two nights at the Fox Theatre in St Louis, Missouri, on 9 and 10 December. Both these shows feature in the 2021 20-CD set *Listen To The River*: a collection that focuses on Dead gigs at the city over the three-year period from 1971 to 1973. The 10 December show was also released as a stand-alone three-CD set titled *Fox Theatre, St. Louis, MO 12-10-71*. As well as the 1971 shows, there are three from October 1972 and a further two from October 1973. As a collection, it's an interesting artefact that chronicles the band's development over a key stage in their career. It also serves as a reminder that, for most fans, seeing The Dead wasn't always about travelling to San Francisco or Madison Square Garden or from show to show in the back of a Volkswagen, but the experience was instead catching them when they played your home town. And given how much they toured, there was every chance that even if you stuck to just one major US city, you'd probably still have the opportunity to see them on a fairly regular basis.

The band closed the year with a show at Winterland in San Francisco. From this show, 'Jam'>'Black Peter' appear on *New Year's Eves At Winterland*, released as a bonus disc with the *Closing Of Winterland* collection.

1972 – Sunshine Daydream

There are many paradoxes with The Dead. They're the definitive San Francisco band, but only lived there a comparatively short time; They're the embodiment of the Summer Of Love and the Haight-Ashbury scene, but quickly moved out. Another is that they're associated with the 1960s, when in fact they probably only reached their artistic peak in the 1970s, and their commercial peak in the 1980s. There are arguments as to *when* they peaked in the 1970s – 1977 makes a good case, as does 1978. But 1972 is certainly a strong contender – with the *Europe '72* tour in April and May, its subsequent live releases, and the *Sunshine Daydream* gig in Veneta, Oregon, there's certainly enough evidence to suggest it. By 1972, they had loosened out the lasso that held their country-rock numbers, and given them room to breathe. They were no longer the hard-jamming acid-rock band of the late-1960s, but had taken the skills from this period and applied them to their newer material, resulting in something unique. It wasn't the easy-listening California rock that the likes of The Eagles would turn into a commercial proposition, nor was it simply repeating the glories of the days of the Fillmores without bringing anything new to the table. The Dead had moved into the new decade with a new lineup and a sound that had its roots in the underground, but had grown into something that didn't fit easily into the new decade's emerging musical genres. It wasn't hard rock or blues-rock; it wasn't progressive rock or singer/songwriter territory, and it wasn't really psychedelic in the way some of the music of the 1960s was. But all these elements were present in what they were creating, and by 1972, they were realising their potential.

In 1972, there were fewer live dates than previous years: one reason being that Pigpen – now back in the band after his illness absence in 1971 – was still very frail. Necessity had meant that the lengthy blues rave-ups he led on stage were out of the set, and his performances were limited to shorter numbers. He was no longer at the centre of the band, and his decline was apparent both onstage and off. Perhaps Pigpen's decreased presence – and the band's subsequent lack of an obvious frontman – encouraged the band members to rely more on their improvisation and performance skills. While the band members certainly had presence on stage, none could possibly compare to Pigpen.

Garcia had spent the end of 1971 recording his first solo album. This meant – in the best 1970s multi-instrumentalist tradition – playing all the instruments himself: pedal steel, bass, keyboards, vocals and guitar. Drums were covered by Kreutzmann. Released in January 1972, the album – simply called *Garcia* – featured a strong selection of Garcia/Hunter songs, with six of the ten tracks going on to become Grateful Dead standards: 'Deal', 'Bird Song', 'Sugaree' and 'Loser' on the first side, and 'To Lay Me Down' and 'The Wheel' on the second. While The Dead were already playing five of these live, 'The Wheel' was an entirely new composition created by Garcia, Hunter and Kreutzmann in the studio. It was a product of the way the album was created – Garcia laying down an acoustic track, Kreutzmann then adding drums, and Garcia overdubbing the other instruments. 'The Wheel' was initially a brief acoustic piece, but with Hunter in the studio quickly putting words together and Kreutzmann giving it the propulsion it needed, a new Grateful Dead classic was grown. If The Grateful Dead have a poor reputation for delivering quality studio albums, their output from 1970 to 1972 – whether as a band or solo artists – shows them very much in control and delivering some of their finest material.

Perhaps it was because Garcia recorded the album without the expectations of delivering a Grateful Dead album, or perhaps because he was free to enjoy himself in the studio, but Garcia's debut solo album is an outstanding collection. He was by now adept at working in the studio and experienced in the available technology, and he took full advantage of the possibilities that it gave him. If the album lacks what the other band members could bring to The Dead, the strength of the songs sustains it, and his guitar and vocals are at their peak. Even the more-experimental pieces on the second side are very much in character with their science-fiction/avant-garde, playful weirdness. Even if they're not as memorable as the other work on *Garcia*, tracks like 'Eep Hour' could have easily made bold film soundtrack pieces. He'd go on to make other solo albums, but this was by far his most successful artistically and commercially, reaching 35 in the *Billboard* chart. A later expanded edition that was released as part of the *All Good Things: Jerry Garcia Studio Sessions* box set in 2004 included alternate takes of 'Sugaree', 'Loser' and 'The Wheel', along with work-in-progress versions of 'Eep Hour' and 'The Wheel'. Had the *Garcia* album been released under The Grateful Dead name, it would probably be regarded as one of their best albums and a worthy follow up to *American Beauty*.

Warner Bros. had offered members of The Dead the opportunity to record solo albums, and Garcia was not the only one to make the most of the opportunity. In 1972, albums followed from Bob Weir and Mickey Hart, who – though no longer a band member – was still very much a member of the extended Grateful Dead family. Weir's album *Ace* was recorded in the first three months of 1972, and its creation was a very different process to Garcia's in that it was a Grateful Dead album in all but name, with every Dead member excluding Pigpen performing on it as Weir's backing band. Like Garcia's album, The Dead would go on to regularly perform almost every song on *Ace* throughout their career.

The songs – perhaps unsurprisingly – take a more country direction than Garcia's album, with every song either written or co-written by Weir. The collection marks a major step in his development as a songwriter, with sharp and memorable songs that would rival the country tunes he loved ('Mexicali Blues'), and rock numbers that wouldn't sound out of place had they been performed by Chuck Berry ('One More Saturday Night'). Hunter co-wrote two songs – 'Greatest Story Ever Told' and 'Playing In The Band' – while others featured John Barlow, who would go on to be Weir's regular songwriting collaborator. 'Mexicali Blues' was already a regular in their set; 'One More Saturday Night' making its live debut with The Dead in October 1971 during Keith Godchaux's first performance with the band. A live version of 'Playing In The Band' had already appeared on the *Skull And Roses* album, and it would appear under the title 'The Main Ten' on Mickey Hart's solo album *Rolling Thunder*: the third part of The Grateful Dead's 1972 solo-album trilogy. 'The Greatest Story Ever Told' also appears there, under the title 'The Pump Song' – it being one of the songs that made its live debut with The Dead during the run of shows at the Capitol Theatre in Port Chester in February 1971. The debut performance can be found on the 50th-anniversary deluxe edition of *American Beauty*. 'Cassidy', a tribute to the birth of a daughter of The Dead's crew members Rex Jackson and his partner Eileen Law, also appears on Weir's album and would be performed long into The Dead's career.

Making their Dead-family debut on the album, was Donna Jean Godchaux – wife of new keyboard player Keith – who would become a full-time band member. The only female member of The Dead ever, Donna had previously worked as a session singer in Alabama, as part of the prestigious Muscle Shoals scene, and performed on recordings including Percy Sledge's 'When A Man Loves A Woman' and Elvis Presley's 'Suspicious Minds'. She sang on Cher's *3614 Jackson Highway* album, appearing on the cover alongside Cher and the other musicians. She married Keith Godchaux in 1970 after moving to California, her husband until then having little knowledge of rock 'n' roll before his wife inspired his interest. She remained in the band until 1979, leaving at the same time as her husband.

Hart's album had a wider cast than Weir or Garcia's, with John Cipollina from Quicksilver Messenger Service on guitar, Stephen Stills, Barry 'The Fish' Melton, Grace Slick and Paul Kantner among them. Weir, Garcia and Lesh are there too. There are two versions of Grateful Dead songs co-written with Weir and Hunter – 'Playing In The Band' and 'The Greatest Story Ever Told' – albeit under different names, while 'Fletcher Carnaby' was a Hart/Hunter co-write. The eye-scorching artwork from San Francisco artists Stanley Mouse and Alton Kelly (one of their finest works), makes it clear that this is a release with its roots, branches, heart and soul firmly in the San Francisco scene. While a solo album from a drummer is a difficult proposition, it's a surprisingly good collection, with instrumentals centred on ethnic percussion, years before the term 'world music' came into general use, other tracks making the most of Hart's talented associates. While two Dead songs feature, they sound very different to The Dead, and 'Fletcher Carnaby' is a song more in the style of late-1960s psychedelic pop than the work The Dead were creating at the time of *Rolling Thunder*'s release.

Apart from his official debut solo album, Garcia's regular gigging with Merl Saunders had led to the release of the album *Heavy Turbulence*. Though it's credited as a Merl Saunders release, Garcia features on every track, playing guitar and singing. Also on the album were John Kahn – who became a long-term Garcia collaborator in the Jerry Garcia Band – and Tom Fogerty, formerly of Creedence Clearwater Revival. Tracks on the album included an instrumental cover of John Lennon's 'Imagine' (apparently the first-released cover of it), and The Band's 'The Night They Drove Old Dixie Down': a song that would be a fixture of the Jerry Garcia Band.

The first live document from 1972 comes from The Academy of Music in New York, where they played a total of seven shows. Released in 2003, *Dick's Picks Volume 30* – their first recordings to feature singer Donna Jean Godchaux – covers the complete 28 March show and pieces from the 25 and 27 March shows. Their gig on 25 March – on disc one – was unusual in that it was a private party booked by the Hells Angels. The band were billed as Jerry Garcia and Friends, with Bo Diddley as support. Diddley performed with The Grateful Dead as his backing band. Five tracks from this set feature on disc one: all are Bo Diddley numbers, including 'Mona' and 'I'm A Man', and there's also a ten-minute jam. The disc also features two unique performances from that night – the songs 'How Sweet It Is (To Be Loved By You) – made famous by Marvin Gaye – and 'Are You Lonely For Me': a late-1960s R&B number by Freddie Scott. It would be the only time The Dead would play these numbers, although 'How Sweet It Is' would later feature in the Jerry Garcia Band's set. Disc one also features a lengthy 'Smokestack Lightning' and 'Playing In The Band' from the 27 March show. The other three discs feature the 28 March performance: both sets and the encore. It's a great show – the content unsurprisingly similar to the material they'd play in their *Europe '72* set, with another unique but brief performance of 'The Sidewalks Of New York', before the 'One More Saturday Night' encore.

Material from the 22 and 23 March shows appeared as the bonus disc that came with pre-orders of the *Rockin' The Rhein With The Grateful Dead* CD set in 2004, including a 22-minute 'Dark Star' from 23 March, and 'Caution (Do Not Stop On Tracks)', 'Jam'>'Uncle Johns Band' from 22 March. For a single disc, that was essentially a promotional giveaway: it's a great collection. *Dave's Picks Volume 14* – released in 2015 – features the 26 March show over three discs, with a collection of tracks from the shows on 21 and 27 March as a bonus disc. With the material spread across several collections, and much of it hard to find, a complete box set of The Academy of Music 1972 shows would make a very fine addition to the band's discography.

Over April and May, they undertook their first proper tour of Europe – 22 shows across the UK, Denmark, France, West Germany, the Netherlands and Luxembourg – with an extensive crew and entourage of family and friends. Their record company decided in advance to record each show professionally with a 16-track recorder, for release as a means to offset the tour expense. It would prove to be a wise decision. The triple *Europe '72* album released in November that year is a stunning document of a band at the peak of their powers. A triple live album was a bold move, but despite the release's apparently extravagant scale, there's not one note surplus to requirement.

One new song that was debuted on the tour, was 'He's Gone': a song originally referring to Lenny Hart's disappearance with a large sum of money that rightfully belonged to the band. Played for the first time in Copenhagen, it's one of their many songs that would take on a different significance over their career, at times being played in tribute to members who died. Despite being their second live album in as many years, the songs were fresh, with many making their first appearance on a Grateful Dead album. The performances were outstanding; the tour's holiday atmosphere, lifting spirits. Rather than simply being a live album that filled the gaps between studio releases, they were proving beyond doubt that the live album could be an artistically-valid release in its own right.

It was the first release to capture Keith and Donna Jean Godchaux's contribution: both bringing new elements and expanding the band's sound considerably. It would also be Pigpen's final released appearance, and despite his issues, his performances on the album – particularly on 'Mr Charlie' (the song he co-wrote with Hunter) – remain authoritative. He made his final appearance with The Dead not long after the European dates, at a show at the Hollywood Bowl in June, before his health problems brought his time with the band to an end.

The *Europe '72* album wasn't the tour's only audio document, even before the 1990s and 21st-century archive releases. A live excerpt of 'Dark Star' from the Empire Pool, Wembley gig on 8 April – titled *'Dark Star....bury'* – filled the first side of the highly collectable *Glastonbury Fayre* triple album released later that year. Appearing alongside Hawkwind, David Bowie, Marc Bolan, Gong and The Pink Fairies, The Dead's appearance cemented their place among their peers of the UK counterculture. They might not have played the UK as regularly as the other acts on *Glastonbury Fayre*, but they were welcome visitors and kindred spirits. They'd never actually play Glastonbury, despite regular rumours. The closest they'd get to actually playing the UK's most famous annual music festival, was a set by Robert Hunter in 1981.

The first archive release from the tour, appeared in the 1990s, with the *Hundred Year Hall* double CD featuring much of the Frankfurt gig: the highlight of this being the outstanding 'Truckin''>'The Other One'>'Comes A Time'>'Sugar Magnolia' sequence. 1999's *So Many Roads (1965-1995)* box set included the version of 'Chinatown Shuffle' from the Rotterdam gig, and later, the 2001 expanded CD release of *Europe '72* added to the original with more tracks from the Empire Pool, Wembley, and Tivoli, Copenhagen shows, along with a track from the Frankfurt show that was left off *Hundred Year Hall*. Further releases would follow: 2002's *Steppin' Out With The Grateful Dead: England '72* was a four-CD set featuring material from London's Empire Pool and Lyceum shows; the Newcastle City Hall and Bickershaw Festival dates. The complete Dusseldorf show emerged in 2004 as the triple CD *Rockin' The Rhein With The Grateful Dead*, featuring bonus tracks from the 24 May Lyceum gig, and a rearranged running order with some of the third-set numbers placed between the first set and the bonus tracks.

Any feelings that running orders had been moved about unnecessarily to accommodate CD running times, or certain tracks had been missed out inappropriately, were finally put to rest in 2011 with the release of *Europe '72: The Complete Recordings*. The massive 73-disc box set comprised all 22 shows remastered, with their original running orders restored where possible. All 7,200 of these limited packages, sold out. A second edition featured the discs without the elaborate packaging, and each of the shows were released individually. A two-CD and four-vinyl-disc *Europe '72 Volume 2* collection featuring tour performances that had been omitted from the original *Europe '72* album, was also issued, and while it makes for a more wallet-friendly release, it also stands as a solid companion to the original.

The 4 May Olympia Paris gig got a special vinyl release the following year, with a 40-minute version of 'Dark Star' making a quite extraordinary album, and 2021 saw a vinyl release of the 3 May Olympia show over six discs. It's a release that hopefully points towards all of the *Europe '72* shows getting a full stand-alone vinyl release. Over the subsequent decades, sending a 16-track recorder over to Europe to document the tour has proven to be a wise move for the record company.

Following their return from Europe, the band resumed live dates in the USA, with a show from The Paramount Northwest Theatre in Seattle, Washington, on 21 July emerging as Volume 10 in The Grateful Dead *Download Series*. Pigpen was now no longer part of the band, having made his final appearance at the Hollywood Bowl on 17 June. Spread over the equivalent of three discs, *Download Series Volume 10* features most of the show, along with bonus tracks from the following night at the same venue. While the highlight is in the second set – with an extraordinary 'He's Gone'>'Truckin''>'Drums'>'The Other One'>'Comes A Time' seeing The Dead move through phases of peak instrumental intensity and soulfulness with ease – the first set contains the earliest released version of 'Stella Blue', which made its live debut in June. Hunter said he originally wrote the song in 1970 at the Chelsea Hotel in New York, Garcia adding the music during the European tour. A powerful song from the start, it became the centrepiece of their next album and an increasingly potent live number as years went by. Also pointing towards their next studio album, sharp ears might pick up a very brief take of 'Weather Report Suite Prelude' before they swing into more familiar territory with 'Me And My Uncle'.

The show that was released as *Dave's Picks Volume 24*, recorded on 25 August at the Berkeley Community Theatre – has the disadvantage that it will always be compared to the show that immediately followed it. However, this should in no way diminish the quality of what's on display in this collection. The first set – over the first two of three discs – brings out some of the songs they'd polished and perfected over the preceding months and were now able to comfortably explore at leisure. 'He's Gone', 'Loser', 'Bird Song', 'Playing In The Band' and the opening 'Cold Rain And Snow' are given room to breathe and take flight. Tighter numbers – whether their own like 'Friend Of The

Devil' or 'Bertha', or covers like 'Promised Land' and 'Beat It On Down The Line' – make it clear that they're never ambling aimlessly, and can pull things together when the song demands it. The second set features a sequence of 'Truckin''>'The Other One'>'Stella Blue', making it absolutely clear that the more-widely-known performances they delivered during *Europe '72* or at their next show, were not the exceptions. While The Dead in later years may have had a reputation for being able to regularly bring the magic but occasionally deliver a dud, this was a band who at their peak were capable of delivering astonishing performances on a nightly basis.

A matter of days later, The Dead played a show widely regard as legendary. While there will always be healthy debate among fans as to which shows were The Dead's finest, their performance at the Old Renaissance Fairgrounds in Veneta, Oregon on 27 August is one of those that is always cited. If they'd blown it at Woodstock, failed to make an impression at Monterey Pop, and Altamont had been a disaster, this show was one when the stars aligned. And not only was it an exceptional show and recorded with what was then state-of-the-art equipment, it was also filmed. Unlike the high-profile events they'd been involved in where they missed the mark, the Field Trip show was very much *their* event, with their audience of friends, family and fans, and on *their* terms. Intended as a benefit for Ken Kesey's family dairy business and organised in a matter of weeks by prankster associates in a beautiful piece of country, The Dead played in intense summer heat, with the sun so hot it was a challenge to keep their instruments in tune.

Finally released in 2013, *Sunshine Daydream* came out as a three-CD set with a DVD of the movie, the three sets each on their own disc. With the exception of 'Sing Me Back Home' – which appeared on the *So Many Roads (1965-1995)* box set in 1999 – the *Sunshine Daydream* versions hadn't been commercially available before. Taken from 16-track tape, the sound quality defies any suggestion that archive releases were left on the shelf for falling below modern recording standards

From the start of the set, the band are on fire – vocals, instruments, pace and song choices – all the pieces fall together perfectly. There can be a tendency among fans to look at the first set as being a warm-up for the main event later in the show, but here they are pin-sharp, with flashes of intense instrumentation. That they make it sound so effortless is little short of astonishing. The second set begins with a version of 'Playing In The Band' where they hit an intensity that's almost terrifying. The third set's 'Dark Star' opener is an extraordinary beast: a piece that easily stands alongside the likes of Miles Davis or John Coltrane for its invention and dexterity. That a piece so far-removed from any regular musical landscape is able to be resolved with a transition into a cover of 'El Paso', shows The Dead as capable of pulling things as sharply into focus as they are of exploring musical tangents. The soulful 'Sing Me Back Home' reveals a band who, despite their earlier inhibitions, have mastered their use of voices: Donna Jean Godchaux's contribution adding another layer of polish.

From old school rock 'n' roll, through country, soul and fiery electric jazz improvisation and back again, the magic and scale of what The Grateful Dead could do is manifest in this release. Almost every song performed could be regarded as the definitive version. Archive or not, *Sunshine Daydream* is one of the finest releases of The Dead's career.

Meanwhile, the weirdness and fundamentally-ramshackle nature of the event was captured in full colour on film. It might lack the finesse of other festival movies of the era, but it successfully captures The Dead at the height of their powers in an appropriately relaxed environment that could hardly be more different to the festivals of the 21st century. There seems to be no security, there are no premium-price areas, and the stage seems to be set in a field with no attempt to block off a backstage area, never mind a VIP area. There's no sponsorship. In fact, it's the absolute opposite: The Dead are playing to benefit a friend's business, rather than distant businesses trying to earn some credibility by funding a music event. Through all this, the audience bakes in the heat and dances in various stages of undress, kids play and dogs wander. Meanwhile, on a rudimentary stage resembling something that could've been built in a back garden, with apparently little in the way of a PA system or lighting, The Dead play for their lives, sweat pouring off them in the Oregon summer heat, while a naked longhaired man grooves to the sounds on top of a tall post behind the stage, hovering above the proceedings like a wingless guardian angel played by Iggy Pop.

There's little added post-production polish. A sequence of the Pranksters driving in their bus through a city, with passers-by greeting them with looks of bemusement and alarm, makes clear the world inhabited by The Dead and their associates was quite different from the one inhabited by most Americans at the time. Later, a handmade collage-like animation sequence added to 'Dark Star', focuses on the strangeness of the world of animals and plants – quite different from the usual *space* imagery associated with the band – but is certainly appropriate for the event's rural setting.

Sunshine Daydream's handmade aesthetic is entirely appropriate for The Dead, and what it might lack in polish, it more than makes up for in authenticity and charm. Though it circulated among fans for decades, the film wasn't released officially until 2013. Given the band's fondness for the film – particularly Garcia – it is a surprise that such a remarkable band document remained effectively on the shelf. One possible reason is the story that the band were invited to a screening of the raw footage shortly after the event, but were left disappointed, having expected to see a finished movie. Whatever the reason, the filming of the show, planted a seed that would bear fruit in a couple of years with *The Grateful Dead Movie*.

The NRPS performance at Veneta – by this time without Garcia as part of the band – was released on CD in 2004 as *Veneta, Oregon 8/27/72*. It was remastered and issued in 2020 under the title *Field Trip*, and was also available as a limited-edition Record Store Day double album.

The *30 Trips Around The Sun* box set included another complete classic 1972 show from Palace Theatre, Waterbury, Connecticut, on 24 September. While its tracklisting might suggest a fairly regular show from this year, the tracklisting alone doesn't do justice to what the band delivered: hitting the same seemingly effortless highs as they'd delivered throughout the year. The peak they were on during and after their European tour had not diminished, with each member continuing to weave their individual magic into an incredible and unique whole. Had this set been released on its own, it would rightly be considered a classic – the disc-three version of 'Dark Star' being a quite extraordinary despatch from the twilight zone, as delicate at times as it is thunderous at others. There really were no *regular* shows in 1972. The set also included one unusual song in their cover of Dolly Parton's 'Tomorrow Is Forever' – originally a duet between Parton and Porter Wagoner, here sung as a duet between Garcia and Donna Jean Godchaux. The song is an obvious extension of the country-rock sound they developed on *Workingman's Dead* and *American Beauty* but could only consider now that Donna was a band member. They performed this song only occasionally in the early-1970s, and this was only the second time this rarity has been officially released: its only other appearance being on *The Grateful Dead Movie Soundtrack* five-disc set released in 2005.

As they had done the two previous years, The Dead brought 1972 to a close at Winterland. An 18-minute version of 'Playing In The Band' from the show appears on the *New Year's Eves At Winterland* bonus disc that accompanied the *The Closing Of Winterland* 4-CD set.

1973 – Here Comes Sunshine

1973 would be another peak year for The Dead, continuing to build on the success they'd enjoyed in 1972. New songs were introduced, Keith and Donna Godchaux were settled in their places in the band, and onstage vigour led to gigs that became lengthy celebrations in venues that increased in size. The quality of The Dead's shows can be seen in the number of them that have subsequently been released. Meanwhile, solo projects began to take shape, and a new record label came into being with a successful new studio album. However, all this positivity unfolded against a backdrop of tragedy, with the band losing one of their key members early in the year.

Dicks's Picks Volume 28 picks up The Dead's live activity in 1973, covering a show from 26 February at Pershing Municipal Auditorium, Lincoln, Nebraska, and one from 28 February at Salt Lake City, Utah, over four discs. A number of songs that first appeared in 1973 make their chronological debut in this collection, including 'Loose Lucy', 'They Love Each Other', 'Row Jimmy' and 'Eyes Of The World'. The first two discs feature the 26 February show, with a number of tracks removed that duplicated material played on the 28th. The set features some intense jamming over 'Dark Star'>'Eyes Of The World' from 26 February, while another version of the song from 28 February features on disc four as part of the sequence 'Truckin''>'The Other One'>'Eyes Of The World'>'Morning Dew'. With the set closing with 'And We Bid You Goodnight', disc four shows the new material sliding into their more established work, effortlessly. The new material was perhaps written more in keeping with where The Dead were musically at the time, and rather than continuing to explore the country or folk-rock sound that their previous albums had covered, the new work lent itself to extended instrumental explorations, with new songs that could easily sit in the first set with more structured pieces, or amidst a lengthy second-set sequence: allowing them even greater flexibility onstage.

The album credits for *Dick's Picks Volume 28* lists Pigpen – at home at the time and gravely ill – as a member of the band 'in spirit'. He was found dead in his apartment on 8 March, at the age of 27. The cause of death was listed as a gastrointestinal haemorrhage, with acute signs of liver disease. While his health had declined in recent years, and his death had seemed likely with his 1971 hospitalisation, his passing came as a devastating blow to the band.

They continued to tour in the immediate aftermath of his death, with shows already lined up on the East Coast: their first gig on 15 March coming just two days after Pigpen's funeral. The 24 March show at the Spectrum, Philadelphia, features on *Dave's Picks Volume 32*. While the first set is a mixture of up-tempo rockers and western numbers – opening with 'Bertha' and 'Beat It On Down The Line' – the inclusion of 'Box Of Rain' can only be seen as significant. In the first set we get the earliest-released versions of 'Wave That Flag' – another of the new Garcia/Hunter songs – and 'Here Comes Sunshine': from the first set, opening the second disc. While this disc features a lengthy 'Playing In The Band' that closed the first set and the first half of the second, the third disc is where things get very interesting. A laid-back 'He's Gone' – a song quickly adopted as a tribute to Pigpen – moves into 'Truckin'', which evolves into a lengthy jam, before crystalising into a remarkably short 'Dark Star' (just over four minutes) and into a mellow cover of 'Sing Me Back Home'. It's an emotional roller coaster that moves up a gear for the set's 'Sugar Magnolia' finale and a 'Johnny B. Goode' encore. It's a hell of a ride, but you're left assured that everything will be alright in the end. Pigpen would've probably wanted it that way.

Dave's Picks Volume 16 chronicles the show just four days later on 28 March at the Springfield Civic Centre, Springfield, Massachusetts. The first set features a rarity with Donna Jean Godchaux taking lead vocals on a version of Loretta Lynn's 'You Aint Woman Enough', along with new songs like 'They Love Each Other', 'Row Jimmy', 'Wave That Flag' and 'Here Comes Sunshine' mixed with established numbers like 'Around And Around', 'Box Of Rain' and 'El Paso'. It's an energetic first set, from its opening 'Cumberland Blues' to its closing 'I Know You Rider'. The second set opens with a cover of 'Promised Land' followed by 'Loose Lucy' – an established cover side by side with a new song – the third disc featuring a sequence of Weir's 'Weather Report Suite Prelude' moving into a 30-minute-plus 'Dark Star', 'Eyes Of The World' and 'Playing In The Band', before 'Johnny B. Goode' closes the show: the third Chuck Berry song of the night. For all that 'Eyes Of The World' was a new song, it was clearly wasting no time making itself right at home.

The following month, the band were in Boston, where they played the final gig of their winter/spring '73 tour at the Boston Garden: released in 2017 as *Dave's Picks Volume 21*. It's an interesting show, as there are fewer of their regular extended jams, instead presenting a show packed with 34 songs ranging from established numbers like 'Box Of Rain' and 'Casey Jones', to fresh-out-of-the-box new material and a wide selection of covers. Again, three Chuck Berry numbers featured in the show, the first set opening with 'Promised Land', 'Around And Around' in the second, and 'Johnny B. Goode' before 'And We Bid You Goodnight' in the encore. The second set's 'Here Comes Sunshine' opens disc three, and it features a lengthy jam into 'Me And Bobby McGee', before a 'Weather Report Suite Prelude' leads into 'Eyes Of The World' and 'China Doll'. It's the earliest released version of 'China Doll', the song having made its debut in February. It's one of Garcia/Hunter's most affecting pieces, and this show brings The Dead's newer material to the foreground, where it absolutely shines.

Three shows from June feature on the 2018-released 19-disc box set *Pacific Northwest '73–'74: The Complete Recordings*. The 1973 shows are from Vancouver on 22 June, Portland, Oregon on 24 June, and Seattle, Washington on 26 June 26, and are presented alongside three complete shows from May 1974. The Vancouver show – over four discs – features a strong 'Bird Song' in the first set, disc two opening with a great 'China Cat Sunflower'>'I Know You Rider', also from the first set. The disc includes the first four numbers of the second set, which opens with 'Here Comes Sunshine', and although it's a new song, it's a perfect piece to set the tone for what's coming. The third disc presents the sequence 'He's Gone'>'Truckin''>'The Other One', the lengthy jam settling into 'Wharf Rat'. It's a perfect second-set run. The Portland show from two days later covers three discs, the third featuring 'Dark Star'>'Eyes Of The World'>'China Doll', where the new songs stand up to the demands of a thorough jam sequence, a bracing 'Sugar Magnolia' coming after 'China Doll'. There's also a performance of the rare 'You Ain't Woman Enough'. The final 1973 contribution to the box comes from the Seattle Centre Arena, the third disc featuring a sequence of 'He's Gone'>'Truckin''>'The Other One'>'Me And Bobby McGee'>'The Other One'>'Sugar Magnolia' that runs for over an hour: 'Me And Bobby McGee' making an unusual central section for 'The Other One'. The three shows all display the magic that permeated the band's performances in 1973, and each would be in their own right a fine example of the band's mastery of their craft. A more-accessible three-CD set *Pacific Northwest '73-'74: Believe It If You Need It* compiles a selection of tracks from the six shows in the box set, the majority of the 1973 content coming from the Vancouver show.

Between Grateful Dead tours, Garcia was, as always, keeping musically busy. He features on the Merl Saunders album *Fire Up* that was released in May 1973, along with Tom Fogerty, John Kahn and Bill Vitt. The Dead's Bill Kreutzmann features on one track taken from a radio broadcast. Like the 1972 *Heavy Turbulence* album, *Fire Up* was credited to Merl Saunders, though the band are essentially the Saunders/Garcia band. Recorded at Fantasy Studios in Berkeley, the album is a funky collection that includes covers of J. J. Cale's 'After Midnight' and 1950s R&B hit 'Lonely Avenue', along with original material. *Fire Up* would be combined with *Heavy Turbulence* for a 1992 CD release under the title *Fire Up Plus,* although the collection is minus a couple of tracks that appeared on the original *Fire Up*.

Two shows with Saunders at the Keystone in Berkeley on 10/11 July 1973 were recorded and released later that year as the double album *Live At Keystone*. With a band again including Kahn on bass and Vitt on drums, the album presents a selection of mostly cover versions, including two Bob Dylan songs, and versions of 'My Funny Valentine' and 'The Harder They Come'. It's worth remembering that the film *The Harder They Come* had only been released the previous year, Garcia being an early fan of reggae. The band gave Garcia the opportunity to tackle a more jazz-informed repertoire than he would've played with The Dead, with some funky interplay between him and Saunders on the Hammond organ. A further volume of unreleased songs from the recordings – titled *Keystone Encores* – was released in 1988 as a CD and two LPs, and the four-CD 2012 set *Keystone Companions* compiled the original *Live At Keystone* album, the later release and some unreleased numbers: the order changed to reflect the original performances.

Bear's Choice – the live album featuring tracks recorded at the Fillmore East in 1970 – was released in July. As well as a celebration of Pigpen's contribution to the band, the release fulfilled their contract with Warner Bros. records, freeing them to establish their own record label. Unlike Garcia, Weir and Hart, Pigpen never completed a solo album. Rough tapes show he certainly had the material and the talent, but it was never to be. A proper Pigpen solo album will always be a lost great Dead album, and this release is likely to be as close to one as there ever will be. Another feature of the album is that it introduced many of the visual icons that would go on to be associated with The Dead, including the 'Stealie' skull with the yin-yang style white lightning flash and red and blue surround, the dancing bears on the rear cover (although it's said they're marching rather than dancing) and the 'Good Ol' Grateful Dead' slogan woven into the front cover design.

It was perhaps a measure of The Dead's following by 1973 that they played Watkins Glen race track – the home of the US Formula 1 Grand Prix – for the Summer Jam event on 28 July alongside the Allman Brothers Band and The Band. A crowd of 600,000 attended the show, setting a record for attendance at a festival. The day before the festival itself, the three bands went on stage for a soundcheck in front of an audience that had already begun to arrive. The Band and The Allmans played a few songs, but The Dead went on to play two full sets for their soundcheck. A jam section they performed in the soundcheck was later released on the *So Many Roads (1965-1995)* box set. The Dead opened the event the following day with another lengthy two-set show, but true to their reputation for doing things on their own terms and not rising to the occasion, most reckon the soundcheck was the outstanding performance of the weekend.

In August, the band were back in the studio recording a new album: *Wake Of The Flood.* It had been three years since their last studio album, new material instead having appeared across live albums or solo releases. What a Dead album released as an immediate follow-up to *American Beauty* would include has long been a source of debate. But in 2015, a collection titled *Ramble On Rose* gave one possible answer, collecting live material from 1971, 1972 and 1973. Given away free with UK music magazine *Uncut*, it included two Pigpen numbers – 'Mr Charlie' and 'Chinatown Shuffle', as well as 'Brown-Eyed Women', 'Looks Like Rain', 'He's Gone', 'Loser', 'Comes A Time', 'Ramble On Rose', 'Black-Throated Wind' and an outtake of 'To Lay Me Down'. Some of the live material came from *Europe '72,* others from elsewhere. It works well as a collection, but it's unlikely to be the final word on the material that didn't make it into the studio in the early-1970s.

Promoted with the promise of 'All new stuff!', *Wake Of The Flood* was their first studio album to feature Keith and Donna Jean Godchaux. But another significant change is that The Dead had since last year been working on the creation of their own record label – Grateful Dead Records – with *Wake Of The Flood* being the first release. The subsidiary label Round Records was also set up for the release of solo projects. With the release of *Bear's Choice*, they'd fulfilled their Warner Bros. contract, and the band felt that by running their own label, they'd be in control of their releases and be able to make a greater profit. With the band playing larger venues requiring larger and more complex sound solutions, they had to employ more staff, meaning more income was required to sustain their business. After many avenues were pursued – some less practical than others – the label's arrangement saw The Dead finance and produce their material, which would then be manufactured and distributed by United Artists Records.

Wake Of The Flood's musical tone is very different to the folk and country flavours of *American Beauty* or *Workingman's Dead*: being a more jazz-rock informed work. It featured seven tracks, most of which were already familiar from having been played live: 'Mississippi Half-Step Uptown Toodeloo', 'Row Jimmy', 'Stella Blue', 'Here Comes Sunshine' and 'Eyes Of The World'. 'Let Me Sing Your Blues Away' was sung by Keith Godchaux, who co-wrote it with Hunter, and made its live debut in September, as did Weir's 'Weather Report Suite' expanded from its instrumental 'Prelude' to a three-part work that took up most of side two: John Anderson co-writing part one with Weir, and John Perry Barlow helping with the writing of Part 2 ('Let It Grow'). The album was recorded in just eleven days at Record Plant in Sausalito, very much on home territory, with The Dead's sound engineer Dan Healy among those at the controls. The album was a commercial success, reaching the *Billboard* top-20. But the album's success, The Dead's growing popularity, and the fact the album was on their own label, meant they also faced new issues such as counterfeit copies also emerging and being sold.

In September, The Dead were back on tour, with the 8 September gig at Nassau Coliseum, Uniondale, New York, being released as *Dave's Picks Volume 38* in 2021. The three-CD set featured the entire gig, with some extra tracks from the previous night. A bonus disc featured much of the previous night's second set. The show included the first performance of two songs from the freshly-recorded but still-to-be-released *Wake Of The Flood* – Keith Godchaux's 'Let Me Sing Your Blues Away' (a song that would only be in the band's repertoire for a number of weeks), and Weir's 'Weather Report Suite' in its entirety: the previous night including the 'Let It Grow' second part only. Another first for The Dead across these shows was the first appearance of Garcia's 'Wolf' guitar: a handmade instrument by luthier Doug Irwin. First played at a Saunders/Garcia show in New York a few days before, Wolf would go on to be Jerry's principal guitar throughout the 1970s. Wolf originally cost Garcia $1,500, and was auctioned in 2002 for $789,500, before it was sold again at auction for charity: raising $1,900,000 for civil rights organisation The Southern Poverty Law Center.

By 1973, Garcia's love of bluegrass led him into another extracurricular activity, with the creation of the band Old And In The Way. Playing alongside Garcia, were Peter Rowan on guitar, Vassar Clements on fiddle, David Grisman on mandolin and John Kahn on bass. Clements was a veteran bluegrass player, having played since the early-1950s with acts like Bill Monroe, and Flatt and

Scruggs. Rowan and Grisman had played together in the band Earth Opera in the late-1960s, with Grisman having contributed mandolin to 'Friend Of The Devil' and 'Ripple' on *American Beauty*. Kahn had been a long-standing musical associate and friend of Garcia, playing at his jam gigs at the Matrix and with the Merl Saunders and Jerry Garcia Band. The band played low key gigs around the Bay Area, in contrast to the ever-growing size of The Dead's shows which were now moving to arena-sized venues rather than theatres or nightclubs. Old And In The Way remained a far more accessible proposition, and didn't require the tons of equipment, logistics and planning The Dead now needed. Garcia would play with Old And In The Way during breaks from touring with The Dead, and a live album – recorded by Bear on 8 October 1973 at the Boarding House in San Francisco – was released on Round Records in 1975. Further albums *That High Lonesome Sound*, *Breakdown* and *Live At The Boarding House* would come out in the 1990s and the 21st century, giving Owsley's original recordings a wider audience.

While Garcia was developing his bluegrass chops in tiny venues close to home, he was still delivering outstanding work with his day job. The Dead were at the Oklahoma State Fair Arena on 19 October: the entire show captured on the three-disc set *Dick's Picks Volume 19*. From an upbeat first set beginning with 'Promised Land' that concludes with 'Playing In The Band' on disc two, they move into a second set that kicks off with 'China Cat Sunflower'>'I Know You Rider', before hitting a sequence on disc three that starts with 'Dark Star' before 'Mind Left Body Jam', 'Morning Dew' and 'Sugar Magnolia'. It's absolutely classic Dead, but they push it further with an encore of 'Eyes Of The World' and 'Stella Blue'. And then there's another encore winding things up with 'Johnny B. Goode'. It's a show that both begins and ends with Chuck Berry covers.

In November, The Dead were back on home soil at Winterland, and the run of three shows was released on the *Winterland 1973: The Complete Recordings* box set of nine discs in 2008. The Winterland run on 9, 10 and 11 November may well be the peak of their 1973 performances. They set a high standard that year, and the three-night run at Winterland captures the essence of the wild spirit they brought to the stage in 1973. If you're looking for a set that encompasses the versatility and virtuosity of The Dead, this box covers it. Over the three nights, songs range from the works of Chuck Berry and Johnny Cash and their own upbeat rockers to exploratory electric jazz improvisation; from deep country to deep space, and from ecstatic outpouring to introspective reflection. The final disc, with its 35-minute version of 'Dark Star' that moves into 'Eyes Of The World' and 'China Doll', is the essence of what's good about The Grateful Dead: the band progressing effortlessly from the further reaches of the strange to wild positivity, and then onto a soulful and fragile number. They finish the set with a rousing 'Sugar Magnolia', before a three-song encore of 'Uncle John's Band' and 'Johnny B. Goode' closing with 'And We Bid You Goodnight'.

A show from just a few nights later, features on the *30 Trips Around The Sun* box set, with the 14 November gig at San Diego Sports Arena across three discs.

The bulk of the second set on disc three is a non-stop sequence that kicks off with 'Truckin'', before 20 minutes worth of 'The Other One' moves into view. They return to' The Other One' after 'Big River', and again for a third time after 'Eyes Of The World', before the sequence resolves with 'Wharf Rat'. The rest of the second set appears at the end of disc two, and given that it's not easy to follow the kind of musical invention and spontaneous performance the band has unleashed, it's a cover of 'Me And My Uncle', 'Going Down The Road Feeling Bad' and 'One More Saturday Night' that brings the audience safely back to earth.

Dave's Picks Volume 5 keeps up the releases from this fertile period, with a show from 17 November at the Pauley Pavilion, Los Angeles. Released in 2013, the three-disc set features the complete show with a second set that features a sequence beginning with 'Playing In The Band', before moving into 'Uncle John's Band', 'Morning Dew', then back into a brief reprise of 'Uncle John's Band', concluding with another 11-minutes plus of 'Playing In The Band'. Pulling off elaborate pieces like this almost verges on showing off, but with The Dead, it never comes across as studied or cynical: more a case of the band enjoying what they are doing because the audience are enjoying it, leading to a virtuous circle that benefits both. You can almost feel the good-natured confusion in a sports arena full of fans wondering, 'Hey, didn't they just play that one?'. Disc three brings the rest of the show, with a 'Stella Blue' that shows how they could just as easily usher in something beautiful; 'Eyes Of The World' and 'Sugar Magnolia' bringing the show to a close with a communal spirit of celebration.

On 21 November, the band were at the Denver Coliseum in Denver, Colorado, for a show that featured on *Road Trips Volume 4 Number 3*. The show is spread over three discs, the final disc including 'Truckin''>'The Other One'>'Stella Blue' from the show at the same venue the night before. The first set on disc one includes 'Here Comes Sunshine' and ends with 'Brokedown Palace', the set ending with a full three-part 'Weather Report Suite' on disc two. The second set includes a version of 'Playing In The Band' that's split into three sections, interspersed with 'El Paso' and 'Wharf Rat', the final part moving into 'Morning Dew'. It's another illustration of the band's easy musical dexterity and imaginative approach to live performance. Disc three concludes the second set, and there's no let up, with a version of 'Truckin'' that sparks a cover of 'Nobody's Fault But Mine' before returning to more familiar ground with 'Going Down The Road Feeling Bad', 'One More Saturday Night' and an encore of 'Uncle John's Band'. A bonus disc featured the band's performance from 6 December at the Public Auditorium in Cleveland, Ohio. A separate disc including a version of 'Dark Star' that runs for almost 45 minutes before melting into 'Eyes Of The World', is a considerable bonus indeed.

Dick's Picks Volume 14 released material from the 30 November and 2 December gigs at the Boston Music Hall, Boston, Massachusetts, over four discs, each show given two discs. Donna Jean Godchaux isn't there, as she was taking time out due to pregnancy. The first night opens with an impressive 'Morning Dew', 'Mexicali Blues' lifting the mood from one of impending apocalypse to one a bit more conducive to fun. The disc concludes with a lengthy 'Playing In The Band', impressive in itself but also giving an indication that there might be more of this kind of playing to come. The second disc makes good this possibility, from 'Here Comes Sunshine' to 'Sugar Magnolia' via 'Weather Report Suite', and a 'Dark Star' jam that runs into 'Eyes Of The World'. This one disc makes it clear why so many fans rate the 1973 version of The Dead. Disc three covers the beginning of the second night: tighter tunes but with some room for a bit of musical tomfoolery after 'Brown-Eyed Woman'. There's another airing of 'Weather Report Suite', and a Garcia gem in the form of 'Wharf Rat'. The final disc covers another powerful sequence, from 'Playing In The Band' into a Jam, then 'He's Gone', 'Truckin'' and 'Stella Blue'. The disc finishes with the 'Morning Dew' encore, bringing the two-night collection to an end the way it began. *Dick's Picks Volume 14* was the last of the series to be released in archivist Dick Latvala's lifetime.

Part of the gig from 4 December 1973 was released as a bonus disc with the *Winterland '73* complete box set. Recorded at Cincinnati Gardens, Cincinnati, Ohio, the disc features four songs from the first set, and the complete second set without the encore. For a single disc, it packs a lot in, with a 'Truckin''>'Stella Blue' from the first set, the second with a memorable 'Eyes Of The World' that goes into a ten-minute 'Space' jam, before resolving in a crisp 'Sugar Magnolia'.

Download Series Volume 8 picks up the band's trail on 10 December at Charlotte Coliseum, Charlotte, North Carolina. Over the equivalent of two discs, it covers most of that night's show, and although a few tracks are trimmed from the first set and one from the second, the material that *is* present makes for a very satisfying listen. The shortened first set takes us through some of their punchier numbers, including 'Bertha', 'Deal' and 'Big River', before embarking on 'Playing In The Band'. If the earlier numbers were short pieces, this track again allows them to stretch their wings and do what they do best. The opening numbers from the second set that follow, are also on the shorter side: including Chuck Berry's 'Promised Land', 'Me And Bobby McGee' and 'Big Railroad Blues'. But by disc two, The Dead let go a bit more, with a sequence of 'Truckin''>'Nobody's Fault But Mine'>'Eyes Of The World' and 'Brokedown Palace'. It's a good show, perhaps not their best in 1973, but the standard that year was pretty high.

It was a show from the end of 1973 that had the honour of being the recording that cracked the vault open, with the gig at the Curtis Hixon Hall in Tampa, Florida on 19 December becoming the very first volume of the *Dick's Picks* archive series. Archivist and curator Dick Latvala – a serious deadhead and tape connoisseur – obviously saw something very special in this show, and he was right. If you're going to start a series of archive releases, best to start on a good foot, and this release certainly does that with an absolute monster of 'Here Comes Sunshine'. As a statement of intent for the rest of the archive releases, it sets the tone perfectly. After an opening like this, the rest of the show has much to live up to, but they manage it with a full 'Weather Report Suite' and lengthy 'Playing In The Band'; disc two featuring 'He's Gone', 'Truckin'' and a cover of 'Nobody's Fault But Mine' – the blues number originally by Blind Willie Johnson that Led Zeppelin recorded for their 1976 album *Presence*. The Dead's version gives way to a lengthy jam, with a brief hint of 'The Other One' in it, before a version of 'Stella Blue' and a closing 'Around And Around'. Donna Jean Godchaux is still absent, as she was giving birth to her and Keith's son Zion at the time. She still got a listing in the credits.

1974 – The Wall Of Sound

It was a situation The Dead referred to as Ouroboros: an ancient symbol of a serpent eating its own tail. By 1974, they were in a strange situation. Increased popularity meant playing bigger venues, but the bigger venues needed better sound systems, which cost more, meaning they had to play bigger venues to cover the cost. They were in a sonic arms race with themselves, chasing their own tail and in danger of destroying what they'd created.

The Dead had leading sound engineers on their team, and led by Owsley, a solution was developed – the Wall of Sound – allowing them to deliver music in the best possible quality in locations like arenas or sports grounds: places that are never best-suited for acoustics. The concept was simple – deliver adequate volume but without distortion: clean sound for the massive venues they were now playing. The Wall of Sound – the largest concert sound system of its time, and one of the biggest ever – featured a massive array of speakers directly behind the band, acting as its own onstage monitor for the musicians, allowing them to hear exactly what the audience heard, rendering the usual onstage monitors redundant. However, this created a different problem, as the sound from behind could be picked up in the microphones, creating a wall of feedback. This was solved by using two microphones with reversed polarity close together; the singer using the top microphone only, the lower picking up the sound of the PA as it was heard on stage. The signals from the two mics were brought together in such a way that any sound that was duplicated in both (the sound from the PA) was cancelled, and the vocals-alone amplified. It seemed a breakthrough and a solution making their live schedule more manageable. The quality of their performances continued to reach new heights, as the amount of archive releases from 1974 attests to.

The Dead had been working on the solution throughout 1973, with smaller-scale versions of the system being tried out – with varying degrees of success – and design work and testing being done on the range of speakers, amps and mics required. The full version of the Wall of Sound made its live debut on 23 March 1974 at the Cow Palace, Daly City, for a gig that was released as *Dick's Picks Volume 24* in 2002. The two-disc set featured most of the show with a few tracks missing, including cowboy's choice numbers like 'Mexicali Blues', 'Tennessee Jed', 'El Paso' and 'Me And My Uncle', and the Garcia numbers 'It Must Have Been The Roses', 'Ship Of Fools' and 'Ramble On Rose', as well as 'Around And Around', 'Casey Jones' and 'One More Saturday Night'. What's included shows the band in great form: disc one featuring Weir's 'Weather Report Suite' in full, and impressive versions of 'Black-Throated Wind' and 'I Know You Rider'. Disc two features a lengthy palindromic sequence of 'Playing In The Band'>'Uncle John's Band'>'Morning Dew'>'Uncle John's Band'>'Playing In The Band', with 'Wharf Rat'>'Sugar Magnolia' as a strong close. If The Dead were under any pressure because of their new sound system, it certainly didn't come across in their performance. Two new songs featured in the show – 'Scarlet Begonias' and 'Cassidy' – classic numbers that would stay in their repertoire for the rest of their career.

Prior to the Cow Palace show in March, a show from the Winterland Arena in San Francisco on 24 February was released as *Dave's Picks Volume 13* in 2015. The full Wall of Sound might not have been deployed yet, but this three-CD set shows that even before it was rolled out, they could cope with larger venues and deliver the goods, even in a converted ice rink. But as ever, they wanted to make things better and take it to the next level. Pioneering as always. The first disc features the first set, 'China Cat Sunflower'>'I Know You Rider' and 'Playing In The Band' challenging the idea that this set was only a place for shorter numbers. The second set features the full version of Weir's 'Weather Report Suite' – centrepiece of the still recent *Wake Of The Flood* – although later years would see Part One dropped. 'It Must Have Been The Roses' makes its earliest appearance, as does 'Ship Of Fools' with some soulful Garcia vocals. While the third disc features a lengthy and inspired 'Dark Star'>'Morning Dew' that would normally attract my full attention, it's the encore of Dylan's 'It's All Over Now, Baby Blue' that I return to: a phenomenal version of one of Dylan's finest. They'd be back at Winterland later in 1974.

At the end of March, The Dead were back in the studio for their second album from Grateful Dead records in just over a year. *From The Mars Hotel* would include many of the Garcia/Hunter songs The Dead had been playing live: 'US Blues', 'China Doll', 'Loose Lucy', 'Scarlet Begonias' and 'Ship Of Fools'. Two Lesh songs – collaborations with poet Robert Petersen – 'Unbroken Chain' and 'Pride Of Cucamonga' are included, though the former wasn't played live until 1995, and the latter, never played live. Weir's contribution 'Money Money' was only played live for a short time, as was 'Loose Lucy'. 'Loose Lucy' would re-emerge in the 1990s, though its reading by then was more tongue-in-cheek. An expanded 2004 version of *From The Mars Hotel* included a different take of 'Loose Lucy', acoustic demos of 'Pride Of Cucamonga' and 'Unbroken Chain', as well as live versions of 'Scarlet Begonias', 'Money Money', 'Wave That Flag' and 'Let It Rock' from the 1973 and 1974 shows later featured on *The Grateful Dead Movie Soundtrack, Dave's Picks Volume 16, Pacific Northwest '73-'74* and *Dave's Picks Volume 34.*

Dave's Picks Volume 9 catches up with the band on 14 May at the Harry Adams Field House in Missoula, Montana. Released in 2014, the three-disc set features a 20-minute-plus version of 'Playing In The Band' at the end of the first set on the second disc, and while the second set opens with 'US Blues' and 'El Paso', it moves on to 'Row Jimmy'. On the third disc, there's a full 'Weather Report Suite' followed by 'Dark Star'>'China Doll': the three numbers showing both the strength of Weir and Garcia's material with an electric jazz-flavoured epic in between. The band are sharp throughout the performance – the shorter western numbers crisp, and the slower numbers given the space to breathe – and the improvised sections really are outstanding.

The Wall Of Sound can be heard in full effect on other releases from May 1974. Two of these are featured in the *Pacific Northwest '73-'74* box set, and have been released as stand-alone items. The 2018 six-LP box set *Portland Memorial Coliseum, Portland, OR, May/19/74*, chronicles that full show, while the limited vinyl release *Playing in the Band, Seattle, Washington, 5/21/74* is an extract from *that* particular gig. Like the *Dark Star* album recorded live at the Olympia in Paris, this album features just one song over two sides: in this instance, a 46-minute version of 'Playing In The Band'. It's the longest version of any single song The Dead recorded. If it's still not enough, the full show is on the *Pacific Northwest '73-'74* box set, along with the Portland Memorial Coliseum show and a gig from Vancouver on 17 May. The record-breaking version of 'Playing In The Band' is also on the three-CD highlights package *Pacific Northwest '73-'74: Believe It If You Need It.*

Another batch of Dead-related solo albums were released or were being worked on in 1974, and while they were important additions to their growing collective discography, they were not perhaps as significant as the raft of solo works that appeared in 1972. Officially titled *Garcia*, his second solo album came out on Round Records: The Grateful Dead Records sub-label for their solo releases. The album is also widely known as *Compliments Of Garcia* or simply *Compliments*, on account of the sticker on the promotional copies that were sent out at the time, helpfully differentiating the collection from his eponymous solo debut. But it's a very different album from his first, the material on it consisting overwhelmingly of cover versions, and only one Robert Hunter/John Kahn original. Songs included Chuck Berry's 'Let It Rock' and The Rolling Stones' 'Let's Spend The Night Together', as well as works by Irving Berlin, Van Morrison and Smokey Robinson. Unlike last time, there were no Dead classics sneaked out on a solo release, and the musicians involved included John Kahn, Ron Tutt and Merl Saunders: mainstays of Garcia's solo act. Although not listed as such, rather than being a solo album, the collection was as much the studio debut of the Jerry Garcia Band, the song choice reflecting the material played by the band, and the release establishing some distance between Garcia's solo career and work with The Dead. A reissue of the album included with the *All Good Things: Jerry Garcia Studio Sessions* box set in 2004, expanded the tracklisting with an additional ten numbers: again mostly covers, but with one studio jam.

If Garcia's second solo album could be accused of playing it safe musically and lacking in the unique blend of weirdness that flavoured much of The Grateful Dead's output, *Seastones* – a release involving Phil Lesh – more than made up for it. *Seastones* was a work by Ned Lagin, created electronically using synthesizers and computers. It's a challenging listen, and while Lesh, Garcia and Hart are included in the sessions along with David Crosby and Grace Slick, their performances are extensively manipulated and processed. As a piece of work, it stands alongside some of the more exploratory work being done at the time in electronics by European artists like Tangerine Dream or Klaus Schultze, and while the use of electronics and computers in a live performance are now established, Lagin and Lesh were among the first to use this technology. 'Seastones' – featuring Lagin and Lesh and occasionally other Dead members – would for a time be a feature of The Dead's 1974 shows. The performance would usually come between The Dead's two sets; at some shows being part of a sequence involving one of the band's largely improvised numbers. Recorded in pieces between 1970 and 1974, *Seastones* was released on The Dead's Round Records label in 1975.

A further significant solo album emerged in 1974, with Dead lyricist Robert Hunter's debut *Tales Of The Great Rum Runners*. Again on Round Records, various Dead team members played on it, Keith and Donna Jean Godchaux, Garcia and Hart all performing. There's a banjo-led version of 'It Must Have Been The Roses' on the album, but other than this, none of the songs on this collection made it into The Dead's repertoire. While it's a decent album that has aged well, it perhaps has more in common with The Dead's late-1960s sound than where they were at in 1975, failing to engage with more-recent Dead fans.

Over three discs, *Dave's Picks Volume 34* records The Dead's gig at the Jai-Alai Fronton in Miami, Florida, on 23 June. A bonus fourth disc features six numbers from the same venue the previous night. Disc one includes The Dead's only airing of Chuck Berry's 'Let It Rock' – a song from Garcia's second solo album – coming between 'Jack Straw' and 'Cumberland Blues'. They'd play Chuck Berry's 'Around And Around' before 'Dark Star' in the second set. That second set begins on disc two with the first performance of *Seastones* from Lagin and Lesh: the electronics moving into a jam that leads into 'Ship Of Fools'. Even though electronic music is now a far-more-familiar concept that it was in 1974, the live *Seastones* experience remains an uncompromising proposition, and as a glimpse into the future of music, it must've left the audience as baffled as the one watching Marty McFly play 'Johnny B. Goode' in the style of Eddie Van Halen and Jimi Hendrix in the movie *Back To The Future*. That a Grateful Dead set could encompass both this and a cover of a Johnny Cash number, is a credit to their wide-ranging influences and abilities. A 'Dark Star' jam (with no vocals) includes a 'Spanish Jam' segment, before moving into 'US Blues' and 'Uncle John's Band' just makes it clear that this is quite an extraordinary show.

Two shows from a few days later are documented on *Dick's Picks Volume 12*: the 26 June gig at Providence Civic Center, Rhode Island, and the 28 June gig at Boston Garden, Boston, Massachusetts. Disc one features most of the second set from 26 June 26, with a jam leading into 'China Cat Sunflower' before another jam into 'I Know You Rider'. There's a short 'Beer Barrel Polka' interlude before they launch into a spectacular sequence of 'Truckin''>'The Other One Jam'>'Spanish Jam'>'Wharf Rat'>'Sugar Magnolia'. The set winds up with a vibrant 'Eyes Of The World' on disc two. The 28 June show then gets under way, the collection including the second set from that night, beginning with a brief taste of that evening's 'Seastones', before moving into the second 'Sugar Magnolia' of the collection. Disc three opens with 'Weather Report Suite' moving in to a lengthy jam that resolves in 'US Blues': the first number of a rock 'n' roll sequence of 'Promised Land', 'Going Down The Road Feeling Bad' and 'Sunshine Daydream'. The set ends with a crystalline 'Ship Of Fools'. The merits of a release that brings together two separate performances rather than one complete show can be argued, but this release showcases an energetic and eclectic band.

The following month, *Dave's Picks Volume 17* picks up a 19 July show from Selland Arena in Fresno, California, with the complete gig over three discs. It's a showcase of just how far The Dead were able to go at that time, with a show that could incorporate cowboy favourites like 'Mexicali Blues', 'El Paso' and 'Me And Bobby McGee' into the first set, with an astonishing 'Playing In The Band' that comes close to 30 minutes in length. There's a 15-minute 'Seastones' interlude between sets, with Lesh and Lagin developing the kind of *Sonic Attack* electronic heavy metal that bands like Hawkwind could only have dreamed of. Similar sounds may have been coming from places like Berlin, with Tangerine Dream and Klaus Schulze pioneering electronic rock, but they never felt the need to include country and western numbers in their set. If The Wall Of Sound PA needed testing to see if it could handle extremes, 'Seastones' was the ideal soundtrack. It's hard to believe it came from essentially the same team that would shortly be delivering a sweet and soulful 'China Doll' towards the end of the set. Disc three brings the meat of the second set with 'He's Gone' and 'US Blues', before 'Weather Report Suite' moves into a jam that develops into 'Eyes Of The World'; 'China Doll' bringing things to a close before the 'One More Saturday Night' encore.

A show from just a few weeks later on 31 July at Dillon Stadium in Hartford, Connecticut, was picked for *Dave's Picks Volume 2*. The three-disc set covers the whole three-set Grateful Dead performance but skips the 'Seastones' interlude between the second and third set. Disc one covers the first set, which after its 'Scarlet Begonias' opener, moves into western territory with 'Me And My Uncle' and 'Brown-Eyed Women', before a diversion south for 'Mississippi Half-Step'. The second set on disc two looks like it will cover similar ground, but following 'Big River', 'Eyes Of The World' takes off. 'China Doll' and 'Ship Of Fools' give Garcia the opportunity to deliver some sweet sounds, while 'Weather Report Suite' again gives the band some wind in their sails. By the third set, we're back out west with 'El Paso', and by the time we're on the third disc, Garcia is again at the mic for 'To Lay Me Down', leading to a powerful 'Truckin'' that moves into two jam sequences, before Garcia brings some peace with a rendition of 'Wharf Rat'. It's a strange show, covering their western catalogue extensively, but intersperses it with some powerful extended numbers and soulful Garcia ballads. *Dave's Picks Volume 2* included a bonus fourth disc with a selection of numbers from the 29 July Capital Centre, Landover, Maryland show. 'Sugaree' and 'Weather Report Suite' are present from the first set, along with the second set sequence of 'He's Gone', 'Truckin'', 'Nobody's Fault But Mine', 'The Other One', 'Spanish Jam' and 'Wharf Rat'. It's far from a complete show, but it delivers some exhilarating playing.

Three shows from August are combined to make the four-disc *Dick's Picks Volume 31* collection – two from the Philadelphia Civic Center on 4/5 August, and the concert from 6 August at Roosevelt Stadium, Jersey City, New Jersey. It's not going to be complete shows by any means, but any collection that kicks off with a 25-minute plus version of 'Playing In The Band' (from 4 August) has immediately got my attention. The rest of the disc includes material from that night, along with five from 5 August. The second disc features much of the second set from 4 August, including the 'Ship Of Fools' opener and a 'Weather Report Suite' that extends into a ten-minute jam before delivering 'Wharf Rat' and 'US Blues'. A slightly abridged second set from 5 August is on disc three, which also features a strong sequence of 'He's Gone',' Truckin'', and a jam that touches on 'The Other One' before embarking into 'Space' again, coming back into focus for 'Stella Blue'. The first set from 6 August dominates disc four, with a powerful reading of 'Eyes Of The World', and a version of 'Playing In The Band' that incorporates 'Scarlet Begonias' before reprising 'Playing In The Band'. 'Uncle John's Band', the second set opener, brings the collection to a close. *Seastones* fans like myself can only hope at some point the three 'Seastones' interludes that missed appearing in this collection, will someday be compiled for a very niche release.

In September, The Dead were back in Europe. But with no major record company subsidising it, and the money coming from their own collective pocket, compared to their visit two years earlier, it was a much more low-key event. They played only four locations – London, Munich, Dijon and Paris – with recordings from three nights at London's Alexandra Palace released as *Dick's Picks Volume 7*, and the 18 September show at the Parc des Expositions in Dijon released as part of the *30 Trips Around The Sun* box set.

Compared to *Europe '72*, the band were not in great shape at all for this tour. They hadn't played together for a month, issues over the logistics of touring with a huge amount of equipment and the expense involved, were becoming a burden. Added to this was considerable tension in the band and crew, particularly regarding drug use getting out of control. Consequently, performances were inconsistent and often below their usual standard. Offstage tales from this tour (beyond the scope of this book) paint the band in a particularly bad light, this perhaps being reflected in their performances.

Dick's Pick's Volume 7 collects the best of their three nights at London's Alexandra Palace on 9, 10 and 11 September, over three discs. It's a strong compilation, disc one with a 'Playing In The Band' from 11 September clocking in at 23 and a half minutes; disc two with a mighty 'Truckin'' followed by a jam into 'Wharf Rat' from 9 September. The third disc – entirely from the 10 September performance – features a lengthy 'Dark Star', a jam, and then into 'Morning Dew'. While these highlights might be familiar to a European audience who'd been digesting *Europe '72* for two years, the collection also includes the more-recent material 'US Blues', 'Weather Report Suite' and 'Stella Blue'.

A further show from the short European tour emerged on the *30 Trips Round The Sun* collection, with the 18 September show from the Parc des Expositions in Dijon presented over three discs. It's possibly the best show of the tour, and if performances had been inconsistent at times, things fell together perfectly here. The Dead are jazzy and relaxed. The first set is a gem from the 'Uncle John's Band' opener to the 'Playing In The Band' that concludes it on disc two; a *Seastones* intermission coming before a second set that includes a by-then-rare 'Caution Jam' that emerges from 'He's Gone'>'Truckin''>'Drums', before moving into 'Ship Of Fools'. Despite the clouds that hovered over the tour, the band barely put a foot wrong here, and it's one of the releases that show The Dead at their intuitive collective best.

If the Wall Of Sound PA system had been a bonus for the audiences, as 1974 progressed, it was apparent that it was also a burden for the band. The massive system was a logistical nightmare, requiring two sets of scaffolding and two crews so that while one was being completed for a show, work would have already begun on the next. The running costs were huge, and the band were getting trapped in a cycle of having to play bigger gigs to fund the equipment they needed to play those shows. Added to this, the additional complication of managing their own record label, meant issues with money and business that they hadn't needed to concern themselves with previously, were now everyday issues. A solution formed in the later months of 1974, with the band deciding to take time out: a chance to step off the hamster wheel and take a breath; an opportunity to recalibrate and reassess their circumstances.

It was a surprisingly bold move, considering the majority of the band's income was dependent on live performances, and the financial risk of running their own record label, which was yet to deliver the anticipated windfall. In hindsight, a temporary reprieve from the rigours of touring made perfect sense, but at the time, there was no assurance that the band would actually reconvene, never mind tour for the next two decades. In the meantime, a series of five October shows at Winterland were arranged, with the possibility in the air that this would indeed be the last time. The decision was made to record the shows and to film them; to document the Wall Of Sound, the scene The Dead had created, and the band at their peak on their home territory. The shows also marked the return of Mickey Hart to the fold – appearing as a guest on the last night, he would go on to resume his role as half of The Dead's eight-limbed Rhythm Devils duo. Time would reveal the shows to have been an artistic success, but in The Dead's own style, it wouldn't quite go to plan at the time – the film cost a fortune and took an age to make; the live album was slated by fans and critics on its release and damaged the band's reputation, and their record company was to collapse just months later.

A live album from the shows had been arranged to subsidise completion of the film, and the task of producing the album fell to Lesh and Owsley: Garcia's time being taken up with making the movie. But a number of faults, errors and poor choices led to a very substandard release. Lesh and Owsley weren't given a full-quality master recording to work with, and didn't have all of the tracks that were recorded, meaning they couldn't access the best song performances. The recording from the Wall Of Sound had many issues, vocals being particularly difficult as a consequence of the unique microphone arrangement. Some vocals had to be re-recorded in the studio, and the drum tracks were distorted. Rather than working on a stereo mix, the album was mixed for quadrophonic, and this was then processed for stereo, resulting in an unclear and muddy sound. Added to this, the track selection was uninspiring – many of the songs already having been released on studio albums by The Dead or on solo albums, and six of the fourteen tracks being covers. It lacked the flow of a regular Dead performance: the songs sitting uncomfortably alongside each other. For a band who'd made much of their reputation on the strength of their live releases, it was a major blunder. The album was out of print for several years as a consequence of Grateful Dead Records folding, and it was probably a blessing in disguise.

With the eventual release of *The Grateful Dead Movie* on DVD, a five-CD box set *The Grateful Dead Movie Soundtrack* was released in 2005, featuring not only the material in the movie, but many unreleased tracks. While not a complete release with all the material performed over the run of shows, and not reflecting the running order of a regular gig, it contains a treasure of great material, whether it was the 'Eyes Of The World'>'China Doll' and 'Playing In The Band' on disc one, the 'The Other One'>'Spanish Jam'>'Mind Left Body Jam'>'The Other One'>'Stella Blue' of disc two, 'Weather Report Suite'>'Jam'>'Dark Star'>'Morning Dew' of disc three, the 'Drums'>'Space'>'Truckin''>'Black Peter' of disc four, or disc five's 'The Other One'>'Wharf Rat'>'Playing In The Band'. There's also a rare appearance of 'Tomorrow Is Forever'. If proof be needed that the 1974 vintage Dead was one of the best incarnations of the band, this box gives a strong argument and rehabilitates the performances in the wake of *Steal Your Face*.

1975 – Unusual Occurrences

For a band that had essentially retired, The Dead remained busy. Alongside solo projects, work on a new album got underway almost immediately at the start of 1975. The process that led to *Blues For Allah* was a very different one to previous albums, and it rewarded them with one of their finest studio albums. If there's a critical consensus that The Dead never really cut it in the studio after the 1960s, *Blues For Allah* makes the case that when they put their minds to it, they certainly *could* cut it. The album not only produced long-standing fan favourites, but it also satisfied critical voices who expected The Dead to up their game in the face of then-contemporary rock acts who put their advanced musicality and artistic aspirations front and centre. Extended versions of 1960s R&B hits or cowboy songs would no longer be enough for a sophisticated mid-1970s audience.

With no income from touring or a record company, a band and all their associates to finance, a lucrative new album was required to keep The Dead's collective head above water. Rather than pay for studio time – with the risks and expense they'd experienced in the past – the decision was made to record the album at Weir's home studio. The setting was more relaxed and informal, and perhaps equally as importantly, from a business point of view, there was no meter running or subsequent bills to settle. In another break with their regular working practices, they didn't take road-tested material into the studio, but worked on new songs from scratch. The new work was created in the studio, sometimes from fragments that members brought to the sessions – whether Garcia's title track or Lesh's instrumental 'King Solomon's Marbles' – which the band then polished and sculpted into their final shape. Others – like 'Help On The Way', 'Slipknot', 'Franklin's Tower' and 'The Music Never Stopped' – were already written but hadn't been aired live yet. They'd go on to be among the highlights of their live shows for years to come.

Blues For Allah is perhaps The Dead's closest release to progressive rock, the title track, in particular, invoking religion, history and contemporary geopolitics in poetic terms; the music soaked through with an otherworldly exoticism. A lesser band would've delivered some vaguely Eastern-sounding clichés with an ersatz Arabic sound, but The Dead developed something on their own terms that encompassed the lofty aspirations of the work, taking what they'd learned from delivering avant-garde explorations on a nightly basis, and condensing it into a powerful package. The Middle Eastern flavour that emerged as the album took shape, would pay dividends a few years later with The Dead's adventure in Egypt.

As an album, it also has a strong overall identity. There are no obvious digressions, no country rambles or blues excursions, and the instrumental numbers work well to showcase the band's skills and musical sophistication without outstaying their welcome. It has a consistency that their studio albums often lacked; there are no obvious Bob or Jerry songs. Instead, it feels like a genuine band effort where each member brings their own vision and combines

89

it into a unique collective whole. It wasn't just *core members* of the band that were delivering something special, as, during the sessions, Mickey Hart again became a full Dead member. While his contribution was credited as 'Percussion and crickets', his in-depth knowledge of ethnic percussion helped subtly shape the album's sound. Elsewhere, Donna Jean Godchaux's contribution went well beyond the backing vocalist role she was normally regarded as having, bringing a unique sound to a predominantly male-dominated genre.

The album's 2004 reissue featured a number of studio jams that give a clear picture of the band's creative process in action. The unreleased song 'Hollywood Cantata' is an early version of 'The Music Never Stopped', featuring lyrics by Robert Hunter. An apparently unhappy Weir asked John Barlow to write alternative lyrics, which, with some changes to the song, became 'The Music Never Stopped'. It's a fascinating look behind the curtain at the album's development.

In March, The Dead took to the stage again, albeit under the name Jerry Garcia And Friends, on 23 March at San Francisco's Kezar Stadium. Their set was part of a benefit for local schools after a decision had been made to cut funding for arts and sport. The event – one of the first large-scale benefit concerts – was intended to draw attention to the issue, and was organised by Dead associate Bill Graham. Named SF SNACK (San Francisco Students Need Athletics, Culture and Kicks), the event featured, among others, Bob Dylan, Santana, Joan Baez, Jefferson Airplane, Neil Young and The Doobie Brothers. While the local authorities reversed their decision to cut the funding a matter of days before the show, it went ahead anyway, and a lesson was learned about how rock music could draw attention to causes and be a force for positive change.

The Dead played a short 45-minute set accompanied by Ned Lagin and Merl Saunders both on keyboards. The title track from *Blues For Allah* got its first public performance, albeit in mostly instrumental form, as the centrepiece of the set. 'Blues For Allah' moves into a lengthy jam based around 'Milking The Turkey', before returning to 'Blues For Allah'. An encore run-through of 'Johnny B. Goode' returned the audience to familiar territory. The set emerged as a bonus disc in the 2004 *Beyond Description* box set of their 1973-1989 output, albeit without the messy but exuberant 'Johnny B. Goode'. The SF SNACK benefit set may be one of The Dead's shorter performances, but it is no less intense for it.

Despite the lack of live dates, the band members remained active. Lesh and Owsley were involved in the thankless task of creating the *Steal Your Face* album from the tapes of the Winterland shows from the end of 1974. Garcia spent much of his time in a film-editing suite working on *The Grateful Dead Movie* using the footage shot the previous year. Meanwhile, Round Records continued its programme of releasing Dead-related solo albums. Ned Lagin's *Seastones* was released in February, and while The Dead audience might've been expected to be more familiar with the extraordinary sounds it contained by the time it was released, it was a step too far into the unknown for many fans, and remains divisive to this day. As commercial solo albums by members of top bands go, it was more John Lennon/Plastic Ono Band than Paul McCartney.

Garcia's *Old And In The Way* album finally came out, although, by this stage, the band was no longer a going concern. Recorded by Owsley in 1973, the album went on to be one of the biggest-selling bluegrass albums ever. Garcia abandoned playing bluegrass in public for many years, but played with Grisman again in the 1990s, releasing a series of albums. Keith and Donna Godchaux's album *Keith & Donna* was released in March, featuring seven of their original songs and two covers: including one of 'River Deep – Mountain High'. The album was recorded in their home; the couple's living room rearranged to act as a studio. Garcia featured on guitar throughout the album, and it's surprising that it remains out of print considering it features key Dead members and a significant appearance from Garcia. Keith and Donna would play live around the San Francisco area in 1975, Kreutzmann joining them on drums for many of the dates, Garcia occasionally sitting in with them. By the start of 1976, they'd put their own band to the side, the pair becoming members of the Jerry Garcia Band while The Grateful Dead resumed playing live. A second album from Robert Hunter was released in 1975: *Tiger Rose*, featuring Garcia on guitar on a number of tracks, and on pedal steel on 'Rose Of Sharon'. With its folk-rock style very different to the sound The Grateful Dead were creating in 1975, and despite his place at the heart of the band's creative core, Hunter's solo career was never the commercial or critical success with Dead fans, as might've been expected.

Bob Weir was indulging in extracurricular activity as a member of the band Kingfish – a group centred around his friend and harmonica player Matt Kelly – who'd appeared on The Dead's *Wake Of The Flood* album – and NRPS alumnus Dave Torbert. Weir had been playing with the band since late-1974 in the San Francisco area. The band's set featured blues and country numbers, and Weir featured on their 1976 debut album – and partially on their 1977 live album – having left the band before its release, as The Dead became active again. Garcia had been performing with his band under the name Legion Of Mary, featuring long-term collaborators Merl Saunders on keyboards, John Kahn on bass and Ron Tutt on drums, augmented with Martin Fierro on saxophone and flute. The live CD *Legion Of Mary: The Jerry Garcia Collection Vol 1* features material from February-July 1975 at various venues, including The Keystone in Berkeley, and the Great American Music Hall in San Francisco. Garcia disbanded Legion Of Mary in August, breaking from Saunders and creating the Jerry Garcia Band featuring Nicky Hopkins on piano and Khan and Tutt. Hopkins was a respected British session musician who'd played with many of the UK's biggest bands of the 1960s, including The Rolling Stones, The Who and The Kinks. Released in 2009, the album *Let It Rock: The Jerry Garcia Collection Vol 2* features the new band live at

Keystone on 17 and 18 November 1975: the set including 'Friend Of The Devil', 'They Love Each Other', 'Sugaree', cover, and several of Hopkins' own numbers.

There was a 17 June at Winterland by 'Jerry Garcia and Friends' (aka The Grateful Dead) – as a benefit for poster artist Bob Fried who had died that year – where they opened with 'Crazy Fingers' (performed in public for the first time), the gig also featuring debuts of 'Help On The Way' and 'Franklin's Tower'. The second set was dominated by 'Blues For Allah': still essentially an instrumental. It remains the only 1975 gig not to have been released officially.

On 13 August, the band performed a low-key invitation-only show at the Great American Music Hall – a small jazz venue in San Francisco – to promote the release of *Blues For Allah*. It was the only time in 1975 that they performed under the name The Grateful Dead. The purpose of the show was to convince record industry executives to give them a distribution deal for their record label; the movie project continuing to eat into their finances, while the lack of live shows meant there was none of their regular income source.

The showcase would become The Dead's first release of an entire show when it was made available in 1991 as the double CD *One From The Vault*. It was an exceptional gig, and an obvious choice for the band's first significant archive release. The show essentially consisted of the entire *Blues For Allah* album, along with other recent material, and it remains one of their finest releases. Opening with the freshly recorded 'Help On The Way'>'Franklin's Tower' must've been a jaw-dropping experience for those in the room. The show moved on with 'The Music Never Stopped', 'It Must Have Been The Roses' and 'Eyes Of The World' into 'King Solomon's Marbles', making it an unusual first set, but one that packs a punch. The second set begins with 'Around And Around' at the end of disc one, disc two picking up with 'Sugaree' and 'Big River'. 'Crazy Fingers' begins a sequence that moves into 'Drums', 'The Other One' and 'Sage & Spirit', before settling into 'Going Down The Road Feeling Bad'. An encore of 'US Blues' would normally suggest the end of the show, but they finish the night instead with 21 minutes of 'Blues For Allah'. If back in 1975 they wanted to convince their audience of the strength of their new material, they certainly managed it. It's a focussed and polished performance that would've convinced anyone that though The Dead may be on a break, they were far from dormant.

The show was broadcast on local FM radio, and quality tapes of the show were widely traded, eventually being released as the bootleg vinyl album *Make Believe Ballroom*, and by the time it was officially released, the show was already a highlight of many Deadhead's tape collections. As an addendum to the show, a rehearsal from the day before, appears on *Beyond Description*, where the band perform 'Showboat': a song from the *Keith & Donna* album. It may not have made it beyond the rehearsal stage, but the rehearsals ensured that The Dead were completely on form for what was a significant gig.

There would be one more show in 1975: a performance at Golden Gate

Park in San Francisco on 28 September, which made it on to the *30 Trips Around The Sun* collection. Like their legendary free local shows during their San-Francisco-based days, the show was announced with short notice. The two-disc set presents a Dead show (one long set in front of a crowd of around 25,000) that has more in common with their normal performances than their other 1975 shows. Disc one opens with 'Help On The Way', which moves into 'Slipknot!', and (unlike later) into 'The Music Never Stopped'. 'Franklin's Tower' – the song that normally ends this trilogy – didn't appear until after another two songs. The set moved on to a lengthy sequence starting with 'Truckin'' and concluding with 'Going Down The Road Feeling Bad'. While they presented several newer numbers at this their final performance of 1975, this was a more familiar Grateful Dead than the one that had played elsewhere that year.

There was no new-year Grateful Dead show in 1975, but the Jerry Garcia Band played at Keystone in Berkeley, with the band's Nicky-Hopkins-era lineup boosted by appearances from Weir, Hart and Matthew Kelly. The show was released in 2014 as *Garcia Live Volume Five*; Weir and Hart featuring on disc two of the two-CD set. It would also be Hopkins' last show with the Jerry Garcia Band: his drink problem leading to erratic performances. The band had already partially recorded a new Jerry Garcia solo album which would be released the following year, although the final songs in the collection featured The Grateful Dead as Garcia's backing band. By 1976, Garcia again focused on The Grateful Dead, while Keith Godchaux took the keyboard position with the Jerry Garcia Band alongside The Grateful Dead.

1976 – Ship Of Fools

If 1975 had given The Dead a much-needed opportunity to recharge their creative batteries, 1976 was a year that would challenge them as much as it inspired them. The activity of Grateful Dead Records continued unabated, with more solo works released. But by the end of the year, the label would collapse, and the experiment with their own independent record company would be over. There would also be a new album, but *Steal Your Face* would probably have been better left on the shelf. But 1976 was the year The Grateful Dead came out of their hibernation and took to the stage again, without the baggage of the Wall Of Sound weighing them down, and with a two-drummer lineup to keep them in time and propel them forward.

Garcia's solo album *Reflections* was partially recorded in December 1975 with the then-current manifestation of the Jerry Garcia Band. But with Nicky Hopkins out of the band, and the album unfinished, measures had to be taken to complete the recording. In the end, Garcia enlisted his Grateful Dead colleagues to record four songs: 'Comes A Time', 'They Love Each Other', 'It Must Have Been The Roses' and 'Might As Well'. The Dead had already performed the first three, while the fourth – 'Might As Well': a song inspired by The Dead's 1970 train tour of Canada – quickly found a place in their shows. Of the four earlier-recorded songs, 'Mission In The Rain' (A song Garcia described as 'autobiographical, but someone else wrote the words') also briefly entered The Dead's repertoire. The song remained a favourite to the extent that it was still included in Weir's Wolf Brothers set in 2021.

Weir featured heavily on the self-titled 1976 debut album by Kingfish. The album's first two songs – 'Lazy Lightning' and 'Supplication' – would be adopted by The Dead, perhaps unsurprisingly, as the two pieces are in a very similar style to what The Dead had created with *Blues For Allah*: sophisticated and jazz informed. The *Kingfish* album cover too, makes the connection – the artist Phillip Garris creating an image similar in design to the one he made for *Blues For Allah*. Weir's association with Kingfish would come to an end with The Dead returning to active service.

Under the name Diga Rhythm Band, Mickey Hart released his second album *Diga*. Hart had joined tabla and percussion virtuoso Zakir Hussain's Tal Vadya Rhythm Band at the Ali Akbar College of Music in San Rafael in 1975, Hussain having appeared on Hart's *Rolling Thunder* album. Hart joined to deepen his knowledge of traditional Indian music, and to gain a better understanding of percussion from an international perspective; the pair renaming the band for the joint album project. Garcia appeared on the album playing guitar on two tracks: The song 'Happiness Is Drumming' would later develop into The Dead song 'Fire On The Mountain'.

The Round Records release schedule had been a busy one and had encouraged Dead members to follow their inspiration in ways that couldn't normally have been accommodated in a band environment. Much that they'd created was fed back into the band, and would become part of the group's overall identity – Phil's experimentation with electronics and computers to create music; Weir's development as a songwriter and performer; Hart's passion to create a new musical vision incorporating non-western percussion; the Godchaux's growth as performers, and Garcia and Hunter's solo work, would all shape the band's development over many years. They were never vanity releases or indulgences. But the commercial environment the albums were released into was precarious, and while The Grateful Dead was a bankable name on a release, the solo projects lacked the same impact. It was never going to be easy to get *Seastones* or *Diga* radio airplay, and *Keith & Donna* or *Kingfish* were unlikely to pick up much of an audience outside their local area or beyond ultra-loyal Deadheads further afield.

The *Steal Your Face* album was released in June, originally intended as the soundtrack for a film that was still some way from completion. The new fans they'd acquired off the sophisticated and sculptured *Blues For Allah* would've been mystified by this sloppy, backwards-looking and musically unambitious collection. That the memorial for a sound system as advanced as the Wall Of Sound was presented in such poor sound quality must've been particularly galling. The album went out of print quickly, a remastered version emerging in 2004. But as a document of the Wall-Of-Sound-era-Dead, it has long been superseded by better archive releases. It was omitted from the *Beyond Description 1973-1989* box set that collected the releases from the second half of their career. *Steal Your Face* was released as a triple album in the UK, the third disc a compilation titled *For Deadheads,* consisting of material that had been released on Grateful Dead Records, including tracks from The Dead, Kingfish, Keith and Donna, Diga Rhythm Band, Garcia, Old And In The Way and The Good Old Boys. Even a free album did little to distract listeners and potential buyers from *Steal Your Face's* shortcomings. Picking up a secondhand copy in the early-1990s felt like a windfall for this fan in Scotland, but it soon became apparent that the photos of The Dead with the Wall Of Sound on the inner gatefold sleeve were the album's high point. It would be the band's final release on Grateful Dead Records, their independent venture coming to an end shortly after.

The Dead hadn't toured since their shows at Winterland in 1974, but the decision to take time out had strengthened the band. They'd removed the shackles of the Wall Of Sound, and had the opportunity to play in smaller, more hospitable venues again, with a less extravagant sound system. Over the summer in 1976, they played more-regular large theatre-sized venues before stepping up to arena-sized venues later in the year. They'd built up a wealth of new material, and while the collapse of Grateful Dead Records and the embarrassment of *Steal Your Face* were still on their minds, resuming live performance gave them the opportunity to move forward, put these issues behind them and focus on what they did best. The Grateful Dead never set out to become business people anyway.

The 9 June show from the Boston Music Hall, Boston, Massachusetts, is the earliest-released of The Dead's 1976 shows, and their third gig since returning from their break. The band played a four-night run at the venue, and the three-disc set *Road Trips Volume 4 Number 5* features the complete gig with bonus tracks from a show at the same venue on 12 June. The show features a number of new and recently-recorded songs alongside more-established material, disc two featuring the second set opening of 'St. Stephen'>'Eyes Of The World'>'Let It Grow', not only illustrating how well the new material sounded alongside tested favourites but also showing how their older material had developed. 'St. Stephen' was quite a different piece with a lighter and more agile touch, while 'Let It Grow' was now unshackled from the rest of 'Weather Report Suite', and all the better for it. Weir's 'Lazy Lighting'>'Supplication' had easily made the transition from Kingfish to The Dead; 'Dancing In The Streets' makes a return to the set in a slightly different form after it was last played in 1971, while a stand-alone 'Franklin's Tower' made an exceptional encore. The bonus tracks from 12 June include 'Mission In The Rain' from the first set, 'The Wheel' and 'Comes A Time' from the second, and a three-song encore. The album would be the final instalment of the *Road Trips* series, *Dave's Picks* replacing it as the vehicle for The Dead's more informal archive releases.

Their June tour was further explored in 2020 with the *June 1976* 15-CD box set, which collected five complete concerts from that month: two shows at the Boston Music Hall on 10/11 June; two at the Beacon Theatre on 14/15 June, and one from the Capitol Theatre on 19 June. The set gives a clear picture of the range of material The Dead now had at their fingertips (newly-recorded numbers from *Blues For Allah*, songs from solo releases, new songs and revitalised older numbers) and the ease with which they could change their set from night to night. There are many highlights, including 11 June's second-set opener of 'St. Stephen'>'Dancing In The Street'>'The Music Never Stopped', and the first set from 19 June on disc 13, where they opened with 'Help On The Way'>'Slipknot!'>'Franklin's Tower'>'The Music Never Stopped', signposting a band with justified confidence in their new material. Weir's 'Lazy Lightning'>'Supplication' finds a comfortable place in the first set, as does Garcia's 'Mission In The Rain', while the new treatment of 'Dancing In The Street' and Weir's arrangement of 'Samson & Delilah', pointed towards the shape of their next studio album.

One of the shows skipped in the June 1976 box set, was the 17 June show at the Capitol Theatre in Passaic, New Jersey, which had already appeared as the bulk of *Dave's Picks Volume 28*. The three-CD set released in 2018 covers the first of their three nights at the venue, with two bonus tracks: 'Sugaree' from 23 June and 'High Time' from 28 June. Like the rest of the early-1976 shows, The Dead are on their toes and pack a lot in – the first set might feature a cover of 'Big River', but they soon move on to songs like 'They Love Each Other', 'Looks Like Rain' and 'Row Jimmy'. The second set, on disc two, features both the triple helping of 'Help On The Way'>'Slipknot!'>'Franklin's Tower' – still very much a new number to the audience – and the more familiar 'Dancing In The Street', while 'Samson & Delilah' brings something entirely new. Disc three opens with 'Lazy Lightning' > 'Supplication' – familiar only to those who followed Weir's Kingfish project during the band's hiatus – but the 'Friend of The Devil' that followed would've been like meeting an old friend again. 'Let It Grow' features a 'Drums' interlude, Garcia's 'Wharf Rat' bringing the set to a classy conclusion. If you'd been waiting since 1974 to see The Dead, a show like this would have everything you'd want: some old favourites and some fresh new material.

The following night's show at the Capitol Theatre, appeared in 2005 as Volume 4 in the *Download Series*, with the show over two discs, a third offering material from their dates in Philadelphia on 21/22 June and Chicago on 28 June. A few of the songs played the previous night, make an appearance: 'Big River', 'Looks Like Rain', 'Row Jimmy' and 'Promised Land' featuring in both first sets; 'Samson & Delilah' in the second. The 18 June show does, however have 'Crazy Fingers' in the first set (an overlooked Garcia gem) and a rare Grateful Dead version of 'Mission In The Rain'. Though the song became a regular for The Jerry Garcia Band, The Dead only played it a handful of times: the second overlooked gem in the set. The second set features a sequence invoking 'St. Stephen', that incorporates 'Not Fade Away' before 'Eyes Of The World' > 'Drums' > 'The Wheel' and 'Sugar Magnolia'. From a perspective of listening to 1980s and 1990s sets, it's interesting to hear 'Not Fade Away' so early in the second set rather than after the 'Drums' > 'Space' sequence, and the 'Drums' section being comparatively short (just over two minutes) despite Hart now back onboard.

In July, The Dead were back in San Francisco for their first shows since their intermission, with six nights at the Orpheum Theatre. *Dave's Picks Volume 18* covers the 17 July gig – the fifth night of the run – over three discs. It includes some additional material from 16 July, and a fourth bonus disc includes more tracks from 16 July. The first-set Garcia classic this time is 'Peggy-O', though the version of 'Sugaree' here is a fine example of the species. The second set begins with 'Samson & Delilah': a tune they seemed to enjoy bringing out during these dates. The set continues on the second disc, with a sequence built around 'The Other One' and 'Eyes Of The World' following 'Comes A Time'. Again, it's a reversal of what would be more common in their later career, 'Comes A Time', the kind of Garcia ballad that would follow a sequence rather than precede it. The third disc includes 'Not Fade Away', the second encore of the night, and at just under fifteen minutes in length, the audience certainly got something they wouldn't have expected. A selection mostly from the first set from 16 July fills the disc, with the second versions of 'Peggy-O' and 'Big River'. The bonus disc takes in most of the second set, with 'Playing In The Band' leading into 'Cosmic Charlie' via a rare performance of the *Blues For Allah* instrumental 'Stronger Than Dirt', then taking further detours before returning for a reprise of the song. A more widely-released version of this set in full, is overdue.

There were a couple of shows after the San Francisco run, and in September, The Dead moved their attention to the East Coast for a series of nine shows. Three of these shows have been released so far, one as *Dave's Pick's Volume 4*, featuring the 24 September gig at the College Of William And Mary in Wiliamsburg, Virginia, and the show from the following night at the Capital Centre, Landover, Maryland, presented alongside one from 28 September at Onondaga County War Memorial, Syracuse, New York, on *Dick's Picks Volume 20*.

The star of *Dave's Picks Volume 4* is probably the first set 'Playing In The Band' that incorporates 'Supplication' that features on disc two, while the other highlight is the disc-three second-set sequence of 'Help On The Way'>'Slipknot!'>'Drums'>'Slipknot!'>'Franklin's Tower'. The 1976 Dead were still flexible about the format of the show, and before things became more rigid, there was room for trying out new things. *Dick's Picks Volume 20* features two shows over four discs, each show losing a track to fit on the release. The 25 September show would be the last time a full version of 'Cosmic Charlie' appeared. It would be teased in 1994, but the 1976 live versions of the *Aoxomoxoa* favourite were its final appearances, though it would eventually be welcomed back by Phil And Friends and other post-Grateful-Dead groupings.

By October, The Dead were in stadium territory, with their shows at Oakland Coliseum Stadium on 9/10 October released as *Dick's Picks Volume 33*, the two complete shows presented over four discs. The two stadium gigs were part of Bill Graham's Day On The Green shows – annual events that helped establish sports stadiums as venues for rock gigs – that ran from 1973 until the early-1990s. Shows in sports stadiums made economic sense. They were more accessible than rural festivals, there were facilities for large crowds already in place, and the ticket prices represented good value-for-money. The stadium gig would become a regular occurrence by the 1980s. The Dead had played Day On The Green in 1974 with the Beach Boys and NRPS, while Kingfish with Bob Weir played it in 1975. The Dead would play there again in 1987. For the 1976 shows, The Dead supported The Who on both nights, the event promoted by memorable tombstone artwork. Garcia had known The Who's Pete Townshend since the Monterey Pop festival, and Townshend was at the time living in the Bay Area.

The Dead's two shows were slightly shorter than usual but still ran over two sets each night, each disc containing a complete set. The first set of the first show opened with a cover of 'Promised Land' followed by a lengthy 'Mississippi Half-Step Uptown Toodeloo', closing with 'Sugaree'. The second set packs a lot in, from 'St. Stephen' into 'Not Fade Away', a brief reprise of 'St. Stephen', and into 'Help On The Way'>'Slipknot!, before moving into 'Drums' and 'Samson & Delilah', a return to 'Slipknot!' and into 'Franklin's Tower'. 'One More Saturday Night' closed the set, with a 'US Blues' encore. It was a set that would've satisfied the most obsessive Deadhead, with the energy that the audience's Who fans would've appreciated. The second day's first set again featured some of The Dead's newer material, their lengthy cover of 'Dancing In The Street' being as familiar to any Mods in The Who crowd as to longtime Dead fans. The second set again covered a lot of ground, the 'Samson & Delilah' opening setting an energetic tone that was maintained by a lengthy 'Playing In The Band' incorporating 'Drums', 'Space', 'The Other One' and 'Stella Blue' before a reprise of the song moved into 'Sugar Magnolia'. An encore of 'Johnny B. Goode' ended the two shows as they'd begun: with a Chuck Berry cover.

At the end of the year, The Dead were back in the Bay Area neighbourhood and headlined a show at the Cow Palace in Daly City: released in 2007 as *Live At Cow Palace*. The show was their first New Year gig since 1972, and the event would become an annual fixture for them. Garcia once commented that he didn't really enjoy playing New Year shows, as the band didn't get the chance to party. But despite that, from this show on, The Dead played a New Year show every year until 1991. It was a return to the Cow Palace – a much larger venue than their usual Winterland and the venue where the Wall Of Sound made its debut. By the end of 1976, the Wall Of Sound was history, The Dead now performing with a smaller but effective PA system that was still technologically ahead of what others were using. The Dead's first set started at just after 10 p.m.. The first set – covered on disc one of the three-CD set – features impressive versions of 'Looks Like Rain' and 'Playing In The Band', the latter a 23-minute set closer as powerful and inventive as any of the versions of this song they performed in 1973 or 1974. The second set kicked off at midnight, the New Year celebrations beginning with 'Sugar Magnolia' and the euphoric 'Eyes Of The World'. Quite why they then went into 'Wharf Rat' – fine version though it is – seems odd given it's a melancholy tale of a down-and-out alcoholic and a bit of a vibe killer. But they move into the more upbeat 'Good Lovin'', and the party spirit revives, maintaining right up to 'Morning Dew': an appropriate tune to wind down in the early hours. Three encores – 'One More Saturday Night', 'Uncle John's Band' and 'And We Bid You Goodnight' – eased the audience into 1977.

Early copies of the album included *The Spirit of '76* bonus disc with eight tracks from shows in September and October, including the show featured on *Dave's Picks Volume 4*. It works well as a collection showing where the band were musically in 1976, with new material like 'The Music Never Stopped' and 'Crazy Fingers' settling well into live performances, and a two-part 'Playing In The Band' sandwiching a live version of Weir's Kingfish number 'Supplication'.

1977 – To Terrapin

In 1977, The Dead would again go through transformations, with a new record company taking them on, a new album finally putting the misstep that was *Steal Your Face* behind them, and a series of live shows widely reckoned to be the finest of their career. The record deal saw them sign to Arista Records: a label that had been interested in getting the band on board for a while. The move secured the band financially following the disaster of Grateful Dead Records and meant a return to the studio, this time with material that they'd been playing live since the previous year, including one of Robert Hunter's most ambitious pieces.

1977 was also the year *The Grateful Dead Movie* was finally released. While no expense had been spared, it underperformed at the box office. The soundtrack had been mixed to be played on a speaker setup that was only available at a limited number of cinemas, meaning only a small proportion of the potential audience got to actually see the movie, and by the time it came out, the band themselves had moved on and the movie was essentially a couple of years past its best. It remains a remarkable piece, capturing the essence of the band at a particular time and place that would never be repeated. Watching it in the 21st century, the quality of the work is apparent, from the cinematography to the editing; the opening animation sequence and the incorporation of documentary elements into the performances. It was released on VHS in 1981, a restored version issued on DVD in 2004 with improved audio options and a second disc of additional performances and interviews. A blu-ray came out in 2011, adding additional commentary on the production of the disc. The DVD sold over 200,000 copies, and it's entirely possible the movie had a bigger audience on DVD and digitally than it originally had in the cinema. It did return to the silver screen in 2011 as a Grateful Dead Meet Up At The Movies event, broadcast to cinemas, repeated in 2017.

The quality of The Dead's live performances in 1977 is reflected in the sheer number that have been released from the archive. The Cornell University show on 8 May is regarded as one of their finest shows, but the quality of the 1977 shows was so high that while the Cornell show may have been a peak, it wasn't an isolated one. It was in fact, a peak that came as part of a mountain range of other highs.

The show from 30 April at the New York Palladium – the second night of a five-night run at the venue – was to become the first volume of The Dead's *Download Series* in 2005. The performance sets out the band's modus operandi for 1977, where they would settle into lengthy grooves, bouncing musical ideas off each other with a relaxed expertise. The band were in a good space, at ease with live performance again, without the need to impress anyone other than themselves, and at the top of their game. The performance is at times a little rough around the edges – there are a couple of tuning breaks as things get sorted – but from the opening 'The Music Never Stopped' to the 'Terrapin Station' encore, there are many shining moments. 'Peggy-O' in the first set sees some classy work from Weir, adding to Garcia's solo, and despite a bumpy start, 'Friend Of The Devil' shows Keith and Donna Godchaux bringing their own special magic in the form of vocals giving Garcia's performance an additional resonance, and piano that matches his guitar-playing for invention and skill. Elsewhere, the version of 'St. Stephen' that includes 'Not Fade Away' and 'Stella Blue' is a second-set highlight. Three songs from the previous night's show at the same venue add the best part of 35 minutes to the third disc's playing time. Aficionados of the occasional tuning breaks were no doubt delighted with the 2021 fan-made collection titled *Tuning '77* – a lengthy collection of onstage pauses, tuning breaks and equipment fixes without any actual music from The Dead. It's worth a listen, but probably only once.

The performance at Barton Hall, Cornell University, Ithica, New York on 8 May, has gone down in legend as one of the best Grateful Dead performances. The three-CD set released in 2017 stands witness for the case. It resolves some of the band paradoxes – Without reigning in the musical experimentation that distinguished them from other acts, The Dead remain approachable throughout this performance, with complex musical ideas woven into the set organically and naturally. The set might not contain many surprises – though there is a 'Lazy Lighting'>'Supplication' in the first set, a 'Scarlet Begonias'>'Fire On The Mountain' and 'St. Stephen' in the second – but each number is played with a rare fluid grace shining through, making even the most familiar number an absolute delight. It's the kind of performance that would remind the most jaded fan why The Dead are so special and one that would convince those unfamiliar with the band that there's something unique here that deserves further investigation. Even with the length of the songs (There's a 16-minute plus 'Dancing In The Street' and a 'Fire On The Mountain' and 'Not Fade Away' that come close to this mark), it doesn't feel like there's any unnecessary playing. Nothing is excessive for its own sake, and there's no sense of the band showboating, but just delivering the songs in the best possible way, letting them breathe naturally, the band serving the music without ego or extravagance. No one is trying to prove what a great musician they are; no one is trying to out-perform the others; they work as a gestalt. Each musician contributes towards the greater whole of the band, each song contributing to the greater whole of the show. The Cornell gig is a definitive example of what The Dead could do.

A box set of eleven discs – *May 1977: Get Shown The Light* – expands the Cornell gig by presenting it alongside the two that preceded it on 5 and 7 May, and the one following on 9 May. These shows put some context around the Cornell gig, making it clear it wasn't an isolated event like the Veneta, Oregon August 1972 show was, but a culmination of elements the band had been employing at the time. Familiarity with the material didn't mean the band treated it as any less deserving of applying their full range of skills, and pieces that could be regarded as musically complex could still shine without unnecessary theatrical adornment. Like the best jazz music, The Dead could be played as background music to a party or listened to intently as part of a musical education. They could certainly have their off nights, but by this point, they were mostly in a good place – renewed from their hiatus, but now settled with their two-drummer lineup again, freshly signed to a new record company, with some of the problems that had befallen them (the Wall Of Sound and Grateful Dead Records), firmly in the past. The new chapter of The Grateful Dead's history looked to be an optimistic one.

The 9 May show at the Memorial Auditorium in Buffalo was released as a stand-alone five-disc vinyl box set in 2020, as a limited edition for Record Store Day. Marketed as 'The contender to Cornell's crown', it makes the case for its versions of 'Help On The Way'>'Slipknot!'>'Franklin's Tower' and 'Comes A Time' being the best ever. Listening to it without Cornell sitting beside it in a box makes it clear it is indeed an outstanding show in its own right.

A second box set covers a further five May gigs over fourteen discs. *May 1977* – released in 2013 – features shows from 11 May at St. Paul Civic Centre, Minnesota, 12/13 May at the Auditorium Theatre, Chicago, 15 May at the St. Louis Arena, Missouri, and the 17 May gig at the University of Alabama, Tuscaloosa. It's a massive, detailed collection that continues their developments with little diminution in returns. The band are comfortable in who they are and what they can do, and while they have little to prove, they continue to strive for improvement and discovery in the songs. The live Dead experience of 1977 may not be about exploring the outer limits of sound or continuing the psychedelic conjuring that made their reputation in the late-1960s, but their continued pushing of the musical boundaries means that new life was breathed into the set every night: each song was given the opportunity to shine like it was being played for the first time. It might not always take shape as well as it might, and this collection might not match the collection that compiled the shows from just a few days before, but the spirit of creativity is always present and being expressed by the hands of experts. And even if things fall a little short of the lofty plateau of the Cornell gig, it's still a live experience few others could come close to.

Dick's Picks Volume 29 picks up the May 1977 trail with a show from the 19th at the Fox Theatre, Atlanta, Georgia, and the 21 May show at the Lakeland Civic Arena, Lakeland, Florida. The release features the two complete concerts over six discs: the only release in the *Dick's Picks* series to include more than four discs. It also includes five bonus tracks from the 11 October gig at the Lloyd Noble Centre in Norman, Oklahoma. More tracks from this show feature on *Road Trips Volume 1 Number 2*.

The first gig is again of the same high standard as the other shows of this immediate era, matching them in passion, sincerity and openness. 'Sugaree' from the first set could be a perfect rendition of the song, Garcia in perfect voice throughout with a tone that matches his playing. While the rest of the set is stellar, the second set – particularly the segment on disc three – takes things to another level with a sequence that begins with 'Terrapin Station' and moves into 'Playing In The Band', before 'Uncle John's Band' hits: starting dramatically with what's normally its closing section, before moving into the song proper. The sequence continues with 'Drums', 'The Wheel' and 'China Doll', before resolving with the reprise of 'Playing In The Band'. The interplay throughout the sequence is astonishing: at times fierce, at times mellow, intense and soulful, as the music apparently plays the band.

The 21 May show is no less inspired – the first set's 'Scarlet Begonias'>'Fire On The Mountain' combination featuring an amazing transition between the songs, with 'Fire On The Mountain' taking on a different rhythm, almost as if the band are somehow playing two songs simultaneously that just happen to fit together perfectly. The second set features a great 'Estimated Prophet', the subsequent sequence featuring 'St. Stephen' and 'Not Fade Away', and while perhaps not as successful as other versions played in May 1977, it remains a powerful listen throughout.

A show from the following day, May 22, at Pembroke Pines in Florida, was released as *Dick's Picks Vol 3*. Dick Latvala had many requests to finally release the Cornell show, but chose to instead release this one early in the series, as be believed it was in fact, better than Cornell. It's a bold claim, but the two-disc collection does present a very strong show from its opening lighthearted 'Funiculi Funicula'. The track listing is arguably better, with 'Help On The Way'>'Slipknot!'>'Franklin's Tower' on disc one, while disc two has a monumental sequence of 'Estimated Prophet' into 'Eyes Of The World', 'Wharf Rat', 'Terrapin Station' and 'Morning Dew'. There's even a gem of a version of 'Sunrise' in the second set, while the first set's 'Sugaree' is close to definitive. The release is a slightly-trimmed version of the show, with a few tracks removed from both sets so it fits on two discs. There's a solid case for issuing it in full, even just to compare the whole show with the Cornell gig.

The final date of the 1977 East Coast tour is represented by the *To Terrapin: Hartford '77* three-CD collection released in 2009. Recorded on 28 May at Hartford Civic Center, Hartford, Connecticut, it opens with a sequence of 'Bertha', 'Good Lovin'' and a version of 'Sugaree' that clocks in at just under 20 minutes. It's a case of quantity as well as quality, though, the set starting strongly and continuing that way for the rest of the show. The second set begins on disc two, but on disc three, it takes flight with 'Estimated Prophet' and 'Playing In The Band'. There's no lengthy 'Drums' piece – it's only a brief minute-and-a-half interlude between a sublime 'Terrapin Station' and a jam-packed 'Not Fade Away', before 'Wharf Rat' and into the reprise of 'Playing In The Band'. 'One More Saturday Night' and the 'US Blues' encore brings things to an upbeat conclusion.

A run of June shows emerged in 2009 as the box set *Winterland June 1977: The Complete Recordings*, covering the shows from 7/8/9 June over nine discs, their second archive release box set of a run of shows from the San Francisco venue. The collection again shows the band's strengths at this stage in their career: confident, fully equipped and delivering from every angle. While The

Dead are regularly portrayed as centred on Garcia – and history to some extent showed this to be the case – in a live environment, it was never a one-man act with a backing band. As this collection and other recordings illustrate, the musicians played together as an ensemble, and in 1977 they were probably at their closest. They would match each other, push the music forward and take the others with them. Weir correctly comments in the accompanying booklet that the shows were the best example of the band playing with a united mind. The band are in synch throughout, the jamming so fluent, it sounds like they're simply communicating in an advanced musical language.

There are many high points across the collection – 'Terrapin Station' and 'Morning Dew' on the first night with the 'Uncle John's Band' encore from that show; 'Estimated Prophet' and 'Eyes Of The World' from the second night, or 'The Other One' and 'Wharf Rat' from the same show, the third night delivering a second set that had room for 'Help On The Way', 'Slipknot!', 'Franklin's Tower' and a 'St. Stephen' that included a version of 'Not Fade Away' and a 'Drums' section, before arriving at 'Terrapin Station'. A box set of three concerts in a row by any other band would inevitably be full of repetition and songs played as recitation rather than performance. But here – as elsewhere – The Dead make each show a unique and joyous occasion. A tenth disc released as a bonus with early purchases, featured material from their 12 May gig at the Auditorium Theatre, Chicago: included in full on the May 1977 box set.

Released in July, the *Terrapin Station* album marked a new chapter for The Grateful Dead. They were with a new record label, were touring again, and following their hiatus were a band reborn. Part of the album deal was that an outside producer had to be involved: the record company wanting the release to be more commercially palatable. The Dead might have been a huge live draw, but it was time to convert that into album sales, or to at least try to. Keith Olsen was given the job, having produced Fleetwood Mac's self-titled 1975 album, which reached number 1, spawned several hit singles and marked the start of a run of massive-selling albums. If this had been Arista's hopes for The Dead, it wouldn't quite go to plan.

The side-long track 'Terrapin Part I' – described as a 'song cycle' – is an ambitious piece, the words composed by Hunter in a single sitting. Synchronously, Garcia, while driving, came up with a melody that he quickly wrote down, that would be the work's central theme. It's the kind of progressive piece that continues their thinking on the title track of *Blues For Allah*, with its overall complexity and individual sections making an elaborate and distinct whole. However, the band were far from impressed with Olsen's decision to add orchestra, choir and strings to the final version. What had already been an elaborate and carefully-constructed piece, became sugarcoated, airbrushed and embellished: Garcia saying Olsen had 'put The Grateful Dead in a dress'. If the studio version erred towards the overelaborate with its orchestration and strings, it remained a live-performance centrepiece for the rest of their career. In a somewhat different form to its studio version,

'Terrapin Station' – normally just the first three sections – became one of The Dead's key pieces.

Elsewhere, the album material is strong. 'Estimated Prophet' – Weir's reflection on some of the dubious self-appointed gurus they encountered – would become a standout live number that demonstrated how the Weir/ Barlow team had progressed as songwriters. They'd come a long way from Bobby Ace's cowboy songs. Again, the album version suffers from some ill-advised and unnecessary embellishment. Lesh's 'Passenger' is a powerful and dynamic rock number that packed a lot into a short piece, and again, had a welcome place in the live set. Donna Godchaux's 'Sunrise' – her first song performed by The Dead – is something of an overlooked gem, understood to be a piece honouring deceased Dead roadie Rex Jackson, in the terms of a Native American ceremony performed by band associate Rolling Thunder. It too would be performed live: all the better for the loss of the studio version's orchestral overkill.

Two covers appear: Weir's arrangement of 'Samson & Delilah' that had featured in their sets since they began touring again, and a cover of 'Dancing In The Street' stylised as 'Dancin' In The Streets'. Though The Dead had performed the Martha and the Vandellas number since their early years, this version was cast in a very different light, the new arrangement filed firmly under 'disco': possibly the most unlikely genre for The Dead. In their defence, the band had always been fans of music of black origin, from blues to funk, gospel to reggae, and had incorporated elements of these in their music throughout their career. But in the late-1970s, many saw *going disco* as the ultimate sellout: putting commercial interests ahead of artistic integrity. For a band who were a borderline progressive-rock act with fans into *serious music*, this was a serious misstep, and the term 'Disco Dead' would be used against them. As it stands, it's a pretty good late-1970s dance track, although it might've been better served as a stand-alone single, and better-received outside the context of a *serious* album.

A 2004 *Terrapin Station* reissue as part of the *Beyond Description* box set added five studio outtakes from the sessions, including the Lesh original 'Equinox' (sung by Garcia, and left off the album due to time constraints), an instrumental 'The Ascent', a version of 'Fire On The Mountain', and covers of 'Peggy-O' and 'Catfish John'. The live version of 'Dancing In The Street' from the Cornell concert is also included. A different version of 'Fire On The Mountain' would be a centrepiece of The Dead's 1978 *Shakedown Street* album.

A show from 3 September at Raceway Park, New Jersey, features in full on *Dick's Picks Volume 15*. The band's live activities had been halted temporarily, due to Hart being injured in a car accident, but demand for their return was huge, and they played to a crowd estimated to be around 150,000: one of the biggest crowds they'd play to. If in 1976 the band had moved to playing smaller shows following their year's absence, they were already back in front of enormous audiences. Highlights here are the disc-two version of 'Eyes Of

The World', and disc three's sequence of 'He's Gone' into 'Not Fade Away' and 'Truckin'', which hadn't been played for over two years – the version of 'Not Fade Away' being particularly outstanding with its distinctive rhythm supporting a lengthy instrumental introduction. Unusually, the set featured 'Terrapin Station' as an encore; Lesh announcing 'And now ladies and gentlemen, we'd like to play a little ditty from our newest album, at your record stores currently'. Perhaps they'd been reminded they should at least make an effort to promote the new album. The release was the first in the series issued following the death of archivist Dick Latvala; a note in the sleeve explaining that Latvala had let colleagues know his plans for future releases, and that the series would continue without him. 36 volumes of *Dick's Picks* would be released, the majority of them after Latvala's death.

Four October concerts are covered in *Road Trips Volume 1 Number 2*: a double CD with a bonus disc, released in 2008. The shows included are from 7 October at the University of New Mexico in Albuquerque; 11 October at the Lloyd Noble Center, Oklahoma; the Hofheinz Pavilion, Houston, Texas on 14 October, and the Baton Rouge Assembly Center, Louisiana on 16 October. The collection has its moments – the 'Help On The Way'>'Slipknot!'>'Franklin's Tower' from disc one; the second disc essentially presenting an extended second set opening with 'Playing In The Band' from the Hofheinz Pavilion, moving into the bulk of the Assembly Center show, before returning to 'Playing In The Band' via 'Brokedown Palace' from the show that opened the disc. Unlike *Road Trips Volume 1 Number 1*, there were no downloads made available of the complete shows.

Dave's Picks Volume 12 picks up the November shows with the full 4 November concert from Colgate University, Hamilton, New York, over two discs. A third disc features around 75 minutes of bonus tracks from 2 November at Seneca College in Toronto. The 4 November show is an upbeat affair, from the 'Bertha' opener and the 'Good Lovin'' that followed. There are a few opportunities for the band and audience to catch their collective breath, with 'It Must Have Been The Roses' and 'Sunrise', before the set ends with an extraordinary 'Let It Grow'. The second set begins with an equipment breakdown, perhaps something overloaded following the power of the first set, and Lesh steps up to the microphone to introduce the band as 'The Jones Gang', every band member now apparently sharing that surname. The band return with 'Samson & Delilah' and 'Cold Rain And Snow', matching the first set's energy levels. The rest of the second set – bookended by 'Playing In The Band' – features 'Iko Iko': a New Orleans Mardi Gras song that would go on to be a fan favourite. Played here for only the fourth time, the song gave rise to the phrase 'Hey now!' being used as a greeting between Dead fans. Originally recorded in 1953, the song was a 1965 hit single for New Orleans girl group The Dixie Cups. Dr. John's version on his 1972 album *Dr. John's Gumbo* is probably the version best known to fans of The Dead.

Other tracks from the Seneca College, Toronto show, are included on *Dick's Picks Volume 34,* alongside a full show from 5 November at the Community War Memorial in Rochester, New York: recorded the night after the show on *Dave's Picks Volume 12.* Like the previous night, the band are in an energetic frame of mind, and Lesh, in particular, is in the driving seat: perhaps a consequence of his onstage goofing during the equipment fault. The second set opens with a bass solo – a strange avant-garde excursion that might've tried the patience of a lesser audience had it been undertaken by a lesser player, but it doesn't overstay its welcome. The band ask the audience to take a step back: perhaps all the better to experience a version of 'Eyes Of The World' that concludes with another Lesh solo. Disc three sees the band return to The Phil Zone for a third time, Lesh joining Hart and Kreutzmann for the 'Drums' segment, before the band moves gradually into 'The Other One'. It's another winner from 1977: a stable full of thoroughbred champions.

A series of four shows at the Winterland in San Francisco concluded what was an exceptional year: commemorated with the three-CD set *Dick's Picks Volume 10.* The release features most of the 29 December show and a selection of tracks from the following night. The 29 December show was easily the best of the run. It opens with a smoking 'Jack Straw', and 'Loser' is another first-set winner, while 'Sugaree' is as sweet as can be. Garcia's vocals are at their soulful best throughout. The second set on disc two sees the band sailing on a mellow sea, but unafraid to summon a lightning storm which breaks at the sequence starting with 'Playing In The Band' before moving into 'China Cat Sunflower': a song that had been out of rotation since 1974. 'China Doll' gives Garcia another opportunity to show that his vocals can be as sweet as his playing, before a rousing 'Not Fade Away' leads back to a concluding chapter of 'Playing In The Band'. The two encores – 'Terrapin Station' and 'Johnny B. Goode' – bring the show to an end on disc three. At the start of the show, Weir introduces The Dead as the Just About Exactly Perfect Brothers Band, and he's not wrong. Four tracks from the 30 December show, fill the disc, but it's unlikely a four-song sequence of 'Estimated Prophet', 'Eyes Of The World', 'St. Stephen' and 'Sugar Magnolia' could really be described as *filler*: the band playing with the same intensity and easy precision that they expressed the previous night.

1978 – Sand Castles And Glass Camels

The start of 1978 saw the release of Bob Weir's second solo album *Heaven Help The Fool*: a very different piece of work to his *Ace* debut. Gone were the other members of The Grateful Dead, as were the country stylings of that earlier work, and a much smoother commercial sound was adopted. With Keith Olsen as producer, it has a slick 1970s studio sound courtesy of top session musicians, including two members of Toto. From the cover portrait of Weir in a pair of flared slacks and holding an acoustic guitar, this is a blow-dried L.A. version of what The Dead could've been like had they fully embraced a soft rock sound. If the album's production and playing is somewhat unengaging, the songs at least have some merit. They might not be well remembered, but Weir was by this point an accomplished songwriter with Barlow. Possibly the album's failure to establish Weir as a serious commercial proposition was that his songs were just too complicated for the easy-on-the-ear demands of commercial radio airplay. Weir/Barlow collaborations dominated the album, and there are two covers: Smokey Robinson's 'I'll Be Doggone' and Little Feat's 'Easy To Slip'. Weir has performed several of the songs he co-wrote for the album in his subsequent career, and The Dead would go on to perform a couple, though they'd be pretty rare occasions. 'This Time Forever' was played on 17 November 1978 at a Bob Weir And Friends show – a band featuring Weir, Lesh, Garcia and Hunter – and the album's title track appeared in acoustic sets in 1980, albeit as an instrumental. 'Salt Lake City' appeared only once in The Dead's set, opening their show in the city in February 1995, as featured on the final volume in the *30 Trips Around The Sun* box set.

The Dead's live activity from January 1978, features on *Dave's Picks Volume 23*, recorded at McArthur Court at the University of Oregon on 22 January. If the 1978 incarnation of The Dead has a bad reputation, this is probably more down to their studio output that year. Their live performances might've lacked the consistency of their 1977 shows, but there's much to commend their live work in 1978. This show features much of the band's strengths, and their ability effortlessly covers ground from old-school rock 'n' roll and country to the furthest reaches of the avant-garde via some challenging pieces in the same gig. In this show, the second set's 'Space' section is an electric sci-fi soundtrack from Garcia – a survey of extraterrestrial planetscapes in a bubbling alien language (with even a nod or two to the *Close Encounters Of The Third Kind* five-note motif) – before 'St. Stephen' rises majestically from the unearthly scene, taking us home, to the familiar rhythms of 'Not Fade Away'. The entire sequence is a lesson in what The Grateful Dead were capable of doing when things fell into place.

The three-CD set *Dick's Picks Volume 18* captures The Dead in February with material from shows on 3 February at Dane County Coliseum, Madison, Wisconsin; 5 February at UNI-Dome, Cedar Falls, Iowa, and two tracks from their 4 February 4. The tracks are put together to give the impression of a complete show. The first disc (which includes songs from all three shows) features a selection from throughout their career – from 'Cold Rain And Snow', right up to 'Passenger' from *Terrapin Station* (at the time their most recent album), and 'Good Lovin'': a cover that would appear on *Shakedown Street* later in 1978. Disc two, entirely from 3 February – features a stunning run of songs showing The Dead at their full late-1970s peak, with 'Estimated Prophet' moving into 'Eyes Of The World', into a 25-minute 'Playing In The Band', 'The Wheel', and a nine-minute reprise of 'Playing In The Band'. The final disc – from 5 February – opens with *Terrapin Station*'s 'Samson & Delilah', before moving into a sequence of 'Scarlet Begonias', a lengthy and still-new 'Fire On The Mountain', followed by 'Truckin'', 'Drums', 'The Other One', 'Wharf Rat', and closing with 'Around And Around': the second Chuck Berry cover of the set. It's an intense performance, with 'Scarlet Begonias'>'Fire On The Mountain' well on the way to its eventual status as live favourite.

Garcia released another solo album in April 1978, although, this time the act was credited as The Jerry Garcia Band. *Cats Under The Stars* was recorded at Club Front: a warehouse in Front Street, San Rafael, the band had acquired as a rehearsal space. With money from Arista Records for the Garcia album, recording studio facilities were installed. Along with Garcia, the band featured Ron Tutt on drums, John Kahn on bass, Keith Godchaux on keyboards, Donna Jean Godchaux on vocals, and Maria Muldaur on backing vocals. It's an accomplished album with a strong selection of songs, without any cover versions. Half of the eight songs bear the respected Garcia/Hunter writing credit; one credited to Hunter, Garcia and Khan. The reggae-flavoured 'Love In The Afternoon' is a Hunter/Khan piece, while the short piece 'Down Home' is a John Kahn composition, and 'Rain' is credited to Donna Godchaux. While not a commercial success, Garcia later claimed it was the favourite of his solo albums, and it's easy to see why. Along with its iconic Stanley Mouse cover art, it has the songs, strong playing, and its own unique band identity. It would be hard to mistake it for a Grateful Dead album, even if it is underpinned with Garcia's distinctive playing and voice throughout. A reissue of the album as part of the *All Good Things: The Jerry Garcia Studio Sessions* box set featured seven rehearsal tracks from November 1976 as bonus tracks. The album's opening track 'Rubin and Cherise' would make it into The Dead's repertoire in 1991, where it would be performed by the band four times. Club Front would go on to become the home of the performing part of The Grateful Dead, offering a rehearsal space for both the band and solo endeavours, a studio, and a place for the band and friends to hang out.

April 1978's live schedule produced several releases, with the 15 April show at the College of William and Mary in Williamsburg, Virginia coming out in January 2021 as *Dave's Picks Volume 37*. It's a three-CD set, the complete show over the first two discs. An appropriately-driving 'Passenger' follows 'Mississippi Half Step' at the start of the first set, 'Passenger' being one of the songs from this era that grew in status as a live number before being dropped off the bus in the early-1980s. The second set features Donna Jean Godchaux's

'Sunrise': a *Terrapin Station* song The Dead had performed since the previous year, that wouldn't last past 1978 in The Dead's set. It sits at the start of a sequence that moves into 'Playing In The Band' before culminating in a very fine 'Morning Dew'. Disc three features a selection of tracks from 18 April, including 'Lazy Lightning'>'Supplication', three others from the first set, and most of the second set, albeit with an edited 'Drums'.

Dave's Picks Volume 15 documents their 22 April show at the Municipal Auditorium, Nashville, Tennessee. Released in 2015, the three-CD set does indeed include 'Tennessee Jed' in the first set, and it's a quality show. To these ears, 1978 Dead has always been a good vintage – the band still capable of brilliance, albeit perhaps not with the same consistency as the previous year – with some great songs at their disposal. Some of their more interesting numbers emerged into their own around this time – 'Terrapin Station', 'Fire On The Mountain', 'Shakedown Street' – while others fell out of use within a short period. This set features 'Lazy Lightning'>'Supplication' – one of those that would fall into disuse in the early-1980s, but, as this release shows, had by this time developed from its Kingfish origins into an absolute gem.

Two days later on 24 April, The Dead were at Horton Fieldhouse, Normal, Illinois, for a show released in 2013 as *Dave's Picks Volume 7*: a three-disc set capturing the end of their spring tour. The Dead's touring throughout their career was noticeably not restricted to the obvious centres of population, with shows taking place regularly in towns that required this puzzled European listener to dig out a map. Perhaps the town's name challenged them to pull out something that went *beyond* normal, the second set featuring some strong playing over an inspired selection of pieces over discs two and three. 'Scarlet Begonias' running into 'Fire On The Mountain' is a real treat. This show features the earliest-released version of Warren Zevon's 'Werewolves Of London', having debuted on 19 April. The song must've made an impression on the band, having only been released in January 1978: one of the rare times The Dead performed a contemporary song. It got a few airings that year before only getting broken out at Halloween shows. Sharp ears might pick up a nod to the Bee Gee's 'Stayin' Alive', before they go into 'Me And My Uncle', which could've been a unique 'Disco Dead' sequence indeed.

Two shows from early May are included in *Dick's Picks Volume 25* – one from 10 May at the Veterans Memorial Coliseum, New Haven, Connecticut, and the show from the following night at Springfield Civic Center, Springfield, Massachusetts. Two tracks have been trimmed from the first night, and three from the second: one of which – 'Peggy-O' – was played on the first night. Immediately you get the impression of the range of material at their fingertips, with two sets each night, 35 songs in total, and other than 'Drums', only one duplication. The first night is the stronger of the two in terms of songs, the second half of the second night focussing more on covers – 'Dancing In The Street', 'Not Fade Away', two Chuck Berry numbers and 'Werewolves Of London' – but, as usual, this only tells half the story. While most of the set consists of early rock 'n' roll classics, The Dead take these numbers as raw material for lengthy jams, every bit as imaginative as the performances of their own numbers the previous night.

A show from a few days later represents 1978 in the *30 trips Around The Sun* collection, recorded at Providence Civic Centre, Providence, Rhode Island on 14 May. The first disc of three, captures the first set, bookended with a lengthy 'Mississippi Uptown Half Step Toodeloo' at the start, and 'Let It Grow' at the end. Heavy with Weir/Barlow compositions like 'Cassidy' and 'Looks Like Rain', any thoughts of Weir being a weaker link in the songwriting chain are quickly dispersed. A triumphant 'Estimated Prophet' from the second set on disc two, shows why this song was deservedly a live Dead staple. A joyous 'Not Fade Away' into 'Going Down The Road Feeling Bad' dominates the third disc, and while this combination can feel dull and overextended at times, here it feels celebratory.

July 1978 saw The Dead perform a series of shows at Colorado's Red Rocks Amphitheatre: the first time they played the venue that would become one of their favourite locations. They played the venue – an open-air amphitheatre built into a massive rock structure surrounded by a park – a total of 20 times in their career. It remained a magical venue even years later, Kreutzmann's Billy and the Kids band playing memorable shows there featuring Billy Strings, in 2021. The Dead's July shows – including two nights at Red Rocks- were collected in the *July 78 Complete* box set in 2016: a twelve-CD collection of five complete shows. The shows included were 1 July at Arrowhead Stadium, Kansas City Missouri; 3 July at St. Paul Civic Arena, St Paul, Minnesota; 5 July at Omaha Civic Auditorium, Omaha, Nebraska, and 7 and 8 July at Red Rocks. The 8 July show would be made available separately as the *Red Rocks 7/8/78* three-CD set. The Dead's 1 July show was an unusual single-set gig, the band playing as part of Willie Nelson's annual Fourth of July Picnic event. Even if it was a non-standard gig, they delivered a set including a lengthy sequence of 'Terrapin Station' into 'Playing In The Band', a 'Drums' interlude into 'Space', into 'Estimated Prophet' and 'The Other One', 'Wharf Rat' and 'Around And Around', before a second Chuck Berry number – 'Johnny B. Goode' – as the encore. The final Red Rocks show features an unusual triple encore of 'Terrapin Station', 'One More Saturday Night' and a closing 'Werewolves Of London'. It wasn't even Halloween.

The Dead's live set was developing into what would become their modus operandi for the rest of their career – a show that incorporated two sets, the first featuring shorter numbers; the cowboy tunes, covers of traditional songs ,and shorter self-penned numbers, the set often ending in a longer piece like 'The Music Never Stopped'. The second set would open with a longer extended work that would be the start of a seamless sequence of several numbers, punctuated by a drum/percussion piece performed by the two drummers: usually referred to as 'Rhythm Devils' or 'Drums' (or 'Time to go to the bar' or 'Time to take a toilet break' by those less tolerant of the band's experimental leanings). This would give way to 'Space', an interlude of improvised guitar music by Garcia and regularly Weir, Lesh and others that would glide into another couple of numbers: often a slow Garcia/Hunter number and an upbeat Weir song, before a shorter number would bring the night to a close. There would usually be one short encore. The format proved to be an effective framework for The Dead. The 'Drums'>'Space' area could be extended or curtailed and could focus on one player or on the interplay between members, and it allowed the band to bring an element of the unexpected to the heart of the performance. The show format also made the set flexible enough to accommodate the band's wide repertoire without it falling into repetition or relying too heavily on one performer or style; there was little danger of a show consisting entirely of cowboy songs or of slow Garcia/Hunter numbers.

From July to August, The Grateful Dead recorded what would become their tenth album *Shakedown Street*. While *Cats Under The Stars* might not have been a major commercial success, the experiment of recording at Club Front had been worthwhile, so, following Garcia's suggestion, the band opted to record the album there. With Arista Records still keen to keep them on a leash, another external producer was brought in: this time Little Feat's Lowell George: a respected musician who was simpatico with The Dead's attitude. The finished album, however, would be controversial. If *Terrapin Station* had raised the spectre of 'Disco Dead' with their version of 'Dancin' In The Streets', the title track showed the band were still capable of surprises that developed into greatness, even in a studio arrangement that didn't necessarily reflect their regular style. *Shakedown Street,* in comparison, had few redeeming features.

Opening with 'Good Lovin'' – a cover they'd performed with Pigpen – *Shakedown Street* presented The Dead as a floundering soft-rock act with few interesting songs. Songs like 'France', If I Had The World To Give (a rare Garcia/Hunter misfire) and Donna Jean Godchaux's 'From The Heart Of Me', could all have been the work of an entirely different and far less interesting band. 'All New Minglewood Blues' was another cover from their early years, and the only worthy tracks are the title song – which would develop into a thunderous live anthem, as would Weir's I Need A Miracle – and Fire On The Mountain: a song that emerged from a track on Hart's *Diga* album. These and 'Stagger Lee' – a retelling of an old folk song – would become established in their set, although, in comparison to Nick Cave's version, The Dead's 'Stagger Lee' comes across as a remarkably polite retelling. With punk and new wave emerging in the USA to reinvigorate rock music with a return to the apparent honesty of basic rock 'n' roll – experimental music moving from progressive rock towards darker post-punk realms – The Dead looked out of time and low on inspiration. Arista had hoped they'd signed the new Fleetwood Mac, Eagles or Steely Dan, without realising they'd scooped up a band whose studio output sounded adrift in a sea of what we would now call soft rock.

One underlying issue with *Shakedown Street* is that the band themselves were not in great shape. There was tension with the Godchauxs by this point, Garcia often frustrated by Keith's playing, and Donna's vocals struggling in the face of the PA. However, more serious issues were emerging, some of the band and their entourage's experimentation with cocaine and heroin leading them into addiction. Garcia was becoming a serious heroin user and – on and off – would remain so for the rest of his life. *Shakedown Street* – with only three Garcia/Hunter songs – showed his inspiration and songwriting skills were on the wane. A 2004 reissue of *Shakedown Street* included the first appearance of three tracks recorded in Egypt – 'Ollin Arageed', 'Fire On The Mountain' and 'Stagger Lee', as well as an outtake of 'Good Lovin'' and a live version of 'All New Minglewood Blues' from November 1978.

While it is deserving of its criticism, I've got a soft spot for *Shakedown Street*, as it was the first Grateful Dead studio album I bought. With many of their albums out of print and being reissued on CD with only limited availability in the UK, a low-priced one that I hadn't heard – bought on the strength of live versions of 'Fire On The Mountain' and the title track – seemed a good deal. Repeated listening left me perplexed that this was the same band whose live tapes had blown me away. The album cover by Gilbert Shelton – one of its most memorable aspects – was intended to reflect some of the 'local colour' of the neighbourhood in San Rafael where the album was recorded. At least the cover's got some swagger.

While 1978 was (on the surface at least) looking like a good year for The Dead – with two solo albums, a new studio album and a series of strong live performances – what they did in September that year would go down in history. For the previous two years, they'd been pursuing an idea – originally from Lesh – for the band to play at the pyramids in Egypt. They had established solid contacts within the US government and with the authorities in Egypt, the agreement being that any money made at the shows to be held at the small outdoor theatre at the foot of the pyramids, would be donated to the Department Of Antiquities – the organisation responsible for the upkeep of the monuments – and to a charity supported by the wife of Egyptian President Anwar Sadat. While Egypt was a conservative Arab country, the visit came at a time of closer relationships between Egypt and the USA, on account of Egypt and Israel working towards a treaty that would be signed between Sadat and Israeli Premier Menachem Begin at meetings facilitated by US President Jimmy Carter at Camp David. The meetings leading to the signing of the Camp David Accord, were being held in secret at the very time the US' most unlikely cultural ambassadors were preparing to take to the stage for three shows at the only surviving wonder of the ancient world.

The Dead hit Egypt with a full entourage of family and friends, with a handful of fans also making the journey. There was time to relax at the hotel, and to explore the area and the landmarks, by car or by camel. The PA and recording truck – on loan from The Who – travelled from London to Cairo. Hundreds of locals, from dignitaries to desert nomads, attended, either in the amphitheatre itself or watching from the desert. The timing was right. The three shows were scheduled for 14, 15 and 16 September 1978, the third taking place beneath a total eclipse of a full moon. The Camp David Accords were signed between Egypt and Israel the following day.

However, the historic nature of the event, and The Grateful Dead's proven ability to repeatedly drop the ball when it counted, perhaps inevitably coincided in Egypt. Lesh – the prime mover behind the project – had spent most of the year drinking heavily; Kreutzmann had broken his wrist, which severely limited his playing, and Keith Godchaux's piano was out of tune. A scheme to wire up the King's Chamber of the pyramid as an echo chamber during the performance, failed. The performances were – despite the setting – subpar. But despite the setbacks, a myth had been established, and while other artists would play historic locations and cut through political barriers – whether it be Jean-Michel Jarre's 1981 concerts in China, or Laibach's 2015 gig in North Korea – The Dead established the high-water mark. There were loose plans for the band to play other world landmarks over the years, but they never came to anything. A planned live album of the Egypt shows was shelved, and European dates that had been pencilled in to coincide with the Egypt dates were cancelled, to allow the band to return home to complete work on *Shakedown Street*.

An album documenting the Egypt dates – *Rocking The Cradle: Egypt 1978* – was eventually released in 2008: a two-disc set compiling the best of the performances, mostly from the final night's show. It's a good, if not spectacular, collection – the second disc's version of the then-new 'Fire On The Mountain' emerging from Nubian master musician Hamza El Din's 'Ollin Arageed' showing both an instinctive understanding of what would later be marketed as world music, and the possibilities of intercultural musical cooperation: something that Dead percussionist Hart would champion throughout his career. The set was accompanied by a DVD of thirteen tracks from the final night's show. While it's an interesting document, the DVD is something of a disappointment given the limitations of 1970s video filming quality in comparison to the magnitude of the event.

The Dead were soon back on home soil, and celebrated their Egypt adventure in October with a five-night run at the Winterland in San Francisco, in front of fans who were unable to make the trip to Egypt: a series of concerts dubbed From Egypt With Love. These shows would be released on the *Road Trips Volume 1 Number 4* collection in 2008: a double CD set with a bonus third disc. The first disc features highlights of the 21 October show, skipping the start of the first set and going straight in with a lengthy 'Sugaree' and three newer numbers: 'Passenger', 'Stagger Lee' and 'I Need A Miracle'. The first disc also includes some second-set highlights, including a lengthy and rare version of 'Got My Mojo Working' featuring harmonica by War's Lee Oskar, who also sits in on the following 'The Other One' and 'Stella Blue'. The second disc, focussing on the 22 October show, opens with Hamza El Din's 'Ollin Arageed' before moving into 'Deal'. A powerful sequence of 'Scarlet Begonias', 'Fire On The Mountain', 'Not Fade Away' and 'Going Down The Road Feeling Bad' dominates the disc, and features guest John Cippolina on guitar. While the *Shakedown Street* version of 'Fire On The Mountain' lacked spark, its live pyrotechnic potential, emerged quickly. A limited third disc added four tracks from 21 October and two from 17 October, including one of only three live outings for 'If I Had The World To Give'. The live version of 'Estimated Prophet' that melts into 'He's Gone', is another highlight. If The Dead missed the mark with their Egypt performance, evidence suggests their run of gigs on home soil shortly after they returned, delivered what they could've done in the shadow of the pyramids. And if The Dead's reputation in 1978 was based on the *Shakedown Street* album, the live *From Egypt With Love* set resets the balance in their favour.

The band returned to Winterland in December for the final time. The former ice skating rink – which had become something of a local home for The Dead, and also a stage for some of the era's biggest names – was scheduled to close at the end of the year, and The Dead brought down the final curtain. While the last few weeks were packed with shows, the final night came on 31 December, with The Dead, New Riders Of The Purple Sage and The Blues Brothers performing. The Dead played three sets and three encores, totalling around five hours; the show released in 2003 as the *The Closing of Winterland* four-disc set and DVD.

Disc one covers the first set, opening with a new-year countdown into 'Sugar Magnolia', and there's a strong song selection including 'Scarlet Begonias', 'Fire On The Mountain' and 'Friend Of The Devil'. While there are a couple of cowboy covers, it's far from the *warm-up* that The Dead's opening set could sometimes be. The set and disc close with 'Sunshine Daydream', which usually acts as a conclusion to 'Sugar Magnolia'. Does this mean the whole first set was essentially an extended version of 'Sugar Magnolia'/'Sunshine Daydream'? Perhaps. Does it mean The Dead have a sense of humour? No doubt about it.

The second set covers disc two and three: 'Terrapin Station' and 'Playing In The Band' being clear highlights that on a regular night would be a peak. Disc three's 20-minute 'Rhythm Devils' followed by 20 minutes of 'Not Fade Away' and ten minutes of 'Around And Around', is probably not to everyone's taste, and it would be fair to say that it does go on a bit. However, the third set on disc four takes us to an even higher level, opening with 'Dark Star' followed by a selection of their finest numbers – 'The Other One', 'Wharf Rat', 'St. Stephen' and 'Good Lovin'' – easily matching their early-1970s performances. 'Dark Star' opens the third set on disc four, making an appearance for the first time since 1974. It would only be performed a handful of times again in the 1970s and 1980s, remaining a rarity until it re-emerged in 1989. 'Dark Star' opens a sequence of classic Grateful Dead, moving into 'The Other One' before a reprise, then into 'Wharf Rat', 'St. Stephen', and finally a lengthy 'Good Lovin''.

Three encores end with 'And We Bid You Goodnight' – a flashback to the *Live/Dead* days – before an early-morning breakfast was served to the audience.

A DVD of the show was released featuring The Dead's entire set, with bonus material including performances from The Blues Brothers and New Riders, recorded originally on two-inch analogue tape. An additional bonus disc of material from the band's previous New Year shows at Winterland accompanied early orders of the DVD. While the show might not be perfect, it's damn close. It could (fairly!) be criticised for being a bit too long, though that might be forgiven in light of the celebratory nature of the occasion. But overall, the set gives a solid account of the appeal of The Grateful Dead. *The Closing of Winterland* album reveals the truth in what Bill Graham once said about the band:

They're not the best at what they do, they're the only ones that do what they do.

1979 – Go To Heaven

Though the first months of 1979 saw The Dead's relentless touring continue – starting with dates across the East Coast, including two nights at New York's Madison Square Garden on 7 and 8 January (the first shows at a venue they'd go on to perform at 52 times in the subsequent sixteen years) – no 1978 performances from any earlier than May have been released.

If the number of archive releases from a particular year are any indication of the quality of The Dead's performances, there's a noticeable downturn in output from 1978 onwards. 1976, 1977 and 1978 were among the peak years for releases, as were 1969-1974. While 1978 has been chronicled in over a dozen collections, from 1979 onwards, the number of releases each year are in single figures, and some years having very few releases at all. In addition to fewer archive issues covering these years, The Dead's contemporary releases dried up, and from 1981 to 1987, there were no new albums – studio or live – on the shelves. Paradoxically, the tailing off of releases (and the underlying suspicion that it was because the music was not as good) coincided with The Dead's popularity growing exponentially. From the sports arenas of the 1970s, they became a regular fixture at stadiums across the USA, touring regularly and attracting a growing audience that led them to being one of the biggest-grossing live acts in the country. With the band playing to their biggest audiences from the 1980s onwards, most contemporary fans will have had their live Grateful Dead experience in this or the following decade. While it seems history looks on these years with disapproval, those attending will vouch for the fact that while there may have been off-nights, the magic was regularly there, and while the flames may not have burned as brightly as they did in previous decades, the light could still be seen in the strangest of places when you looked at it the right way.

The version of The Grateful Dead on the *Live at Hampton Coliseum* double LP (4 May 4 1979) was a significantly different one than was on the many releases from 1978. There was a new lineup: The Godchauxs were both gone, and a new keyboard player was onboard. There were a number of reasons for this – Donna had at times struggled to sing in tune in front of a massive PA, and she didn't contribute onstage when she wasn't singing. There was also the question of whether there really could be a place for a woman in the boy's club that was the band. Keith's playing had in recent years been a source of irritation for some band members, his musical contribution being less than it had been, and his insistence on only playing piano, limiting The Dead's musical palette. Other issues had emerged beyond the stage – tensions in their volatile relationship spilt over into rehearsals and performances, and Keith's reliance on alcohol and drugs – heroin in particular – made his presence uncomfortable. He wasn't the only Dead member using heroin by this point: Garcia was by now a regular user who was suffering the consequences of his addiction. He was spending less time with the band and those around him, becoming more solitary and withdrawn.

Where once he would turn up early for rehearsals because it was something he loved, he'd now be late, distracted and the first to leave: his concentration and interest diminished. The long-term consequences of addiction would come in time. But Keith Godchaux sharing the addiction had an influence on Garcia that the band knew they could do without.

The decision to part company with the Godchauxs had been mulled over for a while and alternatives had been explored; could one go or would both go? How would they even go about sacking them? The issue proved to be easier to deal with than the band initially thought, as it turned out the Godchauxs didn't want to continue with The Dead either. Both wanted out, and although they didn't yet have plans, they knew that splitting from The Dead was the best course of action. The next question was, obviously, who would take Keith Godchaux's place. As was the case when the Godchauxs joined, there was a long list of possible recruits, but they chose Brent Mydland: the keyboardist and backing vocalist for Weir's side project that went on to become Bobby And The Midnites. Mydland – who grew up in the San Francisco Bay Area – had been playing keyboards from a young age before going on to join country rock outfit Silver until the band broke up in 1978, which was when he got in touch with Weir. Mydland – also a distinctive vocalist and skilled songwriter – went on to be The Dead's longest-serving keyboard player.

Keith and Donna played their final show with The Dead on 17 February, and following a few weeks of rehearsals, Mydland made his debut at the end of April, the *Live at Hampton Coliseum* album presenting his third show with the band. It's a measure of his talent that he was able to adapt so quickly to the massive repertoire, ever-changing setlists and improvised performance style. The album features the show highlights rather than the two complete sets, including 'New Minglewood Blues' which was on *Shakedown Street*, and 'Don't Ease Me In', which appeared on their next studio album. Both sound far better in the live setting than in their studio versions. 'Passenger' perhaps sounds more pedestrian without Donna's vocals, but the rest of the collection shows Garcia in fine voice on 'Loser', 'Ship Of Fools' and 'Stella Blue', and Mydland mastering numbers like 'Estimated Prophet', 'Eyes Of The World' and 'Truckin''. The new guy was fitting in like a natural.

Again there is a pause in the live releases until much later in the year. The band were more than active during this period, with a full schedule of shows, including Oakland Arena in August, a return to Red Rocks a few days later, and a further three nights at Madison Square Garden. The Dead were on the road throughout, and there are many potential archive releases among the shows they performed.

There was, however a fascinating side project recorded in 1979, again at Club Front. Director Francis Ford Coppola was a guest at The Dead's New Year's Eve show at the Winterland, and inspired by the performance, he asked Hart and Kreutzmann to record some percussion-based music for his forthcoming Vietnam-war epic *Apocalypse Now*. Hart and Kreutzmann laid a variety of percussion instruments across the rehearsal space, and improvised with other musicans – including Lesh – while an early cut of the movie was screened. This went on over the course of ten days, and the recordings were edited, mixed and assembled into the *Apocalypse Now Sessions: Rhythm Devils Perform River Music* album. Some of the recordings were used in the film and included in the *Apocalypse Now* soundtrack album. While very much an experimental music excursion, and perhaps not for the casual listener, the fact that music like this can be incorporated into a successful commercial film, shows that otherwise-challenging music can be perfectly acceptable to a wide audience; it just depends on the context. While many people would struggle with the idea of listening to a percussion-led Grateful Dead offshoot, they have no such issues when it's part of the score of a favourite movie. Despite Garcia in particular, being a huge fan of cinema, their involvement with it over their career was minimal. Perhaps The Grateful Dead were uncomfortable with the idea of making music-to-order for movies. *Apocalypse Now* shows the possibilities that could emerge when filmmakers took their cues from The Dead's music instead.

The *Apocalypse Now* sessions had other repercussions in The Dead's percussion department, with the creation of specialist instruments giving Hart and Kreutzmann greater opportunity for sonic experimentation. One of these was known as The Beast – essentially a metal rack supporting a variety of different bass drums, allowing Hart and Kreutzmann easy access to a wide variety of bass tones that would've otherwise been out of reach. The Beast was soon incorporated into the 'Drums' section of the show. The other creation was known as The Beam: an eight-foot aluminium girder strung with eight bass piano strings. These were anchored at one end with a tuning nut at the other, so they could all be tuned to D. The strings would then be picked, hit or scraped with anything from fingernails to metal bars. A moveable pickup attached to The Beam then fed the sound to an amplifier via whatever effect units were deemed appropriate. Capable of a wide variety of low-frequency tones, variations of The Beam would be developed over the years.

From July, the band began work on the new studio album *Go To Heaven*, which, like their previous two albums, again involved an external producer. Arista were still hoping for a commercial breakthrough for The Dead, and this time Gary Lyons was chosen, having previously worked with acts including Foreigner and Aerosmith. Recording was done at Club Front, with overdubs at New York's Media Sound studio. Recording went on until January 1980.

Recordings from 1979 live shows resumed in October, with 2007's *Road Trips Volume 1 Number 1* documenting The Dead's Fall Tour of the East Coast. Content from six shows is included over two discs – one track from the 25 October gig at the New Haven Coliseum, four from 6 November at the Spectrum, Philadelphia, two from 8 November at the Capital Centre, Maryland, and two from 11 November at the Crisler Arena, Ann Arbor, Michigan. The collection is dominated by six tracks from 9 November at the Memorial Auditorium, Buffalo, New York. An additional third disc included with early copies features three more tracks from this show, three from the show on 31 October at the Nassau Veterans Memorial Coliseum in Uniondale, New York, and three from the Capital Centre on 8 November.

As the first release in the *Road Trips* series, the collection makes a good case for the compilation of tracks from multiple shows to give a flavour of where the band was at over the course of a tour. 'Alabama Getaway' makes a strong opener, and the sequence from the 9 November show – 'Dancing In The Street', 'Franklin's Tower', 'Wharf Rat', 'I Need A Miracle' and 'Good Lovin'' – makes a strong argument, with disc two's 'Terrapin Station' and 'Playing In The Band' sequence from the 6 November show being the highlight of the collection. 'Shakedown Street' and 'Passenger', appearing side by side at the start of disc two, shows the band in muscular form. It's disappointing perhaps that Weir's 'Lost Sailor', 'Saint Of Circumstance' and 'Althea' were relegated to the bonus disc, as these would've showcased the newer work the band were presenting at their shows. They could easily have been included instead of 'Jack Straw' and 'Deal' or 'Not Fade Away' and 'Morning Dew', but at the end of the day, such editorial decisions have to be made, and the debate about what deserves to be released and how it should be presented, will never end.

It was perhaps to address some of this debate that two of the shows during this run emerged in full as digital downloads a few months later. *Road Trips Full Show: Spectrum 11/5/79* and *Road Trips Full Show: Spectrum 11/5/79* presented two complete concerts, one of which had tracks featured on the first of the *Road Trips* volumes. The first of the two nights (a three-disc set for those who burned it onto physical media) has a strong second set over the second and third discs, incorporating recent material, with 'Althea' and 'Easy To Love You' sitting alongside more established late-1970s work like 'Estimated Prophet' and 'Franklin's Tower'. The extended jam that develops from 'Franklin's Tower' and into 'Drums' and 'Space', resolves into 'Lost Sailor' and 'Saint Of Circumstance', clearly making the case that although they were new, these songs had earned their place in the set. The following night – a two-disc affair – opened with 'Alabama Getaway', and included 'Easy To Love You' in the first set, the second featuring 'Terrapin Station' and 'Playing In The Band', before the improvised section takes us into the more-familiar territory of 'Black Peter' and 'Good Lovin''. They may be recorded on consecutive nights, but they're two quite different shows.

One shows on the East Coast tour that wasn't included in the *Road Trips* collection was later released to represent 1979 in the *30 Trips Around The Sun* collection. The first set – on disc one of three discs – includes Mydland's 'Easy To Love You' and Weir's 'Lost Sailor' and 'Saint Of Circumstance'. The second set is more of a look backwards, from its lengthy 'Dancing In The Street' opener to the brief appearance of 'Caution (Do Not Stop On Tracks)' between 'He's Gone' and 'The Other One'. A lengthy 'Franklin's Tower' is the only representative of their post-1975 output in the second set.

Their early-December shows at the Uptown Theatre, Chicago, feature in *Dave's Picks Volume 31*: a three-disc set released in 2019. While they played three nights at the venue, the 3 December show features in full, with three bonus tracks from the previous night. Perhaps the comparatively-intimate venue, helped – a historic former theatre and movie hall built in the 1920s that they'd play several times – but it's a strong contender for the best release of the 1979-era band, both in terms of performance and track selection. Opening with 'Alabama Getaway', the first set features Weir's 'Lazy Lighting' > 'Supplication' sequence and Garcia's 'Althea'. The second set is alight from the opening 'Scarlet Begonias' via 'Samson & Delilah' to 'Terrapin Station' and 'Playing In The Band'. The third disc presents the 'Space' improvisation moving into 'Lost Sailor' and 'Saint Of Circumstance', 'Wharf Rat' perhaps continuing the maritime theme. An upbeat 'Truckin'' brings the set to a close before a 'Johnny B. Goode' encore: the second Chuck Berry cover of the night. The bonus tracks from the night before are no mere filler – an impressive 'Estimated Prophet', 'Franklin's Tower' and an extended 'Jam' being another rich helping of the seemingly effortless and electric fluid-jazz they were capable of summoning on a nightly basis.

By the end of the year, they were back in home territory, with a run of shows at the Oakland Auditorium. These would be chronicled on two releases: *Dick's Picks Volume 5* and *Road Trips Volume 3 Number 1*. They'd already played the venue in August, when 'Althea' and 'Lost Sailor' were debuted. With the venue now something of a local base for the band, and the run concluding with a New Year's Eve show, it may be surprising that *Dick's Picks Volume 5* features the 26 December show, and the *Road Trips* release features 28 December 28. But as fans who'd being paying attention to The Dead's career could testify, The Dead were more than a little erratic when it came to delivering for a specific occasion. While a New Year's Eve show would become something of a band tradition over the years, it usually coincided with a better show taking place a few nights earlier.

The show that features on the *Dick's Picks* collection was a charity benefit for the Seva Foundation: an organisation founded by Dead associates Ram Dass and Wavy Gravy, to provide eyecare to the developing world and elsewhere. The show is more of a celebration than a showcase, with more old favourites than recent material. From the 'Cold Rain And Snow' opening to the 'Uncle John's Band' second encore, it's a show for the faithful. The second set – over discs two and three – is a solid account of the band's skills. From the 'Uncle John's Band' opening, it's essentially one long sequence that includes 'Estimated Prophet', 'He's Gone', 'The Other One', 'Not Fade Away' and 'Brokedown Palace' interspersed with several jam sequences and a drum section. It concludes, like the first set did, with a Chuck Berry number, although, here we get two: 'Around And Around' and 'Johnny B. Goode'. With two obvious encore numbers already played, the band instead launch into 'Shakedown Street', before finally wrapping up the set up with a coda of 'Uncle John's Band': a flashback to the beginning of the second set.

The 28 December show on *Road Trips Volume 3 Number 1* has a very different flavour. The first set is a noticeably mellow affair: Garcia's 'Sugaree' opening, 'Row Jimmy' and 'High Time' setting a laid-back tone. The second set, however, sees the band revitalised from the start, with 'Alabama Getaway' and 'Greatest Story Ever Told' back to back before 'Terrapin Station' leads into 'Playing In The Band', improvisations and 'Uncle John's Band'. They remain on their toes for 'I Need A Miracle', 'Bertha', 'Good Lovin'' and two encores. Maybe they'd been holding back some energy for the second set. Early copies of the two-disc set had a third bonus disc with tracks from the first and second set of the 30 December show, including the powerful second-set opener of 'Scarlet Begonias', 'Fire On The Mountain' and 'Let It Grow'.

If 1979 had begun with the Godchaux problems coming to a head, by the end of the year it was evident that The Dead were in a better position to face the new decade. *Go To Heaven* may not have brought sales that put them in the same league as Fleetwood Mac or The Eagles, but it *did* show that Mydland had the potential to be a creative asset to the band. He was a powerful new voice on stage and worked well with Garcia in the live environment. His contribution onstage had held things together over what could've been a seriously rocky patch, and he'd helped move the band in a new direction that would ultimately prove commercially successful without diminishing their unique identity.

1980 – Dead Set On Reckoning

The Dead's eleventh studio album *Go To Heaven* was released in April 1980. It only includes two Garcia/Hunter songs – 'Alabama Getaway' and 'Althea' – three by Weir and co-writer Barlow, Mydland bringing two songs to the collection, one of which was co-written with Barlow. There's also a brief percussion instrumental from Kreutzmann and Hart, and a run-through of 'Don't Ease Me In'. The lack of Garcia/Hunter work is noticeable. The fact that they were both great songs, slightly covers the shortage, with 'Althea' in particular an outstanding number from Hunter and a perfect springboard for Garcia's guitar. While 'Alabama Getaway' is a more straightforward rocker, 'Althea' is more reflective, and some of the lyrics can be read in the light of a person's concern for a friend who is doing themselves harm. Garcia was by this point engaged in a serious heroin habit, which could also be seen as one of the reasons his inspiration and creativity were at a low ebb. The three Weir/Barlow numbers – 'Feel Like A Stranger', 'Lost Sailor' and 'Saint Of Circumstance' – were also high-quality numbers, and each were performed regularly. 'Feel Like A Stranger''s reference to a 'long, long, crazy, crazy night' was always met with enthusiasm when played live. Mydland's two numbers were perhaps a more explicit attempt to steer The Dead in a new direction, being more-commercial love songs that wouldn't have sounded out of place performed by a soft-rock crooner like Michael Bolton. Mydland's songs would, however gain a place in the live set, and despite being a recent addition to the band, his input could be seen in other areas, such as with his use of synths.

Despite some good material, the album is an unengaging affair. The cover shows the band posing in white suits and open-neck shirts on a white background, making them look like a Bee Gees tribute act in need of a hairdresser and a blow-dry. Perhaps, like the cover, the content feels like it's been airbrushed too much, and any grit, flavour or substance polished off to make something so digestible it ends up tasting bland. The off-putting cover did them no commercial favours either, presenting The Dead as out of time and seemingly desperate to keep up with a disco trend that had already ended. Those that criticised their previous 'Disco Dead' studio output, saw this as confirmation and didn't feel the need to investigate further by actually listening to the album. Perhaps if the phoenix icon on the rear cover had been on the front – representing the band's revival following the Godchaux's departure – it might've been given a kinder ear. Or if perhaps the band had been presented in their customary un-ironed and unadorned state, it would've felt more like a return to a more-honest rock-based sound, albeit one with some of the polish that would dominate 1980s commercial radio.

Road Trips Volume 3 Number 4 chronicles The Dead's shows on 6 May at Recreation Hall, Pennsylvania State University, and the following night at the hallowed Barton Hall, Cornell University, Ithica, New York. The first of three discs combines material from the first sets of the two shows, and it does make something of an ideal opening set. From its 'Jack Straw' opener onwards, it features some Garcia favourites ('Peggy-O', 'Loser' and 'Row Jimmy'), some Weir cowboy favourites, and 'Cassidy', before a mighty selection of 'Lazy Lightning', 'Supplication', 'Althea', 'Lost Sailor' and 'Saint Of Circumstance'. The second disc features the second set from 6 May; the third disc, most of the second set from 7 May. The 7 May disc edges ahead of the second disc, due to its song selection, opening with a lengthy 'Shakedown Street' into a sequence featuring both 'Playing In The Band' and 'Terrapin Station'. 'Saint Of Circumstance' and 'Black Peter' follow the improvisation section, before a reprise of 'Playing In The Band' leads into 'Good Lovin''.

Two other shows from May 1980 would be combined to make a double CD in 2002, with *Go to Nassau* taking tracks from the 15 and 16 May gigs at Nassau Coliseum, Uniondale, New York. The release approximates the show's running order, incorporating the best performances from the two nights. While perfectionists and completists will obviously prefer a release that features the entire sets from both nights, this compilation gives an effective picture of the band's performances during this era. Six *Go To Heaven* songs are performed across the collection, making the case that the material on the recent studio album was strong enough, and that given a favourable live environment, the songs could soar. 'Jack Straw' and 'Franklin's Tower' from 15 May make a powerful opening on the first disc, with 'Lazy Lightning' and 'Supplication' from the same night making a welcome appearance. If there's a tendency to see this period of The Dead's output as marked by the rise of Weir as a performer and songwriter, Garcia's performance on 'Peggy-O' shows that the subtlety, tone and sheer class he could give a song, are still firmly in place. The magic Garcia could conjure on acoustic-based numbers like this, would be captured more fully later in the year. Disc two opens with five *Go To Heaven* numbers in a row, the first four from 16 May. 'Alabama Getaway' from the previous night follows, despite it being that night's encore. The rest of the disc continues with material from the 15 May show's second set, with a strong 'Playing In The Band' and 'Uncle John's Band' at the centre of proceedings. The 'Brokedown Palace' encore from 16 May would've been nice to have on the album, but you can't have everything.

In July, tragedy again struck the band, with the death of former keyboard player Keith Godchaux in a car crash. Since leaving The Dead in 1979, Keith and Donna Godchaux had relocated to Alabama, still playing occasionally in the San Francisco area. By 1980, they'd formed a new act – The Heart Of Gold Band, featuring Steve Kimock (who would later play alongside former Dead members in The Other Ones) and drummer Greg Anton, who would later form the band Zero with Kimock. Keith Godchaux died before the band had the opportunity to establish themselves. An album was released in 1986, featuring five tracks recorded at a live performance at the Back Door in San Francisco: the band's only performance before Keith Godchaux's death.

Released in 2005, *Download Series Volume 7* presents a three-CD collection of material performed on 3 September at Springfield Civic Centre,

Massachusetts, and the following night at the Providence Civic Centre, Rhode Island. The first night is presented over the equivalent of two discs, the third disc featuring most of the second set of the second night. A first set opening with 'Mississippi Half-Step' going into 'Franklin's Tower' is obviously going to merit investigation, 'Althea', 'Little Red Rooster' and 'Let It Grow' making that decision worthwhile. The second set's 'Saint Of Circumstances' moves into a jam segment before 'Drums' take centre-stage, the first few minutes of this seeing Hart and Kreutzmann joined by Mydland. Opening with 'Supplication Jam' into 'Estimated Prophet', the material from the second night is no filler. The second set sequence carries on into 'Eyes Of The World', 'The Other One' continuing after 'Drums' and 'Space'.

If the structure of the live set had become too stable – a first set of shorter numbers followed by a second set with more improvised pieces – a disruption was called for. In September and October, The Dead performed a short acoustic set ahead of two electric sets each night for a series of concerts at the Warfield in San Francisco, the Saenger Performing Arts Center in New Orleans, and Radio City Music Hall in New York. Unlike their early-1970s acoustic sets, all the band members were involved in the sets – Weir and Garcia on acoustic guitars, Mydland on baby-grand piano, and Hart and Kreutzmann on small drum kits or percussion instruments. Lesh remained in his regular position on bass, playing a more background role at a vastly-reduced volume.

The shows were recorded for release in 1981, with two double albums emerging: the acoustic *Reckoning*, and *Dead Set* representing their electric output. Of the two, *Reckoning* is by far the superior, its blend of Dead originals and traditional numbers making the listener approach both with new ears. 'Dire Wolf' sits alongside 'Jack-A-Roe', 'Been All Around The World' with 'Cassidy', all performed with the ease of songs that have been familiar for decades, or possibly just written recently by a group of West-Coast folkies who went electric. If the electric storm is kept at bay and there's less room for improvisation, it is, however, not a Dead-lite collection – 'China Doll', 'To Lay Me Down' and 'Bird Song' lose none of their soul, and if anything' the immediacy of the setting makes them all the more powerful. It presents The Dead at their most approachable, relaxed and comfortable. It remains the collection to pass on to friends who are interested in The Dead but aren't ready yet for their full psychedelic electric improvisation manifestation.

A 2004 *Reckoning* reissue included a second disc of bonus material – another sixteen tracks that are predominantly alternative versions from Radio City Music Hall, the majority of the original *Reckoning* coming from the Warfield shows. A few tracks that didn't appear on the original are also featured: 'Iko Iko', 'El Paso', 'Little Sadie' and 'Tom Dooley', and instrumentals of 'Heaven Help The Fool' and 'Sage & Spirit'. There's also a rehearsal of 'To Lay Me Down' recorded at Club Front in September. In all, The Dead played 15 nights at the Warfield, and in addition to *Reckoning* and *Dead Set,* a further album of acoustic performances was released in 2019. *The Warfield,*

San Francisco, California, October 9 & 10, 1980 includes the complete acoustic sets from the two nights in the title. Of the nineteen tracks across two discs, only one song wasn't included on the original *Reckoning* release: an acoustic version of Weir's 'Heaven Help The Fool'. Any concerns that there's too much repetition in the content of this release and the expanded version of *Reckoning,* are quickly forgotten. The Dead are playing so well here, fans would happily experience the same set several nights in a row.

Dead Set was recorded at the electric sets of the shows, and while its sister album is one of the highlights of The Dead's discography, this is less so. There was an obvious need for a live Dead collection presenting the new lineup beyond the studio confines, but *Dead Set* only goes part of the way towards meeting this. The individual tracks are good, but the sequencing seems to almost set them against each other rather than presenting the organic flow of a show. 'Samson & Delilah' opens the album, but any momentum it builds is removed by a slow take of 'Friend Of The Devil'. 'New Minglewood Blues' restores the tempo, 'Deal' carries it on, but 'Candyman' deflates the vibe again.

In its favour, *Dead Set* presents an almost streamlined Dead: modern, focussed and wearing the weight of their legacy lightly. The performances are crisp, and there's a freshness about it that you wouldn't expect from a band that had been around so long. There is little by way of improvising, even numbers like 'Franklin's Tower' and 'Fire On The Mountain' having shorter-than-usual running times. There's a brief 'Rhythm Devils' and a short 'Space' segment, although they feel lacking in context. 'Passenger', 'Greatest Story Ever Told' and 'Little Red Rooster' work well in the context of an album that seems more like a compilation, giving a taste of the contemporary Dead live sound to the curious, rather than something more in keeping with their previous live releases.

A 2004 reissue of the album saw the original fifteen tracks supplemented by another ten, and these too are strong takes that give some idea of the difficulty that there must have been in deciding what to exclude from the original album. 'Shakedown Street', 'Let It Grow', 'Sugaree' and 'Lazy Lightning'>'Supplication' could all have deserved a place. Had *Dead Set* originally been issued as a triple CD rather than a double vinyl record, it might've seemed less of a compromise, but the technology was still some years away. Perhaps a fully-expanded version of the album, with some sympathetic sequencing of the tracks, would restore its reputation.

The 1980-vintage Dead features on the *30 Trips Around The Sun* collection with a show from 28 November at Lakeland Civic Center, Lakeland, Florida. The second set opens disc two of the three-disc collection with a sequence beginning with the still-fresh 'Feel Like A Stranger', before moving into the more-vintage 'To Lay Me Down', returning to a Weir-fronted 'Let It Grow', and on into 'Terrapin Station'. At their peak, The Dead were capable of feats like this, sliding effortlessly from a new number into a completely different mood for one of their classics, before again taking things up a gear, with no friction or break in continuity. Songs from completely different places could sit together, their apparent differences forgotten, their unique identities incorporated into a seemingly larger work that was the performance as a whole. The songs could transcend their own existence and limitations, stretched and contorted into new forms that left them identifiable but also constituent parts of a new art. It was at times possible to overlook the complexity of the music being performed in these moments of spontaneous creation; the music served the art as a whole and didn't just exist for its own sake. While *Live/Dead* might be the clearest example of this art, it was a technique that The Dead could pull off to a greater or lesser extent on any good night, and that flow of inspiration can be heard right across this sequence – Just another gem hidden in the landslide of diamonds that is The Dead's archive releases.

1981 – All Around This World

In March, The Dead undertook the first of two 1981 visits to Europe, with shows in London, and one in Essen, Germany, on 28 March. That show was broadcast by German TV channel WDR as a Rock Night special for long-running music show *Rockpalast*, featuring both The Grateful Dead and The Who. The show was also broadcast on BBC 2 in the UK, giving this late-night viewer an opportunity to see The Dead doing their thing on a small black-and-white portable television perched on top of a wardrobe in his bedroom. The Dead's set included Pete Townshend appearing on guitar for 'Not Fade Away', 'Wharf Rat', 'Around And Around' and 'Good Lovin'', while circus act The Flying Karamazov Brothers performed during the 'Drums' section. Some extracts from the show appear on the 2017 *Long Strange Trip* documentary, and the show in full is widely available online: a unique, professionally-shot record of an early-1980s Dead performance. They would return for further European shows in October, playing fourteen concerts, including another four nights at the Rainbow in London.

April saw the release of *Reckoning*: the first of two Grateful Dead live releases in 1981. If The Dead gave the appearance of having a busy release schedule – with a studio album and two live albums in just over a year – it would not last long. *Dead Set* – released in August 1981 – would be their last album until 1987: close to a generation in terms of popular music. The Dead would essentially step away from releasing new material, their focus over these years moving instead to live performance. Many myths would be built about this – The Dead didn't need the money; The Dead were above mere commerce; No studio recording could really capture them, or they were too busy rockin' to deal with *the man*. Things were more mundane; Garcia's heroin use was chipping away at his creativity, and there was little new material forthcoming. Given their reputation for spending time in the studio without much to show for it, it made little economic sense for a record company to throw money at their lack of new material in the hope that it would solve the problem. The constant touring was a necessary survival tactic, ensuring that the band still had the cashflow they needed to continue. It was fortunate that their live performances not only still attracted a massive following but that that following would actually grow over the years between the early-1980s and their next studio release.

The following month's show at Nassau Veterans Memorial Coliseum, Uniondale, New York, featured on *Dick's Picks Volume 13*. First set highlights include 'Alabama Getaway' opening the show, and a vigorous 'Let It Grow'. The second set takes things further, disc three kicking off with a version of 'He's Gone' that moves into 'Caution (Do Not Stop On Tracks)'>'Spanish Jam'. 'Drums' and more jamming continue, before they power into 'The Other One', 'Going Down The Road Feeling Bad' and 'Wharf Rat'. The disc is a perfect example of what The Dead can do when things fall into place perfectly.

The show is also remembered because of Weir dedicating 'He's Gone' to IRA hunger striker Bobby Sands, who'd died the previous day. Although The Dead tended to shy away from explicit involvement in politics – Garcia in particular – they always had an awareness of issues and played benefits for diverse causes, including the Black Panther Party, local theatres and community-support organisations. In 2008, support for Barack Obama's presidential campaign saw Lesh, Hart, Kreutzmann and Weir (and Warren Haynes and Jeff Chimenti, who played with them) invited to the White House with their families.

In May, The Dead were back at Barton Hall at Cornell University, New York, for the final time. While their 1977 show at the venue is remembered as legendary, their 16 May 1981 show is celebrated in the *30 Trips Around The Sun* collection. The three-disc collection opens with 'Feel Like A Stranger' and ends with 'Don't Ease Me In': their engaging with *Go To Heaven* material, a positive sign. The first set is full of classics: 'Passenger' and 'Let It Grow' particularly standing out. The second set runs over two discs, and while the jazzy 'Shakedown Street' on the first disc is a surprise, the sequence on disc three goes further, with a fast 'Spanish Jam' launching a lengthy sequence that includes 'Drums', another jam that develops into 'Truckin'', before a jam themed on 'Nobody's Fault But Mine' moves into 'Stella Blue'. It's an effortless display of musical dexterity and near-telepathic interplay between musicians.

In August' *Dead Set* was released: the live electric collection from their run of shows at the Warfield and Radio City Music Hall the previous year. Until the release of *Without A Net* in 1990, this would be the most up-to-date commercially-available representation of a Grateful Dead gig for the hundreds of thousands who attended the shows in the 1980s.

While there was no Grateful Dead studio album in 1981, Bob Weir had not been putting is feet up, and the previous year he'd formed a new band, Bobby And The Midnites, whose self-titled debut album was released in October. As well as Weir, the band had settled with Brent Mydland on keyboards, former Kingfish member Matt Kelly on harmonica and vocals, Bobby Cochran (formerly of Steppenwolf) on guitar, Alphonso Johnson on bass and Billy Cobham on drums. Cobham had played with both Miles Davis and The Mahavishnu Orchestra. Johnson had been in Weather Report and had previously worked with other jazz musicians, including Cobham, and worked as a solo artist. *Bobby And The Midnites* – produced by *Go To Heaven* producer Gary Lyons – had a jazz-inflected feel, and quite a different sound to Weir's previous solo work. While Bobby And The Midnites would go on to be both a regular live attraction and the focus of Weir's activity between Dead engagements, none of the songs on the album entered The Dead's repertoire.

Dave's Picks Volume 20 features a show from the CU Events Centre, Boulder, Colorado, recorded on 9 December 1981, over three CDs. The first set opened with 'Cold Rain And Snow' and closed with 'I Know You Rider' – two numbers stretching back to their electric folk roots – the selection in between ranging from Weir's country double-punch of 'Mama Tried' and 'Mexicali Blues', to Garcia's 'Bird Song' and 'Candyman'. 'Scarlet Begonias' and 'Fire On The

Mountain' open the second set, 'The Other One' and 'Stella Blue' taking their positions after the improvised 'Space' section. It's noticeable that other than the cover of Willie Dixon's 'Little Red Rooster' – a recent addition to their set – no songs representing their recent studio releases are included in the show. *Terrapin Station*'s 'Estimated Prophet' is the most recent songs in this show, and there's nothing from *Go To Heaven*. The show featured two encores: 'US Blues', and a version of The Rolling Stones' '(I Can't Get No) Satisfaction', making its first appearance on a Dead album. Perhaps they felt the newer material was now so embedded in their repertoire that they no longer needed to give it prominence, or perhaps a tendency to play it safe was beginning to emerge.

1982 – Run For The Roses

By 1982, a significant falloff in releases can be marked. There would be no contemporary releases for a number of years, and so far, the majority of archive releases have not come from this later stage in The Dead's career. It's too easy to generalise that this was a consequence of the decline in Garcia's health. While this did no doubt affect the quality of the band's shows and was obviously linked to the lack of new Garcia/Hunter material, it's only part of the story. Garcia's health was by no means in steady decline in his later years, and while there were times he was significantly under par, there were many occasions when he rallied and enjoyed extended periods in better form.

There are also other factors to take into consideration given that the decade was far from kind to many of The Dead's contemporaries, who found themselves in a critical catch-22 where they'd be criticised for attempting anything new or trying to keep up with the times, or equally criticised for continuing to plough the same furrow they had for decades. Artists like Dylan and The Rolling Stones – both key influences on the early-Dead – struggled in this decade, their situations not helped by weaker material. The crux of the matter was that they lacked focus, as rock 'n' roll was never meant to be a long-term thing, and never originally considered as a *career* with all the expectation and weight that the concept carries. It was difficult for artists to know what was expected of them and how they should respond, and as a consequence, many of the one-time innovators found themselves treading water. The Dead's situation was far from exceptional.

A live recording from 6 April, recorded at the Spectrum, Philadelphia, Pennsylvania, features on *Road Trips Volume 4 Number 4*. The three-CD collection presents the complete show, from its 'Cold Rain And Snow' opener to the 'It's All Over Now, Baby Blue' encore, with supplemental material from both the first and second set of the previous night's show. Despite the caveats about the quality of The Dead's performances over this era, this show finds them focused and on form, with strong interplay between Garcia and Weir throughout. The second set's opening 'Shakedown Street' through to 'Terrapin Station' via 'Lost Sailor' and 'Saint Of Circumstance', shows no letup in quality. If anything, Weir can be seen as stepping up his performance significantly, and coming out from his role as rhythm guitarist, to being an equal frontman. But there's noticeably little new material on offer here. The only new song is a cover of 'Man Smart, Woman Smarter': a song that first appeared in the band's set in 1981. The song – originally a calypso best-known as performed by Harry Belafonte in the 1950s – was first recorded in the 1930s. It remains a popular number in The Dead's repertoire for the rest of their career.

The issue was perhaps more one of consistency. Previous years would see performances just days apart being analysed, dissected and argued over, to determine which was the best. There is great material from the early-1980s, but it's just that there's also a lot of sloppiness creeping in, with missed cues, unimaginative playing, and a feeling that things just aren't fun on stage. But they could deliver a powerful performance all the same. The *30 Trips Around The Sun* collection includes the show from 31 July at Manor Downs, Austin, Texas as the 1982 representative, and again, this is a fine high-energy show. The 'Alabama Getaway' opener into 'Promised Land', shows the former as every bit a classic rock 'n' roll piece as anything Chuck Berry could have come up with, and the second set is really a definitive example of how good they could be, even if in general they were at a low power level.

Dick's Picks Volume 32 focuses on a show from 7 August at Alpine Valley Music Theatre, East Troy, Wisconsin: a double CD documenting the first night of a two-night run at the outdoor venue, the first time they'd played multiple nights there. The opening 'The Music Never Stopped', straight into 'Sugaree' and back into a reprise of 'The Music Never Stopped', features some sweet playing from Garcia. The band are on form throughout a first set which closes with a version of 'Let It Grow' that features the kind of instinctive jamming that wouldn't be out of place in a classic second-set sequence. The actual second set is no anticlimax, with a 'Playing In The Band' sequence that includes 'Drums', 'Space' and 'The Wheel' where the playing is as fine as could be hoped for. If anything, it's a little shorter, a little faster perhaps, but as a performance, it's packed with energy and spontaneous invention.

Garcia released his fourth and what would be his final solo album in November: a collection titled *Run For The Roses*, recorded towards the end of 1981. Accompanied by musical associates Ron Tutt on drums and both Melvin Seals and Merl Saunders on keyboards, it's a lacklustre affair. The title track is an upbeat piece, with Garcia's distinctive playing immediately recognisable. It probably could've fit in with The Dead's repertoire, but it was never included. The other Garcia/Hunter number – 'Valerie' – sounds like an attempt at a Bob Dylan blues number, and while likeable, there's no 'Mission In The Rain' or 'Might As Well' here. 'Midnight Getaway' – a collaboration between Garcia, Hunter and Jerry Garcia Band bass player John Kahn – is as close as there is to a hidden gem here, although, while it comes close, it misses the mark. The cover of The Beatles' 'I Saw Her Standing There' has a very dated reggae style, even for the early-1980s, and while Garcia's vocals and playing are soulful on 'Knockin' On Heaven's Door', the reggae-style chorus makes it best forgotten.

An expanded version of the album included in the Garcia box set *All Good Things: The Jerry Garcia Studio Sessions*, adds a version of 'Fennario' – the traditional song also known as 'Peggy-O' that The Dead performed live – a version of 'Alabama Getaway', covers of Dylan's 'Tangled Up In Blue' and 'Simple Twist Of Fate', The Beatles' 'Dear Prudence', and a different mix of 'Valerie'. An entire album of Beatles and Dylan covers might've ultimately been a better release, while 'Fennario/Peggy-O' – never released by The Dead during their active years but included as an outtake on the re-issue of *Go To Heaven* – would've been an ideal inclusion. It's an interesting song from the perspective of this Scottish Deadhead, given that it's based on a traditional Scottish folk ballad, 'The Bonnie Lass O'Fyvie'. Written in the Scots language, it tells of a soldier travelling from Aberdeen, and passing through the Aberdeenshire village of Fyvie ('Fennario' being an interpretation of the original 'Fyvie-O') where he falls in love with a local girl. This, of course, means that if 'Fennario' is in Aberdeenshire, the song 'Dire Wolf' must also be set there too, making at least three Dead songs set in Scotland: 'Terrapin Station' making reference to events 'Down in Carlisle'. Of course, Fennario gives Hunter a classic could-be-anywhere fictional location for the songs; perhaps it's located in the fictional Bigfoot County, as referred to in the song 'Brown-Eyed Women'. The fact that Robert Hunter's name was originally Robert Burns – the same as Scotland's national poet – until his mother remarried, can't go unnoticed either. 'Fennario/Peggy-O' would be performed live by The Dead until 1995: a link to Garcia and Hunter's folk roots, and a vehicle for Garcia's singing and playing at its most soulful.

Another solo endeavour that was put on tape in 1982-1983, was an album from Brent Mydland. Recorded at Club Front by Mydland's then-partner and Dead sound engineer Betty Cantor-Jackson, the recordings featured guitarist Monty Byrom, bass player Paul Marshall and drummer John Mauceri. While Mydland didn't want the album to be a Grateful Dead project, Garcia apparently appeared on one track, while Jerry Garcia Band bass player John Kahn also contributed. The project fizzled out, with the musician moving on to other things, and the recordings were never released. Among the songs were 'Tons Of Steel' and 'Maybe You Know', which would be performed by The Dead. Others remain in the can, with titles including 'Dreams', 'Inlay It In Your Heart', 'Long Way To Go' and 'See The Other Side'. Mydland's would focus his talent on The Grateful Dead rather than a solo career, allowing him to flourish as both a performer and a songwriter at the heart of the band.

1983 – Throwing Stones

If there were few 1982 archive releases, the same applies to 1983. Three releases from the year have emerged so far, and despite The Dead's overall low point from the early-to-mid-1980s, these show some new points of light in the form of new material starting to emerge.

Further to this, The Dead's rigorous and regular touring schedule was building a unique subculture, with fans now beginning to follow the band on tour, going from show to show in whatever transport they could muster, playing their way through, selling homemade t-shirts, stickers or food. A travelling community of Deadheads was becoming a thing, descending on venues for the duration of a run of shows, camping in the vicinity and setting up a ramshackle mall of amateur vendors and voyagers. While generally good-natured, there could be tension with locals, particularly as drug use was a regular occurrence. While many were there for the music and to see the band, there was a growing number who saw The Dead as little more than an opportunity to party and a licence to indulge in drug use. This would develop into a significant problem in later years.

However, from the vantage point of another continent, these issues were thousands of miles away. Another development was far more interesting: The Dead's openness to allowing the audience to record shows and circulate tapes. While their tolerance of taping and trading (without profit, of course) wasn't new, things went up a gear, with fans being allowed a designated area of the venues to record the shows. At a stroke, the issue of tapers obstructing those who wanted to watch the show, dance or sing, was removed, and the tapers were given a space where they might not have the best view, but would be able to capture the best sound. A small forest of mics on stands would appear at shows, copies of the tapes circulating far and wide, eventually falling into the hands of eager fans on other continents, who might not have been at the shows but were hungry to hear what The Dead were up to in stadiums and sports fields on the other side of the world.

While the supply chain of live tapes was moving into high-production mode in 1983, only a few shows have been released officially. Emerging in 2021, *Dave's Picks Volume 39* features a show from 26 April 26, recorded at the Spectrum in Philadelphia, featuring four new songs, three of them coming consecutively in the first set. First up comes Mydland's 'Maybe You Know' – originally from his solo recordings the previous year – that The Dead would only play live a couple of times, most of these performances coming in April 1983. This is followed immediately by the Garcia/Hunter composition 'West L.A. Fadeaway' that they'd been performing since autumn 1982 – a number that could be read as being about performer John Belushi: a friend of the band who'd died as a consequence of drug abuse, at the Chateau Marmont hotel in L.A., earlier in 1982. It was also possibly a coded warning from Hunter to Garcia, that his behaviour was leading him to the same destination. The first set also includes 'My Brother Esau' – a Weir/Barlow song that was introduced the previous month; a complex number that spans the 'Book Of Genesis', the Vietnam war, Altamont and inter-familial conflict. 'West L.A. Fadeaway' would appear on their next album. 'My Brother Esau' would also be recorded during those sessions. A second Weir/Barlow number titled 'Throwing Stones' features in the second set, sitting in a sequence between 'Morning Dew' and 'Not Fade Away'. It too would feature on their next studio album, though it was still several years away. Bonus tracks included on the release from the 15 April show at the War Memorial Auditorium, Rochester, New York, include another new song: Weir's 'Little Star'. This short jazzy number came up during the second set between 'He's Gone' and 'Drums', and was performed only three times by The Dead in 1983.

Dave's Picks Volume 27 from 2 September at Boise State University Pavilion in Boise, Idaho, documents the only time The Dead played that state. There are only a few states that they never played – Arkansas, Delaware, North and South Dakota and Wyoming – but they did play Alaska in 1980. The Idaho show – over three CDs – opens with a fresh cover of Willie Dixon's 'Wang Dang Doodle', sung by Weir. While the show only features a couple of new numbers, it's no slouch of a performance, with 'Help On The Way'>'Slipknot!'>'Franklin's Tower' starting the second set particularly strongly. 'Throwing Stones' emerges from 'Space' on disc three, the song going on to establish a place for itself in the second part of the second set: a powerful Weir-voiced number that could sit alongside one of Garcia's more soulful pieces or a more upbeat rocker. It's a complicated piece; probably the most overtly-political piece in The Dead's catalogue – but it rises above any simple sloganeering or solutions, and the focus zooms from the global to the personal. Along with some memorable lyrics, the song also offers a platform for some intense and urgent Garcia soloing.

The 14 October gig at the Hartford Civic Centre, Hartford, Connecticut, features on *Dick's Picks Volume 6*, released in 1996. The second set here sees the band hitting the note perfectly, from the 'Fire On The Mountain' opener to the closing 'Sugar Magnolia'. If it's a shade shorter than usual, there's no shortage of content that hits the mark repeatedly, with Garcia engaging fully with a lengthy 'Eyes Of The World' and bringing in a soulful 'Stella Blue' after 'The Other One' and its preceding 'Spanish Jam'.

The album sees the earliest-released appearance of the Garcia/Hunter song 'Keep Your Day Job', played as the closing number of the first set. The song – which made its debut in 1982 – has a unique reputation in The Dead's catalogue as being probably their least-liked song. While its thinking might have been in line with the 1980s yuppie thinking, a song imploring the listener to work hard and focus on their job whether they like it or not, wasn't the kind of thing their audience wanted to hear. Hunter's intentions may have been ironic and humorous, but it comes across as a clumsy managerial, motivational speech. The band eventually stopped playing it in 1986, Hunter admitting that its unpopularity with the fans was the main reason.

While hindsight reveals that many of The Dead's early-1980s shows had their faults, it was these shows that built their audience steadily through the decade, with many of those who attended shows during this era continuing to follow The Dead from then on. The 14 October 1983 show has a particular significance in this respect, as the gig was attended separately by Phish guitarist Trey Anastasio and that band's bass player Mike Gordon. Phish – an act very heavily influenced by The Dead – went on to attract many Dead fans in the 1980s and 1990s, to the present day; Anastasio playing with surviving Dead members in 2015 at the Fare Thee Well: Celebrating 50 Years Of The Grateful Dead concerts.

The show that features on *30 Trips Around The Sun*, from 21 October at the Centrum, Worcester, Massachusetts, shows more new material that would have an even greater impact. Tucked away at the end of the second set following 'I Need A Miracle', comes the earliest-released version of 'Touch Of Grey' – a song that had been part of their repertoire since autumn 1982, and would go on to rewrite The Dead's history upon its release in 1987. It would be a couple of years until the Garcia/Hunter number gained its well-deserved iconic status, but at this moment, it was an upbeat rocker: not a million miles away from songs like 'Bertha' that could close a second set with a defiant flourish. It is, however, fully realised, and not so different from its final form that would become so familiar a few years later. The three-disc set presents a solid performance, and while it might not be a historic one, it hints that – for all that the early-1980s are often regarded as something of a fallow period for The Dead – some new shoots were starting to appear.

1984 – Feel Like A Stranger

The Dead's rocky patch continued into 1984, a year where again there are only a handful of archive releases to represent the shows played. The band were still capable of inspired performances, with Garcia alert and responsive to the other members, pulling imaginative solos out with apparent ease and delivering soulful vocals. But at other times, he would play with his head down, the band members isolated musically from each other, Garcia performing more from memory than from the heart, missing vocal cues and delivering tepid solos. Sets would be shorter, and he would at times seem uncomfortable onstage, disconnected from what was going on, and an unwilling participant in the event.

Released in 2020, *Dave's Picks Volume 35* is so far the only stand-alone release from this year. It features a show from the Philadelphia Civic Centre recorded on 20 April, with bonus tracks from the second set of the show at the same venue the night before making up the three-disc set. 'Feel Like A Stranger' makes an interesting opening number – perhaps Weir expressing something about Garcia's apparent alienation – before a more regular 'Cold Rain And Snow'. It's a busy first set, with Weir at the wheel for much of it, the only significant pause being Garcia's 'It Must Have Been The Roses'. which finds him in strong voice. The second set – even with its shorter duration – is a consistent performance throughout, with Garcia front-and-centre for 'Scarlet Begonias' and 'Fire On The Mountain' at the start. And while Weir's 'Samson & Delilah' and 'I Need A Miracle' are appropriately rocking, Garcia delivers the goods again with a rendition of 'Morning Dew'. If Weir is carrying more weight as a performer, he's up to the job, and fortunately this collection finds Garcia up-to-scratch too. The album sees another appearance of 'Keep Your Day Job' – played as the encore at the 20 April show – and the bonus tracks from 19 April on disc three, include an 'Estimated Prophet'/'Terrapin Station' sequence that shows Weir and Garcia matching each other at the helm for two key numbers from the band's late-1970s songbook.

A second album by Bobby And the Midnites – titled *Where The Beat Meets The Street* – was released in August. While the band had continued in the background, with Weir playing during off-time from The Dead, there had been changes since their previous album, with Alphonso Johnson replaced by ex-Little Feat bass player Kenny Gradney. It's a polished album – as might be expected from one produced by ex-Steely Dan and Doobie Brothers guitarist Jeff 'Skunk' Baxter (who also played guitar and synthesizer on the album) – but it perhaps lacked some of the grit and rawness that fans associated with The Dead. The album was something of a farewell from Bobby And The Midnites, as they would play their final show at the end of September. The band would be Weir's last serious side-project until he began working with bassist Rob Wasserman later in the decade.

The only other live archive release from 1984 comes as part of the *30 Trips Around The Sun* collection, with the show from 12 October at the Augusta Civic Center, Augusta, Maine. The first set alternates between Weir and

Garcia numbers – Weir's work more upbeat, Garcia's more reflective – in a complimentary yin and yang relationship. 'On The Road Again' played alongside 'Jack-a-Roe' (one of the traditional acoustic numbers included on the *Reckoning* album), serves as a reminder of just how good The Dead were at incorporating their folk roots, even this late in their career. Weir again plays a big part in the second set, with 'Lost Sailor' and 'Saint Of Circumstance', while Mydland's 'Don't Need Love' ahead of 'Uncle John's Band' gives the show something of a rarity – 'Don't Need Love' only being performed a few times between 1984 and 1986, and only ever being released on this collection. If Garcia's taken a step back from the microphone to share the duties with Weir, his vocals during this show remain robust and focussed throughout.

Beyond the regular Dead tour dates, other projects were launched in 1984. The Dead set up their own charitable organisation to streamline their benefit gigs – the Rex Foundation: named after their technician Rex Jackson who died in a road accident. Over the rest of their career, The Dead played benefit shows for the foundation, the money raised then being allocated to a range of projects they supported.

Garcia was involved in another film project, this time an attempt to make a film of Kurt Vonnegut's 1959 novel *The Sirens Of Titan*. He worked through 1984 on a screenplay with *Saturday Night Live* writer Tom Davis, completing a first draft in 1985. It never progressed to the screen.

There was an attempt to get some of the new numbers down on tape at Fantasy Records in Berkeley, but the band's overall lack of motivation meant they failed to progress.

While some of these projects bore fruit and others did not, there was something of an ulterior motive in their commissioning, which was to keep Garcia occupied and active. Friends thought his continued drug abuse stemmed from boredom; he was an intelligent, articulate and creative person, but one who could withdraw into self-destructive behaviour if he was without motivation. One other scheme that would prove to be more successful was the idea of making a Grateful Dead video. With home video a growing market, it aligned Garcia's interest in filmmaking with the possibility of creating some new Grateful Dead material without the hurdle of making an actual album.

1985 – The Twilight Zone

By early-1985, Garcia's problems could no longer be ignored, and an intervention was staged, letting him know that his behaviour could not continue as it was, and that treatment was the only option. He reluctantly agreed to seek help, and a change was promised. However, the matter quickly came to a head just days later, when on 18 January while en route to a drug treatment facility, police caught Garcia in Golden Gate Park using drugs in his car. The legal consequences were lenient, but he was obliged to enlist in a programme to quit drugs. This, and his overall health issues, helped motivate his recovery process, and as the year progressed, his drug use tapered off and his general health improved.

The Dead were back performing live from February, and following the March and April dates, work began on the video project that would eventually be released as *So Far*. Garcia worked on the project throughout as co-director, and dealt with the sound mixing. Unlike *The Grateful Dead Movie*, the focus was on the band and the music rather than on the fans and the scene. The Dead were filmed over three days at the Marin Veterans' Memorial Auditorium in San Rafael, California, in rehearsal mode without an audience, running through a number of songs – 'Uncle John's Band', 'Playing In The Band', 'Lady With A Fan', 'Space', 'Rhythm Devils', 'Throwing Stones' and 'Not Fade Away'. They filmed another three days in November, adding some footage from their year-end show at the Oakland Coliseum, and editing-in other visuals.

Another project that came to realisation in 1985, was The Dead's involvement in soundtrack work for a new version of the TV show *The Twilight Zone*. Phil DeGuere – who'd been involved in making the 1972 *Sunshine Daydream* film – had continued to work in the entertainment industry and was producing the show. He had already installed Dead associate Merl Saunders as musical director for the series, and it was suggested that The Dead could contribute background sound and musical themes for the show. There was a mixed reaction among band members, but Hart and Garcia were strongly enthusiastic. While the band's music – mostly the work of Garcia and Hart – featured on a number of episodes, a soundtrack CD credited to The Grateful Dead and Merl Saunders was eventually released, collecting several of their pieces. The Dead's input is mostly short fragments of electronic 'Space'-type soundscapes, and though worthwhile, it might've been better to hear the work in its entirety, rather than as shorter pieces.

A concert from 24 June at the Riverbend Music Centre, Cincinnati, Ohio, is included as a three-disc set in the *30 Trips Around The Sun* set. The first set opens strongly with 'Alabama Getaway' and 'Greatest Story Ever Told', but really takes off with Weir's 'Let It Grow' at the end, the version here going over twelve minutes in length, making it the longest single song they performed that night. At a time when the band seemed to be pulling back from performing lengthy jams, it's all the more remarkable. The second set kicks off the second disc with 'Iko Iko' and 'Samson & Delilah' – two upbeat rhythmic numbers that lead into a lengthy sequence that manages to include three slower Garcia numbers – 'He's Gone', 'Wharf Rat' and 'Comes A Time' – and the return of Weir's 'The Other One' with its 'Cryptical Envelopment' opening and closing sections.

In July, a series of shows at Berkeley's Greek Theatre marking the band's 20th anniversary came as part of a strong run of summer and autumn concerts. The Dead had by this point grown to be one of the biggest live attractions in the USA, selling out the overwhelming majority of their shows, and selling over $11,500,000 worth of tickets during the year. The Greek Theatre had become one of the many venues associated with The Dead. They first played there in 1967, and in the 1980s they played a multiple-night run there every year, the amphitheatre having the advantage of being essentially local, its 8,500-capacity ideal for the size of audience they were attracting, and its outdoor location making a spectacular backdrop.

While tapes marked 'Greek Theatre' or 'Greek Theater' were always treasured by this band of listeners on the other side of the Atlantic, the shows later in the year continued the strong return to form that the band were enjoying. Dick picked one show from 1985 – the 1 November gig at Richmond Coliseum in Virginia – for *Dick's Picks Volume 21*. While the first set is comparatively unadventurous in its song choices, 'Dancing In The Streets' and 'Cold Rain And Snow' make a strong opening, and 'Little Red Rooster' is settling into being a powerful blues groove. The second set finds Garcia in great shape, with 'High Time', 'He's Gone' and 'Comes A Time' all delivered soulfully and with the glorious golden guitar tone that shines like it should. The second set concludes with three strong 1960s covers, and even the encore of 'Keep Your Day Job' couldn't diminish the strong end to the show. The unusual covers that feature on this release, are something the band had been experimenting with since their summer concerts included 'Keep On Growing', originally by Derek And The Dominoes. This show includes the earliest release of 'Gimme Some Lovin'' – originally by The Spencer Davis Group, though probably best known in the USA through its version by Traffic. Others will know it from The Blues Brothers, featuring Dead associate John Belushi. There's also an early recording of the Willie Dixon blues number 'Spoonful', sung by Weir. Dylan's 'She Belongs To Me' is performed: a number The Dead had played in their early years, but which had been more recently in the repertoire of The Jerry Garcia Band. The Dead only performed it a handful of times. Another cover that appears here that was originally part of their earliest sets, is 'Gloria': originally by Them featuring Van Morrison. It would be something of a rarity in the band's set in the 1980s and 1990s, but was always a welcome addition.

The release also includes bonus tracks from their 2 September 1980 gig at the Community War Memorial in Rochester, New York. While it's worth having as bonus material on the third disc – especially given the shorter nature of the performances – it's a puzzling add, given that there would've been content available from shows that were closer chronologically to November 1985, that could've been included. It's no reflection on the quality of the 1980 material, just that it's a little bit out of place here.

The Richmond show was also noted because it was the first significant incidence of gatecrashing at a gig. Hundreds of ticket-less fans gained admission to the arena, and there were confrontations between the police and fans outside the venue. With demand for tickets at an arena that holds over 13,500 people, outstripping supply to the point that gatecrashing and police clampdowns occurred, the band moved to larger stadium venues the following year. As a measure of their growing popularity, The Dead played another New Year's Eve show at the end of 1985, this time at the Oakland Coliseum Arena, as a more accommodating alternative to the previous Oakland Auditorium. The show was broadcast live on radio and cable TV, with an estimated audience of around 500,000 viewers.

1986 – We Will Survive

By the start of 1986, Garcia seemed to be in better health, and his apparent overcoming of his addiction had a knock-on effect on other band members. Others began to tackle their own issues, whether alcohol or cocaine. The change wouldn't affect every member of the band, and in some instances, it would only be temporary, but by the time The Grateful Dead resumed live engagements with a five-night run at the Henry J. Kaiser Convention Centre in Oakland in February, it seemed they were healthier than they'd been for a number of years.

Their performances, however, were still erratic, and the easy interplay between the musicians wasn't as cohesive as it had been. The sets remained shorter, lengthy jam sequences, were fewer and sets tended towards the predictable. That 1986 remains a year documented only by material included in *30 Trips Around The Sun* – despite over 40 shows taking place – makes it clear that not all the problems they'd been experiencing had receded.

The only 1986 show to be released so far, comes from the Cal Expo Amphitheatre in Sacramento, California on 3 May. The entire show fits on a two-disc set: a far more concise experience than the apparently-unconstrained performances that their reputation had been built on. It's still a reasonable performance, albeit one that perhaps falls short of what The Grateful Dead could deliver just a few years before. The first set opens with 'Cold Rain And Snow' and 'The Race Is On'; Garcia's 'High Time' being the only real highlight. The second set opens with a stirring 'Scarlet Begonias' and 'Fire On The Mountain'. The fact that there was space on the first disc for these two second-set numbers, tells its own story as to the opening set's length.

On disc two, 'Man Smart, Woman Smarter' and 'Going Down The Road Feeling Bad' are a spirited combination, and Garcia's 'Comes A Time' hits the mark. It's noticeable that there are no new songs or covers in the set. There's also, unusually, no encore – Lesh explaining, 'Jerry's speakers are totally frozen, his guitar is broken, and my mind is blown, so I don't think we're going to do an encore tonight'. The following night they opened with 'One More Saturday Night', the track they had planned to play as their encore the previous night.

Following their summer stadium dates – where they played on the same bill as Bob Dylan and Tom Petty – things took a dramatic turn for the worse, with Garcia collapsing in a diabetic coma. He had been unwell and dehydrated, the hot summer weather worsening the situation. The gravity of the situation only really emerged publicly some time later, as it became apparent that Garcia had come very close to death. Doctors trying to diagnose his coma, injected him with Valium, to which he was allergic, causing his heart to stop. He was successfully revived and spent 48 hours on a respirator. He did recover, but it took months. On coming out of a coma, he found he had to relearn to play his instrument – a process helped by Merl Saunders, who visited him and encouraged him to regain his strength and his ability to perform. In the meantime, all the band's autumn dates were cancelled so Garcia could undergo the rehabilitation he needed.

Garcia's recovery was remarkable, and in October, he was able to take to the stage again with the Jerry Garcia Band in a San Francisco nightclub. The Dead eventually performed again in December, with a run of three nights at the Oakland Coliseum followed by four nights at the Henry J. Kaiser Convention Centre, including a New Year show. Hunter had been working on a number of new songs while Garcia was recovering, two of which – 'Black Muddy River' and 'When Push Comes To Shove' – appeared in The Dead's sets over these shows. But the song that came out the strongest was the one that opened their first show following Garcia's collapse: 'Touch Of Grey'. The closing line of its chorus – a defiant 'I will survive' – took on a whole new significance in light of the year's events.

1987 – In And Out Of The Dark

The Dead returned to Marin Veterans' Auditorium in San Rafael in January 1987 to finally record a new album. The venue was familiar, as it was where they'd recorded the *So Far* video. The band's equipment was set up on a stage as it would be for a concert (but without an audience), the Le Mobile recording studio parked outside, getting everything down on tape. The environment was a productive one, with the band able to focus on recording the basic tracks without the confining atmosphere of the recording studio, or the distractions of Club Front, where recording sessions could quickly dissolve into a hang-out session.

Unlike their previous three studio albums, the production was kept in-house, with Garcia and Club Front sound-engineer John Cutler working on it. With the songs they were planning to include being familiar from having played them live for several years, the recording process was painless and was completed in just over a week. The band even had time to experiment a little. At one point, they performed with the hall and stage in complete darkness, an experience which gave the album its name. Following the completion of the basic tracks, Garcia and Cutler moved to Club Front in February and March to record vocals and complete the mixing.

The album was finished in May, Arista Records rightly suspecting they had something special on their hands – the first album in seven years from a band who were already headlining stadiums – and who'd recorded a song they were convinced had the potential to be a hit. Arista wanted to make the most of the opportunity, and commissioned a video for 'Touch Of Grey'. Directed by *The Grateful Dead Movie* animator Gary Gutierrez, the video had a simple but effective concept: the band represented by life-size skeletons on stage. The fact that it meant the band themselves didn't have to do too much, suited them perfectly, and they were filmed performing the song in May at Laguna Seca in Monterey after a concert; the audience invited to stay on to watch the skeleton puppets perform. The video first appeared on MTV in June, its humour and unpretentious style, perfect for an audience who were demanding something a bit more sophisticated from music videos without being too challenging. Like the best music videos, it presented a simple idea that was brilliantly done and managed the difficult task of respecting The Dead's legacy, their fans and community, without alienating a potential wider audience. A 30-minute video – *Dead Ringers: The Making Of Touch Of Grey* – was released in 1987, covering the production of the video, directed by Justin Kreutzmann: the son of The Dead's drummer Billy Kreutzmann.

The release of *In The Dark* went on to change everything. Not only did the album achieve sales of over 2,000,000, but the single 'Touch Of Grey' gave them their first *Billboard* top 10 hit single in the USA. Released on 6 July, the album featured seven songs. Four were by Garcia and Hunter – 'Touch Of Grey', 'West L.A. Fadeaway' and the more recent 'When Push Comes To Shove' and 'Black Muddy River'. There were two by Weir and Barlow – 'Throwing

Stones', and 'Hell In A Bucket' co-written with Mydland, and Mydland's own 'Tons Of Steel'. 'My Brother Esau' was released as the B-side of 'Touch Of Grey', and appeared as an extra track on the cassette release of the album. It was included in a 2004 album reissue which added five bonus tracks plus alternative studio recordings of album songs, including 'West L.A. Fadeaway' from the 1984 Fantasy Studios sessions, 'Black Muddy River' and 'When Push Comes To Shove' from Club Front in 1986, and a version of 'Touch Of Grey' from 1982. There's also a live version of 'Throwing Stones' from the 4 July 1987 show at Sullivan Stadium, Foxboro, Massachusetts.

The Foxboro show was the first of six stadium shows during the summer of 1987 where The Dead performed as Bob Dylan's backing band. On each night, The Dead performed their normal two-set show but returned for a further 90-minute set backing Dylan. They'd been rehearsing with Dylan in May, and over a period of three weeks, ran through around 100 songs that could be included in the set. Despite their long-standing familiarity with his material, Dylan was a challenging artist to perform with, as songs would be in unexpected keys, lyrics could be forgotten, and arrangements completely changed without warning. Depending on your affection for Dylan, he was either mercurial or erratic, but he certainly did not make it easy for The Dead to perform at their best. The album *Dylan And The Dead* was released in 1989, documenting the shows, and it remains a controversial addition to both The Dead and Dylan's back catalogues, with some maintaining it marked a low point in the careers of both artists; others suggesting it did in fact capture an inspired hybrid that was always doomed to disappoint purists in either fan base. Dylan's live albums – with perhaps the exception of the 1966 Royal Albert Hall concert presented as Volume Four of his *Bootleg Series* – were always among his least-acclaimed releases. *Dylan And The Dead* did little to change this.

This series of shows also produced The Dead's *View From The Vault, Volume Four*, released as a four-CD set and a DVD in 2003, recorded at the 24 July show at Oakland Stadium and the 26 July show at Anaheim Stadium. The first two discs cover the first night, the opening set featuring two *In The Dark*-era songs – 'My Brother Esau' and 'When Push Come To Shove' – as well as back-catalogue classics like 'Friend Of The Devil' and 'Cassidy'. 'Hell In A Bucket' – another *In The Dark* number – opens the second set that features both 'Playing In The Band' and 'Uncle John's Band', while a cover of Traffic's 'Dear Mr. Fantasy' was establishing itself as a Mydland-voiced favourite. The second night is considered one of their best shows in 1987, and it again features a mix of newer material – 'Tons Of Steel' and 'West L.A. Fadeaway' – alongside established numbers like 'Bird Song' and 'New Minglewood Blues'. There's even a cheeky cover of Dylan's 'When I Paint My Masterpiece'. The second set is a packed sequence that begins with 'Shakedown Street' and ends with 'Throwing Stones' and 'Not Fade Away', via 'Looks Like Rain', 'Terrapin Station', 'The Other One' and 'Stella Blue'. It's a showcase for what the late-

1980s Dead were capable of. And performed in front of an audience that was not entirely their own, it was a set that would easily convince an audience that The Dead were more than up to the challenge of playing with Dylan.

The Dead's two sets at the 12 July show with Dylan at Giants Stadium were released in 2019 as the first two discs of the *Giants Stadium 1987, 1989, 1991* box set chronicling five complete shows at the venue in three separate years. There's only one show from 1987, and given that it was essentially a support slot – albeit they were supporting themselves – it's a shorter show with no encore. Five of the seven *In The Dark* songs are played – only 'Touch Of Grey' and 'Black Muddy River' are missing – and Dylan's 'When I Paint My Masterpiece' makes an appearance to whet the appetite of Dylan fans waiting for their hero's appearance. There's more than enough new material for the recent converts, some favourite covers for those unfamiliar with their output – 'Promised Land', 'Morning Dew' and 'Not Fade Away' – and a few choice back-catalogue cuts for the faithful: 'Loser', 'Bertha', 'Playing In The Band' and 'Stella Blue'. It may not be their most adventurous outing – they're not playing to a home crowd – but they cover a lot of ground and successfully meet the expectations of a varied audience.

If critics were mixed about the merits of Dylan performing with The Dead, there was little doubt the experience was one that made a significant impact on Dylan. His career trajectory in the 1980s had been erratic, starting the decade with the born-again Christianity of *Saved* and *Shot Of Love,* before the critical and artistic resurgence of *Infidels.* But his most recent album was *Knocked Out Loaded*: an underperforming and uninspiring effort. Within two years, he would again be acclaimed, with the release of *Oh Mercy.* Working with The Dead gave Dylan the opportunity to rethink his ideas, focus on what he was doing, and find his inspiration again.

The *So Far* video documentary emerged in 1987, its timing coinciding perfectly with the tidal wave of interest in The Dead. It gave both a behind-the-scenes look at the band and a polished and produced performance video, avoiding the baggage of details that would only be of interest to the most devoted fan, or a live show that only really served as a souvenir for those who were there. While some of the visual effects look dated to a 21st-century viewer, it also capitalised on the growth of home video as a medium that could support more artistic work. The medium was no longer a novelty, and the quality of home entertainment had improved considerably since its introduction (the set was also available on LaserDisc), meaning the viewer experience was more immersive and closer to cinema, while the economics of a video release were more favourable and far less risky for the band. Although they resisted the opportunity to review it simply as *So Far…* so good, The Grateful Dead's excursion into home video was praised by critics.

The show from 1987 included in *30 Trips Around The Sun* comes from Madison Square Garden in New York, recorded on 18 September: the third night of a five-night run at the venue. The show is over two discs, reflecting their shorter performances, the six-song first set opening with an appropriately fiery 'Hell In A Bucket': the only representative of *In The Dark* to appear during the show. The first of three Dylan covers – 'When I Paint My Masterpiece' – appears in the first set before a version of 'Bird Song' (written by Hunter in New York's Chelsea Hotel) brings the first half to a close. An energetic 'Shakedown Street' launched the second set, with the energy levels remaining high for 'Man Smart, Woman Smarter'. 'Terrapin Station' continues the set on the second disc, with the rest of the show a lengthy sequence built around 'Going Down The Road Feeling Bad', 'Morning Dew' and 'Good Lovin'', which includes a brief appearance of 'La Bamba'. Dylan's 'All Along The Watchtower' also features in the set an encore of 'Knockin' On Heaven's Door' bringing the night to a close. The Dylan And The Dead tour may not have made it to New York, but even if he wasn't there in person, Dylan's influence certainly was. On the band's night off during the Madison Square Garden run, Garcia and Weir performed live on the *Late Night With David Letterman* show, playing 'When I Paint My Masterpiece' with the house band, then being interviewed by the host.

The following month, Garcia found himself the unlikely toast of New York, with The Jerry Garcia Band playing a series of 18 shows at the Lunt-Fontanne Theatre on Broadway. The Jerry Garcia band had kept a lower profile than The Dead, predominantly playing smaller venues in San Francisco and wider California. With the surge in interest in The Grateful Dead, promoter Bill Graham saw a unique opportunity. The Broadway shows were different, with an acoustic band – dubbed the Jerry Garcia Acoustic Band – playing a set of traditional and bluegrass songs, followed by the Jerry Garcia Band performing more familiar rock, blues and soul numbers. The Jerry Garcia Acoustic Band included Sandy Rothman – who'd been a member of the Black Mountain Boys with Garcia in 1964 – and David Nelson, with whom Garcia had played in the Wildwood Boys before The Dead. The Jerry Garcia Band bassist John Kahn played acoustic bass with fiddler Kenny Kosek and drummer David Kemper. Garcia's interest in playing traditional music had been rekindled during his period of rehabilitation, and many songs in the band's repertoire were numbers Garcia had played before moving to electric guitar.

A number of recordings of the Broadway performances have emerged in subsequent years. The recording had to be done discretely on account of the venue's policy, which no doubt was what led to the recordings sitting on a shelf for a while despite the obvious demand. In 2004, two collections emerged – *Pure Jerry: Lunt- Fontanne, New York City, October 31, 1987* (a four-disc set with complete matinee and evening acoustic and electric sets on each disc) and *Pure Jerry: Lunt- Fontanne, New York City, The Best Of The Rest, October 15-30, 1987*, with selections from the run of shows over three discs, one featuring acoustic and the other two electric. The first includes an acoustic take of 'Ripple' and electric versions of 'Run For The Roses', 'They Love Each Other', 'Cats Under The Stars', 'Gomorrah' and 'Deal'. The second release includes 'Mission In The Rain'. The covers include a considerable number of well-chosen Dylan songs, including 'Forever Young' and 'Simple Twist OF Fate', along with songs by The Beatles, Van Morrison, Peter Tosh and Jimmy Cliff. The 2015 release *On Broadway: Act One – October 28th 1987* captures a matinee, an evening acoustic set and the evening electric set by the Jerry Garcia Band. It's easily one of the most immediately enjoyable extracurricular Garcia releases, both acoustic and electric obviously taking delight in their craft and making it sound effortless. All three discs overwhelmingly feature covers, the electric band including only two originals: 'Run For The Roses' and 'Gomorrah'. The range and depth of material presented in these releases is a testament to Garcia's wide musical taste and skills, and also makes the obvious case for the benefits of varying the set for each performance.

A number of songs recorded elsewhere in November and December emerged in 1988 as the album *Almost Acoustic*. Recorded at shows at the Warfield Theatre in San Francisco and The Wiltern Theatre in Los Angeles, fans and critics met the collection with praise for both the performance and recording quality. Despite their traditional nature, many of the songs were already familiar to Dead fans, including 'Deep Elem Blues' and 'I've Been All Around The World'. Others were works that had been influences on them, such as the original 'Casey Jones'. A version of 'Ripple' that closed the album made it even sweeter. A further release in 2010 – *Ragged But Right* – included material from the L.A., San Francisco and Broadway shows, selected by band member Sandy Rothman. If the Jerry Garcia Acoustic Band was a short-lived project, its recorded legacy was a wealth of quality material, and Garcia's rekindled interest in traditional music would stay with him for the rest of his life, running in parallel with his day job with The Dead.

Other activities under way in 1987 emerged the following year, with Garcia, Weir and Mydland among the cast of dozens to appear on Bob Dylan's *Down In The Groove* album. In June, the three recorded background vocals for the song 'Silvio': written by Dylan and Hunter. A further Dylan/Hunter collaboration – 'Ugliest Girl In The World' – also appeared on the album, both being songs that Hunter had been working on in 1986 when he delivered 'Black Muddy River' and 'When Push Comes To Shove'. In the years after The Dead, Hunter again collaborated with Dylan, co-writing most of the songs on his 2009 *Together Through Life* album. Meanwhile, in 1987, Hunter had been working on a new solo album titled *Liberty*, which would feature Garcia on guitar.

1988 – Enjoying The Ride

After a few months' rest, The Dead were back on the road in March, with shows on the East Coast and in the Midwest. Venues remained big, and The Dead were up to the challenge of impressing their new audience. A show from 27 March at the Hampton Coliseum in Virginia, was released as Volume 5 of the *Download Series,* and it shows the band in great form: playful and confident, with more jamming returning to the set, and new material appearing. There might've been no *In The Dark* material in the set that night, but there was no shortage of winning performances. From its 'Iko Iko opening', the first set was in a party mood, and a rare performance of Dylan's 'Ballad Of A Thin Man' was an appropriate gift to bring to the event. A 'Let It Grow' that stretched to over eleven and a half minutes, showed a band unafraid to let their improvisational skills blossom, and for the audience to reap the rewards. The second set got off to an even stranger start, with a short 'Space' improvisation that led into their only performance of the Miles Davis classic 'So What'. Their version of the tune may have been under a minute long – perhaps a record for being The Dead's shortest ever live improvisation – but it showed that even in the normally characterless environment of a sports arena, they remained in high spirits. They were no strangers to the venue, and their shows at the venue next year would be particularly memorable. The second set on 27 March 1988 was a great one in its own right, touching on some of their live classics like 'Sugar Magnolia', 'Fire On The Mountain' and 'Estimated Prophet', the 'Space' section taking the audience into an upbeat 'Going Down The Road Feeling Bad' and 'I Need A Miracle', before a peak of 'Dear Mr. Fantasy'. They were playing to their strengths and performing a set that would've impressed anyone in the audience, whether they'd only heard *In The Dark* or had been following their progress for decades.

Two other shows in this run of concerts feature in *Road Trips Volume 4 Number 2*: 31 March and 1 April at the Meadowlands Arena, Rutherford, New Jersey. The three-disc set released in 2011 includes the complete 1 April gig and the complete second set from the previous night, along with the encore and two songs from the first set, over three discs. Opening with 'Mississippi Half-Step Uptown Toodeloo', disc one bounces into the room with a wide April Fool's grin, but they're only a couple of numbers into the set when Garcia pulls out a perfect 'To Lay Me Down' from 'Jack Straw''s cowboy hat. Throughout the show, his solos are on point and the band absolutely shine. The first set's version of 'Ballad Of A Thin Man' also appears on the 2002 *Postcards Of The Hanging* album of The Dead performing Dylan songs. The show features some of their recent material – 'When Push Comes To Shove' in the first set, and 'Throwing Stones' in the second set – sitting comfortably alongside classic material. The collection is a lesson that if in the 1980s the quality of The Grateful Dead's performances could be mixed, they were as capable as ever of producing absolute gems.

The 1988 show that features on *30 Trips Around the Sun,* comes from 3 July at Oxford Plains Speedway, Oxford, Maine. With the first set opening with 'Hell

In A Bucket', and the second with 'Touch Of Grey', *In The Dark* material lights the fuse twice, but the audience are quickly taken into a run-through of gems of The Dead's back catalogue, including 'Bird Song', 'Estimated Prophet' and 'Eyes Of The World'. The new Mydland/Barlow song 'I Will Take You Home' makes its earliest appearance, having been introduced in June 1988. It went on to feature on The Dead's next studio album. The show comes back to earth with 'Dear Mr. Fantasy' and a cover of The Beatles' 'Hey Jude'. Perhaps their inclusion of 1960s covers at this stage in their career was an acknowledgement, for many of their audience, these songs came before their time, and that The Dead – now representatives of that time – wanted to celebrate them. For all their association with the 1960s, The Dead were never a nostalgia act, and their artistic peak certainly didn't just fall within that decade. But their survival as a living link with the music of that decade was something they could not ignore; the USA in the Reagan years was very different from in the late-1960s in so many ways, but The Dead had endured in their own strange way. It seemed only right that they should share some of the treasure they'd been a part of, with their new audience.

Another 1960s survivor who was at the early stages of a career renaissance, was Dylan. His *Down In The Groove* album – featuring two songs co-written with Hunter, one of which featured Garcia, Weir and Mydland on backing vocals – was released at the end of May. While the album was met with critical scorn, Dylan was moving into a new phase, but it was still early days. One of the Hunter tracks – 'Silvio' – was well regarded and released as a single. It would go on to feature in Dylan's live shows and appear on his *Greatest Hits Volume 3* album in 1994. While these songs and six concerts documented with a controversial live album were the most visible aspects of The Dead's work with Dylan, the effect they had on his career, was much more significant. From 1988, Dylan began a tour that would run continuously for much of his career, his performances varying nightly as he dipped into his extensive songbook and a wide selection of covers, with changes and revisions to songs occurring seemingly spontaneously. He learned a lot about remaining a vital and continuously evolving performing artist from The Dead.

In September, their live activity saw them play fewer venues but with longer runs of shows at these locations in a bid to ensure the demand for tickets was met. They played nine nights at Madison Square Garden in New York, the final night being a rainforest benefit that saw them perform with a number of guests, including Suzanne Vega and Bruce Hornsby (both of whom would be involved in future Dead releases), Hall & Oates, former Rolling Stones guitarist Mick Taylor, and Jack Casady from Jefferson Airplane. There would be several unique performances of songs, and while the Hall & Oates and Suzanne Vega numbers might be expected, a version of English singer-songwriter Robyn Hitchcock's 'Chinese Bones' remains a left-field choice and a testimony to The Dead's ability to pull a strange rabbit from the hat at the most unexpected moments.

Robert Hunter's album *Liberty* was released in 1988, with Garcia's guitar gracing the recording. The title song went on to have a life of its own, with The Dead performing a new version from 1993, Garcia changing it from Hunter's original setting. A live version by The Dead appears on the *Ready Or Not* 'last' album, while a studio version appears on Phil And Friends' *There And Back Again* album released in 2002. While 'Liberty' found a new lease of life with The Dead, two other songs on the album that were originally intended for the band, didn't fare so well: 'Bone Alley' and 'Black Shamrock' getting no further than appearances on Hunter's album. Elsewhere, the Jerry Garcia Acoustic Band's *Almost Acoustic* album was released to positive reviews, no doubt educating the post-*In The Dark* fans about Garcia and The Dead's deep folk roots.

Meanwhile, Bob Weir had found a new musical collaborator with whom he'd work extensively. Rob Wasserman was a double-bass player who had worked with acts like Van Morrison and Lou Reed; Wasserman's 1983 album *Solo* winning critical acclaim, and its 1988 follow-up *Duets* getting a Grammy nomination. Weir and Wasserman performed together under that name before using the name Scaring The Children. Live performances from 1988 were released in 1998 as the album *Live*, featuring their versions of Dead songs, including 'Victim Or The Crime', 'Looks Like Rain' and 'Throwing Stones', and songs from Weir's solo catalogue, like 'Heaven Help The Fool', 'Shade Of Grey' and 'This Time Forever'. Weir and Wasserman would go on to form RatDog in 1995: one of the most significant post-Grateful-Dead acts.

Work began on a follow-up to *In The Dark* in the autumn after the tour, with a session at the Marin Veterans' Auditorium arranged in an attempt to see if lightning could strike again. With little to show, they reconvened to the Skywalker Ranch recording studio in Marin County: the facility built by George Lucas, creator of the *Star Wars* movies. Again, there would be no consistent work done, and further recording for a studio album was put on hold until the next year. Two recordings from the studio in 1988 emerged on the *So Many Roads (1965-1995)* box set – the Barlow/Mydland song 'Gentlemen Start Your Engines' – performed live only twice by The Dead – and the Garcia/Hunter number 'Believe It Or Not', which would be performed only a handful of times in 1988 and 1990. Studio sessions would resume in 1989, with a more positive outcome.

1989 – Built To Last

The Dead were back playing live in February, opening their tour on what had become home soil at the Henry J. Kaiser Auditorium in Oakland. If there were only a few archive releases from the previous years, 1989 and 1990 would again see an increased amount of material coming to light: a reflection on the overall quality of their performances. Following Garcia's health crisis in 1987, the band were on an upwards trajectory again. While their unexpected commercial peak in 1987 wouldn't continue (they wouldn't trouble the top 10 singles chart again), the band's popularity as a live attraction had continued to grow, and their performances were particularly sharp, the band apparently unfazed by the venue sizes and the youthful audience they were attracting. Garcia was particularly in a productive zone, MIDI technology giving him a new musical palate to play with and an arsenal of new sounds to experiment with. It might not have always been subtle – digitally-generated trumpets, bells or woodwind sounds appearing in the 'Space' section – but at other times, it added a new colour to familiar work.

The earliest show to be released from 1989 came from the 2 and 3 April shows at Pittsburgh Civic Arena, as *Download Series Volume 9.* Over the equivalent of four discs, both shows are featured in full. A number of songs that would feature on the follow-up to *In The Dark,* are now in the sets, including Weir's 'Victim Or The Crime', Mydland's 'Blow Away' and Garcia/ Hunter's 'Built To Last', having been played since 1988, while Barlow's 'We Can Run' makes its earliest appearance on a release, in the first set of the first night. It's an ecologically-themed number, inspired possibly by the band's involvement with the rainforest benefit show in New York the previous year. Elsewhere in the collection, a sequence including 'The Wheel', 'Dear Mr. Fantasy' and 'Hey Jude', puts the vintage Garcia solo number alongside two of its contemporaries, and the second night's second set with 'Estimated Prophet' and' Crazy Fingers', brings a welcome reggae flavour to proceedings. Had The Dead released a cosmic reggae album in the mid-1970s, it could've been quite an item.

Sessions for a new album resumed in the spring, this time at Club Front with Garcia and John Cutler producing. Instead of the band performing together as they had with *In The Dark,* the album was created by individual members recording their parts on their own, a completed recording eventually being assembled from the various takes. It was a process far removed from the more organic and familiar setting employed to create *In The Dark,* but given they'd already attempted to use the same production method without success the previous year, this method gave them the opportunity to clear whatever had been blocking their creativity.

In February, the *Dylan And The Dead* album was released, with seven songs taken from the summer tour in 1987. Critics were far from convinced by the release, though Bob Dylan live albums have always been something of an acquired taste. I was one of those who scampered out excitedly to buy an import copy when it came out; listened to it a few times and quietly shuffled it to the back of the record collection, despite being a fan of both acts. Although produced by Garcia and John Cutler and with cover art by Dead associate Rick Griffen, it was seen as very much a Dylan release, with no Dead originals among the songs. Dylan's performance throughout was difficult – The Dead doing their best to accommodate his unfocussed and tangential playing – the end result feeling like a jigsaw puzzle where one piece doesn't fit.

The Dead took to the stadium circuit again that summer, in what was becoming something of a regular annual occurrence for them. Again, the number of releases from this period tells something about the quality of their performances. Their 4 July show at Rich Stadium in Orchard Park, New York – close to the city of Buffalo – was released in 2005 as *Truckin' Up To Buffalo*, in both DVD and audio formats. The show was again a concentrated late-1980s-vintage performance, the jamming and improvisation perhaps less free than in earlier years, but still as potent when unleashed. The newer material takes a back seat, with only 'Touch Of Grey' and 'I Will Take You Home' reflecting their recent work. But the rest of the material is well chosen. From the 'Bertha' opening to the closing 'Deal' in the first set, it's a powerful showcase, with both Garcia and Weir giving strong accounts of 'Row Jimmy' and 'Looks Like Rain' for more reflective moments. While 'Touch Of Grey' and 'Man Smart, Woman Smarter' at the start of the second set gives a party mood, there's room for Garcia to launch a 'Ship Of Fools' that hits the spot that only Garcia can. The cover of Dylan's 'All Along The Watchtower' played that night was included in The Dead's album of Dylan covers *Postcards Of The Hanging*, while the version of 'Man Smart, Woman Smarter' appears on the 2004 compilation of Weir's best moments *Weir Here*. Ironically perhaps, the song 'Truckin'' didn't actually feature in their set at all that night in Buffalo.

The band's next concert was three days later on 7 July at the John F. Kennedy Stadium in Philadelphia: emerging in 2010 as a three-CD and DVD set titled *Crimson, White and Indigo*. Doing what The Dead do best, they present a completely different set of songs from the previous night but lay on a performance that's equally strong. 'Hell In A Bucket' and 'Iko Iko' open the show to establish the hedonistic mood; 'Ramble On Rose'. 'Let It Grow' and 'Blow Away' keeping the spirit running. Only Garcia's 'Loser' gives a soulful pause. You can't help but notice the lack of Weir cowboy songs in the opening set. These once seemed to be almost fixed parts of the show, but they've been replaced by more dynamic material and greater flexibility in the running order. Weir still gets the spotlight with 'Little Red Rooster' at this show – 'Walkin' Blues' at the last – and these sharp blues covers have become a welcome addition to the repertoire. The second set opens with a surprise 'Box Of Rain' and a fresh 'Standing On The Moon', before the 'Drums' section shows why it will go on to be one of the new albums most enduring pieces. Disc three shows both Weir and Garcia as equal masters of their craft, with 'The Other One' and 'Wharf Rat' making it clear The Dead can excel in musical avenues that are driving and explorative or soulful and reflective, without a crunching gear change. 'Knockin' On Heaven's Door' brings things to a close: the second Dylan song of the show after 'Stuck Inside Of Mobile With The Memphis Blues Again' in the opening set.

Two nights at Giants Stadium in New Jersey on 9/10 July were their next stop, these shows appearing as the 1989 discs in the *Giants Stadium 1987, 1989, 1991* box set. Unlike the 1987 show in the collection, each of the two 1989 shows has the opportunity to spread over three discs. There's a solid argument that the six discs capturing these two shows are the centrepiece of this box set. The Dead are on fire here, and if there's ever a need to prove just how good The Dead could be in their later years, shows like these would be evidence that wins the case. They were a band who could drop 'I Know You Rider' and 'Don't Ease Me In' – songs they'd been performing since the mid-1960s – into a set alongside new work like 'Built To Last' and 'Foolish Heart', without either sounding out of place; they could cover Dylan with authority and they could own old-school first-generation rock 'n'roll numbers like 'Not Fade Away' with ease. With every show different and every solo loaded with the possibilities of improvisation, they walked a tightrope every night – their high-wire act unafraid to take risks, and instilled with the instinctive confidence that every step would be the right one and every player would be equally focussed on the gravity-defying performance.

It is, of course, possible to criticise the late-1980s/early-1990s Dead. Their sound wasn't to everyone's liking. Some would find them too clinical and polished compared to their early-1970s rough charm and joyous leaps of faith in performance. Others would look back to Pigpen and question any right they had to play the blues without him. Others would struggle with the changes in their sound brought about by technology, whether the booming echo and electronics added to the drums or the MIDI guitar that could sound more like a musical novelty than the golden tones of earlier times. But The Dead were always going to take chances and move forward, and while not every experiment was going to succeed, they would never shy away from letting their spirit of curiosity and playfulness manifest itself. At this point, they'd been playing together for 25 years and were still covering new ground every night with a renewed vigour. To this day, fans debate when The Dead were at their peak. There are many contenders for the honour, and in spite of everything, 1989 and 1990 deserve to be on that list.

Following the two nights at Giants Stadium, The Dead moved on to the RFK Stadium in Washington, D.C. for the nights of 12 and 13 July. These, too, were subsequently released, in 2017 as the six-CD set *Robert F. Kennedy Stadium, Washington, D.C., July 12 & 13, 1989*. Opening the first night with 'Touch Of Grey', the first set included songs featuring all four singers – Garcia, Weir, Mydland and Lesh – who took to the mic for a cover of Dylan's 'Just Like Tom Thumb's Blues'. The second night opened with a different *In The Dark* favourite – 'Hell In A Bucket' – and like the first night, The Dead went on to deliver a focussed and powerful show. The two gigs featured an interesting guest, with Bruce Hornsby sitting in. On the first night, he played accordion on 'Sugaree' – a song normally at home in the first set, for once opening the second set – and accordion and keyboards on the following song 'Man Smart, Woman Smarter'. The next night, he guested in the first set with accordion and vocals on 'Tennessee Jed', and accordion on 'Stuck Inside Of Mobile With The Memphis Blues Again'. Hornsby was a significant star at the time – the debut single 'The Way It Is' by Bruce Hornsby And The Range reaching number 1 in the USA, and the album by the same name becoming a multiplatinum seller. His career had begun while he was a student, in a band with his brother, playing covers of songs by the likes of The Allman Brothers Band and The Dead. Hornsby had appeared on stage with The Dead before, and while many musicians have guested with them, his relationship with them must've been particularly simpatico, because, in just over a year, he would be on stage with them at Madison Square Garden, effectively as a member of the band.

A show from 17 July at the Alpine Valley Music Theatre, East Troy, Wisconsin – one of The Dead's favourite regular outdoor venues – was released on video and DVD in 1997. Titled *Downhill From Here* – perhaps an acknowledgement that this was the band's last peak period or a reference to the venue's steep slope leading to the stage – it features most of the first night of a three-night engagement, along with three songs from July 19. It continues their precise and polished performances from earlier in the tour – some newer material like 'West L.A. Fadeaway' and the then-unreleased 'Built To Last' gracing the first set; 'Standing On The Moon' appearing in the second. There's no shortage of classic Dead in the set, though, with 'Playing In The Band', 'Uncle John's Band' and 'The Wheel' getting an outing in the second set, which closes with a sequence of 'Going Down The Road Feeling Bad', 'Not Fade Away' and a revival of 'And We Bid You Goodnight'. Four of the songs at the end of the 17 July show's first set, don't appear on the release, instead replaced by the final three first-set numbers from the 19 July show. One of the 17 July songs that doesn't appear on the DVD – 'The Music Never Stopped' – appears on the albums *Weir Here* and *Fallout From The Phil Zone*. A version of 'Box Of Rain' from 19 July also appears on this album, while 'Foolish Heart' from 19 July appears as a bonus track on the reissued *Built To Last*.

If triumph was in the air, trouble wasn't far behind. Despite their efforts, crowd trouble and gatecrashing were still an issue – fans becoming collateral damage, between rowdy elements intent on partying without regard for the consequences, and heavy-handed local law enforcement. The Dead had attempted to reduce tensions, by taking steps like playing longer runs at fewer venues, to meet the demand for tickets and to reduce the impact of travelling fans on local communities. The summer venues were made more hospitable environments, with lights and banners intended to take some of the tension out of the atmosphere. It was only a partial success, and while the shows were an artistic achievement, The Dead found themselves unwelcome from playing again at some of their favourite venues.

They took another measure to address the problem, with two *guerrilla gigs* at the Hampton Coliseum, Hampton, Virginia, on 8 and 9 October. The shows were not included in their East Coast tour advance ticket sales, to discourage travelling fans from descending on the venue, and tickets were sold locally from only ten days before the shows, the band being named as 'Formerly The Warlocks'. The Dead travelled with the Le Mobile recording truck during their autumn tour, with the idea that they could collect the material for a live album for release in 1990 – the two Hampton shows released in 2010 as a six-CD box set. While the special measures in place to ensure a positive environment had challenged the audience, their patience and understanding was rewarded by two extraordinary shows. With the release of *Built To Last* just a few weeks away, and the band already delivering a series of memorable shows over the summer, they'd been dusting down some special material for the occasion.

The first night's first set opened with 'Foolish Heart' – the set including a lengthy 'Bird Song' and a cowboy double bill of 'Me And My Uncle' and 'Big River': all very well-played and exciting in their own right. But the second set opener of 'Help On The Way', 'Slipknot!' and 'Franklin's Tower' was the revival that no one anticipated. These favourites had been posted as missing for far too long and were welcomed back with roars of approval. The second night saw things go even further – the second set opening with a sequence of 'Playing In The Band' into 'Uncle John's Band', a brief reprise of 'Playing In The Band', before an unexpected turn straight into the twilight zone with the return of 'Dark Star'. This wasn't the end of the roller coaster ride, as the set moved on to include 'Death Don't Have No Mercy' and a final encore of 'Attics Of My Life': a song they hadn't performed since 1972. The song selection over the two nights was exceptional, but this alone would've meant little had their playing not matched their adventurous choices. But their playing was inspired throughout the shows – Garcia in fine voice, time and time again delivering fluid solos; Weir an effective co-frontman who was capable of bringing his own style and songs that were both distinct from Garcia's contribution but still in keeping with The Dead's overall style; Mydland rising to a new level of creativity in his songwriting, vocals and playing. Some fans may have jokingly still referred to him as 'the new guy', but he'd gradually become an integral part of the band. It was no accident that *Built To Last* – released at the end of October – featured Mydland's name as co-writer on four of the nine songs, his voice front-and-centre for each of these.

If 1989 was an unexpected renaissance after the torpor of the early-to-mid-1980s, the two Formerly The Warlocks shows at Hampton in October 1989 probably marked the peak of their late-career golden age. There would be great shows over the coming years (particularly in 1990), but for consistency and class, the Hampton shows are hard to match.

A show from later in October became 1989's contribution to the *30 Trips Around The Sun* box set, the focus falling on 26 October at the Miami Arena in Florida. The show kicks off in fresh style with 'Foolish Heart' – the first set on disc one of the three-disc set an effective menu serving up the range of the band's back catalogue, including blues ('Little Red Rooster'), country and western ('Me And My Uncle'/'Big River'), folk ('Don't Ease Me In'), and another brand new number: 'Victim Or The Crime'. The second set over the remaining two discs, reveals that the Hampton shows were no flash in the pan – the first disc entrée getting underway with 'Estimated Prophet', a crisp 'Blow Away', before a meaty 'Dark Star' hits the palate, clocking in at just under 30 minutes, then moving into 'Drums'; the final disc progressing into 'Space', 'The Wheel', 'All Along The Watchtower' and 'Stella Blue'. All the key nutritional ingredients are served in the correct proportions with just the right amount of seasoning, the encore of 'And We Bid You Goodnight' leaving a sublime aftertaste.

At the end of the month, *Built To Last* was released: the nine songs on the CD (eight on the vinyl LP) all road-tested since at least earlier that year. Among them there were some *bona fide* classics – 'Foolish Heart' and the title track both feel-good Garcia/Hunter numbers, while Mydland's 'Just A Little Light' and 'Blow Away' are rock numbers that would've easily been standout tracks on many of their lesser studio albums. 'Picasso Moon' is another of Weir's songs that should on paper be overly complex and wordy, but it rocks impressively in its offbeat way. But if there's an ace in the pack, it has to be 'Standing On The Moon' – a Garcia/Hunter ballad that lightly touches on love, geopolitics and humanity, name-checking California, the USA and San Francisco, and dwelling on nostalgia, regret and longing. Matters of the heart take precedence over all glory, achievement and victory, and the narrator – who has reached this peak human achievement – wishes he wasn't isolated and watching endless futile conflicts unfold from a distance when he should be home with the person he's addressing.

A video was made for the album's single 'Foolish Heart', and while it gathered some airplay and MTV attention, it never caught the public imagination the same way 'Touch Of Grey' did. It's a charming-enough video, beginning with a skeleton putting a disc onto an old gramophone, with sepia archive film interspersed with footage of the band performing in a vintage puppet theatre – with some additional speakers – the live footage treated to look similarly vintage. There's some stop-motion animation of regular Dead motifs of cards, roses and hearts, and when they appear in colour, The Dead look particularly polished – Weir in a tux and bow tie, and Garcia with blow-dried hair and a red rose in his lapel. Kreutzmann is notable in his absence for most of the video. A more straightforward 1980s-style studio performance video was made for 'Just A Little Light', Mydland getting most of the camera time amid moody lighting and lots of candles.

Built To Last reach the top-30 in *Billboard:* by any measure, a successful outcome for a band of The Dead's vintage in the face of a very different decade to the one they first came to prominence in. But the album didn't come close to matching the success of *In The Dark*: sales were not as good and reviews were not as positive. The return of The Dead was no longer big news either; unlike *In The Dark, Built To Last* didn't have a 'successful comeback' story to attach to it and, in fact, with *Dylan And The Dead,* they'd already released an album earlier that year to a mostly negative response. *Built To Last* itself, while polished and with material that was good enough, also lacked some of the vitality that had made *In The Dark* a pleasure to listen to. With the band members recording their parts separately in the studio, assembling the final recording from the various takes, it's no surprise that the easy spontaneity and interplay that made their live shows special events, is missing from the final release.

An expanded version of the album released as part of the *Beyond Description (1973-1989)* box set, included a live version of 'Foolish Heart' from the 19 July 1989 Alpine Valley show, 'Blow Away' from the John F. Kennedy Stadium in Philadelphia on 7 July, and a version of 'California Earthquake (Whole Lotta Shakin' Goin' On)' from The Spectrum in Philadelphia on 20 October. The live versions of the studio tracks on the album show some of what *Built To Last* was lacking – it was ironic that the band released a studio album that failed to capture their spirit at a time when their live performances were particularly outstanding. While by no means a bad album, given some of their previous releases, perhaps the biggest disappointment associated with *Built To Last* is that it was, in fact, their last studio album.

1990 – Without A Net

The roll that The Dead were on would continue into 1990. However, cracks were beginning to show. In December, Mydland was admitted to hospital after suffering an overdose, although he was well enough to play at the four end-of-the-year shows at the Oakland Coliseum. But it drew attention to a deeper issue he was struggling with. While his playing was on fire, he was wracked by a difficult family life, and plagued with self-doubt over his place in the band: his increased involvement in the last album and its subsequent lukewarm reception, taken personally. Garcia's heroin habit was re-emerging, and though it was not as serious as it had been in previous years, it was a particular cause for concern. Shows resumed at Oakland Arena at the end of February, and if *Built To Last* hadn't won over the critics or the wider public, it had little effect on the quality of The Dead's performances or the size of the audience they were attracting.

Their plans to follow up *Built To Last* with a live album, were already underway, with recordings from 1989 already in the can. These would be added to recordings from the spring-1990 run, to create the album *Without A Net*. They knew that their popularity stemmed from their live shows – and that this was where their artistry flourished – so it seemed an obvious move. The thinking behind *Without A Net,* was to release a collection that was closer in form to an actual Dead show, with a first and second set over two CDs. *Without A Net* was their first release to take advantage of the longer running time offered by CD, the two-disc format fitting the length of their regular live performances at the time. Instead of presenting a single show, producers John Cutler and Phil Lesh decided to create an idealised show – though without the 'Drums' and 'Space' section – using a collection of seventeen songs recorded at different shows from late-1989 and spring 1990. It's a sharp selection, a clear highlight being the version of 'Eyes Of The World' from Nassau Coliseum on 29 March that has a guest appearance from jazz saxophonist Branford Marsalis. It's arguably their greatest performance of one of the key songs in their repertoire. Elsewhere, the recently returned 'Help On The Way'>'Slipknot!'>'Franklin's Tower' sounds remarkably fresh and revitalised.

While *Without A Net* took a flavour of the shows played on the autumn 1989 and spring 1990 tours, later releases emerged, including every date of the spring 1990 tour. Their gig from 15 March came out in 1997 as *Terrapin Station (Limited Edition)* – a triple-CD released to raise funds for a proposed San Francisco venue/museum/music-centre to celebrate The Dead's legacy: which was in development at the time, althoug the idea eventually stalled. Two tracks from this release featured on *Without A Net*. The show – played on Lesh's 50th birthday – features a cover of the Beatles song 'Revolution' as an encore: one of Lesh's favourite songs. The show from the following night at the Capital Centre, Landover, Maryland, and shows from 19, 22, 26, 30 March and 2 April are covered in the 18-disc 2012 box set *Spring 1990*. The collection is an absolute showcase of The Dead at their spring-1990 peak – a wide selection of songs from recent albums *In The Dark* and *Built To Last*, like 'Touch Of Grey', 'Hell In A Bucket', 'Picasso Moon' and 'We Can Run'; back-catalogue classics like 'Truckin'', 'Stella Blue', 'I Know You Rider' and 'Attics Of My Life', and well-considered covers like 'Dear Mr. Fantasy', 'Hey Jude' and 'The Last Time' carrying something of the 1960s to the audience: many of whom were not even born when these songs first came out. Bonus tracks across the set come from the 24 March show at the Knickerbocker Arena, Albany, New York, which, combined with tracks released elsewhere (on 1996's *Dozin' At The Nick*, *Without A Net* and 2002's *Postcards Of The Hanging*), complete the material from that show.

The two-CD collection *Spring 1990: So Glad You Made It*, collects 20 songs from the box set, giving a flavour of the magic that the band were conjuring on a nightly basis on the tour. It's a worthwhile collection to introduce The Dead to a listener unfamiliar with their output, and it serves as an appetizer that inevitably leads to consumption of more of the spring-1990 delicacies.

Dozin' At The Knick covers the three nights they played at the Knickerbocker Arena on 24, 25 and 26 March. The three-disc set sits like a companion piece to *Without A Net*, in that it's arranged to give the impression of being a complete show, albeit one that this time includes the 'Drums' and 'Space' sections. The collection covers both recent material like 'Hell In A Bucket' and 'Blow Away', and gems like 'And We Bid You Goodnight' and 'Black Peter', although, 'And We Bid You Goodnight' seems slightly in the wrong place appearing halfway through the third disc. However, having a third disc allows the collection a bit more room to breathe than *Without A Net* had, meaning there's room for a 'Playing In The Band', 'Uncle John's Band', and 'Terrapin Station' complete with its 'Lady With A Fan' introductory passage. Mydland's deserved place at the centre of the band's new-found brio can be seen clearly in his four songs, and his contribution throughout. His playing in the spring-1990 shows was one of the factors that pushed The Dead that bit further. On a nightly basis, he not only excelled in performing his own material, but he matched Garcia with his creativity, fire, imaginative solos and band interplay. While on the surface, he'd dealt with the issues that troubled him at the end of the previous year, he was more likely channelling them into his music.

Dozin' At The Knick features much of the 24 March show, and with 26 March in full on the *Spring 1990* box set, the 25 March show would appear on the second box set chronicling 1990, titled *Spring 1990 (The Other One)*. This collection – released in 2014 – covers eight shows over 23 discs: the dates fitting alongside the gigs released in the *Spring 1990* box. This box features the shows from 14, 18, 21, 25, 28, 29 March, and 1 and 3 April. If there's suspicion that this is a roundup of second-rate shows from the tour, a listen quickly puts that fear to rest. Although, given the running time of the material on offer, a quick listen easily extends into a matter of days. From the opening 'Cold Rain And Snow' from 14 March at the Capital Centre, Landover, Maryland, to 'And We Bid You Goodnight' from 3 April at the Omnia, Atlanta, Georgia, the band

Above: Psychedelic cowboys: The Grateful Dead, 1970. (L-R): Bill Kreutzmann, Ron 'Pigpen' McKernan, Bob Weir, Mickey Hart, Phil Lesh (Front): Jerry Garcia. *(Public domain)*

Right: Altamont: The Dead were involved in organising the festival and were scheduled to play but pulled out on the day. *(Unknown, CC BY-SA 2.0)*

Below: Wall Of Sound: The Grateful Dead's pioneering PA system brought quality sound to arena-sized venues in 1974. *(Mary Ann Mayer, CC BY-SA 4.0)*

Left: The self-titled debut album from *1967. (Warner Bros. Records)*)

Below: *Anthem Of The Sun*. A studio album interwoven with live material. *(Warner Bros. Records)*

Above: *Aoxomoxoa*: Experiments in the studio with 16-track *recording*. *(Warner Bros. Records)*

Right: *Live/Dead*. A groundbreaking live recording captured The Dead's unique live sound. *(Warner Bros. Records)*

Right: *Workingman's Dead*. Regarded as one of their most successful, with a country-based approach and a polished sound. *(Warner Bros. Records)*

Below: *American Beauty*. This collection continued The Dead's success in the studio in 1970. *(Warner Bros. Records)*

Above: *The Grateful Dead* aka *Skull And Roses*. This live album introduced several key new songs. *(Warner Bros. Records)*

Left: *Europe '72*. This ambitious triple live album showcased the Dead's improvisation skills. *(Warner Bros. Records)*

Left: Bob Weir performs
with Kingfish in 1975
(David Gans, CC BY 2.0)

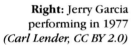

Right: Jerry Garcia
performing in 1977
(Carl Lender, CC BY 2.0)

Left: Jerry Garcia and
Mickey Hart at Red Rocks
Amphitheatre, Colorado,
1987. *(Mark L Knowles,
CC BY-SA 3.0)*

Right: Jerry Garcia playing his iconic 'Wolf' guitar. *(Carl Lender, CC BY 2.0)*

Left: The Grateful Dead backed Bob Dylan at six stadium shows in 1987. The subsequent live album had a mixed response.

Right: Bob Weir at the mic as The Grateful Dead play at the Zenith in Paris during the Europe '90 tour. *(John Kilbride)*

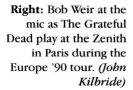

Left: *Bear's Choice*. A live collection looked back at Pigpen following his death in 1973. *(Warner Bros. Records)*

Below: *Wake Of The Flood*. The first studio release featuring the band's new lineup. *(Grateful Dead Records)*

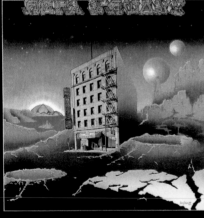

Above: *From The Mars Hotel:* The second release on The Dead's own record label. *(Grateful Dead Records)*

Right: *Blues For Allah*. Recorded while the band took time off from touring in 1975. *(Grateful Dead Records)*

Right: *Steal Your Face.* The disappointing live album from their 1974 'farewell' shows. *(Grateful Dead Records)*

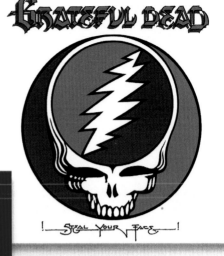

Below: *Terrapin Station.* A new start on a new label featured strong material but had production issues. *(Arista Records)*

Above: *Shakedown Street.* Some songs would become favourites, but this was another patchy collection. *(Arista Records)*

Left: *Go To Heaven.* The first album with Brent Mydland and better than the cover suggested. *(Arista Records)*

Left: Bob Weir, guitarist and vocalist with The Dead, in 1993. Weir brought his love of country music to the band.

Right: Phil Lesh, bass player and occasional vocalist, pictured in 1993. Lesh was a music scholar before he joined The Dead.

Left: Vince Welnick, The Dead's keyboard player from 1990 - 1995, following the death of Brent Mydland.

Right: Mickey Hart, one of The Dead's two 'Rhythm Devils' drummers, who introduced world music textures to the band.

Left: Jerry Garcia, The Dead's iconic frontman, with drummer Billy Kreutzmann, who played with The Dead throughout their career.

Right: Keyboard player Bruce Hornsby stepped in as a temporary member in 1990 and performed over 100 shows with The Dead.

GRATEFUL DEAD

R E C K O N I N G

Left: *Reckoning.* A live album of acoustic performances informed by the band's interest in folk music. *(Arista Records)*

Below: *Dead Set.* An electric collection that didn't quite capture the appeal of The Dead's live performances in the 1980s. *(Arista Records)*

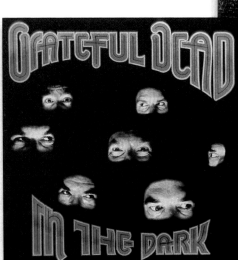

Above: *In The Dark.* This studio album delivered a hit single, mainstream commercial success and a whole new audience. *(Arista Records)*

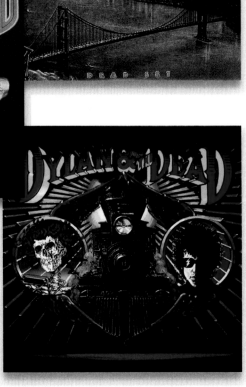

Right: *Dylan And The Dead.* The Dead backed Bob Dylan, but the live album failed to show either at their best. *(Columbia Records)*

Right: *Built To Last*. The final studio album featured strong songs but lacked the spirit of past triumphs. *(Arista Records)*

Below: *Without A Net*. Strong later-period live performances edited together to present an 'ideal show.' *(Arista Records)*

Above: *Infrared Roses*. An experimental work that focuses on the 'Drums' and 'Space' improvised performances from their live shows. *(Grateful Dead Records)*

Left: *Greyfolded*. An intriguing sound collage created from 100 versions of 'Dark Star' from 1968 – 1993. *(Plumderphonics)*

Left: The Fillmore West, formerly The Carousel, The Dead's 'home' venue in San Francisco. *(Davygrvy, CC BY-SA 3.0)*

Right: Radio City Music Hall. Landmark New York venue where tracks for Reckoning and Dead Set were recorded. *(Ajay Suresh, CC BY 2.0)*

Left: Haight-Ashbury. The San Francisco neighbourhood was at the centre of the counterculture of the 1960s. *(Daniel Schwen, CC BY-SA 2.5)*

Right: *One From The Vault.* The Dead's
first vault release presented a show
from 1975. *(Grateful Dead Records)*

Below: *Ladies And Gentlemen...*
The Grateful Dead. Peak-era 1971
performances at the Fillmore East, New
York. *(Grateful Dead Records)*

The Grateful Dead

cordially invite you
to a
rare and important musical performance
at
The Great American Music Hall
859 O'Farrell Street
Date: August 13, 1975   Time: 9:00 p.m.

This invitation admits one

Grateful Dead • Birth Of The Dead

Above: *Birth Of The Dead.* A
compilation of early recordings, rarities
and live performances. *(Rhino Records)*

Left: *The Closing Of Winterland.* A
New Year's Eve celebration marked the
San Francisco venue closing its doors.
(Rhino Records)

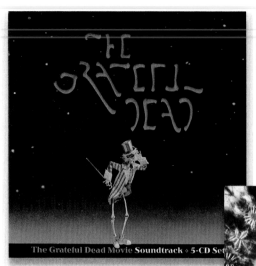

The Grateful Dead Movie Soundtrack ❖ 5-CD Set

Left: *The Grateful Dead Movie Soundtrack.* The Dead's 'farewell' gigs from 1974 finally get the audio release they deserved. *(Grateful Dead Records)*

Below: *Sunshine Daydream.* One of The Dead's greatest shows gets released on CD and DVD over 40 years after it was recorded. *(Rhino Records)*

Above: *Wake Up To Find Out.* This live album captures an intense 1990 show with Branford Marsalis guesting on saxophone. *(Rhino Records)*

Right: *Cornell 5/8/77.* The archive release of what many consider The Dead's greatest performance. *(Rhino Records)*

Right: *Dick's Picks Volume Four.* The Dead's 1970 shows at the Fillmore East were powerful performances. *(Grateful Dead Records)*

Below: *Dick's Picks Volume Eight:* Acoustic and electric sets showcase the range of The Dead's ability. *(Grateful Dead Records)*

Above: *Road Trips Vol 1 No 4:* The Dead deliver quality performances that circumstances in Egypt made difficult. *(Grateful Dead Records)*

Left: *Dave's Picks Vol 14.* Highlights of The Dead's New York shows ahead of the Europe '72 tour. *(Rhino Records)*

Left: *Ready Or Not.* Live recordings of songs that would have featured on a final studio release. *(Rhino Records)*

Right: Bob Weir in 2020 – solo artist and a key member of Dead & Co. *(Thekingdekalb, CC BY-SA 4.0)*

Left: Bob Weir plays in Amsterdam with Ratdog in 2002. *(John Kilbride)*

are firing on all cylinders, and it's evident that the high-water mark shows on the previous *Spring 1990* box set were not exceptions, this box showing that the overall standard was consistently high throughout the run. There are many moments included here that capture the special magic that they conjured – perhaps a gem from earlier in their career, like 'Crazy Fingers', 'To Lay Me Down', 'Dark Star' or 'Loose Lucy' brought out again to an audience who may have never heard them live before; maybe a Dylan classic like 'All Along The Watchtower', 'Knockin' On Heaven's Door' or 'Quinn The Eskimo' (performed with a mix of respect and reinvention only possible because Dylan was practically a member of the band), or one of their covers, whether a blues number like 'Spoonful' or 'Little Red Rooster', or a 1960s flashback like 'Morning Dew', 'Revolution' or 'The Weight'. There's a vast amount on offer here, and like the previous *Spring 1990* box, it's a culmination of what The Dead were doing in the previous decade, brought into focus, polished, and played with panache.

The 29 March show at the Nassau Coliseum in Uniondale, New York, also got a well-deserved stand-alone release under the title *Wake Up To Find Out* simultaneous to the release of *Spring 1990 (The Other One)*. While 'Bird Song' from the first set, and second set opener 'Eyes Of The World' had both been released before – on the *So Many Roads (1965-1995)* box set and *Without A Net* respectively – the entire show is extraordinary. Invited by Lesh, Branford Marsalis sat in on saxophone with the band for 'Bird Song' in the first set, and was invited to join them for the entire second set, resulting in some extraordinary playing. Marsalis not only added bold new textures, his playing coaxed the rest of the band into new dimensions. Marsalis was an experienced master jazz player who was up for a challenge and capable of not only fitting in with what the band were doing, but was able to interact with them in a way that few outside their immediate circle were able to. Not only was the playing during this show elevated beyond what they'd been playing on tour so far (and what they'd been playing recently was among their absolute best), the song choice was beyond compare. From 'Eyes Of The World', the second set moved into 'Estimated Prophet' and a rare performance of 'Dark Star'. There's just under 20 minutes of one of The Dead's finest free explorations, before a 'Drums' interlude; disc three covering the subsequent 'Space' improvisation, before a reprise of 'Dark Star'. 'The Wheel', 'Throwing Stones' and 'Love Light' bring the show back to earth before a 'Knockin' On Heaven's Door' encore. It's hard to imagine a better framework for an artist like Marsalis to contribute his work. While unquestionably a peak late-period Dead show, I suspect that in years to come, this show will be looked upon as one of their all-time best.

The Dead were back on the road again almost immediately after the spring tour – the 2002 DVD and three-CD release *View From The Vault, Volume Three* recording their 16 June show at the Shoreline Amphitheatre, Mountain View, California. Opening with 'Let The Good Times Roll' was an appropriate choice, setting the tone for the second night of a three-show run in their local Bay

Area neighbourhood. While The Dead released a number of commercial videos in their active years, they were always more reticent about video, and while taping and trading were encouraged, video was not. Fortunately, they captured a number of shows themselves professionally, as they were filmed when providing live images for the giant video screens at the shows.

The 22,000-plus-capacity Shoreline Amphitheatre venue is a particularly auspicious one for the band, as it was built in collaboration with longtime Dead associate and music promoter Bill Graham. Graham knew The Dead would be the ideal act for the outdoor lakeside venue, and helped design it, ensuring that it resembled – from the air at least – The Dead's iconic *Steal Your Face* logo. A quick check on Google Maps using satellite view does indeed reveal an approximation of what must be one of the largest band logos anywhere on Earth. The Dead had been scheduled to open the venue in 1986, but Garcia's health meant the show was cancelled. They played the venue for the first time in October 1987, and returned there every year until 1995. The three-CD release *View From The Vault, Volume Three* includes six bonus tracks from their 3 October 1987 gig.

A show from 8 July at Three Rivers Stadium in Pittsburgh was released as the first in the *View From The Vault* series in 2000. It, too, is a crisp show, this and *View From The Vault, Volume Three* complimenting the *Spring 1990* releases well. The band here are still very much on form. Perhaps there are fewer surprises in the setlist, but a fiery second set (on disc two) opening with 'Samson & Delilah' moving into 'Eyes Of The World', 'Estimated Prophet' and 'Terrapin Station', is always welcome. Three bonus tracks from 6 July are appended to the third disc, with Garcia in full soulful effect on 'Standing On The Moon', 'He's Gone', and a lengthy jam.

A further two summer shows were released in autumn 2021 as *Dave's Picks Volume 40*, consisting of the 18 and 19 July shows at the Deer Creek Music Centre, Noblesville, Indiana. The four-disc set includes the entire sets from both nights, although without the second-night encore. From the opening 'Help On The Way'>'Slipknot!'>'Franklin's Tower' sequence of the opening night. it's absolutely clear that the magic of the spring tour was still in play. The set includes a crystal sharp 'Peggy-O', and what would be the last performance of Mydland's 'Easy To Love You'. The second set's 'Terrapin Station' followed by 'The Other One' by way of 'Drums' and a set-closing 'Morning Dew', are just about perfect. The band are in high gear throughout, playing with an intricacy that's so fluent, it doesn't appear to be complicated at all. The second night's show plays out over the third and fourth discs, and again The Dead cook up something hot, with more recent songs featuring – including Weir's 'Picasso Moon' in the first set, and 'Victim Or The Crime' opening the second, ahead of 'Foolish Heart'. But there's room for a serving of classics: whether 'Althea' or 'Row Jimmy' in the first set, or 'Playing In The Band' or 'China Doll' in the second. There's a Dylan double-play with a definitive take on 'Desolation Row' in the first set, and a fiery 'All Along The Watchtower' in the second.

But the band's resurgence was not to last. The tour finished on 23 July, and on 26 July, Brent Mydland died in his California home of a drug overdose: the third Grateful Dead keyboard player to die. There's a convincing argument that The Dead never really recovered from the death of Mydland, and that although they continued with considerable success, they never reached the consistent peaks they'd achieved in 1989 and 1990. The band already had dates scheduled for the rest of the year, including their first European tour since 1981, and were keen not to lose the momentum they'd achieved in the last year. With hindsight, taking time out would've perhaps been a wiser decision – recovering rather than rushing into things – but the beast that the band had become needed to be fed and needed to keep moving. A new keyboard player had to be found urgently before September dates in the Midwest and on the East Coast – including six nights at Madison Square Garden – and engagements across Europe in October.

Bruce Hornsby had not only opened for The Dead with his band, and sat in with them onstage, but he'd been a long-time fan. Approached by the band, he suggested instead a temporary position until a full-time replacement for Mydland could be found. Names were discussed – from those already part of the extended Dead family, to others beyond, and a shortlist was eventually drawn up. Vince Welnick – a former member of theatrical art punks The Tubes, going on to play with Todd Rundgren – was the eventual choice: a capable musician who could cope in a wide variety of musical situations, and a singer with the right kind of voice for The Dead. Welnick had to undergo a steep learning process so he was up to speed with a repertoire of over 100 songs. To familiarise him with their work, he was sent a series of live tapes of their 1989 and 1990 shows, and he learnt his parts from those. Fortunately, as well as being a talented musician, he was a fast learner.

The Dead's return to Madison Square Garden features on *Dick's Picks Volume 9,* released in 1997. The three-CD set features the complete 16 September 16 show: the third night of their six-night run at the venue. The dates before the New York run featured Welnick on keyboards alone, but these shows marked the start of Hornsby's long-term involvement with the band. It's a tall order to so abruptly fill the vacated place on stage, and in such difficult circumstances. But Welnick and Hornsby were up to the challenge – Hornsby on piano, bringing a star quality to the proceedings, trading licks with Garcia without stealing any of the band's thunder, while Welnick's place is more than deserved. It's worth remembering that Welnick had almost two separate roles in the band, his contribution being very different when Hornsby was on stage, compared to times when Welnick was the only keyboard player.

From the 'Hell In A Bucket' and 'Cold Rain And Snow' opening, the band are itching to show what they can do, and they deliver a show that – while very different from their recent performances in late 1989, spring and summer – was of a similar, if not better, quality. If their situation following the death of Mydland was difficult, they dug deep into their collective musical resources, and were able to deliver something special. The set had an obvious difference in that there were no Mydland songs performed, but other than that, they could still cover a significant amount of material. Two Dylan songs feature: 'Queen Jane Approximately' in the first set, and 'It's All Over Now, Baby Blue' in the encore. But if there's a highlight here, it's in the second set, where a moody 'Looks Like Rain' moves into 'He's Gone': a song laden with significance under the circumstances. Garcia's tone is majestic; all the sorrow and the warmth are there, the music carrying into a lengthy and celebratory jam that moves into the 'Drums' and 'Space' area, before resolving into 'Standing On The Moon'. It may have been a then-recent Garcia/Hunter composition, but it's every bit as affecting as any of their vintage pieces, and in the context, absolutely perfect. It's hard to imagine a dry eye in the house. But beyond the song choices, the band's playing is fluent and dexterous throughout, the new lineup bringing a freshness to proceedings, with new ideas and different approaches constantly emerging. There's almost an impatience at times to stretch out and do something new, and if there are raw emotions, they're cut through with a simultaneous joy: perhaps a realisation that – despite the setbacks, loss and grief – things can still continue, albeit in a different way, and their friend and bandmate's legacy is worthy of being celebrated.

The September 1990 Madison Square Garden run also provided the source material for *Road Trips Volume 2 Number 1*, with material from 18, 19 and 20 September collected on two discs. A third bonus disc features a selection of tracks from the first and second sets of the 18 September show. There's always an argument that collections like this that don't present full shows, don't do justice to the band's artistry, but releases like *Road Trips Volume 2 Number 1* concentrate the magic of the three shows, in one container. You don't always need to hear another version of 'Loose Lucy', 'Big River' or 'El Paso'. The central two-disc collection opens with the first three numbers of the 20 September show's second set – an upbeat 'Truckin'', 'China Cat Sunflower' and 'I Know You Rider', before moving on to the first half of the 19 September second set. Disc two takes us back to the second half of the second set on 20 September, with an absolute monster of a sequence: a 'Jam' going into 'Dark Star', 'Playing In The Band', a reprise of 'Dark Star' into 'Throwing Stones', 'Touch Of Grey' and 'Love Light'. Juxtaposing some of their recent work with one of their most cherished (and most difficult) pieces, is a bold proposition, and throwing in one of Pigpen's signature numbers just confirms their apparent audacity. Their confidence seems to know no bounds. Their original keyboard player Pigpen may have died long before Mydland, but he is now forever one of The Grateful Dead, as is Mydland.

The September run coincided with the release of the double live CD *Without A Net*, compiling recordings from October 1989 to April 1990. Despite being a contemporary release rather than an archive recording, the death of Mydland meant the album no longer represented the band as it currently was. Despite that, The Dead's popularity as a live act was enough to put the album into the *Billboard* top-50 and for it to sell over 500,000 copies in its first week of release. The album is dedicated to Clifton Hanger: the assumed name Mydland used when he checked into hotels on tour.

Following the Madison Square Garden run, The Dead's next stop was Europe, for their first tour since 1981. With a new album to promote, and with many fans willing to make the trip from the USA to Europe (meaning there was a guaranteed audience to follow the band on a short tour with dates in Sweden, Germany, France and England), it made economic and artistic sense. The European media had only been able to follow the story of The Grateful Dead's apparent return to commercial success from a distance, and the opportunity to see what the fuss was about, was not to be missed. At the opening night in Stockholm, however, jet lag quickly dispelled any hope that they'd simply pick up where their triumphant New York run left off. But they managed to shake this off, and the tour progressed across Germany, with shows in Essen – the scene of their 1981 live *Rockpalast* broadcast – two nights in Berlin, and gigs in Frankfurt and Hamburg.

They played the first of two nights at the Zénith arena in Paris on 27 October, the show released as the 1990 volume in the *30 Trips Around The Sun* collection. While there was a considerable American contingent in the audience, in common with all the dates of the tour named Europe '90 in recognition of *Europe '72*, the shows gave the opportunity for fans in Europe to be part of the live Grateful Dead experience again. Some were veterans of European dates going back to the early-1970s; others had not yet had the opportunity at all to see them live, despite having listened to them and followed their movements from a distance for years.

That was the category I fell into, and the two nights in Paris and three subsequent nights at London's Wembley Arena gave me my first opportunity to finally see The Grateful Dead. There had been rumours for years that they were planning to tour over here – some of these more credible than others: whether live appearances at Stonehenge or Glastonbury, or maybe a stadium tour with Dylan, or maybe with Yes. But inevitably, it was always no. Hawkwind remained unchallenged for the Stonehenge headline slot; Glastonbury had moved on from its underground roots to becoming a corporate-sponsored rite-of-passage for well-heeled young things to establish their boho credentials. But the Europe '90 tour actually happened, and despite everything – including the possibility of the whole tour being cancelled – my girlfriend (now wife) and I found ourselves at the Zénith area in the Parc de la Villette for the shows there. We'd travelled from Scotland via overnight bus to London, and by hovercraft across the channel to get there; my brother picking up tickets for the first night, when he was in the city some months earlier. In those pre-internet days, undertakings like this required organisation and planning. Our budget only stretched to the Paris-and-London leg of the tour, with cheap accommodation and hasty sightseeing during the days, but after listening to

The Dead studiously on live tapes, secondhand vinyl and a handful of CDs for around five years, it was worth the wait. The venue – an arena located in a park developed in the 1980s, housing museums, halls, theatres, canals, sculptures and playparks – might not have been a vintage-and-storied Paris music hall like L'Olympia, but for the 1990-vintage Grateful Dead, it was a perfect location.

The 27 October show was probably the best night of the tour. By London, Garcia's voice was rough, but throughout this show, he hits a sweet soulful spot. From 'Sugaree' in the first set to 'Stella Blue' in the second via 'Bird Song' and 'Crazy Fingers', he's on form vocally and on guitar. Hornsby and Welnick are playing together solidly, complimenting each other in a way similar to Hart and Kreutzmann on the drums. The second Paris show may have had a more adventurous running order with Hornsby's 'Stander On The Mountain' making its debut (It would only be played three times), and Lesh taking to the mic for 'Box Of Rain' complete with a quick introduction in French, but the show – released on *30 Trips Around The Sun* – delivered everything this fan had been waiting and hoping for. I'd see The Dead with Garcia live a few more times (the second night in Paris and the subsequent three nights in London), and while there would be a 'Dark Star' in London and a 'Werewolves Of London' encore for Halloween, the thrill of that first concert was hard to match, and to me at least, a great choice for an archive release.

Every fan who saw them live will have their own special show – whether their first, one that involved a particular performance, or one that's linked to a particular memory. And while the release of archive recordings might not capture an entire event, it at least ensures the music can be experienced again – and even if it's only a small part of the magic, it's a magic that can be so powerful, even the smallest drop of it remains potent.

1990 would be their final European tour. Reconvening in the USA, Garcia came into contact again with his former Old And In The Way bandmate David Grisman: rekindling Garcia's love for acoustic and bluegrass music. In the years following Old And In The Way, Grisman had established himself as one of America's foremost mandolin players: his keynote sound, a melange of bluegrass, folk and jazz that he dubbed Dawg Music. He'd also founded his own label: Acoustic Disc. Thanks to Garcia, The Grateful Dead's Rex Foundation had awarded Grisman a grant for his contribution to music. After arranging to meet up, Garcia came over to Grisman's house and suggested they begin recording new material using Grisman's home studio, to be released on Grisman's label.

It was one of several extracurricular activities that Garcia undertook in 1990, the highest-profile being his appearance on two tracks on Bruce Hornsby And The Range's *A Night On The Town* album: playing guitar on 'Barren Ground' and the single 'Across The River': a song that reached the *Billboard* top-20. Less commercial was his involvement with 'word jazz' performer Ken Nordine, who'd released several jazz/spoken-word crossover albums in the late-1950s and 1960s. Garcia had been a fan of his 'beat' stylings, and while Nordine had made a successful career as a voice-over artist for commercials and cinema, Garcia approached him to host the radio broadcast of The Dead's New Year show at the Oakland Coliseum, Nordine recording an improvised piece with Garcia, Hart and Egyptian musician Hamza El Din. The Branford Marsalis Quartet supported them at the show, Marsalis sitting in with The Dead during their set. If 1990 had seen both high points and lows in The Grateful Dead's career, the year would go out with a measure of the good-natured experimental weirdness that they could do like no one else could.

1991 – Drums 'n' Space

While Garcia and Grisman made their live debut in early February at the
Warfield in San Francisco, The Grateful Dead also returned to live activity
that month, with shows throughout March, April, May and June. Compared
to 1990, there's a notable falling away in the amount of material that's been
made available. The first recordings to emerge from 1991 – two tracks from
the second set of the show on 31 March at Greensboro Coliseum, Greensboro,
North Carolina – appeared as bonus tracks on *Dick's Picks Volume 17*.

A CD released in April – *Deadicated: A Tribute To The Grateful Dead* – gave
a snapshot of some of the artists who acknowledged The Dead as an influence.
The artists cover a wide range of genres, from Dwight Yoakam's country take
on 'Truckin'', to Burning Spear's old-school reggae version of 'Estimated
Prophet', via singer-songwriters, including Suzanne Vega's performances
of 'China Doll' and 'Cassidy', Elvis Costello's version of 'Ship Of Fools' and
Warren Zevon's cover of 'Casey Jones'. Bruce Hornsby And The Range perform
'Jack Straw'. Many of the acts have a loose association with The Dead; Suzanne
Vega sharing a stage with them at their rainforest benefit gig in 1988; Zevon's
'Werewolves Of London' a live favourite performed by The Dead. Elvis Costello
was a long-term fan who'd played on stage with Garcia, and was in the
audience when The Dead played in England in 1972. The collection gives an
idea of the cross-genre and cross-generational appeal that The Dead enjoyed
in the early-1990s; their music a thread that bound seemingly-disparate acts
like New Orleans gris-gris rhythm and blues master Dr, John and early-1990s
alternative rock headliners Jane's Addiction. Some of the versions work better
than others (The Cowboy Junkies version of 'To Lay Me Down' is exceptional),
but The Dead's material is strong enough to endure even the less-successful
covers by Midnight Oil and Jane's Addiction. Proceeds from the album sales
went towards rainforest and indigenous rights organisations.

The first proper archive album from The Dead's vault also emerged in April,
with *One From The Vault* presenting their 1975 show at the Great American
Music Hall. While The Dead had accumulated a collection of recordings of
previous performances, they'd previously been reticent in releasing these,
despite there being an obvious market, as seen by the unofficial *Vintage Dead*
and *Historic Dead* releases, and the *Bear's Choice* album. While archive
releases are now commonplace, in the early-1990s, acts were only beginning
to realise the potential. A couple of factors made archive releases a worthwhile
proposition – there were opportunities with the medium that weren't there
in previous decades, a three-CD set easily accommodating a lengthy show in
a cost-effective way that vinyl couldn't, and a realisation that archive material
wouldn't distract from contemporary releases but could actually work in the
favour of an artist's reputation. Releasing an archive recording that was better
than anything an act was releasing at the time, wouldn't necessarily show up
the thinness of their current material, but instead could act as a reminder of
their greatness. While Bob Dylan's 1990 release *Under The Red Sky* was not a

critical or artistic success, his 1991 *Bootleg Series Volumes 1-3* box reminded critics and audience what the fuss was about in the first place.

The Dead's 1975 show was an obvious choice for the first archive release. The recording and performance were exceptional, while the band and material on the album were unlikely to be confused with the manifestation of The Dead that was currently touring. The release complimented what The Dead were doing, rather than distracted from it, while also keeping up the momentum of official Grateful Dead releases (There hadn't been a studio album since 1989's tepid *Built To Last*, and there was no sign of a new one on the horizon), and *One From The Vault* was sufficiently different to *Without A Net,* so there was little possibility of confusing the customer.

The first full archive release from 1991 came out in 2001: the 14 June gig at RFK Stadium in Washington, D.C., released as both a three-CD set and a DVD: *View From The Vault, Volume Two.* If shows earlier in the year had been hit-or-miss, their summer stadium shows were more consistently high quality. Hornsby's presence in the band was making a significant difference to shows, his playing adding new textures and his drive pushing the music into new areas. He could easily match Garcia on stage, both coaxing him forward and supporting him as the situation determined. The Dead were settling into their new lineup, and if Welnick so far didn't have the same stage presence or songs that Mydland had, Hornsby more than made up for it.

The DVD is the only commercially released stand-alone video of a full show featuring the Hornsby/Welnick lineup. As a bonus, the DVD features a version of 'Box Of Rain' from July 1990, and a video for the song 'Liberty' using a live recording from 1994. Meanwhile, the CD includes three bonus tracks from the 12 July 1990 gig at RFK Stadium: 'Victim Or The Crime', 'Foolish Heart' and 'Dark Star'. As a selection of bonus tracks, it's a generous helping – with 'Dark Star' clocking in at just under 25 minutes – of the band at their 1990-prime.

The band's next stop was at Giants Stadium, East Rutherford, New Jersey, for two nights on 16/17 June, both of which make up the 1991 part of the *Giants Stadium 1987, 1989, 1991* box set. The two sets feature in full, the 17 June show also included on video as a DVD/blu-ray. The two 1991 shows were the only live show The Dead recorded on 48-track. They show that by this stage, The Dead were a confident and polished act, and the stadium audiences they'd attracted on the back of *In The Dark* were still there, even if its successor hadn't hit the same commercial heights. But more than this, they'd achieved it without diluting the essence that made them unique. It may have been a professional stadium engagement, but they could never be mistaken for U2. They were still capable of pulling off surprises in terms of performance and song choices: the 16 June show managing to open with Weir's recent angular number 'Picasso Moon' and closing with Lesh's *American Beauty* classic 'Box Of Rain' as the encore.

While 1991 hadn't seen much by way of new material in the set, the 17 June show includes a reappearance of 'New Speedway Boogie': a song that returned to their set earlier in the year after being on the shelf since 1970. The 17 June show also features a 'Dark Star' like no other, appearing no less than four times during the show. It makes a surprise (if brief) appearance in the first set, another two short appearances in the second set sequence over disc two (as a short bridge between 'Ship Of Fools' and 'Truckin''), and a brief passage between 'New Speedway Boogie' and 'Uncle John's Band', which finally morphs into a fuller version of the legendary piece. It's not the longest 'Dark Star' – as it's only just over eight minutes before 'Drums' takes the spotlight – but it's very welcome after the teasing throughout the set. The second set continues over disc two, with 'Space', 'China Doll' and 'Playing In The Band'. The jams and the solos may be shorter, but they're certainly there and they sparkle as they should, and the performances make it clear that the 1991 incarnation of The Dead had a sense of fun and no shortage of playfulness. The 17 June show – the best of the two nights – was released as a stand-alone three-CD set titled *Saint Of Circumstance*, and it makes a strong case for why The Dead were one of the biggest live acts in the USA in the early-1990s.

The *Jerry Garcia/David Grisman* album was released in August – an acoustic/bluegrass collection that emerged organically from Garcia's renewed working relationship with the mandolin player; the album quickly coming together in Grisman's home studio after they began playing together again in 1990. While the album contains many older and traditional pieces, whether 1950's blues number 'The Thrill Is Gone', Hoagy Carmichael's 'Rockin' Chair' or Irving Berlin's 'Russian Lullaby', there are a few of their own compositions: 'Grateful Dawg', a piece that draws on each other's musical background; a Grisman number 'Dawg's Waltz', and a cover of The Dead's 'Friend Of The Devil'. One significant track, is 'Arabia' – an instrumental that could be seen as an extension of The Dead's *Blues For Allah*-era interest in North Africa, or a reflection on the then-contemporary Gulf War, with a musical nod to Cuban revolutionary Che Guevara, incorporating a theme from folk song 'Hasta Siempre, Comandante'. A striking old-style black and white video was made for 'The Thrill Is Gone', introducing some older music to a younger audience, with some success, the album getting nominated for a Grammy.

The same month saw a significant release from the Jerry Garcia Band, in the shape of a two-CD self-titled live album. Garcia hadn't released a solo rock album since 1982's *Run For The Roses* (at best a disappointing release), but there are no such reservations about *Jerry Garcia Band*. Recorded in 1990 at the Warfield in San Francisco, it presents a selection of covers, including soul, R&B and pieces by Dylan, The Band, Peter Tosh and Los Lobos. There's only one Dead number: a version of 'Deal'. The Jerry Garcia Band had been operating in parallel with Garcia's *day job* with The Dead, performing to a mostly local audience in the San Francisco area in more intimate venues, allowing Garcia the opportunity to perform some of his personal favourite songs without the weight of expectation that The Dead carried. Dates were arranged around The Dead's schedule, the band consisting of longtime members John Kahn, Melvin Seals and David Kemper on drums, with Jackie LaBranch and Gloria Jones on backing vocals. The band were nimble, and capable of showcasing the more soulful side of Garcia's work; his voice and playing every bit as on-point in this recording as it was during The Dead's recent creative peak in 1990. It's a hugely enjoyable collection, and while it's a more relaxed experience than The Grateful Dead, Garcia's playing is sharp and the band are responsive, and it remains possibly the definitive Jerry Garcia Band live showcase.

If The Dead's shows over the summer were a success, the autumn dates were more erratic in quality. It had become apparent during the tour, that Garcia's drug problem had made a return, leading to the band quickly staging an intervention. Despite his anger, Garcia agreed to enrol in a withdrawal programme. He also spoke to *Rolling Stone* about the possibility of The Dead taking six months off, as he felt the band were in a rut and needed to refresh things with some new material and more time for rehearsals with the new lineup. He felt it wasn't fun performing, that the loss of Mydland had taken a toll on them, and that they needed to regroup and find their enthusiasm again. It was a positive move, acknowledging a problem and devising a solution to address it. Needless to say, it didn't happen, and the relentless touring continued unabated.

In September, they played nine nights at Madison Square Garden in New York, the show from 10 September chosen as the 1991 show on the *30 Trips Around The Sun* box set. It's an obvious choice, as the band are in a good place, from a thunderous 'Shakedown Street' opening the first set, to a second set opening with 'Help On The Way', 'Slipknot!' and 'Franklin's Tower', with Dark Star bookending the 'Drums'/'Space' sequence. Hornsby plays up a storm, but guest Branford Marsalis adds some special sauce to the proceedings. Hornsby spoke about the Madison Square Garden shows being the first time he became aware of Garcia's drug problems and was irritated by how it affected the quality of the performance; he confronted Garcia about his uninspiring playing, and demanded that he up his game. But while some of the performances that September may have been mediocre, the 10 September show was as inspiring as could be hoped for: Garcia and Marsalis trading licks while Hornsby pushed them on to greater heights.

From New York, The Dead moved on to Boston for a six-night run at the Boston Gardens: a series of gigs some fans regard as the band's last great run of shows. *Dick's Picks Volume 17* – released in 2000 – chronicles the 25 September gig over three discs, with two bonus tracks from March 1991. Opening the first set with the 'Help On The Way'>'Slipknot!'>'Franklin's Tower' trilogy, it's a show that combines some fine playing with a strong song selection. 'Crazy Fingers' makes a welcome appearance in the second set, as does 'Terrapin Station', but the interesting gem tucked into the show after the 'Space section', is a cover of Paul McCartney's 'That Would Be Something' from his 1970 debut solo album *McCartney*. It was The Dead's first performance of the song, and they'd go on to play it sixteen times until 1995. While The Dead and The Beatles never crossed paths, there was something of a mutual admiration borne out by McCartney's short film from 1995 *Grateful Dead: A Photofilm,* made using still images taken by his late wife Linda during her photography career. McCartney had begun work on the project before Garcia's death and had been hoping to show it to him. McCartney had made a brief visit to San Francisco in April 1967, and on finding The Grateful Dead not home, hung out with Jefferson Airplane who were rehearsing at The Fillmore. The Dead, and Garcia as a solo artist, would play many Beatles songs in their career, but performing 'That Would Be Something' – more of deep cut in the McCartney discography – showed that their affection for his work and their knowledge of his discography, was profound.

A new Grateful Dead album was on the racks in early November, albeit a very different release from their previous live albums or studio collections. If *Without A Net* had been structured to create an imaginary Grateful Dead show from a variety of recordings over 1989 and 1990, it was far from a complete live-Dead experience, as there was no attempt to include 'Drums' or 'Space'. *Infrared Roses* filled that gap; a compilation of the 'Drums' and 'Space' sequences from 1989 and 1990 restructured and edited together into an almost hour-long experimental sonic piece. Producer Bob Bralove – who'd introduced and developed the band's MIDI technology – curated the album, with Robert Hunter providing segment titles. There are no songs, just improvisation, and a sound journey that begins with a drum circle playing outside the hall, to Hart and Kreutzmann creating a rhythmic piece. Other sections feature different combinations of The Dead improvising together: at times Garcia, Lesh and Weir; other times Hornsby and Welnick. One track features Branford Marsalis playing in the band. For what could be a challenging listen, the album works surprisingly well, if at times Garcia's MIDI excursions can get a bit tiresome. For an experimental piece from a rock act, it's no *Metal Machine Music,* and it makes it clear how conservative many mainstream releases are when something that's as comparatively approachable as this is seen as wildly left-field by critics.

It's almost a digital version of what jazz artists had previously done – creating a new work by editing together material from a variety of sessions or live performances, with elements juxtaposed to bring new contrasts and textures that encourage the listener to consider the work in a new light. There's an argument that it's a more-considered and curated approach to the experimental cut-up method pioneered by beat author William S. Burroughs, using existing material to create a new work that brings to light the underlying elements of the source material that may have been hidden. In this instance, it brings to light the playful weirdness at the heart of The Grateful Dead that could be overlooked by the cowboy songs, soulful ballads and cover versions on the surface. It's hard to imagine a similar band green-lighting a project like this at the peak of their commercial success, never mind it being the work of an act that had been performing for 25 years. A short video – *Infrared Sightings*

– was released commercially to accompany the album, albeit featuring digital animation that now looks as dated as Garcia's *computer art* album cover.

The Dead suffered another major blow at the end of October, with the death of promoter and long-standing champion of the band Bill Graham in a helicopter crash. Graham may have been a controversial figure at times – a businessman in the centre of a music and social scene that purported to have no truck with such capitalist trappings – but without his efforts and dedication, the San Francisco scene would never have enjoyed the level of success it did. Poster artists, musicians and fans, all had a lot to thank him for. As well as running legendary venues like The Fillmore and Winterland, Graham pioneered both the use of sports stadiums to hold concerts, and the large-scale charity benefit gig. Above all, he championed The Dead throughout their career, giving them the opportunity to perform on celebrated stages in their early career, to the creation of the Shoreline Amphitheatre: an outdoor venue in the heart of Silicon Valley, built loosely in the shape of a giant Grateful Dead 'stealie' logo. With the death of Bill Graham, The Dead lost both a trusted business associate and the close friend they referred to as 'Uncle Bobo'.

Graham was commemorated in probably the most appropriate way: a memorial concert, on 2 November at Golden Gate Park. Along with The Dead, other acts associated with Graham, played, including Santana, and Crosby, Stills, Nash & Young. Journey, Tracy Chapman, Jackson Browne and Joe Satriani were also on the bill. The Dead's set included appearances from John Popper of Blues Traveler on harmonica for 'Wang Dang Doodle', John Fogerty from Creedence Clearwater Revival on 'Born On The Bayou', 'Green River', 'Bad Moon Rising' and 'Proud Mary', and Neil Young on a version of Dylan's 'Forever Young'. Given the historic occasion and the number of unique performances, The Dead's performance has been widely circulated unofficially and bootlegged, but has not yet had an official release.

The Dead concluded 1991 with a New Year run of shows at the Oakland Coliseum. The tradition of the New Year gigs had been one of Bill Graham's innovations, and the shows – particularly the New Year's Eve performance – had become an annual celebration, broadcast, and enjoyed by both the committed and the curious, far beyond the walls of the Coliseum. While many would make the pilgrimage, and the faithful would always insist that the New Year show was never the best night of the run, the event had become for many a fixture of the festive celebrations. With the death of Bill Graham, however, 1991 would be The Dead's final New Year show.

1992 – Tomorrow Never Knows

The Grateful Dead's live return at the end of February at the Oakland Coliseum featured new material, with the songs 'So Many Roads', 'Corrina', 'Way To Go Home' and 'Wave To The Wind' all making their debuts over the three-night run. 'So Many Roads' – a Garcia/Hunter composition – would not only become a live favourite with audiences but would come to be regarded as one of the pair's finest pieces. 'Corrina' – by Weir, Hart and Hunter – provided a piece that developed into a platform for extended jamming in many of their 1990s performances. 'Way To Go Home' – co-written by Welnick, Bralove and Hunter – made it clear that Vince wasn't just in the band to fill in for Hornsby, but was capable of contributing to the creation of the kind of idiosyncratic rock that could sit comfortably shoulder-to-shoulder with their more-established songs. 'Wave To The Wind', a work by Hunter and Lesh – isn't quite so fondly recalled, and its absence in the posthumous 'final album' live collection *Ready Or Not*, perhaps shows it was never really a contender. 'Wave To The Wind' doesn't actually appear on any of The Dead's archive releases at all: a fate that even 'Keep Your Day Job' avoided.

There are only a couple of releases chronicling The Dead in 1992, and the first of these comes from their spring tour, when they played the Copps Coliseum in Hamilton, Ontario, Canada, which appears in *30 Trips Around The Sun*. The 1992 Spring Tour wasn't regarded as a particularly good one, but this show was above average for that time. Opening with 'Hell In A Bucket', 'Althea' and Willie Dixon's blues number 'The Same Thing', the first set is a concise one that plays relatively safe: only a twelve-minute-plus version of 'Bird Song' introducing some extended playing. The second set on discs two and three gets livelier, from the 'Shakedown Street' opening into 'Man Smart, Woman Smarter', before a 'Dark Star' heralds a sequence of around 50 minutes that runs through 'Drums', 'Space' and The Other One, resolving with a sharp 'Standing On The Moon'. It's this jazzy and fluid sequence – with Garcia both soulful and inventive, while Hornsby and Welnick mesh together perfectly – that probably lifts the show above the others of this era. It's noticeable, however, that there are none of the new songs included in the show, although their set the following night – the second of two shows at the venue – featured 'So Many Roads', 'Long Way To Go Home' and 'Corrina'. Perhaps playing in their comfort zone on the first night without the concern about how the new material would fit in, helped ensure a better show.

In May, the *Two From The Vault* album was released. While there was still no *regular* release from The Dead, the pace of material coming saw no sign of slowing. Like the first *Vault* release, the two-CD set was unlikely to be mistaken for new product, the material consisting firmly of their late-1960s repertoire. Like its predecessor, it made clear that there was a significant demand for archive releases, and while there would not be another (final) *...From The Vault* release until 2007, the vault door was open and the releases would continue for decades.

From May, The Dead played a series of West Coast and East Coast stadiums and outdoor arenas – the version of 'So Many Roads' from the Star Lake Amphitheatre, Pennsylvania on 23 June, and the performance of 'Way To Go Home' from the Deer Creek Music Centre in Indiana on 28 June, both appearing on the *Ready Or Not* live collection of 'final album' songs. By the summer tour, Hornsby had left his temporary position in the band, the decision justified by the fact Welnick was now settled in his place, and the band had completed the transition to a new post-Mydland lineup. Other factors, such as Hornsby's wife having given birth to twins earlier in the year, and Garcia's playing no longer being the inspiration it was when Hornsby joined, played a significant part in his decision. He would still occasionally sit in with The Dead, even making an appearance on the summer tour.

Those dates were widely regarded as an improvement on the spring shows in terms of musical quality, new covers featuring in the sets, including The Who's 'Baba O'Riley' and The Beatles' 'Tomorrow Never Knows': both already audience favourites and performed with verve as encores. The Dead's 'Casey Jones' also made a reappearance in the set. Another innovation on the summer tour was the introduction of in-ear monitors for the band – so they no longer had to be exposed to excessive volume while performing and were able to hear their instruments clearly. Having been performing for decades in front of a massive sound system had done significant damage to the hearing of several band members, and this system was intended to stop the deterioration. However, one side-effect of this was that it meant that while the musician could hear his own performance, he wasn't able to focus on what the other musicians were playing. Given how important this is when playing an improvised piece, it was an obstacle to the group developing their once-easy and spontaneous onstage interplay.

Following the tour and July dates with the Jerry Garcia Band, Garcia's health again brought serious concern. With symptoms similar to the diabetic coma that almost killed him in 1986, he was diagnosed with lung disease and an enlarged heart. He'd been unfit for some time; overweight and easily tired, his on/off drug habit and his junk food diet contributing to his overall decline. Measures were taken, a health programme was adopted, changes made to his diet and alternative therapy remedies introduced. The Grateful Dead dates that had been arranged for the autumn were cancelled, as were shows by The Jerry Garcia Band, and Garcia was given the time he needed to get back into shape. By the time he was back on stage at the end of October with The Jerry Garcia Band, he was looking better, had lost weight, and seemed to be enjoying performing, no longer a hunched figure motionless behind a microphone.

The Dead resumed live dates in December, with two shows each in Colorado and Arizona, and five nights at the Oakland Coliseum. *Dick's Picks Volume 27* records the show on 16 December, with four bonus tracks from the following night's show. With no New Year show, these were the closest to their festive tradition. While the December shows had seen the introduction of The Beatles'

'Rain' into the set, and the return of 'Here Comes Sunshine', neither feature on *Dick's Picks Volume 27*, nor do any of the new Dead songs introduced that year. Instead, it's a run-through of favourites; a revitalised Garcia contributing strongly on vocals on 'Row Jimmy' and 'Stella Blue', and with some strong playing on a 'Dark Star' that emerges out of the 'Drums' and 'Space' sequence, before moving into Dylan's 'All Along The Watchtower'. The four bonus tracks on disc three – from 17 December – are 'Throwin' Stones' and 'Not Fade Away' from the end of the second set' with the two-song encore of 'Baba O'Riley' and 'Tomorrow Never Knows'. *Dick's Picks Volume 27* might be the volume that comes closest to the end of the band's career, but it ends on a positive note.

1993 – Days Between

Like 1992, only a couple of 1993 releases have emerged so far. While the performances may have lacked some of the magic of previous years, The Dead remained a massive commercial proposition. In 1993 they were the highest-grossing touring act of the year, bringing in just over $45,000,000: a position they also held in 1991 with just under $35,000,000. Side ventures – from Cherry Garcia ice cream to ties based on Garcia's artwork – were massive sellers. The Dead were still a big deal, and even if they didn't rely on chart success or MTV-play to attract an audience, their cultural presence was pervasive. Even here in the UK it had become possible to purchase their albums without hefty import charges, and High-Street shops actually sold t-shirts and posters. They might not be household names beyond a select few households like the one I grew up in, but they were far from the underground phenomenon they'd been in the 1970s.

While The Dead as a live attraction was a lucrative proposition, there was still no follow-up to *Built To Last*. In February 1993, rehearsal sessions released on the *So Many Roads (1965-1995)* box set include the Garcia/Hunter numbers 'Lazy River Road' and 'Days Between': two songs that sit easily among the pair's best work. They also run through 'Eternity' (the Weir/Wasserman and Willie Dixon number), and cover 'Whiskey In The Jar': the traditional Irish song made popular by Thin Lizzy and, later, Metallica. Another new song that soon featured in their live set, was 'Liberty': a new Garcia arrangement of the title track of Hunter's 1987 album. Their dates at the Oakland Coliseum Arena at the end of the month saw many of these songs making their first public appearance, along with a Lesh-sung cover of Robbie Robertson's 'Broken Arrow'.

An East Coast spring tour brought them to North Carolina on 25 March – when the version of 'Lazy River Road' that appears on *Ready Or Not* was recorded – and then on to the Knickerbocker Arena on 27 March. This show appears as the 1993 representative on *30 trips Around The Sun*: one of only two complete shows released from 1993. It's a decent three-disc set, if perhaps thin on any major substance. The first set's 'Peggy-O' is a beauty, the second set moves brightly through 'Eyes Of the World', 'Estimated Prophet' and 'Comes a Time', the comparatively fresh 'Corrina' moving into the 'Drums' section. However, 'Days Between' sitting in the *Garcia-slow-number slot* before the *uplifting-set-closer slot*, makes it clear what an outstanding song this is. If 'Stella Blue' is a song that matured and took on more resonance as the years moved on, 'Days Between' landed fully-formed and perfect: the right song at the right time. With its mature and enigmatic pause for reflection, and its refusal to give easy answers, 'Days Between' effortlessly shut down any suspicions among some fans that Hunter and Garcia's work was behind them by the 1990s. If Garcia was caricatured as a carefree happy-hippy dancing bear, the grinning skull of mortality beneath, was never far from the surface – 'Days Between' a *memento mori* like 'Death Don't Have No Mercy', that has its place in life's multicoloured tapestry as much as any celebration does.

Another show highlight – albeit a very different mood – is the encore of 'I Fought The Law' – a hit for the Bobby Fuller Four in 1966, but perhaps better known in a cover version by The Clash. There may not seem to be much common ground between The Dead and English punk rock legends The Clash, but an outlaw anthem united them. While performed a few dozen times as an encore, it's the only time it's ever been released. It might not be classic Dead by any means, but it can't help to raise a smile.

In April, Bruce Hornsby's solo album *Harbor Lights* was released: the first album released under his own name without 'and The Range' post-nominal. Garcia appears on guitar on two tracks: 'Passing Through' and 'Pastures Of Plenty'. It's a collection with a distinctly jazzy flavour, with guests including Pat Metheny and Branford Marsalis. While there's a song called 'China Doll', it's a Hornsby song that only shares a title with Hunter and Garcia's piece. 'Rainbow's Cadillac' would eventually be performed live by Dead alumni The Other Ones on their *The Strange Remain* album. 'Pastures Of Plenty' – the album's closing number – has a strong extended instrumental passage with Garcia and Hornsby complementing each other with an easy confidence.

A second Dead release from 1993 emerged in 2009 as *Road Trips Volume 2 Number 4*, featuring content from the 26 and 27 May shows at Cal Expo Amphitheatre, Sacramento, California: the final two nights of a three-night run at the venue. As with other releases in the *Road Trips* series, it's a digest of the two shows over two discs, with some extra material appearing on a limited bonus disc. The first disc has four tracks from the first set from 26 May, along with a very satisfying pre-'Space' sequence of 'Box Of Rain', 'Victim Or The Crime', 'Crazy Fingers' and 'Playing In The Band', while disc two presents the rest of the set but without 'Space', including the reprise of 'Playing In The Band' and the 'Liberty' encore. Five tracks from the first set of the 27 May show – including the 'Shakedown Street' opener – fill the disc. Frustratingly, the bonus disc has some good material from 27 May's second set: the opening 'Picasso Moon', running into a twelve-minute-plus 'Fire On The Mountain'. 'Cassidy' runs into 'Uncle John's Band', which itself moves into a reprise of 'Cassidy', and their version of Van Morrison's 'Gloria' – the second night's encore – is also there. Three tracks from the 26th make up the disc, including 'Broken Arrow'. 'Wave To The Wind' was originally performed between 'Fire On The Mountain' and 'Cassidy', but even here – possibly its most likely appearance – it misses the cut. It's a pleasant enough listen, although, with more-recent releases tending towards full shows, it's frustrating for the fan who wants to experience the show even with its imperfections.

At the end of October, The Dead's vault releases entered a new phase, with the release of *Dick's Picks Volume 1*. The two-CD set chronicled a show from December 1973 that had been selected by Dead archivist Dick Latvala. It differed from previous vintage releases, in that instead of being sourced from a multitrack recording, it came from a basic two-track recording, which meant post-production work on the recording was limited – the collection, (like all the others in the series) warning the listener not to expect the same sound quality as they might experience with other releases, with the historical value of the recording outweighing whatever technical failings it may have. The album also had a more low-key release than previous vintage releases, the majority of copies being sold directly from the band's merchandise arm rather than via retail outlets. Its minimal-though-distinctive packaging also helped keep the band's outlay down and the profit margin worthwhile. Its success – and the subsequent success of other volumes in the *Dick's Picks* series – led the way for more of these basic recordings to be released over subsequent decades, though the packaging would get a bit more elaborate.

Another October issue was the second release by Garcia/Grisman. Titled *Not For Kids Only,* it's a collection of traditional songs predominantly for youngsters. With songs like 'There Ain't No Bugs On Me' and 'Hopalong Peter', it's a long way from The Grateful Dead's usual output, although, one of the numbers – 'Teddy Bear's Picnic' – at least once appeared as a brief tuning piece during a Grateful Dead show. Garcia and Grisman made an appearance on *The Late Show* in September, during The Dead's six-night run at Madison Square Garden in New York, performing 'Friend Of The Devil', Grisman having played mandolin on the song's original *American Beauty* recording.

Garcia and Grisman's relaxed jamming together with a cast of others, and with easy access to Grisman's recording, meant they quickly built up a substantial collection of recordings, some of which were released posthumously. One recorded in February 1993 at Grisman's Dawg studio, became known as *The Pizza Tapes*. Recorded with bass player Tony Rice, over two nights the trio performed a selection of traditional and bluegrass numbers, and covers of Miles Davis and Bob Dylan numbers, the recordings first becoming available via The Grateful Dead tape trading community after Garcia apparently tipped a pizza delivery boy with a copy of the recordings. Grisman finally released a slice of the recordings in 2000 as a 75-minute CD, and an extended three-CD Extra Large Edition with previously unreleased takes came out in 2010, both on Grisman's Acoustic Disc label. Both editions present a hot and fresh selection.

Unlike 1992, The Dead were able to undertake a full live schedule this year. The lack of releases perhaps reflects that the quality was still erratic; the performances often uninspiring. By the early-1990s, live shows by major commercial acts tended to be slickly-produced affairs, with little room in the live environment for deviation from a carefully-curated MTV-friendly image, whether the band was a heritage act like The Rolling Stones or a then vogue-ish pop phenomenon like New Kids On The Block. The Dead weren't above using some of the new technology – teleprompters helped with forgotten lyrics, and giant screens helped the audiences see what was happening on stage – but they retained an attitude few other bands had, where the music took the central role. Not many stadium acts would leave room for improvisation, never mind celebrate it. Few would be flexible enough to play different sets every night, often with a loose sketch of what the performance would involve before taking the stage. In an increasingly sterile stadium and arena environment, The Dead still took musical risks, and though things didn't come together perfectly at time, other times they would. They were still performing without a net; So what if things weren't perfect all the time? One day it will please us to remember even this, as ancient poet Virgil might've said after a mediocre show at the Greek Theatre.

1994 – Every Leaf Is Turning

The latter-day Dead archive releases continue to be thin pickings in 1994. They were back on stage in February at the Oakland Coliseum, and the by-now seemingly regular rota of tours, continued. If Garcia's health and his on/off drug abuse are blamed for inconsistent and uninspiring shows, it's not the whole story. Garcia was physically fragile in his later years, but other things had crept in to take away some of the magic that the band had in their earlier years. All the members were older, with all the associated issues that age brings. While they were musically close – the original core lineup of Garcia, Weir, Lesh, Hart and Kreutzmann maintaining a live schedule few acts of their status would tolerate, giving them an intuitive understanding of their fellow band members' playing – they were all settled in their own lives with their own priorities: children, partners, homes and lives outside the band. If their playing didn't always mesh together as organically as it had in the 1970s, it's perhaps a reflection that the band wasn't always the main focus of their lives anymore.

Other responsibilities had imposed themselves on the band, with The Dead's touring income necessary to pay the wages of the crew, and to sustain the lifestyles they and the band had become accustomed to. If there was no Wall Of Sound to pay for, there were still constant overheads, flights, hotels and health insurance that needed constant attention. Garcia's hoped-for break in the early-1990s to get the band out of the musical rut he felt they were in, had come to nothing. The audiences continued to come. For many, the shows remained almost religious experiences; for others, it was an excuse to party, while older tie-dyed-in-the-wool heads might grumble that it wasn't like it used to be. Crowd problems like gatecrashing and drug use hadn't gone away, and serious incidents continued to plague the community.

In January, The Dead were inducted into the Rock and Roll Hall Of Fame: band members except Garcia appearing at the induction ceremony in New York. Garcia – who had an aversion to formal events and awards – was represented by a cardboard cutout. Also, Garcia – whose personal relationships had always been fairly chaotic – remarried in February, just ahead of the band undertaking their February dates.

During the spring dates, Garcia's performances continued to be erratic. His playing was often well below par: complicated passages were simplified, his playing would lag behind the rest of the band, and he'd miss cues or forget lyrics. But he was still capable of delivering a stellar performance at times, particularly on ballads: the slower tempo seemingly suiting his pace of playing. Garcia could at times play to his normal standard, and many of his shortcomings were covered by the other band members, but the only release from this period is a live version of 'Liberty', recorded on the first night of two at the Omni in Atlanta on 30 March, released in the *So Many Roads (1965-1995)* box set.

After The Dead tour, Garcia embarked on dates with the Jerry Garcia Band in May. At a show in Arizona, he took a break after five songs and collapsed backstage. On returning home, a reoccurrence of his diabetes was diagnosed, and another attempt was made to instil healthy habits and a better diet. Over and above this, Garcia had been complaining about a loss of feeling in his fingertips – a consequence of carpal tunnel syndrome – had been given exercises to alleviate the problem, and was also looking for a lighter guitar, to reduce the strain.

There would be little time to recuperate, with The Dead back on the road from early June. Garcia remained in poor shape, hunched over a microphone with a listless demeanour on stage, his playing below standard. There were occasional flashes of inspiration, but the tour wasn't greeted with the usual enthusiasm, and many fans expressed grave concern about Garcia's health. Again, recordings released from this tour remain sparse, with only a version of 'Way To Go Home' from 31 July at Auburn Hill, Michigan, emerging on *So Many Roads (1965-1995)*. By the time The Dead reached the East Coast, word of the substandard performances over the summer had affected ticket sales, and their by-now regular runs at the Boston Gardens and Madison Square Garden (six nights each) failed to sell out in advance. Perhaps this brought matters into focus for the band, or perhaps it was just that playing familiar venues they'd previously enjoyed, had a positive effect on them, but the standard of the performances did improve.

The 1 October show at Boston Gardens – the fourth night of the run there – is the only complete show from 1994 to be released, coming as part of the *30 Trips Around The Sun* set. Opening the first set with the 'Help On The Way'/'Slipknot!'/'Franklin's Tower' trilogy, it's a respectable if unspectacular show. There are points when Garcia's guitar would be expected to ring out confidently, but the absence of any definitive playing comes as a surprise. He's there and you can hear him, but there doesn't seem to be coordination or vision, and where he would previously have sparkled consistently, there are sparks that only occasionally come close to igniting. The capability of the rest of the band does much to minimise any shortcomings, deftly sustaining The Grateful Dead live experience. If Garcia is unfocussed and off-track at times, Weir, Lesh and Welnick's playing remains fluent throughout. There are no classic versions of songs on this collection – 'So Many Roads' makes an appearance in the first set, but the vocals sound disinterested and Garcia's playing uninvolved. 'Scarlet Begonias' opens the second set on disc two, and although it's upbeat, it doesn't really convince that it's fun. 'Terrapin Station' is far from first-class transportation, providing instead a bus-replacement service, and Garcia shows up late for his vocals in 'Stella Blue'. On the whole, the show isn't great, but there are moments that remind us of the greatness of The Grateful Dead – Garcia's singing in 'Stella Blue' when it eventually comes in; Weir repeatedly hitting the mark during the show, with 'Walkin' Blues', his cowboy double-feature of 'Me And My Uncle' and 'Big River' in the first set' and the closing 'One More Saturday Night'.

Two tracks from the Madison Square Garden run also emerged, with 'Liberty' – the encore from 14 October – appearing as the opening track on *Ready Or*

Not. 'Days Between' from the 18 October show's second set, appears as the closing track on the three-CD edition of the *Long Strange Trip* soundtrack album. The fact that two tracks from these gigs were chosen for auspicious places on two significant posthumous releases reflects their quality: particularly the version of 'Days Between'. Despite regularly turning in disappointing work, Garcia could still be inspired both vocally and instrumentally, particularly with the ballads. The version of 'Days Between' here is perfect; his voice is sweet yet weary, the guitar-playing and tone absolutely nailing the sentiment.

In November, the band stepped into a studio to capture the new material for a new album. There had been discussions since the previous year, but Garcia's opinion was that it should be postponed until they had much more new material to choose from. The subsequent year hadn't seen much by way of new compositions; Garcia's muse proving to be as elusive as it was in the early-1980s when his drug habit began to take hold. They held twelve days of sessions at The Site studio in West Marin, recording basic tracks for the new material, but the endeavour was fairly fruitless. Welnick voiced unhappiness with the studio sound and quality of their performances, while Garcia's enthusiasm for the recording was low: arriving late or not showing up, making a bare minimum of contribution.

If the studio wasn't a conducive environment for a new Grateful Dead album, another emerged in 1994 from a very different source. *Grayfolded* was the result of Canadian experimental composer and producer John Oswald creating a new work using existing recordings of the band performing 'Dark Star', taken from throughout their career. Oswald had pioneered a technique he called 'Plunderphonics', using recordings as the source material for a composition where different elements would be juxtaposed and edited together to reveal similarities and differences. Oswald took his inspiration from William S. Burroughs' cut-up technique, but using sound – familiar pieces of music in particular – as his building blocks rather than text. Previously, he'd worked (unofficially) with material by Michael Jackson, The Doors and Led Zeppelin. Lesh was aware of Oswald's work from his 1989 *Plunderphonics* album – a collection he gave away so as to avoid copyright issues – and suggested the project to him. For the *Grayfolded* project, he used 100 different versions of 'Dark Star' from every lineup of the band, and produced a two-CD set. Recordings from different eras blended into each other; vocals recorded decades apart became a choir; The Dead's most exploratory piece going on a journey to a strange destination.

Like the *Infrared Roses* collection, it's a bold step into the twilight zone, and a challenging listen, but one that retains a sense of fun. Part of Oswald's Plunderphonics ethos is that the original has to be recognisable in the finished work, rather than just being a sample laid over new material. While two discs of remixed and processed recordings of a lengthy and explorative instrumental might not be something that would normally trouble the pop charts, it wasn't entirely beyond what The Dead had been doing previously in their career

– with *Anthem Of The Sun* being a composite of studio and live recordings, edited and blended into a new whole, or the studio experimentation that went on during the creation of *Aoxomoxoa*. *Grayfolded* remains a strange and rewarding listening experience, and it's possibly significant that The Dead's final new release while they were together was perhaps one of their strangest ever.

The end of the year saw The Dead back on home ground, with a run of four shows at Oakland Coliseum in December, before four more shows in L.A. closed the year. For the Oakland shows, the band teased the possibility of performing 'St. Stephen' in their soundcheck, but it never emerged during the shows. What did emerge was the version of 'Days Between' from 11 December that would be included in the *Ready Or Not* album: the closing track on the live collection of songs that could've made their final studio album.

1995 – Dark Star Crashes

1995 was the year the curtain finally came down. While 1994 had been a difficult one for the band artistically, commercially, it had been a considerable success. Despite there being no new studio album, The Dead were at the peak of their success as a live attraction, even if the shows were not of the quality they had previously been. Garcia's health had given both those associated with the band, and their fans, considerable cause for concern, but he'd pulled back into shape before and come back with stronger performances. Similarly, while the November studio sessions had not resulted in a new album, the process had rarely been a straightforward one for The Dead. The recording of *Built To Last* had, after all, involved sessions at Marin County Civic Centre and Skywalker Ranch before sessions at Front Street completed the process. While some dates may not have sold out, they'd been touring relentlessly, and even the most loyal fan base could become jaded. While there had been issues, there was a feeling that things could still work out. The assumption that the final years of The Grateful Dead were a downward spiral on account of Garcia's drug issues and the relentless demands of touring, takes a far-too-simple view of the situation, the narrative inevitably informed by hindsight.

There remained no sign of the promised break in their live schedule – arenas and stadiums requiring to be booked considerably in advance – and the wheel began to turn again in February, with dates in Utah and three shows at the Coliseum in Oakland. The Salt Lake City show from 21 February – the final night of the three-night run at the Delta Center – was issued in the *30 Trips Around The Sun* collection: the only full 1995 gig to be released. The first set opens with The Dead's only performance of 'Salt Lake City': a track from Weir's *Heaven Help The Fool* album. 'Friend Of The Devil', with its reference to spending the night in Utah, followed. It's a strong first set, with Lesh's version of 'Broken Arrow', and Weir on acoustic guitar for 'Black-Throated Wind'. Garcia's 'So Many Roads', follows, making it clear that, had it been written in the mid-1970s, it would easily be regarded as one of their classics. The second set might lack the surprise of a song making its debut, but it too had its unexpected twists, with a version of Willie Dixon's 'I Just Want To Make Love To You' making its first appearance since 1984, and Dylan's 'Visions Of Johanna' reappearing after being absent since 1986: an onstage teleprompter helping Garcia with Dylan's poetic and lengthy lyrics. From the 'Foolish Heart' opener to the 'Sugar Magnolia' final number and 'Liberty' encore, it's a solid performance. Garcia's in good voice, and his playing is confident and distinctive. While it might be far from vintage Dead, it's a much better release than might be expected given the poor reputation of their output over their final years.

The tour dates continued, but there would be no further full-show releases from 1995. A version of 'Visions Of Johanna' recorded at The Spectrum in Philadelphia on 18 March appeared on the *Fallout From The Phil Zone* collection, while 'Samba In The Rain' from The Omni in Atlanta on 30 March

appears on *Ready Or Not*. A live version of 'Eternity' recorded on 2 April at
the Pyramid in Memphis, Tennessee, is also on that posthumous collection.
The tour wasn't without its highlights, including Hornsby sitting in on grand
piano for the entire 23 March show at Charlotte, North Carolina, and their
cover of Al Green's 'Take Me To The River' making its debut in Memphis: Al
Green's hometown. Perhaps the biggest surprise was the appearance of Lesh's
'Unbroken Chain': a song from their 1974 *From The Mars Hotel* album that
they'd never played live until 19 March 1995 in Philadelphia. Fans who'd been
waiting a matter of decades to hear it performed live were not disappointed.

In May, The Dead returned to The Site to continue recording a studio
album, but the sessions over ten days didn't yield much. Garcia again wasn't
particularly interested, and didn't get around to recording definitive guitar
or vocal tracks. Elsewhere, he did get more involved with a writing project: a
book – *Harrington Street* – recalling in illustrations and anecdotes, his growing
up in San Francisco. The book would be finished by his widow and published
posthumously.

Garcia's performances in 1995 were still inconsistent. At times his playing
was sharp, imaginative and upbeat, but at others, he lacked energy, his
attention wandering and his playing sloppy. These issues continued into the
band's summer stadium tour, which began in June, with Dylan supporting on
several dates, though this time not actually performing with The Dead. The
shows had a number of problems beyond Garcia, with crowd trouble and
gatecrashing. Deer Creek – a popular venue with the fans, that they played on
2 July – was a tense show after police informed the band of a credible threat
that Garcia would be shot during the concert. With security stepped up, Garcia
rose to the occasion by performing 'Dire Wolf', with its 'Don't murder me'
lyrics. But despite the increased security presence, thousands of ticket-less
fans broke down a fence and swarmed into the show, police deploying tear gas
and pepper spray to maintain order. The second night's show was cancelled.
The tour resumed in Missouri, with two nights at the Riverport Amphitheatre.
While things went better than at Deer Creek, over 100 fans were injured when
a campsite porch collapsed after the first night's concert. Again, The Dead were
making the news, but for the wrong reasons.

Two nights at Soldier Field in Chicago brought the tour to its conclusion.
No one at the time realised that they would be The Dead's final shows. The
performances were far from perfect, but the version of 'Visions Of Johanna'
from the 8 July show – which made it onto the *Garcia Plays Dylan* collection –
presents a powerful version of the song: Garcia's vocals and playing confident
and strong. The final night was again an uneven performance. The show might
be remembered as historic – the last stand of a legendary band, Garcia facing
the end of the road. But again, hindsight gives weight to things that perhaps
don't always deserve it. Garcia may have been in poor physical shape – a
man in his mid-50s who looked and acted more like a man in his mid-70s –
but opening the show with 'Touch Of Grey' and its 'We will survive' refrain

wasn't the act of a man who suspected his time was fast running out. Fans and historians might scour the setlist for details they see as significant – Did the performance of 'Unbroken Chain' mean they subconsciously knew it would be their last tour?; Did singing Dylan's 'When I Paint My Masterpiece' signify that Garcia thought he'd completed his art? None of these – or countless other fanciful speculations – add any mystique to the show. However, the version of 'So Many Roads' from the second set – released as the title track and final song on the *So Many Roads (1965-1995)* box set – is genuinely outstanding. As before, Garcia was lifted in his performance of one of the ballads, and this time there seemed to be a recognition of his frailty from the audience, an awareness of the song's expression of the fragility of things, and acceptance of the transitory nature of life.

Garcia's final number was 'Black Muddy River': another ponderous and thoughtful number that reflected on the end of things, performed as the encore. Lesh had other ideas, and didn't want the tour to close on a downbeat number, and he led the band into 'Box Of Rain'. A recording of this song was included on a CD that accompanied early copies of Lesh's 2005 autobiography *Searching For The Sound*. While an undisputed classic of The Dead's back-catalogue, it was also a song with a considerable emotional weight, as, despite its upbeat and hopeful nature, it was a song written after Lesh asked Hunter to help him compose a song for his father, who at the time had terminal cancer and was in a nursing home. The song's final lines – 'Such a long, long time to be gone/And such a short time to be here' – resonate powerfully in the circumstances of the performance and also echo those of the traditional song 'Little Birdie', performed by Garcia and the Sleepy Valley Hog Stompers in 1962: 'A short time to stay here and a long time to be gone'.

A week after the tour ended, Garcia and Grisman recorded a cover of Jimmie Rodgers' 'Blue Yodel No. 9 (Standing On The Corner)' for a Jimmie Rogers tribute album that would also contain contributions from stars like Bob Dylan, Bono, Van Morrison, Willie Nelson and Mary Chapin Carpenter. It was Garcia's last recording session, the album coming out in 1997.

Garcia headed to the Betty Ford Clinic for a detox programme: his first lengthy residential attempt to finally come off heroin. Although he only lasted for two weeks of the month-long programme, he was said to be in good form, optimistic and positive. He was, however, made aware of his overall physical frailty and poor health. Garcia checked in to a rehab facility in Marin County on 8 August, planning to stay for three weeks, keeping his plans secret from most of The Grateful Dead organisation and even from his wife. On finding out, she visited him, and with permission, took him out for a meal and returned him to the centre. In the early hours of the morning of 9 August, Garcia was found to have died in his sleep, the cause of his death listed as a heart attack. The long, strange trip was over.

Furthur

It would take months for The Grateful Dead to confirm the inevitable: that following the death of Garcia, the band was no more. A memorial service was held in Golden Gate Park on 13 August, thousands of fans attending the event to hear speeches from his family, friends and band members. Rumours and speculation about the band's future circulated, until the surviving band members confirmed they had no intention of continuing as The Grateful Dead. Despite being a band that had no real frontman, that had been Garcia's role all along. Even though he'd always been the last one to accept being in a position of leadership, Garcia had been The Dead's *de facto* leader throughout, and for a band that never really subscribed to a cult of personality, Garcia was too big a personality to replace.

But it would take years for the band to finally say goodbye, with a series of concerts in 2015 that culminated in three shows at Soldier Field in Chicago: the scene of the final Dead concert. *Fare Thee Well: Celebrating 50 Years Of The Grateful Dead* saw Weir, Lesh, Hart and Kreutzmann, alongside Bruce Hornsby, Phish guitarist Trey Anastasio and keyboard player Jeff Chimenti, celebrate the band's legacy with two shows at Santa Clara's Levi Stadium on 27/28 June, and three at Soldier Field on 3, 4 and 5 July. The shows were released in a variety of formats – a 12-disc box set chronicling the complete run of Soldier Field shows; a three-disc set of the 5 July 5 with two additional DVDs or blu-rays, and a two-disc best-of collection of performances from the three nights. It may not have been The Grateful Dead as such, but the event had a celebratory atmosphere and a sense of achievement that – despite everything – The Dead were still a part of American music, and was a timely reminder that, despite Garcia's passing, the music never actually stopped. There may have been reservations among fans – Was Anastasio the most appropriate choice? Was the song selection appropriate and could the former band members do their legacy justice? There was a considerable weight of expectation, but The Dead's music carried it off, and while the recordings might not be the first thing a fan reaches for, they remain a reminder of The Dead's unique status. *Fare Thee Well* represented a healing of animosity between band members that had been an on/off element of the post-Dead years, and was also a celebration of Garcia's legacy and a reminder that The Dead had never really gone away.

Garcia's death didn't mean the end of the band members' careers. From then until the present day, they've pursued a variety of projects, working with each other in different combinations, and with an evolving cast of new collaborators, bringing fresh blood and new ideas into the ever-expanding Grateful Dead family. Acts like The Other Ones, The Dead, Furthur, Phil and Friends, Ratdog and Dead & Company, have kept The Grateful Dead's fire burning; all different in their own ways, but all working more or less in line with the style established by The Dead. And like The Dead, the former members' subsequent bands have put their focus on live performance, but there have still been a number of significant releases.

Weir's band Ratdog – an extension of his work with Wasserman – was already on the road when Garcia died. Originally a side-project, Weir's band would be one of the most consistent of the post-Dead solo acts, constantly touring and eventually releasing both studio and live recordings. Alongside Wasserman, key band members included keyboard player Jeff Chimenti and guitarist Mark Karan; the lineup going through some changes over the years they were active until 2014. Their studio collection *Evening Moods* was released in 2000, featuring a number of new songs that the band played along with material originally by The Dead. Most were group compositions, with regular Weir collaborator John Perry Barlow involved. The song 'Corrina' – originally a late-period Dead number by Weir, Hart and Hunter – features on the album, Hart himself appearing as a guest on three tracks. Ratdog went on to release a double live 2001 CD *Live At Roseland,* featuring a number of songs that were on *Evening Moods*, alongside covers of Dead classics like 'The Music Never Stopped', 'Friend Of The Devil' and 'The Other One'. While the majority of Dead songs on the collection were ones that Weir performed, the version of 'Mission In The Rain' – originally from a Garcia solo album – is outstanding.

The 2004 compilation *Weir Here* focuses on his career, with material from his solo albums, Kingfish, Bobby and The Midnites and Ratdog, along with performances of The Grateful Dead with Weir in the driving seat. The collection has one studio and one live disc, the live Dead material including previously unreleased tracks among the material from live archive albums. Weir's career was also examined in the documentary *The Other One: The Long Strange Trip Of Bob Weir* in 2014.

Weir released a solo album in 2016 – *Blue Mountain* – his third solo album following *Heaven Help The Fool*. It features new western-styled material befitting the more mature artist. Collaborators include contemporary Americana singer-songwriter Josh Ritter, and Josh Kaufman, who produced the album. It's possibly Weir's most successful solo album that's not called *Ace*. More recently, Weir has been performing as Bob Weir and Wolf Bros – a trio of Weir, bassist Don Was and former Ratdog drummer Jay Lane, with a live album, *Live In Colorado* being released in February 2022 featuring Dead favourites 'New Speedway Boogie' and 'Lost Sailor'/'Saint Of Circumstance' among the eight tracks. It was recorded at Red Rocks Amphitheatre and the Gerald R. Ford Amphitheatre in July 2021.

From 1998, Lesh performed as leader of Phil Lesh And Friends – an act with a lineup that has at times changed on an almost nightly basis, allowing all kinds of experimentation and new musical ideas to emerge. Phil takes The Dead's idea of creating something new every night to another level by almost constantly playing with a changing cast of characters, although at times they've had periods of relative stability. Following The Dead's precedent, staying across live recordings of the band have been an essential part of keeping up with the Leshes, helped by a number of Instant Live releases and downloads. The band's first proper release was the live double *Love Will See You Through,*

189

recorded in June 1999 at the Warfield in San Francisco – the band including former Jefferson Airplane guitarist Jorma Kaukonen, along with Steve Kimock, who'd played guitar with Keith and Donna Godchaux and Kingfish. Pete Sears – formerly of Jefferson Starship and Hot Tuna – played keyboards, and former member of The Tubes Prairie Prince was on drums. The album doesn't stray far from The Grateful Dead's loose formula, with a number of Dead songs – including 'Friend Of The Devil', 'Franklin's Tower' and 'St. Stephen' – and covers performed by The Dead, like 'Dancing In The Street', 'Big Boss Man' and 'Broken Arrow'. The second disc features 'Good Shepherd' – a traditional number performed by Jefferson Airplane and released on their *Volunteers* album that was arranged and sung by Kaukonen. It's followed by the first of two lengthy jams on the album, the second following a version of The Dead's 'New Potato Caboose', before a lengthy 'St. Stephen' brings the album to a worthy conclusion.

The studio album *There And Back Again* came out in 2002, featuring one of the longer-running and most celebrated lineups of the band, with Warren Haynes and Jimmy Herring on guitar, John Molo on drums and Rob Barraco on keyboards. Three of the songs – 'Celebration', 'No More Do I' and 'Rock-n-Roll Blues' – are co-written by Lesh and Hunter; a fourth – 'Night Of A Thousand Stars' – also credits Haynes, while 'Again And Again' is credited to Herring and Hunter. A version of 'Liberty' – the Garcia/Hunter song that was both the title track of Hunter's 1987 solo album and one of the songs intended for The Dead's final studio album – also features. The album was met with a mixed response, perhaps failing to satisfy those who wanted more emphasis on the band's jamming than on the songs which – despite their heritage – didn't compare favourably with the familiarity of The Dead's output. Simply put, some listeners only wanted to hear the old stuff. Undertaking a studio album was a gamble, and perhaps one that would've worked for The Dead, as their audience would've been quicker to accept the songs as in-development sketches or continued live improvement, rather than a finished item. Critics were less accommodating to a debut album by a less-familiar act. A limited version of the album featured a second disc with a studio version of 'Passenger' and live versions of 'St. Stephen' from April 2002 with Derek Trucks, 'Dark Star' from New Year's Eve 2001, and 'The Eleven' from March 2002.

A live release from Phil And Friends – *Live At The Warfield* – came out in 2006, including a DVD with different tracks. The band is slightly different, with Molo and Barraco still onboard, but with John Scofield and Larry Campbell on guitars. Joan Osborne adds vocals, and Greg Osby brings saxophone to the band. It's a different sound from their studio album and first live collection, and it has a strong track listing. Obviously centred on Dead material, there are versions of 'Shakedown Street' and 'Cosmic Charlie' on disc one, while the second has 'Dark Star', 'Morning Dew', and a version of 'The Other One' that involves a return to 'Dark Star' before 'Box Of Rain' closes the disc. The DVD features more classic Dead tunes, including 'Uncle John's Band', 'St Stephen',

'The Eleven' and the trilogy of 'Help On The Way', 'Slipknot!' and 'Franklin's Tower'. The band performs some of The Dead's most iconic work with the kind of verve that you wish The Dead themselves were able to muster consistently in their later years.

Phil and Friends remain a going concern, Lesh having also established the Terrapin Crossroads music venue at a former seafood restaurant in San Rafael in 2012. While The Dead's project to create a museum or venue in San Francisco eventually came to nothing, Lesh created a vibrant venue that The Dead community could call their own, with regular live performances from Phil And Friends and other sympathetic musicians. With a bar and restaurant, it was a regular haunt for local fans and a place of pilgrimage for those further afield. It lasted until November 2021, when it was confirmed that it would close, though leaving open the possibility it might reopen elsewhere.

Other former Dead members continued to work following the demise of the band. Welnick joined Weir's RatDog for a while, although the troubled keyboard player was not in the band for long. Serious health problems, including cancer and emphysema, led to depression and a suicide attempt. Following successful treatment and therapy, he formed the band Missing Man Formation, who went on to release a self-titled album in 1998. Included was 'Samba In The Rain': the song he co-wrote with Robert Hunter, that was performed by The Dead. Another song, 'Golden Days', was a tribute to Garcia. The band performed live around San Francisco, their sets including many Dead numbers and covers. Welnick died in 2006.

Mickey Hart's career as a major figure in world music continued, and he also continued to perform with other former Dead members. His 1996 *Mystery Box* album saw his world-influenced percussion alongside vocal act The Mint Juleps, on a collection of songs co-written with Robert Hunter, the song 'Only The Strange Remain' featuring on the live album by The Other Ones. His following albums were more percussion-based, 1998's *Supralingua* featuring percussion grooves with vocal collaborations. It's a powerful soundscape: the production challenging and forward-looking. His 1999 *Spirit Into Sound* album was a sister to his *Spirit Into Sound: The Magic Of Music* book that was published that year. His 2007 *Global Drum Project* won a Grammy Award for the Best Contemporary World Music Album. Hart has continued to pursue interesting avant-garde ideas, and present them in a way that is accessible. *Mysterium Tremedum* from 2012 has Hart and other musicians play along with sounds created by computers, having processed light, radio waves and radiation from objects like stars and galaxies, and transformed them into sound. 2013's *Superorganism* takes the sound source much closer to home, with musicians playing along to sounds generated from Hart's brain waves. Both these albums feature lyrics written by Robert Hunter. Hart's most recent release – 2017's *RAMU* – features a synthesizer that combines electronic drum sounds with sound samples, bringing a wide range of sounds together in a surprising and entertaining piece. Among the samples, are work by Jerry Garcia on guitar and synth guitar. Of all the former Dead musicians, Hart has probably remained the closest to the spirit of experimental weirdness and fun at the heart of the band.

Relations between the former members of The Grateful Dead have not always been harmonious, and at times, things have gotten plain ugly, but every family has its issues. Over time, some of these are resolved, others emerge, and these too are forgiven, forgotten or set aside. Since 1995 there have been various incarnations of bands featuring more than one member of the band – The Other Ones, The Dead, Furthur and the currently-active Dead & Company have all been projects involving several former members of The Dead performing a selection of their repertoire, these groups touring and often performing alongside the solo careers of the former members.

The first post-Dead grouping that went on the road came about in 1998, when Weir, Lesh, Hart and Hornsby toured under the name The Other Ones. In 1996, a tour was organised to fill the void with no Dead tour taking place: the Furthur Festival, involving Weir's Ratdog, Hart's Mystery Box, Bruce Hornsby, Hot Tuna and Los Lobos. While it was a successful series of shows – perhaps on account of the demand for a Dead-related event still being strong – a tour the following year, again featuring Weir, Hart and Hornsby, along with Hunter, was headlined by The Black Crowes: perhaps a step too far away from the core Dead fans' tastes. The 1998 Furthur tour was a different matter, with The Other Ones making their appearance with Mark Karan and Steve Kimock on guitar, John Molo on drums and Dave Ells on sax. Their set was essentially Dead numbers, with some changes to accommodate new members. A live album – the two-CD set *The Strange Remain* – was released in 1999: a strong collection that showed the new band more than capable of filling the space left by The Dead. Opening with 'St. Stephen' and 'The Eleven' was a bold move, but one that couldn't help but convince. The set also included Hornsby's 'White-Wheeled Limousine' and 'Rainbow's Cadillac', 'Corrina' from the later days of The Dead, the Hart/Hunter numbers 'Only The Strange Remain' and 'Baba Jingo', and 'Banyan Tree': a Weir/Hart/Hunter number. The collection was a great balance of less-familiar numbers with classic Dead, indicating that the band not only had a rich history, but also the potential to still produce some new surprises. 'Banyan Tree' in particular could've been a classic Dead number from their later years.

The Other Ones were to undergo regular lineup changes: Kreutzmann joining in 2000 while Lesh and Molo stepped out, Alphonso Johnson joining on bass. In 2002, Lesh rejoined, Jimmy Herring taking guitar duties, Rob Barraco and Jeff Chimenti taking over from Hornsby, and Susan Tedeschi joining on vocals. By 2003, they decided to rename the act The Dead – Joan Osborne replacing Susan Tedeschi, former Allman Brothers Band guitarist Warren Haynes coming onboard in 2004. They'd return in 2008 in support of the Obama presidential campaign, eventually playing at one of his inauguration balls. A tour was held in 2009, following which Weir and Lesh decided to form a new band under the name Furthur, which continued until 2014. While there was only the one release by The Other Ones – and The Dead and Furthur didn't release any commercial product – the bands were followed closely by fans, the tape trading networks of the 1970s and 1980s now online and exchanging files, the shows remaining interesting by not only incorporating classic Dead material, but supplemented with new cover versions and guest appearances from the now much-wider pool of Dead-associated musicians, along with bigger names like Elvis Costello and Branford Marsalis.

While the Fare Thee Well shows in 2015 marked the final performances of Lesh, Weir, Hart and Kreutzmann together, a new band came into being shortly after. Dead & Company features Weir, Hart and Kreutzmann, but with Oteil Burbridge – formerly of The Allmans – on bass, RatDog's Jeff Chimenti on keyboards, and solo artist John Mayer on guitar. Mayer had become aware of The Dead, and he invited Weir to perform with him on *The Late Late Show* in 2015. A one-off show in October 2015 at Madison Square Garden led to a full tour, and more dates followed in 2016. They've continued to tour every year since, and although 2020 dates were cancelled on account of COVID-19, shows resumed in May 2021. While, again, they have not released any studio material, their shows have been released on CD and on streaming platforms. So far, Dead & Company are fulfilling the 'built to last' promise of the final Grateful Dead studio album.

Even before The Grateful Dead finally left the stage, the significance of their recorded body of work had become apparent, with several archive releases emerging while they were still touring. But in the subsequent decades, these releases have not only maintained the band's reputation and their following, but they've caused many to reassess the band's work and consider it in different ways that may not have been apparent at the time. With distance and hindsight, new perspectives emerge as some of the negative attributes that surrounded The Dead fade from memory.

Foremost among the posthumous releases is 2019's *Ready Or Not*: a collection that approximates what a final Grateful Dead album might have been like. Featuring nine of their later songs, they're taken from live performances in the 1990s, including two from the same show at Madison Square Garden in 1994. Had they completed a studio follow-up to *Built To Last,* these songs would've probably been included. They had begun work in 1992, but the sessions didn't progress far, and the recordings were far from complete, with no vocals from Garcia on the numbers he would've sung and only basic guitar work laid down. Any attempt to complete the album by surviving band members would've made Garcia's lack of involvement apparent, and using a replacement guitarist would've been beyond the pale. Consequently, live versions of the unreleased songs were used. Fans will forever debate what should've been included (some later songs such as 'Wave To The Wind' and 'Childhood's End' are missing) and whether the best versions were used, but *Ready Or Not* probably gives as close a picture as we'll likely ever get of a final

Dead album. Some pieces sparkle: 'So Many Roads' and 'Days Between' are as good as anything on an *official* release. 'Samba In The Rain' and 'Corrina', less so. The particularly ugly cover, cheapens what should've been a more respectful release.

Another earlier sketch of what this final album might've been like, can be found on the *So Many Roads (1965-1995)* five-CD collection released in 1999. Disc five features live versions of 'Way To Go Home' and 'Liberty', rehearsals of 'Lazy River Road', 'Eternity', 'Days Between', 'Whiskey In The Jar', and a live take of 'So Many Roads' from their final show in 1995. While the live versions of the songs on *Ready Or Not* are more finished, there's a real charm in hearing the rehearsals, especially 'Whiskey In The Jar'. The rest of the *So Many Roads (1965-1995)* collection merits the admission price, with the material that spans their career from early Emergency Crew demos to their final show, being mostly previously unreleased, some of its contents coming out on later releases. It's a great cross-section of their career and includes material that still hasn't appeared elsewhere.

One of the first themed collections of live Dead material was 1997's *Fallout From The Phil Zone*, with live tracks spanning from 1967's *In The Midnight Hour* to 1995's *Visions of Johanna,* over two discs. If Lesh, perhaps unfairly, was criticised for his track selection for *Steal Your Face*, he more than made up for it here. Opening with 'Dancing In The Street' from 12 April 1970 – the Fillmore West show where they were supported by Miles Davis – the collection features both covers and original Dead songs, with the exception of 'The Music Never Stopped', the selection of Dead material centring on the songs created during their *Workingman's Dead/American Beauty* period. If there's a standout track, it has to be the version of 'In The Midnight Hour' recorded at Dance Hall, Rio Nido on 3 September 1967. In the sleeve notes, Phil comments that it's the longest version of the track he was able to find in the archives. At just over 30 minutes long, it's close enough in playing time to follow 'Dark Star' and 'Playing In The Band' as a one-track album release. The only song written by Lesh himself in the collection is the closing track 'Box Of Rain': recorded in 1989. Some of the material has since appeared on other releases: *Dave's Picks Volume 30, Road Trips Vol ume 3 Number 3, May '77* and *Weir Here*. Other subsequent releases have featured additional tracks from the shows that material on this collection originated from, such as *Dick's Picks Volume 26, Dick's Picks Volume35, Road Trips Volume 1 Number 3* and *Downhill From Here*. For other tracks, this release is their only official outing. This, and the fact it was curated by Lesh – giving insight into the moments when a key band member thought they were at their best – makes it a popular release among fans.

If *Fallout From The Phil Zone* was held together by the common thread of Phil's choice, the theme of 2002's *Postcards Of The Hanging* was more obvious – the collection billed on its cover as Grateful Dead Perform The Songs Of Bob Dylan: perhaps a nod to the 1979 *The Byrds Play Dylan* album. *Dylan And*

The Dead may have been a disappointment as an album, but The Dead's love of Dylan's art has been there since Hunter and Garcia began frequenting folk clubs in the early-1960s, and Dylan covers have been a staple of The Dead's live sets throughout their career. The material included is predominantly from 1980s performances, but also includes a rare performance of 'It Takes A Lot To Laugh, It Takes A Train To Cry' dating from June 1973 at RFK Stadium and featuring members of the Allman Brothers Band, and 'Desolation Row': an unreleased track from the *Without A Net/Spring 1990* Knickerbocker Arena, New York gig on 24 March 1990. A rehearsal version of 'Man Of Peace' from 1987, featuring Dylan himself on vocals, closes the set and ensures the album's place in every Dylan fanatic's collection. The majority of the versions on the album have not been released elsewhere, and the sharp selection of Dylan songs featured – the majority originally appearing on *Bringing It All Back Home* or *Highway 61 Revisit*ed – helps rehabilitate the perception of the relationship between Dylan and The Dead that the *Dylan And The Dead* album failed to reflect.

A sister release to *Postcards Of The Hanging*, is the 2005-released double CD set *Garcia Plays Dylan,* which brings together previously unreleased live material by Garcia/Saunders, Legion Of Mary and The Jerry Garcia Band. There are also three late-period Grateful Dead performances of Dylan covers from 1989, 1990 and their final show in 1995, for good measure. The selection of Dylan material is wider than on *Postcards Of The Hanging*, with songs originally on *Planet Waves, John Wesley Harding, Blood On The Tracks, Blonde On Blonde, Street Legal* and others, while two songs – 'It's All Over Now, Baby Blue' and 'It Takes A Lot To Laugh, It Takes A Train To Cry' – appear on both, albeit in different versions. Jerry's choice of covers – whether with The Dead or in his solo projects – reveals he had the taste of a genuine Dylan fan. 'The Wicked Messenger' – performed by Legion Of Mary in 1975 and clocking in at over thirteen minutes – is a particular treat on this album, while versions of 'Senor (Tales Of Yankee Power)' and 'Visions Of Johanna' are underrated Dylan gems given the opportunity to shine. Garcia's reading of 'Positively 4th Street' – arguably Dylan at his most cynical – is carried off with aplomb.

There have been many multiple-disc box sets released in the years since The Dead left the stage, most capturing runs of shows over a particular time or place, but there's one that takes a far broader picture. Released in 2015 to mark the band's 50th anniversary, *30 Trips Around The Sun* collects one show from each of the 30 years the band were active. If, at the time of its release, *Europe '72* was regarded as an extravagant package, with three vinyl discs and colour insert, *30 Trips Around The Sun* took things to the extreme. Consisting of a full 80 discs of music, with a playing time of 73 hours, the complete package has more in common with a piece of furniture than any regular release. On top of the discs, there's a scroll, a book and a 7' single that features 'Caution (Do Not Stop On Tracks)' from their 1965 session, and 'Box Of Rain': the final song performed by the band at their final show in 1995. The shows included in this collection are discussed in the appropriate years in this book, and while some tracks did emerge in other places, the overwhelming majority of the content is exclusive to *30 Trips Around The Sun*. It's a quite extraordinary item, and was released in an edition of 6,500; a further thousand released as a USB stick with the music as FLAC and MP3 files. You'll have to look on online auction sites and the regularly-updated Discogs list of 'most expensive CDs' to track it down and also have a good relationship with your credit card provider to fund it. A more wallet-friendly four-disc compilation titled *30 Trips Around The Sun: The Definitive Live Story 1965-1995*, takes one track from each show and presents them in chronological order.

For most of the time they were active, only 1974's *Skeletons From the Closet: The Best Of The Grateful Dead* and the *What A Long Strange Trip It's Been* double album from 1977, served as 'greatest hits' collections. Perhaps not actually having any actual hits until years later was a factor. Both albums featured material from their Warner Bros. albums, and were released after they'd left the label, both collections serving as useful catch-up items for the new fans who weren't around when the material was originally released. *What A Long Strange Trip It's Been was* particularly useful by including on the discs inside its distinctive Rick Griffin gatefold sleeve, the single versions of 'Dark Star' and its B-side 'Born Cross-Eyed': both comparatively rare tracks to locate in the pre-internet late-1970s and 1980s.

Two more recent compilations are *The Best Of The Grateful Dead* and *The Best Of The Grateful Dead Live*: two separate two-discs sets that take a retrospective look at The Dead's output. The first, released in 2015, takes a chronological run through The Dead's studio back-catalogue, from 'The Golden Road (To Unlimited Devotion)' to 'Standing On The Moon', with one or more tracks from every album. The latter, from 2018, features live material predominantly from the live releases that came out during their career, but with tracks from *One From The Vault, Cornell 5/8/77, Crimson White And Indigo, Truckin' Up To Buffalo* and *So Many Roads (1965-1995)*. If you've got a friend who's curious about The Dead's reputation as a live band, it's as good a place as any for them to dip their feet before jumping into deeper water.

However, if there's one definitive Grateful Dead compilation, it has to be the soundtrack to the *Long Strange Trip* documentary. While not officially a compilation album *per se* (It is, after all, a soundtrack), it ticks all the boxes and delivers much more than it needs to: favourites, career-high points, rarities and a hit single. It's the kind of wide-ranging collection that encompasses both the studio version of 'Touch Of Grey' and an unreleased version of 'Dark Star' from the Fillmore East in 1970, without either seeming out of place. Over the three-disc set, there are tracks from the Château d'Hérouville in France from 1971, unreleased versions of 'Dear Mr. Fantasy' and 'Hey Jude' from 1989 during their peak stadium years, a live 'Stella Blue' from 1981, and 'Days Between' from 1994, unavailable elsewhere. The rest of the music has been expertly curated, with the content focusing (perhaps wisely) on live material from *Live/*

Dead, Sunshine Daydream, Cornell 5/8/77 and *Europe '72,* as well as studio material from *American Beauty, Workingman's Dead* and *In The Dark.* It's probably the only compilation that gives an indication of the scale and depth of The Grateful Dead's legacy.

Which brings us to the *Long Strange Trip* documentary series: a six-part series that featured on Amazon Prime in 2017. Directed by Amir Bar-Lev, it includes extraordinary footage from throughout The Dead's career, and features contributions from all the surviving significant figures in The Dead's story: musicians, managers, family, associates and fans. Weir, Lesh, Hart, Kreutzmann and Donna Jean Godchaux are all represented, along with archive footage of Garcia. Footage, including *Europe '72,* an early tip to England for the Hollywood Festival, home movies and archive footage from other sources, and photographs, illustrate the story. It doesn't shy away from some of the darker issues that surrounded the band. If, at times, it doesn't look great (the scenes outside the shows, the behaviour of the entourage or the state of Garcia), it's probably just an accurate reflection. It makes the case that the band went downhill after the death of Mydland; Garcia, in particular, under intense pressure to ensure the band continued, to the cost of his personal relationships, his drug dependency progressively consuming him. It simplifies and streamlines the narrative, but that's often how film works. It does, however, do it very well indeed. The montage over 'Death Don't Have No Mercy' towards the end is a powerful piece of cinema.

It won't be the last word on The Dead or on Garcia. While other films documented The Dead at the time – whether *The Grateful Dead Movie* or any of the video releases – a forthcoming high-profile biopic will cast more light on Garcia's life and legacy, and on the music and the artistry of The Grateful Dead. Meanwhile – whether in the archive releases or in the live performances of the former band members or their wider community – their songs continue to fill the air.

Appendix One – Contemporary live and studio releases and unfinished final album in order of release dates

The Grateful Dead (1967)
Personnel:
Jerry ('Captain Trips') Garcia: guitar, vocals
Bill The Drummer (Kreutzmann): drums, percussion
Phil Lesh: bass, vocals
Pigpen (Ron McKernan): keyboards, harmonica, vocals
Bob Weir: guitar, vocals
Recorded at RCA Studio A, Los Angeles and Coast Recorders, San Francisco, January 1967.
Produced by David Hassinger.
Release date: March 1967
Running time: 34:53
'The Golden Road (To Unlimited Devotion)' (McGannahan Skjellyfetti), 'Beat It On Down The Line' (Jesse Fuller), 'Good Morning, Little School Girl' (H.G. Demarais), 'Cold Rain And Snow' (McGannahan Skjellyfetti), 'Sittin' On Top Of The World' (Jacobs, Carter), 'Cream Puff War' (Jerry Garcia), 'Morning Dew' (Dobson, Rose), 'New, New Minglewood Blues' (McGannahan Skjellyfetti), 'Viola Lee Blues' (Noah Lewis)
2001 reissue bonus tracks: 'Alice D. Millionaire' (Grateful Dead), 'Overseas Stomp (Lindbergh Hop or The Lindy Hop)' (Jones, Shade) 'Tastebud' (Ron McKernan), 'Death Don't Have No Mercy' (Edited studio take) (Davis), 'Viola Lee Blues' (Edited version) (Noah Lewis), 'Viola Lee Blues' (Live) (Noah Lewis)
2017 50th Anniversary bonus CD (Recorded live at Garden Auditorium Vancouver, British Columbia July 29/30, 1966)
'Standing On The Corner' (Grateful Dead), 'I Know You Rider' (trad.), 'Next Time You See Me (Forest, Harvey), 'Sittin' On Top Of The World' (Jacobs, Carter), 'You Don't Have To Ask' (Grateful Dead), 'Big Boss Man' (Dixon, Smith), 'Stealin'' (Gus Cannon), 'Cardboard Cowboy' (Phil Lesh), 'It's All Over Now, Baby Blue' (Bob Dylan), 'Cream Puff War' (Garcia), 'Viola Lee Blues' (Noah Lewis), 'Beat It On Down The Line' (Jesse Fuller), 'Good Mornin' Little Schoolgirl' (H.G. Demarais), 'Cold Rain And Snow' (Obray Ramsey), 'One Kind Favor' (Blind Lemon Jefferson), 'Hey Little One' (Burnette, De Vorzon), 'New, New Minglewood Blues' (McGannahan Skjellyfetti)

Anthem Of The Sun (1968)
Personnel:
Jerry Garcia: lead guitar, acoustic guitar, kazoo, vibraslap
Mickey Hart: drums, orchestra bells, gong, chimes, crotales, prepared piano, finger cymbals
Bill Kreutzmann: drums, orchestra bells, gong, chimes, crotales, pared piano, finger cymbals
Phil Lesh: bass guitar, trumpet, harpsichord, guiro, kazoo, piano, timpani,
Ron McKernan: organ and celesta, claves,
Bob Weir: rhythm guitar, 12-string guitar, acoustic guitar, kazoo
Additional personnel:
Tom Constanten: prepared piano, piano, electronic tape
Recorded at RCA Victor Studio A, Hollywood (September 1967), American Recording Company, Studio City (October 1967), Century Sound Studio, New York (December 1967),

Olmstead Sound Studios, New York (December 1967). Live recordings from November 1967, January 1968 and February 1968). Produced by Grateful Dead and David Hassinger
Released July 1968
Running time: 38:57
'That's It For The Other One' l) 'Cryptical Envelopment' (Garcia) Il) 'Quadlibet For Tender Feet' (Garcia, Kreutzmann, Lesh, McKernan, Weir) lll) 'The Faster We Go, The Rounder We Get' (Kreutzmann, Weir) IV) 'We Leave The Castle' (Constanten), 'New Potato Caboose' (Lesh, Petersen), Born Cross-Eyed (Weir), 'Alligator' (Lesh, McKernan, Hunter), 'Caution (Do Not Stop On Tracks) (Garcia, Kreutzmann, Lesh, McKernan, Weir)
2001 reissue bonus tracks: 'Alligator' (Lesh, McKernan, Hunter), 'Caution (Do Not Stop On Tracks)' (live) (Garcia, Kreutzmann, Lesh, McKernan, Weir), 'Feedback' (live) (Grateful Dead), 'Born Cross-Eyed' (single version) (Weir),
2018 50th Anniversary Deluxe Edition bonus CD (Recorded live at Winterland Ballroom, San Francisco, October 22, 1967)
'Morning Dew' (Dobson, Rose), 'New Potato Caboose'   (Lesh, Petersen), 'It Hurts Me Too' (James, Sehorn) 'Cold Rain And Snow' (trad.), 'Turn On Your Lovelight' (Scott, Malone), 'Beat It On Down The Line' (Jesse Fuller), 'That's It For The Other One' (Garcia, Weir, Kreutzmann)

Aoxomoxoa (1969)

Personnel:
Tom Constanten: keyboards
Jerry Garcia: guitar, vocals
Mickey Hart: drums, percussion
Bill Kreutzmann: drums, percussion
Phil Lesh: bass, vocals
Ron McKernan: Pigpen
Bob Weir: guitar, vocals
Additional personnel:
John 'Marmaduke' Dawson, David Nelson, Peter Grant, Wendy, Debbie, Mouse
Recorded at Pacific Recording, San Mateo, and Pacific High Recording, San Francisco, September 1968 – March 1969. Produced by Grateful Dead.
Release date: June 1969
Running time: 36:00
'St. Stephen' (Garcia, Lesh, Hunter), 'Dupree's Diamond Blues' (Garcia, Hunter), 'Rosemary' (Garcia, Hunter), 'Doin' That Rag' (Garcia, Hunter), 'Mountains Of The Moon' (Garcia, Hunter), 'China Cat Sunflower' (Garcia, Hunter), 'What's Become Of The Baby' (Garcia, Hunter), 'Cosmic Charlie' (Garcia, Hunter)
2001 reissue bonus tracks (Pacific Recording Studios, August 13 1968): 'Clementine Jam' (Garcia, Hart, Kreutzmann, Lesh, McKernan, Weir), 'Nobody's Spoonful Jam'(Garcia, Hart, Kreutzmann, Lesh, McKernan, Weir), 'The Eleven Jam' (Garcia, Hart, Kreutzmann, Lesh, McKernan, Weir), 'Cosmic Charlie' (live) (Garcia, Hunter)
2019 50th Anniversary Deluxe Edition bonus CD (Recorded live at Avalon Ballroom, San Francisco January 24-26, 1969)
'New Potato Caboose' (Lesh, Petersen), 'Dupree's Diamond Blues' (Garcia, Hunter), 'Doin' That Rag' (Garcia, Hunter), 'Alligator'(Lesh, McKernan, Weir) 'Caution (Do Not Stop On Tracks)' (Garcia, Hart, Kreutzmann, Lesh, McKernan, Weir), 'Feedback' (Garcia, Hart, Kreutzmann, Lesh, McKernan, Weir), 'And We Bid You Goodnight' (trad.), 'Clementine' (Lesh, Hunter), 'Death Don't Have No Mercy' (Rev. Gary Davis)

Live/Dead (1969)
Personnel:
Tom Constanten: organ
Jerry Garcia: guitar, vocals
Mickey Hart: drums, percussion
Bill Kreutzmann: drums, percussion
Phil Lesh: electric bass, vocals
Ron 'Pigpen' McKernan: vocals, congas, organ on 'Death Don't Have No Mercy'
Bob Weir: guitar, vocals
Recorded live on January 26, February 27 and March 2, 1969, at the Avalon Ballroom and the Fillmore West, San Francisco. Produced by Grateful Dead, Bob Matthews, Betty Cantor.
Release date: November 1969
Running time: 75:07
'Dark Star' (Garcia, Hart, Hunter, Kreutzmann, Lesh, McKernan, Weir), 'St. Stephen' (Garcia, Lesh, Hunter), 'The Eleven' (Hunter, Lesh), 'Turn On Your Lovelight' (Malone, Scott), 'Death Don't Have No Mercy' (Rev. Gary Davis), 'Feedback' (Constanten, Garcia, Hart, Kreutzmann, Lesh, McKernan, Weir), 'And We Bid You Goodnight' (trad, arr. by Grateful Dead)
2001 reissue bonus tracks: 'Dark Star' (single version) (Garcia, Hunter) *'Live/Dead* radio promo'

Workingman's Dead (1970)
Personnel:
Tom Constanten: keyboards (re-issue bonus live material tracks 2 – 6 only)
Jerry Garcia: lead guitar, pedal steel guitar, banjo, vocals
Mickey Hart: drums, percussion (except 50th anniversary live discs)
Bill Kreutzmann: drums, percussion
Phil Lesh: bass, vocals
Ron 'Pigpen' McKernan: keyboards, harmonica, vocals, lead vocals on 'Easy Wind'
Bob Weir: guitar, vocals
Additional personnel:
David Nelson: Acoustic guitar on 'Cumberland Blues'
Recorded at Pacific High Recording, San Francisco, February 1970. Produced by Bob Matthews, Betty Cantor and Grateful Dead.
Release date: June 1970
Running time: 35:33
'Uncle John's Band' (Garcia, Hunter), 'High Time' (Garcia, Hunter), 'Dire Wolf' (Garcia, Hunter), 'New Speedway Boogie' (Garcia, Hunter), 'Cumberland Blues' (Garcia, Lesh, Hunter), 'Black Peter' (Garcia, Hunter), 'Easy Wind' (Hunter), 'Casey Jones' (Garcia, Hunter)
2001 reissue bonus tracks: 'New Speedway Boogie' (alternate mix) (Garcia, Hunter), 'Dire Wolf' (live) (Garcia, Hunter), 'Black Peter' (live) (Garcia, Hunter), 'Easy Wind' (live) (Hunter), 'Cumberland Blues' (live) (Garcia, Hunter), 'Mason's Children' (live) 'Garcia, Lesh, Weir, Hunter), 'Uncle John's Band' (live) (Garcia, Hunter), Radio promo
2020 50th Anniversary Deluxe Edition bonus CDs (Recorded live at Capitol Theatre, Port Chester, New York, February 21, 1971)
'Cold Rain And Snow' (trad.), 'Me And Bobby McGee' (Kristofferson, Foster), 'Loser' (Garcia, Hunter), 'Easy Wind' (Hunter), 'Playing In The Band' (Weir, Hart, Hunter), 'Bertha' (Garcia, Hunter), 'Me And My Uncle' (John Phillips), 'Ripple' (false start) (Garcia, Hunter),

'Ripple' (Garcia, Hunter), 'Next Time You See Me' (Forest, Harvey), 'Sugar Magnolia' (Weir, Hunter), 'Greatest Story Ever Told' (Weir, Hunter), 'Johnny B. Goode' (Chuck Berry), 'China Cat Sunflower' (Garcia, Hunter), 'I Know You Rider' (trad.), 'Bird Song' (Garcia, Hunter), 'Cumberland Blues' (Garcia, Lesh, Hunter), 'I'm A King Bee' (Slim Harpo), 'Beat It On Down The Line' (Jesse Fuller), 'Wharf Rat' (Garcia, Hunter), 'Truckin'' (Garcia, Lesh, Weir, Hunter), 'Casey Jones' (Garcia, Hunter), 'Good Lovin'' (Resnick, Clark), 'Uncle John's Band' (Garcia, Hunter)

American Beauty (1970)

Personnel:
Jerry Garcia: guitar, pedal steel, piano, vocals
Mickey Hart : percussion
Robert Hunter: songwriter
Bill Kreutzmann: drums
Phil Lesh: bass, guitar, piano, vocals
Pigpen (Ron McKernan): harmonica, vocals
Bob Weir: guitar, vocals
Additional personnel:
David Grisman: mandolin on 'Friend Of The Devil', 'Ripple'
Ned Lagin: piano on 'Candyman'
David Nelson: electric guitar on 'Box Of Rain'
Dave Torbert: bass guitar on 'Box Of Rain'
Howard Wales: organ on 'Candyman', 'Truckin''; piano on 'Brokedown Palace'
Recorded live at Wally Heider Studios, San Francisco, August- September 1970. Produced by Grateful Dead, co-produced by Steve Barncard.
Release date: September 1971
Running time: 42:21
'Box Of Rain' (Lesh, Hunter), 'Friend Of The Devil' (Garcia, Dawson, Hunter), 'Sugar Magnolia' (Weir, Hunter), 'Operator' (McKernan), 'Candyman' (Garcia, Hunter), 'Ripple' (Garcia, Hunter), 'Brokedown Palace' (Garcia, Hunter), 'Till The Morning Comes' (Garcia, Hunter), 'Attics Of My Life' (Garcia, Hunter), 'Truckin'' (Garcia, Lesh, Weir, Hunter)
2001 reissue bonus tracks: 'Truckin'' (Single Version) (Garcia, Lesh, Weir, Hunter), 'Friend Of The Devil' (live) (Garcia, Dawson, Hunter), 'Candyman' (live) (Garcia, Hunter), 'Till the Morning Comes' (live), 'Attics Of My Life' (live) (Garcia, Hunter), 'Truckin'' (live) (Garcia, Lesh, Weir, Hunter), [hidden tracks]: 'Ripple' (Single Edit) (Garcia, Hunter), American Beauty radio promo
2020 50th Anniversary Deluxe Edition bonus CDs (Recorded live at Capitol Theatre, Port Chester, New York, February 18, 1971)
'Bertha' (Garcia, Hunter), 'Truckin'' (Garcia, Lesh, Weir, Hunter), 'It Hurts Me Too' (James, Red), 'Loser' (Garcia, Hunter), 'Greatest Story Ever Told' (Weir, Hunter), 'Johnny B. Goode' (Chuck Berry), 'Mama Tried' (Merle Haggard), 'Hard to Handle' (Isbell, Jones, Redding), 'Dark Star' (Hunter, Garcia, Mickey Hart, Kreutzmann, Lesh, McKernan, Weir), 'Wharf Rat' (Garcia, Hunter), 'Dark Star' (Hunter, Garcia, Mickey Hart, Kreutzmann, Lesh, McKernan, Weir), 'Me And My Uncle' (John Phillips), 'Casey Jones' (Garcia, Hunter), 'Playing In The Band' (Weir, Hart, Hunter), 'Me And Bobby McGee' (Kristofferson, Foster), 'Candyman' (Garcia, Hunter), 'Big Boss Man' (Dixon, Smith), 'Sugar Magnolia' (Weir, Hunter), 'St. Stephen' (Hunter, Garcia, Lesh), 'Not Fade Away' (Holly, Petty) 'Goin' Down the Road Feeling Bad' (trad.), 'Not Fade Away' (Holly, Petty), 'Uncle John's Band' (Garcia, Hunter)

Grateful Dead (AKA Skull And Roses) (1971)

Personnel:
Jerry Garcia: lead guitar, vocals
Bill Kreutzmann: drums
Phil Lesh: bass guitar, vocals
Ron 'Pigpen ' McKernan): organ harmonica, vocals
Bob Weir: rhythm guitar, vocals
Additional personnel:
Merl Saunders: organ on 'Bertha', 'Playing In The Band' and 'Wharf Rat'
Recorded live at Winterland Ballroom, Fillmore East and Hammerstein Ballroom, March 24, April 5-6 and April 26-29, 1970. Produced by Grateful Dead with Betty Cantor and Bob Matthews.
Release date: November 1970
Running time: 76:26
'Bertha' (Garcia, Hunter), 'Mama Tried' (Merle Haggard), 'Big Railroad Blues' (Noah Lewis), 'Playing In The Band' (Weir, Hunter), 'The Other One' (Weir, Kreutzmann), 'Me And My Uncle' (John Phillips), 'Big Boss Man' (Dixon, Smith), 'Me And Bobby McGee' (Foster, Kristofferson), 'Johnny B. Goode' (Chuck Berry), 'Wharf Rat'(Garcia, Hunter), 'Not Fade Away/Goin' Down the Road Feeling Bad' (Holly, Petty/trad.)
2001 reissue bonus tracks: (recorded live at Hammerstein Ballroom, April 6 1971): 'Oh, Boy!'(Petty, Bill, West), 'I'm A Hog for You' (Leiber, Stoller), *Grateful Dead* radio spot'
2021 50th Anniversary Deluxe Edition bonus CD (recorded live at the Fillmore West July 2, 1971): 'Good Lovin'' (Clark, Resnick), 'Sing Me Back Home' (Merle Haggard) 'Mama Tried' (Merle Haggard), 'Cryptical Envelopment' (Garcia) 'Drums' (Kreutzmann), 'The Other One' (Weir, Kreutzmann), 'Big Boss Man' (Smith, Dixon), 'Not Fade Away' (Holly, Petty), 'Goin' Down The Road Feeling Bad' (trad.), 'Not Fade Away' (Holly, Petty)

Europe '72 (1972)

Personnel:
Jerry Garcia: lead guitar, vocals, pedal steel guitar, organ
Donna Jean Godchaux: vocals
Keith Godchaux: piano
Robert Hunter: songwriter
Bill Kreutzmann: drums, percussion
Phil Lesh: bass guitar, vocals
Ron 'Pigpen' McKernan: organ, harmonica, vocals
Bob Weir: rhythm guitar, vocals
Recorded by Betty Cantor, Janet Furman, Bob Matthews, Rosie, Wizard April – May 1972.
Mixed by Betty Cantor, Bob Matthews
Release date: November 1972
Running time: 109:35
'Cumberland Blues' (Garcia, Lesh, Hunter), 'He's Gone' (Garcia, Hunter), 'One More Saturday Night' (Weir), 'Jack Straw' (Weir, Hunter), 'You Win Again' (Hank Williams), 'China Cat Sunflower' (Garcia, Hunter), 'I Know You Rider' (trad.), 'Brown Eyed Women' (Garcia, Hunter), 'Hurts Me Too' (James, Sehorn), 'Ramble On Rose '(Garcia, Hunter), 'Sugar Magnolia' (Weir, Hunter), 'Mr. Charlie' (McKernan, Hunter), 'Tennessee Jed' (Garcia, Hunter), 'Truckin'' (Garcia, Lesh, Weir, Hunter), 'Epilogue' (Grateful Dead), 'Prelude' (Grateful Dead), 'Morning Dew' (Rose, Dobson)

2003 reissue bonus tracks: 'The Stranger (Two Souls In Communion)' (McKernan), 'Looks Like Rain' (Weir, Barlow), 'Good Lovin'' (Resnick, Clark), 'Caution (Do Not Stop On Tracks)', (Garcia, Kreutzmann, Lesh, McKernan, Weir), 'Who Do You Love (Ellas McDaniel), 'Caution (Do Not Stop On Tracks)', (Garcia. Kreutzmann, Lesh, McKernan, Weir) 'Good Lovin'' (Resnick, Clark), 'Yellow Dog Story' (trad.)

History Of The Grateful Dead, Volume One (Bear's Choice) (1973)
Personnel:
Jerry Garcia: acoustic guitar, lead guitar, vocals
Bill Kreutzmann: drums
Phil Lesh: bass
Ron 'Pigpen' McKernan: acoustic guitar, organ, harmonica, percussion vocals
Bob Weir: acoustic guitar, electric guitar, vocals
Recorded live at the Fillmore East in New York City on February 13 and 14, 1970. Produced by Owsley Stanley.
Release date: July 1973
Running time: 47:28
'Katie Mae' (Lightnin' Hopkins), 'Dark Hollow' (Bill Browning), 'I've Been All Around This World' (trad.), 'Wake Up Little Susie' (Bryant, Bryant), 'Black Peter' (Garcia, Hunter), 'Smokestack Lightning' (Howlin' Wolf), 'Hard To Handle' (Bell, Jones, Redding)
2001 re-issue bonus tracks: 'Good Lovin'' (Clark, Resnick), 'Big Boss Man' (Smith, Dixon), 'Smokestack Lightning' (Howlin' Wolf), 'Sitting On Top Of The World' (Chatmon, Vinson)

Wake Of The Flood (1973)
Personnel:
Jerry Garcia: guitar, pedal steel guitar, vocals
Donna Jean Godchaux: vocals
Keith Godchaux: keyboards, vocals
Bill Kreutzmann: drums
Phil Lesh: bass guitar
Bob Weir: guitar, vocals
Additional personnel:
Bill Atwood: trumpet
Vassar Clements: violin
Joe Ellis: trumpet
Martin Fierro: saxophone (alto, tenor)
Sarah Fulcher: vocals
Matthew Kelly: harmonica
Frank Morin: saxophone (tenor)
Pat O'Hara: trombone
Doug Sahm: bajo sexto
Benny Velarde: timbales
Recorded at The Record Plant, Sausalito, California in August 1973. Produced by Grateful Dead.
Release date: October 1973
Running time: 45:34
'Mississippi Half-Step Uptown Toodeloo' (Garcia, Hunter), 'Let Me Sing Your Blues Away' (Godchaux, Hunter), 'Row Jimmy' (Garcia, Hunter), 'Stella Blue' (Garcia, Hunter), 'Here Comes Sunshine' (Garcia, Hunter), 'Eyes Of The World' (Garcia, Hunter), 'Weather Report

Suite': l) 'Prelude' (Weir), ll) 'Part I' (Eric Andersen, Weir), lll) 'Part II (Let it Grow)' (Barlow, Weir)

2004 reissue bonus tracks: 'Eyes Of The World' (live) (Garcia, Hunter), 'Weather Report Suite' (acoustic demo) (Weir, Andersen, Barlow), 'China Doll' (outtake) (Garcia, Hunter)

From The Mars Hotel (1974)

Personnel:
Jerry Garcia: guitar, pedal steel guitar, vocals
Donna Jean Godchaux: vocals
Keith Godchaux: keyboards, vocals
Bill Kreutzmann: drums
Phil Lesh: bass guitar
Bob Weir: guitar, vocals
Additional personnel:
Ned Lagin: synthesizers on 'Unbroken Chain'
John McFee: pedal steel guitar on 'Pride Of Cucamonga'
Recorded at CBS Studios, San Francisco, California in March and April 1974. Produced by Grateful Dead.
Release date: June 1974
Running time: 37:26

'U.S. Blues' (Garcia, Hunter), 'China Doll (Garcia, Hunter), Unbroken Chain (Lesh, Petersen), 'Loose Lucy' (Garcia, Hunter), 'Scarlet Begonias' (Garcia, Hunter), 'Pride Of Cucamonga' (Lesh, Petersen), 'Money Money' (Weir, Barlow), 'Ship Of Fools' (Garcia, Hunter)

2004 reissue bonus tracks: 'Loose Lucy' (alternate take) (Garcia, Hunter), 'Scarlet Begonias' (live) (Garcia, Hunter). 'Money Money' (live) (Weir, Barlow), 'Wave That Flag' (live) (Garcia, Hunter), 'Let It Rock' (live) (Chuck Berry), 'Pride Of Cucamonga' (acoustic demo) (Lesh, Petersen), Unbroken Chain (acoustic demo) (Lesh, Petersen)

Blues for Allah (1975)

Personnel:
Jerry Garcia: guitar, vocals
Donna Jean Godchaux: vocals
Keith Godchaux: keyboards, vocals
Mickey Hart: percussion, crickets
Bill Kreutzmann: drums, percussion
Phil Lesh: bass guitar
Bob Weir: guitar, vocals
Additional personnel:
Steve Schuster: flute, reeds
Recorded at Ace's, Mill Valley, California, February – May 1975. Produced by Grateful Dead.
Release date: September 1975
Running time: 44:13

Help On The Way' (Garcia, Hunter), 'Slipknot!' (Garcia, Godchaux, Kreutzmann, Lesh, Weir), Franklin's Tower (Garcia, Kreutzmann, Hunter), 'King Solomon's Marbles': l) 'Stronger Than Dirt' (Lesh), ll) 'Milkin' the Turkey' (Hart, Kreutzmann, Leash), 'The Music Never Stopped' (Weir, Barlow), 'Crazy Fingers' (Garcia, Hunter), 'Sage And Spirit' (Weir), 'Blues For Allah' (Garcia, Hunter), 'Sand Castles And Glass Camels' (Garcia, Godchaux, Godchaux, Hart, Kreutzmann), 'Unusual Occurrences In The Desert'

2004 reissue bonus tracks: 'Groove #1' (instrumental outtake) (Garcia, Godchaux, Hart, Kreutzmann, Lesh, Weir), Groove #2 (instrumental outtake) (Garcia, Godchaux, Hart, Kreutzmann, Lesh, Weir), Distorto (instrumental outtake) (Garcia), A to E Flat Jam (instrumental outtake) (Garcia, Godchaux, Hart, Kreutzmann, Lesh, Weir), Proto 18 Proper (instrumental outtake) (Garcia, Godchaux, Hart, Kreutzmann, Lesh, Weir), Hollywood Cantata (studio outtake) (Hunter, Weir)

Steal Your Face (1976)

Personnel:
Jerry Garcia: guitar, vocals
Donna Jean Godchaux: vocals
Keith Godchaux: keyboards, vocals
Mickey Hart: drums on 'Promised Land'
Bill Kreutzmann: drums
Phil Lesh: bass guitar
Bob Weir: guitar, vocals
Recorded live at the Winterland Ballroom, San Francisco on October 17 – 20, 1974.
Produced by Grateful Dead.
Release date: June 1976
Running time: 84:13
'Promised Land' (Chuck Berry), 'Cold Rain and Snow' (trad.), 'Around And Around' (Chuck Berry), 'Stella Blue' (Garcia, Hunter), 'Mississippi Half-Step Uptown Toodeloo' (Garcia, Hunter) 'Ship Of Fools' (Garcia, Hunter), 'Beat It On Down the Line' (Jesse Fuller), 'Big River' (Johnny Cash), 'Black-Throated Wind' (Barlow, Weir), 'U.S. Blues' (Garcia, Hunter), 'El Paso' (Marty Robbins), 'Sugaree' (Garcia, Hunter), 'It Must Have Been the Roses' (Hunter), 'Casey Jones' (Garcia, Hunter)

Terrapin Station (1977)

Personnel:
Jerry Garcia: guitar, vocals
Donna Jean Godchaux: vocals
Keith Godchaux: keyboards, pianos, synthesizers, vocals
Mickey Hart: drums, vibes
Bill Kreutzmann: drums
Phil Lesh: bass guitar
Bob Weir: guitar, vocals
Additional personnel
Paul Buckmaster: orchestral arrangements
The English Choral
The Martyn Ford Orchestra
Tom Scott: lyricon, saxophones on 'Estimated Prophet'
Recorded November 2, 1976 – May 8, 1977 at Sound City Studios, Van Nuys, California and at Automated Sound Studios, New York City. Additional recording at AIR Studios, London; Trident Studios, London; Abbey Road Studios, London. Produced by Keith Olsen.
Release date: July 1977
Running time: 35:38
'Estimated Prophet' (Weir, Barlow), 'Dancin' In The Streets' (Stevenson, Gaye, Hunter), 'Passenger' (Lesh, Monk), 'Samson And Delilah' (trad.), 'Sunrise' (Donna Godchaux), 'Terrapin Part 1': 'Lady With A Fan' (Garcia, Hunter), 'Terrapin Station' (Garcia, Hunter),

'Terrapin' (Garcia, Hunter), 'Terrapin Transit' (Hart, Kreutzmann), 'At A Siding' (Hart, Hunter), 'Terrapin Flyer' (Hart, Kreutzmann), 'Refrain' (Garcia)
2004 reissue bonus tracks: 'Peggy-O' (trad.), 'The Ascent' ((Garcia, Godchaux, Hart, Kreutzmann, Lesh, Weir), 'Catfish John (McDill, Reynolds), Equinox (Lesh), 'Fire On The Mountain' (Hart, Hunter), 'Dancin' In The Streets '(live) (Stevenson, Gaye, Hunter)

Shakedown Street (1978)
Personnel:
Jerry Garcia: guitar, vocals
Donna Jean Godchaux: vocals
Keith Godchaux: keyboards, vocals
Mickey Hart: drums, percussion
Bill Kreutzmann: drums, percussion
Phil Lesh: bass guitar
Bob Weir: guitar, vocals
Additional Personnel:
Jordan Amarantha: percussion
Lowell George: vocal on 'Good Lovin'' (outtake)
Matthew Kelly: harmonica
Steve Schuster: horn on 'From The Heart Of Me'
Recorded July – August 1978 at Club Front, San Rafael, California. Produced by Lowell George.
Release date: November 1978
Running time: 39:04
'Good Lovin'' (Clark, Resnick), 'France', (Hart, Hunter, Weir), 'Shakedown Street' (Garcia, Hunter), 'Serengetti' (Hart, Kreutzmann), 'Fire On The Mountain' (Hart, Hunter), 'I Need A Miracle' (Weir, Barlow), 'From The Heart Of Me' (Godchaux), 'Stagger Lee' (Garcia, Hunter), 'All New Minglewood Blues' (Noah Lewis), 'If I Had The World To Give' (Garcia, Hunter)
2004 reissue bonus tracks: 'Good Lovin'' (outtake), 'Ollin Arageed' (live in Egypt) (Hamza El Din), 'Fire On The Mountain' (live in Egypt) (Hart, Hunter), 'Stagger Lee' (live in Egypt) (Garcia, Hunter), 'All New Minglewood Blues' (live) (Noah Lewis)

Go To Heaven (1980)
Personnel:
Jerry Garcia: guitar, vocals
Mickey Hart: drums
Bill Kreutzmann: drums
Phil Lesh: bass guitar
Brent Mydland: keyboards, vocals
Bob Weir: guitar, vocals
Recorded July 1979 – January 1980 at Club Front, San Rafael, California. Produced by Gary Lyons.
Release date: April 1980
Running time: 38:19
'Alabama Getaway' (Garcia, Hunter), 'Far From Me' (Mydland), 'Althea' (Garcia, Hunter), 'Feel Like A Stranger' (Weir, Barlow), 'Lost Sailor' (Weir, Barlow), 'Saint Of Circumstance' (Weir, Barlow), 'Antwerp's Placebo (The Plumber)' (Hart, Kreutzmann), 'Easy To Love You' (Mydland, Barlow), 'Don't Ease Me In' (trad.)
2004 reissue bonus tracks: 'Peggy-O' (trad.), 'What'll You Raise' (Garcia, Hunter), 'Jack-

A-Roe' (trad.), 'Althea' (live) (Garcia, Hunter), 'Lost Sailor' (live) (Weir, Barlow), 'Saint of Circumstance' (Weir, Barlow)

Reckoning (1981)
Personnel:
Jerry Garcia: guitar, vocals
Mickey Hart: drums
Bill Kreutzmann: drums
Phil Lesh: bass guitar
Brent Mydland: keyboards, vocals
Bob Weir: guitar, vocals
Recorded live Sept 25 – October 31 at the Warfield Theatre, San Francisco and at the Radio City Music Hall, New York City. Produced by Dan Healy, Betty Cantor-Jackson and Jerry Garcia.
Release date: April 1981
Running time: 72:21
'Dire Wolf' (Garcia, Hunter), 'The Race Is On' (Don Rollins), 'Oh Babe, It Ain't No Lie' (Elizabeth Cotten), 'It Must Have Been the Roses' (Hunter), 'Dark Hollow' (Bill Browning), 'China Doll' (Garcia, Hunter), 'Been All Around This World' (trad.), 'Monkey And The Engineer' (Jesse Fuller), 'Jack-A-Roe' (trad.), 'Deep Elem Blues' (trad.), 'Cassidy' (Weir, Barlow), 'To Lay Me Down' (Garcia, Hunter), 'Rosalie McFall' (Charlie Monroe), 'On the Road Again'(trad.), 'Bird Song' (Garcia, Hunter), 'Ripple' (Garcia, Hunter)
 2004 reissue bonus disc: 'To Lay Me Down' (Studio Rehearsal) (Garcia, Hunter), 'Iko Iko' (Crawford, Hawkins, Hawkins, Johnson), 'Heaven Help The Fool' (instrumental) (Weir, Barlow), 'El Paso' (Marty Robbins), 'Sage And Spirit' (Weir), 'Little Sadie' (trad.), 'It Must Have Been The Roses' (alternate live version) (Hunter), 'Dark Hollow' (alternate live version), 'Jack-A-Roe' (alternate live version)(trad.), 'Cassidy' (alternate live version) (Weir, Barlow), 'China Doll' (alternate live version) (Garcia, Hunter), 'Monkey And The Engineer' (alternate live version) (Jesse Fuller), 'Oh Babe It Ain't No Lie' (alternate live version) (Cotten), 'Ripple' (alternate live version) (Garcia, Hunter), 'Tom Dooley' (trad.), 'Deep Elem Blues' (alternate live version) (trad.)

Dead Set (1981)
Personnel:
Jerry Garcia: guitar, vocals
Mickey Hart: drums
Bill Kreutzmann: drums
Phil Lesh: bass guitar
Brent Mydland: keyboards, vocals
Bob Weir: guitar, vocals
Recorded live Sept 25 – October 31 at the Warfield Theatre, San Francisco and at the Radio City Music Hall, New York City. Produced by Dan Healy, Betty Cantor-Jackson and Jerry Garcia.
Release date: August 1981
Running time: 73:51
'Samson And Delilah' (trad.), 'Friend Of The Devil' (Garcia, Dawson, Hunter), 'New Minglewood Blues' (trad.), 'Deal' (Garcia, Hunter), 'Candyman' (Garcia, Hunter), 'Little Red Rooster' (Willie Dixon), 'Loser' (Garcia, Hunter), 'Passenger' (Lesh, Monk), 'Feel Like A Stranger' (Weir, Barlow), 'Franklin's Tower' (Garcia, Kreutzmann, Hunter), 'Rhythm Devils'

(Hart, Kreutzmann), 'Space' (LP and later CDs only), (Lesh, Mydland, Hart, Kreutzmann), 'Fire On The Mountain' (Hart, Hunter), 'Greatest Story Ever Told' (Hart, Weir, Hunter), 'Brokedown Palace' (Garcia, Hunter)
2004 reissue bonus disc: 'Let It Grow' (Weir, Barlow), 'Sugaree' (Garcia, Hunter), 'C.C. Rider' (trad.), 'Row Jimmy' (Garcia, Hunter), 'Lazy Lightnin'' (Weir, Barlow), 'Supplication' (Weir, Barlow). 'High Time' (Garcia, Hunter), 'Jack Straw' (Weir, Hunter), 'Shakedown Street' (Garcia, Hunter), 'Not Fade Away' (Hardin, Petty)

In The Dark (1987)
Personnel:
Jerry Garcia: guitar, vocals
Mickey Hart: drums, percussion
Bill Kreutzmann: drums
Phil Lesh: bass
Brent Mydland: keyboards, vocals
Bob Weir: guitar, vocals
Recorded January 1987 at Marin Veterans Memorial Auditorium, San Rafael, California.
Produced by Jerry Garcia and John Cutler.
Release date: July 1987
Running time: 40:37
'Touch Of Grey' (Garcia, Hunter), 'Hell In A Bucket' (Barlow, Weir), 'When Push Comes To Shove' (Garcia, Hunter), 'West L.A. Fadeaway' (Garcia, Hunter), 'Tons Of Steel' (Mydland), 'Throwing Stones' (Barlow, Weir), 'Black Muddy River'(Garcia, Hunter),
2004 reissue bonus disc: 'My Brother Esau' ('Touch Of Grey' b-side) (Weir, Barlow), 'West L.A. Fadeaway' (alternate version) (Garcia, Hunter), 'Black Muddy River' (studio outtake) (Garcia, Hunter), 'When Push Comes to Shove' (studio outtake) (Garcia, Hunter), 'Touch Of Grey' (studio outtake) (Garcia, Hunter), 'Throwing Stones' (live) (Barlow, Weir)

Dylan And The Dead (1989)
Personnel:
Bob Dylan: guitar, vocals
Jerry Garcia: guitar, vocals
Mickey Hart: drums
Bill Kreutzmann: drums
Phil Lesh: bass guitar
Brent Mydland: keyboards, vocals
Bob Weir: guitar, vocals
Recorded live in July 1987, Produced by John Cutler and Jerry Garcia
Release date: February 1989
Running time: 43:07
'Slow Train' (Bob Dylan), 'I Want You' (Bob Dylan), 'Gotta Serve Somebody' (Bob Dylan), 'Queen Jane Approximately' (Bob Dylan), 'Joey' (Dylan, Levy), 'All Along The Watchtower' (Bob Dylan), 'Knockin' On Heaven's Door' (Bob Dylan)

Built To Last (1989)
Personnel:
Jerry Garcia: guitar, vocals
Mickey Hart: drums, percussion
Bill Kreutzmann: drums

Phil Lesh: bass
Brent Mydland: keyboards, vocals
Bob Weir: guitar, vocals
Recorded February – October 1989 at Club Front, San Rafael, California. Produced by John Cutler and Jerry Garcia
Release date: October 1989
Running time: 49:52
'Foolish Heart' (Garcia, Hunter), 'Just A Little Light' (Barlow, Mydland), 'Built To Last' (Garcia, Hunter), 'Blow Away' (Barlow, Mydland), 'Victim Or The Crime' (Graham, Weir), 'We Can Run' (Barlow, Mydland), 'Standing On The Moon' (Garcia, Hunter), 'Picasso Moon' (Barlow, Bralove, Weir), 'I Will Take You Home' (Barlow, Mydland)
2004 reissue bonus material: 'Foolish Heart' (live) (Garcia, Hunter), 'Blow Away' (live) (Barlow, Mydland), 'California Earthquake (Whole Lotta Shakin' Goin' On)' (live) (Rodney Crowell)

Without A Net (1990)
Personnel:
Jerry Garcia: guitar, vocals
Mickey Hart: drums
Bill Kreutzmann: drums
Phil Lesh: bass, vocals
Brent Mydland: keyboards, vocals
Bob Weir: guitar, vocals
Recorded live October 1989 – April 1990. Produced by John Cutler and Phil Lesh
Release date: September 1990
Running time: 131:56
'Feel Like A Stranger' (Barlow, Weir), 'Mississippi Half-Step Uptown Toodeloo' (Garcia, Hunter), 'Walkin' Blues' (Robert Johnson), 'Althea' (Garcia, Hunter), 'Cassidy' (Barlow, Weir), 'Bird Song' (Garcia, Hunter), 'Let It Grow' (Barlow, Weir), 'China Cat Sunflower'/'I Know You Rider' (Hunter, Garcia/trad.), 'Looks Like Rain' (Barlow, Weir), 'Eyes Of The World' (Garcia, Hunter), 'Victim Or The Crime' (Graham, Weir), 'Help On The Way/Slipknot!/Franklin's Tower' (Hunter, Garcia/Grateful Dead/Hunter, Garcia, Kreutzmann) 'One More Saturday Night' (Weir), 'Dear Mr. Fantasy' (Capaldi, Winwood, Wood)

Infrared Roses (1991)
Personnel:
Jerry Garcia: guitar, synthesizer, electronic percussion
Mickey Hart: drums
Bill Kreutzmann: drums
Phil Lesh: bass, synthesizer
Brent Mydland: keyboards, rattles, synthesizer, tom-tom
Bob Weir: guitar, marimba, synthesizer
Vince Welnick: synthesizer
Additional personnel:
Deadheads on 'Crowd Scuplture'
Willie Green lll: kick, snare, hat on 'Post-Modern Highrise Table Top Stomp'
Dan Healy: processing on 'Sparrow Hawk Row'
Bob Bralove: drum machine on 'River Of Nine Sorrows'
Branford Marsalis: saxophone on 'Apollo At The Ritz'

Recorded live 1989 -1990. Produced by Bob Bralove
Release date: November 1991
Running time: 58:18
'Crowd Sculpture' (Bralove), 'Parallelogram' (Hart, Kreutzmann), 'Little Nemo In Nightland' (Bralove, Garcia, Lesh, Weir), 'Riverside Rhapsody' (Garcia, Hart, Kreutzmann, Lesh, Mydland, Weir), 'Post-Modern Highrise Table Top Stomp' (Garcia, Green, Hart, Kreutzmann, Lesh, Mydland, Weir), 'Infrared Roses' (Bralove, Garcia, Lesh, Mydland, Weir), 'Silver Apples Of The Moon' (Hornsby, Welnick), 'Speaking In Swords' (Bralove, Hart, Kreutzmann), 'Magnesium Night Light' (Garcia, Lesh, Mydland, Weir), 'Sparrow Hawk Row' (Bralove, Garcia, Healy, Hart, Kreutzmann, Lesh, Mydland, Weir), 'River Of Nine Sorrows' (Bralove, Hart, Kreutzmann), 'Apollo At The Ritz' (Garcia, Hart, Kreutzmann, Lesh, Marsalis, Mydland, Weir)

Grayfolded (1994/1995)
Personnel:
Tom Constanten: keyboards
Jerry Garcia: lead guitar , vocals
Donna Jean Godchaux: vocals
Keith Godchaux: keyboards
Mickey Hart: drums
Bruce Hornsby: piano, keyboard, vocals
Bill Kreutzmann: drums
Phil Lesh: bass, vocals
Ron 'Pigpen' McKernan: keyboards, vocals, harmonica, percussion
Brent Mydland: keyboards, vocals
John Oswald: arranger
Bob Weir: rhythm guitar, vocals
Vince Welnick: keyboards, vocals
Recorded live 1968 -1993. Produced by John Oswald
Release date: First disc: 'Transitive Axis' 1994, second disc 'Mirror Ashes' 1995
Running time: 109:53
'Transitive Axis': 'Novature (Formless Nights Fall)' (Skyjellyfetti, Oswald), 'Pouring Velvet' (Skyjellyfetti, Oswald), 'In Revolving Ash Light' (Skyjellyfetti, Oswald), 'Clouds Cast' (Skyjellyfetti, Oswald), 'Through' (Skyjellyfetti, Oswald), 'Fault Forces' (Skyjellyfetti, Oswald), 'The Phil Zone' (Skyjellyfetti, Oswald), 'La Estrella Oscura' (Skyjellyfetti, Oswald), 'Recedes (While We Can)' (Skyjellyfetti, Oswald), 'Mirror Ashes': 'Fold' (Skyjellyfetti, Oswald), 'Transilience'(Skyjellyfetti, Oswald), '73rd Star Bridge Sonata' (Skyjellyfetti, Oswald), 'Cease Tone Beam' (Skyjellyfetti, Oswald), 'The Speed of Space' (Skyjellyfetti, Oswald), 'Dark Matter Problem/Every Leaf Is Turning' (Skyjellyfetti, Oswald), 'Foldback Time' (Skyjellyfetti, Oswald)

Ready Or Not (2019) [unreleased final album compiled from live recordings]
Personnel:
Jerry Garcia: guitar, vocals
Mickey Hart: drums
Bill Kreutzmann: drums
Phil Lesh: bass, vocals
Bob Weir: guitar, vocals

Vince Welnick: keyboards, vocals
Recorded live June 1992 – April 1995. Produced by Grateful Dead, produced for release by David Lemieux.
Release date: November 2019
Running time: 75:53
'Liberty' (Garcia, Hunter), 'Eternity' (Weir, Wasserman, Dixon), 'Lazy River Road' (Garcia, Hunter), 'Samba In The Rain' (Welnick, Hunter), 'So Many Roads' (Garcia, Hunter), 'Way To Go Home' (Welnick, Bralove, Hunter), 'Corrina' (Weir, Hart, Hunter), 'Easy Answers' (Hunter, Bralove, Weir, Welnick, Wasserman), 'Days Between' (Garcia, Hunter)

Appendix Two – Archive releases in order of recording date

1965
Birth Of The Dead (2003)
Personnel:
Jerry Garcia: guitar, vocals
Bill Kreutzmann: drums
Phil Lesh: bass guitar, vocals
Ron McKernan: organ, harmonica, vocals
Bob Weir: guitar, vocals
Additional personnel:
Jon Hendricks: vocals on 'Fire In The City'
Recorded: Tracks one to six; November 1965, Golden Gate Recorders, San Francisco.
Produced by Tom Donahue and Bobby Mitchell. Tracks seven to sixteen; June 1966 Buena
Vista Studio, San Francisco and Western Recordings, San Francisco. Producer/engineer:
Gene Estribou. Track seventeen; March 1967, Columbus Recorders, San Francisco.
Producer/arranger: Jon Hendricks. Tracks eighteen to 31 recorded in 1966 at the Fillmore
Auditorium in San Francisco. Engineers: Owsley Stanley and Rock Scully.
Release date: March 2003
Running time: 126:57
'Early Morning Rain' (Gordon Lightfoot), 'I Know You Rider' (trad.), 'Mindbender
(Confusion's Prince)' (Garcia, Lesh), 'The Only Time Is Now' (Grateful Dead), 'Caution
(Do Not Stop On Tracks)' (Grateful Dead), 'Can't Come Down' (Grateful Dead), 'Stealin''
(Instrumental) (Gus Cannon), 'Stealin'' (with vocals) (Gus Cannon), 'Don't Ease Me In'
(instrumental) (trad.), 'Don't Ease Me In' (with vocals) (trad.), 'You Don't Have to Ask'
(Grateful Dead), 'Tastebud' (instrumental) (Ron McKernan), 'Tastebud' (with vocals) (Ron
McKernan), 'I Know You Rider' (trad.), 'Cold Rain And Snow' (instrumental) (trad.), 'Cold
Rain And Snow' (with vocals) (trad.), 'Fire In The City' (Peter Krug), 'Viola Lee Blues'
(Noah Lewis), 'Don't Ease Me In' (trad.), 'Rain In My Heart' (Naomi Neville), 'Sitting On
Top Of The World' (Vinson, Chatmon), 'It's All Over Now, Baby Blue' (Bob Dylan), 'I'm
A King Bee' (James Moore), 'Big Boss Man' (Dixon, Smith), 'Standing On The Corner'
(Grateful Dead), 'In The Pines' (Bryant, McMichen), 'Nobody's Fault But Mine' (Johnson),
'Next Time You See Me' (Forest, Harvey), 'One Kind Favor' (Hopkins, Taub), 'He Was A
Friend Of Mine' (trad.), 'Keep Rolling By' (trad.)

1966
Rare Cuts And Oddities 1966 (2005)
Personnel:
Jerry Garcia: guitar, vocals
Bill Kreutzmann: drums
Phil Lesh: electric bass, vocals
Ron 'Pigpen' McKernan: harmonica, vocals, organ
Bob Weir: guitar, vocals
Original recordings producer: Owsley Stanley. Track nine producer: Grateful Dead.
Compilation producer: David Lemieux. Tracks one-six and ten recorded early 1966. Tracks
seven-eight recorded March 1966. Track nine recorded late 1966. Tracks eleven-thirteen

recorded live February/March 1966. Tracks fourteen-fifteen recorded live at the Fillmore Auditorium, San Francisco, July 3 1966. Tracks sixteen-eighteen recorded live at the Danish Centre, Los Angeles, March 12 1966
Release date: March 2005
Running time: 78: 31
'Walking The Dog' (Rufus Thomas), 'You See A Broken Heart' (Pigpen), 'The Promised Land' (Chuck Berry), 'Good Lovin'' (Resnick, Clark), 'Standing On The Corner' (Grateful Dead), 'Cream Puff War' (Garcia), 'Betty And Dupree' (trad.), 'Stealin'' (Gus Cannon), 'Silver Threads And Golden Needles' (Reynolds, Rhondes), 'Not Fade Away' (Holly, Petty), 'Big Railroad Blues' (Noah Lewis), 'Sick And Tired' (Bartholomew, Kenner), 'Empty Heart' (Jagger, Jones, Richards, Watts, Wyman), 'Gangster Of Love' (Johnny 'Guitar' Watson), 'Don't Mess Up A Good Thing' (Oliver Sain), 'Hey Little One' (Burnette, De Vorzon), 'I'm A King Bee' (Slim Harpo), 'Caution (Do Not Stop On Tracks)' (Grateful Dead)

July 29 1966, P.N.E. Garden Aud., Vancouver Canada (2017)
Personnel:
Jerry Garcia: lead guitar, vocals
Bill Kreutzmann: drums
Phil Lesh: bass guitar, vocals
Ron 'Pigpen' McKernan: organ, harmonica, vocals
Bob Weir: rhythm guitar, vocals
Recorded live at the P.N.E. Garden Auditorium, Vancouver, British Columbia, Canada July 29, 1966 (tracks one-thirteen). Tracks fourteen-seventeen recorded at same venue on July 30, 1966) Produced by Grateful Dead, produced for release by David Lemieux. Recording by Owsley Stanley.
Release date: April 2017
'Standing On The Corner' (Garcia, Weir, McKernan, Lesh, Kreutzmann), 'I Know You Rider' (trad.), 'Next Time You See Me' (Forest, Harvey), 'Sittin' On Top Of The World' (Jacobs, Carter), 'You Don't Have To Ask' (Garcia, Weir, McKernan, Lesh, Kreutzmann), 'Big Boss Man' (Dixon, Smith), 'Stealin'' (Gus Cannon), 'Cardboard Cowboy' (Lesh), 'It's All Over Now, Baby Blue' (Bob Dylan), 'Cream Puff War' (Garcia), 'Viola Lee Blues' (Noah Lewis), 'Beat It On Down The Line' (Jesse Fuller), 'Good Mornin' Little Schoolgirl' (Sonny Boy Williamson), 'Cold Rain And Snow' (trad.), 'One Kind Favor' (Bihari, Hopkins), 'Hey Little One' (Burnette, De Vorzon), 'New, New Minglewood Blues' (Garcia, Weir, McKernan, Lesh, Kreutzmann)

Vintage Dead (1970)
Personnel:
Jerry Garcia: lead guitar, vocals
Bill Kreutzmann: drums
Phil Lesh: bass guitar, vocals
Ron 'Pigpen' McKernan: organ, harmonica, vocals
Bob Weir: rhythm guitar, vocals
Recorded live at the Avalon Ballroom, San Francisco, September 1966. Production and engineering: Robert Cohen. Editing and remixing: Richard Delvy.
Release date: October 1970
Running time: 39:50
'I Know You Rider' (trad.), 'It Hurts Me Too' (Elmore James), 'It's All Over Now, Baby Blue' (Bob Dylan), 'Dancing In The Street' (Gaye, Hunter, Stevenson), 'In The Midnight Hour' (Cropper, Pickett)

Historic Dead (1971)
Personnel:
Jerry Garcia: lead guitar, vocals
Bill Kreutzmann: drums
Phil Lesh: bass guitar, vocals
Ron 'Pigpen' McKernan: organ, harmonica, vocals,
Bob Weir: rhythm guitar, vocals
Recorded live at the Avalon Ballroom, San Francisco, September 1966. Production and engineering: Robert Cohen. Editing and remixing: Richard Delvy.
Release date: June 1971
Running time: 28:51
'Good Morning Little Schoolgirl' (Sonny Boy Williamson), 'Lindy' (Jones, Shade), 'Stealin'' (Cannon, Shade), 'The Same Thing' (Willie Dixon)

1967
Shrine Exposition Hall, Los Angeles, CA 11/10/1967 (2016)
Personnel:
Jerry Garcia: guitar, vocals
Mickey Hart: drums
Bill Kreutzmann: drums
Phil Lesh: bass, vocals
Ron 'Pigpen' McKernan: organ, harmonica, percussion, vocals
Bob Weir: guitar, vocals
Recorded live at the Shrine Exposition Hall in Los Angeles, California on November 10 1967. Produced for release by David Lemieux.
Release date: January 2016
Running time: 1:37:06
'Viola Lee Blues' (Noah Lewis), 'It Hurts Me Too' (Elmore James) 'Beat It On Down The Line' (Jesse Fuller), 'Morning Dew' (Dobson, Rose), 'Good Morning Little Schoolgirl' (Sonny Boy Williamson), 'That's It For The Other One: 'Cryptical Envelopment' (Garcia); 'The Other One' (Kreutzmann, Weir); 'Cryptical Envelopment' (reprise) (Garcia), 'New Potato Caboose' (Lesh, Petersen), 'Alligator' (Lesh, McKernan, Hunter), 'Caution (Do Not Stop On Tracks)' (part 1)(Garcia, Kreutzmann, Lesh, McKernan, Weir), 'Caution (Do Not Stop On Tracks) (part 2)' (Garcia, Kreutzmann, Lesh, McKernan, Weir)

1968
Road Trips Vol.2 No. 2 (2009)
Personnel:
Jerry Garcia: lead guitar, vocals
Mickey Hart: drums
Bill Kreutzmann: drums
Phil Lesh: electric bass, vocals
Ron 'Pigpen' McKernan: organ, vocals
Bob Weir: rhythm guitar, vocals
Recorded live at the Carousel Ballroom, San Francisco, on February 14 1968. Recorded by Dan Healy
Release date: March 2009
Running time: 156:48

'(Walk Me Out In The) Morning Dew' (Dobson, Rose), 'Good Morning Little School Girl' (Sonny Boy Williamson), 'Dark Star' (Grateful Dead, Hunter), 'China Cat Sunflower' (Garcia, Hunter), 'The Eleven' (Hunter, Lesh), 'Turn On Your Love Light' (Scott, Malone), [Bonus Material]: Viola Lee Blues' (Noah Lewis) [Eureka, California Jan. 20, 1968], Beat It On Down The Line' (Jesse Fuller) [Seattle, Washington, Jan. 23 1968], 'It Hurts Me Too' (Elmore James) [Seattle, Washington, Jan. 23 1968], 'Dark Star' (Grateful Dead, Hunter) (Portland, Oregon Feb. 2 1968], That's It For The Other One' (Garcia, Kreutzmann, Lesh, McKernan, Weir), 'New Potato Caboose' (Lesh, Petersen), 'Born Cross-Eyed' (Weir), 'Spanish Jam ' (The Grateful Dead), 'Alligator' (Lesh, McKernan, Hunter), 'Caution (Do Not Stop On Tracks)' (Garcia, Kreutzmann, Lesh, McKernan, Weir), 'Feedback' (Garcia, Kreutzmann, Lesh, McKernan, Weir), 'In The Midnight Hour' (Cropper, Pickett), [Bonus Disc: recorded live in January, 1968] 'Viola Lee Blues' (Noah Lewis) [Seattle, Washington, Jan. 23 1968], 'Good Morning Little School Girl' (Sonny Boy Williamson) [Eureka, California Jan. 20, 1968], 'New Potato Caboose' (Lesh, Petersen) [Eugene, Oregon Jan. 30, 1968], 'Dark Star' (Grateful Dead, Hunter) [Seattle, Washington, Jan. 23 1968], 'China Cat Sunflower' [Seattle, Washington, Jan. 23 1968, 'The Eleven' (Hunter, Lesh) [Seattle, Washington, Jan. 23 1968], 'Turn On Your Love Light' (Scott, Malone) [Seattle, Washington, Jan. 23 1968]

Download Series Vol. 6 (2005)
Personnel:
Jerry Garcia: lead guitar, vocals
Mickey Hart: drums
Bill Kreutzmann: drums
Phil Lesh: electric bass
Ron 'Pigpen' McKernan: vocals, organ, harmonica, percussion
Bob Weir: rhythm guitar, vocals
Recorded live at the Carousel Ballroom in San Francisco, on March 17, 1968. Recorded by Dan Healy.
Release date: October 2005
Running time: 77:43
'Turn On Your Lovelight' (Scott, Malone), 'That's It For The Other One' (Garcia, Kreutzmann, Weir), 'New Potato Caboose' (Petersen, Lesh), 'China Cat Sunflower' (Garcia, Hunter), 'The Eleven' (Hunter, Lesh), 'Caution (Do Not Stop On Tracks)' (Grateful Dead), 'Feedback' (Grateful Dead)

Two From The Vault (1992)
Personnel:
Jerry Garcia: guitar, vocals
Mickey Hart: percussion
Bill Kreutzmann: percussion
Phil Lesh: bass, vocals
Ron 'Pigpen' McKernan: keyboard, harmonica, vocals
Bob Weir: guitar, vocals
Recorded live at the Shrine Auditorium in Los Angeles, California on August 24 1968.
Produced by Dan Healy.
Release date: May 1992
Running time: 109:11
'Good Morning, Little Schoolgirl' (Sonny Boy Williamson), 'Dark Star' (Garcia, Lesh, McKernan, Weir, Hart, Kreutzmann, Hunter), 'St. Stephen' (Garcia, Lesh, Hunter), 'The Eleven'

(Lesh, Hunter), 'Death Don't Have No Mercy' (Rev. Gary Davis), 'That's It For The Other One' (Garcia, Kreutzmann, Weir), 'New Potato Caboose' (Lesh, Petersen), 'Turn On Your Lovelight' (Scott, Malone), '(Walk Me Out in The) Morning Dew' (Dobson, Rose), [Bonus tracks on 2007 edition, recorded August 23, 1968:] 'Alligator' (McKernan, Lesh, Hunter), 'Caution (Do Not Stop On Tracks)' (McKernan, Grateful Dead), 'Feedback' (Grateful Dead)

1969
Live at the Fillmore East 2-11-69 (1997)
Personnel:
Tom Constanten: organ
Jerry Garcia: lead guitar, vocals
Mickey Hart: drums
Bill Kreutzmann: drums
Phil Lesh: bass guitar. vocals
Ron 'Pigpen' McKernan: percussion, harmonica, vocals
Bob Weir: rhythm guitar, vocals
Recorded live at the Fillmore East, New York City, on February 11 1969. Produced and mixed by John Cutler and Phil Lesh.
Release date: October 1997
Running time: 2:01:14
'Good Morning Little Schoolgirl' (Sonny Boy Williamson), 'Cryptical Envelopment' (Garcia), 'The Other One' (Weir, Kreutzmann), 'Cryptical Envelopment' (Garcia), 'Doin' That Rag' (Garcia, Hunter), 'I'm A King Bee' (Moore), 'Turn On Your Lovelight' (Scott, Malone), 'Hey Jude' (Lennon, McCartney), Introduction by Bill Graham, 'Dupree's Diamond Blues' (Garcia, Hunter), 'Mountains Of The Moon' (Garcia, Hunter), 'Dark Star' (Garcia, Kreutzmann, Lesh, McKernan, Weir, Hunter), 'St. Stephen' (Garcia, Lesh, Hunter), 'The Eleven' (Lesh), 'Drums' (Kreutzmann, Hart), 'Caution (Do Not Stop On Tracks)' (Grateful Dead), 'Feedback' (Grateful Dead), 'And We Bid You Goodnight' (trad.)

Dick's Picks Vol.22 (2001)
Personnel:
Jerry Garcia: lead guitar, vocals
Bill Kreutzmann: drums
Phil Lesh: electric bass, vocals
Ron 'Pigpen' McKeran: organ, harmonica, percussion, vocals
Bob Weir: rhythm guitar, vocals
Recorded live at the Kings Beach Bowl, Kings Beach, California on February 23 and 24 1968.
Recorded by Dan Healy.
Release date: June 2001
Running time: 146:53
'Viola Lee Blues' (Noah Lewis), 'It Hurts Me Too' (Elmore James), 'Dark Star' (Hunter, Garcia, Hart, Kreutzmann, Lesh, McKernan, Weir), 'China Cat Sunflower' (Garcia, Hunter), 'The Eleven' (Hunter, Lesh), 'Turn On Your Lovelight' (Malone, Scott), 'Born Cross-Eyed' (Weir), 'Spanish Jam' (Grateful Dead), [Following are from February 24, 1968] 'Morning Dew' (Dobson, Rose), 'Good Morning Little Schoolgirl' (Sonny Boy Williamson), 'That's It For The Other One' (Garcia, Kreutzmann, Weir), 'New Potato Caboose' (Petersen, Lesh), 'Alligator' (Hunter, McKernan, Lesh), 'China Cat Sunflower' (Garcia, Hunter), 'The Eleven' (Hunter, Lesh), 'Alligator' (McKernan, Lesh), 'Caution (Do Not Stop On Tracks)', (Grateful Dead), 'Feedback' (Grateful Dead)

Fillmore West 1969: The Complete Recordings (2005)

Personnel:
Tom Constanten: keyboards
Jerry Garcia: lead guitar, vocals
Mickey Hart: drums
Bill Kreutzmann: drums
Phil Lesh: bass guitar. vocals
Ron 'Pigpen' McKernan: keyboards, vocals, harmonica, percussion
Bob Weir: guitar, vocals
Recorded live at the Fillmore West, San Francisco, on February 27 – March 2, 1969.
Produced by David Lemieux.
Release date: November 2005

February 27, 1969
'Good Morning Little Schoolgirl' (Sonny Boy Williamson), 'Doin' That Rag' (Garcia, Hunter), 'That's It For The Other One' (Garcia, Kreutzmann, Weir), 'Dupree's Diamond Blues' (Garcia, Hunter), 'Mountains Of The Moon' (Garcia, Hunter), 'Dark Star' (Hunter, Garcia, Hart, Kreutzmann, Lesh, Pigpen, Weir), 'St. Stephen' (Hunter, Garcia, Lesh), 'The Eleven' (Hunter, Lesh), 'Turn On Your Lovelight' (Scott, Malone), 'Cosmic Charlie' (Garcia, Hunter)

February 28, 1969
'(Walk Me Out In The) Morning Dew' (Dobson, Rose), 'Good Morning Little School Girl' (Williamson), 'Doin' That Rag' (Garcia, Hunter), 'I'm A King Bee' (Slim Harpo), 'Turn On Your Lovelight' (Scott, Malone), 'That's It For The Other One' (Garcia, Kreutzmann, Weir), 'Dark Star' (Hunter, Garcia, Hart, Kreutzmann, Lesh, Pigpen, Weir), 'St. Stephen' (including William Tell Bridge)' (Hunter, Garcia, Lesh), 'The Eleven' (Hunter, Lesh), 'Death Don't Have No Mercy' (Rev. Gary Davis), 'Alligator' (Hunter, Pigpen, Lesh), 'Drums' (Hart, Kreutzmann), 'Jam' (Grateful Dead), 'Caution (Do Not Stop On Tracks)' (Grateful Dead), 'Feedback' (Grateful Dead), 'And We Bid You Goodnight' (trad.)

March 1, 1969
'That's It For The Other One' (Garcia, Kreutzmann, Weir), 'New Potato Caboose' (Petersen, Lesh), Doin' That Rag' (Garcia, Hunter), 'Cosmic Charlie' (Garcia, Hunter), 'Dupree's Diamond Blues' (Garcia, Hunter), 'Mountains Of The Moon' (Garcia, Hunter), 'Dark Star' (Hunter, Garcia, Hart, Kreutzmann, Lesh, Pigpen, Weir), 'St. Stephen' (Hunter, Garcia, Lesh), 'The Eleven' (Hunter, Lesh), 'Turn On Your Lovelight' (Scott, Malone), 'Hey Jude' (Lennon, McCartney)

March 2, 1969
'Dark Star' (Hunter, Garcia, Hart, Kreutzmann, Lesh, Pigpen, Weir), 'St. Stephen' (Hunter, Garcia, Lesh), 'The Eleven' (Hunter, Lesh), 'Turn On Your Lovelight' (Scott, Malone), 'Doin' That Rag' (Garcia, Hunter), 'That's It For The Other One' (Garcia, Kreutzmann, Weir), 'Death Don't Have No Mercy' (Rev. Gary Davis), 'Morning Dew' (Dobson, Rose), 'Alligator' (Hunter, Pigpen, Lesh), 'Drums' (Hart, Kreutzmann), 'Jam' (Grateful Dead), 'Caution (Do Not Stop On Tracks)' (Grateful Dead), 'Feedback' (Grateful Dead), 'And We Bid You Goodnight' (trad.)

Bonus disc
'Caution (Do Not Stop On Tracks)' (Grateful Dead) [Recorded at Fillmore East New York City, June 14, 1968], 'He Was A Friend Of Mine' (trad.) [Recorded at Fillmore West, San Francisco, June 8, 1969], 'China Cat Sunflower' (Garcia, Hunter) [Recorded at Fillmore West, San Francisco, June 8, 1969], 'New Potato Caboose' (Lesh, Peterson) [Recorded at Fillmore West, San Francisco, June 8, 1969], 'China Cat Sunflower' (Garcia, Hunter) [Recorded at

217

Fillmore West, San Francisco, February 7, 1970], 'I Know You Rider' (trad.) [Recorded at Fillmore West, San Francisco, February 7, 1970], 'High Time' (Garcia, Hunter) [Recorded at Fillmore West, San Francisco, February 7, 1970]

Fillmore West 1969 (2005)
Personnel:
Tom Constanten: keyboards
Jerry Garcia: lead guitar, vocals
Mickey Hart: drums
Bill Kreutzmann: drums
Phil Lesh: bass guitar. vocals
Ron 'Pigpen' McKernan: keyboards, vocals, harmonica, percussion
Bob Weir: guitar, vocals
Recorded live at the Fillmore West, San Francisco, on February 27 – March 2, 1969.
Produced by David Lemieux.
Release date: November 2005
Running time: 203:01
'Morning Dew' (Dobson, Rose), 'Good Morning Little Schoolgirl' (Sonny Boy Williamson), 'Doin' That Rag' (Garcia, Hunter), 'I'm A King Bee' (James Moore), 'Cosmic Charlie' (Garcia, Hunter), 'Turn On Your Lovelight' (Scott, Malone), 'Dupree's Diamond Blues' (Garcia, Hunter), 'Mountains Of The Moon' (Garcia, Hunter), 'Dark Star' (Garcia, Hart, Kreutzmann, Lesh, McKernan, Weir, Hunter), 'St. Stephen' (Garcia, Lesh, Hunter), 'The Eleven' (Lesh, Hunter), 'Death Don't Have No Mercy' (Rev. Gary Davis), 'That's It For The Other One' I) 'Cryptical Envelopment' (Garcia) II) 'The Other One' (Weir, Kreutzmann), III) 'Cryptical Envelopment' (Garcia), 'Alligator'(Lesh, McKernan, Hunter), 'Drums' (Hart, Kreutzmann), 'Jam' (Grateful Dead), 'Caution (Do Not Stop On Tracks)' (Grateful Dead), 'Feedback' (Grateful Dead), 'And We Bid You Goodnight' (trad.)

Fillmore West 1969: February 27th (2018)
Personnel:
Tom Constanten: keyboards
Jerry Garcia: lead guitar, vocals
Mickey Hart: drums
Bill Kreutzmann: drums
Phil Lesh: bass guitar. vocals
Ron 'Pigpen' McKernan: keyboards, vocals, harmonica, percussion
Bob Weir: guitar, vocals
Recorded live at the Fillmore West, San Francisco, on February 27, 1969. Produced for release by David Lemieux.
Release date: April 2018
Running time: 1:57:59
'Good Morning Little Schoolgirl' (Sonny Boy Williamson), 'Doin' That Rag' (Garcia, Hunter), 'That's It For The Other One' l) 'Cryptical Envelopment' (Garcia), ll) 'The Other One' (Weir, Kreutzmann), lll) 'Cryptical Envelopment' (Garcia), 'Dupree's Diamond Blues' (Garcia, Hunter), 'Mountains Of The Moon' (Garcia, Hunter), 'Dark Star' (Garcia, Hart, Kreutzmann, Lesh, McKernan, Weir, Hunter), 'St. Stephen' (Garcia, Lesh, Hunter), 'The Eleven' (Lesh, Hunter), 'Turn On Your Lovelight' (Scott, Malone), 'Cosmic Charlie' (Garcia, Hunter)

Fillmore West 1969: February 28th (2019)

Personnel:
Tom Constanten: keyboards
Jerry Garcia: lead guitar, vocals
Mickey Hart: drums
Bill Kreutzmann: drums
Phil Lesh: bass guitar. vocals
Ron 'Pigpen' McKernan: keyboards, vocals, harmonica, percussion
Bob Weir: guitar, vocals
Recorded live at the Fillmore West, San Francisco, on February 28, 1969. Produced for
release by David Lemieux.
Release date: July 2019
Running time: 2:48:13
'Morning Dew' (Dobson, Rose), 'Good Morning Little School Girl' (Sonny Boy Williamson),
'Doin' That Rag' (Garcia, Hunter), 'I'm A King Bee' (Slim Harpo), 'Turn On Your Lovelight'
(Scott, Malone), 'That's It For The Other One' l) 'Cryptical Envelopment' (Garcia) ll) 'The
Other One' (Garcia, Kreutzmann, Weir), lll) 'Cryptical Envelopment' (Garcia), 'Dark Star'
(Hunter, Garcia, Hart, Kreutzmann, Lesh, Pigpen, Weir), 'St. Stephen' (Hunter, Garcia, Lesh),
'The Eleven' (Hunter, Lesh), 'Death Don't Have No Mercy' (Rev. Gary Davis), 'Alligator'
(Hunter, Pigpen, Lesh), 'Drums' (Hart, Kretzmann), 'Jam' (Grateful Dead), 'Caution (Do Not
Stop On Tracks)' (Grateful Dead), 'Feedback' (Grateful Dead) , 'And We Bid You Goodnight'
(trad.)

Download Series Vol. 12 (2006)

Personnel:
Tom Constanten: keyboards
Jerry Garcia: lead guitar, vocals
Mickey Hart: drums
Bill Kreutzmann: drums
Phil Lesh: electric bass
Ron 'Pigpen' McKernan: percussion, harmonica, vocals
Bob Weir: rhythm guitar, vocals
Recorded live at the Washington University in St. Louis, Missouri, on April 17, 1969.
Recorded by Owsley Stanley
Release date: April 2006
Running time: 120:43
'Hard To Handle' (Redding, Jones, Isbell), 'Morning Dew' (Dobson, Rose), 'Good Morning
Little Schoolgirl' (Sonny Boy Williamson, 'Dark Star' (Garcia, Hart, Kreutzmann, Lesh,
McKernan, Weir, Hunter), 'St. Stephen' (Garcia, Lesh, Hunter), 'I Know It's A Sin' (Reed,
Reed), 'St. Stephen' (Garcia, Lesh, Hunter), 'Turn On Your Lovelight' (Malone, Scott),
'That's It For The Other One' (Garcia, Kreutzmann, Weir), 'Caution (Do Not Stop On
Tracks)' (Grateful Dead), [Following are bonus tracks from Avalon Ballroom rehearsals,
San Francisco, January 23 1969]: 'The Eleven' (Lesh, Hunter), 'Dupree's Diamond Blues'
(Garcia, Hunter)

Dick's Picks Volume 26 (2002)

Personnel:
Tom Constanten: organ
Jerry Garcia: guitar, vocals

Mickey Hart: drums
Bill Kreutzmann: drums
Phil Lesh: electric bass guitar, vocals
Ron 'Pigpen' McKernan: harmonica, percussion, vocals
Bob Weir: guitar, vocals
Recorded live at Electric Theater in Chicago, Illinois on April 26 1969 and at the Labor
Temple in Minneapolis, Minnesota, on April 29 1969. Recorded by Owsley Stanley.
Release date: October 2002
Running time: 142:01
'Dupree's Diamond Blues' (Garcia, Hunter),' Mountains Of The Moon' (Garcia, Hunter),
'China Cat Sunflower' (Garcia, Hunter), 'Doin' That Rag' (Garcia, Hunter), 'Cryptical
Envelopment' (Garcia), 'The Other One' (Weir, Kreutzmann), 'The Eleven' (Lesh, Hunter),
'The Other One' (Weir, Kreutzmann), 'I Know It's A Sin' (Jimmy Reed), [Following are from
April 27, 1969] 'Turn On Your Lovelight' (Malone, Scott), 'Me And My Uncle' (John Phillips),
'Sittin' On Top Of The World' (Carter, Jacobs), 'Dark Star' (Garcia, Hart, Kreutzmann, Lesh,
McKernan, Weir, Hunter), 'St. Stephen' (Garcia, Lesh, Hunter), 'The Eleven' (Lesh, Hunter)
'Turn On Your Lovelight' (Malone, Scott), 'Morning Dew' (Dobson, Rose)

Road Trips Vol.4 No.1 (2010)

Personnel:
Tom Constanten: keyboards
Jerry Garcia: lead guitar, vocals
Mickey Hart: drums
Bill Kreutzmann: drums
Phil Lesh: electric bass, vocals
Ron 'Pigpen' McKernan: vocals, percussion
Bob Weir: rhythm guitar, vocals
Recorded live at the Big Rock Pow-Wow Festival on May 23 and 24, 1969. Recorded by
Owsley Stanley.
Release date: November 2010
Running time: 184:83
'Hard To Handle' (Otis Redding), 'Dark Star' (Garcia, Hart, Kreutzmann, Lesh, McKernan,
Weir, Hunter), 'St. Stephen' (Garcia, Lesh, Hunter), 'The Eleven' (Garcia, Lesh, Hunter),
'Turn On Your Lovelight' (Malone, Scott), Introduction, 'Turn On Your Lovelight' (Malone,
Scott), 'Doin' That Rag' (Garcia, Hunter), 'He Was A Friend Of Mine' ('Just A Hand To
Hold') (Mark Spoelstra), 'China Cat Sunflower' (Garcia, Hunter), 'The Eleven' (Garcia, Lesh,
Hunter), 'Death Don't Have No Mercy' (Rev. Gary Davis), 'Morning Dew' (Dobson, Rose),
'Me And My Uncle' (John Phillips)' 'Yellow Dog Story' (Weir), 'Alligator' (Lesh, McKernan,
Hunter), 'Drums' (Hart, Kreutzmann), 'St. Stephen' (Garcia, Lesh, Hunter), 'Feedback'
(Grateful Dead), 'We Bid You Goodnight' (trad.)

Dick's Picks Vol.16 (2000)

Personnel:
Tom Constanten: keyboards
Jerry Garcia: lead guitar, vocals
Mickey Hart: drums
Bill Kreutzmann: drums
Phil Lesh: bass, vocals
Ron 'Pigpen' McKernan: harmonica, percussion, vocals

Bob Weir: rhythm guitar, vocals
Recorded live at the Fillmore Auditorium in San Francisco on November 7/8 1969. Recorded by Owsley Stanley.
Release date: March 2000
Running time: 191:00
'Good Morning Little Schoolgirl' (Sonny Boy Williamson), 'Casey Jones' (Garcia, Hunter), 'Dire Wolf' (Garcia, Hunter), 'Easy Wind' (Hunter), 'China Cat Sunflower' (Garcia, Hunter), 'I Know You Rider' (trad.), 'High Time' (Garcia, Hunter), 'Mama Tried' (Merle Haggard), 'Good Lovin'' (Clark, Resnick), 'Cumberland Blues' (Garcia, Hunter, Lesh), 'Dark Star' (Grateful Dead, Hunter), 'The Other One' (Kreutzmann, Weir), 'Dark Star' (Grateful Dead, Hunter), 'Uncle John's Band Jam' (Garcia, Hunter), 'Dark Star' (Grateful Dead, Hunter), 'St. Stephen' (Garcia, Hunter, Lesh), 'The Eleven' (Hunter, Lesh), 'Caution (Do Not Stop On Tracks)' (Garcia, Kreutzmann, Lesh, Weir), 'The Main Ten' (Hart), 'Caution (Do Not Stop On Tracks)' (Garcia, Kreutzmann, Lesh, Weir), 'Feedback' (Grateful Dead), 'We Bid You Goodnight' (trad.), 'Turn On Your Love Light' (Malone, Scott) [From November 7, 1969]

Dave's Picks Vol.10 (2014)
Personnel:
Tom Constanten: keyboards
Jerry Garcia: lead guitar, vocals
Mickey Hart: drums
Bill Kreutzmann: drums
Phil Lesh: electric bass, vocals
Ron 'Pigpen' McKernan: harmonica, percussion vocals
Bob Weir: guitar, vocals
Recorded live at the Thelma music venue in Los Angeles, California, on December 12, 1969. Recorded by Owsley Stanley.
Release date: May 2014
Running time: 193:46
'Cold Rain And Snow' (trad.), 'Me And My Uncle' (John Phillips), 'Easy Wind' (Hunter), 'Cumberland Blues' (Garcia, Lesh, Hunter), 'Black Peter' (Garcia, Hunter), 'Next Time You See Me' (Harvey, Forest), 'China Cat Sunflower' (Garcia, Hunter), 'I Know You Rider' (trad.), 'Turn On Your Lovelight' (Scott, Malone), 'Hard To Handle' (Redding, Isbell, Jones), 'Casey Jones' (Garcia, Hunter), 'Mama Tried' (Merle Haggard), 'High Time' (Garcia, Hunter), 'Dire Wolf' (Garcia, Hunter), 'Good Lovin'' (Clark, Resnick), 'I'm A King Bee' (James Moore), 'Uncle John's Band' (Garcia, Hunter), 'He Was A Friend Of Mine' (trad.), 'Alligator' (Lesh, McKernan, Hunter), 'Drums' (Hart, Kreutzmann), 'Alligator' (Lesh, McKernan, Hunter), 'Caution (Do Not Stop On Tracks)' (Grateful Dead), 'Feedback' (Grateful Dead), 'And We Bid You Goodnight' (trad.), [Bonus disc: recorded live at Thelma, Los Angeles, California, on December 11, 1969]: 'Dark Star' (Garcia, Hart, Kreutzmann, Lesh, McKernan, Weir, Hunter), 'St. Stephen' (Garcia, Lesh, Hunter), 'The Eleven' (Lesh, Hunter), 'Cumberland Blues' (Garcia, Lesh, Hunter), 'That's It For The Other One: Cryptical Envelopment' (Garcia); 'Drums' (Hart, Kreutzmann); 'The Other One' (Weir, Kreutzmann); 'Cryptical Envelopment' (Garcia), 'Cosmic Charlie' (Garcia, Hunter)

Dave's Picks Vol.6 (2013)
Personnel:
Tom Constanten: keyboards (Fillmore concert)
Jerry Garcia: lead guitar, vocals

Mickey Hart: drums and percussion
Bill Kreutzmann: drums and percussion
Phil Lesh: bass guitar, vocals
Ron 'Pigpen' McKernan: keyboards (Fox Theatre concert), harmonica, vocals
Bob Weir: rhythm guitar, vocals
Recorded live at the Fillmore Auditorium in San Francisco, on December 20, 1969, and at the Fox Theatre in St Louis on February 2, 1970. Recorded by Owsley Stanley.
Release date: May 2013
Running time: 228:24
[February 2, 1970 – Fox Theatre]: 'Casey Jones' (Garcia, Hunter), 'Mama Tried' (Merle Haggard), 'Hard To Handle' (Isbell, Jones, Redding), 'Cold Rain And Snow' (trad.), 'Black Peter' (Garcia, Hunter), 'Cumberland Blues' (Garcia, Lesh, Hunter), 'Dark Star' (Garcia, Hunter, Hart, Kreutzmann, Lesh, McKernan, Weir), 'St. Stephen' (Garcia, Lesh, Hunter), 'Mason's Children', (Garcia, Hunter, Lesh, Weir), 'Good Lovin'' (Clark, Resnick), 'Uncle John's Band' (Garcia, Hunter), 'Turn On Your Lovelight' (Scott, Malone), 'Not Fade Away' (Petty, Hardin), 'Turn On Your Lovelight' (Scott, Malone) 'And We Bid You Goodnight' (trad.)
[Fillmore Auditorium December 20, 1969]: 'Dark Star' (Garcia, Hart, Hunter, Kreutzmann, Lesh, McKernan, Weir), 'St. Stephen' (Garcia, Lesh, Hunter), 'The Eleven' (Lesh, Hunter), 'New Speedway Boogie' (Garcia, Hunter), 'Turn On Your Lovelight' (Scott, Malone), 'Mason's Children' (Garcia, Hunter, Lesh, Weir), 'China Cat Sunflower' (Garcia, Hunter), 'I Know You Rider' (trad.), 'High Time' (Garcia, Hunter), 'Me And My Uncle' (John Phillips), 'Hard To Handle' (Isbell, Jones, Redding), 'Cumberland Blues' (Garcia, Hunter, Lesh), [Bonus Disc: Fillmore Auditorium December 21, 1969]: 'Smokestack Lightning' (Chester Burnett), 'New Speedway Boogie', (Garcia, Hunter) 'Dire Wolf' (Garcia, Hunter), 'Mason's Children' (Garcia, Hunter, Lesh, Weir), 'China Cat Sunflower' (Garcia, Hunter), 'I Know You Rider' (trad.), 'Black Peter' (Garcia, Hunter), 'Good Lovin'' (Clark, Resnick), 'Drums' (Hart, Kreutzmann), 'The Other One' (Kreutzmann, Weir), 'Cumberland Blues' (Garcia, Hunter, Lesh)

1970
Dave's Picks Vol. 30 (2019)
Personnel:
Tom Constanten: keyboards
Jerry Garcia: guitar, vocals
Mickey Hart: drums
Bill Kreutzmann: drums
Phil Lesh: bass, vocals
Ron 'Pigpen' McKernan: harmonica, percussion, vocals
Bob Weir: rhythm guitar, vocals
Recorded live at the Fillmore East in New York City, on January 2, 1970 (early and late shows) along with bonus material and a bonus disc from the same venue the following night. Recorded by Owsley Stanley.
Release date: May 2019
Running time: 228:41
[January 2, 1970, early show]: 'Mason's Children' (Garcia, Weir, Lesh, Hunter), 'Casey Jones' (Garcia, Hunter), 'Black Peter' (Garcia, Hunter), 'Mama Tried' (Merle Haggard), 'Hard to Handle' (Redding, Bell, Jones), 'Cumberland Blues' (Garcia, Lesh, Hunter), 'That's It For The Other One': I. 'Cryptical Envelopment' (Garcia); II. 'Drums' (Hart, Kreutzmann); III. 'The Other One' (Weir, Kreutzmann); IV. 'Cryptical Envelopment' (Garcia), 'Cosmic Charlie'

(Garcia, Hunter), [January 2, 1970, late show]: 'Uncle John's Band' (Garcia, Hunter), 'High Time' (Garcia, Hunter), Dire Wolf' (Garcia, Hunter), 'Easy Wind' (Hunter), 'China Cat Sunflower' (Garcia, Hunter), 'I Know You Rider' (trad.), 'Good Lovin'' (Clark, Resnick), 'Me And My Uncle' (John Phillips), 'Monkey And The Engineer' (Jesse Fuller), [Bonus tracks from January 3, 1970]: 'Morning Dew' (Dobson, Rose), 'Big Boss Man' (Smith, Dixon), 'Dancing In The Street' (Stevenson, Gaye, Hunter), 'St. Stephen' (Garcia, Lesh, Hunter), 'In The Midnight Hour' (Cropper, Pickett), [January 2, 1970, late show contd.]: 'Dark Star' (Garcia, Hart, Kreutzmann, Lesh, McKernan, Weir, Hunter), 'St. Stephen' (Garcia, Lesh, Hunter), 'The Eleven' (Lesh, Hunter), 'Turn On Your Lovelight' (Scott, Malone), [Bonus disc recorded on January 3, 1970]: 'Cold Rain And Snow' (trad.), 'Alligator' (Lesh, McKernan, Hunter), 'Drums' (Hart, Kreutzmann), 'Alligator'(Lesh, McKernan, Hunter), 'Feedback' (Grateful Dead), 'Casey Jones' (Garcia, Hunter), 'Mason's Children' (Garcia, Weir, Lesh, Hunter), 'That's It For The Other One': I. 'Cryptical Envelopment' (Garcia); II. 'Drums' (Hart, Kreutzmann); III. 'The Other One' (Weir, Kreutzmann); IV. 'Cryptical Envelopment' (Garcia), 'Cosmic Charlie' (Garcia, Hunter), 'Uncle John's Band ' (Garcia, Hunter)

Download Series Vol. 2 (2005)
Personnel:
Tom Constanten: keyboards
Jerry Garcia: lead guitar, vocals
Mickey Hart: drums
Bill Kreutzmann: drums
Phil Lesh: electric bass
Ron 'Pigpen' McKernan: vocals, percussion
Bob Weir: rhythm guitar, vocals
Recorded live at Springer's Inn, Gresham, Oregon, on January 18, 1970. Recorded by Bear.
Release date: June 2005
Running time: 79.47
'Cold Rain And Snow' (trad.), 'Big Boss Man' (Dixon, Smith), 'Mason's Children' (Hunter, Garcia, Lesh, Weir), 'Black Peter' (Garcia, Hunter), 'Dancing In The Street' (Gaye, Hunter, Stevenson), 'Good Lovin'' (Clark, Resnick), 'China Cat Sunflower' (Garcia, Hunter), 'I Know You Rider' (trad.), 'Turn On Your Lovelight' (Malone, Scott)

Dave's Picks Vol.19 (2016)
Personnel:
Tom Constanten: keyboards
Jerry Garcia: guitar, vocals
Mickey Hart: drums
Bill Kreutzmann: drums
Phil Lesh: bass, vocals
Ron 'Pigpen' McKernan: harmonica, percussion, vocals
Bob Weir: guitar, vocals
Recorded live at the Honolulu Civic Auditorium in Honolulu, Hawaii, on January 23, 1970.
Additional tracks from January 24 1970. Recorded by Owsley Stanley
Release date: August 2016
Running time: 190:20
'China Cat Sunflower' (Garcia, Hunter), 'I Know You Rider' (trad.), 'Black Peter' (Garcia, Hunter), 'The Yellow Dog Story' (Weir), 'Hard To Handle' (Redding, Isbell, Jones), 'Mama Tried' (Merle Haggard), 'Casey Jones' (Garcia, Hunter), 'Dire Wolf' (Garcia, Hunter), 'Good

Lovin'" (Clark, Resnick). 'That's It For The Other One: Cryptical Envelopment' (Garcia); 'Drums' (Hart, Kreutzmann); 'The Other One' (Weir, Kreutzmann) 'Cryptical Envelopment' (Garcia), 'Dark Star' (Garcia, Hart, Kreutzmann, Lesh, McKernan, Weir, Hunter), 'St. Stephen' (Garcia, Lesh, Hunter), 'Turn On Your Lovelight' (Scott, Malone), [January 24, 1970]: 'Cumberland Blues' (Garcia, Lesh, Hunter), 'Cold Rain And Snow' (trad.), 'Me And My Uncle' (John Phillips), 'I'm A King Bee' (James Moore), 'Mason's Children' (Garcia, Weir, Lesh, Hunter), 'Black Peter' (Garcia, Hunter), 'Good Lovin'" (Clark, Resnick), 'Feedback' (Grateful Dead), 'And We Bid You Goodnight' (trad.), 'Dancing In The Street' (Stevenson, Gaye, Hunter)

Grateful Dead Download Series: Family Dog At The Great Highway (2005)

Personnel:
Jerry Garcia: lead guitar, vocals
Mickey Hart: drums, percussion
Bill Kreutzmann: drums
Phil Lesh: bass, backing vocals
Ron 'Pigpen' McKernan: organ, percussion, harmonica, vocals
Bob Weir: rhythm guitar, vocals
Recorded live at Family Dog at the Great Highway, in San Francisco, California on February 4, 1970. Mastering by Jeffrey Norman
Release date: December 2005
Running time: 79:43
'Hard To Handle' (Redding, Jones, Isbell), 'Black Peter' (Garcia, Hunter), 'Me And My Uncle' (John Phillips), 'China Cat Sunflower' (Garcia, Hunter), 'I Know You Rider' (trad.), 'St. Stephen' (Garcia, Lesh, Hunter), 'Not Fade Away' (Petty, Holly), 'St. Stephen' (Garcia, Lesh, Hunter), 'In The Midnight Hour' (Pickett, Cropper), [Following are bonus tracks from October 5, 1970]: 'Dancing In The Street' (Gaye, Stevenson, Hunter), 'Monkey And The Engineer' (Jesse Fuller), 'Good Lovin' ' (Resnick, Clark)

Dick's Picks Vol.4 (1996)

Personnel:
Jerry Garcia: lead guitar, vocals
Mickey Hart: drums
Bill Kreutzmann: drums
Phil Lesh: bass
Ron 'Pigpen' McKernan: organ, percussion, vocals
Bob Weir: guitar, vocals
Recorded live at the Fillmore East, New York City, February 13 and February 14, 1970.
Recorded by Owsley Stanley.
Release date: February 1996
Running time: 189:46
'Introduction' (Zacherle), 'Casey Jones' (Garcia, Hunter), 'Dancing In The Street' (Stevenson, Gaye, I. Hunter), 'China Cat Sunflower' (Garcia, Hunter), 'I Know You Rider' (trad.), 'High Time' (Garcia, Hunter), 'Dire Wolf' (Garcia, Hunter), 'Dark Star' (Garcia, Hart, Kreutzmann, Lesh, McKernan, Weir, Hunter), 'That's It For The Other One' (Grateful Dead), 'Turn On Your Love Light' (Malone, Scott), 'Alligator' (Lesh, McKernan, Hunter), 'Drums' (Hart, Kreutzmann), 'Me And My Uncle' (John Phillips), 'Not Fade Away' (Hardin, Petty), 'Mason's Children' (Garcia, Lesh, Weir, Hunter), 'Caution (Do Not Stop On Tracks)' (Grateful Dead), 'Feedback' (Grateful Dead), 'We Bid You Goodnight' (trad.)

Family Dog at the Great Highway, San Francisco, CA 4/18/70 (2013)
Personnel:
Jerry Garcia: lead guitar, vocals
Mickey Hart: drums, percussion
Bill Kreutzmann: drums
Phil Lesh: bass, backing vocals
Ron 'Pigpen' McKernan: organ, percussion, harmonica, vocals
Bob Weir: rhythm guitar, vocals
Additional personnel:
John Dawson, David Nelson
Recorded live at Family Dog at the Great Highway in San Francisco, California on April 18, 1970. Recorded by Owsley Stanley
Release date: December 2005
Running time: 72:39
'I Know You Rider' (trad.), 'Don't Ease Me In' (trad.), 'Silver Threads And Golden Needles' (Reynolds, Rhodes), 'Friend Of The Devil' (Garcia, Dawson, Hunter), 'Deep Elem Blues' (trad.), 'Wake Up Little Susie' (Bryant, Bryant), 'Candyman' (Garcia, Hunter), 'Cumberland Blues' (Garcia, Lesh, Hunter), 'New Speedway Boogie' (Garcia, Hunter), 'Me And My Uncle' (John Phillips), 'Mama Tried' (Merle Haggard), 'Katie Mae' (Lightnin' Hopkins), Ain't It Crazy (The Rub)' (Lightnin' Hopkins), 'Roberta' (trad.), 'Bring Me My Shotgun' (Lightnin' Hopkins), 'The Mighty Flood' (trad.), 'Black Snake' (Lightnin' Hopkins)

Dick's Picks Vol.8 (1997)
Personnel:
Jerry Garcia: acoustic guitar (first set, except Cumberland Blues) lead electric guitar (Cumberland Blues, second and third set), vocals
Mickey Hart: drums, percussion
Bill Kreutzmann: drums, percussion
Phil Lesh: electric bass, vocals
Ron 'Pigen' McKernan: organ, harmonica, vocals
Bob Weir: acoustic guitar (first set) rhythm electric guitar (second and third sets), vocals
Additional musicians:
John 'Marmaduke' Dawson: vocals on 'Cold Jordan'
David Nelson: acoustic guitar on 'Cumberland Blues', mandolin on 'Cold Jordan'
Recorded live at Harpur College, Binghamton, New York, May 2 1970. Recorded by Bob Matthews.
Release date: June 1997
Running time: 176:38
'Don't Ease Me In' (trad.), 'I Know You Rider' (trad.), 'Friend Of The Devil' (Garcia, Dawson, Hunter), 'Dire Wolf' (Garcia, Hunter), 'Beat It On Down The Line' (Jesse Fuller), 'Black Peter' (Garcia, Hunter), 'Candyman' (Garcia, Hunter), 'Cumberland Blues' (Garcia, Hunter, Lesh), 'Deep Elem Blues' (trad.), 'Cold Jordan' (trad.), 'Uncle John's Band' (Garcia, Hunter) 'St. Stephen' (Garcia, Hunter, Lesh), 'Cryptical Envelopment' (Garcia), 'Drums' (Hart, Kreutzmann), 'The Other One' (Weir, Kreutzmann), 'Cryptical Envelopment' (Garcia), 'Cosmic Charlie' (Garcia, Hunter), 'Casey Jones' (Garcia, Hunter), 'Good Lovin'' (Resnick, Clark), 'It's A Man's World' (Brown, Jones, Newsome), 'Dancing In The Streets' (Stevenson, Gaye, Hunter), 'Morning Dew' (Dobson, Rose), 'Viola Lee Blues' (Noah Lewis), 'We Bid You Goodnight' (trad.)

Road Trips Vol.3 No. 3 (2010)

Personnel:
Jerry Garcia: lead guitar, vocals
Mickey Hart: drums
Bill Kreutzmann: drums
Phil Lesh: electric bass, vocals
Ron 'Pigpen' McKernan: vocals, organ, percussion, harmonica, acoustic guitar
Bob Weir: rhythm guitar, vocals
Additional personnel:
John Dawson: harmony vocals on 'A Voice From On High' and 'Cold Jordan'
David Nelson: mandolin on 'A Voice From On High' and 'Cold Jordan'
Recorded live at the Fillmore East in New York City on May 15, 1970 (early and late shows).
Recording by Bob Matthews.
Release date: June 2010
Running time: 230:29
'Don't Ease Me In' (trad.), 'I Know You Rider' (trad.), 'Ain't It Crazy (The Rub)' (Lightnin'
Hopkins), 'Long Black Limousine' (Stovall, George), 'New Speedway Boogie' (Garcia,
Hunter) 'Casey Jones' (Garcia, Hunter), 'St. Stephen' (Garcia, Phil Lesh, Hunter), 'That's It
For The Other One' (Garcia, Kreutzmann, Lesh, McKernan, Weir), 'Cosmic Charlie' (Garcia,
Hunter), 'New Minglewood Blues' (Noah Lewis), 'Deep Elem Blues' (trad.), 'The Ballad
Of Casey Jones' (trad.), 'Silver Threads And Golden Needles' (Rhodes, Reynolds), 'Black
Peter' (Garcia, Hunter)', 'Friend Of The Devil' (Garcia, Dawson, Hunter), 'Uncle John's
Band' (Garcia, Hunter), 'She's Mine' (Lightnin' Hopkins), 'Katie Mae' (Lightnin' Hopkins),
'A Voice From On High' (Bill Monroe), 'China Cat Sunflower' (Garcia, Hunter), 'I Know You
Rider' (trad.), 'Cumberland Blues' (Garcia, Lesh, Hunter), 'Hard To Handle' (Isbell, Jones,
Redding), 'Morning Dew' (Dobson, Rose), 'Dire Wolf' (Garcia, Hunter), 'Good Lovin'‘
(Clark, Resnick), 'Dark Star' (Garcia, Hart, Kreutzmann, Lesh, McKernan, Weir, Hunter), 'St.
Stephen' (Garcia, Lesh, Hunter), 'Not Fade Away' (Holly, Petty), 'Turn On Your Love Light'
(Scott, Malone), 'Cold Jordan' (trad.), [Bonus Disc recorded at the Fillmore East, New York,
on May 15, 1970]: 'Friend Of The Devil' (Garcia, Dawson, Hunter), 'Candyman' (Garcia,
Hunter), 'Cumberland Blues' (Garcia, Lesh, Hunter), 'Cold Jordan' (trad.), 'Easy Wind'
(Hunter), 'Attics Of My Life' (Garcia, Hunter), 'Beat It On Down The Line' (Jesse Fuller),
'Next Time You See Me' (Forest, Harvey), [Following Recorded at Meramec Community
College, Kirkwood, Missouri on May 14, 1970]: 'New Speedway Boogie' (Garcia, Hunter),
'St. Stephen' (Garcia, Lesh, Hunter), 'Not Fade Away' (Holly, Petty), 'Turn On Your Lovelight'
(Scott, Malone)

1971
Three From The Vault (2007)

Personnel:
Jerry Garcia: lead guitar, vocals
Bill Kreutzmann: drums and percussion
Phil Lesh: bass guitar, vocals
Ron 'Pigpen' McKernan: keyboards, harmonica, percussion, vocals
Bob Weir: rhythm guitar, vocals
Recorded live at the Capitol Theatre in Port Chester, New York on February 19, 1971.
Produced by Grateful Dead, recorded by Bob Matthews and Betty Cantor.
Release date: June 2007
Running time: 142:42

Two Ditties: 'The Merry-Go-Round Broke Down' (Friend, Franklin), 'Spring Song' (Mendelssohn), 'Truckin'' (Garcia, Lesh, Weir, Hunter), 'Loser' (Garcia, Hunter), 'Cumberland Blues' (Garcia, Lesh, Hunter), 'It Hurts Me Too' (James, Red), 'Bertha' (Garcia, Hunter), 'Playing In The Band' (Weir, Hart, Hunter), 'Dark Hollow' (Bill Browning), 'Smokestack Lightning' (Howlin' Wolf), 'China Cat Sunflower' (Garcia, Hunter), 'I Know You Rider' (trad.), 'Greatest Story Ever Told' (Weir, Hunter), 'Johnny B. Goode' (Chuck Berry), 'Bird Song' (Garcia, Hunter), 'Easy Wind' (Hunter), 'Deal' (Garcia, Hunter), 'Cryptical Envelopment' (Garcia), 'Drums', (Kreutzmann), 'The Other One' (Weir, Kreutzmann), 'Wharf Rat' (Garcia, Hunter, 'Good Lovin'' (Resnick, Clark), 'Casey Jones' (Garcia, Hunter)

Ladies And Gentlemen... The Grateful Dead (2000)
Personnel:
Jerry Garcia: lead guitar, vocals
Bill Kreutzmann: drums
Phil Lesh: electric bass. vocals
Ron 'Pigpen' McKernan: organ, percussion, harmonica, vocals
Bob Weir: rhythm guitar, vocals
Additional personnel:
Tom Constanten: keyboards (disc 3, tracks 6-10)
Recorded live at the Fillmore East in New York City, on April 25, 1971 – April 29, 1971.
Produced by David Lemieux.
Release date: October 2000
Running time: 296:44
'Truckin'' (Hunter, Garcia, Lesh, Weir), 'Bertha' (Garcia, Hunter), 'Next Time You See Me' (Forest, Harvey), 'Beat It On Down The Line' (Jesse Fuller), 'Bird Song' (Garcia, Hunter), 'Dark Hollow' (Bill Browning), 'I Second That Emotion' (Cleveland, Robinson), 'Me And My Uncle' (John Phillips), 'Cumberland Blues' (Hunter, Garcia, Lesh), 'Good Lovin'' ' (Clark, Resnick), 'Drums' (Kreutzmann), 'Good Lovin' ' ' (Clark, Resnick), 'Sugar Magnolia' (Hunter, Weir), 'Loser' (Garcia, Hunter), 'Ain't It Crazy (The Rub)' (Lightnin' Hopkins), 'El Paso' (Marty Robbins), 'I'm A King Bee' (Slim Harpo), 'Ripple' (Garcia, Hunter), 'Me And Bobby McGee' (Foster, Kristofferson), 'Uncle John's Band' (Garcia, Hunter), 'Turn On Your Lovelight' (Malone, Scott), 'China Cat Sunflower' (Garcia, Hunter), 'I Know You Rider' (trad.), 'It Hurts Me Too' (Elmore James), 'Sing Me Back Home' (Merle Haggard), 'Hard To Handle' (Isbell, Jones, Redding), 'Dark Star' (Hunter, Garcia, Hart, Kreutzmann, Lesh, McKernan, Weir), 'St. Stephen' (Hunter, Garcia, Lesh), 'Not Fade Away' (Holly, Petty), 'Goin' Down The Road Feeling Bad' (trad.), 'Not Fade Away' (Holly, Petty), 'Morning Dew' (Dobson, Rose), 'New Minglewood Blues' (trad.), 'Wharf Rat' (Garcia, Hunter), 'Alligator' (Hunter, McKernan, Lesh), 'Drums' (Kreutzmann), 'Jam' (Grateful Dead), 'Goin' Down The Road Feeling Bad' (trad.), 'Cold Rain And Snow' (trad.), 'Casey Jones' (Garcia, Hunter), 'In The Midnight Hour' (Cropper, Pickett), 'And We Bid You Goodnight' (trad.)

Winterland: May 30th 1971 (2012)
Personnel:
Jerry Garcia: lead guitar, vocals
Bill Kreutzmann: drums
Phil Lesh: electric bass. vocals
Ron 'Pigpen' McKernan: organ, harmonica, percussion, vocals
Bob Weir: rhythm guitar, vocals
Recorded live at the Winterland Ballroom in San Francisco, California, on May 30, 1971.

Produced for release by David Lemieux and Mason Williams.
Release date: November 2012
Running time: 68:29
'Sugar Magnolia' (Weir, Hunter), 'Cumberland Blues' (Garcia, Lesh, Hunter), 'Big Boss Man' (Smith, Dixon), 'Me And My Uncle' (John Phillips), 'Deal' (Garcia, Hunter), 'Truckin'' (Garcia, Lesh, Weir, Hunter), 'Turn On Your Lovelight' (Scott, Malone), 'Uncle John's Band' (Garcia, Hunter), 'Casey Jones' (Garcia, Hunter), Johnny B. Goode' (Chuck Berry)

Road Trips Vol. 1 No. 3 (2008)

Personnel:
Jerry Garcia: lead guitar, vocals
Bill Kreutzmann: drums
Phil Lesh: electric bass, vocals
Ron 'Pigpen' McKernan: organ, percussion, vocals
Bob Weir: rhythm guitar, vocals
Recorded live at Yale Bowl, New Haven, Connecticut on July 31, 1971, and at the Auditorium Theatre, Chicago, Illinois on August 23, 1971. Recorded by Rex Jackson.
Release date: June 2008
Running time: 154:52
[Recorded at Yale Bowl, New Haven, Connecticut, July 31, 1971]: 'Big Railroad Blues' (Noah Lewis), 'Hard To Handle' (Redding, Bell, Jones), 'Me And Bobby McGee' (Kristofferson, Foster), 'Dark Star' (Garcia, Hart, Kreutzmann, Lesh, McKernan, Weir, Hunter), 'Bird Song' (Garcia, Hunter), 'Not Fade Away' (Holly, Petty), 'Goin' Down The Road Feeling Bad' (trad.), 'Not Fade Away' (Holly, Petty), 'Uncle John's Band' (Garia, Hunter), 'Johnny B. Goode' (Chuck Berry), [Recorded at Auditorium Theatre, Chicago, Illinois, August 23, 1971]: 'China Cat Sunflower' (Garcia, Hunter), 'I Know You Rider' (trad.), 'Truckin'' (Garcia, Lesh, Weir, Hunter), 'Sugaree' (Garcia, Hunter), 'Cryptical Envelopment' (Garcia), 'Drums' (Kreutzmann), 'The Other One' (Weir, Kreutzmann), 'Me And My Uncle' (John Phillips), 'The Other One' (Weir, Kreutzmann), 'Cryptical Envelopment' (Garcia), 'Wharf Rat' (Garcia, Hunter), 'Sugar Magnolia' (Weir, Hunter), [Bonus Disc recorded at Hollywood Palladium, Hollywood, California, August 6, 1971]: 'Bertha' (Garcia, Hunter), 'Mr. Charlie' (McKernan, Hunter), 'Cumberland Blues' (Garcia, Lesh, Hunter), 'Brokedown Palace' (Garcia, Hunter), 'Hard To Handle' (Redding, Bell, Jones), [Recorded at Yale Bowl, New Haven, Connecticut, July 31, 1971]: 'Sing Me Back Home' (Merle Haggard), 'Big Boss Man' (Dixon, Smith), [Recorded at Terminal Island Correctional Facility, San Pedro, California, August 4, 1971]: 'Not Fade Away' (Holly, Petty), 'Goin' Down The Road Feeling Bad' (trad.), 'Turn On Your Lovelight' (Scott, Malone)

Dick's Picks Vol 35 (2005)

Personnel:
Jerry Garcia: lead guitar, vocals
Bill Kreutzmann: drums
Phil Lesh: electric bass, vocals
Ron 'Pigpen' McKernan: vocals, harmonica, organ, percussion
Bob Weir: rhythm guitar, vocals
Recorded live at Golden Hall in San Diego, California, on August 7, 1971 and at the Auditorium Theatre in Chicago, Illinois, on August 24, 1971, and bonus tracks recorded at the Hollywood Palladium in Hollywood, California, on 6, 1971. Recorded by Rex Jackson
Release date: June 2005

Running time: 290:56
[August 7 1971:] 'Big Railroad Blues' (Noah Lewis), 'El Paso' (Marty Robbins), 'Mr.
Charlie' (McKernan, Hunter), 'Sugaree' (Garcia, Hunter), 'Mama Tried' (Merle Haggard),
'Bertha' (Garcia, Hunter), 'Big Boss Man' (Smith, Dixon), 'Promised Land' (Chuck Berry),
'Hard To Handle' (Jones, Bell, Redding), 'Cumberland Blues' (Garcia, Lesh, Hunter),
'Casey Jones' (Garcia, Hunter), 'Truckin'' (Garcia, Lesh, Weir, Hunter), 'China Cat
Sunflower' (Garcia, Hunter), 'I Know You Rider' (trad.), 'Next Time You See Me' (Harvey,
Forest), 'Sugar Magnolia' (Weir, Hunter), 'Sing Me Back Home' (Merle Haggard), 'Me
And My Uncle' (John Phillips), 'Not Fade Away' (Hardin, Petty), 'Goin' Down The Road
Feeling Bad' (trad.), 'Jam' (Grateful Dead), 'Johnny B. Goode' (Chuck Berry), [August 24
1971:] 'Uncle John's Band' (Garcia, Hunter), 'Playing In The Band' (Weir, Hart, Hunter),
'Loser' (Garcia, Hunter), 'It Hurts Me Too' (Elmore James), 'Cumberland Blues' (Garcia,
Lesh, Hunter), 'Empty Pages' (McKernan), 'Beat It On Down The Line' (Jesse Fuller),
'Brown-Eyed Women' (Garcia, Hunter), 'St Stephen' (Garcia, Lesh, Hunter), 'Not Fade
Away' (Hardin, Petty), 'Goin' Down The Road Feeling Bad' (trad.), 'Not Fade Away'
(reprise) (Hardin, Petty), 'Me And Bobby McGee' (Kristofferson, Foster), 'Big Boss Man'
(Smith, Dixon), 'Brokedown Palace' (Garcia, Hunter), 'Good Lovin'' (Resnick, Clark)
[Bonus tracks from Aug 6 1971:] 'The Other One' (Weir, Kreutzmann) 'Me And My Uncle'
(John Phillips), 'The Other One' (Weir, Kreutzmann), 'Deal' (Garcia, Hunter), 'Sugar
Magnolia' (Weir, Hunter), 'Morning Dew' (Dobson, Rose), 'Turn On Your Love Light'
(Scott, Malone)

Dave's Picks Vol.3 (2012)
Personnel:
Jerry Garcia: lead guitar, vocals
Keith Godchaux: keyboards
Bill Kreutzmann: drums
Phil Lesh: electric bass, vocals
Bob Weir: rhythm guitar, vocals
Recorded live at the Auditorium Theatre in Chicago, Illinois, on October 22, 1971. Recorded
by Rex Jackson.
Release date: August 2012
Running time: 3:23:11
'Bertha' (Garcia, Hunter), 'Me And My Uncle' (John Phillips), 'Tennessee Jed' (Garcia,
Hunter), 'Jack Straw' (Weir, Hunter), 'Loser' (Garcia, Hunter), 'Playing In The Band' (Weir,
Hart, Hunter), 'Sugaree' (Garcia, Hunter), 'Beat It On Down The Line' (Jesse Fuller), 'Black
Peter' (Garcia, Hunter), 'Mexicali Blues' (Weir, Barlow), 'Cold Rain And Snow' (trad.), 'Me
And Bobby McGee' (Kristofferson, Foster), 'Comes A Time' (Garcia, Hunter), 'One More
Saturday Night' (Weir), 'Ramble On Rose' (Garcia, Hunter), 'Cumberland Blues' (Garcia,
Phil Lesh, Hunter), 'That's It For The Other One: Cryptical Envelopment' (Garcia), 'Drums'
(Bill Kreutzmann), 'The Other One' (Weir, Kreutzmann), 'Cryptical Envelopment' (Garcia),
'Deal' (Garcia, Hunter), 'Sugar Magnolia' (Weir, Hunter), 'Casey Jones' (Garcia, Hunter),
'Johnny B. Goode' (Chuck Berry), [Bonus tracks recorded at Auditorium Theatre in Chicago
on October 21, 1971]: 'Truckin'' (Garcia, Lesh, Weir, Hunter), 'Big Railroad Blues' (Noah
Lewis), 'The Frozen Logger' (James Stevens), 'Dark Star' (Garcia, Hart, Kreutzmann, Lesh,
McKernan, Weir, Hunter), 'Sittin' On Top Of The World' (Jacobs, Carter), 'Dark Star' (Garcia,
Hart, Kreutzmann, Lesh, McKernan, Weir, Hunter), 'Me And Bobby McGee' (Kristofferson,
Foster), 'Brown-Eyed Women' (Garcia, Hunter), 'St. Stephen' (Garcia, Lesh, Hunter),
'Johnny B. Goode' (Chuck Berry)

Download Series Vol. 3 (2005)

Personnel:
Jerry Garcia: lead guitar, vocals
Keith Godchaux: keyboards
Bill Kreutzmann: drums
Phil Lesh: electric bass, vocals
Bob Weir: rhythm guitar, vocals
Recorded live at The Palestra in Rochester, New York, on October 26, 1971. Recorded by Rex Jackson.
Release date: July 2005
Running time: 140.42
'Bertha' (Garcia, Hunter), 'Playing In The Band' (Hunter, Hart, Bob Weir), 'Sugaree' (Garcia, Hunter), 'Me And My Uncle' (John Phillips), 'Tennessee Jed' (Garcia, Hunter), 'Jack Straw' (Hunter, Weir), 'Big Railroad Blues' (Noah Lewis), 'Me And Bobby McGee' (Foster, Kristofferson), 'Cumberland Blues' (Hunter, Garcia, Lesh), 'Cold Rain And Snow' (trad.), 'Mexicali Blues' (Barlow, Weir), 'Loser' (Garcia, Hunter), 'El Paso' (Marty Robbins), 'Comes A Time' (Garcia, Hunter), 'One More Saturday Night' (Weir), 'Ramble On Rose' (Garcia, Hunter), 'Sugar Magnolia' (Hunter, Weir), 'Truckin'' (Hunter, Garcia, Lesh), 'Drums' (Kreutzmann), 'The Other One' (Kreutzmann, Weir), 'Johnny B. Goode' (Chuck Berry)

Dick's Picks Vol.2 (1995)

Personnel:
Jerry Garcia: lead guitar, vocals
Keith Godchaux: keyboards
Bill Kreutzmann: percussion
Phil Lesh: bass, vocals
Bob Weir: guitar, vocals
Recorded live at the Ohio Theatre in Columbus, Ohio, on October 31 1971. Recorded by Rex Jackson
Release date: March 1995
Running time: 58:19
'Dark Star Jam' (Garcia, Hart, Kreutzmann, Lesh, McKernan, Weir, Hunter), 'Sugar Magnolia' (Weir, Hunter), 'St. Stephen' (Garcia, Lesh, Hunter), 'Not Fade Away' (Petty, Hardin), 'Goin' Down The Road Feeling Bad' (trad.), 'Not Fade Away' (Petty, Hardin)

Road Trips Vol.3 No. 2 (2010)

Personnel:
Jerry Garcia: lead guitar, vocals
Keith Godchaux: piano
Bill Kreutzmann: drums
Phil Lesh: electric bass, vocals
Bob Weir: rhythm guitar, vocals
Recorded live at Austin Memorial Auditorium in Austin, Texas on November 15, 1971.
Recording by Rex Jackson.
Release date: February 2010
Running time: 151:41
'Truckin'' (Garcia, Lesh, Weir, Hunter), 'Bertha' (Garcia, Hunter), 'Playing In The Band' (Weir, Hunter), 'Deal' (Garcia, Hunter), 'Jack Straw' (Weir, Hunter), 'Loser' (Garcia,

Hunter), 'Beat It On Down The Line' (Jesse Fuller), 'Dark Star' (Garcia, Hunter), 'El Paso' (Marty Robbins), 'Dark Star' (Garcia, Hunter), 'Casey Jones' (Garcia, Hunter), 'One More Saturday Night' (Weir), 'Me And My Uncle' (John Phillips), 'Ramble On Rose' (Garcia, Hunter), 'Mexicali Blues' (Weir, Barlow), 'Brokedown Palace' (Garcia, Hunter), 'Me And Bobby McGee' (Kristofferson, Foster), 'Cumberland Blues' (Garcia, Lesh, Hunter), 'Sugar Magnolia' (Weir, Hunter), 'You Win Again' (Hank Williams), 'Not Fade Away' (Holly, Petty), 'Jam', 'Goin' Down The Road Feeling Bad' (trad.) 'Not Fade Away' (Holly, Petty), 'Johnny B. Goode' (Chuck Berry), [Bonus Disc recorded live at Texas Christian University, Fort Worth, Texas, November 14, 1971]: 'China Cat Sunflower' (Garcia, Hunter), 'I Know You Rider' (trad.), 'Sugaree' (Garcia, Hunter). 'Truckin'' (Garcia, Lesh, Weir, Hunter), 'Drums' (Kreutzmann), 'The Other One' (Weir, Kreutzmann), 'Me And My Uncle' (John Phillips), 'The Other One' (Weir, Kreutzmann), 'Wharf Rat' (Garcia, Hunter), 'Sugar Magnolia' (Weir, Hunter)

Dave's Picks Vol. 26 (2018)
Personnel:
Jerry Garcia: guitar, vocals
Keith Godchaux: keyboards
Bill Kreutzmann: drums
Phil Lesh: bass, vocals
Ron 'Pigpen' McKernan: organ, harmonica, vocals (on December 14, 1971 tracks)
Bob Weir: rhythm guitar, vocals
Recorded live at the Albuquerque Civic Auditorium in Albuquerque, New Mexico, on November 17, 1971, with bonus material recorded at Hill Auditorium in Ann Arbor, Michigan on December 14, 1971. Recorded by Rex Jackson.
Release date: April 2018
Running time: 223:36
'Truckin'' '(Garcia, Lesh, Weir, Hunter), 'Sugaree' (Garcia, Hunter), 'Beat It On Down The Line' (Jesse Fuller), 'Tennessee Jed' (Garcia, Hunter), 'El Paso' (Marty Robbins), 'Big Railroad Blues' (Noah Lewis), 'Jack Straw' (Weir, Hunter), 'Deal' (Garcia, Hunter), 'Playing In The Band' (Weir, Hart, Hunter), 'Cumberland Blues' (Garcia, Lesh, Hunter), 'Me And Bobby McGee' (Kristofferson, Foster), 'You Win Again' (Hank Williams), 'Mexicali Blues' (Weir, Barlow), 'Casey Jones' (Garcia, Hunter), 'One More Saturday Night' (Weir), 'Ramble On Rose' (Garcia, Hunter), 'Sugar Magnolia' (Weir, Hunter),' Cryptical Envelopment' (Garcia), 'Drums' (Kreutzmann), 'The Other One' (Weir, Kreutzmann), 'Me And My Uncle' (John Phillips), 'The Other One' (Weir, Kreutzmann), 'Wharf Rat' (Garcia, Hunter), 'Not Fade Away' (Holly, Petty), 'Goin' Down The Road Feeling Bad' (trad.), 'Not Fade Away' (Holly, Petty), [Bonus material from December 14, 1971]: 'Truckin'' (Garcia, Lesh, Weir, Hunter), 'Sugaree' (Garcia, Hunter), 'Mr. Charlie' (McKernan, Hunter), 'Beat It On Down The Line' (Jesse Fuller), 'Loser' (Garcia, Hunter), 'Next Time You See Me' (Harvey, Forest), 'El Paso' (Marty Robbins), 'Big Railroad Blues' (Noah Lewis), 'Me And My Uncle' (John Phillips), 'Run Rudolph Run' (Marks, Brodie), 'Big Boss Man' (Smith, Dixon), 'You Win Again' (Williams), 'Not Fade Away' (Holly, Petty), 'Goin' Down The Road Feeling Bad' (trad.), 'Not Fade Away' (Holly, Petty), [Bonus disc from December 14, 1971]: 'Jack Straw' (Weir, Hunter), 'Tennessee Jed' (Garcia, Hunter), 'Black Peter' (Garcia, Hunter), 'Playing In The Band' (Weir, Hart, Hunter), 'Casey Jones' (Garcia, Hunter), 'Mexicali Blues' (Weir, Barlow), 'Cryptical Envelopment' (Garcia), 'Drums' (Kreutzmann), 'The Other One' (Weir, Kreutzmann), 'Wharf Rat' (Garcia, Hunter), 'Sugar Magnolia' (Weir, Hunter)

Dave's Picks Vol. 22 (2017)

Personnel:
Jerry Garcia: guitar, vocals
Keith Godchaux: keyboards
Bill Kreutzmann: drums
Phil Lesh: bass, vocals
Ron 'Pigpen' McKernan: organ, harmonica, vocals
Bob Weir: guitar, vocals
Recorded live at the Felt Forum in New York City on December 7, 1971. Bonus tracks recorded live on December 6, 1971. Recorded by Rex Jackson.
Release date: May 2017
Running time: 3:51:05
'Cold Rain And Snow' (trad.), 'Beat It On Down The Line' (Jesse Fuller), 'Mr. Charlie' (McKernan, Hunter), 'Sugaree' (Garcia, Hunter), 'Jack Straw' (Weir, Hunter), 'Next Time You See Me' (Harvey, Forest), 'Tennessee Jed' (Garcia, Hunter), 'El Paso' (Marty Robbins), 'Brokedown Palace' (Garcia, Hunter), 'Run Rudolph Run' (Marks, Brodie), 'You Win Again' (Hank Williams), 'Cumberland Blues' (Garcia, Lesh, Hunter), 'Casey Jones' (Garcia, Hunter), 'Sugar Magnolia' (Weir, Hunter), 'Ramble On Rose' (Garcia, Hunter), 'Big Boss Man' (Smith, Dixon), 'Mexicali Blues' (Weir, Barlow), 'Brown-Eyed Women' (Garcia, Hunter), 'Me And My Uncle' (John Phillips), 'Smokestack Lightning' (Chester Burnett), 'Deal' (Garcia, Hunter), 'Truckin'' (Garcia, Lesh, Weir, Hunter), 'Not Fade Away' (Petty, Hardin), 'Going Down The Road Feelin' Bad' (trad.), 'Not Fade Away' (Petty, Hardin), 'One More Saturday Night' (Weir), [Bonus Tracks: Recorded live, December 6, 1971]: 'Big Railroad Blues' (Noah Lewis), 'Me And My Uncle' (John Phillips), 'Ramble On Rose' (Garcia, Hunter), 'Playing In The Band' (Weir, Hart, Hunter), 'Cryptical Envelopment' (Garcia), 'Drums' (Kreutzmann), 'The Other One' (Weir, Kreutzmann), 'Me And Bobby McGee' (Kristofferson, Foster), 'The Other One' (Weir), 'Wharf Rat' (Garcia, Hunter), 'One More Saturday Night' (Weir), 'Uncle John's Band' (Garcia, Hunter), [Bonus disc: recorded December 6, 1971]: 'Truckin'' (Garcia, Lesh, Weir, Hunter), 'Loser' (Garcia, Hunter), 'Mr. Charlie' (McKernan, Hunter), 'Jack Straw' (Weir, Hunter), 'China Cat Sunflower' (Garcia, Hunter), 'I Know You Rider' (trad.), 'Tennessee Jed' (Garcia, Hunter), 'Mexicali Blues' (Weir, Barlow), 'Black Peter' (Garcia, Hunter), 'Casey Jones' (Garcia, Hunter)

Fox Theatre, St. Louis, MO 12-10-71 (2021)

Personnel:
Jerry Garcia: guitar, vocals
Keith Godchaux: keyboards
Bill Kreutzmann: drums
Phil Lesh: bass, vocals
Ron 'Pigpen' McKernan: keyboards, harmonica, vocals
Bob Weir: guitar, vocals
Recorded live at the Fox Theatre in St. Louis, Missouri, on December 10, 1971. Recorded by Rex Jackson.
Release date: October 2021
Running time: 183:37
'Bertha' (Garcia, Hunter), 'Me And My Uncle' (John Phillips), 'Mr. Charlie' (McKernan, Hunter), 'Loser' (Garcia, Hunter), 'Beat It On Down The Line' (Jesse Fuller), 'Sugaree' (Garcia, Hunter), 'Jack Straw' (Bob Weir, Hunter), 'Next Time You See Me' (Harvey, Forest), 'Tennessee Jed' (Garcia, Hunter), 'El Paso' (Marty Robbins), 'Big Railroad Blues' (Noah

Lewis), 'Casey Jones' (Garcia, Hunter), 'Good Lovin'' (Clark, Resnick), 'Brokedown Palace' (Garcia, Hunter), 'Playing In The Band' (Weir, Hart, Hunter), 'Run Rudolph Run' (Marks, Brodie), 'Deal' (Garcia, Hunter), Sugar Magnolia' (Weir, Hunter), 'Comes A Time' (Garcia, Hunter), 'Truckin'' (Garcia, Lesh, Weir, Hunter), 'Drums' (Kreutzmann), 'The Other One' (Weir, Kreutzmann), 'Sittin' On Top Of The World' (Carter, Jacobs), 'The Other One' (Weir, Kreutzmann), 'Not Fade Away' (Petty, Hardin), 'Goin' Down The Road Feeling Bad' (trad.), 'Not Fade Away' (Petty, Hardin), 'One More Saturday Night' (Weir)

1972
Dave's Picks Vol.14 (2015)
Personnel:
Jerry Garcia: guitar, vocals
Keith Godchaux: piano
Bill Kreutzmann: drums
Phil Lesh: electric bass, vocals
Ron 'Pigpen' McKernan: organ, harmonica, percussion, vocals
Bob Weir: guitar, vocals
Recorded at the Academy of Music in New York City, on March 26, 1972. Recorded by Rex Jackson.
Release date: May 2015
Running time: 192:42
'Greatest Story Ever Told' (Weir, Hart, Hunter), 'Cold Rain And Snow' (trad.), 'Chinatown Shuffle' (McKernan), 'Black-Throated Wind' (Weir, Barlow), 'You Win Again' (Hank Williams), 'Mr. Charlie' (McKernan, Hunter), 'Jack Straw' (Weir, Hunter), 'Loser' (Garcia, Hunter), 'Looks Like Rain' (Weir, Barlow), 'Big Railroad Blues' (Noah Lewis), 'Big Boss Man' (Smith, Dixon), 'Playing In The Band' (Weir, Hart, Hunter), 'El Paso' (Marty Robbins), 'Good Lovin'' (Clark, Resnick), 'Truckin'' (Garcia, Lesh, Weir, Hunter), 'Drums' (Kreutzmann), 'The Other One' (Weir, Kreutzmann), 'Me And My Uncle' (John Phillips), 'The Other One' (Weir, Kreutzmann), 'Wharf Rat' (Garcia, Hunter), 'Sugar Magnolia' (Weir, Hunter), 'The Stranger (Two Souls in Communion)' (McKernan), 'Not Fade Away' (Petty, Hardin), 'Goin' Down The Road Feeling Bad' (trad.), 'Not Fade Away' (Petty, Hardin), [Bonus Disc: Recorded live at Academy of Music, New York City, March 27, 1972]: 'Bertha' (Garcia, Hunter), 'Brown-Eyed Women' (Garcia, Hunter), 'China Cat Sunflower' (Garcia, Hunter), 'I Know You Rider' (trad.), 'Cumberland Blues' (Garcia, Lesh, Hunter), [Following recorded live at Academy of Music, New York City, March 21, 1972]: 'Truckin'' (Garcia, Lesh, Weir, Hunter), 'Drums' (Kreutzmann), 'The Other One' (Weir, Kreutzmann), 'Wharf Rat' (Garcia, Hunter)

Dick's Picks Vol. 30 (2003)
Personnel:
Jerry Garcia: guitar, vocals
Donna Godchaux: vocals
Keith Godchaux: piano
Bill Kreutzmann: drums
Phil Lesh: electric bass, vocals
Ron 'Pigpen' McKernan: harmonica, organ, percussion, vocals
Bob Weir: guitar, vocals
Additional musician:
Bo Diddley: guitar, vocals

Recorded live at the Academy of Music in New York City on March 28, 1972 with tracks from March 25, 1972, and March 27 at the same venue. Recorded by Betty Cantor-Jackson. Release date: October 2003
Running time: 265:34
'Bo Diddley' (Bo Diddley) [Bo Diddley backed by The Grateful Dead, March 25 1972], 'I'm A Man (Mannish Boy)' (Bo Diddley) [Bo Diddley backed by The Grateful Dead, March 25 1972], 'I've Seen Them All' (Bo Diddley) [Bo Diddley backed by The Grateful Dead, March 25 1972], 'Jam' (Bo Diddley, Grateful Dead) [Bo Diddley backed by The Grateful Dead, March 25 1972], 'Mona' (Bo Diddley) [Bo Diddley backed by The Grateful Dead, March 25 1972], 'How Sweet It Is (To Be Loved By You)' (Holland, Dozier, Holland) [March 25 1972], 'Are You Lonely For Me' (Bert Berns) [March 25 1972], 'Smokestack Lightnin'' (Howlin' Wolf) [March 25 1972], 'Playing In The Band' (Hunter, Hart, Weir) [March 27 1972], [Following from March 28 1972] 'Truckin'' (Hunter, Garcia, Lesh, Weir), 'Tennessee Jed' (Garcia, Hunter), 'Chinatown Shuffle' (Pigpen), 'Black-Throated Wind' (Barlow, Weir), 'You Win Again' (Hank Williams), 'Mr. Charlie' (Hunter, Pigpen), 'Mexicali Blues' (Barlow, Weir), 'Brokedown Palace' (Garcia, Hunter), 'Next Time You See Me' (Forest, Harvey), 'Cumberland Blues' (Hunter, Garcia, Lesh), 'Looks Like Rain' (Barlow, Weir), 'Big Railroad Blues' (Noah Lewis), 'El Paso' (Marty Robbins), 'China Cat Sunflower' (Garcia, Hunter), 'I Know You Rider' (trad.), 'Casey Jones' (Garcia, Hunter), 'Playing In The Band' (Hunter, Hart, Weir), 'Sugaree' (Garcia, Hunter), 'The Stranger (Two Souls In Communion)' (Pigpen), 'Sugar Magnolia' (Hunter, Weir), 'The Other One' (Kreutzmann, Weir), 'It Hurts Me Too' (Elmore James), 'Not Fade Away' (Holly, Petty), 'Goin' Down The Road Feelin' Bad' (trad.), 'Not Fade Away' (Holly, Petty), 'The Sidewalks Of New York' (Blake, Lawlor), 'One More Saturday Night' (Weir)

Steppin' Out With The Grateful Dead: England '72 (1972)

Personnel:
Jerry Garcia: lead guitar, vocals, pedal steel guitar, organ
Donna Jean Godchaux: vocals
Keith Godchaux: piano
Robert Hunter: songwriter
Bill Kreutzmann: drums, percussion
Phil Lesh: bass guitar, vocals
Ron 'Pigpen' McKernan: organ, harmonica, vocals
Bob Weir: rhythm guitar, vocals
Compilation producer: David Lemieux Recording: Bob Matthews, Betty Cantor, Dennis Leonard, Janet Furman – April/May 1972. Mixed by Jeffrey Norman
Release date: July 2002
Running time: 5:14:05
'Cold Rain And Snow' (Grateful Dead), 'Greatest Story Ever Told' (Weir, Hart, Hunter), 'Mr. Charlie' (McKernan, Hunter), 'Sugaree' (Garcia, Hunter), 'Mexicali Blues' (Weir, Barlow), 'Big Boss Man' (Dixon, Smith), 'Deal' (Garcia, Hunter), 'Jack Straw' (Weir, Hunter), 'Big Railroad Blues' (Noah Lewis), 'Hurts Me Too' (James, Sehorn), 'China Cat Sunflower' (Garcia, Hunter), 'I Know You Rider' (trad.), 'Happy Birthday To You' (Hill), 'Playing In The Band' (Weir, Hart, Hunter), 'Good Lovin'' (Clark, Resnick), 'Ramble On Rose' (Garcia, Hunter), 'Black-Throated Wind' (Weir, Barlow), 'Sitting On Top Of The World' (Carter, Jacobs), 'Comes A Time' (Garcia, Hunter), 'Turn On Your Lovelight' (Malone, Scott), 'Goin' Down The Road Feeling Bad' (trad.) 'Not Fade Away' (Petty, Hardin), 'Hey Bo Diddley' (Ellas

McDaniel), 'Not Fade Away' (Petty, Hardin), 'Rockin' Pneumonia And The Boogie Woogie Flu' (Huey 'Piano' Smith), 'Black Peter' (Garcia, Hunter), 'Chinatown Shuffle' (McKernan), 'Truckin'' (Garcia, Lesh, Weir, Hunter), 'Drums' (Kreutzmann), 'The Other One' (Weir, Kreutzmann), 'El Paso' (Marty Robbins), 'The Other One' (Weir, Kreutzmann), 'Wharf Rat' (Garcia, Hunter), 'One More Saturday Night' (Bob Weir), 'Uncle John's Band' (Garcia, Hunter), 'The Stranger (Two Souls In Communion)' (McKernan) 'Dark Star' (Garcia, Hart, Kreutzmann, Lesh, McKernan, Weir, Hunter), 'Sugar Magnolia' (Weir, Hunter), 'Caution (Do Not Stop On Tracks), (Grateful Dead), 'Brokedown Palace' (Garcia, Hunter)

Europe '72 Volume 2 (2011)
Personnel:
Jerry Garcia: lead guitar, vocals, pedal steel guitar, organ
Donna Jean Godchaux: vocals
Keith Godchaux: piano
Bill Kreutzmann: drums, percussion
Phil Lesh: bass guitar, vocals
Ron 'Pigpen' McKernan: organ, harmonica, vocals
Bob Weir: rhythm guitar, vocals
Recorded by Betty Cantor, Janet Furman, Bob Matthews, Rosie, Wizard April – May 1972
Produced by David Lemieux
Release date: September 2011
Running time: 155:01
'Bertha' (Garcia, Hunter), 'Me And My Uncle' (John Phillips), 'Chinatown Shuffle' (McKernan), 'Sugaree' (Garcia, Hunter), 'Beat It On Down The Line' (Jesse Fuller), 'Loser' (Garcia, Hunter), 'Next Time You See Me' (Harvey, Forest), 'Black- Throated Wind' (Weir, Barlow), 'Dire Wolf' (Garcia, Hunter), 'Greatest Story Ever Told' (Weir, Hart, Hunter), 'Deal' (Garcia, Hunter), 'Good Lovin'' (Resnick, Clark), 'Playing In The Band' (Weir, Hart, Hunter), 'Dark Star' (Garcia, Hart, Kreutzmann, Lesh, McKernan, Weir, Hunter), 'Drums' (Kreutzmann), 'The Other One' (Weir, Kreutzmann), 'Sing Me Back Home' (Merle Haggard), 'Not Fade Away' (Petty, Hardin), 'Goin' Down The Road Feeling Bad' (trad.), 'Not Fade Away' (Petty, Hardin)
Vinyl edition bonus track: 'Big Railroad Blues' (Noah Lewis)

Europe '72: The Complete Recordings (2011)
Personnel:
Jerry Garcia: lead guitar, vocals, pedal steel guitar, organ
Donna Jean Godchaux: vocals
Keith Godchaux: piano
Bill Kreutzmann: drums, percussion
Phil Lesh: bass guitar, vocals
Ron 'Pigpen' McKernan: organ, harmonica, vocals
Bob Weir: rhythm guitar, vocals
Recorded by Betty Cantor, Janet Furman, Bob Matthews, Rosie, Wizard April – May 1972.
Produced by David Lemieux
Release date: September 2011
Running time: 70:47:25
Vol.1: Empire Pool, Wembley, London, England, April 7, 1972
'Greatest Story Ever Told' (Weir, Hart, Hunter), 'Sugaree' (Garcia, Hunter), 'Chinatown Shuffle' (McKernan), 'Me And My Uncle' (John Phillips), 'China Cat Sunflower' (Garcia,

Hunter), 'I Know You Rider' (trad.), 'Big Boss Man' (Smith, Dixon), 'Black-Throated Wind' (Weir, Barlow), 'Loser' (Garcia, Hunter), 'Mr. Charlie' (McKernan, Hunter), 'Beat It On Down The Line' (Jesse Fuller), 'Tennessee Jed' (Garcia, Hunter), 'Playing In The Band' (Weir, Hart, Hunter), 'Truckin'' (Garcia, Lesh, Weir, Hunter), 'Drums' (Kreutzmann), 'The Other One' (Weir, Kreutzmann), 'El Paso' (Marty Robbins), 'The Other One' (Weir, Kreutzmann) 'Wharf Rat' (Garcia, Hunter), 'Ramble On Rose' (Garcia, Hunter), 'Sugar Magnolia' (Weir, Hunter), 'Not Fade Away' (Petty, Hardin), 'Goin' Down The Road Feeling Bad' (trad.), 'Not Fade Away' (Petty, Hardin), 'One More Saturday Night' (Weir)

Vol.2: Empire Pool, Wembley, London, England, April 8, 1972
'Bertha' (Garcia, Hunter), 'Me And My Uncle' (John Phillips), 'Mr. Charlie' (McKernan, Hunter), 'Deal' (Garcia, Hunter), 'Black-Throated Wind' (Weir, Barlow), 'Next Time You See Me' (Harvey, Forest), 'Cumberland Blues' (Garcia, Lesh, Hunter), 'The Yellow Dog Story' (trad.), 'Brown-Eyed Women' (Garcia, Hunter), 'Beat It On Down The Line' (Jesse Fuller), 'Tennessee Jed' (Garcia, Hunter), 'Playing in The Band' (Weir, Hart, Hunter), 'Good Lovin'' (Clark, Resnick), 'Looks Like Rain' (Weir, Barlow), 'Casey Jones' (Garcia, Hunter), 'Truckin'' (Garcia, Lesh, Weir, Hunter), 'Big Railroad Blues' (Noah Lewis), 'Hurts Me Too' (James, Sehorn), 'Dark Star' (Garcia, Hart, Kreutzmann, Lesh, McKernan, Weir, Hunter), 'Sugar Magnolia' (Weir, Hunter), 'Caution (Do Not Stop On Tracks)', (Grateful Dead), 'One More Saturday Night' (Weir)

Vol. 3: City Hall, Newcastle, England, April 11, 1972
'Greatest Story Ever Told' (Weir, Hart, Hunter), 'Deal' (Garcia, Hunter), 'Mr. Charlie' (McKernan, Hunter), 'Black-Throated Wind' (Weir, Barlow), 'Tennessee Jed' (Garcia, Hunter), 'Big Boss Man' (Smith, Dixon), 'Beat It On Down The Line' (Jesse Fuller), 'Sugaree' (Garcia, Hunter), 'Jack Straw' (Weir, Hunter), 'Chinatown Shuffle' (McKernan), 'China Cat Sunflower' (Garcia, Hunter), 'I Know You Rider' (trad.), 'Playing In The Band' (Weir, Hart, Hunter), 'Next Time You See Me' (Harvey, Forest), 'Brown-Eyed Women' (Garcia, Hunter), 'Looks Like Rain' (Weir, Barlow), 'Big Railroad Blues' (Noah Lewis), 'Casey Jones' (Garcia, Hunter), 'Good Lovin'' (Clark, Resnick), 'Ramble On Rose' (Garcia, Hunter), 'Truckin'' (Garcia, Lesh, Weir, Hunter), 'Drums' (Kreutzmann), 'The Other One' (Weir, Kreutzmann), 'Comes A Time' (Garcia, Hunter), 'Sugar Magnolia' (Weir, Hunter), 'Brokedown Palace' (Garcia, Hunter), 'One More Saturday Night' (Bob Weir)

Vol. 4: Tivoli Concert Hall, Copenhagen, Denmark, April 14, 1972
'Bertha' (Garcia, Hunter), 'Me And My Uncle' (John Phillips), 'Mr. Charlie' (McKernan, Hunter), 'You Win Again' (Hank Williams), 'Black-Throated Wind' (Weir, Barlow), 'Chinatown Shuffle' (McKernan), 'Loser' (Garcia, Hunter), 'Me And Bobby McGee' (Kristofferson, Foster), 'Cumberland Blues' (Garcia, Lesh, Hunter), 'Playing In The Band' (Weir, Hart, Hunter), 'Tennessee Jed' (Garcia, Hunter), 'El Paso' (Marty Robbins), 'Big Boss Man' (Smith, Dixon), 'Beat It On Down The Line' (Jesse Fuller), 'Casey Jones' (Garcia, Hunter), 'Truckin'' (Garcia, Lesh, Weir, Hunter), 'Hurts Me Too' (James, Sehorn), 'Brown-Eyed Women' (Garcia, Hunter), 'Looks Like Rain' (Weir, Barlow), 'Dark Star' (Garcia, Hart, Kreutzmann, Lesh, McKernan, Weir, Hunter), 'Sugar Magnolia' (Weir, Hunter), 'Good Lovin'' (Clark, Resnick), 'Caution (Do Not Stop On Tracks)' (Grateful Dead), 'Good Lovin'' (Clark, Resnick), 'Ramble On Rose' (Garcia, Hunter), 'Not Fade Away' (Petty, Hardin), 'Goin' Down The Road Feeling Bad' (trad.), 'Not Fade Away' (Petty, Hardin), 'One More Saturday Night' (Weir)

Vol. 5: Stakladen, Aarhus, Denmark April 16 1972
'Greatest Story Ever Told' (Weir, Hart, Hunter), 'Sugaree' (Garcia, Hunter), 'Chinatown Shuffle' (McKernan) 'Black-Throated Wind' (Weir, Barlow), 'Tennessee Jed' (Garcia, Hunter), 'Mr. Charlie' (McKernan, Hunter), 'Beat It On Down The Line' (Jesse Fuller), 'China Cat Sunflower' (Garcia, Hunter), 'I Know You Rider' (trad.), 'Mexicali Blues' (Weir,

Barlow), 'Loser' (Garcia, Hunter), 'Next Time You See Me' (Harvey, Forest), 'Playing In The Band' (Weir, Hart, Hunter), 'Dire Wolf' (Garcia, Hunter), 'Good Lovin'' (Clark, Resnick), 'Cumberland Blues' (Garcia, Lesh, Hunter), 'El Paso' (Marty Robbins), 'Deal' (Garcia, Hunter), 'Truckin'' (Garcia, Lesh, Weir, Hunter), 'Jam' (Grateful Dead), 'The Other One' (Weir, Kreutzmann), 'Me And My Uncle' (John Phillips), 'The Other One' (Weir, Kreutzmann), 'Not Fade Away' (Petty, Hardin), 'Goin' Down The Road Feeling Bad' (trad.), 'Not Fade Away' (Petty, Hardin)

Vol 6: Tivoli Concert Hall, Copenhagen, Denmark, April 17, 1972
'Cold Rain And Snow' (trad.), 'Me And Bobby McGee' (Kristofferson, Foster), 'Chinatown Shuffle' (McKernan), 'China Cat Sunflower' (Garcia, Hunter), 'I Know You Rider' (trad.), 'Jack Straw' (Weir, Hunter), 'He's Gone' (Garcia, Hunter), 'Next Time You See Me' (Harvey, Forest), 'Black-Throated Wind' (Weir, Barlow), 'Casey Jones' (Garcia, Hunter), 'Mr. Charlie' (McKernan, Hunter), 'Playing In The Band' (Weir, Hart, Hunter), 'Sugaree' (Garcia, Hunter), 'One More Saturday Night' (Weir), 'Hurts Me Too' (James, Sehorn), 'Ramble On Rose' (Garcia, Hunter), 'El Paso' (Marty Robbins), 'Big Railroad Blues' (Noah Lewis), 'Truckin'' (Garcia, Lesh, Weir, Hunter), 'Dark Star' (Garcia, Hart, Kreutzmann, Lesh, McKernan, Weir, Hunter), 'Sugar Magnolia' (Weir, Hunter), 'Caution (Do Not Stop On Tracks)' (Grateful Dead), 'Johnny B. Goode' (Chuck Berry)

Vol 7: Beat Club, Bremen, West Germany, April 21, 1972
'Bertha' (Garcia, Hunter), 'Playing In The Band' (Weir, Hart, Hunter), 'Mr. Charlie' (McKernan, Hunter), 'Sugaree' (Garcia, Hunter), 'One More Saturday Night' (Weir), 'Playing In The Band' (Weir, Hart, Hunter), 'Beat It On Down The Line' (Jesse Fuller), 'Truckin'' (Garcia, Lesh, Weir, Hunter), 'Drums' (Kreutzmann), 'The Other One' (Weir, Kreutzmann)

Vol 8: Rheinhalle, Dusseldort, West Germany, April 24, 1972
'Truckin'' (Garcia, Lesh, Weir, Hunter), 'Tennessee Jed' (Garcia, Hunter), 'Chinatown Shuffle' (McKernan), 'Black-Throated Wind' (Weir, Barlow), 'China Cat Sunflower' (Garcia, Hunter), 'I Know You Rider' (trad.), 'Mr. Charlie' (McKernan, Hunter), 'Beat It On Down The Line' (Jesse Fuller), 'Loser' (Garcia, Hunter), 'Playing In The Band' (Weir, Hart, Hunter), 'Next Time You See Me' (Harvey, Forest). 'Me And Bobby McGee' (Kristofferson, Foster), 'Good Lovin'' (Clark, Resnick), 'Casey Jones' (Garcia, Hunter), 'Dark Star' (Garcia, Hart, Kreutzmann, Lesh, McKernan, Weir, Hunter), 'Me And My Uncle' (John Phillips) 'Dark Star' (Garcia, Hart, Kreutzmann, Lesh, McKernan, Weir, Hunter), 'Wharf Rat' (Garcia, Hunter), 'Sugar Magnolia' (Weir, Hunter) 'He's Gone' (Garcia, Hunter), 'Hurts Me Too' (James, Sehorn), 'El Paso' (Marty Robbins), 'Not Fade Away' (Petty, Hardin), 'Goin' Down The Road Feeling Bad' (trad.), 'Not Fade Away' (Petty, Hardin), 'One More Saturday Night' (Weir)

Vol 9: Jahrhunderthalle, Frankfurt, West Germany, April 26, 1972
'Bertha' (Garcia, Hunter), 'Me And My Uncle' (John Phillips), 'Mr. Charlie' (McKernan, Hunter), 'He's Gone' (Garcia, Hunter), 'Black-Throated Wind' (Weir, Barlow), 'Next Time You See Me' (Harvey, Forest), 'China Cat Sunflower' (Garcia, Hunter), 'I Know You Rider' (trad.), 'Jack Straw' (Weir, Hunter), 'Big Railroad Blues' (Noah Lewis), 'Playing In The Band' (Weir, Hart, Hunter), 'Chinatown Shuffle' (McKernan), 'Loser' (Garcia, Hunter), 'Beat It On Down The Line' (Jesse Fuller) 'You Win Again' (Hank Williams), 'El Paso' (Marty Robbins), 'Tennessee Jed' (Garcia, Hunter), 'Greatest Story Ever Told' (Weir, Hart, Hunter), 'The Stranger (Two Souls In Communion)' (McKernan), 'Casey Jones' (Garcia, Hunter), 'Good Lovin'' (Clark, Resnick) 'Dire Wolf' (Garcia, Hunter), 'Truckin'' (Garcia, Lesh, Weir, Hunter), 'Drums' (Kreutzmann), 'The Other One' (Weir, Kreutzmann), 'Comes A Time' (Garcia, Hunter), 'Sugar Magnolia' (Weir, Hunter), 'Lovelight' (Scott, Malone), 'Goin' Down The Road Feeling Bad' (trad.), 'One More Saturday Night' (Weir)

Vol 10: Musikhalle, Hamburg, West Germany, April 29, 1972

'Playing In The Band' (Weir, Hart, Hunter), 'Sugaree' (Garcia, Hunter), 'Mr. Charlie' (McKernan, Hunter), 'Black-Throated Wind' (Weir, Barlow), 'China Cat Sunflower' (Garcia, Hunter), 'I Know You Rider' (trad.), 'Big Boss Man' (Smith, Dixon), 'Jack Straw' (Weir, Hunter), 'Loser' (Garcia, Hunter), 'Chinatown Shuffle' (McKernan), 'Me And My Uncle' (John Phillips), 'Big Railroad Blues' (Noah Lewis), 'Good Lovin'' (Clark, Resnick), 'Casey Jones' (Garcia, Hunter), 'Greatest Story Ever Told' (Weir, Hart, Hunter), 'He's Gone'(Garcia, Hunter), 'Next Time You See Me' (Harvey, Forest), 'Dark Star' (Garcia, Hart, Kreutzmann, Lesh, McKernan, Weir, Hunter), 'Sugar Magnolia' (Weir, Hunter), 'Caution (Do Not Stop On Tracks)' (Grateful Dead), 'One More Saturday Night' (Weir), 'Uncle John's Band' (Garcia, Hunter)

Vol 11: Olympia Theatre, Paris, France, May 3, 1972

'Bertha' (Garcia, Hunter), 'Me And My Uncle' (John Phillips), 'Mr. Charlie' (McKernan, Hunter), 'Sugaree' (Garcia, Hunter), 'Black-Throated Wind' (Weir, Barlow) 'Chinatown Shuffle' (McKernan), 'China Cat Sunflower' (Garcia, Hunter), 'I Know You Rider' (trad.), 'Beat It On Down The Line' (Jesse Fuller), 'He's Gone' (Garcia, Hunter), 'Next Time You See Me' (Harvey, Forest), 'Playing In The Band' (Weir, Hart, Hunter), 'Tennessee Jed' (Garcia, Hunter), 'Good Lovin'' (Clark, Resnick), 'Sing Me Back Home' (Merle Haggard), 'Casey Jones' (Garcia, Hunter),' Greatest Story Ever Told' (Weir, Hart, Hunter), 'Ramble On Rose' (Garcia, Hunter), 'Hurts Me Too' (James, Sehorn), 'Truckin'' (Garcia, Lesh, Weir, Hunter), 'The Other One' (Weir, Kreutzmann), 'Drums' (Kreutzmann), 'The Other One' (Weir, Kreutzmann), 'Me And Bobby McGee' (Kristofferson, Foster), 'The Other One' (Weir, Kreutzmann), 'Wharf Rat' (Garcia, Hunter), 'Jack Straw' (Weir, Hunter), 'Sugar Magnolia' (Weir, Hunter), 'Not Fade Away' (Petty, Hardin), 'Goin' Down The Road Feeling Bad' (trad.), 'Not Fade Away' (Petty, Hardin), 'One More Saturday Night' (Weir)

Vol 12: Olympia Theatre, Paris, France, May 4, 1972

'Greatest Story Ever Told' (Weir, Hart, Hunter), 'Deal' (Garcia, Hunter), 'Mr. Charlie' (McKernan, Hunter), 'Beat It On Down The Line' (Jesse Fuller), 'Brown-Eyed Women' (Garcia, Hunter), 'Chinatown Shuffle' (McKernan), 'Playing In The Band' (Weir, Hart, Hunter), 'You Win Again' (Hank Williams), 'Hurts Me Too' (James, Sehorn), 'He's Gone' (Garcia, Hunter), 'El Paso' (Marty Robbins), 'Big Railroad Blues' (Noah Lewis), 'The Stranger (Two Souls In Communion)' (McKernan), 'Casey Jones' (Garcia, Hunter), 'Good Lovin'' (Clark, Resnick), 'Next Time You See Me' (Harvey, Forest), 'Ramble On Rose' (Garcia, Hunter), 'Jack Straw' (Weir, Hunter), 'Dark Star' (Garcia, Hart, Kreutzmann, Lesh, McKernan, Weir, Hunter), 'Drums' (Kreutzmann), 'Dark Star' (Garcia, Hart, Kreutzmann, Lesh, McKernan, Weir, Hunter), 'Sugar Magnolia' (Weir, Hunter), 'Sing Me Back Home' (Merle Haggard),' Mexicali Blues' (Weir, Barlow), 'Big Boss Man' (Smith, Dixon), 'Uncle John's Band' (Garcia, Hunter), 'Goin' Down The Road Feeling Bad' (trad.), 'Not Fade Away' (Petty, Hardin), 'One More Saturday Night' (Weir)

Vol 13: Bickershaw Festival, Wigan, England, May 7, 1972

'Truckin'' (Garcia, Lesh, Weir, Hunter), 'Sugaree' (Garcia, Hunter), 'Mr. Charlie' (McKernan, Hunter), 'Beat It On Down The Line' (Jesse Fuller), 'He's Gone' (Garcia, Hunter), 'Chinatown Shuffle' (McKernan), 'China Cat Sunflower' (Garcia, Hunter), 'I Know You Rider' (trad.), 'Black-Throated Wind' (Weir, Barlow), 'Next Time You See Me' (Harvey, Forest), 'Happy Birthday To You' (Hill, Hill), 'Playing In The Band' (Weir, Hart, Hunter), 'Tennessee Jed' (Garcia, Hunter), 'Good Lovin'' (Clark, Resnick), 'Casey Jones' (Garcia, Hunter), 'Greatest Story Ever Told' (Weir, Hart, Hunter), 'Big Boss Man' (Smith, Dixon), 'Ramble On Rose' (Garcia, Hunter), 'Jack Straw' (Weir, Hunter), 'Dark Star' (Garcia, Hart, Kreutzmann, Lesh, McKernan, Weir, Hunter), 'Drums' (Kreutzmann), 'The Other One' (Weir,

Kreutzmann), 'Sing Me Back Home' (Merle Haggard), 'Sugar Magnolia' (Weir, Hunter), 'Turn On Your Lovelight' (Scott, Malone), 'Goin' Down The Road Feeling Bad' (trad.), 'Not Fade Away' (Petty, Hardin), 'One More Saturday Night' (Weir)

Vol 14: Concertbebouw, Amsterdam, The Netherlands, May 10 1972
'Bertha' (Garcia, Hunter), 'Me And My Uncle' (John Phillips), 'Mr. Charlie' (McKernan, Hunter), 'China Cat Sunflower' (Garcia, Hunter), 'I Know You Rider' (trad.), 'Black-Throated Wind' (Weir, Barlow), 'Loser' (Garcia, Hunter), 'Next Time You See Me' (Harvey, Forest), 'El Paso' (Marty Robbins), 'He's Gone' (Garcia, Hunter), 'Chinatown Shuffle' (McKernan), 'Playing In The Band' (Weir, Hart, Hunter), 'Big Railroad Blues' (Noah Lewis), 'Jack Straw' (Weir, Hunter), 'Tennessee Jed' (Garcia, Hunter), 'Big Boss Man' (Smith, Dixon), 'Greatest Story Ever Told' (Weir, Hart, Hunter), 'Casey Jones' (Garcia, Hunter), 'Truckin'' (Garcia, Lesh, Weir, Hunter), 'Drums' (Kreutzmann), 'The Other One' (Weir, Kreutzmann), 'Me And Bobby McGee' (Kristofferson, Foster), 'The Other One' (Weir, Kreutzmann), 'Wharf Rat' (Garcia, Hunter), 'Beat It On Down The Line' (Jesse Fuller), 'The Stranger (Two Souls in Communion)' (McKernan), 'Ramble On Rose' (Garcia, Hunter), 'Sing Me Back Home' (Merle Haggard), 'Sugar Magnolia' (Weir, Hunter), 'Not Fade Away' (Petty, Hardin), 'Goin' Down The Road Feeling Bad' (trad.), 'Not Fade Away' (Petty, Hardin)

Vol 15: Grote Zaal, De Doelen, Rotterdam, The Netherlands, May 11 1972
'Playing In The Band' (Weir, Hart, Hunter), 'Sugaree' (Garcia, Hunter), 'Mr. Charlie' (McKernan, Hunter), 'Black-Throated Wind' (Weir, Barlow), 'Deal' (Garcia, Hunter), 'Chinatown Shuffle' (McKernan), 'Mexicali Blues' (Weir, Barlow), 'China Cat Sunflower' (Garcia, Hunter), 'I Know You Rider' (trad.), 'Hurts Me Too' (James, Sehorn), 'Beat It On Down The Line' (Jesse Fuller), 'Brown-Eyed Women' (Garcia, Hunter), 'Jack Straw' (Weir, Hunter), 'Big Railroad Blues' (Noah Lewis), 'Good Lovin'' (Clark, Resnick), 'Casey Jones' (Garcia, Hunter), 'Morning Dew' (Dobson, Rose), 'Me And My Uncle' (John Phillips), 'The Stranger (Two Souls In Communion)' (McKernan), 'El Paso' (Marty Robbins), 'Tennessee Jed' (Garcia, Hunter), 'Next Time You See Me' (Harvey, Forest), 'Dark Star' (Garcia, Hart, Kreutzmann, Lesh, McKernan, Weir, Hunter), 'Drums' (Kreutzmann), 'Dark Star' (Garcia, Hart, Kreutzmann, Lesh, McKernan, Weir, Hunter), 'Sugar Magnolia' (Weir, Hunter), 'Caution (Do Not Stop On Tracks)', (Grateful Dead), 'Truckin'' (Garcia, Lesh, Weir, Hunter), 'Uncle John's Band' (Garcia, Hunter)

Vol 16: Lille Fairgrounds, Lille, France May 13 1972
Tuning Rap, 'Bertha' (Garcia, Hunter), 'Black-Throated Wind' (Weir, Barlow), 'Chinatown Shuffle' (McKernan), 'Loser' (Garcia, Hunter), 'Beat It On Down The Line' (Jesse Fuller), 'Mr. Charlie' (McKernan, Hunter), 'China Cat Sunflower' (Garcia, Hunter), 'I Know You Rider' (trad.), 'Me And My Uncle' (John Phillips), 'Big Railroad Blues' (Noah Lewis), 'Next Time You See Me' (Harvey, Forest), 'Playing In The Band' (Weir, Hart, Hunter), 'Sugaree' (Garcia, Hunter), 'Mexicali Blues' (Weir, Barlow), Casey Jones (Garcia, Hunter), 'Truckin'' (Garcia, Lesh, Weir, Hunter), 'Drums' (Kreutzmann), 'The Other One' (Weir, Kreutzmann), 'He's Gone' (Garcia, Hunter), 'Hurts Me Too' (James, Sehorn), 'Sugar Magnolia' (Weir, Hunter), 'Not Fade Away' (Petty, Hardin), 'Goin' Down The Road Feeling Bad' (trad.), Not Fade Away' (Petty, Hardin), 'One More Saturday Night' (Weir)

Vol 17: La Grande Salle Du Grand Theatre, Luxembourg, May 16, 1972
'Big River' (Johnny Cash) 'Sugar Magnolia' (Weir, Hunter), 'Bertha' (Garcia, Hunter), 'Me And My Uncle' (John Phillips), 'Mr. Charlie' (McKernan, Hunter), 'Sugaree' (Garcia, Hunter), 'Black-Throated Wind' (Weir, Barlow), 'Chinatown Shuffle' (McKernan), 'China Cat Sunflower' (Garcia, Hunter), 'I Know You Rider' (trad.), 'Beat It On Down The Line' (Jesse Fuller), 'It Hurts Me Too' (James, Sehorn), 'Tennessee Jed' (Garcia, Hunter), 'Playing In The Band' (Weir, Hart, Hunter), 'Promised Land' (Chuck Berry), 'Truckin'' (Garcia, Lesh,

Weir, Hunter), 'Drums' (Kreutzmann), 'The Other One' (Weir, Kreutzmann), 'Sing Me Back Home' (Merle Haggard), 'Sugar Magnolia' (Weir, Hunter), 'Not Fade Away' (Petty, Hardin), 'Goin' Down The Road Feeling Bad' (trad.), 'Not Fade Away' (Petty, Hardin), 'One More Saturday Night' (Weir)

Vol 18: Kongressaal, Munich, West Germany, May 18, 1972

'Truckin'' (Garcia, Lesh, Weir, Hunter), 'Sugaree' (Garcia, Hunter), 'Mr. Charlie' (McKernan, Hunter), 'Jack Straw' (Weir, Hunter), 'Tennessee Jed' (Garcia, Hunter), 'Chinatown Shuffle' (McKernan), 'Black-Throated Wind' (Weir, Barlow), 'China Cat Sunflower' (Garcia, Hunter), 'I Know You Rider' (trad.), 'El Paso' (Marty Robbins), 'Hurts Me Too' (James, Sehorn), 'You Win Again' (Hank Williams), 'Playing In The Band' (Weir, Hart, Hunter), 'Good Lovin'' (Clark, Resnick), 'Casey Jones' (Garcia, Hunter), 'Sitting On Top Of The World' (Carter, Jacobs), 'Me And My Uncle' (John Phillips), 'Ramble On Rose' (Garcia, Hunter), 'Beat It On Down The Line' (Jesse Fuller), 'Dark Star' (Garcia, Hart, Kreutzmann, Lesh, McKernan, Weir, Hunter), 'Morning Dew' (Dobson, Rose), 'Drums' (Kreutzmann), 'Sugar Magnolia' (Weir, Hunter), 'Sing Me Back Home' (Merle Haggard), 'One More Saturday Night' (Weir)

Vol 19: Lyceum Theatre, London, England May 23, 1972

'Promised Land' (Chuck Berry), 'Sugaree' (Garcia, Hunter), 'Mr. Charlie' (McKernan, Hunter), 'Black-Throated Wind' (Weir, Barlow), 'Tennessee Jed' (Garcia, Hunter), 'Next Time You See Me' (Harvey, Forest), 'Jack Straw' (Weir, Hunter), 'China Cat Sunflower' (Garcia, Hunter), 'I Know You Rider' (trad.), 'Me And My Uncle' (John Phillips), 'Chinatown Shuffle' (McKernan), 'Big Railroad Blues' (Noah Lewis), 'The Stranger (Two Souls in Communion)' (McKernan), 'Playing In The Band' (Weir, Hart, Hunter), 'Sitting On Top Of The World' (Carter, Jacobs), 'Rockin' Pneumonia And The Boogie Woogie Flu' (Huey 'Piano' Smith), 'Mexicali Blues' (Weir, Barlow), 'Good Lovin'' (Clark, Resnick), 'Casey Jones' (Garcia, Hunter), 'Ramble On Rose' (Garcia, Hunter), 'Dark Star' (Garcia, Hart, Kreutzmann, Lesh, McKernan, Weir, Hunter), 'Morning Dew' (Dobson, Rose), 'He's Gone' (Garcia, Hunter), 'Sugar Magnolia' (Weir, Hunter), 'Comes A Time' (Garcia, Hunter), 'Goin' Down The Road Feeling Bad' (trad.) 'Not Fade Away' (Petty, Hardin), 'Hey Bo Diddley' (Bo Diddley), 'Not Fade Away' (Petty, Hardin), 'Uncle John's Band' (Garcia, Hunter)

Vol 20: Lyceum Theatre, London, England May 24, 1972

'Cold Rain And Snow' (trad.), 'Beat It On Down The Line' (Jesse Fuller), 'Mr. Charlie' (McKernan, Hunter), 'Deal' (Garcia, Hunter), 'Me And My Uncle' (John Phillips), 'Hurts Me Too' (James, Sehorn), 'Dire Wolf' (Garcia, Hunter), 'Black-Throated Wind' (Weir, Barlow), 'Chinatown Shuffle' (McKernan), 'China Cat Sunflower' (Garcia, Hunter), 'I Know You Rider' (trad.), 'Playing In The Band' (Weir, Hart, Hunter), 'You Win Again' (Hank Williams), 'Jack Straw' (Weir, Hunter),' Casey Jones' (Garcia, Hunter), 'Rockin' Pneumonia And The Boogie Woogie Flu' (Huey 'Piano' Smith), 'Mexicali Blues' (Weir, Barlow), 'Black Peter' (Garcia, Hunter), 'Truckin'' (Garcia, Lesh, Weir, Hunter), 'Drums' (Kreutzmann), 'The Other One' (Weir, Kreutzmann), 'Sing Me Back Home' (Merle Haggard), 'Sugar Magnolia' (Weir, Hunter), 'Turn On Your Lovelight' (Scott, Malone), 'The Stranger' (Two Souls in Communion) (McKernan), 'One More Saturday Night' (Weir)

Vol 21: Lyceum Theatre, London, England, May 25, 1972

'Promised Land' (Chuck Berry), 'Brown-Eyed Women' (Garcia, Hunter), 'Big Boss Man' (Smith, Dixon), 'Black-Throated Wind' (Weir, Barlow), 'Tennessee Jed' (Garcia, Hunter), 'Mr. Charlie' (McKernan, Hunter), 'Jack Straw' (Weir, Hunter), 'China Cat Sunflower' (Garcia, Hunter), 'I Know You Rider' (trad.), 'Me And Bobby McGee' (Kristofferson, Foster), 'Good Lovin'' (Clark, Resnick), 'Playing In The Band' (Weir, Hart, Hunter), 'Brokedown Palace' (Garcia, Hunter), 'Casey Jones' (Garcia, Hunter), 'Me And My Uncle' (John Phillips), 'Big Railroad Blues' (Noah Lewis), 'Chinatown Shuffle' (McKernan), 'Ramble On Rose' (Garcia,

Hunter), 'Uncle John's Band' (Garcia, Hunter), 'Wharf Rat' (Garcia, Hunter), 'Dark Star' (Garcia, Hart, Kreutzmann, Lesh, McKernan, Weir, Hunter), 'Sugar Magnolia' (Weir, Hunter), 'Comes A Time' (Garcia, Hunter), 'El Paso' (Marty Robbins), 'Sitting On Top Of The World' (Carter, Jacobs), 'Goin' Down The Road Feeling Bad' (trad.) 'One More Saturday Night' (Weir)

Vol 22: Lyceum Theatre, London, England, May 26, 1972

'Promised Land' (Chuck Berry), 'Sugaree' (Garcia, Hunter), 'Mr. Charlie' (McKernan, Hunter), 'Black-Throated Wind' (Weir, Barlow), 'Loser' (Garcia, Hunter), 'Next Time You See Me' (Harvey, Forest), 'El Paso' (Marty Robbins), 'Dire Wolf' (Garcia, Hunter), 'The Stranger (Two Souls In Communion)' (McKernan), 'Playing In The Band' (Weir, Hart, Hunter), 'He's Gone' (Garcia, Hunter), 'Cumberland Blues' (Garcia, Lesh, Hunter), 'Jack Straw' (Weir, Hunter), 'Chinatown Shuffle' (McKernan), 'China Cat Sunflower' (Garcia, Hunter), 'I Know You Rider' (trad.), 'Not Fade Away' (Petty, Hardin), 'Goin' Down The Road Feeling Bad' (trad.), 'Not Fade Away' (Petty, Hardin), 'Truckin'' (Garcia, Lesh, Weir, Hunter), 'The Other One' (Weir, Kreutzmann), 'Drums' (Kreutzmann), 'The Other One' (Weir, Kreutzmann), 'Morning Dew' (Dobson, Rose), 'The Other One' (Weir, Kreutzmann), 'Sing Me Back Home' (Merle Haggard), 'Me And My Uncle' (John Phillips), 'Ramble On Rose' (Garcia, Hunter), 'Sugar Magnolia (Weir, Hunter), 'Casey Jones' (Garcia, Hunter), 'One More Saturday Night' (Weir)

Rockin' The Rhein With The Grateful Dead (2004)

Personnel:
Jerry Garcia: guitar, vocals
Donna Jean Godchaux: vocals
Keith Godchaux: piano
Bill Kreutzmann: drums
Phil Lesh: bass guitar, vocals
Ron 'Pigpen' McKernan: organ, harmonica, percussion, vocals
Bob Weir: guitar (rhythm), vocals
Recorded live at Rheinhallen in Düsseldorf, West Germany, on April 24, 1972. Produced by John Cutler and Phil Lesh.
Release date: May 2004
Running time: 227:02

'Truckin'' (Garcia, Hunter, Lesh, Weir), 'Tennessee Jed' (Garcia, Hunter), 'Chinatown Shuffle' (McKernan), 'Black-Throated Wind' (Barlow, Weir), 'China Cat Sunflower' (Garcia, Hunter), 'I Know You Rider' (trad.), 'Mr. Charlie' (Hunter, McKernan), 'Beat It On Down The Line' (Jesse Fuller), 'Loser' (Garcia, Hunter), 'Playing In The Band' (Hart, Weir, Hunter), 'Next Time You See Me' (Forest, Harvey), 'Me And Bobby McGee' (Foster, Kristofferson), 'Good Lovin'' (Clark, Resnick), 'Casey Jones' (Garcia, Hunter), 'He's Gone' (Garcia, Hunter), 'Hurts Me Too' (James, Sehorn), 'El Paso' (Marty Robbins), 'Turn On Your Love Light' (Malone, Scott) [Bonus track recorded live at the Lyceum Theatre, London, England, May 24, 1972]: 'The Stranger (Two Souls In Communion)' (McKernan) [Bonus track recorded live at the Lyceum Theatre, London, England, May 24, 1972]: 'Dark Star' (Grateful Dead, Hunter), 'Me And My Uncle' (John Phillips), 'Dark Star' (Grateful Dead, Hunter), 'Wharf Rat' (Garcia, Hunter), 'Sugar Magnolia' (Hunter, Weir), 'Not Fade Away' (Holly, Petty), 'Goin' Down The Road Feeling Bad' (trad.), 'Not Fade Away' (Holly, Petty), 'One More Saturday Night' (Weir) [Bonus Disc recorded at the Academy of Music, New York City March 22 and 23, 1972]: 'Playing In The Band' (Weir, Hart, Hunter), 'Sugar Magnolia' (Weir, Hunter), 'Caution (Do Not Stop On Tracks)' (Grateful Dead), 'Jam' (Grateful Dead), 'Uncle John's Band' (Garcia, Hunter), 'Dark Star' (Garcia, Hart, Kreutzmann, McKernan, Lesh, Weir, Hunter)

Hundred Year Hall (1995)

Personnel:
Jerry Garcia: guitar, vocals
Donna Jean Godchaux: vocals
Keith Godchaux: piano
Bill Kreutzmann: drums
Phil Lesh: bass guitar, vocals
Ron 'Pigpen' McKernan: harmonica, vocals, organ
Bob Weir: rhythm guitar, vocals
Recorded live at the Jahrhunderthalle in Frankfurt, West Germany, on April 26, 1972.
Produced by John Cutler and Phil Lesh.
Release date: September 1995
Running time: 142:23
'Bertha' (Garcia, Hunter), 'Me And My Uncle' (John Phillips), 'Next Time You See Me' (Forest, Harvey), 'China Cat Sunflower' (Garcia, Hunter), 'I Know You Rider' (trad.), 'Jack Straw' (Bob Weir, Hunter), 'Big Railroad Blues' (Noah Lewis), 'Playing In The Band' (Weir, Hart, Hunter), 'Turn On Your Love Light' (Malone, Scott), 'Goin' Down The Road Feeling Bad'(trad.), 'One More Saturday Night' (Weir), 'Truckin'' (Garcia, Weir, Lesh, Hunter), 'The Other One' (Weir, Kreutzmann), 'Comes A Time' (Garcia, Hunter), 'Sugar Magnolia' (Weir, Hunter)

Dark Star (2012)

Personnel:
Jerry Garcia: lead guitar, vocals, pedal steel guitar, organ
Donna Jean Godchaux: vocals
Keith Godchaux: piano
Bill Kreutzmann: drums, percussion
Phil Lesh: bass guitar, vocals
Ron 'Pigpen' McKernan: organ, harmonica, vocals
Bob Weir: rhythm guitar, vocals
Recorded on May 4, 1972, at the Olympia Theatre, Paris, France. Produced by Grateful Dead
Mixed by Jeffrey Norman
Release date: April 2012
Running time: 39:27
'Dark Star' (Garcia, Hart, Kreutzmann, Lesh, McKernan, Weir, Hunter), 'Drums' (Kreutzmann), 'Dark Star' (Garcia, Hart, Kreutzmann, Lesh, McKernan, Weir, Hunter)

Download Series Vol. 10 (2006)

Personnel:
Jerry Garcia: lead guitar, vocals
Donna Jean Godchaux: vocals
Keith Godchaux: piano
Bill Kreutzmann: drums
Phil Lesh: electric bass, vocals
Bob Weir: rhythm guitar, vocals
Recorded live at the Paramount Northwest Theatre in Seattle, Washington, on July 21, 1972.
Mastering by Jeffrey Norman.
Release date: February 2006
Running time: 231:16
'Sugaree' (Garcia, Hunter), 'Black-Throated Wind' (Weir, Barlow), 'Cumberland Blues'

(Garcia, Lesh, Hunter), 'Me And Bobby McGee' (Kristofferson, Foster), 'Loser' (Garcia, Hunter), 'Mexicali Blues' (Weir, Barlow), 'China Cat Sunflower' (Garcia, Hunter), I Know You Rider' (trad.), 'Beat It On Down The Line' (Jesse Fuller), 'Stella Blue' (Garcia, Hunter), 'Playing In The Band' (Weir, Hart, Hunter), 'Tennessee Jed' (Garcia, Hunter), 'Casey Jones' (Garcia, Hunter), 'Me And My Uncle' (John Phillips), 'Deal' (Garcia, Hunter), 'Jack Straw' (Weir, Hunter), 'He's Gone' (Garcia, Hunter), 'Truckin' ' (Garcia, Lesh, Weir, Hunter), 'Drums' (Kreutzmann), 'The Other One' (Weir, Kreutzmann), 'Comes A Time' (Garcia, Hunter), 'Sugar Magnolia' (Weir, Hunter), 'Ramble On Rose' (Garcia, Hunter), 'Goin' Down The Road Feeling Bad' (trad.), Not Fade Away' (Hardin, Petty), [Bonus tracks recorded at the Paramount Northwest Theatre on July 22, 1972]: 'You Win Again' (Hank Williams), 'Bird Song' (Garcia, Hunter), 'Playing In The Band' (Weir, Hart, Hunter), 'Morning Dew' (Dobson, Rose), 'Uncle John's Band' (Garcia, Hunter), 'One More Saturday Night' (Weir)

Dave's Picks Vol 24 (2017)
Personnel:
Jerry Garcia: guitar, vocals
Donna Jean Godchaux: vocals
Keith Godchaux: keyboards
Bill Kreutzmann: drums
Phil Lesh: bass, vocals
Bob Weir: guitar, vocals
Recorded live at the Berkeley Community Theatre in Berkeley, California, on August 25, 1972. Recorded by Owsley Stanley.
Release date: November 2017
Running time: 165.01
'Cold Rain And Snow' (trad.), 'Black-Throated Wind' (Weir, Barlow), 'He's Gone' (Garcia, Hunter), 'Beat It On Down The Line' (Jesse Fuller), 'Loser' (Garcia, Hunter), 'El Paso' (Marty Robbins), 'Black Peter' (Garcia, Hunter), 'Jack Straw' (Weir, Hunter), 'Friend Of The Devil' (Garcia, Dawson, Hunter), 'Promised Land' (Chuck Berry), 'Bird Song' (Garcia, Hunter), 'Playing In The Band' (Weir, Hart, Hunter), 'Bertha' (Garcia, Hunter), 'Truckin'' (Garcia, Lesh, Weir, Hunter), 'The Other One' (Weir, Kreutzmann), 'Stella Blue' (Garcia, Hunter), 'One More Saturday Night' (Weir), 'Sugar Magnolia' (Weir, Hunter)

Sunshine Daydream (2013)
Personnel:
Jerry Garcia: guitar, vocals
Donna Jean Godchaux: vocals
Keith Godchaux: keyboards
Bill Kreutzmann: drums
Phil Lesh: bass, vocals
Bob Weir: guitar, vocals
Recorded live at the Old Renaissance Faire Grounds in Veneta, Oregon, on August 28, 1972.
Produced for release by David Lemieux.
Release date: September 2013
Running time: 176:04
Introduction, 'Promised Land' (Chuck Berry), 'Sugaree' (Garcia, Hunter), 'Me And My Uncle' (John Phillips), 'Deal' (Garcia, Hunter), 'Black-Throated Wind' (Weir, Barlow), 'China Cat Sunflower' (Garcia, Hunter), 'I Know You Rider' (trad.), 'Mexicali Blues' (Weir, Barlow), 'Bertha' (Garcia, Hunter), 'Playing in The Band' (Weir, Mickey Hart, Hunter), 'He's Gone'

(Garcia, Hunter), 'Jack Straw' (Weir, Hunter), 'Bird Song' (Garcia, Hunter), 'Greatest Story Ever Told' (Weir, Hart, Hunter), 'Dark Star' (Garcia, Hart, Kreutzmann, Lesh, McKernan, Weir, Hunter), 'El Paso' (Marty Robbins), 'Sing Me Back Home' (Merle Haggard), 'Sugar Magnolia' (Weir, Hunter), 'Casey Jones' (Garcia, Hunter), 'One More Saturday Night' (Weir)

Dick's Picks Vol.23 (2001)

Personnel:
Jerry Garcia: lead guitar, vocals
Donna Jean Godchaux: vocals
Keith Godchaux: piano
Bill Kreutzmann: drums
Phil Lesh: electric bass, vocals
Bob Weir: rhythm guitar, vocals
Recorded live at the Baltimore Civic Center in Baltimore. September 17, 1972. Recorded by Owsley Stanley.
Release date: October 2001
Running time: 206:35
'Promised Land' (Chuck Berry), 'Sugaree' (Garcia, Hunter), 'Black-Throated Wind' (Barlow, Weir), 'Friend Of The Devil' (Dawson, Hunter, Garcia), 'El Paso' (Marty Robbins), 'Bird Song' (Garcia, Hunter), 'Big River' (Johnny Cash), 'Tennessee Jed' (Garcia, Hunter), 'Mexicali Blues' (Barlow, Weir), 'China Cat Sunflower' (Garcia, Hunter), 'I Know You Rider' (trad.), 'Playing In The Band' (Hunter, Hart, Weir), 'Casey Jones' (Garcia, Hunter), 'Truckin'' (Hunter, Garcia, Lesh, Weir), 'Loser' (Garcia, Hunter), 'Jack Straw' (Hunter, Weir), 'Mississippi Half-Step Uptown Toodleloo' (Garcia, Hunter), 'Me And My Uncle' (John Phillips), 'He's Gone' (Garcia, Hunter), 'The Other One' (Kreutzmann, Weir), 'Sing Me Back Home' (Merle Haggard), 'Sugar Magnolia' (Hunter, Weir), 'Uncle John's Band' (Garcia, Hunter)

Dick's Picks Vol 36 (2005)

Personnel:
Jerry Garcia: lead guitar, vocals
Donna Jean Godchaux: vocals
Keith Godchaux: keyboards
Bill Kreutzmann: drums
Phil Lesh: electric bass, vocals
Bob Weir: rhythm guitar, vocals
Recorded live at The Spectrum in Philadelphia, Pennsylvania, on September 21, 1972, with bonus tracks recorded at Folsom Field in Boulder, Colorado, on September 3, 1972. Recorded by Owsley Stanley.
Release date: October 2005
'Promised Land' (Chuck Berry), 'Bird Song' (Garcia, Hunter), 'El Paso' (Marty Robbins), 'China Cat Sunflower' (Garcia, Hunter), 'I Know You Rider' (trad.), 'Black-Throated Wind' (Weir, Barlow), 'Big Railroad Blues' (Noah Lewis), 'Jack Straw' (Weir, Hunter), 'Loser' (Garcia, Hunter), 'Big River' (Johnny Cash), 'Ramble On Rose' (Garcia, Hunter), 'Cumberland Blues' (Garcia, Phil Lesh, Hunter), 'Playing In The Band' (Weir, Hart, Hunter), 'He's Gone' (Garcia, Hunter), 'Truckin'' (Garcia, Lesh, Weir, Hunter), 'Black Peter' (Garcia, Hunter), 'Mexicali Blues' (Weir, Barlow), 'Dark Star' (Garcia, Hart, Kreutzmann, Lesh, McKernan, Weir, Hunter), 'Morning Dew' (Dobson, Rose), 'Beat It On Down The Line' (Jesse Fuller), 'Mississippi Half-Step Uptown Toodeloo' (Garcia, Hunter), 'Sugar Magnolia' (Weir, Hunter), 'Friend Of The Devil' (Garcia, Dawson, Hunter), 'Not Fade Away' (Holly,

Petty), 'Goin' Down The Road Feeling Bad' (trad.), 'Not Fade Away' (reprise) (Hardin, Petty), 'One More Saturday Night' (Weir) [Following from September 3, 1972]: 'He's Gone' (Garcia, Hunter), 'The Other One' (Weir, Kreutzmann), 'Wharf Rat' (Garcia, Hunter)

Dick's Picks Vol.11 (1998)
Personnel:
Jerry Garcia: lead guitar, vocals
Donna Godchaux: vocals
Keith Godchaux: keyboards
Bill Kreutzmann: drums, percussion
Phil Lesh: bass, vocals
Bob Weir: guitar, vocals
Recorded live at the Stanley Theater, Jersey City, September 27, 1972. Recorded by Owsley Stanley and Bob Matthews.
Release Date: June 1998
Running time: 183:22
'Morning Dew' (Dobson, Rose), 'Beat It On Down The Line' (Jesse Fuller), 'Friend Of The Devil' (Garcia, Dawson, Hunter), 'Black-Throated Wind' (Barlow, Weir), 'Tennessee Jed' (Garcia, Hunter), 'Mexicali Blues' (Barlow, Weir), 'Bird Song' (Garcia, Hunter), 'Big River' (Johnny Cash), 'Brokedown Palace' (Garcia, Hunter), 'El Paso' (Marty Robbins), 'China Cat Sunflower' (Garcia, Hunter), 'I Know You Rider' (trad.), 'Playing In The Band' (Hart, Hunter, Weir), 'He's Gone' (Garcia, Hunter), 'Me And My Uncle' (John Phillips), 'Deal' (Garcia, Hunter), 'Greatest Story Ever Told' (Hart, Hunter, Weir), 'Ramble On Rose' (Garcia, Hunter), 'Dark Star' (Grateful Dead, Hunter), 'Cumberland Blues' (Garcia, Hunter, Lesh), 'Attics Of My Life' (Garcia, Hunter), 'Promised Land' (Chuck Berry), 'Uncle John's Band' (Garcia, Hunter), 'Casey Jones' (Garcia, Hunter), 'Around And Around' (Chuck Berry)

Light Into Ashes (2021)
Personnel:
Jerry Garcia: guitar, vocals
Donna Jean Godchaux: vocals
Keith Godchaux: keyboards
Bill Kreutzmann: drums,
Phil Lesh: bass guitar, vocals
Bob Weir: rhythm guitar, vocals
Recorded live at the Fox Theatre, St Louis, October 18, 1972. Produced by David Lemieux
Release date: October 2021
'Playing In The Band' (Weir, Hart, Hunter), 'Drums' (Kreutzmann), 'Dark Star (beginning)' (Garcia, Hart, Kreutzmann, Lesh, McKernan, Weir, Hunter), 'Dark Star (conclusion)' (Garcia, Hart, Kreutzmann, Lesh, McKernan, Weir, Hunter), 'Morning Dew' (Dobson, Rose), 'Playing In The Band' (Weir, Hart, Hunter)

Dave's Picks Vol. 11 (2014)
Personnel:
Jerry Garcia: lead guitar, vocals
Donna Jean Godchaux: vocals
Keith Godchaux: keyboards
Bill Kreutzmann: drums
Phil Lesh: electric bass, vocals

Bob Weir: guitar, vocals
Recorded live at the Century II Convention Center in Wichita, Kansas, on November 17, 1972. Recorded by Owsley Stanley.
Release date: August 2014
Running time: 229:37
'Promised Land' (Chuck Berry), 'Sugaree' (Garcia, Hunter), 'Me And My Uncle' (John Phillips), 'Tennessee Jed' (Garcia, Hunter), 'Black-Throated Wind' (Weir, Barlow), 'Bird Song' (Garcia, Hunter), 'Jack Straw' (Weir, Hunter), 'Box Of Rain' (Lesh, Hunter), 'Don't Ease Me In' (trad.), 'Beat It On Down The Line' (Jesse Fuller), 'Brown-Eyed Women' (Garcia, Hunter), 'Big River' (Johnny Cash), 'China Cat Sunflower' (Garcia, Hunter), 'I Know You Rider' (trad.), 'Around And Around' (Chuck Berry), 'Casey Jones' (Garcia, Hunter), 'Cumberland Blues' (Garcia, Lesh, Hunter), 'El Paso' (Marty Robbins), 'He's Gone' (Garcia, Hunter), 'Truckin'' (Garcia, Lesh, Weir, Hunter), 'The Other One' (Weir, Kreutzmann), 'Brokedown Palace' (Garcia, Hunter), 'Sugar Magnolia' (Weir, Hunter), 'Uncle John's Band' (Garcia, Hunter), 'Johnny B. Goode' (Chuck Berry) [Bonus tracks: Recorded at Oklahoma City Music Hall, Oklahoma City, Oklahoma on November 15, 1972]: 'Playing In The Band' (Weir, Hart, Hunter), 'Wharf Rat' (Garcia, Hunter), 'Not Fade Away' (Petty, Hardin), 'Goin' Down The Road Feeling Bad' (trad.), 'Not Fade Away' (Petty, Hardin)

Houston, Texas 11-18-1972 (2014)
Personnel:
Jerry Garcia: guitar, vocals
Donna Jean Godchaux: vocals
Keith Godchaux: keyboards
Bill Kreutzmann: drums
Phil Lesh: electric bass, vocals
Bob Weir: rhythm guitar, vocals
Recorded live at Hofheinz Pavilion in Houston, Texas, on November 18, 1972. Original recording produced by Owsley Stanley.
Release date: November 2014
Running time: 79:54
'Bertha' (Garcia, Hunter), 'Greatest Story Ever Told' (Weir, Hart, Hunter), 'He's Gone' (Garcia, Hunter), 'Jack Straw' (Weir, Hunter), 'Deal' (Garcia, Hunter), 'Playing In The Band' (Weir, Hart, Hunter), 'Mississippi Half-Step Uptown Toodeloo' (Garcia, Hunter), 'Sugar Magnolia' (Weir, Hunter)

1973
Dick's Picks Vol. 28 (2003)
Personnel:
Jerry Garcia: guitar, vocals
Donna Godchaux: vocals
Keith Godchaux: piano
Bill Kreutzmann: drums, percussion
Phil Lesh: electric bass, vocals
Bob Weir: guitar, vocals
Pigpen: in spirit
Recorded live at the Pershing Municipal Auditorium in Lincoln, Nebraska, on February 26, 1973, and at the Salt Palace in Salt Lake City, Utah, on February 28 1973. Recorded by Bill Candelario.

Release date: April 2003
Running time: 304:05
'The Promised Land' (Chuck Berry), 'Loser' (Garcia, Hunter), 'Jack Straw' (Hunter, Weir), 'Don't Ease Me In' (trad.), 'Looks Like Rain' (Barlow, Weir), 'Loose Lucy' (Garcia, Hunter), 'Beer Barrel Polka' (Brown, Timm, Vejvoda, Zeman), 'Big Railroad Blues' (Noah Lewis), 'Playing In The Band' (Hunter, Hart, Weir), 'They Love Each Other' (Garcia, Hunter), 'Big River' (Johnny Cash), 'Tennessee Jed' (Garcia, Hunter), 'Greatest Story Ever Told' (Hunter, Hart, Weir), 'Dark Star' (Hunter, Garcia, Hart, Kreutzmann, Lesh, Pigpen, Weir), 'Eyes Of The World' (Garcia, Hunter), 'Mississippi Half-Step Uptown Toodleloo' (Garcia, Hunter), 'Me And My Uncle' (John Phillips), 'Not Fade Away' (Holly, Petty), 'Goin' Down The Road Feelin' Bad' (trad.) 'Not Fade Away' (Holly, Petty), [Following from February 28, 1973]: 'Cold Rain And Snow' (trad.), 'Beat It On Down The Line' (Jesse Fuller), 'They Love Each Other' (Garcia, Hunter), 'Mexicali Blues' (Barlow, Weir), 'Sugaree' (Garcia, Hunter), 'Box Of Rain' (Hunter, Lesh), 'El Paso' (Marty Robbins), 'He's Gone' (Garcia, Hunter), 'Jack Straw' (Hunter, Weir), 'China Cat Sunflower' (Garcia, Hunter), 'I Know You Rider' (trad.), 'Big River' (Johnny Cash), 'Row Jimmy' (Garcia, Hunter), 'Truckin'' (Hunter, Garcia, Lesh, Weir), 'The Other One' (Kreutzmann, Weir), 'Eyes Of The World' (Garcia, Hunter), 'Morning Dew' (Dobson, Rose), 'Sugar Magnolia'(Hunter, Weir), 'We Bid You Goodnight' (trad.)

Dave's Picks Vol. 32 (2019)
Personnel:
Jerry Garcia: lead guitar, vocals
Donna Jean Godchaux: vocals
Keith Godchaux: keyboards
Bill Kreutzmann: drums
Phil Lesh: bass, vocals
Bob Weir: guitar, vocals
Recorded live at the Spectrum in Philadelphia on March 24, 1973. Recorded by Rex Jackson and Kidd Candelario.
Release date: November 2019
Running time: 228:26
'Bertha' (Garcia, Hunter), 'Beat It On Down The Line' (Jesse Fuller), 'Don't Ease Me In' (trad.), 'The Race Is On' (Don Rollins), 'Cumberland Blues' (Garcia, Lesh, Hunter), 'Box Of Rain' (Lesh, Hunter), 'Row Jimmy' (Garcia, Hunter), 'Jack Straw' (Weir, Hunter), 'They Love Each Other' (Garcia, Hunter), 'Mexicali Blues' (Weir, Barlow), 'Tennessee Jed' (Garcia, Hunter), 'Looks Like Rain' (Weir, Barlow), 'Wave That Flag' (Garcia, Hunter), 'El Paso' (Marty Robbins), 'Here Comes Sunshine' (Garcia, Hunter), 'Me And Bobby McGee' (Kristofferson, Foster), 'Loser' (Garcia, Hunter), 'Playing In The Band' (Weir, Hart, Hunter), 'Promised Land' (Chuck Berry), 'China Cat Sunflower' (Garcia, Hunter), 'I Know You Rider' (trad.), 'Big River' (Johnny Cash), 'Stella Blue' (Garcia, Hunter), 'Me And My Uncle' (John Phillips), 'He's Gone' (Garcia, Hunter) , 'Truckin'' (Garcia, Lesh, Weir, Hunter), 'Jam' (Grateful Dead), 'Dark Star' (Garcia, Hart, Kreutzmann, Lesh, McKernan, Weir, Hunter), 'Sing Me Back Home' (Merle Haggard), 'Sugar Magnolia' (Weir, Hunter), Johnny B. Goode' (Chuck Berry)

Dave's Picks Vol. 16 (2015)
Personnel:
Jerry Garcia: guitar, vocals
Donna Jean Godchaux: vocals
Keith Godchaux: keyboards

Bill Kreutzmann: drums
Phil Lesh: bass, vocals
Bob Weir: guitar, vocals
Recorded live at the Springfield Civic Centre in Springfield, Massachusetts on March 28, 1973. Recorded by Kidd Candelario.
Release date: November 2015
Running time: 210:22
'Cumberland Blues' (Garcia, Lesh, Hunter), 'Here Comes Sunshine' (Garcia, Hunter), 'Mexicali Blues' (Weir, Barlow), 'Wave That Flag' (Garcia, Hunter), 'Beat It On Down The Line' (Jesse Fuller), 'Loser' (Garcia, Hunter), 'Jack Straw' (Weir, Hunter), 'Box Of Rain' (Lesh, Hunter), 'They Love Each Other' (Garcia, Hunter), 'El Paso' (Marty Robbins), 'Row Jimmy' (Garcia, Hunter), 'Around And Around' (Chuck Berry), 'Brown-Eyed Women' (Garcia, Hunter), 'You Ain't Woman Enough' (Loretta Lynn), 'Looks Like Rain' (Weir, Barlow), 'China Cat Sunflower' (Garcia, Hunter), 'I Know You Rider' (trad.), 'Promised Land' (Chuck Berry), 'Loose Lucy' (Garcia, Hunter), 'Me And My Uncle' (John Phillips), 'Don't Ease Me In' (trad.), 'The Race Is On' (Don Rollins), 'Stella Blue' (Garcia, Hunter), 'Big River' (Johnny Cash), 'Mississippi Half-Step Uptown Toodeloo' (Garcia, Hunter), 'Weather Report Suite Prelude' (Weir), 'Dark Star' (Garcia, Hart, Kreutzmann, Lesh, McKernan, Weir, Hunter), 'Eyes Of The World' (Garcia, Hunter), 'Playing In The Band' (Weir, Hart, Hunter), 'Johnny B. Goode' (Chuck Berry)

Dave's Picks Vol. 21 (2017)
Personnel:
Jerry Garcia: guitar, vocals
Donna Jean Godchaux: vocals
Keith Godchaux: keyboards
Bill Kreutzmann: drums
Phil Lesh: bass, vocals
Bob Weir: guitar, vocals
Recorded live at Boston Garden in Boston, Massachusetts, on April 2, 1973. Recorded by Rex Jackson.
Release date: February 2017
Running time: 217:06
'Promised Land' (Chuck Berry), 'Deal' (Garcia, Hunter), 'Mexicali Blues' (Weir, Barlow), 'Brown-Eyed Women' (Garcia, Hunter), 'Beat It On Down The Line' (Jesse Fuller), 'Row Jimmy' (Garcia, Hunter), 'Looks Like Rain' (Weir, Barlow), 'Wave That Flag' (Garcia, Hunter), 'Box Of Rain' (Lesh, Hunter), 'Big River' (Johnny Cash), 'China Cat Sunflower' (Garcia, Hunter), 'I Know You Rider' (trad.), 'You Ain't Woman Enough' (Loretta Lynn), 'Jack Straw' (Weir, Hunter), 'Don't Ease Me In' (trad.), 'Playing In The Band' (Weir, Hart, Hunter), 'Ramble On Rose' (Garcia, Hunter), 'Me And My Uncle' (John Phillips), 'Mississippi Half-Step Uptown Toodeloo' (Garcia, Hunter), 'Greatest Story Ever Told' (Weir, Hart, Hunter), 'Loose Lucy' (Garcia, Hunter), 'El Paso' (Marty Robbins), 'Stella Blue' (Garcia, Hunter), 'Around And Around' (Chuck Berry), 'Here Comes Sunshine' (Garcia, Hunter), 'Jam' (Grateful Dead), 'Me And Bobby McGee' (Kristofferson, Foster), 'Weather Report Suite: Prelude' (Weir), 'Eyes Of The World' (Garcia, Hunter), 'China Doll' (Garcia, Hunter), 'Sugar Magnolia' (Weir, Hunter), 'Casey Jones' (Garcia, Hunter), 'Johnny B. Goode' (Chuck Berry), 'And We Bid You Goodnight' (trad.)

Pacific Northwest '73–'74: The Complete Recordings (2018)
Personnel:
Jerry Garcia: lead guitar, vocals

Donna Jean Godchaux: vocals
Keith Godchaux: keyboards
Bill Kreutzmann: drums
Phil Lesh: bass, vocals
Bob Weir: rhythm guitar, vocals
Recorded live at venues in the Pacific Northwest in 1973 and 1974. Produced for release by David Lemieux.
Release date: September 2018

P.N.E. Coliseum, Vancouver, British Columbia, June 22, 1973
'Bertha' (Garcia, Hunter), 'Beat It On Down The Line' (Jesse Fuller), 'Deal' (Garcia, Hunter), 'Mexicali Blues' (Weir, Barlow), 'Box Of Rain' (Lesh, Hunter), 'Bird Song' (Garcia, Hunter), 'The Race Is On' (Don Rollins), 'Sugaree' (Garcia, Hunter), 'Looks Like Rain' (Weir, Barlow), 'Row Jimmy' (Garcia, Hunter), 'Jack Straw' (Weir, Hunter), 'China Cat Sunflower' (Garcia, Hunter), 'I Know You Rider' (trad.), 'Big River' (Johnny Cash), 'Tennessee Jed' (Garcia, Hunter), 'Playing In The Band' (Weir, Hart, Hunter), 'Here Comes Sunshine' (Garcia, Hunter), 'Promised Land' (Chuck Berry), 'Brown-Eyed Women' (Garcia, Hunter), 'El Paso' (Marty Robbins), 'Black Peter' (Garcia, Hunter), 'Greatest Story Ever Told' (Weir, Hunter), 'Big Railroad Blues' (Noah Lewis), 'He's Gone' (Garcia, Hunter), 'Truckin'' (Garcia, Lesh, Weir, Hunter), 'The Other One' (Weir, Kreutzmann), 'Wharf Rat' (Garcia, Hunter), 'Sugar Magnolia' (Weir, Hunter), 'Casey Jones' (Garcia, Hunter), 'Johnny B. Goode' (Chuck Berry)

Portland Memorial Coliseum, Portland, Oregon, June 24, 1973
'Promised Land' (Chuck Berry), 'Loser' (Garcia, Hunter), 'Mexicali Blues' (Weir, Barlow), 'They Love Each Other' (Garcia, Hunter), 'Looks Like Rain' (Weir, Barlow), 'Box Of Rain' (Lesh, Hunter), 'Big Railroad Blues' (Noah Lewis), 'Jack Straw' (Weir, Hunter), 'Sugaree' (Garcia, Hunter), 'The Race Is On' (Don Rollins), 'Row Jimmy' (Garcia, Hunter), 'Beat It On Down The Line' (Jesse Fuller), 'China Cat Sunflower' (Garcia, Hunter), 'I Know You Rider' (trad.), 'Around And Around' (Chuck Berry), 'Mississippi Half-Step Uptown Toodeloo' (Garcia, Hunter), 'You Ain't Woman Enough' (Loretta Lynn), 'El Paso' (Marty Robbins), 'Stella Blue' (Garcia, Hunter), 'Greatest Story Ever Told' (Weir, Hunter), 'Bertha' (Garcia, Hunter), 'Big River' (Johnny Cash), 'Dark Star' (Garcia, Hart, Kreutzmann, Lesh, McKernan, Weir, Hunter), 'Eyes Of The World' (Garcia, Hunter), 'China Doll' (Garcia, Hunter), 'Sugar Magnolia' (Weir, Hunter), 'One More Saturday Night' (Weir)

Seattle Center Arena, Seattle, Washington, June 26, 1973
'Casey Jones' (Garcia, Hunter), 'Greatest Story Ever Told' (Weir, Hunter), 'Brown-Eyed Women' (Garcia, Hunter), 'Jack Straw' (Weir, Hunter), 'Box Of Rain' (Lesh, Hunter), 'Deal' (Garcia, Hunter), 'Mexicali Blues' (Weir, Barlow), 'You Ain't Woman Enough' (Loretta Lynn), 'Row Jimmy' (Garcia, Hunter), 'The Race Is On' (Don Rollins), 'China Cat Sunflower' (Garcia, Hunter), 'I Know You Rider' (trad.), 'Beat It On Down The Line' (Jesse Fuller), 'Loser' (Garcia, Hunter), 'Playing In The Band' (Weir, Hart, Hunter), 'Bertha' (Garcia, Hunter), 'Promised Land' (Chuck Berry), 'They Love Each Other' (Garcia, Hunter), 'El Paso' (Marty Robbins), 'Black Peter' (Garcia, Hunter), 'Big River' (Johnny Cash), 'Here Comes Sunshine' (Garcia, Hunter), 'Me And My Uncle' (John Phillips), 'He's Gone' (Garcia, Hunter), 'Truckin'' (Garcia, Lesh, Weir, Hunter), 'The Other One' (Weir, Kreutzmann), 'Me And Bobby McGee' (Kris Kristofferson), 'The Other One' (Weir, Kreutzmann), 'Sugar Magnolia' (Weir, Hunter), 'Johnny B. Goode' (Chuck Berry)

P.N.E. Coliseum, Vancouver, British Columbia, May 17, 1974
'Promised Land' (Chuck Berry), 'Deal' (Garcia, Hunter), 'The Race Is On' (Don Rollins), 'Ramble On Rose' (Garcia, Hunter), 'Jack Straw' (Weir, Hunter), 'Dire Wolf' (Garcia, Hunter), 'Beat It On Down The Line' (Jesse Fuller), 'Loose Lucy' (Garcia, Hunter), 'Big

River' (Johnny Cash), 'It Must Have Been The Roses' (Hunter), 'Mexicali Blues' (Weir, Barlow), 'Row Jimmy' (Garcia, Hunter), 'Playing In The Band' (Weir, Hart, Hunter), 'U.S. Blues' (Garcia, Hunter), 'Me And My Uncle' (John Phillips), 'Ship Of Fools' (Garcia, Hunter), 'Money Money' (Weir, Barlow), 'China Cat Sunflower' (Garcia, Hunter), 'I Know You Rider' (trad.), 'Greatest Story Ever Told' (Weir, Hunter), 'Sugaree' (Garcia, Hunter), 'Truckin'' (Garcia, Lesh, Weir, Hunter), 'Nobody's Fault But Mine' (trad.), 'Eyes Of The World' (Garcia, Hunter), 'China Doll' (Garcia, Hunter), 'Sugar Magnolia' (Weir, Hunter)

Portland Memorial Coliseum, Portland, Oregon, May 19, 1974
'Mississippi Half-Step Uptown Toodeloo' (Garcia, Hunter), 'Mexicali Blues' (Weir, Barlow), Big Railroad Blues' (Noah Lewis), 'Black-Throated Wind' (Weir, Barlow), 'Scarlet Begonias' (Garcia, Hunter), 'Beat It On Down The Line' (Jesse Fuller), 'Tennessee Jed' (Garcia, Hunter), 'Me And Bobby McGee' (Kristofferson), 'Sugaree' (Garcia, Hunter), 'Jack Straw' (Weir, Hunter), 'It Must Have Been The Roses' (Hunter), 'El Paso' (Marty Robbins), 'Loose Lucy' (Garcia, Hunter), 'Money Money' (Weir, Barlow), 'China Cat Sunflower' (Garcia, Hunter), 'I Know You Rider' (trad.), 'Promised Land' (Chuck Berry), 'Bertha' (Garcia, Hunter), 'Greatest Story Ever Told' (Weir, Hunter), 'Ship Of Fools' (Garcia, Hunter), 'Weather Report Suite' (Weir, Andersen), 'Wharf Rat' (Garcia, Hunter), 'Big River' (Johnny Cash), 'Peggy-O' (trad.), 'Truckin'' (Garcia, Lesh, Weir, Hunter), 'Jam' (Grateful Dead), 'Not Fade Away' (Holly, Petty), 'Goin' Down The Road Feeling Bad' (trad.), 'One More Saturday Night' (Weir), 'U.S. Blues' (Garcia, Hunter)

Hec Edmundson Pavilion, Seattle, Washington, May 21, 1974
'Me And My Uncle' (John Phillips), 'Brown-Eyed Women' (Garcia, Hunter), 'Beat It On Down The Line' (Jesse Fuller), 'Deal' (Garcia, Hunter), 'Mexicali Blues' (Weir, Hunter), 'It Must Have Been The Roses' (Hunter), 'The Race Is On' (Don Rollins), 'Scarlet Begonias' (Garcia, Hunter), 'El Paso' (Marty Robbins), 'Row Jimmy' (Garcia, Hunter), 'Money Money' (Weir, Barlow), 'Ship Of Fools' (Garcia, Hunter), 'Weather Report Suite' (Weir, Andersen), 'China Doll' (Garcia, Hunter), 'Playing In The Band' (Weir, Hart, Hunter), 'U.S. Blues' (Garcia, Hunter), 'Big River' (Johnny Cash), 'Stella Blue' (Garcia, Hunter), 'Around And Around' (Chuck Berry), 'Eyes Of The World' (Garcia, Hunter), 'Wharf Rat' (Garcia, Hunter), 'Sugar Magnolia' (Weir, Hunter), 'Johnny B. Goode' (Chuck Berry)

Pacific Northwest '73–'74: Believe It If You Need It (2018)

Personnel:
Jerry Garcia: lead guitar, vocals
Donna Jean Godchaux: vocals
Keith Godchaux: keyboards
Bill Kreutzmann: drums
Phil Lesh: bass, vocals
Bob Weir: rhythm guitar, vocals
Recorded live at venues in the Pacific Northwest in 1973 and 1974. Produced for release by David Lemieux.
Release date: September 2018
Running time: 234:30
'China Cat Sunflower' (Garcia, Hunter), 'I Know You Rider' (trad.), 'Bird Song' (Garcia, Hunter), 'Box Of Rain' (Lesh, Hunter), 'Brown-Eyed Women' (Garcia, Hunter), 'Truckin'' (Garcia, Lesh, Weir, Hunter), 'Jam' (Grateful Dead), 'Not Fade Away' (Holly, Petty), 'Goin' Down The Road Feeling Bad' (trad.), 'One More Saturday Night' (Weir) 'Here Comes Sunshine' (Garcia, Hunter), 'Eyes Of The World' (Garcia, Hunter), 'China Doll' (Garcia, Hunter), 'Playing In The Band' (Weir, Hart, Hunter), 'Sugaree' (Garcia, Hunter), 'He's

Gone' (Garcia, Hunter), 'Truckin'' (Garcia, Lesh, Weir, Hunter), 'The Other One' (Weir, Kreutzmann), 'Wharf Rat' (Garcia, Hunter), 'Sugar Magnolia' (Weir, Hunter)

Dave's Picks Vol. 38 (2020)
Personnel:
Jerry Garcia: guitar, vocals
Donna Jean Godchaux: vocals
Keith Godchaux: keyboards
Bill Kreutzmann: drums
Phil Lesh: bass
Bob Weir: guitar, vocals
Recorded live at Nassau Coliseum in Uniondale, New York, on September 8, 1973. Recorded by Kidd Candelario
Release date: April 2021
Running time: 229:22
'Bertha' (Garcia, Hunter), 'Me And My Uncle' (John Phillips), 'Sugaree' (Garcia, Hunter), 'Beat It On Down The Line' (Jesse Fuller), 'Tennessee Jed' (Garcia, Hunter), 'Looks Like Rain' (Weir, Barlow), 'Brown-Eyed Women' (Garcia, Hunter), 'Jack Straw' (Weir, Hunter), 'Row Jimmy' (Garcia, Hunter), 'Weather Report Suite': 'Prelude' (Weir); 'Part I' (Weir, Eric Andersen; 'Part II (Let It Grow)' (Weir, Hunter), 'Eyes Of The World' (Garcia, Hunter), 'China Doll' (Garcia, Hunter), 'Greatest Story Ever Told' (Weir, Hart, Hunter), 'Ramble On Rose' (Garcia, Hunter), 'Big River' (Johnny Cash), 'Let Me Sing Your Blues Away' (Godchaux, Hunter), 'China Cat Sunflower' (Garcia, Hunter), I Know You Rider' (trad.), 'El Paso' (Marty Robbins), 'Bird Song' (Garcia, Hunter)) [Bonus track recorded at Nassau Coliseum on September 7, 1973], 'He's Gone' (Garcia, Hunter), 'Truckin'' (Garcia, Lesh, Weir, Hunter), 'Not Fade Away' (Petty, Holly) 'Goin' Down The Road Feeling Bad' (trad.), 'Not Fade Away' (Petty, Hardin), 'Stella Blue' (Garcia, Hunter), 'One More Saturday Night' (Weir), 'Playing In The Band' (Weir, Hart, Hunter) [Bonus track recorded at Nassau Coliseum on September 7, 1973], [Bonus disc recorded at Nassau Coliseum on September 7, 1973]: 'Here Comes Sunshine' (Garcia, Hunter), 'Let It Grow' (Weir, Barlow), 'Stella Blue' (Garcia, Hunter), 'Truckin'' (Garcia, Lesh, Weir, Hunter), 'Drums' (Kreutzmann), 'The Other One Jam' (Weir, Kreutzmann), 'Eyes Of The World' (Garcia, Hunter), 'Sugar Magnolia' (Weir, Hunter)

Dick's Picks Vol. 19 (2000)
Personnel:
Jerry Garcia: guitar, vocals
Donna Jean Godchaux: vocals
Keith Godchaux: piano
Bill Kreutzmann: drums
Phil Lesh: bass guitar, vocals
Bob Weir: rhythm guitar, vocals
Recorded live at the Fairgrounds Arena in Oklahoma City, Oklahoma, on October 19, 1973. Recorded by Bill Candelario.
Release date: October 2000
Running time: 188:34
'Promised Land' (Chuck Berry), 'Sugaree' (Garcia, Hunter), 'Mexicali Blues' (Weir, Barlow), 'Tennessee Jed' (Garcia, Hunter), 'Looks Like Rain' (Weir, Barlow), 'Don't Ease Me In' (trad.), 'Jack Straw' (Weir, Hunter), 'They Love Each Other' (Garcia, Hunter), 'El Paso' (Marty Robbins), 'Row Jimmy' (Garcia, Hunter), 'Playing In The Band' (Weir, Hart, Hunter),

'China Cat Sunflower' (Garcia, Hunter), 'I Know You Rider' (trad.), 'Me And My Uncle' (John Phillips), 'Mississippi Half-Step Uptown Toodeloo' (Garcia, Hunter), 'Big River' (Johnny Cash), Dark Star' (Garcia, Kreutzmann, Lesh, McKernan, Weir, Hunter), 'Mind Left Body Jam' (Grateful Dead), 'Morning Dew' (Dobson, Rose), 'Sugar Magnolia' (Weir, Hunter), 'Eyes Of The World' (Garcia, Hunter), 'Stella Blue' (Garcia, Hunter), 'Johnny B. Goode' (Chuck Berry)

Winterland 1973: The Complete Recordings (2008)

Personnel:
Jerry Garcia: guitar, vocals
Donna Jean Godchaux: vocals
Keith Godchaux: piano
Bill Kreutzmann: drums
Phil Lesh: electric bass guitar
Bob Weir: rhythm guitar, vocals
Recorded live at Winterland Ballroom, San Francisco, California, on November 9 – 11, 1973.
Box set produced by David Lemieux and Jeffrey Norman.
Release date: April 2008
Running time: 9:30:04

November 9, 1973
'Promised Land' (Chuck Berry), 'Brown-Eyed Woman' (Garcia, Hunter), 'Me And Bobby McGee' (Kristofferson, Foster), 'They Love Each Other' (Garcia, Hunter), 'Black-Throated Wind' (Weir, Barlow), 'Don't Ease Me In' (trad.), 'Mexicali Blues' (Weir, Barlow), 'Row Jimmy' (Garcia, Hunter), 'The Race Is On' (Don Rollins), 'China Cat Sunflower' (Garcia, Hunter), 'I Know You Rider' (trad.), 'Playing In The Band' (Weir, Hart, Hunter), 'Here Comes Sunshine' (Garcia, Hunter), 'Me And My Uncle' (John Phillips), 'To Lay Me Down' (Garcia, Hunter), 'Big River' (Johnny Cash), 'Mississippi Half-Step Uptown Toodeloo' (Garcia, Hunter), 'Greatest Story Ever Told' (Weir, Hunter), 'Bertha' (Garcia, Hunter), 'Weather Report Suite' (Weir, Andersen, Barlow), 'Eyes Of The World' (Garcia, Hunter), 'China Doll' (Garcia, Hunter), 'Around And Around' (Chuck Berry), 'Goin' Down The Road Feeling Bad' (trad.), 'Johnny B. Goode' (Chuck Berry)

November 10, 1973
'Bertha' (Garcia, Hunter), 'Jack Straw' (Weir, Hunter), 'Loser' (Garcia, Hunter), 'Looks Like Rain' (Weir, Barlow), 'Deal' (Garcia, Hunter), 'Mexicali Blues' (Weir, Barlow), 'Tennessee Jed' (Garcia, Hunter), 'El Paso' (Marty Robbins), 'Brokedown Palace' (Garcia, Hunter), 'Beat It On Down The Line' (Jesse Fuller), 'Row Jimmy' (Garcia, Hunter), 'Weather Report Suite' (Weir, Andersen, Barlow), 'Playing In The Band' (Weir, Hart, Hunter), 'Uncle John's Band' (Garcia, Hunter), 'Morning Dew' (Dobson, Rose), 'Uncle John's Band' (Garcia, Hunter), 'Playing In The Band' (Weir, Hart, Hunter), 'Big River' (Johnny Cash), 'Stella Blue' (Garcia, Hunter), 'Truckin'' (Garcia, Phil Lesh, Weir, Hunter), 'Wharf Rat' (Garcia, Hunter), 'Sugar Magnolia' (Weir, Hunter), 'One More Saturday Night' (Weir), 'Casey Jones' (Garcia, Hunter)

November 11, 1973
'Promised Land' (Chuck Berry), 'Bertha' (Garcia, Hunter), 'Greatest Story Ever Told' (Weir, Hunter), 'Sugaree' (Garcia, Hunter), 'Black-Throated Wind' (Weir, Barlow), 'To Lay Me Down' (Garcia, Hunter), 'El Paso' (Marty Robbins), 'Ramble On Rose' (Garcia, Hunter), 'Me And Bobby McGee' (Kristofferson, Foster), 'China Cat Sunflower' (Garcia, Hunter), 'I Know You Rider' (trad.), 'Me And My Uncle' (John Phillips), 'Loose Lucy' (Garcia, Hunter), 'Weather Report Suite' (Weir, Andersen, Barlow), 'Mississippi Half-Step Uptown Toodeloo'

(Garcia, Hunter), 'Big River' (Johnny Cash), 'Dark Star' (Garcia, Lesh, Weir, Bill Kreutzmann, Keith Godchaux, Hunter), 'Eyes Of The World' (Garcia, Hunter), 'China Doll' (Garcia, Hunter), 'Sugar Magnolia' (Weir, Hunter), 'Uncle John's Band' (Garcia, Hunter), 'Johnny B. Goode' (Chuck Berry), 'And We Bid You Goodnight' (trad.)
Bonus Disc recorded live at Cincinnati Gardens, Cincinnati, Ohio on December 4, 1973:
'China Cat Sunflower' (Garcia, Hunter), 'I Know You Rider' (trad.), 'Truckin' ' (Garcia, Lesh, Weir, Hunter), 'Stella Blue' (Garcia, Hunter) 'Eyes Of The World' (Garcia, Hunter), 'Space' (Garcia, Lesh, Weir, Kreutzmann, Godchaux), 'Sugar Magnolia' (Weir, Hunter), 'Goin' Down The Road Feeling Bad' (trad.), 'Casey Jones' (Garcia, Hunter)

Dave's Picks Vol.5 (2013)
Personnel:
Jerry Garcia: lead guitar, vocals
Donna Jean Godchaux: vocals
Keith Godchaux: keyboards
Bill Kreutzmann: drums
Phil Lesh: electric bass, vocals
Bob Weir: rhythm guitar, vocals
Recorded live at Pauley Pavilion, UCLA in Los Angeles, California, on November 17, 1973.
Recorded by Kidd Candelario.
Release date: Feb 2013
Running time: 3:07:46
'Me And My Uncle' (John Phillips), 'Here Comes Sunshine' (Garcia, Hunter), 'Looks Like Rain' (Weir, Barlow), 'Deal' (Garcia, Hunter), 'Mexicali Blues' (Weir, Barlow), 'Tennessee Jed' (Garcia, Hunter), 'The Race Is On' (George Jones), 'China Cat Sunflower' (Garcia, Hunter), 'I Know You Rider' (trad.), 'Big River' (Johnny Cash), 'Brown-Eyed Women' (Garcia, Hunter), 'Around And Around' (Chuck Berry), 'Row Jimmy' (Garcia, Hunter), 'Jack Straw' (Weir, Hunter), 'Ramble On Rose' (Garcia, Hunter), 'Playing In The Band' (Weir, Hart, Hunter), 'Uncle John's Band' (Garcia, Hunter), 'Morning Dew' (Dobson, Rose), 'Uncle John's Band' (Garcia, Hunter), 'Playing In The Band' (Weir, Hart, Hunter), 'Stella Blue' (Garcia, Hunter), 'El Paso' (Marty Robbins), 'Eyes Of The World' (Garcia, Hunter), 'Sugar Magnolia' (Weir, Hunter), 'Casey Jones' (Garcia, Hunter)

Road Trips Vol 4 No. 3 (2011)
Personnel:
Jerry Garcia: lead guitar, vocals
Donna Jean Godchaux: vocals
Keith Godchaux: keyboards
Bill Kreutzmann: drums
Phil Lesh: electric bass, vocals
Bob Weir: rhythm guitar, vocals
Recorded live at Denver Coliseum in Denver, Colorado, on November 21, 1973. Recorded by Kidd Candelario.
Release date: April 2011
Running time: 224:22
'Me And My Uncle' (John Phillips), 'Sugaree' (Garcia, Hunter), 'Jack Straw' (Weir, Hunter), 'Dire Wolf' (Garcia, Hunter), 'Black-Throated Wind' (Weir, Barlow), 'Big Railroad Blues' (Noah Lewis), 'Mexicali Blues' (Weir, Barlow), 'They Love Each Other' (Garcia, Hunter),

'Looks Like Rain' (Weir, Barlow), 'Here Comes Sunshine' (Garcia, Hunter), 'Big River' (Johnny Cash), 'Brokedown Palace' (Garcia, Hunter), 'Weather Report Suite' l) 'Prelude' (Weir), ll) 'Part 1' (Weir, Andersen), lll) 'Let It Grow' (Weir, Barlow), 'Mississippi Half-Step Uptown Toodeloo' (Garcia, Hunter), 'Playing In The Band' (Weir, Hart, Hunter), 'El Paso' (Marty Robbins), 'Playing In The Band' (Weir, Hart, Hunter), 'Wharf Rat' (Garcia, Hunter), 'Playing In The Band' (Weir, Hart, Hunter), 'Morning Dew' (Dobson, Rose), 'Truckin'' (Garcia, Lesh, Weir, Hunter), 'Nobody's Fault but Mine' (trad.), 'Goin' Down The Road Feeling Bad' (trad.), 'One More Saturday Night' (Weir), 'Uncle John's Band' (Garcia, Hunter), [Bonus tracks recorded at Denver Coliseum in Denver, Colorado on November 20, 1973]: 'Truckin'' (Garcia, Lesh, Weir, Hunter), 'The Other One' (Weir, Kreutzmann), 'Stella Blue' (Garcia, Hunter), [Bonus Disc: Recorded at Public Auditorium, Cleveland, Ohio, December 6, 1973]: 'Greatest Story Ever Told' (Hart, Weir, Hunter), 'China Cat Sunflower' (Garcia, Hunter), 'I Know You Rider' (trad.), 'Dark Star' (Garcia, Hart, Kreutzmann, Lesh, McKernan, Weir, Hunter), 'Eyes Of The World' (Garcia, Hunter)

Dick's Picks Vol.14 (1999)

Personnel:
Jerry Garcia: lead guitar, vocals
Keith Godchaux: keyboards
Bill Kreutzmann: drums
Phil Lesh: electric bass, vocals
Bob Weir: rhythm guitar, vocals
Recorded live at Boston Music Hall in Boston, Massachusetts, November 30 and December 2, 1973. Recorded by Bill Candelario.
Release date: June 1999
Running time: 279:00
'(Walk Me Out In The) Morning Dew' (Dobson, Rose), 'Mexicali Blues' (Weir, Barlow), 'Dire Wolf' (Garcia, Hunter), 'Black-Throated Wind' (Weir, Barlow), 'Don't Ease Me In' (trad.), 'Big River' (Johnny Cash), 'They Love Each Other' (Garcia, Hunter), 'Playing In The Band' (Weir, Hart, Hunter), 'Here Comes Sunshine' (Garcia, Hunter), 'Weather Report Suite' (Weir, Anderson, Barlow), 'Dark Star Jam' (Grateful Dead, Hunter), 'Eyes Of The World' (Garcia, Hunter), 'Sugar Magnolia' (Hunter, Weir), [Following from December 2, 1973]: 'Cold Rain And Snow' (trad.), 'Beat It On Down The Line' (Jesse Fuller), 'Brown-Eyed Women/The Merry-Go-Round Broke Down/Beer Barrel Polka' (Brown, Franklin, Friend, Garcia, Hunter, Timm, Vejvoda, Zeman), 'Jack Straw' (Hunter, Weir), 'Ramble On Rose' (Garcia, Hunter), 'Weather Report Suite' (Anderson, Barlow, Weir), 'Wharf Rat' (Garcia, Hunter), 'Mississippi Half-Step Uptown Toodleloo' (Garcia, Hunter), 'Playing In The Band' (Weir, Hart, Hunter), 'Jam' (Grateful Dead), 'He's Gone' (Garcia, Hunter), 'Truckin'' (Garcia, Lesh, Weir, Hunter), 'Stella Blue' (Garcia, Hunter), '(Walk Me Out In The) Morning Dew' (Dobson, Rose)

Download Series Vol. 8 (2005)

Personnel:
Jerry Garcia: lead guitar, vocals
Keith Godchaux: keyboards
Bill Kreutzmann: drums
Phil Lesh: electric bass
Bob Weir: rhythm guitar, vocals
Recorded live at the Charlotte Coliseum in Charlotte, North Carolina, on December 10, 1973. Recorded by Kidd Candelario.

Release date: December 2005
Running time: 149:15
'Bertha' (Garcia, Hunter), 'Mexicali Blues' (Weir, Barlow), 'Deal' (Garcia, Hunter), 'Big
River' (Johnny Cash), 'Don't Ease Me In' (trad.), 'Playing In The Band' (Weir, Hart,
Hunter), 'Promised Land' (Chuck Berry), 'Peggy-O' (trad.), 'Row Jimmy' (Garcia, Hunter),
'Me And Bobby McGee' (Kristofferson, Foster), 'Big Railroad Blues' (Noah Lewis).
'Truckin' ' (Garcia, Lesh, Weir, Hunter), 'Nobody's Fault But Mine' (Blind Willy Johnson),
'Eyes Of The World' (Garcia, Hunter), 'Brokedown Palace' (Garcia, Hunter), 'China Cat
Sunflower' (Garcia, Hunter), 'I Know You Rider' (trad.), 'Sugar Magnolia' (Weir, Hunter),
'Goin' Down The Road Feeling Bad' (trad.), 'Sunshine Daydream' (Weir, Hunter), 'Casey
Jones' (Garcia, Hunter)

Dick's Picks Vol. 1 (1993)
Personnel:
Jerry Garcia: lead guitar, vocals
Donna Jean Godchaux: giving birth
Keith Godchaux: keyboards
Bill Kreutzmann: drums
Phil Lesh: bass, vocals
Bob Weir: rhythm guitar, vocals
Recorded live at Curtis Hixon Hall in Tampa, Florida, on December 19, 1973. Produced and
recorded by Kidd Candelario.
Release date: October 1993
Running time: 125:03
'Here Comes Sunshine' (Garcia, Hunter), 'Big River' (Johnny Cash), 'Mississippi Half-Step
Uptown Toodeloo' (Garcia, Hunter), 'Weather Report Suite' (Andersen, Weir, Barlow),
'Big Railroad Blues' (Noah Lewis), 'Playing In The Band' (Weir, Hart, Hunter), 'He's Gone'
(Garcia, Hunter), 'Truckin'' (Garcia, Weir, Lesh, Hunter), 'Nobody's Fault But Mine '(Blind
Willie Johnson), 'Jam' (Garcia, Godchaux, Kreutzmann, Lesh, Weir), 'The Other One' (Weir,
Kreutzmann), 'Jam' (Garcia, Godchaux, Kreutzmann, Lesh, Weir), 'Stella Blue' (Garcia,
Hunter), 'Around And Around' (Chuck Berry)

1974
Dave's Picks Vol. 13 (2015)
Personnel:
Jerry Garcia: guitar, vocals
Donna Jean Godchaux: vocals
Keith Godchaux: keyboards
Bill Kreutzmann: drums
Phil Lesh: bass, vocals
Bob Weir: guitar, vocals
Recorded at the Winterland Arena in San Francisco, California, on February 24, 1974.
Recorded by Kidd Candelario.
Release date: February 2015
Running time: 213:30
'U.S. Blues' (Garcia, Hunter), 'Mexicali Blues' (Weir, Barlow), 'Brown-Eyed Women'
(Garcia, Hunter), 'Beat It On Down The Line' (Jesse Fuller), 'Candyman' (Garcia, Hunter),
'Jack Straw' (Weir, Hunter), 'China Cat Sunflower' (Garcia, Hunter), 'I Know You Rider'
(trad.), 'El Paso' (Marty Robbins), 'Loser' (Garcia, Hunter), 'Playing In The Band' (Weir,

Hart, Hunter), 'Cumberland Blues' (Garcia, Hunter), 'It Must Have Been The Roses' (Hunter), 'Big River' (Johnny Cash), 'Bertha' (Garcia, Hunter), 'Weather Report Suite': l) 'Prelude' (Weir); ll) 'Part I' (Weir, Andersen); lll) 'Part II (Let It Grow)' (Weir, Barlow), 'Row Jimmy' (Garcia, Hunter), 'Ship Of Fools' (Garcia, Hunter), 'Promised Land' (Chuck Berry), 'Dark Star' (Garcia, Hart, Kreutzmann, Lesh, McKernan, Weir, Hunter), 'Morning Dew' (Dobson, Rose), 'Sugar Magnolia' (Weir, Hunter), 'Not Fade Away' (Petty, Hardin), 'Goin' Down The Road Feeling Bad' (trad.), 'Not Fade Away' (Petty, Hardin), 'It's All Over Now, Baby Blue' (Bob Dylan)

Dick's Picks Vol.24 (2002)
Personnel:
Jerry Garcia: lead guitar, vocals
Donna Jean Godchaux: vocals
Keith Godchaux: keyboards
Bill Kreutzmann: drums
Phil Lesh: bass guitar, vocals
Bob Weir: rhythm guitar, vocals
Recorded live at Cow Palace in Daly City, California, March 23, 1974. Recorded by Bill Candelario.
Release date: February 2002
Running time: 151:17
'U.S. Blues' (Garcia, Hunter), 'Promised Land' (Chuck Berry), 'Brown-Eyed Women' (Garcia, Hunter), 'Black-Throated Wind' (Barlow, Weir), 'Scarlet Begonias' (Garcia, Hunter), 'Beat It On Down The Line' (Jesse Fuller), 'Deal' (Garcia, Hunter), 'Cassidy' (Barlow, Weir), 'China Cat Sunflower' (Garcia, Hunter), 'I Know You Rider' (trad.), 'Weather Report Suite' (Andersen, Barlow, Weir), 'Playing In The Band' (Hunter, Hart, Weir), 'Uncle John's Band' (Garcia, Hunter), 'Morning Dew' (Dobson, Rose), 'Uncle John's Band' (Garcia, Hunter), 'Playing In The Band' (Hunter, Hart, Weir), 'Big River' (Johnny Cash), 'Bertha' (Garcia, Hunter), 'Wharf Rat' (Garcia, Hunter), 'Sugar Magnolia' (Hunter, Weir)

Dave's Picks Vol. 9 (2014)
Personnel:
Jerry Garcia: guitar, vocals
Donna Jean Godchaux: vocals
Keith Godchaux: keyboards
Bill Kreutzmann: drums
Phil Lesh: electric bass, vocals
Bob Weir: guitar, vocals
Recorded live at the Harry Adams Field House in Missoula, Montana, on May 14, 1974. Recorded by Kidd Candelario
Release date: February 2014
Running time: 181:52
'Bertha' (Garcia, Hunter), 'Me And My Uncle' (John Phillips), 'Loser' (Garcia, Hunter), 'Black-Throated Wind' (Weir, Barlow), 'Scarlet Begonias' (Garcia, Hunter), 'It Must Have Been The Roses' (Hunter), 'Jack Straw' (Weir, Hunter), 'Tennessee Jed' (Garcia, Hunter), 'Mexicali Blues' (Weir, Barlow), 'Deal' (Garcia, Hunter), 'Big River' (Johnny Cash), 'Brown-Eyed Women' (Garcia, Hunter), 'Playing In The Band' (Weir, Hart, Hunter), 'U.S. Blues' (Garcia, Hunter), 'El Paso' (Marty Robbins), 'Row Jimmy' (Garcia, Hunter), 'Weather Report Suite:' l) 'Prelude' (Weir), ll) 'Part I' (Weir, Eric Andersen), lll) 'Part II (Let It Grow)' (Weir,

Barlow), 'Dark Star' (Garcia, Hart, Kreutzmann, Lesh, McKernan, Weir, Hunter), 'China Doll' (Garcia, Hunter), 'Promised Land' (Chuck Berry), 'Not Fade Away' (Petty, Hardin), 'Goin' Down The Road Feeling Bad' (trad.), 'One More Saturday Night' (Weir)

Portland Memorial Coliseum 5/19/1974 (2018)

Personnel:
Jerry Garcia: guitar, vocals
Donna Jean Godchaux: vocals
Keith Godchaux: keyboards
Bill Kreutzmann: drums
Phil Lesh: bass, vocals
Bob Weir: guitar, vocals
Recorded live at Portland Memorial Coliseum on May 19, 1974. Produced for release by David Lemieux.
Release date: November 2018
'Mississippi Half-Step Uptown Toodeloo' (Garcia, Hunter), 'Mexicali Blues' (Weir, Barlow), 'Big Railroad Blues' (Noah Lewis), 'Black-Throated Wind' (Weir, Barlow), 'Scarlet Begonias' (Garcia, Hunter), 'Beat It On Down The Line' (Jesse Fuller), 'Tennessee Jed' (Garcia, Hunter), 'Me And Bobby McGee' (Kristofferson, Foster), 'Sugaree' (Garcia, Hunter), 'Jack Straw' (Weir, Hunter), 'It Must Have Been The Roses' (Hunter), 'El Paso' (Marty Robbins), 'Loose Lucy' (Garcia, Hunter), 'Money Money' (Weir, Barlow), 'China Cat Sunflower' (Garcia, Hunter), 'I Know You Rider' (trad.), 'Promised Land' (Chuck Berry), 'Bertha' (Garcia, Hunter), 'Greatest Story Ever Told' (Weir, Hunter), 'Ship Of Fools' (Garcia, Hunter), 'Weather Report Suite' (Weir, Andersen), 'Wharf Rat' (Garcia, Hunter), 'Big River' (Johnny Cash), 'Peggy-O' (trad.), 'Truckin'' (Garcia, Lesh, Weir, Hunter), 'Jam' (Grateful Dead), 'Not Fade Away' (Holly, Petty), 'Goin' Down The Road Feeling Bad' (trad.), 'One More Saturday Night' (Weir), 'U.S. Blues' (Garcia, Hunter)

Playing In The Band, Seattle, Washington, 5/21/74 (2018)

Personnel:
Jerry Garcia: guitar, vocals
Donna Jean Godchaux: vocals
Keith Godchaux: keyboards
Bill Kreutzmann: drums
Phil Lesh: bass, vocals
Bob Weir: guitar, vocals
Recorded live at Hec Edmundson Pavilion in Seattle, Washington on May 21, 1974. Produced for release by David Lemieux.
Release date: November 2018
Running time: 46:24
'Playing In The Band' (Weir, Hart, Hunter), 'Playing In The Band' (continued) (Weir, Hart, Hunter)

Road Trips Vol.2 No. 3 (2009)

Personnel:
Jerry Garcia: lead guitar, vocals
Donna Jean Godchaux: vocals
Keith Godchaux: keyboards
Bill Kreutzmann: drums

Phil Lesh: electric bass, vocals
Bob Weir: rhythm guitar, vocals
Recorded live at Iowa State Fairgrounds, Des Moines, Iowa, on June 16, 1974, and at
Freedom Hall, Louisville, Kentucky, on June 18, 1974. Recorded by Kidd Candelario.
Release date: June 2009
Running time: 158:42
[State Fairgrounds, Des Moines, Iowa June 16, 1974]: 'China Cat Sunflower' (Garcia,
Hunter), 'I Know You Rider' (trad.). 'The Race Is On' (Don Rollins), 'Eyes Of The World'
(Garcia, Hunter), 'Big River' (Johnny Cash), 'U.S. Blues' (Garcia, Hunter), 'Playing In
The Band' (Weir, Hart, Hunter), [Freedom Hall, Louisville, Kentucky June 18, 1974]:
'Loose Lucy' (Garcia, Hunter), 'Eyes Of The World' (Garcia, Hunter), 'China Doll' (Garcia,
Hunter), 'Weather Report Suite' (Weir, Andersen, Barlow), 'Jam' (Grateful Dead), 'The
Other One' (Weir), 'It's A Sin Jam' (Grateful Dead), 'Stella Blue' (Garcia, Hunter), [Bonus
Disc]: Morning Dew' (Dobson, Rose) [Freedom Hall, Louisville, Kentucky June 18, 1974],
'Around And Around' (Chuck Berry) [Freedom Hall, Louisville, Kentucky June 18, 1974],
'Deal' (Garcia, Hunter) [State Fairgrounds, Des Moines, Iowa June 16, 1974], 'Greatest
Story Ever Told' (Weir, Hunter) [State Fairgrounds, Des Moines, Iowa June 16, 1974],
'Truckin'' (Garcia, Lesh, Weir, Hunter) [State Fairgrounds, Des Moines, Iowa June 16,
1974], 'Nobody's Fault But Mine Jam' (Grateful Dead) [State Fairgrounds, Des Moines,
Iowa June 16, 1974], 'Wharf Rat' (Garcia, Hunter) [State Fairgrounds, Des Moines, Iowa
June 16, 1974], 'Goin' Down The Road Feeling Bad' (trad.), [State Fairgrounds, Des
Moines, Iowa June 16, 1974],'Sugar Magnolia' (Weir, Hunter) [Freedom Hall, Louisville,
Kentucky June 18, 1974]

Dave's Picks Vol. 34 (2020)
Personnel:
Jerry Garcia: lead guitar, vocals
Donna Jean Godchaux: vocals
Keith Godchaux: keyboards
Bill Kreutzmann: drums
Phil Lesh: bass, vocals
Bob Weir: guitar, vocals
Additional personnel:
Ned Lagin: keyboards on 'Seastones' and during the second set.
Recorded live at the Jai-Alai Fronton in Miami, Florida, on June 23, 1974. Recorded by Kidd
Candelario
Release date: May 2020
Running time: 180:09
'Ramble On Rose' (Garcia, Hunter), 'Black-Throated Wind' (Weir, Barlow), 'Mississippi
Half-Step Uptown Toodeloo' (Garcia, Hunter), 'Beat It On Down The Line' (Jesse
Fuller), 'Row Jimmy' (Garcia, Hunter), 'Jack Straw' (Weir, Hunter), 'Let It Rock' (Chuck
Berry), 'Cumberland Blues' (Garcia, Lesh, Hunter), 'El Paso' (Marty Robbins), 'To Lay
Me Down' (Garcia, Hunter), 'Weather Report Suite': 1) 'Prelude' (Weir); 2) 'Part I' (Weir,
Eric Andersen): 3) 'Part II (Let It Grow)' (Weir, Hunter), 'China Doll' (Garcia, Hunter),
'Seastones' (Lagin, Lesh), 'Jam' (Grateful Dead), 'Ship Of Fools' (Garcia, Hunter), 'Big
River' (Johnny Cash), 'Black Peter' (Garcia, Hunter), 'Around And Around' (Chuck
Berry), 'Dark Star Jam' (Garcia, Hart, Kreutzmann, Lesh, McKernan, Weir, Hunter),
'Spanish Jam' (Grateful Dead), 'U.S. Blues' (Garcia, Hunter), 'Uncle John's Band'
(Garcia, Hunter), 'One More Saturday Night' (Weir), 'Casey Jones' (Garcia, Hunter),

[Bonus disc recorded live at Jai-Alai Fronton, June 22, 1974]: 'Playing In The Band' (Weir, Hart, Hunter), 'China Cat Sunflower' (Garcia, Hunter), 'I Know You Rider' (trad.), 'Eyes Of The World' (Garcia, Hunter), 'Wharf Rat' (Garcia, Hunter), 'Sugar Magnolia' (Weir, Hunter)

Dick's Picks Vol.12 (1998)

Personnel:
Jerry Garcia: lead guitar, vocals
Donna Godchaux: vocals
Keith Godchaux: keyboards
Bill Kreutzmann: drums, percussion
Phil Lesh: bass, vocals
Bob Weir: guitar, vocals
Recorded live at Providence Civic Center, Providence, Rhode Island, June 26, 1974, and at Boston Garden, Boston, Massachusetts, June 28 1974. Recorded by Bill Candelario.
Release date: October 1998
Running time: 204:51
'Jam' (Grateful Dead), 'China Cat Sunflower' (Garcia, Hunter), 'Mind Left Body Jam' (Grateful Dead), 'I Know You Rider' (trad.) 'Beer Barrel Polka' (Brown, Timm, Vejvoda, Zeman), 'Truckin'' (Garcia, Weir, Lesh, Hunter), 'The Other One Jam' (Grateful Dead), 'Spanish Jam' (Grateful Dead), 'Wharf Rat' (Garcia, Hunter), 'Sugar Magnolia' (Weir, Hunter), 'Eyes Of The World' (Garcia, Hunter) [Following from June 28, 1974, Boston Garden]: 'Seastones' (Lesh, Lagin), 'Sugar Magnolia' (Weir, Hunter), 'Scarlet Begonias' (Garcia, Hunter), 'Big River' (Johnny Cash), 'To Lay Me Down' (Garcia, Hunter), 'Me And My Uncle' (John Phillips), 'Row Jimmy' (Garcia, Hunter), 'Weather Report Suite': 1) 'Prelude' (Weir), 2) 'Part 1' (Weir, Eric Andersen), 3) 'Let It Grow' (Weir, Barlow), 'Jam' (Grateful Dead), 'U.S. Blues' (Garcia, Hunter), 'Promised Land' (Chuck Berry), 'Goin' Down The Road Feeling Bad' (trad.), 'Sunshine Daydream' (Weir, Hunter), 'Ship Of Fools' (Garcia, Hunter)

Dave's Picks Vol. 17 (2016)

Personnel:
Jerry Garcia: lead guitar, vocals
Donna Jean Godchaux: vocals
Keith Godchaux: keyboards
Bill Kreutzmann: drums
Phil Lesh: electric bass, vocals
Bob Weir: rhythm guitar, vocals
Additional personnel:
Ned Lagin: synthesiser and electronic keyboards on 'Seastones'
Recorded live at Selland Arena in Fresno, California, on July 19, 1974. Recorded by Kidd Candelario.
Release date: February 2016
Running time: 197:29
'Bertha' (Garcia, Hunter), 'Mexicali Blues' (Weir, Barlow), 'Deal' (Garcia, Hunter), 'Beat It On Down The Line' (Jesse Fuller), 'Row Jimmy' (Garcia, Hunter), 'Me And Bobby McGee' (Kristofferson, Foster), 'Scarlet Begonias' (Garcia, Hunter), 'El Paso' (Marty Robbins), 'Tennessee Jed' (Garcia, Hunter), 'Playing In The Band' (Weir, Hart, Hunter), 'Seastones' (Lesh, Lagin), 'Brown-Eyed Women' (Garcia, Hunter), 'Me And My Uncle'

(John Phillips), 'It Must Have Been The Roses' (Hunter), 'Jack Straw' (Weir, Hunter), 'He's Gone' (Garcia, Hunter), 'U.S. Blues' (Garcia, Hunter), 'Weather Report Suite': 1) 'Prelude' (Weir); 2) 'Part 1' (Weir, Andersen) 2) 'Let It Grow' (Weir, Barlow), 'Jam' (Grateful Dead), 'Eyes Of The World' (Garcia, Hunter), 'China Doll' (Garcia, Hunter), 'One More Saturday Night' (Weir)

Dave's Picks Vol.2 (2012)
Personnel:
Jerry Garcia: lead guitar, vocals
Donna Jean Godchaux: vocals
Keith Godchaux: keyboards
Bill Kreutzmann: drums
Phil Lesh: electric bass, vocals
Bob Weir: rhythm guitar, vocals
Recorded live at Dillon Stadium in Hartford, Connecticut, on July 31, 1974. Recorded by Kidd Candelario.
Release date: May 2012
Running time: 216:40
'Scarlet Begonias' (Garcia, Hunter), 'Me And My Uncle' (John Phillips), 'Brown Eyed Women' (Garcia, Hunter), 'Beat It On Down The Line' (Jesse Fuller), 'Mississippi Half-Step Uptown Toodeloo' (Garcia, Hunter), 'It Must Have Been The Roses' (Hunter), 'Mexicali Blues' (Weir, Barlow), 'Row Jimmy' (Garcia, Hunter), 'Jack Straw' (Weir, Hunter), 'China Cat Sunflower' (Garcia, Hunter), 'I Know You Rider' (trad.), 'Around And Around' (Chuck Berry), 'Bertha' (Garcia, Hunter), 'Big River' (Johnny Cash), 'Eyes Of The World' (Garcia, Hunter), 'China Doll' (Garcia, Hunter), 'Promised Land' (Chuck Berry), 'Ship Of Fools' (Garcia, Hunter), 'Weather Report Suite: l)'Prelude' (Weir); 2) 'Part 1' (Weir, Andersen); lll) 'Let It Grow' (Weir, Barlow), 'El Paso' (Marty Robbins), 'Ramble On Rose' (Garcia, Hunter), 'Greatest Story Ever Told' (Weir, Hart, Hunter), 'To Lay Me Down' (Garcia, Hunter), 'Truckin'' (Garcia, Lesh, Weir, Hunter), 'Mind Left Body Jam' (Grateful Dead), 'Spanish Jam' (Grateful Dead), 'Wharf Rat' (Garcia, Hunter), 'U.S. Blues' (Garcia, Hunter), 'One More Saturday Night' (Weir), 'Uncle John's Band' (Garcia, Hunter) [Bonus disc-recorded at Capital Centre, Landover, Maryland July 29 1974]: 'Sugaree' (Garcia, Hunter), 'Weather Report Suite:' l) 'Prelude' (Weir); ll) 'Part 1' (Weir, Andersen); lll) 'Let It Grow' (Weir, Barlow), 'He's Gone' (Garcia, Hunter), 'Truckin'' (Garcia, Lesh, Weir, Hunter), 'Nobody's Fault But Mine' (trad.), 'The Other One' (Weir, Kreutzmann), 'Spanish Jam' (Grateful Dead), 'Wharf Rat' (Garcia, Hunter)

Dick's Picks Vol.31 (2004)
Personnel:
Jerry Garcia: guitar, vocals
Donna Godchaux: vocals
Keith Godchaux: piano
Bill Kreutzmann: drums
Phil Lesh: electric bass, vocals
Bob Weir: guitar, vocals
Recorded live at the Philadelphia Civic Center in Philadelphia, Pennsylvania on August 4 and 5, 1974, and at Roosevelt Stadium in Jersey City, New Jersey on August 6, 1974. Recorded by Bill Candelario.
Release date: March 2004

Running time: 295:34
'Playing In The Band' (Hunter, Hart, Weir) [August 4 1974], 'Scarlet Begonias' (Garcia, Hunter) [August 5 1974], 'Jack Straw' (Hunter, Weir), [August 4 1974], 'Peggy-O' (trad.) [August 4 1974], 'Me And Bobby McGee' (Foster, Kristofferson) [August 5 1974], 'China Cat Sunflower' (Garcia, Hunter) [August 5 1974], 'I Know You Rider' (trad.) [August 5 1974], 'Around And Around' (Chuck Berry) [August 5 1974], 'Ship Of Fools' (Garcia, Hunter) [August 4 1974], 'Loose Lucy' (Garcia, Hunter) [August 4 1974], 'Weather Report Suite:' l) 'Prelude' (Weir); ll) 'Part I' (Andersen, Weir); lll) 'Part II: Let It Grow' (Barlow, Weir) [August 4 1974], 'Jam' (Grateful Dead) [August 4 1974], 'Wharf Rat' (Garcia, Hunter) [August 4 1974] 'U.S. Blues' (Garcia, Hunter) [August 4 1974], 'Sugar Magnolia/Sunshine Daydream' (Hunter, Weir) [August 4 1974], 'Casey Jones' (Garcia, Hunter) [August 4 1974], 'Mississippi Half-Step Uptown Toodeloo' (Garcia, Hunter) [August 5 1974], 'It Must Have Been The Roses' (Hunter) [August 5 1974], 'Big River' (Johnny Cash) [August 5 1974], 'He's Gone' (Garcia, Hunter) [August 5 1974], 'Truckin'' (Hunter, Garcia, Lesh, Weir) [August 5 1974], 'Jam' (Grateful Dead) [August 5 1974], 'The Other One Jam' (Grateful Dead) [August 5 1974], 'Space' (Grateful Dead) [August 5 1974], 'Stella Blue' (Garcia, Hunter) [August 5 1974], 'One More Saturday Night' (Weir)[August 5 1974], [Following from August 6, 1974]: 'Eyes Of The World' (Garcia, Hunter), 'Playing In The Band' (Hunter, Hart, Weir), 'Scarlet Begonias' (Garcia, Hunter), 'Playing In The Band' (Hunter, Hart, Weir), 'Uncle John's Band' (Garcia, Hunter)

Dick's Picks Vol.7 (1997)
Personnel:
Jerry Garcia: lead guitar, vocals
Donna Jean Godchaux: vocals
Keith Godchaux: keyboards
Bill Kreutzmann: drums
Phil Lesh: electric bass, vocals
Bob Weir: guitar, vocals
Recorded live at Alexandra Palace in London, England, on September 9-11 1974. Recorded by Bill Candelario.
Release date: March 1997
Running time: 212:57
'Scarlet Begonias' (Garcia, Hunter), 'Mexicali Blues' (Barlow, Weir), 'Row Jimmy' (Garcia, Hunter), 'Black-Throated Wind' (Barlow, Weir), 'Mississippi Half-Step Uptown Toodleloo' (Garcia, Hunter), 'Beat It On Down The Line' (Jesse Fuller), 'Tennessee Jed' (Garcia, Hunter), 'Playing In The Band' (Hart, Hunter, Weir), 'Weather Report Suite' (Anderson, Barlow, Weir), 'Stella Blue' (Garcia, Hunter), 'Jack Straw' (Hunter, Weir), 'Brown-Eyed Women' (Garcia, Hunter), 'Big River' (Johnny Cash), 'Truckin'' (Garcia, Hunter, Lesh, Weir), 'Wood Green Jam' (Grateful Dead), 'Wharf Rat' (Garcia, Hunter), 'Me And My Uncle' (John Phillips), 'Not Fade Away' (Holly, Petty), 'Dark Star' (Grateful Dead, Hunter), 'Spam Jam' (Grateful Dead), '(Walk Me Out in the) Morning Dew' (Dobson, Rose), 'U.S. Blues' (Garcia, Hunter)

The Grateful Dead Movie Soundtrack (2005)
Personnel:
Jerry Garcia: lead guitar, vocals
Donna Jean Godchaux: vocals
Keith Godchaux: keyboards, piano

Mickey Hart: drums on disc five
Bill Kreutzmann: drums
Phil Lesh: bass guitar, vocals
Bob Weir: rhythm guitar, vocals
Recorded live at Winterland Ballroom, San Francisco, on October 16 – 20, 1974. Produced by David Lemieux and Jeffrey Norman.
Release date: March 2005
Running time: 387:54
'U.S. Blues' (Garcia, Hunter), 'One More Saturday Night' (Weir), 'China Cat Sunflower' (Garcia, Hunter), 'I Know You Rider' (trad.), 'Eyes Of The World' (Garcia, Hunter), 'China Doll' (Garcia, Hunter), 'Playing In The Band' (Hunter, Hart, Weir), 'Scarlet Begonias' (Garcia, Hunter), 'He's Gone' (Garcia, Hunter), 'Jam' (Grateful Dead), 'Weirdness' (Grateful Dead), 'The Other One' (Kreutzmann, Weir), 'Spanish Jam' (Grateful Dead). 'Mind Left Body Jam' (Grateful Dead), 'The Other One' (Kreutzmann, Weir), 'Stella Blue' (Garcia, Hunter), 'Casey Jones' (Garcia, Hunter), 'Weather Report Suite' l) 'Prelude' (Weir), ll) 'Part I' (Andersen, Weir), lll) 'Part II: Let It Grow' (Barlow, Weir), 'Jam' (Grateful Dead), 'Dark Star' (Hunter, Garcia, Hart, Kreutzmann, Lesh, Pigpen, Weir), 'Morning Dew' (Dobson, Rose), 'Not Fade Away' (Holly, Petty), 'Goin' Down The Road Feeling Bad' (trad.), 'Uncle John's Band' (Garcia, Hunter), 'Big Railroad Blues' (Noah Lewis), 'Tomorrow Is Forever' (Parton, Wagoner), 'Sugar Magnolia' (Hunter, Weir), 'He's Gone' (Garcia, Hunter), 'Caution Jam' (Grateful Dead), 'Drums' (Kreutzmann), 'Space' (Grateful Dead), 'Truckin' ' (Hunter, Garcia, Lesh, Weir), 'Black Peter' (Garcia, Hunter), 'Sunshine Daydream' (Hunter, Weir), 'Playing In The Band' (Hunter, Hart, Weir), 'Drums' (Hart, Kreutzmann), 'Not Fade Away' (Holly, Petty), 'Drums' (Hart, Kreutzmann), 'The Other One' (Kreutzmann, Weir), 'Wharf Rat' (Garcia, Hunter), 'Playing In The Band' (Hunter, Hart, Weir), 'Johnny B. Goode' (Chuck Berry), 'Mississippi Half-Step Uptown Toodeloo' (Garcia, Hunter), 'And We Bid You Goodnight' (trad.)

1975
One From The Vault (1991)
Personnel:
Jerry Garcia: guitar, vocals
Donna Jean Godchaux
Keith Godchaux: keyboards, vocals
Mickey Hart: percussion and crickets
Bill Kreutzmann: drums and percussion
Phil Lesh: bass guitar, vocals
Bob Weir: guitar, vocals
Recorded live at the Great American Music Hall, San Francisco, California on August 13, 1975. Produced by Dan Healy
Release date: April 1991
Running time: 121:51
'Introduction by Bill Graham', 'Help On The Way/Slipknot!' (Garcia, Hunter), 'Franklin's Tower' (Garcia, Kreutzmann, Hunter), 'The Music Never Stopped' (Weir, Barlow), 'It Must Have Been The Roses' (Hunter), 'Eyes Of The World/Drums' (Garcia, Hunter), 'King Solomon's Marbles' (Lesh), 'Around And Around' (Chuck Berry), 'Sugaree' (Garcia, Hunter), 'Big River' (Johnny Cash), 'Crazy Fingers/Drums' (Garcia, Hunter), 'The Other One' (Weir, Kreutzmann), 'Sage And Spirit' (Weir), 'Goin' Down The Road Feeling Bad' (trad.), 'U.S. Blues' (Garcia, Hunter), 'Blues For Allah' (Garcia, Hunter)

1976
Road Trips Vol 4 No. 5 (2011)
Personnel:
Jerry Garcia: lead guitar, vocals
Donna Jean Godchaux: vocals
Keith Godchaux: keyboards
Mickey Hart: drums
Bill Kreutzmann: drums
Phil Lesh: electric bass
Bob Weir: rhythm guitar, vocals
Recorded live at the Boston Music Hall in Boston, Massachusetts, on June 9, 1976. Produced for release by David Lemieux and Blair Jackson.
Release date: November 2011
Running time: 220:40
'Cold Rain And Snow' (trad.), 'Cassidy' (Weir, Barlow), 'Scarlet Begonias' (Garcia, Hunter), 'The Music Never Stopped' (Weir, Barlow), 'Crazy Fingers' (Garcia, Hunter), 'Big River' (Johnny Cash), 'They Love Each Other' (Garcia, Hunter), 'Looks Like Rain' (Weir, Barlow), 'Ship Of Fools' (Garcia, Hunter), 'Promised Land' (Chuck Berry), 'St. Stephen' (Garcia, Lesh, Hunter), 'Eyes Of The World' (Garcia, Hunter), 'Let It Grow' (Weir, Barlow), 'Brown-Eyed Women' (Garcia, Hunter), 'Lazy Lightning' (Weir, Barlow), 'Supplication' (Weir, Barlow), 'High Time' (Garcia, Hunter), 'Samson And Delilah' (trad.), 'It Must Have Been The Roses' (Hunter), 'Dancing In The Streets' (Stevenson, Gaye, Hunter), 'Wharf Rat' (Garcia, Hunter), 'Around And Around' (Chuck Berry), 'Franklin's Tower' (Garcia, Kreutzmann, Hunter), [Bonus tracks recorded at Boston Music Hall, June 12 1976]: 'Mission In The Rain' (Garcia, Hunter), 'The Wheel' (Garcia, Hunter), 'Comes A Time' (Garcia, Hunter), 'Sugar Magnolia' (Weir, Hunter), 'U.S. Blues' (Garcia, Hunter), 'Sunshine Daydream' (Weir, Hunter)

June 1976 (2020)
Personnel:
Jerry Garcia: lead guitar, vocals
Donna Jean Godchaux: vocals
Keith Godchaux: keyboards
Mickey Hart: drums
Bill Kreutzmann: drums
Phil Lesh: bass
Bob Weir: guitar, vocals
Recorded live at the Boston Music Hall, the Beacon Theatre, New York City, and the Capitol Theatre in Passaic, New Jersey, on June 10 – June 19, 1976. Produced for release by David Lemieux.
Release date: March 2020
Boston Music Hall, June 10, 1976
'Promised Land' (Chuck Berry), 'Sugaree' (Garcia, Hunter), 'Cassidy' (Weir, Barlow), 'They Love Each Other' (Garcia, Hunter), 'The Music Never Stopped' (Weir, Barlow), 'Brown-Eyed Women' (Garcia, Hunter), 'Lazy Lightning' (Weir, Barlow), 'Supplication' (Weir, Barlow), 'Row Jimmy' (Garcia, Hunter), 'Big River' (Johnny Cash), 'Mission In The Rain' (Garcia, Hunter), 'Looks Like Rain' (Weir, Barlow), 'Might As Well' (Garcia, Hunter), 'Samson And Delilah' (trad.), 'Help On The Way' (Garcia, Hunter), 'Slipknot!' (Garcia, Godchaux, Kreutzmann, Lesh, Weir), 'Franklin's Tower' (Garcia, Kreutzmann, Hunter), 'Let It Grow' (Weir, Barlow), 'Friend Of The Devil' (Garcia, Dawson, Hunter), 'Playing In The Band' (Weir,

Hart, Hunter), 'Dancing In The Street' (Stevenson, Gaye, I. J. Hunter), 'U.S. Blues' (Garcia, Hunter)

Boston Music Hall, June 11, 1976
'Might As Well' (Garcia, Hunter), 'Mama Tried' (Merle Haggard), 'Tennessee Jed' (Garcia, Hunter), 'Cassidy' (Weir, Barlow), 'Candyman' (Garcia, Hunter), 'Big River' (Johnny Cash), 'Scarlet Begonias' (Garcia, Hunter), 'Looks Like Rain' (Weir, Barlow), 'It Must Have Been The Roses' (Hunter), 'Lazy Lightning' (Weir, Barlow), 'Supplication' (Weir, Barlow), 'Brown-Eyed Women' (Garcia, Hunter), 'Promised Land' (Chuck Berry), 'St. Stephen' (Garcia, Lesh, Hunter), 'Dancing in The Street' (Stevenson, Gaye, I. J. Hunter), 'The Music Never Stopped' (Weir, Barlow), 'Ship Of Fools' (Garcia, Hunter), 'Samson And Delilah' (trad.), 'Sugaree' (Garcia, Hunter), 'Sugar Magnolia' (Weir, Hunter), 'Eyes Of The World' (Garcia, Hunter), 'Stella Blue' (Garcia, Hunter), 'Sunshine Daydream' (Weir, Hunter), 'Johnny B. Goode' (Chuck Berry)

Beacon Theatre, June 14, 1976
'Cold Rain And Snow' (trad.), 'Mama Tried' (Merle Haggard), 'Row Jimmy' (Garcia, Hunter), 'Cassidy' (Weir, Barlow), 'Brown-Eyed Women' (Garcia, Hunter), 'Big River' (Johnny Cash), 'Might As Well' (Garcia, Hunter), 'Lazy Lightning' (Weir, Barlow), 'Supplication' (Weir, Barlow), 'Tennessee Jed' (Garcia, Hunter), 'Playing In The Band' (Weir, Hart, Hunter), 'The Wheel' (Garcia, Hunter), 'Samson And Delilah' (trad.), 'High Time' (Garcia, Hunter), 'The Music Never Stopped' (Weir, Barlow), 'Crazy Fingers' (Garcia, Hunter), 'Dancing In The Street' (Stevenson, Gaye, I. J. Hunter), 'Cosmic Charlie' (Garcia, Hunter), 'Help On The Way' (Garcia, Hunter), 'Slipknot!' (Garcia, Godchaux, Kreutzmann, Lesh, Weir), 'Franklin's Tower' (Garcia, Kreutzmann, Hunter), 'Around And Around' (Chuck Berry), 'U.S. Blues' (Garcia, Hunter)

Beacon Theatre, June 15, 1976
'Promised Land' (Chuck Berry), 'Sugaree' (Garcia, Hunter), 'Cassidy' (Weir, Barlow), 'Candyman' (Garcia, Hunter), 'The Music Never Stopped' (Weir, Barlow), 'It Must Have Been The Roses' (Hunter), 'Looks Like Rain' (Weir, Barlow), 'Tennessee Jed' (Garcia, Hunter), 'Let It Grow' (Weir, Barlow), 'Might As Well' (Garcia, Hunter), 'St. Stephen' (Garcia, Lesh, Hunter), 'Not Fade Away' (Holly, Petty), 'Stella Blue' (Garcia, Hunter), 'Samson And Delilah' (trad.), 'Friend Of The Devil' (Garcia, Dawson, Hunter), 'Dancing In The Street' (Stevenson, Gaye, I. J. Hunter), 'The Wheel' (Garcia, Hunter), 'Sugar Magnolia' (Weir, Hunter), 'Scarlet Begonias' (Garcia, Hunter), 'Sunshine Daydream' (Weir, Hunter), 'Johnny B. Goode' (Chuck Berry)

Capitol Theatre, June 19, 1976
'Help On The Way' (Garcia, Hunter), 'Slipknot!' (Garcia, Godchaux, Kreutzmann, Lesh, Weir), 'Franklin's Tower' (Garcia, Kreutzmann, Hunter), 'The Music Never Stopped' (Weir, Barlow), 'Brown-Eyed Women' (Garcia, Hunter), 'Cassidy' (Weir, Barlow), 'They Love Each Other' (Garcia, Hunter), 'Looks Like Rain' (Weir, Barlow), 'Tennessee Jed' (Garcia, Hunter), 'Playing In The Band' (Weir, Hart, Hunter), 'Might As Well' (Garcia, Hunter), 'Samson And Delilah' (trad.), 'High Time' (Garcia, Hunter), 'Let It Grow' (Weir, Barlow), 'Dancing In The Street' (Stevenson, Gaye, I. J. Hunter), 'Cosmic Charlie' (Garcia, Hunter), 'Around And Around' (Chuck Berry), 'Goin' Down The Road Feeling Bad' (trad.), 'One More Saturday Night' (Weir), 'Not Fade Away' (Holly, Petty)

Dave's Picks Vol. 28 (2018)
Personnel:
Jerry Garcia: guitar, vocals
Donna Jean Godchaux: vocals

Keith Godchaux: keyboards
Mickey Hart: drums
Bill Kreutzmann: drums
Phil Lesh: bass
Bob Weir: rhythm guitar, vocals
Recorded live at the Capitol Theatre, in Passaic, New Jersey on June 17, 1976. Recorded by Betty Cantor-Jackson.
Release date: October 2018
Running time: 193:18
'Cold Rain And Snow' (trad.), 'Big River' (Johnny Cash), 'They Love Each Other' (Garcia, Hunter), 'Cassidy' (Weir, Barlow), 'Tennessee Jed' (Garcia, Hunter), 'Looks Like Rain' (Weir, Barlow), 'Row Jimmy' (Garcia, Hunter), 'The Music Never Stopped' (Weir, Barlow), 'Scarlet Begonias' (Garcia, Hunter), 'Promised Land' (Chuck Berry), 'Help On The Way' (Garcia, Hunter), 'Slipknot!' (Garcia, Godchaux, Kreutzmann, Lesh, Weir), 'Franklin's Tower' (Hunter, Garcia, Kreutzmann), 'Dancing In The Street' (Stevenson, Gaye, Hunter), 'Samson And Delilah' (trad.), 'Ship Of Fools' (Garcia, Hunter), 'Lazy Lightning' (Weir, Barlow), 'Supplication' (Weir, Barlow), 'Friend Of The Devil' (Garcia, Hunter), 'Let It Grow' (Weir, Barlow), 'Drums' (Hart, Kreutzmann), 'Let It Grow' (Weir, Barlow), 'Wharf Rat' (Garcia, Hunter), 'Around And Around' (Chuck Berry), [Bonus track recorded at Tower Theatre, Upper Darby, Pennsylvania, June 23, 1976]: 'Sugaree' (Garcia, Hunter), [Bonus track recorded at Auditorium Theatre, Chicago, Illinois, June 28, 1976]: 'High Time' (Garcia, Hunter)

Download Series Vol. 4 (2005)

Personnel:
Jerry Garcia: lead guitar, vocals
Donna Jean Godchaux: vocals
Keith Godchaux: keyboards
Mickey Hart: drums
Bill Kreutzmann: drums
Phil Lesh: electric bass
Bob Weir: rhythm guitar, vocals
Recorded live at the Capitol Theatre in Passaic, New Jersey, on June 18, 1976. Recorded by Betty Cantor-Jackson.
Release date: August 2005
Running time: 209.45
'The Music Never Stopped' (Barlow, Weir), 'Sugaree' (Garcia, Hunter), 'Mama Tried' (Merle Haggard). 'Crazy Fingers' (Garcia, Hunter), 'Big River' (Johnny Cash), 'Brown-Eyed Women' (Garcia, Hunter), 'Looks Like Rain' (Barlow, Weir), 'Row Jimmy' (Garcia, Hunter), 'Cassidy' (Barlow, Weir), 'Mission In The Rain' (Garcia, Hunter), 'Promised Land' (Chuck Berry), 'Samson And Delilah' (trad.), 'St. Stephen' (Hunter, Garcia, Lesh), 'Not Fade Away' (Holly, Petty), 'St. Stephen' (Hunter, Garcia, Lesh), 'Eyes Of The World' (Garcia, Hunter), 'Drums' (Hart, Kreutzmann), 'The Wheel' (Garcia, Hunter), 'Sugar Magnolia' (Hunter, Weir), 'U.S. Blues' (Garcia, Hunter), [Bonus tracks recorded at the Tower Theatre, Philadelphia, on June 21, 1976] 'Scarlet Begonias' (Garcia, Hunter), 'Lazy Lightnin' ' (Weir, Barlow), 'Supplication' (Weir, Barlow), 'Candyman' (Garcia, Hunter) [Bonus tracks recorded at the Tower Theatre, Philadelphia, on June 22, 1976] 'Playing In The Band' (Weir, Mickey Hart, Hunter), 'Drums' (Hart, Kreutzmann), 'The Wheel' (Garcia, Hunter), 'Playing In The Band' (Weir, Mickey Hart, Hunter), 'High Time' (Garcia, Hunter)

Dave's Picks Vol.18 (2016)
Personnel:
Jerry Garcia: guitar, vocals
Donna Jean Godchaux: vocals
Keith Godchaux: keyboards
Mickey Hart: drums
Bill Kreutzmann: drums
Phil Lesh: bass
Bob Weir: guitar, vocals
Recorded live at the Orpheum Theatre in San Francisco, California, on July 17, 1976.
Recorded by Betty Cantor-Jackson
Release date: May 2016
Running time: 207:05
'Promised Land' (Chuck Berry), 'Mississippi Half-Step Uptown Toodeloo' (Garcia, Hunter), 'Mama Tried' (Merle Haggard), 'Deal' (Garcia, Hunter), 'New Minglewood Blues' (trad.), 'Peggy-O' (trad.), 'Big River' (Johnny Cash), 'Sugaree' (Garcia, Hunter), 'Johnny B. Goode' (Chuck Berry), 'Samson And Delilah' (trad.), 'Comes A Time' (Garcia, Hunter), 'Drums' (Hart, Kreutzmann), 'The Other One' (Weir, Kreutzmann), 'Space' (Garcia, Lesh, Weir) 'Eyes Of The World' (Garcia, Hunter), 'Jam' (Grateful Dead), 'The Other One' (Weir, Kreutzmann), 'Goin' Down The Road Feeling Bad' (trad.), 'One More Saturday Night' (Weir), 'U.S. Blues' (Garcia, Hunter), 'Not Fade Away' (Petty, Hardin). [Bonus tracks: recorded at Orpheum Theatre, July 16, 1976]: 'Big River' (Johnny Cash), 'Brown-Eyed Women' (Garcia, Hunter), 'Looks Like Rain' (Weir, Barlow), 'Peggy-O' (trad.), 'The Music Never Stopped' (Weir, Barlow), 'Scarlet Begonias' (Garcia, Hunter), 'U.S. Blues' (Garcia, Hunter), [bonus disc: recorded at Orpheum Theatre, July 16, 1976]: 'Playing In The Band' (Weir, Hart, Hunter), 'Cosmic Charlie' (Garcia, Hunter), 'Spanish Jam' (Grateful Dead), 'Drums' (Hart, Kreutzmann), 'The Wheel' (Garcia, Hunter, Kreutzmann), 'Playing In The Band' (Weir, Hart, Hunter), 'High Time' (Garcia, Hunter), 'Sugar Magnolia' (Weir, Hunter)

Dave's Picks Vol.4 (2012)
Personnel:
Jerry Garcia: lead guitar, vocals
Donna Jean Godchaux: vocals
Keith Godchaux: keyboards
Mickey Hart: drums
Bill Kreutzmann: drums
Phil Lesh: electric bass,
Bob Weir: rhythm guitar, vocals
Recorded live at the College of William and Mary in Williamsburg, Virginia, on September 24, 1976. Recorded by Dan Healy.
Release date: November 2012
Running time: 161:36
'Promised Land' (Chuck Berry), 'Deal' (Garcia, Hunter), 'Cassidy' (Weir, Barlow), 'Sugaree' (Garcia, Hunter), 'Looks Like Rain' (Weir, Barlow), 'Row Jimmy' (Garcia, Hunter), 'Big River' (Johnny Cash), 'Tennessee Jed' (Garcia, Hunter), 'Playing In The Band' (Weir, Mickey Hart, Hunter), 'Supplication' (Weir, Barlow), 'Playing In The Band' (Weir, Hart, Hunter), 'Might As Well' (Garcia, Hunter), 'Samson And Delilah' (trad.), 'Loser' (Garcia, Hunter), 'New Minglewood Blues' (trad.), 'Help On The Way' (Garcia, Hunter), 'Slipknot!' (Garcia, Lesh, Weir, Kreutzmann, Godchaux), 'Drums' (Hart, Kreutzmann), 'Slipknot!' (Garcia, Lesh, Weir,

Kreutzmann, Godchaux), 'Franklin's Tower' (Garcia, Kreutzmann, Hunter), 'The Music Never Stopped' (Weir, Barlow), 'Stella Blue' (Garcia, Hunter), 'Around And Around' (Chuck Berry), 'U.S. Blues' (Garcia, Hunter)

Dick's Picks Vol.20 (2001)

Personnel:
Jerry Garcia: guitar, vocals
Donna Jean Godchaux: vocals
Keith Godchaux: piano, vocals
Mickey Hart: drums
Bill Kreutzmann: drums
Phil Lesh: electric bass
Bob Weir: rhythm guitar, vocals
Recorded live at the Capital Centre in Landover, Maryland, on September 25, 1976, and at the Onondaga County War Memorial in Syracuse, New York, on September 28 1976. Recorded by Dan Healy.
Release date: January 2001
Running time: 5:06:09
'Bertha' (Garcia, Hunter), 'New Minglewood Blues' (Noah Lewis), 'Ramble On Rose' (Garcia, Hunter), 'Cassidy' (Weir, Barlow), 'Brown-Eyed Woman' (Garcia, Hunter), 'Mama Tried' (Merle Haggard), 'Peggy-O' (trad.), 'Loser' (Garcia, Hunter), 'Let It Grow' (Weir, Barlow), 'Sugaree' (Garcia, Hunter), 'Lazy Lightning' (Weir, Barlow), 'Supplication' (Weir, Barlow), 'Mississippi Half-Step Uptown Toodeloo' (Garcia, Hunter), 'Dancing In The Street' (Gaye, Hunter, Stevenson), 'Cosmic Charlie' (Garcia, Hunter), 'Scarlet Begonias' (Garcia, Hunter), 'St. Stephen' (Garcia, Lesh, Hunter), 'Not Fade Away' (Petty, Hardin), 'Drums' (Hart, Kreutzmann), 'Jam' (Grateful Dead), 'St. Stephen' (Garcia, Lesh, Hunter), 'Sugar Magnolia' (Weir, Hunter) [Following from September 28, 1976]: 'Cold Rain And Snow' (trad.), 'Big River' (Johnny Cash), 'Cassidy' (Weir, Barlow), 'Tennessee Jed' (Garcia, Hunter), 'New Minglewood Blues' (Noah Lewis), 'Candyman' (Garcia, Hunter), 'It's All Over Now' (Womack, Womack), 'Friend Of The Devil' (Garcia, Dawson, Hunter), 'Let It Grow' (Weir, Barlow), 'Goin' Down The Road Feeling Bad' (trad.), 'Playing In The Band' (Weir, Hart, Hunter), 'The Wheel' (Garcia, Hunter), 'Samson And Delilah' (trad.), 'Jam' (Grateful Dead), 'Comes A Time' (Garcia, Hunter), 'Drums' (Hart, Kreutzmann), 'Eyes Of The World' (Garcia, Hunter), 'Orange Tango Jam' (Grateful Dead), 'Dancing In The Street' (Gaye, Hunter, Stevenson), 'Playing In The Band' (Weir, Hart, Hunter), 'Johnny B. Goode' (Chuck Berry)

Dick's Picks Volume 33 (2004)

Personnel:
Jerry Garcia: guitar, vocals
Donna Jean Godchaux: vocals
Keith Godchaux: piano
Mickey Hart: drums
Bill Kreutzmann: drums
Phil Lesh: electric bass
Bob Weir: rhythm guitar, vocals
Recorded live at Oakland Coliseum Stadium in Oakland, California, on October 9 and October 10, 1976. Recorded by Betty Cantor-Jackson.
Release date: November 2004

Running time: 310.02
[October 9 1976:] 'Promised Land' (Chuck Berry), 'Mississippi Half-Step Uptown Toodeloo' (Garcia, Hunter), 'Cassidy' (Weir, Barlow), 'Tennessee Jed' (Garcia, Hunter), 'Looks Like Rain' (Weir, Barlow), 'They Love Each Other' (Garcia, Hunter), 'New Minglewood Blues' (trad.), 'Scarlet Begonias' (Garcia, Hunter), 'Lazy Lightnin'' (Weir, Barlow), 'Supplication' (Weir, Barlow), 'Sugaree' (Garcia, Hunter), 'St. Stephen' (Garcia, Lesh, Hunter), 'Not Fade Away' (Holly, Petty), 'St. Stephen' (reprise) (Garcia, Lesh, Hunter), 'Help On The Way' (Garcia, Hunter), 'Slipknot!' (Garcia, Godchaux, Kreutzmann, Lesh, Weir), 'Drums' (Hart, Kreutzmann), 'Samson And Delilah' (trad.), 'Slipknot!' (reprise) (Garcia, Godchaux, Kreutzmann, Lesh, Weir), 'Franklin's Tower' (Garcia, Kreutzmann, Hunter), 'One More Saturday Night' (Weir), 'U.S. Blues' (Garcia, Hunter), [October 10, 1976]: 'Might As Well' (Garcia, Hunter), 'Mama Tried' (Merle Haggard), 'Ramble On Rose' (Garcia, Hunter), 'Cassidy' (Weir, Barlow), 'Deal' (Garcia, Hunter), 'El Paso' (Marty Robbins), 'Loser' (Garcia, Hunter), 'Promised Land' (Chuck Berry), 'Friend Of The Devil' (Garcia, Dawson, Hunter), 'Dancing In The Streets' (Stevenson, Gaye, Hunter), 'Wharf Rat' (Garcia, Hunter), 'Dancing In The Streets' (reprise) (Stevenson, Gaye, Hunter), 'Samson And Delilah' (trad.), 'Brown-Eyed Woman' (Garcia, Hunter), 'Playing In The Band' (Weir, Hart, Hunter), 'Drums' (Hart, Kreutzmann), 'The Wheel' (Garcia, Kreutzmann, Hunter), 'Space' (Garcia, Lesh, Weir), 'The Other One' (Weir, Kreutzmann), 'Stella Blue' (Garcia, Hunter), 'Playing In The Band' (reprise) (Weir, Hart, Hunter), 'Sugar Magnolia' (Weir, Hunter), 'Johnny B. Goode' (Chuck Berry)

Live at the Cow Palace (2007)

Personnel:
Jerry Garcia: guitar, vocals
Donna Jean Godchaux: vocals
Keith Godchaux: piano
Mickey Hart: drums
Bill Kreutzmann: drums
Phil Lesh: electric bass
Bob Weir: guitar, vocals
Recorded live at the Cow Palace in Daly City, California on December 31, 1976. Produced by David Lemieux and James Austin.
Release date: January 2007
Running time: 190:25
'The Promised Land' (Chuck Berry), 'Bertha' (Garcia, Hunter), 'Mama Tried' (Merle Haggard), 'They Love Each Other' (Garcia, Hunter), 'Looks Like Rain' (Barlow, Weir), 'Deal' (Garcia, Hunter), 'Playing In The Band' (Hunter, Hart, Weir), 'Sugar Magnolia' (Hunter, Weir), 'Eyes Of The World' (Garcia, Hunter), 'Wharf Rat' (Garcia, Hunter), 'Good Lovin'' (Resnick, Clark), 'Samson And Delilah' (trad.), 'Scarlet Begonias' (Garcia, Hunter), 'Around And Around' (Chuck Berry), 'Help On The Way' (Garcia, Hunter), 'Slipknot!' (Garcia, Godchaux, Kreutzmann, Lesh, Weir), 'Drums' (Hart, Kreutzmann), 'Not Fade Away' (Holly, Petty), 'Morning Dew' (Dobson, Rose), 'One More Saturday Night' (Weir), 'Uncle John's Band' (Garcia, Hunter), 'We Bid You Goodnight' (trad.) [Bonus Disc: *Spirit Of '76*]: 'The Music Never Stopped' (Weir, Barlow), 'Crazy Fingers' (Garcia, Hunter) [recorded live at Boston Music Hall, Boston, on June 9, 1976], 'Let It Grow' (Weir, Barlow), 'Might As Well' (Garcia, Hunter) [recorded live at Riverfront Coliseum, Cincinnati, Ohio, on October 2, 1976], 'Playing In The Band' (Weir, Hart, Hunter) 'Supplication' (Weir, Barlow), 'Playing In The Band' (Weir, Hart, Hunter) [recorded live at the College Of William And Mary, Williamsburg, Virginia, on September 24, 1976], 'Scarlet Begonias' (Garcia, Hunter)

[recorded live at Mershon Auditorium, Columbus, Ohio on September 30, 1976]

1977
Dave's Picks Vol. 29 (2019)

Personnel:
Jerry Garcia: guitar, vocals
Donna Jean Godchaux: vocals
Keith Godchaux: keyboards
Mickey Hart: drums
Bill Kreutzmann: drums
Phil Lesh: bass
Bob Weir: rhythm guitar, vocals
Recorded live at Swing Auditorium in San Bernardino, California, on February 26, 1977.
Recorded by Betty Cantor-Jackson.
Release date: February 2019
Running time: 197:51
'Terrapin Station' (Garcia, Hunter), 'New Minglewood Blues' (trad.), 'They Love Each Other' (Garcia, Hunter), 'Estimated Prophet' (Weir, Barlow), 'Sugaree' (Garcia, Hunter), 'Mama Tried' (Merle Haggard), 'Deal' (Garcia, Hunter), 'Playing In The Band' (Weir, Hart, Hunter), 'The Wheel' (Garcia, Kreutzmann, Hunter), 'Playing In The Band' (Weir, Hart, Hunter), 'Samson And Delilah' (trad.), 'Tennessee Jed' (Garcia, Hunter), 'The Music Never Stopped' (Weir, Barlow), 'Help On The Way' (Garcia, Hunter), 'Slipknot!' (Garcia, Godchaux, Kreutzmann, Lesh, Weir), 'Franklin's Tower' (Garcia, Hunter, Kreutzmann), 'Promised Land' (Chuck Berry), 'Eyes Of The World' (Garcia, Hunter), 'Dancing In The Street' (Stevenson, Gaye, Hunter), 'Around And Around' (Chuck Berry), 'U.S. Blues' (Garcia, Hunter), [Bonus tracks recorded at Robertson Gym, University of California, Santa Barbara, California on February 27, 1977]: 'Morning Dew' (Dobson, Rose), 'Sugar Magnolia' (Weir, Hunter), 'Johnny B. Goode' (Chuck Berry)

Capitol Theatre, Passaic, NJ, 4/25/77 (2016)

Personnel:
Jerry Garcia: guitar, vocals
Donna Jean Godchaux: vocals
Keith Godchaux: keyboards
Mickey Hart: drums
Bill Kreutzmann: drums
Phil Lesh: electric bass
Bob Weir: guitar, vocals
Recorded live at Capitol Theatre, Passaic, New Jersey, on April 25, 1977. Produced for release by David Lemieux.
Release date: April 2016
Running time: 2:33:52
'New Minglewood Blues' (trad.), 'Deal' (Garcia, Hunter), 'Mama Tried' (Merle Haggard), 'They Love Each Other' (Garcia, Hunter), 'Looks Like Rain' (Weir, Barlow), 'Peggy-O' (trad.), 'Lazy Lightning' (Weir, Barlow), 'Supplication' (Weir, Barlow), 'Ship Of Fools' (Garcia, Hunter), 'Estimated Prophet' (Weir, Barlow), 'Brown-Eyed Women' (Garcia, Hunter), 'The Music Never Stopped' (Weir, Barlow), 'U.S. Blues' (Garcia, Hunter), 'Scarlet Begonias' (Garcia, Hunter), 'Fire On The Mountain' (Hart, Hunter), 'Samson And Delilah' (trad.), 'Terrapin Station' (Garcia, Hunter), 'Playing In The Band' (Weir, Hart, Hunter),

'Drums' (Hart, Kreutzmann), 'Wharf Rat' (Garcia, Hunter), 'Playing In The Band' (Weir, Hart, Hunter)

Download Series Vol. 1 (2005)

Personnel:
Jerry Garcia: lead guitar, vocals
Donna Jean Godchaux: vocals
Keith Godchaux: keyboards
Mickey Hart: drums
Bill Kreutzmann: drums
Phil Lesh: electric bass
Bob Weir: rhythm guitar, vocals
Recorded live at New York City Palladium on April 30, 1977. Recorded by Betty Cantor-Jackson
Release date: May 2005
Running time: 189.08
The Music Never Stopped' (Barlow, Weir), 'Bertha' (Garcia, Hunter), 'It's All Over Now' (Womack, Womack), 'Deal' (Garcia, Hunter), 'Mama Tried' (Merle Haggard), 'Me And My Uncle' (John Phillips), 'Peggy-O' (trad.), 'Looks Like Rain' (Barlow, Weir), 'Mississippi Half Step Uptown Toodeloo' (Garcia, Hunter), 'Promised Land' (Chuck Berry), 'Scarlet Begonias' (Garcia, Hunter), 'Fire On The Mountain' (Hunter, Hart), 'Good Lovin'' (Clark, Resnick), 'Friend Of The Devil' (Dawson, Hunter, Garcia), 'Estimated Prophet' (Barlow, Weir), 'St. Stephen' (Hunter, Garcia, Lesh), 'Not Fade Away' (Holly, Petty), 'Stella Blue' (Garcia, Hunter), 'St. Stephen' (Hunter, Garcia, Lesh), 'One More Saturday Night' (Weir), 'Terrapin Station' (Garcia, Hunter) [Bonus tracks from New York City's Palladium, April 29, 1977]: 'Sugaree' (Garcia, Hunter) 'Scarlet Begonias' (Garcia, Hunter), 'Goin' Down The Road Feeling Bad' (trad.)

May 1977: Get Shown the Light (2017)

Personnel:
Jerry Garcia: guitar, vocals
Donna Jean Godchaux: vocals
Keith Godchaux: keyboards
Mickey Hart: drums
Bill Kreutzmann: drums
Phil Lesh: bass
Bob Weir: guitar, vocals
Recorded live May 5, 7, 8, and 9, 1977. Produced for release by David Lemieux.
Release date: May 2017
Veterans Memorial Coliseum, New Haven, Connecticut, May 5, 1977
'Promised Land' (Chuck Berry), 'Sugaree' (Garcia, Hunter), 'Mama Tried' (Merle Haggard), 'El Paso' (Marty Robbins), 'Tennessee Jed' (Garcia, Hunter), 'Looks Like Rain' (Weir, Barlow), 'Deal' (Garcia, Hunter), 'Lazy Lightning' (Weir, Barlow), 'Supplication' (Weir, Barlow), 'Peggy-O' (trad.), 'The Music Never Stopped' (Weir, Barlow), 'Bertha' (Garcia, Hunter), 'Estimated Prophet' (Weir, Barlow), 'Scarlet Begonias' (Garcia, Hunter), 'Fire On The Mountain' (Hart, Hunter), 'Good Lovin'' (Clark, Resnick), 'St. Stephen' (Garcia, Lesh, Hunter), 'Sugar Magnolia' (Weir, Hunter), 'Johnny B. Goode' (Chuck Berry)
Boston Garden, Boston, Massachusetts, May 7, 1977
'Bertha' (Garcia, Hunter), 'Cassidy' (Weir, Barlow), 'Deal' (Garcia, Hunter), 'Jack Straw' (Weir, Hunter), 'Peggy-O' (trad.), 'New Minglewood Blues' (trad.), 'Mississippi Half-Step

Uptown Toodeloo' (Garcia, Hunter), 'Big River' (Johnny Cash), 'Tennessee Jed' (Garcia, Hunter), 'The Music Never Stopped' (Weir, Barlow), 'Terrapin Station' (Garcia, Hunter), 'Samson And Delilah' (trad.), 'Friend Of The Devil' (Garcia, Dawson, Hunter), 'Estimated Prophet' (Weir, Barlow), 'Eyes Of The World' (Garcia, Hunter), 'Drums' (Hart, Kreutzmann), 'The Wheel' (Garcia, Hunter, Kreutzmann), 'Wharf Rat' (Garcia, Hunter), 'Around And Around' (Chuck Berry), 'U.S. Blues' (Garcia, Hunter)

Barton Hall, Ithaca, New York, May 8, 1977
'New Minglewood Blues' (trad.), 'Loser' (Garcia, Hunter), 'El Paso' (Marty Robbins), 'They Love Each Other' (Garcia, Hunter), 'Jack Straw' (Weir, Hunter), 'Deal' (Garcia, Hunter), 'Lazy Lightning' (Weir, Barlow), 'Supplication' (Weir, Barlow), 'Brown-Eyed Women' (Garcia, Hunter), 'Mama Tried' (Merle Haggard), 'Row Jimmy' (Garcia, Hunter), 'Dancing In The Street' (Stevenson, Gaye, I. J. Hunter), 'Scarlet Begonias' (Garcia, Hunter), 'Fire On The Mountain' (Hart, Hunter), 'Estimated Prophet' (Weir, Barlow), 'St. Stephen' (Garcia, Lesh, Hunter), 'Not Fade Away' (Petty, Hardin), 'St. Stephen' (Garcia, Lesh, Hunter), 'Morning Dew' (Dobson, Rose), 'One More Saturday Night' (Weir)

Buffalo Memorial Auditorium, Buffalo, New York, May 9, 1977
'Help On The Way' (Garcia, Hunter), 'Slipknot' (Garcia, Godchaux, Kreutzmann, Lesh, Weir), 'Franklin's Tower' (Garcia, Hunter), 'Cassidy' (Weir, Barlow), 'Brown-Eyed Women' (Garcia, Hunter), 'Mexicali Blues' (Weir, Barlow), 'Tennessee Jed' (Garcia, Hunter), 'Big River' (Johnny Cash), 'Peggy-O' (trad.), 'Sunrise' (Donna Jean Godchaux), 'The Music Never Stopped' (Weir, Barlow), 'Bertha' (Garcia, Hunter), 'Good Lovin'' (Clark, Resnick), 'Ship Of Fools' (Garcia, Hunter), 'Estimated Prophet' (Weir, Barlow), 'The Other One' (Weir, Kreutzmann), 'Drums' (Hart, Kreutzmann), 'Not Fade Away' (Petty, Hardin), 'Comes A Time' (Garcia, Hunter), 'Sugar Magnolia' (Weir, Hunter. 'Uncle John's Band' (Garcia, Hunter)

Cornell 5/8/77 (2017)
Personnel:
Jerry Garcia: guitar, vocals
Donna Jean Godchaux: vocals
Keith Godchaux: keyboards
Mickey Hart: drums
Bill Kreutzmann: drums
Phil Lesh: bass
Bob Weir: guitar, vocals
Recorded live at Barnton Hall, Cornell University, Ithaca, New York, on May 8 1977.
Produced for release by David Lemieux.
Release date: May 2017
'New Minglewood Blues' (trad.), 'Loser' (Garcia, Hunter), 'El Paso' (Marty Robbins), 'They Love Each Other' (Garcia, Hunter), 'Jack Straw' (Weir, Hunter), 'Deal' (Garcia, Hunter), 'Lazy Lightning' (Weir, Barlow), 'Supplication' (Weir, Barlow), 'Brown-Eyed Women' (Garcia, Hunter), 'Mama Tried' (Merle Haggard), 'Row Jimmy' (Garcia, Hunter), 'Dancing In The Street' (Stevenson, Gaye, I. J. Hunter), 'Scarlet Begonias' (Garcia, Hunter), 'Fire On The Mountain' (Hart, Hunter), 'Estimated Prophet' (Weir, Barlow), 'St. Stephen' (Garcia, Lesh, Hunter), 'Not Fade Away' (Petty, Hardin), 'St. Stephen' (Garcia, Lesh, Hunter), 'Morning Dew' (Dobson, Rose), 'One More Saturday Night' (Weir)

Buffalo 5/9/77 (2020)
Personnel:
Jerry Garcia: guitar, vocals

Donna Jean Godchaux: vocals
Keith Godchaux: keyboards
Mickey Hart: drums
Bill Kreutzmann: drums
Phil Lesh: electric bass
Bob Weir: guitar, vocals
Recorded live at Buffalo Memorial Auditorium, Buffalo, New York, on May 9, 1977. Produced by David Lemieux.
Release date: October 2020
Running time: 2:41:16
'Help On The Way' (Garcia, Hunter), 'Slipknot' (Garcia, Godchaux, Kreutzmann, Lesh, Weir), 'Franklin's Tower' (Garcia, Hunter), 'Cassidy' (Weir, Barlow), 'Brown-Eyed Women' (Garcia, Hunter), 'Mexicali Blues' (Weir, Barlow), 'Tennessee Jed' (Garcia, Hunter), 'Big River' (Johnny Cash), 'Peggy-O' (trad.), 'Sunrise' (Donna Jean Godchaux), 'The Music Never Stopped' (Weir, Barlow), 'Bertha' (Garcia, Hunter), 'Good Lovin'' (Clark, Resnick), 'Ship Of Fools' (Garcia, Hunter), 'Estimated Prophet' (Weir, Barlow), 'The Other One' (Weir, Kreutzmann), 'Drums' (Hart, Kreutzmann), 'Not Fade Away' (Petty, Hardin), 'Comes A Time' (Garcia, Hunter), 'Sugar Magnolia' (Weir, Hunter. 'Uncle John's Band' (Garcia, Hunter)

May 1977 (2013)
Personnel:
Jerry Garcia: lead guitar, vocals
Donna Jean Godchaux: vocals
Keith Godchaux: keyboards
Mickey Hart: drums
Bill Kreutzmann: drums
Phil Lesh: bass guitar
Bob Weir: rhythm guitar, vocals
Recorded live May 11 – May 17, 1977. Produced for release by David Lemieux.
Release date: June 2013
St. Paul Civic Center, Saint Paul, Minnesota, May 11, 1977
'Promised Land' (Chuck Berry), 'They Love Each Other' (Garcia, Hunter), 'Big River' (Johnny Cash), 'Loser' (Garcia, Hunter), 'Looks Like Rain' (Weir, Barlow), 'Ramble On Rose' (Garcia, Hunter), 'Jack Straw' (Weir, Hunter), 'Peggy-O' (trad.), 'El Paso' (Marty Robbins), 'Deal' (Garcia, Hunter), 'Lazy Lightning' (Weir, Barlow), 'Supplication' (Weir, Barlow), 'Sugaree' (Garcia, Hunter), 'Samson And Delilah' (trad.), 'Brown-Eyed Women' (Garcia, Hunter), 'Estimated Prophet' (Weir, Barlow), 'Scarlet Begonias' (Garcia, Hunter), 'Fire On The Mountain' (Hart, Hunter), 'Good Lovin'' (Clark, Resnick), 'Uncle John's Band' (Garcia, Hunter), 'Space' (Garcia, Godchaux, Lesh, Weir), 'Wharf Rat' (Garcia, Hunter), 'Around And Around' (Chuck Berry), 'Brokedown Palace' (Garcia, Hunter)
Auditorium Theatre, Chicago, Illinois, May 12, 1977
'Bertha' (Garcia, Hunter), 'Me And My Uncle' (John Phillips), 'Tennessee Jed' (Garcia, Hunter), 'Cassidy' (Weir, Barlow), 'Peggy-O' (trad.), 'Jack Straw' (Weir, Hunter), 'They Love Each Other' (Garcia, Hunter), 'New Minglewood Blues' (Noah Lewis), 'Mississippi Half-Step Uptown Toodeloo' (Garcia, Hunter), 'Dancing In The Street' (Gaye, I.J. Hunter, Stevenson), 'Samson And Delilah' (trad.), 'Brown-Eyed Women' (Garcia, Hunter), 'Estimated Prophet' (Weir, Barlow), 'Sunrise' (Godchaux), 'Terrapin Station' (Garcia, Hunter), 'Playing In The Band' (Weir, Hart, Hunter), 'Drums' (Hart, Kreutzmann), 'Not

Fade Away' (Hardin, Petty), 'Comes A Time' (Garcia, Hunter), 'Playing In The Band' (Weir, Hart, Hunter), 'Johnny B. Goode' (Chuck Berry)

Auditorium Theatre, Chicago, Illinois, May 13, 1977
'The Music Never Stopped' (Weir, Barlow), 'Ramble On Rose' (Garcia, Hunter), 'Cassidy' (Weir, Barlow), 'Brown-Eyed Women' (Garcia, Hunter), 'New Minglewood Blues' (Noah Lewis), 'Friend Of The Devil' (Garcia, John Dawson, Hunter), 'El Paso' (Marty Robbins), 'Jack-A-Roe' (trad.), 'Looks Like Rain' (Weir, Barlow), 'Scarlet Begonias' (Garcia, Hunter), 'Fire On The Mountain' (Hart, Hunter), 'Samson And Delilah' (trad.), 'Bertha' (Garcia, Hunter), 'Estimated Prophet' (Weir, Barlow), 'Drums' (Hart, Kreutzmann), 'The Other One' (Weir, Kreutzmann), 'Stella Blue' (Garcia, Hunter), 'Goin' Down The Road Feeling Bad' (trad.) [June 8, 1977], 'One More Saturday Night' (Weir) [May 28, 1977], 'U.S. Blues' (Garcia, Hunter)

St. Louis Arena, St. Louis, Missouri, May 15, 1977
'Bertha' (Garcia, Hunter), 'Good Lovin'' (Clark, Resnick), 'Row Jimmy' (Garcia, Hunter), 'New Minglewood Blues' (trad.), 'Tennessee Jed' (Garcia, Hunter), 'Lazy Lightning' (Weir, Barlow), 'Supplication' (Weir, Barlow), 'Jack-A-Roe' (trad.), 'Passenger' (Lesh, Monk), 'Brown-Eyed Women' (Garcia, Hunter), 'Dancing In The Street' (Gaye, Ivy Jo Hunter, Stevenson), 'Estimated Prophet' (Weir, Barlow), 'Eyes Of The World' (Garcia, Hunter), 'Drums' (Hart, Kreutzmann), 'Samson And Delilah' (trad.), 'Ship Of Fools' (Garcia, Hunter), 'St. Stephen' (Garcia, Lesh, Hunter), 'Iko Iko' (Crawford, Hawkins, Hawkins, Johnson), 'Not Fade Away' (Hardin, Petty), 'Sugar Magnolia' (Weir, Hunter), 'Uncle John's Band' (Garcia, Hunter)

University of Alabama, Tuscaloosa, Alabama, May 17, 1977
'New Minglewood Blues' (trad.), 'Mississippi Half-Step Uptown Toodeloo' (Garcia, Hunter), 'El Paso' (Marty Robbins), 'They Love Each Other' (Garcia, Hunter), 'Jack Straw' (Weir, Hunter), 'Jack-A-Roe' (trad.), 'Looks Like Rain' (Weir, Barlow), 'Tennessee Jed' (Garcia, Hunter), 'Passenger' (Lesh, Monk), 'High Time' (Garcia, Hunter), 'Big River' (Johnny Cash), 'Sunrise' (Godchaux), 'Scarlet Begonias' (Garcia, Hunter), 'Fire On The Mountain' (Hart, Hunter), 'Samson And Delilah' (trad.), 'Bertha' (Garcia, Hunter), 'Good Lovin'' (Clark, Resnick), 'Brown-Eyed Women' (Garcia, Hunter), 'Estimated Prophet' (Weir, Barlow), 'Terrapin Station' (Garcia, Hunter), 'Playing In The Band' (Weir, Hart, Hunter), 'Drums' (Hart, Kreutzmann), 'Wharf Rat' (Garcia, Hunter), 'Playing In The Band' (Weir, Hart, Hunter), 'Sugar Magnolia' (Weir, Hunter)

Dick's Picks Vol. 29 (2003)

Personnel:
Jerry Garcia: guitar, vocals
Donna Godchaux: vocals
Keith Godchaux: keyboards
Mickey Hart: drums
Bill Kreutzmann: drums
Phil Lesh: electric bass,
Bob Weir: guitar, vocals
Recorded live at the Fox Theatre in Atlanta, Georgia, on May 19 1977 and at the Lakeland Civic Center in Lakeland, Florida, on May 21 1977. Recorded by Betty Cantor-Jackson.
Release date: July 2003
Running time: 420:26
'The Promised Land' (Chuck Berry), 'Sugaree' (Garcia, Hunter), 'El Paso' (Marty Robbins), 'Peggy-O' (trad.), 'Looks Like Rain' (Barlow, Weir), 'Row Jimmy' (Garcia, Hunter), 'Passenger' (Monk, Lesh), 'Loser' (Garcia, Hunter), 'Dancing In The Streets' (Gaye, I. J. Hunter, Stevenson), 'Samson And Delilah' (trad.), 'Ramble On Rose' (Garcia, Hunter), 'Estimated

Prophet' (Barlow, Weir), 'Not Fade Away' (Holly, Petty) [Bonus track from October 11, 1977], 'Wharf Rat' (Garcia, Hunter) [Bonus track from October 11, 1977], 'Around And Around' (Chuck Berry) [Bonus track from October 11, 1977], 'Lady With A Fan/Terrapin Station' (Garcia, Hunter), 'Playing In The Band' (Hunter, Mickey Hart, Weir), 'Uncle John's Band' (Garcia, Hunter), 'Drums' (Hart, Kreutzmann), 'The Wheel' (Garcia, Hunter), 'China Doll' (Garcia, Hunter), 'Playing In The Band' (Hunter, Hart, Weir), [Following from May 21, 1977] 'Bertha' (Garcia, Hunter), 'Me And My Uncle' (John Phillips), 'They Love Each Other' (Garcia, Hunter), 'Cassidy' (Barlow, Weir), 'Jack-A-Roe' (trad.), 'Jack Straw' (Hunter, Weir), 'Tennessee Jed' (Garcia, Hunter), 'New Minglewood Blues' (trad.), 'Row Jimmy' (Garcia, Hunter), 'Passenger' (Monk, Lesh), 'Scarlet Begonias' (Garcia, Hunter), 'Fire On The Mountain' (Hunter, Hart), 'Samson And Delilah' (trad.), 'Brown-Eyed Women' (Garcia, Hunter), 'Dancing In The Streets' (Gaye, Hunter, Stevenson) [Bonus track from October 11, 1977], 'Dire Wolf' (Garcia, Hunter) [Bonus track from October 11, 1977], 'Estimated Prophet' (Barlow, Weir), 'He's Gone' (Garcia, Hunter), 'Drums' (Hart, Kreutzmann), 'The Other One' (Kreutzmann, Weir), 'Comes A Time' (Garcia, Hunter), 'St. Stephen' (Hunter, Garcia, Lesh), 'Not Fade Away' (Holly, Petty), 'St. Stephen' (Hunter, Garcia, Lesh), 'One More Saturday Night' (Weir)

Dick's Picks Vol.3 (1995)

Personnel:
Jerry Garcia: lead guitar, vocals
Donna Jean Godchaux: vocals
Keith Godchaux: keyboards
Mickey Hart: drums
Bill Kreutzmann: drums
Phil Lesh: bass
Bob Weir: guitar, vocals
Recorded live at the Sportatorium in Pembroke Pines, Florida, on May 22, 1977. Recorded by Betty Cantor-Jackson.
Release date: November 1995
Running time: 137:54
'Funiculì, Funiculà' (Luigi Denza), 'The Music Never Stopped' (Barlow, Weir), 'Sugaree' (Garcia, Hunter), 'Lazy Lightning' (Barlow, Weir), 'Supplication' (Barlow, Weir), 'Dancing In The Street' (Gaye, Hunter, Stevenson), 'Help On The Way' (Garcia, Hunter), 'Slipknot!' (Grateful Dead), 'Franklin's Tower' (Hunter, Kreutzmann), 'Samson And Delilah' (trad.), 'Sunrise' (Donna Godchaux), 'Estimated Prophet' (Barlow, Weir), 'Eyes Of The World' (Garcia, Hunter), 'Wharf Rat' (Garcia, Hunter), 'Terrapin Station' (Garcia, Hunter), 'Morning Dew' (Dobson, Rose)

Dave's Picks Vol.1 (2012)

Personnel:
Jerry Garcia: lead guitar, vocals
Donna Jean Godchaux: vocals
Keith Godchaux: keyboards
Mickey Hart: drums
Bill Kreutzmann: drums
Phil Lesh: electric bass
Bob Weir: rhythm guitar, vocals
Recorded live at the Mosque in Richmond, Virginia, May 25 1977. Recorded by Betty Cantor-Jackson

Release date: February 2012
Running time: 168:16
'Mississippi Half-Step Uptown Toodeloo' (Garcia, Hunter), 'Jack Straw' (Weir, Hunter), 'They Love Each Other' (Garcia, Hunter), 'Mexicali Blues' (Weir, Barlow), 'Peggy-O' (trad.), 'Cassidy' (Weir, Barlow), 'Loser' (Garcia, Hunter), 'Lazy Lightning' (Weir, Barlow), 'Supplication' (Weir, Barlow), 'Brown-Eyed Women' (Garcia, Hunter), 'Promised Land' (Chuck Berry), 'Scarlet Begonias' (Garcia, Hunter), 'Fire On The Mountain' (Mickey Hart, Hunter), 'Estimated Prophet' (Weir, Barlow), 'He's Gone' (Garcia, Hunter), 'Drums' (Hart, Kreutzmann), 'The Other One' (Weir, Kreutzmann), 'Wharf Rat' (Garcia, Hunter), 'The Other One' (Weir, Kreutzmann), 'The Wheel' (Garcia, Hunter), 'Around And Around' (Chuck Berry), 'Johnny B. Goode' (Chuck Berry)

To Terrapin: Hartford '77 (2009)
Personnel:
Jerry Garcia: guitar, vocals
Donna Jean Godchaux: vocals
Keith Godchaux: piano
Mickey Hart: drums
Bill Kreutzmann: drums
Phil Lesh: electric bass
Bob Weir: guitar, vocals
Recorded live at the Hartford Civic Center in Hartford, Connecticut, on May 28, 1977. Produced for release by David Lemieux.
Release date: April 2009
Running time: 182:19
'Bertha' (Garcia, Hunter), 'Good Lovin'' (Resnick, Clark), 'Sugaree' (Garcia, Hunter), 'Jack Straw' (Weir, Hunter), 'Row Jimmy' (Garcia, Hunter), 'New Minglewood Blues' (Noah Lewis), 'Candyman' (Garcia, Hunter), 'Passenger' (Lesh, Monk), 'Brown-Eyed Women' (Garcia, Hunter), 'Promised Land' (Chuck Berry), 'Samson And Delilah' (trad.), 'Tennessee Jed' (Garcia, Hunter), 'Estimated Prophet' (Barlow, Weir), 'Playing In The Band' (Hunter, Hart, Weir), 'Terrapin Station' (Garcia, Hunter), 'Drums' (Hart, Kreutzmann), 'Not Fade Away' (Holly, Petty), 'Wharf Rat' (Garcia, Hunter), 'Playing In The Band' (Hunter, Hart, Weir), 'One More Saturday Night' (Weir), 'U.S. Blues' (Garcia, Hunter)

Winterland June '77 – The Complete Recordings (2009)
Personnel:
Jerry Garcia: lead guitar, vocals
Donna Jean Godchaux: vocals
Keith Godchaux: keyboards
Mickey Hart: drums
Bill Kreutzmann: drums
Phil Lesh: electric bass
Bob Weir: rhythm guitar, vocals
Recorded live at the Winterland Ballroom, San Francisco, June 7 – 9, 1977. Box set produced for release by David Lemieux.
Release date: October 2009
Running time: 182:19
June 7, 1977
'Bertha' (Garcia, Hunter), 'Jack Straw' (Weir, Hunter), 'Tennessee Jed' (Garcia, Hunter),

'Looks Like Rain' (Weir, Barlow), 'Peggy-O' (trad.), 'Funiculi Funiculà' (Luigi Denza), 'El Paso' (Marty Robbins), 'Friend Of The Devil' (Garcia, Dawson, Hunter), 'The Music Never Stopped' (Weir, Barlow), 'Scarlet Begonias' (Garcia, Hunter), 'Fire On The Mountain' (Hart, Hunter), 'Good Lovin'' (Resnick, Clark), 'Candyman' (Garcia, Hunter), 'Estimated Prophet' (Weir, Barlow), 'He's Gone' (Garcia, Hunter), 'Drums' (Kreutzmann, Hart), 'Samson And Delilah' (trad.), 'Terrapin Station' (Garcia, Hunter), '(Walk Me Out In The) Morning Dew' (Dobson, Rose), 'Around And Around' (Chuck Berry), 'Uncle John's Band (Garcia, Hunter), 'U.S. Blues' (Garcia, Hunter)

June 8, 1977
'New Minglewood Blues' (Noah Lewis), 'Sugaree' (Garcia, Hunter), 'Mexicali Blues' (Weir, Barlow), 'Row Jimmy' (Garcia, Hunter), 'Passenger' (Lesh, Monk), 'Sunrise' (Godchaux), 'Brown-Eyed Women' (Garcia, Hunter), 'It's All Over Now' (Womack, Womack), 'Jack-A-Roe' (trad.), 'Lazy Lightnin' ' (Weir, Barlow), 'Supplication' (Weir, Barlow), 'Bertha' (Garcia, Hunter), 'Good Lovin'' (Clarke, Resnick), 'Ramble On Rose' (Garcia, Hunter), 'Estimated Prophet' (Weir, Barlow), 'Eyes Of The World' (Garcia, Hunter), 'Drums' (Kreutzmann, Hart), 'The Other One' (Grateful Dead), 'Wharf Rat' (Garcia, Hunter), 'Not Fade Away' (Holly, Petty), 'Goin' Down The Road Feeling Bad' (trad.), 'Johnny B. Goode' (Chuck Berry), 'Brokedown Palace' (Garcia, Hunter)

June 9, 1977
'Mississippi Half-Step Uptown Toodeloo' (Garcia, Hunter), 'Jack Straw' (Weir, Hunter), 'They Love Each Other' (Garcia, Hunter), 'Cassidy' (Weir, Barlow), 'Sunrise' (Godchaux), 'Deal' (Garcia, Hunter), 'Looks Like Rain' (Weir, Barlow), 'Loser' (Garcia, Hunter), 'The Music Never Stopped' (Weir, Barlow), 'Samson And Delilah' (trad.), 'Funiculì Funiculà' (Turco, Denza), 'Help On The Way' (Garcia, Hunter), 'Slipknot!' (Garcia, Hunter), 'Franklin's Tower' (Garcia, Hunter, Kreutzmann), 'Estimated Prophet' (Weir, Barlow), 'St. Stephen' (Garcia, Lesh, Hunter), 'Not Fade Away' (Holly, Petty), 'Drums' (Kreutzmann, Hart), 'St. Stephen' (Garcia, Lesh, Hunter), 'Terrapin Station' (Garcia, Hunter), 'Sugar Magnolia' (Weir, Hunter), 'U.S. Blues' (Garcia, Hunter), 'One More Saturday Night' (Weir)

Bonus Disc: Selections from Auditorium Theatre, Chicago, Illinois, May 12, 1977
'Mississippi Half-Step Uptown Toodeloo' (Garcia, Hunter), 'Dancing In The Street' (Gaye, I J Hunter, Stevenson), 'Terrapin Station' (Garcia, Hunter), 'Playing In The Band' (Weir, Hart, Hunter), 'Drums' (Kreutzmann, Hart), 'Not Fade Away' (Holly, Petty), 'Comes A Time' (Garcia, Hunter), 'Playing In The Band' (Weir, Hart, Hunter)

Dick's Picks Vol.15 (1999)
Personnel:
Jerry Garcia: lead guitar, vocals
Donna Jean Godchaux: vocals
Keith Godchaux: keyboards
Bill Kreutzmann: drums
Mickey Hart: drums'
Phil Lesh: bass, vocals
Bob Weir: guitar, vocals
Recorded live at Raceway Park in Englishtown, New Jersey, on September 3 1977. Recorded by Betty Cantor-Jackson.
Release date: October 1999
Running time: 176:43
'Introduction' (Scher), 'Promised Land' (Chuck Berry), 'They Love Each Other' (Garcia, Hunter), 'Me And My Uncle' (John Phillips), 'Mississippi Half-Step Uptown Toodleloo'

(Garcia, Hunter), 'Looks Like Rain' (Weir, Barlow), 'Peggy-O' (trad.), 'New Minglewood Blues' (Noah Lewis), 'Friend Of The Devil' (Garcia, Dawson, Hunter), 'The Music Never Stopped' (Weir, Barlow), 'Bertha' (Garcia, Hunter), 'Good Lovin'' (Clark, Resnick), 'Loser' (Garcia, Hunter), 'Estimated Prophet' (Barlow, Weir), 'Eyes Of The World' (Garcia, Hunter), 'Samson And Delilah' (Rev. Gary Davis), 'He's Gone' (Garcia, Hunter), 'Not Fade Away' (Holly, Petty), 'Truckin'' (Garcia, Lesh, Weir, Hunter), 'Terrapin Station' (Garcia, Hunter)

Road Trips Vol. 1 No. 2 (2008)
Personnel:
Jerry Garcia: lead guitar, vocals
Donna Godchaux: vocals
Keith Godchaux: keyboards
Mickey Hart: drums
Bill Kreutzmann: drums
Phil Lesh: electric bass
Bob Weir: rhythm guitar, vocals
Recorded live at venues in New Mexico, Oklahoma, Texas and Louisiana, October 7- 16, 1977. Recorded by Betty Cantor Jackson
Release date: February 2008
Running time: 158:20
'Let It Grow' (Weir, Barlow), 'Sugaree' (Garcia, Hunter), 'The Music Never Stopped' (Weir, Barlow), 'Mississippi Half-Step Uptown Toodeloo' (Garcia, Hunter), 'El Paso' (Marty Robbins), 'Help On the Way' (Garcia, Hunter), 'Slipknot!' (Garcia, Godchaux, Lesh, Weir), 'Franklin's Tower' (Garcia, Kreutzmann, Hunter), 'Playing In The Band' (Weir, Hart, Hunter), 'Drums' (Hart, Kreutzman), 'The Other One' (Weir), 'Good Lovin'' (Resnick, Clark), 'Terrapin Station' (Garcia, Hunter), 'Black Peter' (Garcia, Hunter), 'Around And Around' (Chuck Berry), 'Brokedown Palace' (Garcia, Hunter), 'Playing In The Band reprise' (Weir, Hart, Hunter), [Bonus Disc]: 'Scarlet Begonias' (Garcia, Hunter), 'Fire On The Mountain' (Hart, Hunter), 'Estimated Prophet' (Weir, Barlow), 'Loser' (Garcia, Hunter), 'Sunrise' (Donna Godchaux), 'Iko Iko' (James Crawford), 'The Wheel' (Garcia, Kreutzmann, Hunter), 'Wharf Rat' (Garcia, Hunter), 'Sugar Magnolia' (Weir, Hunter)

Dave's Picks Vol 33 (2020)
Personnel:
Jerry Garcia: lead guitar, vocals
Donna Jean Godchaux: vocals
Keith Godchaux: keyboards
Mickey Hart: drums
Bill Kreutzmann: drums
Phil Lesh: bass, vocals
Bob Weir: guitar, vocals
Recorded live at Evans Field House at Northern Illinois University in DeKalb, Illinois, on October 29, 1977. Recorded by Betty Cantor-Jackson.
Release date: January 2020
Running time: 196:22
'Might As Well' (Garcia, Hunter), 'Jack Straw' (Weir, Hunter), 'Dire Wolf' (Garcia, Hunter), 'Looks Like Rain' (Weir, Barlow), 'Loser' (Garcia, Hunter), 'El Paso' (Marty Robbins), 'Ramble On Rose' (Garcia, Hunter), 'New Minglewood Blues' (trad.), 'It Must Have Been The Roses' (Hunter), 'Bertha' (Garcia, Hunter), 'Good Lovin'' (Clark, Resnick), 'Friend Of The Devil'

(Garcia, Dawson, Hunter), 'Estimated Prophet' (Weir, Barlow), 'Eyes Of The World' (Garcia, Hunter), 'Space' (Garcia, Lesh, Weir), 'St. Stephen' (Garcia, Lesh, Hunter), 'Not Fade Away' (Petty, Holly), 'Black Peter' (Garcia, Hunter), 'Sugar Magnolia' (Weir, Hunter), 'One More Saturday Night' (Weir)

Dave's Picks Vol. 12 (2014)
Personnel:
Jerry Garcia: lead guitar, vocals
Donna Jean Godchaux: vocals
Keith Godchaux: keyboards
Mickey Hart: drums
Bill Kreutzmann: drums
Phil Lesh: electric bass, vocals
Bob Weir: guitar, vocals
Recorded at Colgate University in Hamilton, New York, on November 4, 1977, with bonus tracks recorded at the Seneca College Field House in Toronto, Ontario, Canada on November 2, 1977. Recorded by Betty Cantor-Jackson.
Release date: November 2014
Running time: 233:12
'Bertha' (Garcia, Hunter), 'Good Lovin'' (Resnick, Clark), 'Brown-Eyed Women' (Garcia, Hunter), 'Cassidy' (Weir, Barlow), 'It Must Have Been The Roses' (Hunter), 'Sunrise' (Godchaux), 'New Minglewood Blues' (trad.), 'Dupree's Diamond Blues' (Garcia, Hunter), 'Let It Grow' (Weir, Barlow), 'Jones Gang Introduction', 'Samson And Delilah' (trad.), 'Cold Rain And Snow' (McGannahan Skjellyfetti), 'Playing In The Band' (Weir, Hart, Hunter), 'Eyes Of The World' (Garcia, Hunter), 'Estimated Prophet' (Weir, Barlow), 'The Other One' (Weir, Kreutzmann), 'Drums' (Hart, Kreutzmann), 'Iko Iko' (Crawford, Hawkins, Hawkins, Johnson), 'Stella Blue' (Garcia, Hunter), 'Playing In The Band' (Weir, Hart, Hunter), 'Johnny B. Goode' (Chuck Berry), [Bonus tracks: recorded live at Seneca College Feld House November 2, 1977]: 'Promised Land' (Chuck Berry), 'They Love Each Other' (Garcia, Hunter), 'Me And My Uncle' (John Phillips), 'Big River' (Johnny Cash), Candyman (Garcia, Hunter), 'Looks Like Rain' (Weir, Barlow), 'Ramble On Rose' (Garcia, Hunter), 'Scarlet Begonias' (Garcia, Hunter), 'Fire On The Mountain' (Hart, Hunter), 'Terrapin Station' (Garcia, Hunter)

Dick's Picks Vol. 34 (2005)
Personnel:
Jerry Garcia: lead guitar, vocals
Donna Jean Godchaux: vocals
Keith Godchaux: keyboards
Mickey Hart: drums
Bill Kreutzmann: drums
Phil Lesh: electric bass, vocals
Bob Weir: rhythm guitar, vocals
Recorded live at the Community War Memorial in Rochester, New York on November 5, 1977 with bonus tracks recorded at the Seneca College Field House in Toronto, Ontario, Canada on November 2, 1977. Recorded by Betty Cantor-Jackson
Release date: February 2005
Running time: 210:52
'New Minglewood Blues' (trad.), 'Mississippi Half-Step Uptown Toodeloo' (Garcia, Hunter),

'Looks Like Rain' (Weir, Barlow), 'Dire Wolf' (Garcia, Hunter), 'Mama Tried' (Merle Haggard), 'Big River' (Johnny Cash), 'Candyman' (Garcia, Hunter), 'Jack Straw' (Weir, Hunter), 'Deal' (Garcia, Hunter), 'Phil Solo' (Lesh), 'Take A Step Back' (Grateful Dead), 'Eyes Of The World' (Garcia, Hunter), 'Samson And Delilah' (trad.), 'It Must Have Been The Roses' (Hunter), 'Might As Well' (Garcia, Hunter) [November 2, 1977], 'Estimated Prophet' (Weir, Barlow)[November 2, 1977], 'St. Stephen' (Garcia, Lesh, Hunter)[November 2, 1977], 'Truckin'' (Garcia, Lesh, Weir, Hunter)[November 2, 1977], 'Around And Around' (Chuck Berry) [November 2, 1977], 'Estimated Prophet' (Weir, Barlow), 'He's Gone' (Garcia, Hunter), 'Rhythm Devils' (Hart, Kreutzmann), 'The Other One' (Weir, Kreutzmann), 'Black Peter' (Garcia, Hunter), 'Sugar Magnolia' (Weir, Hunter), 'One More Saturday Night' (Weir), [Bonus tracks from November 2, 1977] 'Lazy Lightnin'' (Weir, Barlow), 'Supplication' (Weir, Barlow)

Dave's Picks Vol. 25 (2018)

Personnel:
Jerry Garcia: guitar, vocals
Donna Jean Godchaux: vocals
Keith Godchaux: keyboards
Mickey Hart: drums
Bill Kreutzmann: drums
Phil Lesh: bass, vocals
Bob Weir: guitar, vocals
Recorded live at Broome County Veterans Memorial Arena in Binghamton, New York, on November 6, 1977. Recorded by Betty Cantor-Jackson.
Release date: January 2018
Running time: 166:07
'Mississippi Half-Step Uptown Toodeloo' (Garcia, Hunter), 'Jack Straw' (Weir, Hunter), 'Tennessee Jed' (Garcia, Hunter), 'Mexicali Blues' (Weir, Barlow), 'Me And My Uncle' (John Phillips), 'Friend Of The Devil' (Garcia, Hunter), 'New Minglewood Blues' (trad.), 'Dupree's Diamond Blues' (Garcia, Hunter), 'Passenger' (Lesh, Monk), 'Dire Wolf' (Garcia, Hunter), 'The Music Never Stopped' (Weir, Barlow), 'Samson And Delilah' (trad.), 'Sunrise' (Godchaux), 'Scarlet Begonias' (Garcia, Hunter), 'Fire On The Mountain' (Hart, Hunter), 'Good Lovin'' (Clark, Resnick), 'St. Stephen' (Garcia, Lesh, Hunter), 'Drums' (Hart, Kreutzmann), 'Not Fade Away' (Holly, Petty), 'Wharf Rat' (Garcia, Hunter), 'St. Stephen' (Garcia, Lesh, Hunter), 'Truckin'' (Garcia, Weir, Lesh, Hunter), 'Johnny B. Goode' (Chuck Berry)

Dick's Picks Vol.10 (1998)

Personnel:
Jerry Garcia: lead guitar, vocals
Donna Godchaux: vocals
Keith Godchaux: keyboards
Mickey Hart: drums, percussion
Bill Kreutzmann: drums, percussion
Phil Lesh: bass guitar
Bob Weir: rhythm guitar, vocals
Recorded live at Winterland Arena, San Francisco, on December 29 1977.
Recorded by Betty Cantor-Jackson
Release date: February 1998
Running time: 197:59

'Jack Straw' (Hunter, Weir). 'They Love Each Other' (Garcia, Hunter), 'Mama Tried' (Merle Haggard), 'Loser' (Garcia, Hunter), 'Looks Like Rain' (Barlow, Weir), 'Tennessee Jed' (Garcia, Hunter), 'New Minglewood Blues' (trad.), 'Sugaree' (Garcia, Hunter), 'Promised Land' (Chuck Berry), 'Bertha' (Garcia, Hunter), 'Good Lovin'' (Clark, Resnick), 'Playing In The Band' (Hunter, Hart, Weir), 'China Cat Sunflower' (Garcia, Hunter), 'I Know You Rider' (trad.), 'China Doll' (Garcia, Hunter), 'Playing Jam' (Hart, Weir), 'Drums' (Hart, Kreutzmann), 'Not Fade Away' (Holly, Petty), 'Playing In The Band' (Hunter, Hart, Weir), 'Terrapin Station' (Garcia, Hunter), 'Johnny B. Goode' (Chuck Berry), [Bonus tracks: December 30 1977]: 'Estimated Prophet' (Barlow, Weir), 'Eyes Of The World' (Garcia, Hunter), 'St. Stephen' (Hunter, Garcia, Lesh), 'Sugar Magnolia' (Hunter, Weir)

1978
Dave's Picks Vol. 23 (2017)
Personnel:
Jerry Garcia: guitar, vocals
Donna Jean Godchaux: vocals
Keith Godchaux: keyboards
Mickey Hart: drums
Bill Kreutzmann: drums
Phil Lesh: bass, vocals
Bob Weir: guitar, vocals
Recorded live at McArthur Court at the University of Oregon in Eugene, Oregon, on January 22, 1978. Recorded by Betty Cantor-Jackson.
Release date: August 2017
Running time: 167:54
'New Minglewood Blues' (trad.), 'Dire Wolf' (Garcia, Hunter), 'Cassidy' (Weir, Barlow), 'Peggy-O' (trad.), 'El Paso' (Marty Robbins), 'Tennessee Jed' (Garcia, Hunter), 'Jack Straw' (Weir, Hunter), 'Row Jimmy' (Garcia, Hunter), 'The Music Never Stopped' (Weir, Barlow), 'Bertha' (Garcia, Hunter), 'Good Lovin'' (Clark, Resnick), 'Ship Of Fools' (Garcia, Hunter), 'Samson And Delilah' (trad.), 'Terrapin Station' (Garcia, Hunter), 'Drums' (Hart, Kreutzmann), 'The Other One' (Weir, Kreutzmann), 'Space' (Garcia, Lesh, Weir), 'St. Stephen' (Garcia, Lesh, Hunter), 'Not Fade Away' (Petty, Hardin), 'Around And Around' (Chuck Berry), 'U.S. Blues' (Garcia, Hunter)

Dick's Picks Vol.18 (2000)
Personnel:
Jerry Garcia: guitar, vocals
Donna Jean Godchaux: vocals
Keith Godchaux: keyboards
Mickey Hart: drums
Bill Kreutzmann: drums
Phil Lesh: bass, vocals
Bob Weir: guitar, vocals
Recorded live at the Dane County Coliseum in Madison, Wisconsin, on February 3, 1978, and at the UNI-Dome in Cedar Falls, Iowa, on February 5, 1978. Two songs are from February 4 1978. Recorded by Betty Cantor-Jackson.
Release date: June 2000
Running time: 228:32
'Bertha' (Garcia, Hunter), 'Good Lovin'' (Clark, Resnick), 'Cold Rain And Snow' (trad.),

'New Minglewood Blues' (trad.) 'They Love Each Other' (Garcia, Hunter), 'It's All Over Now' (Womack, Womack), 'Dupree's Diamond Blues' (Garcia, Hunter), 'Looks Like Rain' (Weir, Barlow), 'Brown-Eyed Women' (Garcia, Hunter), 'Passenger' (Lesh, Monk), 'Deal' (Garcia, Hunter), 'The Music Never Stopped' (Weir, Barlow), 'Estimated Prophet' (Weir, Barlow), 'Eyes Of The World' (Garcia, Hunter), 'Playing In The Band' (Weir, Mickey Hart, Hunter), 'The Wheel' (Garcia, Kreutzmann, Hunter), 'Playing In The Band' (Weir, Hart, Hunter), 'Johnny B. Goode' (Chuck Berry), 'Samson And Delilah' (trad.), 'Scarlet Begonias' (Garcia, Hunter), 'Fire On The Mountain' (Hart, Hunter), 'Truckin'' (Garcia, Lesh, Weir, Hunter), 'Drums' (Hart, Kreutzmann), 'The Other One' (Weir, Kreutzmann), 'Wharf Rat' (Garcia, Hunter), 'Around And Around' (Chuck Berry)

Dave's Picks Vol. 37 (2021)
Personnel:
Jerry Garcia: guitar, vocals
Donna Jean Godchaux: vocals
Keith Godchaux: keyboards
Mickey Hart: drums
Bill Kreutzmann: drums
Phil Lesh: bass
Bob Weir: guitar, vocals
Recorded live at the College of William and Mary in Williamsburg, Virginia, on April 15, 1978, with bonus tracks recorded at the Civic Arena in Pittsburgh, Pennsylvania, recorded on April 18 1978. Recorded by Betty Cantor-Jackson
Release date: January 2021
Running time: 233:00
'Mississippi Half-Step Uptown Toodeloo' (Garcia, Hunter) 'Passenger' (Lesh, Monk), 'Friend Of The Devil' (Garcia, Dawson, Hunter), 'El Paso' (Marty Robbins), 'Brown-Eyed Women' (Garcia, Hunter), 'Let It Grow' (Weir, Barlow), 'Deal' (Garcia, Hunter), 'Bertha' (Garcia, Hunter), 'Good Lovin'' (Clark, Resnick), 'Candyman' (Garcia, Hunter), 'Sunrise' (Godchaux), 'Playing In The Band' (Weir, Hart, Hunter), 'Rhythm Devils' (Hart, Kreutzmann), 'Not Fade Away' (Petty, Hardin), Morning Dew' (Dobson, Rose), 'Around And Around' (Chuck Berry), 'One More Saturday Night' (Weir), [Bonus tracks recorded on April 18, 1978]: 'Lazy Lightning' (Weir, Barlow), 'Supplication' (Weir, Barlow), 'Sugaree' (Garcia, Hunter), 'Tennessee Jed' (Garcia, Hunter), 'Scarlet Begonias' (Garcia, Hunter), 'Dancing In The Street' (Stevenson, Gaye, Hunter), 'Rhythm Devils' (Hart, Kreutzmann). 'Samson And Delilah' (trad.), 'Terrapin Station' (Garcia, Hunter), 'Around and Around' (Chuck Berry)

Dave's Picks Vol. 15 (2015)
Personnel:
Jerry Garcia: guitar, vocals
Donna Jean Godchaux: vocals
Keith Godchaux: keyboards
Mickey Hart: drums, percussion
Bill Kreutzmann: drums, percussion
Phil Lesh: bass, vocals
Bob Weir: guitar, vocals
Recorded at the Municipal Auditorium in Nashville, Tennessee, on April 22, 1978. Recorded by Betty Cantor-Jackson.
Release date: August 2015

Running time: 164:14
'Bertha' (Garcia, Hunter), 'Good Lovin'' (Resnick, Clark), 'Candyman' (Garcia, Hunter), 'Looks Like Rain' (Weir, Barlow), 'Tennessee Jed' (Garcia, Hunter), 'Jack Straw' (Weir, Hunter), 'Peggy-O' (trad.), 'New Minglewood Blues' (trad.), 'Deal' (Garcia, Hunter), 'Lazy Lightning' (Weir, Barlow), 'Supplication' (Weir, Barlow), 'It Must Have Been The Roses' (Hunter), 'Estimated Prophet' (Weir, Barlow), 'Eyes Of The World' (Garcia, Hunter), 'Rhythm Devils' (Hart, Kreutzmann), 'Not Fade Away' (Petty, Hardin), 'Wharf Rat' (Garcia, Hunter), 'Sugar Magnolia' (Weir, Hunter), 'One More Saturday Night' (Weir)

Dave's Picks Vol 7 (2013)

Personnel:
Jerry Garcia: lead guitar, vocals
Donna Jean Godchaux: vocals
Keith Godchaux: keyboards
Mickey Hart: drums and percussion
Bill Kreutzmann: drums and percussion
Phil Lesh: bass guitar, vocals
Bob Weir: rhythm guitar, vocals
Recorded live at the Horton Field House, Illinois State University, in Normal, Illinois on April 24, 1978. Recorded by Betty Cantor-Jackson.
Release date: August 2013
Running time: 169:21
'Promised Land' (Chuck Berry), 'Ramble On Rose' (Garcia, Hunter), 'Me And My Uncle' (John Phillips), 'Big River' (Johnny Cash), 'Friend Of The Devil' (Garcia, Hunter), 'Cassidy' (Weir, Barlow), 'Brown-Eyed Women' (Garcia, Hunter), 'Passenger' (Lesh, Monk), 'It Must Have Been The Roses' (Hunter), 'The Music Never Stopped' (Weir, Barlow), 'Scarlet Begonias' (Garcia, Hunter), 'Fire On The Mountain' (Hart, Hunter), 'Good Lovin'' (Clark, Resnick), 'Terrapin Station' (Garcia, Hunter), 'Rhythm Devils' (Hart, Kreutzmann), 'Space' (Garcia, Godchaux, Lesh, Weir), 'Not Fade Away' (Holly, Petty), 'Black Peter' (Garcia, Hunter), 'Around And Around' (Chuck Berry), 'Werewolves Of London' (Marinell, Wachtel, Zevon)

Dick's Picks Vol. 25 (2002)

Personnel:
Jerry Garcia: lead guitar, vocals
Donna Jean Godchaux: vocals
Keith Godchaux: piano
Mickey Hart: drums
Bill Kreutzmann: drums
Phil Lesh: electric bass guitar, vocals
Bob Weir: rhythm guitar, vocals
Recorded live at Veteran's Memorial Coliseum in New Haven, Connecticut on May 10, 1978, and at the Springfield Civic Center Arena in Springfield, Massachusetts, on May 11 1978. Recorded by Owsley Stanley and Betty Cantor-Jackson.
Release date: July 2002
Running time: 309:53
'Jack Straw' (Hunter, Weir), 'They Love Each Other' (Garcia, Hunter), 'Cassidy' (Barlow, Weir), 'Ramble On Rose' (Garcia, Hunter), 'Me And My Uncle' (John Phillips), 'Big River' (Johnny Cash), 'Peggy-O' (trad.), 'Let It Grow' (Barlow, Weir), 'Deal' (Garcia,

Hunter), 'Bertha' (Garcia, Hunter), 'Good Lovin'' (Clark, Resnick), 'Estimated Prophet' (Barlow, Weir), 'Eyes Of The World' (Garcia, Hunter), 'Drums' (Hart, Kreutzmann), 'The Other One' (Kreutzmann, Weir), 'Wharf Rat' (Garcia, Hunter), 'Sugar Magnolia/ Sunshine Daydream' (Hunter, Weir), [Following tracks are from May 11, 1978] 'Cold Rain And Snow' (trad.), 'Beat It On Down The Line' (Jesse Fuller), 'Friend Of The Devil' (Dawson, Hunter, Garcia), 'Looks Like Rain' (Barlow, Weir), 'Loser' (Garcia, Hunter), 'New Minglewood Blues' (trad.), 'Tennessee Jed' (Garcia, Hunter), 'Lazy Lightnin'' (Barlow, Weir), 'Supplication' (Barlow, Weir), 'Scarlet Begonias' (Garcia, Hunter), 'Fire On The Mountain' (Hunter, Hart), 'Dancing In The Streets' (Gaye, Hunter, Stevenson), 'Drums' (Hart, Kreutzmann), 'Not Fade Away' (Holly, Petty), 'Stella Blue' (Garcia, Hunter), 'Around And Around' (Chuck Berry), 'Werewolves Of London' (Marinell, Wachtel, Zevon), 'Johnny B. Goode' (Chuck Berry)

July 1978: The Complete Recordings (2016)
Personnel:
Jerry Garcia: guitar, vocals
Donna Jean Godchaux: vocals
Keith Godchaux: keyboards
Mickey Hart: drums
Bill Kreutzmann: drums
Phil Lesh: bass
Bob Weir: guitar, vocals
Recorded live July 1 – 8, 1978. Produced for release by David Lemieux.
Release date: May 2016
Running time: 744:51
Arrowhead Stadium, Kansas City, Missouri, July 1, 1978
'Bertha' (Garcia, Hunter), 'Good Lovin'' (Resnick, Clark), 'Tennessee Jed' (Garcia, Hunter), 'Jack Straw' (Weir, Hunter), 'Friend Of The Devil' (Garcia, Dawson, Hunter), 'Me And My Uncle' (John Phillips), 'Big River' (Johnny Cash), 'Terrapin Station' (Garcia, Hunter, Kreutzmann, Hart), 'Playing In The Band' (Weir, Hart, Hunter), 'Rhythm Devils' (Hart, Kreutzmann), 'Space' (Garcia, Phil Lesh, Weir, Godchaux), 'Estimated Prophet' (Weir, Barlow), 'The Other One' (Weir, Kreutzmann), 'Wharf Rat' (Garcia, Hunter), 'Around And Around' (Chuck Berry), 'Johnny B. Goode' (Chuck Berry)
St. Paul Civic Center Arena, St. Paul, Minnesota, July 3, 1978
'New Minglewood Blues' (trad.), 'Loser' (Garcia, Hunter), 'Looks Like Rain' (Weir, Barlow), 'Ramble On Rose' (Garcia, Hunter), Mexicali Blues' (Weir, Barlow), 'Mama Tried' (Merle Haggard), 'Peggy-O' (trad.), 'Cassidy' (Weir, Barlow), 'Deal' (Garcia, Hunter), 'The Music Never Stopped' (Weir, Barlow), 'Scarlet Begonias' (Garcia, Hunter), 'Fire On The Mountain' (Hart, Hunter), 'Dancing In The Street' (Gaye, Hunter, Stevenson), 'Rhythm Devils' (Hart, Kreutzmann), 'Not Fade Away' (Hardin, Petty), 'Stella Blue' (Garcia, Hunter), 'Sugar Magnolia' (Weir, Hunter), 'Werewolves Of London' (Marinell, Wachtel, Zevon)
Omaha Civic Auditorium, Omaha, Nebraska, July 5, 1978
'Sugaree' (Garcia, Hunter), 'Beat It On Down The Line' (Jesse Fuller), 'They Love Each Other' (Garcia, Hunter), 'Looks Like Rain' (Weir, Barlow), 'Dire Wolf' (Garcia, Hunter), 'It's All Over Now' (Womack, Womack), 'Candyman' (Garcia, Hunter), 'Lazy Lightning' (Weir, Barlow), 'Supplication' (Weir, Barlow), 'Deal' (Garcia, Hunter), 'Samson And Delilah' (trad.), 'Ship Of Fools' (Garcia, Hunter), 'Estimated Prophet' (Weir, Barlow), 'Eyes Of The World' (Garcia, Hunter), 'Rhythm Devils' (Hart, Kreutzmann), 'Space' (Garcia, Lesh, Weir, Godchaux), 'Wharf Rat' (Garcia, Hunter), 'Truckin'' (Garcia, Lesh, Weir, Hunter), 'Iko Iko'

(Crawford, Hawkins, Hawkins, Johnson), 'Around And Around' (Chuck Berry), 'Promised Land' (Chuck Berry)

Red Rocks Amphitheatre, Morrison, Colorado, July 7, 1978
'Jack Straw' (Weir, Hunter), 'Candyman' (Garcia, Hunter), 'Me And My Uncle' (John Phillips), 'Big River' (Johnny Cash), 'Friend Of The Devil' (Garcia, Dawson, Hunter), 'Cassidy' (Weir, Barlow), 'Tennessee Jed' (Garcia, Hunter), 'Passenger' (Lesh, Monk), 'Peggy-O' (trad.), 'The Music Never Stopped' (Weir, Barlow), 'Cold Rain And Snow' (trad.), 'Beat It On Down The Line' (Jesse Fuller), 'Scarlet Begonias' (Garcia, Hunter), 'Fire On The Mountain' (Hart, Hunter), 'Dancing In The Street' (Gaye, Hunter, Stevenson), 'Rhythm Devils' (Hart, Kreutzmann) 'Space' (Garcia, Lesh, Weir, Godchaux), 'Not Fade Away' (Hardin, Petty), 'Black Peter' (Garcia, Hunter), 'Around And Around' (Chuck Berry), 'U.S. Blues' (Garcia, Hunter), 'Johnny B. Goode' (Chuck Berry)

Red Rocks Amphitheatre, Morrison, Colorado, July 8, 1978
'Bertha' (Garcia, Hunter), 'Good Lovin'' (Resnick, Clark), 'Dire Wolf' (Garcia, Hunter), 'El Paso' (Marty Robbins), 'It Must Have Been The Roses' (Hunter), 'New Minglewood Blues' (trad.), 'Ramble On Rose' (Garcia, Hunter), 'Promised Land' (Chuck Berry), 'Deal' (Garcia, Hunter), 'Samson And Delilah' (trad.), 'Ship Of Fools' (Garcia, Hunter), 'Estimated Prophet' (Weir, Barlow), 'The Other One' (Weir, Kreutzmann), 'Eyes Of The World' (Garcia, Hunter), 'Rhythm Devils' (Hart, Kreutzmann), 'Space' (Garcia, Godchaux, Lesh, Weir), 'Wharf Rat' (Garcia, Hunter), 'Franklin's Tower' (Garcia, Hunter, Kreutzmann), 'Sugar Magnolia' (Weir, Hunter), 'Terrapin Station' (Garcia, Hunter, Kreutzmann, Hart), 'One More Saturday Night' (Weir), 'Werewolves Of London' (Marinell, Wachtel, Zevon)

Red Rocks: 7/8/78 (2016)
Personnel:
Jerry Garcia: guitar, vocals
Donna Jean Godchaux: vocals
Keith Godchaux: keyboards
Mickey Hart: drums
Bill Kreutzmann: drums
Phil Lesh: bass
Bob Weir: guitar, vocals
Recorded live at Red Rocks Amphitheatre, Morrison, Colorado, on July 8, 1978. Produced for release by David Lemieux.
Release date: May 2016
Running time: 170:08
'Bertha' (Garcia, Hunter), 'Good Lovin'' (Resnick, Clark), 'Dire Wolf' (Garcia, Hunter), 'El Paso' (Marty Robbins), 'It Must Have Been The Roses' (Hunter), 'New Minglewood Blues' (trad.), 'Ramble On Rose' (Garcia, Hunter), 'Promised Land' (Chuck Berry), 'Deal' (Garcia, Hunter), 'Samson And Delilah' (trad.), 'Ship Of Fools' (Garcia, Hunter), 'Estimated Prophet' (Weir, Barlow), 'The Other One' (Weir, Kreutzmann), 'Eyes Of The World' (Garcia, Hunter), 'Rhythm Devils' (Hart, Kreutzmann), 'Space' (Garcia, Godchaux, Lesh, Weir), 'Wharf Rat' (Garcia, Hunter), 'Franklin's Tower' (Garcia, Hunter, Kreutzmann), 'Sugar Magnolia' (Weir, Hunter), 'Terrapin Station' (Garcia, Hunter, Kreutzmann, Hart), 'One More Saturday Night' (Weir), 'Werewolves Of London' (Marinell, Wachtel, Zevon)

Rocking the Cradle: Egypt 1978 (2008)
Personnel:
Jerry Garcia: lead guitar, vocals

Donna Jean Godchaux: vocals
Keith Godchaux: keyboards
Mickey Hart: drums
Bill Kreutzmann: drums
Phil Lesh: bass guitar
Bob Weir: rhythm guitar, vocals
Additional personnel:
Hamza El Din: vocals, oud, tar, hand-clapping on 'Ollin Arageed'
The Nubian Youth Choir: vocals, hand-clapping, tar on 'Ollin Arageed'
Recorded live at the Giza Pyramid Complex, Egypt, on September 15 – 16, 1978. Produced by David Lemieux.
Release date: September 2008
Running time: 145:48
'Jack Straw' (Hunter, Weir), 'Row Jimmy' (Garcia, Hunter), 'New Minglewood Blues' (Noah Lewis), 'Candyman' (Garcia, Hunter), 'Looks Like Rain' (Barlow, Weir), 'Stagger Lee' (Garcia, Hunter), 'I Need A Miracle' (Barlow, Weir), 'It's All Over Now' (Womack, Womack), 'Deal' (Garcia, Hunter), 'Ollin Arageed' (Hamza El Din), 'Fire On The Mountain' (Hunter, Hart), 'Iko Iko' (James 'Sugar Boy' Crawford), 'Shakedown Street' (Garcia, Hunter), 'Drums' (Hart, Kreutzmann), 'Space' (Garcia, Godchaux, Lesh, Weir), 'Truckin' ' (Hunter, Garcia, Lesh, Weir), 'Stella Blue' (Garcia, Hunter), 'Around And Around' (Chuck Berry)

Road Trips Vol. 1 No. 4 (2008)

Personnel:
Jerry Garcia: lead guitar, vocals
Donna Jean Godchaux: vocals
Keith Godchaux: keyboards
Mickey Hart: drums
Bill Kreutzmann: drums
Phil Lesh: electric bass
Bob Weir: rhythm guitar, vocals
Additional personnel:
Hamza El Din: oud, vocals on 'Ollin Arageed'
John Cipollina: guitar on 'Not Fade Away' and 'Goin' Down The Road Feeling Bad'
Lee Oskar: harmonica on 'Got My Mojo Working', 'The Other One', Stella Blue' and 'Sugar Magnolia'
Recorded live at Winterland Arena in San Francisco, California, on October 21 and 22, 1978. Compilation produced by David Lemieux and Blair Jackson.
Release date: September 2008
Running time: 159:36
'Sugaree' (Garcia, Hunter), 'Passenger' (Lesh, Monk), 'Stagger Lee' (Garcia, Hunter), 'I Need A Miracle' (Weir, Barlow), 'Got My Mojo Working' (Preston Foster), 'The Other One' (Weir), 'Stella Blue' (Garcia, Hunter) 'Sugar Magnolia' (Weir, Hunter), 'U.S. Blues' (Garcia, Hunter), 'Ollin Arageed' (Hamza El Din), 'Deal' (Garcia, Hunter), 'Peggy-O' (trad.), 'Jack Straw' (Weir, Hunter), 'Scarlet Begonias' (Garcia, Hunter), 'Fire On The Mountain' (Hart, Hunter), 'Not Fade Away' (Petty, Holly), 'Goin' Down The Road Feeling Bad' (trad.), [Bonus Disc: Recorded live at Winterland on October 21, 1978]: 'Bertha' (Garcia, Hunter), 'Good Lovin'' (Resnick, Clark), 'Estimated Prophet' (Weir, Barlow), 'He's Gone' (Garcia, Hunter), [Recorded live at Winterland on October 17, 1978]: 'If I Had The World To Give' (Garcia, Hunter), 'Around And Around' (Chuck Berry)

The Closing Of Winterland (2003)
Personnel:
Jerry Garcia: guitar, vocals
Donna Jean Godchaux: vocals
Keith Godchaux: piano
Mickey Hart: drums, percussion
Bill Kreutzmann: drums, percussion
Phil Lesh: electric bass, vocals
Bob Weir: guitar, vocals
Additional personnel:
Dan Aykroyd: midnight countdown
John Cipollina: guitar
Greg Errico: drums
Bill Graham: master of ceremonies
Matthew Kelly: harmonica
Ken Kesey: thunder machine
Lee Oskar: harmonica
Recorded live at Winterland Arena, San Francisco, on December 31, 1978. Produced by David Lemieux.
Release date: December 2003
Running time: 250:12
'Sugar Magnolia' (Weir, Hunter), 'Scarlet Begonias' (Garcia, Hunter), 'Fire On The Mountain' (Hart, Hunter), 'Me And My Uncle' (John Phillips), 'Big River' (Johnny Cash), 'Friend Of The Devil' (Garcia, Dawson, Hunter), 'It's All Over Now' (Womack, Womack), 'Stagger Lee' (Garcia, Hunter), 'From The Heart Of Me' (Donna Godchaux), 'Sunshine Daydream' (Weir, Hunter), 'Samson And Delilah' (trad.), 'Ramble On Rose' (Garcia, Hunter), 'I Need A Miracle' (Weir, Barlow), 'Terrapin Station' (Garcia, Hunter), 'Playing In The Band' (Weir, Hart, Hunter), 'Rhythm Devils' (Hart, Kreutzmann), 'Not Fade Away' (Petty, Holly), 'Around And Around' (Chuck Berry), 'Dark Star' (Garcia, Hart, Kreutzmann, Lesh, McKernan, Weir, Hunter), 'The Other One' (Weir, Kreutzmann), 'Dark Star' (Garcia, Hart, Kreutzmann, Lesh, McKernan, Weir, Hunter), 'Wharf Rat' (Garcia, Hunter), 'St. Stephen' (Garcia, Lesh, Hunter), 'Good Lovin'' (Clark, Resnick), 'Casey Jones' (Garcia, Hunter), 'Johnny B. Goode' (Chuck Berry), 'And We Bid You Goodnight' (trad.)
Bonus disc: 'New Year's Eves at Winterland'
'Easy Wind' (Hunter) [December 31, 1970], 'Jam' (Grateful Dead), 'Black Peter' (Garcia, Hunter) [December 31, 1971], 'Playing In The Band' (Weir, Hart, Hunter) [December 31, 1972], 'Lazy Lightning' (Weir, Barlow), 'Supplication' (Weir, Barlow), 'Sugar Magnolia' (Weir, Hunter), 'Scarlet Begonias', 'Fire On The Mountain' (Hart, Hunter) [December 31, 1977]

1979
Live at Hampton Coliseum (2014)
Personnel:
Jerry Garcia: guitar, vocals
Mickey Hart: drums
Bill Kreutzmann: drums
Phil Lesh: bass
Brent Mydland: keyboards, vocals
Bob Weir: guitar, vocals

Recorded live at Hampton Coliseum in Hampton, Virginia, on May 4, 1979. Produced for release by David Lemieux.
Release date: April 2014
Running time: 1:39:06
'Loser' (Garcia, Hunter), 'New Minglewood Blues' (trad.), 'Don't Ease Me In' (trad.), 'Passenger' (Lesh, Monk), 'I Need A Miracle' (Weir, Barlow, 'Bertha' (Garcia, Hunter), 'Good Lovin'' (Clark, Resnick), 'Ship Of Fools' (Garcia, Hunter), 'Estimated Prophet' (Weir, Barlow), 'Eyes Of The World' (Garcia, Hunter), 'Truckin'' (Garcia, Lesh, Weir, Hunter), 'Stella Blue' (Garcia, Hunter), 'Around And Around' (Chuck Berry)

Road Trips Vol.1 No.1 (2007)

Personnel:
Jerry Garcia: guitar, vocals
Mickey Hart: drums
Bill Kreutzmann: drums
Phil Lesh: bass
Brent Mydland: keyboards, vocals
Bob Weir: guitar, vocals
Recorded live on the 1979 East Coast fall tour; October 25 – November 10, 1979. Recorded by Dan Healy.
Release date: November 2007
Running time: 156:26
'Alabama Getaway' (Garcia, Hunter), 'Promised Land' (Chuck Berry), 'Jack Straw' (Weir, Hunter), 'Deal' (Garcia, Hunter), 'Dancing In The Street' (Stevenson, Gaye, Hunter), 'Franklin's Tower' (Garcia, Kreutzmann, Hunter), 'Wharf Rat' (Garcia, Hunter), 'I Need A Miracle' (Weir, Barlow), 'Bertha' (Garcia, Hunter), 'Good Lovin'' (Resnick, Clark), 'Shakedown Street' (Garcia, Hunter), 'Passenger' (Lesh, Monk), 'Terrapin Station' (Garcia, Hunter), 'Playing In The Band' (Weir, Hart, Hunter), 'Not Fade Away' (Holly, Petty), 'Morning Dew' (Dobson, Rose), [Bonus Disc]: 'China Cat Sunflower' (Garcia, Hunter), 'I Know You Rider' (trad.), 'Lost Sailor' (Weir, Barlow), 'Saint Of Circumstance' (Weir, Barlow), 'Jam' (Grateful Dead), 'Althea' (Garcia, Hunter), 'Estimated Prophet' (Weir, Barlow), 'He's Gone' (Garcia, Hunter), 'Jam' (Grateful Dead) (Garcia, Hunter)

Road Trips Full Show: Spectrum 11/5/79 (2008)

Personnel:
Jerry Garcia: lead guitar, vocals
Mickey Hart: drums
Bill Kreutzmann: drums
Phil Lesh: electric bass
Brent Mydland: keyboards, vocals
Bob Weir: rhythm guitar, vocals
Recorded live at the Spectrum, in Philadelphia, Pennsylvania, on November 5, 1979.
Recorded by Dan Healy.
'China Cat Sunflower' (Garcia, Hunter), 'I Know You Rider' (trad.), 'Cassidy' (Weir, Barlow), 'Friend Of The Devil' (Garcia, Dawson, Hunter), 'El Paso' (Marty Robbins), 'Stagger Lee' (Garcia, Hunter), 'Passenger' (Lesh, Monk), 'Peggy-O' (trad.), 'The Music Never Stopped' (Weir, Barlow), 'Althea' (Garcia, Hunter), 'Easy To Love You' (Mydland, Barlow), 'Eyes Of The World' (Garcia, Hunter), 'Estimated Prophet' (Weir, Barlow), 'Franklin's Tower' (Garcia, Kreutzmann, Hunter), 'Jam' (Grateful Dead), 'Drums' (Grateful Dead), 'Space' (Grateful

Dead), 'Lost Sailor' (Weir, Barlow), 'Saint Of Circumstance' (Weir, Barlow), 'Sugar Magnolia' (Weir, Hunter), 'Casey Jones' (Garcia, Hunter)

Road Trips Full Show: Spectrum 11/6/79 (2008)

Personnel:
Jerry Garcia: lead guitar, vocals
Mickey Hart: drums
Bill Kreutzmann: drums
Phil Lesh: electric bass
Brent Mydland: keyboards, vocals
Bob Weir: rhythm guitar, vocals
Recorded live at the Spectrum, in Philadelphia, Pennsylvania, on November 6, 1979.
Recorded by Dan Healy.
'Alabama Getaway' (Garcia, Hunter), 'Promised Land' (Chuck Berry), 'Tennessee Jed' (Garcia, Hunter), 'Me And My Uncle' (John Phillips), 'Mexicali Blues' (Weir, Barlow), 'Candyman' (Garcia, Hunter), 'Easy To Love You' (Mydland, Barlow), 'Looks Like Rain' (Weir, Barlow), 'Jack-A-Roe' (trad.), 'Jack Straw' (Weir, Hunter), 'Deal' (Garcia, Hunter), 'Terrapin Station' (Garcia, Hunter), 'Playing In The Band' (Weir, Hart, Hunter), 'Drums' (Grateful Dead), 'Space' (Grateful Dead), 'Black Peter' (Garcia, Hunter), 'Good Lovin' ' (Clarke, Resnick), 'U.S. Blues' (Garcia, Hunter)

Dave's Picks Vol. 31 (2019)

Personnel:
Jerry Garcia: lead guitar, vocals
Mickey Hart: drums
Bill Kreutzmann: drums
Phil Lesh: bass
Brent Mydland: keyboards, vocals
Bob Weir: rhythm guitar, vocals
Recorded live at the Uptown Theatre in Chicago, Illinois, on December 3, 1979. Recorded by Dan Healy.
Release date: July 2019
Running time: 217:24
'Alabama Getaway' (Garcia, Hunter), 'Promised Land' (Chuck Berry), 'Brown-Eyed Women' (Garcia, Hunter), 'El Paso' (Marty Robbins), 'Ramble On Rose' (Garcia, Hunter), 'It's All Over Now' (Womack, Womack), 'Jack-A-Roe' (trad.), 'Lazy Lightning' (Weir, Barlow), 'Supplication' (Weir, Barlow), 'Althea' (Garcia, Hunter), 'The Music Never Stopped' (Weir, Barlow), 'Scarlet Begonias' (Garcia, Hunter), 'Fire On The Mountain' (Hart, Hunter), 'Samson And Delilah' (trad.), 'Terrapin Station' (Garcia, Hunter), 'Playing In The Band' (Weir, Hart, Hunter), 'Drums' (Hart, Kreutzmann),'Space' (Garcia, Lesh, Weir), 'Lost Sailor' (Weir, Barlow), 'Saint Of Circumstance' (Weir, Barlow), 'Wharf Rat' (Garcia, Hunter), 'Truckin'' (Garcia, Lesh, Weir, Hunter), 'Johnny B. Goode' (Chuck Berry), [Bonus tracks recorded live at Uptown Theatre, December 4, 1979]: 'Estimated Prophet' (Weir, Barlow), Franklin's Tower' (Garcia, Kreutzmann, Hunter), 'Jam' (Grateful Dead)

Dick's Picks Vol.5 (1996)

Personnel:
Jerry Garcia: lead guitar, vocals
Mickey Hart: drums
Bill Kreutzmann: drums

Phil Lesh: bass
Brent Mydland: keyboards, vocals
Bob Weir: guitar, vocals
Recorded live at the Oakland Auditorium Arena, Oakland, California, on December 26 1979.
Recorded by Betty Cantor-Jackson
Release date: May 1996
Running time: 176:06
'Cold Rain And Snow' (trad.), 'C.C. Rider' (trad.), 'Dire Wolf' (Garcia, Hunter), 'Me And My Uncle' (John Phillips), 'Big River' (Johnny Cash), 'Brown-Eyed Women' (Garcia, Hunter), 'New Minglewood Blues' (trad.), 'Friend Of The Devil' (Garcia, Dawson, Hunter), 'Looks Like Rain' (Weir, Barlow), 'Alabama Getaway' (Garcia, Hunter), 'Promised Land' (Chuck Berry), 'Uncle John's Band' (Garcia, Hunter), 'Estimated Prophet' (Barlow, Weir), 'Jam 1' (Grateful Dead), 'He's Gone' (Garcia, Hunter), 'The Other One' (Weir, Kreutzmann), 'Drums' (Hart, Kreutzmann), 'Drums' (Hart, Kreutzmann), 'Jam 2' (Grateful Dead), 'Not Fade Away' (Petty, Hardin), 'Brokedown Palace' (Garcia, Hunter), 'Around And Around' (Chuck Berry), 'Johnny B. Goode' (Chuck Berry), 'Shakedown Street' (Garcia, Hunter), 'Uncle John's Band' (Garcia, Hunter)

Road Trips Vol.3 No. 1 (2009)
Personnel:
Jerry Garcia: lead guitar, vocals
Mickey Hart: drums
Bill Kreutzmann: drums
Phil Lesh: electric bass, vocals
Brent Mydland: keyboard, vocals
Bob Weir: rhythm guitar, vocals
Recorded live at the Oakland Auditorium in Oakland, California on December 28 1979.
Produced by Grateful Dead.
Release date: November 2009
Running time: 152:32
'Sugaree' (Garcia, Hunter), 'Mama Tried' (Merle Haggard), 'Mexicali Blues' (Weir, Barlow), 'Row Jimmy' (Garcia, Hunter), 'It's All Over Now' (Womack, Womack), 'High Time' (Garcia, Hunter), 'The Music Never Stopped' (Weir, Barlow), 'Alabama Getaway' (Garcia, Hunter), 'Greatest Story Ever Told' (Weir, Hart, Hunter), 'Terrapin Station' (Garcia, Hunter), 'Playing In The Band' (Weir, Hart, Hunter), 'Rhythm Devils' (Hart, Kreutzmann), 'Space' (Grateful Dead), 'Uncle John's Band' (Garcia, Hunter), 'I Need A Miracle' (Weir, Barlow), 'Bertha' (Garcia, Hunter), 'Good Lovin'' (Resnick, Clark), 'Casey Jones' (Garcia, Hunter), 'One More Saturday Night' (Weir), [Bonus Disc recorded on December 30, 1979]: 'New Minglewood Blues' (Noah Lewis), 'Candyman' (Garcia, Hunter), 'Ramble On Rose' (Garcia, Hunter), 'Lazy Lightning' (Weir, Barlow), 'Supplication' (Weir, Barlow), 'Scarlet Begonias' (Garcia, Hunter), 'Fire On The Mountain' (Hart, Hunter), 'Let It Grow' (Weir, Barlow), 'Truckin'' (Garcia, Phil Lesh, Weir, Hunter), 'Wharf Rat' (Garcia, Hunter)

1980
Road Trips Vol.3 No. 4 (2010)
Personnel:
Jerry Garcia: lead guitar, vocals
Mickey Hart: drums
Bill Kreutzmann: drums

Phil Lesh: electric bass
Brent Mydland: keyboards, vocals
Bob Weir: rhythm guitar, vocals
Recorded live at Recreation Hall, Pennsylvania State University and at Barton Hall, Cornell University, Ithaca, New York on May 6-7, 1980. Recording by Dan Healy.
Release date: June 2010
Running time: 237:03
'Jack Straw' (Weir, Hunter), 'Peggy-O' (trad.), 'Me And My Uncle' (John Phillips), 'Big River' (Johnny Cash), 'Loser' (Garcia, Hunter), 'Cassidy' (Weir, Barlow), 'Row Jimmy' (Garcia, Hunter), 'Lazy Lightning' (Weir, Barlow), 'Supplication' (Weir, Barlow), 'Althea' (Garcia, Hunter), 'Lost Sailor' (Weir, Barlow), 'Saint Of Circumstance' (Weir, Barlow), 'China Cat Sunflower' (Garcia, Hunter), 'I Know You Rider' (trad.), 'Feel Like A Stranger' (Weir, Barlow), 'He's Gone' (Garcia, Hunter), 'The Other One' (Weir, Kreutzmann), 'Rhythm Devils' (Hart, Kreutzmann), 'Space' (Garcia, Lesh, Weir), 'Wharf Rat' (Garcia, Hunter), 'Around And Around' (Chuck Berry), 'Johnny B. Goode' (Chuck Berry), 'Shakedown Street' (Garcia, Hunter), 'Bertha' (Garcia, Hunter), 'Playing In The Band' (Weir, Hart, Hunter), 'Terrapin Station' (Garcia, Hunter), 'Rhythm Devils' (Hart, Kreutzmann), 'Space' (Garcia, Lesh, Weir), 'Saint Of Circumstance' (Weir, Barlow), 'Black Peter' (Garcia, Hunter), 'Playing In The Band' (Weir, Hart, Hunter), 'Good Lovin'' (Clark, Resnick)

Go to Nassau (2002)

Personnel:
Jerry Garcia: guitar, vocals
Mickey Hart: drums, percussion
Bill Kreutzmann: drums
Phil Lesh: electric bass
Brent Mydland: keyboards, vocals
Bob Weir: guitar, vocals
Recorded live at Nassau Coliseum in Uniondale, New York, on May 15 and May 16, 1980. Compilation produced for release by David Lemieux.
Release date: October 2002
Running time: 156:03
'Jack Straw' (Hunter, Weir), 'Franklin's Tower' (Hunter, Garcia, Kreutzmann), 'New Minglewood Blues' (trad.), 'High Time' (Garcia, Hunter), 'Lazy Lightnin'' (Barlow, Weir), 'Supplication' (Barlow, Weir), 'Peggy-O' (trad.), 'Far From Me' (Mydland), 'Looks Like Rain' (Barlow, Weir), 'China Cat Sunflower' (Garcia, Hunter), 'I Know You Rider' (trad.), 'Feel Like A Stranger' (Barlow, Weir), 'Althea' (Garcia, Hunter), 'Lost Sailor' (Barlow, Weir), 'Saint Of Circumstance' (Barlow, Weir), 'Alabama Getaway' (Garcia, Hunter), 'Playing In The Band' (Hunter, Hart, Weir), 'Uncle John's Band' (Garcia, Hunter), 'Drums' (Hart, Kreutzmann), 'Space' (Grateful Dead), 'Not Fade Away' (Holly, Petty), 'Goin' Down The Road Feeling Bad' (trad.), 'Good Lovin'' (Resnick, Clark)

Download Series Vol. 7 (2005)

Personnel:
Jerry Garcia: lead guitar, vocals
Mickey Hart: drums
Bill Kreutzmann: drums
Phil Lesh: electric bass
Brent Mydland: keyboards, vocals
Bob Weir: rhythm guitar, vocals

Recorded live at the Springfield Civic Center in Springfield, Massachusetts, on September 3, 1980, and at Providence Civic Center in Providence, Rhode Island, on September 4 1980. Recorded by Dan Healy.
Release date: October 2005
Running time: 238:20
'Mississippi Half-Step Uptown Toodeloo' (Garcia, Hunter), 'Franklin's Tower' (Garcia, Kreutzmann, Hunter), 'Mama Tried' (Merle Haggard), 'Mexicali Blues' (Weir, Barlow), 'Althea' (Garcia, Hunter), 'Little Red Rooster' (Willie Dixon), 'Candyman' (Garcia, Hunter), 'Easy To Love You' (Mydland, Barlow), 'Let It Grow' (Weir, Barlow), 'Deal' (Garcia, Hunter), 'Feel Like A Stranger' (Weir, Barlow), 'High Time' (Garcia, Hunter), 'Lost Sailor' (Weir, Barlow), 'Saint Of Circumstance' (Weir, Barlow), 'Jam' (Grateful Dead), 'Drums with Brent' (Hart, Kreutzmann, Mydland), 'Rhythm Devils' (Hart, Kreutzmann), 'Space' (Garcia, Lesh, Weir), 'He's Gone' (Garcia, Hunter), 'Truckin' ' (Garcia, Lesh, Weir, Hunter), 'Black Peter' (Garcia, Hunter), 'Around And Around' (Chuck Berry), 'Johnny B. Goode' (Chuck Berry) 'Brokedown Palace' (Garcia, Hunter), [Following recorded at Providence Civic Center, Providence, on September 4, 1980]: 'Supplication Jam' (Weir, Barlow), 'Estimated Prophet' (Weir, Barlow), 'Eyes Of The World' (Garcia, Hunter), 'Rhythm Devils' (Hart, Kreutzmann), 'Space' (Garcia, Lesh, Weir), 'The Other One' (Weir, Kreutzmann), 'Wharf Rat' (Garcia, Hunter), 'Goin' Down The Road Feeling Bad' (trad.), 'Good Lovin' ' (Resnick, Clark), 'U.S. Blues' (Garcia, Hunter)

The Warfield, San Francisco, California, October 9 And 10, 1980 (2019)
Personnel:
Jerry Garcia: acoustic guitar, vocals
Mickey Hart: drums
Bill Kreutzmann: drums
Phil Lesh: electric bass
Brent Mydland: piano, harpsichord, vocals
Bob Weir: acoustic guitar, vocals
Recorded live at the Warfield, San Francisco, California, October 9 and 10, 1980.
Compilation produced for release by David Lemieux.
Release date: April 2019
Running time: 1:36:41
[Disc one: October 9, 1980]
'Dire Wolf' (Garcia, Hunter), 'Dark Hollow' (Bill Browning), 'I've Been All Around This World' (trad.), 'Cassidy' (Weir, Barlow), 'China Doll' (Garcia, Hunter), 'On The Road Again' (Rev. Gary Davis), 'Bird Song' (Garcia, Hunter), 'The Race Is On' (Don Rollins), 'Oh Babe, It Ain't No Lie' (Elizabeth Cotten), 'Ripple' (Garcia, Hunter)
[Disc two: October 10, 1980]
'On The Road Again' (Davis), 'It Must Have Been The Roses' (Hunter), 'Monkey And The Engineer' (Jesse Fuller), 'Jack-A-Roe' (trad.), 'Dark Hollow' (Bill Browning), 'To Lay Me Down' (Garcia, Hunter), 'Heaven Help The Fool' (Weir, Barlow), 'Bird Song' (Garcia, Hunter), 'Ripple' (Garcia, Hunter)

Dave's Picks Vol 8 (2013)
Personnel:
Jerry Garcia: guitar, vocals
Mickey Hart: drums
Bill Kreutzmann: drums

Phil Lesh: electric bass
Brent Mydland: keyboards, vocals
Bob Weir: guitar, vocals
Recorded live at the Fox Theatre in Atlanta, Georgia, on November 30 1980. Recorded by Dan Healy
Release date: November 2013
Running time: 188:03
'Feel Like A Stranger' (Weir, Barlow), 'Loser' (Garcia, Hunter), 'Cassidy' (Weir, Barlow), 'Ramble On Rose' (Garcia, Hunter), 'Little Red Rooster' (Willie Dixon), 'Bird Song' (Garcia, Hunter), 'Me And My Uncle' (John Phillips), 'Big River' (Johnny Cash), 'It Must Have Been The Roses' (Hunter), 'Lost Sailor' (Weir, Barlow), 'Saint Of Circumstance' (Weir, Barlow), 'Deal' (Garcia, Hunter), 'Scarlet Begonias' (Garcia, Hunter), 'Fire On The Mountain' (Hart, Hunter), 'Samson And Delilah' (trad.), 'Ship Of Fools' (Garcia, Hunter), 'Playing In The Band' (Weir, Hart, Hunter), 'Drums' (Hart, Kreutzmann), 'Space' (Garcia, Lesh, Weir), 'The Wheel' (Garcia, Kreutzmann, Hunter), 'China Doll' (Garcia, Hunter), 'Around And Around' (Chuck Berry), 'Johnny B. Goode' (Chuck Berry), 'Uncle John's Band' (Garcia, Hunter)

1981
Dick's Picks Vol.13 (1999)
Personnel:
Jerry Garcia: lead guitar, vocals
Mickey Hart: drums
Bill Kreutzmann: percussion
Phil Lesh: bass, vocals
Brent Mydland: keyboards, vocals
Bob Weir: guitar, vocals
Recorded live at Nassau Veterans Memorial Coliseum in Uniondale, New York, May 6 1981. Recorded by Dan Healy.
Release date: March 1999
Running time: 206:55
'Alabama Getaway' (Garcia, Hunter), 'Greatest Story Ever Told' (Hart, Hunter, Weir), 'They Love Each Other' (Garcia, Hunter), 'Cassidy' (Barlow, Weir), 'Jack-A-Roe' (trad.), 'Little Red Rooster' (Willie Dixon), 'Dire Wolf' (Garcia, Hunter), 'Looks Like Rain' (Barlow, Weir), 'Big Railroad Blues' (Noah Lewis), 'Let It Grow'(Barlow, Weir), 'Deal' (Garcia, Hunter), 'New Minglewood Blues' (trad.), 'High Time' (Garcia, Hunter), 'Lost Sailor' (Barlow, Weir), 'Saint Of Circumstance' (Barlow, Weir) [Hidden tracks-recorded at Nassau Veterans Memorial Coliseum, Uniondale, New York, November 1, 1979]: 'Scarlet Begonias' (Garcia, Hunter), 'Fire On The Mountain' (Hart, Hunter)] 'He's Gone' (Garcia, Hunter), 'Caution/Spanish Jam' (Grateful Dead), 'Drums' (Hart, Kreutzmann), 'Jam' (Grateful Dead), 'The Other One' (Grateful Dead), 'Goin' Down The Road Feeling Bad' (trad.),'Wharf Rat' (Garcia, Hunter), 'Good Lovin'' (Clark, Resnick), 'Don't Ease Me In' (trad.)

Dave's Picks Vol.20 (2016)
Personnel:
Jerry Garcia: guitar, vocals
Mickey Hart: drums
Bill Kreutzmann: drums
Phil Lesh: bass
Brent Mydland: keyboards, vocals

Bob Weir: guitar, vocals
Recorded live at the CU Events Center in Boulder, Colorado, on December 9, 1981.
Recorded by Dan Healy.
Release date: November 2016
Running time: 182:07
'Cold Rain And Snow' (trad.), 'Jack Straw' (Weir, Hunter), 'Friend Of The Devil' (Garcia, Dawson, Hunter), 'Little Red Rooster' (Willie Dixon), 'Bird Song' (Garcia, Hunter), 'Mama Tried' (Merle Haggard), 'Mexicali Blues' (Weir, Barlow), 'Candyman' (Garcia, Hunter), 'Cassidy' (Weir, Barlow), 'Looks Like Rain' (Weir, Barlow), 'China Cat Sunflower' (Garcia, Hunter), 'I Know You Rider' (trad.), 'Scarlet Begonias' (Garcia, Hunter), 'Fire On The Mountain' (Hart, Hunter), 'Estimated Prophet' (Weir, Barlow), 'He's Gone' (Garcia, Hunter), 'Drums' (Hart, Kreutzmann), 'Space' (Garcia, Phil Lesh, Weir), 'The Other One' (Weir, Kreutzmann), 'Stella Blue' (Garcia, Hunter), 'Around And Around' (Chuck Berry), 'Good Lovin'' (Clark, Resnick), 'U.S. Blues' (Garcia, Hunter), '(I Can't Get No) Satisfaction' (Jagger, Richards)

1982
Road Trips Vol 4 No. 4 (2011)
Personnel:
Jerry Garcia: lead guitar, vocals
Mickey Hart: drums
Bill Kreutzmann: drums
Phil Lesh: electric bass
Brent Mydland: keyboards, vocals
Bob Weir: rhythm guitar, vocals
Recorded at the Spectrum in Philadelphia, Pennsylvania, on April 6, 1982. Recorded by Dan Healy.
Release date: August 2011
Running time: 222:42
'Cold Rain And Snow' (trad.), 'Promised Land' (Chuck Berry), 'Candyman' (Garcia, Hunter), 'C.C. Rider' (trad.), 'Brown-Eyed Women' (Garcia, Hunter), 'Mama Tried' (Merle Haggard), 'Mexicali Blues' (Weir, Barlow), 'Big Railroad Blues' (Noah Lewis), 'Looks Like Rain' (Weir, Barlow), 'Jack-A-Roe' (trad.), 'It's All Over Now' (Womack, Womack), 'Might As Well' (Garcia, Hunter), 'Shakedown Street' (Garcia, Hunter), 'Lost Sailor' (Weir, Barlow), 'Saint Of Circumstance' (Weir, Barlow), 'Terrapin Station' (Garcia, Hunter), 'Rhythm Devils' (Hart, Kreutzmann), 'Space' (Garcia, Phil Lesh, Weir), 'Deep Elem Blues' (trad.) [Bonus track from April 5 1982], 'Althea' (Garcia, Hunter)[Bonus track from April 5 1982], 'Man Smart, Woman Smarter' (Norman Span)[Bonus track from April 5 1982], 'Truckin'' (Garcia, Lesh, Weir, Hunter), 'The Other One' (Weir, Kreutzmann), 'Morning Dew' (Dobson, Rose), 'Sugar Magnolia' (Weir, Hunter), 'It's All Over Now, Baby Blue' (Bob Dylan), [Bonus tracks recorded at the Spectrum, Philadelphia on April 5 1982]: 'Bertha' (Garcia, Hunter), 'Playing In The Band' (Weir, Hart, Hunter), 'Ship Of Fools' (Garcia, Hunter), 'Playing In The Band' (Weir, Hart, Hunter)

Dick's Picks Vol. 32 (2004)
Personnel:
Jerry Garcia: guitar, vocals
Mickey Hart: drums
Bill Kreutzmann: drums
Phil Lesh: electric bass

Brent Mydland: keyboards, vocals
Bob Weir: rhythm guitar, vocals
Recorded live at the Alpine Valley Music Theatre in East Troy, Wisconsin, on August 7, 1982.
Recorded by Dan Healy
Release date: July 2004
Running time: 156:40
'The Music Never Stopped' (Weir, Barlow), 'Sugaree' (Garcia, Hunter), 'The Music Never Stopped' (reprise) (Weir, Barlow), 'Me And My Uncle' (John Phillips), 'Big River' (Johnny Cash), 'It Must Have Been The Roses' (Hunter), 'C.C. Rider' (trad.), 'Ramble On Rose' (Garcia, Hunter), 'Beat It On Down The Line' (Jesse Fuller), 'On The Road Again' (trad.), 'Althea' (Garcia, Hunter), 'Let It Grow' (Weir, Barlow), 'U.S. Blues' (Garcia, Hunter), 'China Cat Sunflower' (Garcia, Hunter), 'I Know You Rider' (trad.), 'Man Smart, Woman Smarter' (Norman Span), 'Ship Of Fools' (Garcia, Hunter), 'Playing In The Band' (Weir, Mickey Hart, Hunter), 'Drums' (Hart, Kreutzmann), 'Space' (Garcia, Lesh, Weir), 'The Wheel' (Garcia, Kreutzmann, Hunter), 'Playing In The Band' (reprise) (Weir, Hart, Hunter), 'Morning Dew' (Dobson, Rose), 'One More Saturday Night' (Weir)

1983
Dave's Picks Vol. 39 (2021)
Personnel:
Jerry Garcia: guitar, vocals
Mickey Hart: drums
Bill Kreutzmann: drums
Phil Lesh: bass
Brent Mydland: keyboards, vocals
Bob Weir: guitar, vocals
Recorded live at the Spectrum in Philadelphia, Pennsylvania, on April 26, 1983. Recorded by Dan Healy.
Release date: July 2021
Running time: 231:42
'Shakedown Street' (Garcia, Hunter), 'New Minglewood Blues' (trad.), 'They Love Each Other' (Garcia, Hunter), 'Me And My Uncle' (John Phillips), 'Mexicali Blues' (Weir, Barlow), 'Maybe You Know' (Mydland), 'West L.A. Fadeaway' (Garcia, Hunter), 'My Brother Esau' (Weir, Barlow), 'It Must Have Been The Roses' (Hunter), 'Let It Grow' (Weir, Barlow), 'Help On The Way' (Garcia, Hunter), Slipknot!' (Garcia, Godchaux, Kreutzmann, Lesh, Weir), 'Franklin's Tower' (Garcia, Kreutzmann, Hunter), 'Man Smart, Woman Smarter' (Norman Span), 'Drums' (Hart, Kreutzmann) 'Space' (Garcia, Lesh, Weir) [Bonus track recorded at the Spectrum, Philadelphia, Pennsylvania, April 25, 1983], 'The Wheel' (Garcia, Hunter) [Bonus track recorded at the Spectrum, Philadelphia, Pennsylvania, April 25, 1983], 'Playing In The Band' (Weir, Hart, Hunter) [Bonus track recorded at the Spectrum, Philadelphia, Pennsylvania, April 25, 1983], 'Goin' Down The Road Feeling Bad' (trad.) [Bonus track recorded at the Spectrum, Philadelphia, Pennsylvania, April 25, 1983], 'Sugar Magnolia' (Weir, Hunter) [Bonus track recorded at the Spectrum, Philadelphia, Pennsylvania, April 25, 1983], '(I Can't Get No) Satisfaction' (Jagger, Richards) [Bonus track recorded at the Spectrum, Philadelphia, Pennsylvania, April 25, 1983], 'Space' (Garcia, Lesh, Weir), 'Truckin'' (Garcia, Lesh, Weir, Hunter), 'Morning Dew' (Dobson, Rose), 'Throwing Stones' (Weir, Barlow), 'Not Fade Away' (Petty, Hardin), 'U.S. Blues' (Garcia, Hunter) [Bonus tracks recorded at the War Memorial Auditorium, Rochester, New York on April 15, 1983]: 'He's Gone' (Garcia, Hunter), 'Little Star' (Weir)

Dave's Picks Vol. 27 (2018)

Personnel:
Jerry Garcia: guitar, vocals
Mickey Hart: drums
Bill Kreutzmann: drums
Phil Lesh: bass, vocals
Brent Mydland: keyboards, vocals
Bob Weir: rhythm guitar, vocals
Recorded live at Boise State University Pavilion in Boise, Idaho on September 2, 1983.
Recorded by Dan Healy.
Release date: July 2018
Running time: 182:10
'Wang Dang Doodle' (Willie Dixon), 'Jack Straw' (Weir, Hunter), 'They Love Each Other' (Garcia, Hunter), 'Mama Tried' (Merle Haggard), 'Big River' (Johnny Cash), 'Brown-Eyed Women' (Garcia, Hunter), 'New Minglewood Blues' (trad.), 'Big Railroad Blues' (Noah Lewis), 'Looks Like Rain', (Weir, Barlow), 'Deal' (Garcia, Hunter), 'Help On The Way' (Garcia, Hunter), 'Slipknot!' (Garcia, Godchaux, Kreutzmann, Lesh, Weir), 'Franklin's Tower' (Garcia, Kreutzmann, Hunter), 'Estimated Prophet' (Weir, Barlow), 'Eyes Of The World' (Garcia, Hunter), 'Jam' (Grateful Dead), 'Drums' (Hart, Kreutzmann), 'Space' (Garcia, Lesh, Weir), 'Throwing Stones' (Weir, Barlow), 'Goin' Down The Road Feeling Bad' (trad.), 'Black Peter' (Garcia, Hunter), 'Sugar Magnolia' (Weir, Hunter), It's All Over Now, Baby Blue' (Bob Dylan)

Dick's Picks Vol.6 (1996)

Personnel:
Jerry Garcia: lead guitar, vocals
Mickey Hart: drums
Bill Kreutzmann: drums
Phil Lesh: electric bass, vocals
Brent Mydland: keyboards, vocals
Bob Weir: guitar, vocals
Recorded live at Hartford Civic Center in Hartford, Connecticut, on October 14 1983.
Recorded by Dan Healy.
Release date: October 1996
Running time: 177:41
'Alabama Getaway' (Garcia, Hunter), 'Greatest Story Ever Told' (Hart, Hunter, Weir), 'They Love Each Other' (Garcia, Hunter), 'Mama Tried (Merle Haggard), 'Big River' (Johnny Cash), 'Althea' (Garcia, Hunter), 'C.C. Rider' (trad.) 'Tennessee Jed' (Garcia, Hunter), 'Hell In A Bucket' (Barlow, Weir), 'Keep Your Day Job' (Garcia, Hunter), 'Scarlet Begonias' (Garcia, Hunter), 'Fire On The Mountain' (Hart, Hunter), 'Estimated Prophet' (Barlow, Weir), 'Eyes Of The World' (Garcia, Hunter), 'Drums' (Hart, Kreutzmann), 'Spanish Jam' (Grateful Dead), 'The Other One' (Kreutzmann, Weir), 'Stella Blue' (Garcia, Hunter), 'Sugar Magnolia' (Hunter, Weir), 'U.S. Blues' (Garcia, Hunter)

1984
Dave's Picks Vol. 35 (2020)

Personnel:
Jerry Garcia: guitar, vocals

Mickey Hart: drums
Bill Kreutzmann: drums
Phil Lesh: bass,
Brent Mydland: keyboards, vocals
Bob Weir: guitar, vocals
Recorded live at the Philadelphia Civic Center in Philadelphia, Pennsylvania, on April 20, 1984. Recorded by Dan Healy
Release date: July 2020
Running time: 230:30
'Feel Like A Stranger' (Weir, Barlow), 'Cold Rain And Snow' (trad.), 'Beat It On Down The Line' (Jesse Fuller), 'Cumberland Blues' (Garcia, Lesh, Hunter), 'Little Red Rooster' (Willie Dixon), 'Brown-Eyed Women' (Garcia, Hunter), 'My Brother Esau' (Weir, Barlow), 'It Must Have Been The Roses' (Hunter), 'Let It Grow' (Weir, Barlow), 'Scarlet Begonias' (Garcia, Hunter) 'Fire On The Mountain'(Hart, Hunter), 'Samson And Delilah' (trad.), 'Drums' (Hart, Kreutzmann), 'Space' (part 1) (Garcia, Lesh, Weir), 'The Wheel' (Garcia, Hunter, Kreutzmann) [Bonus track from April 19, 1984], 'Wharf Rat' (Garcia, Hunter) [Bonus track from April 19, 1984], 'Sugar Magnolia' (Weir, Hunter) [Bonus track from April 19, 1984], 'Space' (part 2) (Garcia, Lesh, Weir), 'I Need A Miracle' (Weir, Barlow), 'Morning Dew' (Dobson, Rose), 'Around And Around' (Chuck Berry), 'Johnny B. Goode' (Chuck Berry), 'Keep Your Day Job' (Garcia, Hunter) [Bonus tracks recorded at the Philadelphia Civic Centre on April 19, 1984]: 'China Cat Sunflower' (Garcia, Hunter), 'I Know You Rider' (trad.), 'Estimated Prophet' (Weir, Barlow), 'Terrapin Station' (Garcia, Hunter)

1985
Dick's Picks Vol.21 (2001)
Personnel:
Jerry Garcia: lead guitar, vocals
Mickey Hart: drums
Bill Kreutzmann: drums
Phil Lesh: electric bass, vocals
Brent Mydland: keyboards, vocals
Bob Weir: rhythm guitar, vocals
Recorded live at Richmond Coliseum in Richmond, Virginia on November 1, 1985. Recorded by Dan Healy.
Release date: March 2001
Running time: 187:24
'Dancing In The Streets' (Gaye, Hunter, Stevenson), 'Cold Rain And Snow' (trad.), 'Little Red Rooster' (Willie Dixon), 'Stagger Lee' (Garcia, Hunter), 'Me And My Uncle' (John Phillips), 'Big River' (Johnny Cash), 'Brown-Eyed Woman' (Garcia, Hunter), 'Jack Straw' (Hunter, Weir), 'Don't Ease Me In' (trad.), 'Samson And Delilah' (trad.), 'High Time' (Garcia, Hunter), 'He's Gone' (Garcia, Hunter), 'Spoonful' (Willie Dixon), 'Comes A Time' (Garcia, Hunter), 'Lost Sailor' (Barlow, Weir), 'Drums' (Hart, Kreutzmann), 'Space' (Garcia, Lesh, Weir), 'Saint Of Circumstance' (Barlow, Weir), 'Gimme Some Lovin'' (Davis, Winwood, Winwood), 'She Belongs To Me' (Bob Dylan), 'Gloria' (Van Morrison), 'Keep Your Day Job' (Garcia, Hunter) [Bonus tracks recorded live September 2, 1980] 'Space' (Garcia, Lesh, Weir), 'Iko Iko' (James Crawford), 'Morning Dew' (Dobson, Rose), 'Sugar Magnolia' (Hunter, Weir)

1987
Dave's Picks Vol. 36 (2020)
Personnel:
Jerry Garcia: guitar, vocals
Mickey Hart: drums
Bill Kreutzmann: drums
Phil Lesh: bass, vocals
Brent Mydland: keyboards, vocals
Bob Weir: guitar, vocals
Recorded live at the Hartford Civic Center in Hartford, Connecticut, on March 26 and 27, 1987. Recorded by Dan Healy and Don Pearson
Release date: October 2020
Running time: 275:54
'In The Midnight Hour' (Cropper, Pickett), 'Cold Rain And Snow' (trad.), 'C.C. Rider' (trad.), 'Row Jimmy' (Garcia, Hunter), 'My Brother Esau' (Weir, Barlow), 'When Push Comes To Shove' (Garcia, Hunter), 'Desolation Row' (Bob Dylan), 'Bird Song' (Garcia, Hunter), 'Promised Land' (Chuck Berry), 'China Cat Sunflower' (Garcia, Hunter), 'I Know You Rider' (trad.), 'Looks Like Rain' (Weir, Barlow), 'He's Gone' (Garcia, Hunter), 'Drums' (Hart, Kreutzmann), 'Space' (Garcia, Lesh, Weir), 'I Need A Miracle' (Weir, Barlow), 'Black Peter' (Garcia, Hunter), 'Around And Around' (Chuck Berry), 'Good Lovin'' (Clark, Resnick), 'The Mighty Quinn' (Bob Dylan) [March 27, 1987]: 'Alabama Getaway' (Garcia, Hunter), 'Greatest Story Ever Told' (Weir, Hart, Hunter), 'West L.A. Fadeaway' (Garcia, Hunter), 'Little Red Rooster' (Willie Dixon), 'Brown-Eyed Women' (Garcia, Hunter), 'Beat It On Down The Line' (Jesse Fuller), 'Tennessee Jed' (Garcia, Hunter), 'The Music Never Stopped' (Weir, Barlow), 'Touch Of Grey' (Garcia, Hunter), 'Samson And Delilah' (trad.), 'Cumberland Blues' (Garcia, Hunter, Lesh), 'Estimated Prophet' (Weir, Barlow), 'Eyes Of The World' (Garcia, Hunter), 'Drums' (Hart, Kreutzmann), 'Space' (Garcia, Lesh, Weir), 'Uncle John's Band' (Garcia, Hunter), 'Morning Dew' (Dobson, Rose), 'Johnny B. Goode' (Chuck Berry)

View from the Vault, Vol. 4 (2003)
Personnel:
Jerry Garcia: guitar, vocals
Mickey Hart: drums, percussion
Bill Kreutzmann: drums, percussion
Phil Lesh: bass, vocals
Brent Mydland: keyboards, vocals
Bob Weir: guitar, vocals
Recorded live at Oakland Stadium on July 24, 1987 and at Anaheim Stadium on July 26, 1987. Produced by David Lemieux.
Release date: April 2003
Running time: 4:26:21
Oakland Stadium, Oakland, California, July 24, 1987
'Funiculi Funiculà' (Luigi Denza), 'Jack Straw' (Weir, Hunter) 'Mississippi Half-Step Uptown Toodeloo' (Garcia, Hunter), 'My Brother Esau' (Weir, Barlow), 'Friend Of The Devil' (Garcia, Dawson, Hunter), 'Me And My Uncle' (John Phillips), 'Big River' (Johnny Cash), 'When Push Comes To Shove' (Garcia, Hunter), 'Far From Me' (Mydland), 'Cassidy' (Weir, Barlow), 'Deal' (Garcia, Hunter), 'Hell In A Bucket' (Weir, Barlow), 'Scarlet Begonias' (Garcia, Hunter), 'Playing In The Band' (Weir, Hart, Hunter), 'Drums' (Kreutzmann, Hart), 'Space' (Grateful

Dead), 'Uncle John's Band' (Garcia, Hunter), 'Dear Mr. Fantasy' (Capaldi, Winwood, Wood), 'I Need A Miracle' (Weir, Barlow), 'Bertha' (Garcia, Hunter), 'Sugar Magnolia' (Weir, Hunter)
Anaheim Stadium, Anaheim, California, July 26, 1987
'Iko Iko' (James Crawford), 'New Minglewood Blues' (Noah Lewis), 'Tons Of Steel' (Mydland), 'West L.A. Fadeaway' (Garcia, Hunter), 'When I Paint My Masterpiece' (Bob Dylan), 'Mexicali Blues' (Weir, Barlow), 'Bird Song' (Garcia, Hunter), 'Promised Land' (Chuck Berry), 'Shakedown Street' (Garcia, Hunter), 'Looks Like Rain' (Weir, Barlow), 'Terrapin Station' (Garcia, Hunter), 'Drums' (Kreutzmann, Hart), 'Space' (Grateful Dead), 'The Other One' (Weir, Kreutzmann), 'Stella Blue' (Garcia, Hunter), 'Throwing Stones' (Weir, Barlow), 'Not Fade Away' (Holly, Petty).

1988
Download Series Vol. 5 (2005)
Personnel:
Jerry Garcia: lead guitar, vocals
Mickey Hart: drums
Bill Kreutzmann: drums
Phil Lesh: electric bass
Brent Mydland: keyboards, vocals
Bob Weir: rhythm guitar, vocals
Recorded live at the Hampton Coliseum in Hampton, Virginia, on March 27, 1988. Recorded by Dan Healy
Release date: September 2005
Running time: 142.31
'Iko Iko' (Crawford, Hawkins, Hawkins, Johnson), 'Little Red Rooster' (Willie Dixon), 'Stagger Lee' (Garcia, Hunter), 'Ballad Of A Thin Man' (Bob Dylan), 'Cumberland Blues' (Garcia, Lesh, Hunter), 'Me And My Uncle' (John Phillips), 'To Lay Me Down' (Garcia, Hunter), 'Let It Grow' (Weir, Barlow), 'Space' (Garcia, Lesh, Weir), 'So What' (Miles Davis), 'Sugar Magnolia' (Weir, Hunter), 'Scarlet Begonias' (Garcia, Hunter), 'Fire On The Mountain' (Hart, Hunter), 'Estimated Prophet' (Weir, Barlow), 'Eyes Of The World' (Garcia, Hunter), 'Rhythm Devils' (Hart, Kreutzmann), 'Space' (Garcia, Lesh, Weir), 'Goin' Down The Road Feeling Bad' (trad.), 'I Need A Miracle' (Weir, Barlow), 'Dear Mr. Fantasy' (Capaldi, Winwood, Wood), 'Sunshine Daydream' (Weir, Hunter), 'U.S. Blues' (Garcia, Hunter)

Road Trips Vol 4 No. 2 (2011)
Personnel:
Jerry Garcia: lead guitar, vocals
Mickey Hart: drums
Bill Kreutzmann: drums
Phil Lesh: electric bass, vocals
Brent Mydland: keyboards, vocals
Bob Weir: rhythm guitar, vocals
Recorded live at the Brendan Byrne Arena in East Rutherford, New Jersey, on March 31 and April 1, 1988. Recorded by Dan Healy.
Release date: February 2011
Running time: 237:34
'Mississippi Half-Step Uptown Toodeloo' (Garcia, Hunter), 'Jack Straw' (Weir, Hunter), 'To Lay Me Down' (Garcia, Hunter), 'Ballad Of A Thin Man' (Bob Dylan), 'When Push Comes To Shove' (Garcia, Hunter), 'New Minglewood Blues' (trad.), 'Cumberland Blues' (Garcia, Lesh,

Hunter), 'Deal' (Garcia, Hunter), 'When I Paint My Masterpiece' (Dylan), 'Let It Grow' (Weir, Barlow), 'Brokedown Palace' (Garcia, Hunter), 'Scarlet Begonias' (Garcia, Hunter), 'Fire On The Mountain' (Hart, Hunter), 'Samson And Delilah' (trad.), 'Terrapin Station' (Garcia, Hunter), 'Rhythm Devils' (Hart, Kreutzmann), 'Space' (Garcia, Lesh, Weir), 'Goin' Down The Road Feeling Bad' (trad.), 'I Need A Miracle' (Weir, Barlow), 'Dear Mr. Fantasy' (Capaldi, Wood, Winwood), 'Hey Jude' (Lennon, McCartney), 'All Along The Watchtower' (Bob Dylan), 'Knockin' On Heaven's Door' (Bob Dylan), 'China Cat Sunflower' (Garcia, Hunter), 'I Know You Rider' (trad.), 'Estimated Prophet' (Weir, Barlow), 'Eyes Of The World' (Garcia, Hunter), 'Rhythm Devils' (Hart, Kreutzmann), 'Space' (Garcia, Lesh, Weir), 'The Other One' (Weir, Kreutzmann), 'Wharf Rat' (Garcia, Hunter), 'Throwing Stones' (Weir, Barlow), 'Not Fade Away' (Petty, Hardin)

1989
Download Series Vol. 9 (2006)
Personnel:
Jerry Garcia: lead guitar, vocals
Mickey Hart: drums
Bill Kreutzmann: drums
Phil Lesh: electric bass, vocals
Brent Mydland: keyboards, vocals
Bob Weir: rhythm guitar, vocals
Recorded live at Pittsburgh Civic Arena on April 2 and 3, 1989. Recorded by Dan Healy.
Release date: January 2006
Running time: 289:13
'Iko Iko' (Crawford, B. Hawkins, R. Hawkins, Johnson), 'Little Red Rooster' (Willie Dixon), 'Dire Wolf' (Garcia, Hunter), 'It's All Over Now' (Womack, Womack), 'We Can Run' (Mydland, Barlow), 'Brown-Eyed Women' (Garcia, Hunter), 'Queen Jane Approximately' (Bob Dylan), 'Tennessee Jed' (Garcia, Hunter), 'The Music Never Stopped' (Weir, Barlow), 'It's All Over Now, Baby Blue' (Bob Dylan), 'Shakedown Street' (Garcia, Hunter), 'Man Smart, Woman Smarter' (Norman Span), 'Foolish Heart' (Garcia, Hunter), 'Rhythm Devils' (Hart, Kreutzmann), 'Space' (Garcia, Lesh, Hunter), 'The Wheel' (Garcia, Hunter), 'Dear Mr. Fantasy' (Winwood, Capaldi, Wood), 'Hey Jude' (Lennon, McCartney), 'Around And Around' (Chuck Berry), 'Goin' Down The Road Feeling Bad' (trad.), 'Turn On Your Lovelight' (Scott, Malone), [Following from April 3, 1989]: 'Greatest Story Ever Told' (Weir, Barlow), 'Bertha' (Garcia, Hunter), 'Walking Blues' (Johnson), 'Jack-A-Roe' (trad.), 'El Paso' (Marty Robbins), 'Built To Last' (Garcia, Hunter), 'Victim Or The Crime' (Weir, Graham), 'Just Like Tom Thumb's Blues' (Bob Dylan), 'Don't Ease Me In' (trad. arr. By Grateful Dead), 'Blow Away' (Mydland, Barlow), 'Johnny B. Goode' (Chuck Berry), 'Black Muddy River' (Garcia, Hunter), 'Estimated Prophet' (Weir, Barlow), 'Crazy Fingers' (Garcia, Hunter), 'Uncle John's Band' (Garcia, Hunter), 'Rhythm Devils' (Hart, Kreutzmann), 'Space' (Garcia, Lesh, Weir), 'Gimme Some Lovin' ' (Winwood, Winwood, Davis), 'I Need A Miracle' (Weir, Barlow), 'Stella Blue' (Garcia, Hunter), 'Sugar Magnolia' (Weir, Hunter)

Truckin' Up To Buffalo (2005)
Personnel:
Jerry Garcia: guitar, vocals
Mickey Hart: drums, percussion
Bill Kreutzmann: drums, percussion
Phil Lesh: electric bass, vocals

Brent Mydland: keyboards, Hammond B3, vocals
Bob Weir: guitar, vocals
Recorded live at Rich Stadium in Orchard Park on July 4, 1989. Executive producers Jimmy Edwards and James Austin.
Release date: July 2005
Running time: 157:05
'Bertha' (Garcia, Hunter), 'Greatest Story Ever Told' (Hunter, Hart, Weir), 'Cold Rain And Snow' (trad.), 'Walkin' Blues' (Robert Johnson), 'Row Jimmy' (Garcia, Hunter), 'When I Paint My Masterpiece' (Bob Dylan), 'Stagger Lee' (Garcia, Hunter), 'Looks Like Rain' (Barlow, Weir), 'Deal' (Garcia, Hunter), 'Touch Of Grey' (Garcia, Hunter), 'Man Smart, Woman Smarter' (Norman Span), 'Ship Of Fools' (Garcia, Hunter), 'Playing In The Band' (reprise) (Hunter, Hart, Weir), 'Terrapin Station' (Garcia, Hunter), 'Drums' (Hart, Kreutzmann), 'Space' (Garcia, Lesh, Weir), 'I Will Take You Home' (Mydland), 'All Along The Watchtower' (Dylan), 'Morning Dew' (Dobson, Rose), 'Not Fade Away' (Holly, Petty), 'U.S. Blues' (Garcia, Hunter)

Crimson White And Indigo (2010)

Personnel:
Jerry Garcia: guitar, vocals
Mickey Hart: drums, percussion
Bill Kreutzmann: drums, percussion
Phil Lesh: electric bass, vocals
Brent Mydland: keyboards, Hammond B3, vocals
Bob Weir: guitar, vocals
Recorded live at John F. Kennedy Stadium in Philadelphia on July 7, 1989. Producer: David Lemieux.
Release date: April 2010
Running time: 174:58
'Hell In A Bucket' (Weir, Barlow), Iko Iko' (James 'Sugar Boy' Crawford), 'Little Red Rooster' (Willie Dixon), 'Ramble On Rose' (Garcia, Hunter), Stuck Inside Of Mobile With The Memphis Blues Again' (Bob Dylan), 'Loser' (Garcia, Hunter), 'Let It Grow' (Weir, Barlow), 'Blow Away' (Mydland, Barlow), 'Box Of Rain' (Lesh, Hunter), 'Scarlet Begonias' (Garcia, Hunter), 'Fire On The Mountain' (Hart, Hunter), 'Estimated Prophet' (Weir, Barlow), 'Standing On The Moon' (Garcia, Hunter), 'Rhythm Devils' (Hart, Kreutzmann), 'Space' (Garcia, Lesh, Weir), 'The Other One' (Weir, Kreutzmann), 'Wharf Rat' (Garcia, Hunter), 'Turn On Your Love Light' (Scott, Malone), 'Knockin' On Heaven's Door' (Bob Dylan)

Robert F. Kennedy Stadium, Washington, D.C., July 12 & 13, 1989 (2017)

Personnel:
Jerry Garcia: guitar, vocals
Mickey Hart: drums
Bill Kreutzmann: drums
Phil Lesh: bass, vocals
Brent Mydland: keyboards, vocals
Bob Weir: guitar, vocals
Additional personnel:
Bruce Hornsby: accordion on 'Sugaree' and 'Stuck Inside Of Mobile With The Memphis Blues Again', accordion and keyboards on 'Man Smart, Woman Smarter', accordion and

vocals on 'Tennessee Jed'
Recorded live at Robert F. Kennedy Stadium, Washington, D.C. on July 12 and 13, 1989.
Produced for release by David Lemieux.
Release date: November 2017
Running time: 324:57

July 12, 1989
'Touch Of Grey' (Garcia, Hunter), 'New Minglewood Blues' (trad.), 'Mississippi Half-Step Uptown Toodeloo' (Garcia, Hunter), 'Just Like Tom Thumb's Blues' (Bob Dylan), 'Far From Me' (Mydland), 'Cassidy' (Weir, Barlow), 'Friend Of The Devil' (Garcia, Dawson, Hunter), 'Promised Land' (Chuck Berry), 'Sugaree' (Garcia, Hunter), 'Man Smart, Woman Smarter' (Norman Span), 'Ship Of Fools' (Garcia, Hunter), 'Estimated Prophet' (Weir, Barlow), 'Eyes Of The World' (Garcia, Hunter), 'Drums' (Hart, Kreutzmann), 'Space' (Garcia, Lesh, Weir), 'I Need A Miracle' (Weir, Barlow), 'Dear Mr. Fantasy' (Capaldi, Wood, Winwood), 'Black Peter' (Garcia, Hunter), 'Turn On Your Lovelight' (Scott, Malone), 'Black Muddy River' (Garcia, Hunter)

July 13, 1989
'Hell in A Bucket' (Weir, Mydland, Barlow), 'Cold Rain And Snow' (trad.), 'Little Red Rooster' (Willie Dixon), 'Tennessee Jed' (Garcia, Hunter), 'Stuck Inside Of Mobile With The Memphis Blues Again' (Bob Dylan), 'To Lay Me Down' (Garcia, Hunter), 'Let It Grow' (Weir, Barlow), 'He's Gone' (Garcia, Hunter), 'Looks Like Rain' (Weir, Barlow), 'Terrapin Station' (Garcia, Hunter), 'Drums' (Hart, Kreutzmann), 'Space' (Garcia, Lesh, Weir), 'I Will Take You Home' (Mydland, Barlow), 'The Other One' (Weir, Kreutzmann), 'Wharf Rat' (Garcia, Hunter), 'Throwing Stones' (Weir, Barlow), 'Good Lovin'' (Clark, Resnick), 'U.S. Blues' (Garcia, Hunter)

Formerly the Warlocks (2010)

Personnel:
Jerry Garcia: lead guitar, vocals
Mickey Hart: drums
Bill Kreutzmann: drums
Phil Lesh: electric bass, vocals
Brent Mydland: keyboards, vocals
Bob Weir: rhythm guitar, vocals
Recorded live at the Hampton Coliseum in Hampton, Virginia, on October 8 and October 9, 1989. Recorded by John Cutler.
Release date: September 2010
Running time: 327:23

October 8, 1989
'Foolish Heart' (Garcia, Hunter), 'Walkin' Blues' (Robert Johnson), 'Candyman' (Garcia, Hunter), 'Me And My Uncle' (John Philips), 'Big River' (Johnny Cash), 'Stagger Lee' (Garcia, Hunter), 'Queen Jane Approximately' (Bob Dylan), 'Bird Song' (Garcia, Hunter), 'Promised Land' (Chuck Berry), 'Help On The Way' (Garcia, Hunter), 'Slipknot!' (Garcia, Godchaux, Hart, Kreutzmann, Lesh, Weir), 'Franklin's Tower' (Garcia, Kreutzmann, Hunter), 'Victim Or The Crime' (Weir, Graham), 'Eyes Of The World' (Garcia, Hunter), 'Rhythm Devils' (Hart, Kreutzmann), 'Space' (Garcia, Lesh, Weir), 'I Need A Miracle' (Weir, Barlow), 'The Wheel' (Garcia, Hunter), 'Gimme Some Lovin'' (Winwood, Davis, Winwood), 'Morning Dew' (Dobson, Rose), 'And We Bid You Goodnight' (trad.)

October 9, 1989
'Feel Like A Stranger' (Weir, Barlow), 'Built To Last' (Garcia, Hunter), 'Little Red Rooster'

(Willie Dixon), 'Ramble On Rose' (Garcia, Hunter), 'We Can Run' (Mydland, Barlow), 'Jack-A-Roe' (trad.), 'Stuck Inside Of Mobile With The Memphis Blues Again (Bob Dylan), 'Row Jimmy' (Garcia, Hunter), 'The Music Never Stopped' (Weir, Barlow), 'Playing In The Band' (Weir, Hart, Hunter), 'Uncle John's Band' (Garcia, Hunter), 'Playing In The Band' (Weir, Hart, Hunter), 'Dark Star' (Garcia, Hart, Kreutzmann, Lesh, McKernan, Weir, Hunter), 'Rhythm Devils' (Hart, Kreutzmann), 'Space' (Garcia, Lesh, Weir), 'Death Don't Have No Mercy' (Rev. Gary Davis), 'Dear Mr. Fantasy' (Capaldi, Wood, Winwood), 'Hey Jude' (Lennon, McCartney), 'Throwing Stones' (Weir, Barlow), 'Good Lovin' ' (Clark, Resnick), 'Attics Of My Life' (Garcia, Hunter)

Nightfall Of Diamonds (2001)

Personnel:
Jerry Garcia: lead guitar, vocals
Mickey Hart: drums, percussion
Bill Kreutzmann: drums, percussion
Phil Lesh: bass, vocals
Brent Mydland: Hammond organ, keyboards, vocals
Bob Weir: rhythm guitar, vocals
Recorded live at Meadowlands Arena in East Rutherford on October 16, 1989. Engineered by John Cutler.
Release date: September 2001
Running time: 140:39
'Picasso Moon' (Barlow, Bralove, Weir), 'Mississippi Half-Step Uptown Toodelloo' (Garcia, Hunter), 'Feel Like A Stranger' (Barlow, Weir), 'Never Trust A Woman' (Mydland), 'Built To Last' (Garcia, Hunter), 'Stuck Inside Of Mobile With The Memphis Blues Again' (Bob Dylan), 'Let It Grow' (Barlow, Weir), 'Deal' (Garcia, Hunter), 'Dark Star' (Hunter, Garcia, Hart, Kreutzmann, Lesh, McKernan, Weir), 'Playing In The Band' (Hunter, Hart, Weir), 'Uncle John's Band' (Garcia, Hunter), 'Jam' (Grateful Dead), 'Drums' (Hart, Kreutzmann), 'Space' (Garcia, Lesh, Weir), 'I Will Take You Home' (Mydland), 'I Need A Miracle' (Barlow, Weir), 'Dark Star' (Hunter, Garcia, Hart, Kreutzmann, Lesh, McKernan, Weir), 'Attics Of My Life' (Garcia, Hunter), 'Playing In The Band' (Hunter, Hart, Weir), 'And We Bid You Goodnight' (trad.)

1990
Spring 1990 (The Other One) (2014)

Personnel:
Jerry Garcia: lead guitar, vocals
Mickey Hart: drums
Bill Kreutzmann: drums
Phil Lesh: electric bass, vocals
Brent Mydland: keyboards, vocals
Bob Weir: rhythm guitar, vocals
Additional personnel:
Branford Marsalis: saxophone on March 29, 1990, concert
Recorded live on the Spring 1990 tour March 14-April 3, 1990. Produced for release by David Lemieux. Recorded by John Cutler.
Release date: Sept 2014
Capital Centre, Landover, Maryland, March 14, 1990
'Cold Rain And Snow' (trad.), 'Feel Like A Stranger' (Weir, Barlow), 'Never Trust A Woman' (Mydland), 'Mama Tried' (Merle Haggard), 'Big River' (Johnny Cash), 'Loose Lucy' (Garcia,

Hunter), 'Stuck Inside Of Mobile With The Memphis Blues Again' (Bob Dylan), 'Row Jimmy' (Garcia, Hunter), 'Let It Grow' (Weir, Barlow), 'Crazy Fingers' (Garcia, Hunter), 'Playing In The Band' (Weir, Hart, Hunter), 'Uncle John's Band' (Garcia, Hunter), 'Jam' (Grateful Dead), 'Drums' (Hart, Bill Kreutzmann), 'Space' (Garcia, Lesh, Mydland, Weir), 'Dear Mr. Fantasy' (Winwood, Wood, Capaldi), 'I Need A Miracle' (Weir, Barlow), 'Black Peter' (Garcia, Hunter), 'Turn On Your Lovelight' (Scott, Malone), 'Black Muddy River' (Garcia, Hunter),

Hartford Civic Center, Hartford, Connecticut, March 18, 1990
'Shakedown Street' (Garcia, Hunter), 'Little Red Rooster' (Willie Dixon), 'Stagger Lee' (Garcia, Hunter), 'Me And My Uncle' (John Phillips), 'Mexicali Blues' (Weir, Barlow), 'Friend Of The Devil' (Garcia, Dawson, Hunter), 'Just A Little Light' (Mydland, Barlow), 'When I Paint My Masterpiece' (Bob Dylan), 'Ramble On Rose' (Garcia, Hunter), 'The Music Never Stopped' (Weir, Barlow), 'Iko Iko' (James Crawford), 'Looks Like Rain' (Weir, Barlow), 'He's Gone' (Garcia, Hunter), 'Truckin'' (Garcia, Lesh, Weir, Hunter), 'Spoonful' (Willie Dixon), 'Drums' (Hart, Kreutzmann), 'Space' (Garcia, Lesh, Mydland, Weir), 'The Wheel' (Garcia, Hunter), 'All Along The Watchtower' (Bob Dylan) 'Morning Dew' (Dobson, Rose), 'U.S. Blues' (Garcia, Hunter)

Copps Coliseum, Hamilton, Ontario, March 21, 1990
'Mississippi Half-Step Uptown Toodeloo' (Garcia, Hunter), 'New Minglewood Blues' (trad.), 'Far From Me' (Mydland), 'Queen Jane Approximately' (Bob Dylan), 'Loose Lucy' (Garcia, Hunter), 'Victim Or The Crime' (Weir, Graham), 'Standing On The Moon' (Garcia, Hunter), 'Promised Land' (Chuck Berry), 'Hey Pocky Way' (Modeliste, Neville, Nocentelli, Porter Jr.), 'Crazy Fingers' (Garcia, Hunter), 'Cumberland Blues' (Garcia, Lesh, Hunter), 'Estimated Prophet' (Weir, Barlow), 'He's Gone' (Garcia, Hunter), 'Drums' (Hart, Kreutzmann), 'Space' (Garcia, Lesh, Mydland, Weir), 'I Need A Miracle' (Weir, Barlow), 'Wharf Rat' (Garcia, Hunter), 'Throwing Stones' (Weir, Barlow), 'Turn On Your Lovelight' (Scott, Malone), 'Knockin' On Heaven's Door' (Bob Dylan)

Knickerbocker Arena, Albany, New York, March 25, 1990
'Greatest Story Ever Told' (Weir, Hart, Hunter), 'Touch Of Grey' (Garcia, Hunter), 'Wang Dang Doodle' (Willie Dixon), 'Never Trust A Woman' (Mydland), 'Jack-A-Roe' (trad.), 'When I Paint My Masterpiece' (Bob Dylan), 'Bird Song' (Garcia, Hunter), 'Let It Grow' (Weir, Barlow), 'Eyes Of The World' (Garcia, Hunter), 'Samson And Delilah', 'Crazy Fingers' (Garcia, Hunter), 'Truckin'' (Garcia, Lesh, Weir, Hunter), 'Spoonful' (Willie Dixon), 'Drums' (Hart, Kreutzmann), 'Space' (Garcia, Lesh, Mydland, Weir), 'I Will Take You Home' (Mydland), 'Goin' Down The Road Feeling Bad' (trad.), 'Black Peter' (Garcia, Hunter), 'Around And Around' (Chuck Berry), 'Quinn The Eskimo' (Bob Dylan)

Nassau Coliseum, Uniondale, New York, March 28, 1990
'Cold Rain And Snow' (trad.), 'New Minglewood Blues' (trad.), 'Easy to Love You' (Mydland), 'High Time' (Garcia, Hunter), 'Queen Jane Approximately' (Bob Dylan), 'Loose Lucy' (Garcia, Hunter), 'Cassidy' (Weir, Barlow), 'Deal' (Garcia, Hunter), 'Foolish Heart' (Garcia, Hunter), 'Looks Like Rain' (Weir, Barlow), 'Cumberland Blues' (Garcia, Lesh, Hunter), 'The Weight' (Robbie Robertson), 'Hey Pocky Way' (Modeliste, Neville, Nocentelli, Porter), 'Drums' (Hart, Kreutzmann), 'Space' (Garcia, Lesh, Mydland, Weir), 'The Other One' (Weir, Kreutzmann), 'Wharf Rat' (Garcia, Hunter), 'Good Lovin'' (Clark, Resnick), 'Revolution' (Lennon, McCartney)

Nassau Coliseum, Uniondale, New York, March 29, 1990
'Jack Straw' (Weir, Hunter), 'Bertha' (Garcia, Hunter), 'We Can Run' (Mydland, Barlow), 'Ramble On Rose' (Garcia, Hunter), 'When I Paint My Masterpiece' (Bob Dylan), 'Bird Song' (Garcia, Hunter), 'Promised Land' (Chuck Berry), 'Eyes Of The World' (Garcia, Hunter), 'Estimated Prophet' (Weir, Barlow), 'Dark Star' (Garcia, Hart, Kreutzmann, Lesh, McKernan,

303

Weir, Hunter), 'Drums' (Hart, Kreutzmann), 'Space' (Garcia, Lesh, Mydland, Weir), 'Dark Star' (Garcia, Hart, Kreutzmann, Lesh, McKernan, Weir, Hunter), 'The Wheel' (Garcia, Hunter), 'Throwing Stones' (Weir, Barlow), 'Turn On Your Lovelight' (Scott, Malone), 'Knockin' On Heaven's Door' (Bob Dylan)

The Omni, Atlanta, Georgia, April 1, 1990
'Touch Of Grey' (Garcia, Hunter), 'Walkin' Blues' (Robert Johnson), 'Just A Little Light' (Mydland), 'Candyman' (Garcia, Hunter), 'Me And My Uncle' (John Phillips), 'Big River' (Johnny Cash), 'Althea' (Garcia, Hunter), 'Victim Or The Crime' (Weir, Graham), 'To Lay Me Down' (Garcia, Hunter), 'The Music Never Stopped' (Weir, Barlow), 'China Cat Sunflower' (Garcia, Hunter), 'I Know You Rider' (trad.), 'Ship Of Fools' (Garcia, Hunter), 'Man Smart, Woman Smarter' (Norman Span), 'Drums' (Hart, Kreutzmann), 'Space' (Garcia, Lesh, Mydland, Weir), 'Dear Mr. Fantasy' (Winwood, Wood, Capaldi), 'Hey Jude' (Lennon, McCartney), 'Truckin'' (Garcia, Lesh, Weir, Hunter), 'Stella Blue' (Garcia, Hunter), 'Sugar Magnolia' (Weir, Hunter), 'It's All Over Now, Baby Blue' (Bob Dylan)

The Omni, Atlanta, Georgia, April 3, 1990
'Shakedown Street' (Garcia, Hunter), 'Hell In A Bucket' (Weir, Mydland, Barlow), 'Sugaree' (Garcia, Hunter), 'We Can Run' (Mydland, Barlow), 'When I Paint My Masterpiece' (Bob Dylan), 'Row Jimmy' (Garcia), 'Picasso Moon' (Weir, Bralove, Barlow), 'Tennessee Jed' (Garcia, Hunter), 'Promised Land' (Chuck Berry), Estimated Prophet' (Weir, Barlow), 'Scarlet Begonias' (Garcia, Hunter), 'Crazy Fingers' (Garcia, Hunter), 'Playing In The Band' (Weir, Hart, Hunter), 'Drums' (Hart, Kreutzmann), 'Space' (Garcia, Lesh, Mydland, Weir), 'I Will Take You Home' (Mydland), 'Goin' Down The Road Feeling Bad' (trad.), 'Throwing Stones' (Weir, Barlow),'Not Fade Away' (Petty, Hardin), 'We Bid You Goodnight' (trad.)

Terrapin Station (Limited Edition) (1997)
Personnel:
Jerry Garcia: guitar, vocals
Mickey Hart: drums, percussion
Bill Kreutzmann: drums, percussion
Phil Lesh: bass, vocals
Brent Mydland: keyboards, vocals
Bob Weir: guitar, vocals
Recorded live at the Capital Centre in Landover, Maryland, on March 15, 1990. Recorded by John Cutler.
Release date: September 1997
Running time: 169:18
'Jack Straw' (Hunter, Weir), 'Sugaree' (Garcia, Hunter), 'Easy to Love You' (Barlow, Mydland), 'Walkin' Blues' (Robert Johnson), 'Althea' (Garcia, Hunter), 'Just Like Tom Thumb's Blues' (Bob Dylan), 'Tennessee Jed' (Garcia, Hunter), 'Cassidy' (Barlow, Weir), 'Don't Ease Me In' (trad.), 'China Cat Sunflower' (Garcia, Hunter), 'I Know You Rider' (trad.), 'Samson And Delilah' (trad.), 'Terrapin Station' (Garcia, Hunter), 'Mock Turtle Jam' (Grateful Dead), 'Drums' (Hart, Kreutzmann), 'And' (Bralove, Hart, Kreutzmann), 'Space' (Garcia, Lesh, Mydland, Weir), 'I Will Take You Home' (Mydland), 'Wharf Rat' (Garcia, Hunter), 'Throwing Stones' (Barlow, Weir), 'Not Fade Away' (Hardin, Petty), 'Revolution' (Lennon, McCartney)

Spring 1990 (2012)
Personnel:
Jerry Garcia: lead guitar, vocals

Mickey Hart: drums
Bill Kreutzmann: drums
Phil Lesh: electric bass, vocals
Brent Mydland: keyboards, vocals
Bob Weir: rhythm guitar, vocals
Recorded live on the Spring 1990 tour March 16-April 2, 1990. Produced for release by David Lemieux. Recorded by John Cutler
Release date: Aug 2012

Capital Centre, Landover, Maryland, March 16, 1990
'Let The Good Times Roll' (Sam Cooke), 'Touch Of Grey' (Garcia, Hunter), 'New Minglewood Blues' (trad.),'Peggy-O' (trad.), 'Queen Jane Approximately' (Bob Dylan), 'Loser' (Garcia, Hunter), 'Black-Throated Wind' (Weir, Barlow), 'Bird Song' (Garcia, Hunter), 'Blow Away' (Mydland, Barlow) 'Scarlet Begonias' (Garcia, Hunter), 'Estimated Prophet' (Weir, Barlow), 'Ship Of Fools' (Garcia, Hunter), 'Man Smart, Woman Smarter' (Norman Span), 'Jam' (Garcia, Hart, Kreutzmann, Lesh, Mydland, Weir), 'Drums' (Hart, Kreutzmann), 'Space' (Garcia, Lesh, Mydland, Weir), 'The Other One' (Weir, Kreutzmann), 'Stella Blue' (Garcia, Hunter), 'Sugar Magnolia' (Weir, Hunter), 'The Last Time' (Jagger, Richards)

Hartford Civic Center, Hartford, Connecticut, March 19, 1990
'Hell In A Bucket' (Weir, Mydland, Barlow), 'Bertha' (Garcia, Hunter), 'We Can Run' (Mydland, Barlow), 'Jack-A-Roe' (trad.), 'Picasso Moon' (Weir, Bralove, Barlow), 'Brown-Eyed Women' (Garcia, Hunter), 'It's All Over Now' (Womack, Womack), 'Deal' (Garcia, Hunter), 'Box Of Rain' (Lesh, Hunter), 'Foolish Heart' (Garcia, Hunter), 'Playing In The Band' (Weir, Hart, Hunter), 'Eyes Of The World' (Garcia, Hunter), 'Drums' (Hart, Kreutzmann), 'Space' (Garcia, Lesh, Mydland, Weir), 'China Doll' (Garcia, Hunter), 'Gimme Some Lovin'' (Winwood, Davis, Winwood), 'Goin' Down The Road Feeling Bad' (trad.), 'Around And Around' (Chuck Berry), 'Brokedown Palace' (Garcia, Hunter)

Copps Coliseum, Hamilton, Ontario, March 22, 1990
'Feel Like A Stranger' (Weir, Barlow), 'West L. A. Fadeaway' (Garcia, Hunter), 'Easy To Love You' (Mydland, Barlow), 'Beat It On Down The Line' (Jesse Fuller), 'It Must Have Been The Roses' (Hunter), 'The Last Time' (Jagger, Richards), 'Picasso Moon' (Weir, Bralove, Barlow), 'Don't Ease Me In' (trad.), 'Scarlet Begonias' (Garcia, Hunter), 'Fire On The Mountain' (Hart, Hunter), 'Samson And Delilah' (trad.), 'Believe It Or Not' (Garcia, Hunter), 'Truckin'' (Garcia, Lesh, Weir, Hunter), 'Drums' (Hart, Kreutzmann), 'Space' (Garcia, Lesh, Mydland, Weir) 'The Other One' (Weir, Kreutzmann), 'Hey Jude' (Lennon, McCartney), 'Dear Mr. Fantasy' (Winwood, Wood, Capaldi), 'Hey Jude' (Lennon, McCartney), Sugar Magnolia' (Weir, Hunter), 'It's All Over Now, Baby Blue' (Bob Dylan)

Knickerbocker Arena, Albany, New York, March 26, 1990
'Hell In A Bucket' (Weir, Mydland, Barlow), 'Dupree's Diamond Blues' (Garcia, Hunter), 'Just A Little Light' (Mydland, Barlow), 'Black-Throated Wind' (Weir, Barlow), 'Big Railroad Blues' (Noah Lewis), 'Picasso Moon' (Weir, Bralove, Barlow), 'Row Jimmy' (Garcia, Hunter), Blow Away' (Mydland, Barlow),'Built To Last' (Garcia, Hunter), Victim Or The Crime' (Weir, Graham), 'China Cat Sunflower' (Garcia, Hunter), 'I Know You Rider' (trad.), Man Smart, Woman Smarter' (Norman Span), 'Drums' (Hart, Kreutzmann), 'Space' (Garcia, Lesh, Mydland, Weir), 'I Need A Miracle' (Weir, Barlow), 'Dear Mr. Fantasy' (Winwood, Wood, Capaldi), 'Gimme Some Lovin'' (Winwood, Davis, Winwood), 'Morning Dew' (Dobson, Rose), 'Brokedown Palace' (Garcia, Hunter), [Bonus tracks recorded at the Knickerbocker Arena on March 24, 1990]: 'Let The Good Times Roll' (Sam Cooke), 'Help On The Way' (Garcia, Hunter), 'Slipknot!' (Garcia, Godchaux, Kreutzmann, Lesh, Weir), 'Franklin's Tower' (Garcia, Kreutzmann, Hunter), 'Loser' (Garcia, Hunter), 'Tennessee Jed' (Garcia, Hunter)

Nassau Coliseum, Uniondale, New York, March 30, 1990
'Help On The Way' (Garcia, Hunter), 'Slipknot!' (Garcia, Godchaux, Kreutzmann, Lesh, Weir), 'Franklin's Tower' (Garcia, Kreutzmann, Hunter), 'Little Red Rooster' (Willie Dixon), 'Dire Wolf' (Garcia, Hunter), 'It's All Over Now' (Womack, Womack), 'Just Like Tom Thumb's Blues' (Bob Dylan), 'Picasso Moon' (Weir, Bralove, Barlow), 'Don't Ease Me In' (trad.), 'Iko Iko' (James Crawford), 'Playing In The Band' (Weir, Hart, Hunter), 'China Doll' (Garcia, Hunter), 'Uncle John's Band' (Garcia, Hunter), 'Terrapin Station' (Garcia, Hunter), 'Drums' (Hart, Kreutzmann), 'Space' (Garcia, Lesh, Mydland, Weir), 'I Need A Miracle' (Weir, Barlow), 'Gimme Some Lovin'' (Winwood, Davis, Winwood), 'Standing On The Moon' (Garcia, Hunter), 'Not Fade Away' (Petty, Hardin), 'Attics Of My Life' (Garcia, Hunter)

The Omni, Atlanta, Georgia. April 2, 1990
'Feel Like A Stranger' (Weir, Barlow), 'Mississippi Half-Step Uptown Toodeloo' (Garcia, Hunter), 'The Weight' (Robbie Robertson), 'Queen Jane Approximately' (Bob Dylan), 'Easy To Love You' (Mydland, Barlow), 'Brown-Eyed Women' (Garcia, Hunter), 'Let It Grow' (Weir, Barlow), 'Foolish Heart' (Garcia, Hunter), 'Looks Like Rain' (Weir, Barlow), 'He's Gone' (Garcia, Hunter), 'The Last Time' (Jagger, Richards), 'Drums' (Hart, Kreutzmann), 'Space' (Garcia, Lesh, Mydland, Weir), 'The Other One' (Weir, Kreutzmann), 'Death Don't Have No Mercy' (Rev. Gary Davis), Around And Around' (Chuck Berry), 'Good Lovin'' (Resnick, Clark), 'Black Muddy River' (Garcia, Hunter)

Dozin' At The Knick (1996)

Personnel:
Jerry Garcia: guitar, vocals
Mickey Hart: drums
Bill Kreutzmann: drums
Phil Lesh: bass guitar
Brent Mydland: keyboards, vocals
Bob Weir: guitar, vocals
Recorded live at the Knickerbocker Arena in Albany, New York, on March 24 – 26, 1990.
Produced by John Cutler and Phil Lesh.
Release date: October 1996
'Hell In A Bucket' (Barlow, Mydland, Weir), 'Dupree's Diamond Blues' (Garcia, Hunter), 'Just A Little Light' (Barlow, Mydland), 'Walkin' Blues' (Robert Johnson), 'Jack-A-Roe' (trad.), 'Never Trust A Woman' (Mydland), 'When I Paint My Masterpiece' (Bob Dylan), 'Row Jimmy' (Garcia, Hunter), 'Blow Away' (Barlow, Mydland), 'Playing In The Band' (Hunter, Hart, Weir), 'Uncle John's Band' (Garcia, Hunter), 'Lady With A Fan' (Garcia, Hunter), 'Terrapin Station' (Garcia, Hunter), 'Mud Love Buddy Jam' (Grateful Dead), 'Drums' (Hart, Kreutzmann), 'Space' (Garcia, Lesh, Weir), 'Space' (Garcia, Lesh, Weir), 'The Wheel' (Garcia, Hunter), 'All Along The Watchtower' (Bob Dylan), 'Stella Blue' (Garcia, Hunter), 'Not Fade Away' (Holly, Petty), 'And We Bid You Goodnight' (trad.), 'Space' (Garcia, Lesh, Mydland, Weir), 'I Will Take You Home' (Mydland), 'Goin' Down The Road Feeling Bad' (trad.), 'Black Peter' (Garcia, Hunter), 'Around And Around' (Chuck Berry), 'Brokedown Palace' (Garcia, Hunter)

Wake Up to Find Out (2014)

Personnel:
Jerry Garcia: lead guitar, vocals
Mickey Hart: drums
Bill Kreutzmann: drums
Phil Lesh: electric bass, vocals

Brent Mydland: keyboards, vocals
Bob Weir: rhythm guitar, vocals
Additional personnel:
Branford Marsalis: Saxophone on 'Bird Song', second set and encore.
Recorded live at Nassau Coliseum in Uniondale, New York, on March 29, 1990. Produced for release by David Lemieux.
Release date: September 2014
Running time: 152:06
'Jack Straw' (Weir, Hunter), 'Bertha' (Garcia, Hunter), 'We Can Run' (Mydland, Barlow), 'Ramble On Rose' (Garcia, Hunter), 'When I Paint My Masterpiece' (Bob Dylan), 'Bird Song' (Garcia, Hunter), 'Promised Land' (Chuck Berry), 'Eyes Of The World' (Garcia, Hunter), 'Estimated Prophet' (Weir, Barlow), 'Dark Star' (Garcia, Hart, Kreutzmann, Lesh, McKernan, Weir, Hunter), 'Drums' (Hart, Kreutzmann), 'Space' (Garcia, Lesh, Weir), 'Dark Star' (Garcia, Hart, Kreutzmann, Lesh, McKernan, Weir, Hunter), 'The Wheel' (Garcia, Hunter, Kreutzmann), 'Throwing Stones' (Weir, Barlow), 'Turn On Your Lovelight' (Scott, Malone), 'Knockin' On Heaven's Door' (Bob Dylan)

View From The Vault Vol. 3 (2002)

Personnel:
Jerry Garcia: lead guitar, vocals
Mickey Hart: drums, percussion
Bill Kreutzmann: drums, percussion
Phil Lesh: bass guitar, vocals
Brent Mydland: Hammond organ, keyboards, vocals
Bob Weir: rhythm guitar, vocals
Recorded live at the Shoreline Amphitheatre in Mountain View, California, on June 16, 1990. Recorded by Dan Healy.
Release date: August 2002
Running time: 202:46
Let The Good Times Roll' (Sam Cooke), 'Truckin'' (Hunter, Garcia, Lesh, Weir), 'Touch Of Grey' (Garcia, Hunter), 'Mama Tried' (Merle Haggard), 'Big River' (Johnny Cash), 'Friend Of The Devil' (Dawson, Hunter, Garcia), 'Cassidy' (Barlow, Weir), 'Big Boss Man' (Dixon, Smith), 'One More Saturday Night' (Weir), 'China Cat Sunflower' (Garcia, Hunter), 'I Know You Rider' (trad.), 'We Can Run' (Barlow, Mydland), 'Estimated Prophet' (Barlow, Weir), 'Terrapin Station' (Garcia, Hunter), 'Jam' (Grateful Dead), 'Space' (Grateful Dead), 'Drums' (Hart, Kreutzmann), 'China Doll' (Garcia, Hunter), 'Sugar Magnolia' (Hunter, Weir), 'It's All Over Now, Baby Blue' (Bob Dylan), [Bonus tracks recorded at Shoreline Amphitheatre on October 3, 1987]: 'Hey Pocky Way' (Modeliste, Neville, Nocentelli, Porter), 'New Minglewood Blues' (Noah Lewis), 'Candyman' (Garcia, Hunter), 'When I Paint My Masterpiece' (Bob Dylan), 'West L.A. Fadeaway' (Garcia, Hunter), 'My Brother Esau' (Barlow, Weir)

View From The Vault (2000)

Personnel:
Jerry Garcia: lead guitar, vocals
Mickey Hart: drums, percussion
Bill Kreutzmann: drums, percussion
Phil Lesh: bass guitar, vocals
Brent Mydland: Hammond organ, keyboards, vocals

Bob Weir: rhythm guitar, vocals
Recorded live at Three Rivers Stadium in Pittsburgh on July 8, 1990, on July 8, 1990.
Recorded by Dan Healy.
Release date: June 2000
Running time: 211:16
'Touch Of Grey' (Garcia, Hunter), 'Greatest Story Ever Told' (Hunter, Hart, Weir), 'Jack-A-Roe' (trad.), 'New Minglewood Blues' (trad.), 'Row Jimmy' (Garcia, Hunter), 'Mama Tried' (Merle Haggard), 'Mexicali Blues' (Barlow, Weir), 'Just Like Tom Thumb's Blues' (Bob Dylan), 'Let It Grow' (Barlow, Weir), 'Samson And Delilah' (trad.), 'Eyes Of The World' (Garcia, Hunter), 'Estimated Prophet' (Barlow, Weir), 'Terrapin Station' (Garcia, Hunter), 'Jam' (Grateful Dead), 'Drums' (Hart, Kreutzmann), 'Space' (Garcia, Lesh, Weir), 'I Need A Miracle' (Barlow, Weir), 'Wang Dang Doodle' (Willie Dixon), 'Black Peter' (Garcia, Hunter), 'Throwing Stones' (Barlow, Weir), 'Turn On Your Lovelight' (Malone, Scott), 'Knockin' On Heaven's Door' (Bob Dylan), [Bonus tracks from July 6, 1990]: 'Standing On the Moon' (Garcia, Hunter), 'He's Gone' (Garcia, Hunter), 'KY Jam' (Grateful Dead)

Dave's Picks Vol. 40 (2021)

Personnel:
Jerry Garcia: guitar, vocals
Mickey Hart: drums
Bill Kreutzmann: drums
Phil Lesh: bass, vocals
Brent Mydland: keyboards, vocals
Bob Weir: guitar, vocals
Recorded live at Deer Creek Music Center in Noblesville, Indiana, on July 18 and 19, 1990.
Recorded by Dan Healy.
Release date: October 2021
Running time: 309:26
'Help On The Way' (Garcia, Hunter), 'Slipknot!' (Garcia, Godchaux, Kreutzmann, Lesh, Weir), 'Franklin's Tower' (Garcia, Kreutzmann, Hunter), 'New Minglewood Blues' (trad.), 'Easy To Love You' (Mydland, Barlow), 'Peggy-O' (trad.), 'When I Paint My Masterpiece' (Bob Dylan), 'Brown-Eyed Women' (Garcia, Hunter), 'Cassidy' (Weir, Barlow), 'Deal' (Garcia, Hunter), 'China Cat Sunflower' (Garcia, Hunter), I Know You Rider' (trad.), 'Looks Like Rain' (Weir, Barlow), 'Terrapin Station' (Garcia, Hunter), 'Jam' (Grateful Dead), 'Drums' (Hart, Kreutzmann), 'Space' (Garcia, Lesh, Weir) , 'The Other One' (Weir, Kreutzmann), 'Morning Dew' (Dobson, Rose), 'The Weight' (Robbie Robertson), [Following from July 19, 1990]: 'Jack Straw' (Weir, Hunter), 'They Love Each Other' (Garcia, Hunter), 'Desolation Row' (Bob Dylan), 'Row Jimmy' (Garcia, Hunter), 'Picasso Moon' (Weir, Barlow, Bralove), 'Althea' (Garcia, Hunter), 'Promised Land' (Chuck Berry), 'Victim Or The Crime' (Weir, Graham), 'Foolish Heart' (Garcia, Hunter), 'Playing In The Band' (Weir, Hart, Hunter), 'China Doll' (Garcia, Hunter), 'Uncle John's Band' (Garcia, Hunter), 'Drums' (Hart, Kreutzmann), 'Space' (Garcia, Lesh, Weir), 'All Along The Watchtower' (Bob Dylan), 'Black Peter' (Garcia, Hunter), 'Not Fade Away' (Petty, Hardin)

Dick's Picks Vol.9 (1997)

Personnel:
Jerry Garcia: lead guitar, vocals
Mickey Hart: drums, percussion
Bruce Hornsby: accordion, piano, synthesiser, vocals

Bill Kreutzmann: drums, percussion
Phil Lesh: bass guitar, vocals
Bob Weir: rhythm guitar, vocals
Vince Welnick: keyboards, vocals
Recorded live at Madison Square Garden, New York City, on September 16, 1990. Recorded by Dan Healy.
Release date: October 1997
Running time: 179:48
'Hell In A Bucket' (Weir, Mydland, Barlow), 'Cold Rain And Snow' (trad.), 'Little Red Rooster' (Willie Dixon), 'Stagger Lee' (Garcia, Hunter), 'Queen Jane Approximately' (Bob Dylan), 'Tennessee Jed' (Garcia, Hunter), 'Cassidy' (Weir, Barlow), 'Deal' (Garcia, Hunter), 'Samson And Delilah' (trad.), 'Iko Iko' (James Crawford), 'Looks Like Rain' (Weir, Barlow), 'He's Gone' (Garcia, Hunter), 'No MSG Jam' (Grateful Dead), 'Drums' (Kreutzmann, Hart), 'Space' (Grateful Dead), 'Standing On The Moon' (Garcia, Hunter), 'Lunatic Preserve' (Grateful Dead), 'I Need A Miracle' (Weir, Barlow), 'Morning Dew' (Dobson, Rose), 'It's All Over Now, Baby Blue' (Bob Dylan)

Road Trips Vol.2 No. 1 (2008)

Personnel:
Jerry Garcia: lead guitar, vocals
Mickey Hart: drums
Bruce Hornsby: piano, accordion, vocals
Bill Kreutzmann: drums
Phil Lesh: electric bass, vocals
Bob Weir: rhythm guitar, vocals
Vince Welnick: keyboards, vocals
Recorded live at Madison Square Garden, New York City on September 18 – 20, 1990. Recorded by Dan Healy.
Release date: December 2008
Running time: 154:54
'Truckin'' (Garcia, Lesh, Weir, Hunter), 'China Cat Sunflower' (Garcia, Hunter), 'I Know You Rider' (trad.), 'Playing In The Band' (Weir, Hart, Hunter), 'Ship Of Fools' (Garcia, Hunter), 'Playing In The Band' (Weir, Hart, Hunter), 'Uncle John's Band' (Garcia, Hunter), 'Let it Grow' (Weir, Barlow), 'Jam' (Grateful Dead), 'Jam' (Grateful Dead), 'Dark Star' (Garcia, Hart, Kreutzmann, Lesh, McKernan, Weir, Hunter), 'Playing In The Band' (Weir, Hart, Hunter), 'Dark Star' (Garcia, Hart, Kreutzmann, Lesh, McKernan, Weir, Hunter), 'Throwing Stones' (Weir, Barlow), 'Touch Of Grey' (Garcia, Hunter), 'Turn On Your Love Light' (Scott, Malone), 'Knockin' On Heaven's Door' (Bob Dylan), [Bonus Disc: recorded on September 18, 1990]: 'Mississippi Half-Step Uptown Toodeloo' (Garcia, Hunter), 'Picasso Moon' (Weir, Barlow, Bralove), 'To Lay Me Down' (Garcia, Hunter), 'Eyes Of The World' (Garcia, Hunter), 'Estimated Prophet' (Weir, Barlow), 'Foolish Heart' (Garcia, Hunter), 'Jam' (Grateful Dead)

1991
View From The Vault, Vol, 2 (2001)

Personnel:
Jerry Garcia: lead guitar, vocals
Mickey Hart: drums, percussion
Bruce Hornsby: accordion, piano, synthesizer, vocals
Bill Kreutzmann: drums, percussion

Phil Lesh: bass guitar, vocals
Brent Mydland: keyboards, vocals (July 12, 1990, bonus material)
Bob Weir: rhythm guitar, vocals
Vince Welnick: keyboards, vocals
Recorded live at Robert F. Kennedy Stadium in Washington, D.C on June 14 1991. Recorded by Dan Healy.
Release date: June 2001
Running time: 207:44
'Cold Rain And Snow' (trad.), 'Wang Dang Doodle' (Willie Dixon), 'Jack-A-Roe' (trad.), 'Big River' (Johnny Cash), 'Maggie's Farm' (Bob Dylan), 'Row Jimmy' (Garcia, Hunter), 'Black-Throated Wind' (Barlow, Weir), 'Tennessee Jed' (Garcia, Hunter), 'The Music Never Stopped' (Barlow, Weir), 'Help On The Way' (Garcia, Hunter), 'Slipknot!' (Grateful Dead), 'Franklin's Tower' (Hunter, Garcia, Kreutzmann), 'Estimated Prophet' (Barlow, Weir), 'Dark Star' (Hunter, Garcia, Mickey Hart, Kreutzmann, Lesh, McKernan, Weir), 'Drums' (Hart, Kreutzmann), 'Space' (Garcia, Lesh, Weir), 'Stella Blue' (Garcia, Hunter), 'Turn On Your Love Light' (Malone, Scott), 'It's All Over Now, Baby Blue' (Bob Dylan) [Bonus tracks from Robert F. Kennedy Stadium, July 12, 1990]: 'Victim Or The Crime' (Graham, Weir), 'Foolish Heart' (Garcia, Hunter), 'Dark Star' (Hunter, Garcia, Hart, Kreutzmann, Lesh, McKernan, Weir)

Saint Of Circumstance (2019)

Personnel:
Jerry Garcia: guitar, vocals
Mickey Hart: drums
Bruce Hornsby: keyboards, vocals
Bill Kreutzmann: drums
Phil Lesh: bass, vocals
Bob Weir: guitar, vocals
Vince Welnick: keyboards, vocals
Recorded live at Giants Stadium in East Rutherford, New Jersey, on June 17, 1991. Produced for release by David Lemieux.
Release date: September 2019
'Eyes Of The World' (Garcia, Hunter), 'Walkin' Blues' (Johnson), 'Brown-Eyed Women' (Garcia, Hunter), 'Dark Star' (Garcia, Hart, Kreutzmann, Lesh, McKernan, Weir, Hunter), 'When I Paint My Masterpiece' (Bob Dylan), 'Loose Lucy' (Garcia, Hunter), 'Cassidy' (Weir, Barlow), 'Might As Well' (Garcia, Hunter), 'Saint Of Circumstance' (Weir, Barlow), 'Ship Of Fools' (Garcia, Hunter), Dark Star' (Garcia, Hart, Kreutzmann, Lesh, McKernan, Weir, Hunter), 'Truckin'' (Garcia, Lesh, Weir, Hunter), 'New Speedway Boogie' (Garcia, Hunter), 'Dark Star' (Garcia, Hart, Kreutzmann, Lesh, McKernan, Weir, Hunter), 'Uncle John's Band' (Garcia, Hunter), 'Dark Star' (Garcia, Hart, Kreutzmann, Lesh, McKernan, Weir, Hunter), 'Drums' (Hart, Kreutzmann), 'Space' (Garcia, Lesh, Weir), 'China Doll' (Garcia, Hunter), 'Playing In The Band' (Weir, Hart, Hunter), 'Sugar Magnolia' (Weir, Hunter), 'The Weight' (Robbie Robertson)

Download Series Vol. 11 (2006)

Personnel:
Jerry Garcia: lead guitar, vocals
Mickey Hart: drums, percussion
Bruce Hornsby: piano, accordion, vocals
Bill Kreutzmann: drums, percussion

Phil Lesh: electric bass
Bob Weir: rhythm guitar, vocals
Vince Welnick: keyboards, vocals
Recorded live at the Pine Knob Music Theatre in Clarkston, Michigan, on June 20, 1991.
Mastering by Jeffrey Norman.
Release date: March 2006
Running time: 215:30
'Touch Of Grey' (Garcia, Hunter), 'Greatest Story Ever Told' (Weir, Hart, Hunter), 'Peggy-O'
(trad.), 'Mexicali Blues' (Weir, Barlow), 'Maggie's Farm' (Bob Dylan), 'Bird Song' (Garcia,
Hunter), 'Scarlet Begonias' (Garcia, Hunter) [Bonus track recorded at Pine Knob Music
Theatre June 19, 1991], 'Fire On The Mountain' (Hart, Hunter) [Bonus tracks recorded
at Pine Knob Music Theatre June 19, 1991], 'Throwing Stones' (Weir, Barlow), 'Iko Iko'
(Crawford, Hawkins, Hawkins, Johnson), 'All Along The Watchtower' (Bob Dylan), 'Standing
On The Moon' (Garcia, Hunter), 'He's Gone' (Garcia, Hunter), 'Rhythm Devils' (Hart,
Kreutzmann), 'Space' (Garcia, Lesh, Weir), 'The Wheel' (Garcia, Hunter), 'I Need A Miracle'
(Weir, Barlow), 'Wharf Rat' (Garcia, Hunter), 'Throwing Stones' (Weir, Barlow), 'Not Fade
Away' (Petty, Hardin), 'Brokedown Palace' (Garcia, Hunter), [Bonus tracks recorded at Pine
Knob Music Theatre June 19, 1991]: 'Stella Blue' (Garcia, Hunter), 'The Other One' (Weir,
Kreutzmann), 'Johnny B. Goode' (Chuck Berry)

Dick's Picks Vol.17 (2000)

Personnel:
Jerry Garcia: lead guitar, vocals
Mickey Hart: drums
Bruce Hornsby: keyboard, accordion, vocals
Bill Kreutzmann: drums
Phil Lesh: bass, vocals
Bob Weir: rhythm guitar, vocals
Vince Welnick: keyboards, vocals
Recorded live at Boston Garden in Boston, Massachusetts, on September 25, 1991.
Additional tracks from March 31, 1991. Recorded by Dan Healy.
Release date: April 2000
Running time: 194:11
'Help On The Way' (Garcia, Hunter), 'Slipknot!' (Garcia, Godchaux, Kreutzmann, Lesh,
Weir), 'Franklin's Tower' (Garcia, Hunter, Kreutzmann), 'Walkin' Blues' (Robert Johnson),
'It Must Have Been The Roses' (Hunter), 'Dire Wolf' (Garcia, Hunter), 'Queen Jane
Approximately' (Bob Dylan), 'Tennessee Jed' (Garcia, Hunter), 'The Music Never Stopped'
(Barlow, Weir), 'Victim Or The Crime' (Graham, Weir), 'Crazy Fingers' (Garcia, Hunter),
'Playing In The Band' (Hart, Hunter, Weir), 'Terrapin Station' (Garcia, Hunter), 'Boston Clam
Jam' (Grateful Dead), Drums (Hart, Kreutzmann), 'Space' (Grateful Dead), 'That Would
Be Something' (Paul McCartney), 'Playing In The Band' (Hart, Hunter, Weir), 'China Doll'
(Garcia, Hunter), 'Throwing Stones' (Barlow, Weir), 'Not Fade Away' (Holly, Petty), 'The
Mighty Quinn (Quinn The Eskimo)' (Bob Dylan), [Bonus tracks from March 31, 1991]:
'Samson And Delilah' (trad.), 'Eyes Of The World' (Garcia, Hunter)

1992
Dick's Picks Vol 27 (2003)

Personnel:
Jerry Garcia: guitar, vocals

Mickey Hart: drums, percussion
Bill Kreutzmann: drums, percussion
Phil Lesh: electric bass guitar, vocals
Bob Weir: guitar, vocals
Vince Welnick: keyboards, vocals
Recorded live at the Oakland Coliseum Arena in Oakland, California, on December 16, 1992.
Recorded by Dan Healy.
Release date: January 2003
Running time: 196:21
'Feel Like A Stranger' (Barlow, Weir), 'Brown-Eyed Women' (Garcia, Hunter), 'The Same Thing' (Willie Dixon), 'Loose Lucy' (Garcia, Hunter), 'Stuck Inside Of Mobile With The Memphis Blues Again' (Bob Dylan), 'Row Jimmy' (Garcia, Hunter), 'Let It Grow' (Barlow, Weir), 'Shakedown Street' (Garcia, Hunter), 'Samson And Delilah' (trad.), 'Ship Of Fools' (Garcia, Hunter), 'Playing In The Band' (Hunter, Mickey Hart, Weir), 'Drums' (Hart, Kreutzmann), 'Space' (Garcia, Phil Lesh, Weir), 'Dark Star' (Hunter, Garcia, Hart, Kreutzmann, Lesh, Pigpen, Weir), 'All Along The Watchtower' (Bob Dylan), 'Stella Blue' (Garcia, Hunter), 'Good Lovin'' (Resnick, Clark), 'Casey Jones' (Garcia, Hunter) [Bonus tracks from December 17, 1992]: 'Throwing Stones' (Barlow, Weir), 'Not Fade Away' (Holly, Petty), 'Baba O'Riley' (Pete Townshend), 'Tomorrow Never Knows' (Lennon, McCartney)

1993
Road Trips Vol.2 No. 4 (2009)
Personnel:
Jerry Garcia: lead guitar, vocals
Mickey Hart: drums
Bill Kreutzmann: drums
Phil Lesh: electric bass, vocals
Bob Weir: rhythm guitar, vocals
Vince Welnick: keyboards, vocals
Recorded live at the Cal Expo Amphitheatre in Sacramento, California, on May 26 – 27, 1993.
Compilation produced by David Lemieux and Blair Jackson.
Release date: August 2009
Running time: 152:06
'Samson And Delilah' (trad.), 'Here Comes Sunshine' (Garcia, Hunter), 'Walkin' Blues' (trad.), 'Deal' (Garcia, Hunter), 'Box Of Rain' (Lesh, Hunter), 'Victim Or The Crime' (Weir, Graham), 'Crazy Fingers' (Garcia, Hunter), 'Playing In The Band' (Hart, Weir, Hunter), 'Rhythm Devils' (Hart, Kreutzmann), 'Corrina' (Hart, Weir, Hunter), 'Playing In The Band' (Hart, Weir, Hunter), 'China Doll' (Garcia, Hunter), 'Around And Around' (Chuck Berry), 'Liberty' (Garcia, Hunter), 'Shakedown Street' (Garcia, Hunter), 'The Same Thing' (Willie Dixon), 'Dire Wolf' (Garcia, Hunter), 'High Time' (Garcia, Hunter), 'When I Paint My Masterpiece' (Bob Dylan). [Bonus Disc recorded May 26 – 27 1993]: 'Picasso Moon' (Weir, Barlow, Bralove), 'Fire On The Mountain' (Hart, Hunter), 'Cassidy' (Weir, Barlow), 'Uncle John's Band' (Garcia, Hunter), 'Cassidy' (Weir, Barlow), 'Gloria' (Van Morrison), 'Broken Arrow' (Robbie Robertson), 'Ramble On Rose' (Garcia, Hunter), 'Stuck Inside Of Mobile With The Memphis Blues Again' (Dylan)

Appendix Three – Collections with unreleased material from different years by release date

Fallout from the Phil Zone (1997)
Personnel:
Tom Constanten: organ
Jerry Garcia: lead guitar, vocals
Keith Godchaux: keyboards
Mickey Hart: drums
Bill Kreutzmann: drums
Phil Lesh: bass guitar, vocals
Ron 'Pigpen' McKernan: harmonica, organ, vocals
Brent Mydland: keyboards, vocals
Bob Weir: rhythm guitar, vocals
Vince Welnick: keyboards
Recorded live 1967 -1995. Produced by Phil Lesh and John Cutler
Release date: June 1997
Running time: 2:03:52
'Dancing In The Street' (Gaye, I. J. Hunter, Stevenson) 'New Speedway Boogie' (Hunter,
Garcia), 'Viola Lee Blues' (Noah Lewis), 'Easy Wind' (Hunter), 'Mason's Children' (Hunter,
Garcia, Lesh, Weir), 'Hard To Handle' (Isbell, Jones, Redding), 'The Music Never Stopped'
(Barlow, Weir), 'Jack-A-Roe' (trad.), 'In The Midnight Hour' (Cropper, Pickett), 'Visions Of
Johanna' (Bob Dylan), 'Box Of Rain' (Hunter, Lesh)

So Many Roads (1965-1990) (1999)
Personnel:
Jerry Garcia: lead guitar, vocals (1965-1995)
Bill Kreutzmann: drums (1965-1995)
Phil Lesh: bass guitar, vocals (1965-1995)
Bob Weir: guitar, vocals (1965-1995)
Ron 'Pigpen' McKernan: keyboards, harmonica, vocals (1965-Jul 17 1972)
Mickey Hart: drums (Sept 29, 1967-Feb 18, 1971; Oct 20 1974-1995)
Tom Constanten: keyboards (Nov 23, 1968-Jan 30, 1970)
Keith Godchaux: keyboards, vocals (Oct 19, 1971-Feb 17 1979)
Donna Jean Godchaux: vocals (Dec 31,1971-Feb 17 1979)
Brent Mydland: keyboards, vocals (Apr 22, 1979-Jul 23, 1990)
Vince Welnick: keyboards, vocals (Sept 7 1990-1995)
Bruce Hornsby: piano, accordion, vocals (Sept 15, 1990-Mar 24, 1992)
Ned Lagin: keyboards (on 'Beautiful Jam' and 'Dark Star Jam'
Recorded at various locations 1965-1995
Release date: November 1999
Running time: 386:22
'Can't Come Down' (Grateful Dead), 'Caution (Do Not Step On Tracks' (Grateful Dead)
[Studio recordings, November 3 1965], 'You Don't Have To Ask' (Grateful Dead) [Live,
Fillmore Auditorium, San Francisco July 16 1966], 'On The Road Again' (trad.) [Live,
Los Angeles, March 12 1966], 'Cream Puff War' (Garcia) [Live, Fillmore Auditorium, San
Francisco July 16 1966], 'I Know You Rider' (trad.) [Live, Avalon Ballroom, San Francisco,
1966], 'The Same Thing' (Willie Dixon) [Live, Winterland Arena, San Francisco, March

18 1967], 'Dark Star>China Cat Sunflower>The Eleven' (Grateful Dead, Hunter) [Live, Carousel Ballroom, San Francisco, March 16 1968], 'Clementine' (Lesh, Hunter) [Live, Crystal Ballroom, Portland, Oregon, February 2 1968], 'Mason's Children' (Garcia, Hunter) ['*Workingman's Dead*' studio outtake, Feb 1970], 'To Lay Me Down' (Garcia, Hunter) ['*American Beauty*' studio outtake, Summer 1970], 'That's It For The Other One' (Grateful Dead) [Live, Fillmore West, San Francisco, February 27, 1969], 'Beautiful Jam' (Grateful Dead) [Live, Capitol Theatre, Port Chester, New York, February 18 1971], 'Chinatown Shuffle' (McKernan) [Live, Civic Hall, Rotterdam, The Netherlands May 11 1972], 'Sing Me Back Home' (Merle Haggard) [Live, County Fairgrounds, Veneta, Oregon August 27 1972], 'Watkins Glen Soundcheck Jam' (Grateful Dead) [Live, Grand Prix Race Course, Watkins Glen, New York, July 27 1973], 'Dark Star Jam' (Grateful Dead) 'Spanish Jam' (Grateful Dead) 'US Blues' (Garcia, Hunter) [Live, Jai Alai Fronton, Miami, June 23 1974], 'Eyes Of The World' (Garcia, Hunter) [Live, Winterland Arena, San Francisco, October 19 1974], 'The Wheel' (Garcia, Hunter) [Live, Auditorium Theater, Chicago, Illinois, June 29 1976], 'Stella Blue' (Garcia, Hunter) [Live, Rupp Arena, Lexington, Kentucky April 21 1978], 'Estimated Prophet' (Barlow, Weir) [Live, Red Rocks Amphitheatre, Morrison, Colorado, August 12 1979], 'The Music Never Stopped' (Barlow, Weir) [Live, Warfield Theatre, San Francisco, October 14 1980], 'Shakedown Street' (Garcia, Hunter) [Live, San Francisco Civic Auditorium, San Francisco, December 31 1984], 'Cassidy' (Weir, Barlow) [Live, Meadowlands Arena, East Rutherford, New Jersey November 10 1985], 'Hey Pocky Way' (Modeliste, Neville, Nocentelli, Porter) [Live, Greensboro Coliseum, Greensboro, North Carolina, March 31 1989], 'Believe It Or Not' (Garcia, Hunter) ['*Built To Last*' studio outtake, 1989], 'Playing In The Band' (Hart, Hunter, Weir) [Live, Laguna Seca, Monterey, California, July 29 1988], 'Gentlemen Start Your Engines' (Barlow, Mydland) ['*Built To Last*' studio outtake, 1989], 'Death Don't Have No Mercy' (Rev. Gary Davis) [Live, Shoreline Amphitheatre, Mountain View, California, September 29 1989], 'Scarlet Begonias' (Garcia, Hunter) 'Fire On The Mountain' (Hart, Hunter) [Live, Copps Coliseum, Hamilton, Ontario, March 22 1990], 'Bird Song' (Garcia, Hunter) [Live, Nassau Coliseum, Uniondale, New York, March 29 1990], 'Jam Out Of Terrapin' (Grateful Dead) [Live, Richfield Coliseum, Richfield Township, Ohio, August 8 1990], 'Terrapin Station' (Garcia, Hunter) [Live, Madison Square Gardens, New York, September 12 1991], 'Jam Out Of Foolish Heart' (Grateful Dead) [Live, Madison Square Gardens, New York, September 18 1990], 'Way To Go Home' (Bralove, Hunter, Welnick) [Live, The Palace, Auburn Hills, Michigan, July 31 1994], 'Liberty' (Garcia, Hunter), [Live, The Omni, Atlanta, Georgia, March 30 1994] 'Lazy River Road' (Garcia, Hunter), 'Eternity' (Dixon, Wasserman, Weir) [Studio rehearsals for unfinished studio album, February 18 1993], 'Jam Into Days Between' (Grateful Dead) [Studio rehearsals for unfinished studio album, February 9 1993], 'Days Between' (Garcia, Hunter), [Studio rehearsals for unfinished studio album, February 18 1993], 'Whiskey In The Jar' (trad.) [Studio rehearsals for unfinished studio album February 16 1993], 'So Many Roads' (Garcia, Hunter) [Live, Soldier Field, Chicago, Illinois, July 9 1995]

Postcards Of The Hanging (2002)

Personnel:
Jerry Garcia: lead guitar, vocals
Bob Weir: rhythm guitar, vocals
Phil Lesh: bass guitar, vocals
Brent Mydland: keyboards, organ, vocals (except track 6)
Mickey Hart: drums
Bill Kreutzmann: drums

Keith Godchaux: piano (track 6)
Additional personnel:
Dickey Betts: guitar (track 6)
Bob Dylan: acoustic guitar, vocals (track 11)
Butch Trucks: drums (track 6)
Recorded live at various venues 1973-1990. Track 11 from Dylan And The Dead tour
rehearsal, June 1987. Engineered by John Cutler and Bill Candelario
Release date: March 2002
Running time: 75:39
'When I Paint My Masterpiece' (Bob Dylan), 'She Belongs to Me' (Bob Dylan), 'Just Like Tom
Thumb's Blues' (Bob Dylan), 'Maggie's Farm' (Bob Dylan), 'Stuck Inside Of Mobile With The
Memphis Blues' Again (Bob Dylan), 'It Takes a Lot to Laugh, It Takes a Train to Cry' (Bob
Dylan), 'Ballad Of A Thin Man' (Bob Dylan), 'Desolation Row' (Bob Dylan), 'All Along The
Watchtower' (Bob Dylan), 'It's All Over Now, Baby Blue' (Bob Dylan), 'Man Of Peace' (Bob
Dylan), 'Queen Jane Approximately' [bonus track] (Bob Dylan), 'Quinn the Eskimo (Mighty
Quinn)' [bonus track] (Bob Dylan)

30 Trips Around The Sun (2015)
Personnel
Jerry Garcia: guitar, vocals
Bob Weir: guitar, vocals
Ron 'Pigpen' McKernan: organ, harmonica, percussion, vocals
Bill Kreutzmann: drums
Phil Lesh: bass, vocals
Mickey Hart: drums
Tom Constanten: keyboards
Keith Godchaux: keyboards
Donna Jean Godchaux: vocals
Brent Mydland: keyboards, vocals
Vince Welnick: keyboards, vocals
Additional musicians
Bruce Hornsby: piano, vocals
Branford Marsalis: saxophone
Ned Lagin: synthesizer
Matt Kelly: guitar
Release date: October 2015
Running time: 74:05:24
July 3, 1966: Fillmore Auditorium, San Francisco, California
'Nobody's Fault But Mine' (trad.) 'Dancing In The Street' (Stevenson, Gaye, Hunter), 'I
Know You Rider' (trad.), 'He Was A Friend of Mine' (Mark Spoelstra), 'Next Time You See
Me' (Harvey, Forest), 'Viola Lee Blues' (Noah Lewis), 'Big Boss Man' (Smith, Dixon), 'Sitting
On Top of the World' (Carter, Jacobs), 'Keep Rolling By' (trad.), 'New, New Minglewood
Blues' (trad.), 'Cold Rain And Snow' (trad.), 'Tastebud' (McKernan), Beat It On Down the
Line' (Jesse Fuller), 'Cream Puff War' (Garcia), 'Don't Mess Up A Good Thing' (Oliver Sain),
'Cardboard Cowboy' (Lesh), 'Gangster Of Love' (John Watson), 'You Don't Have To Ask'
(Garcia, Kreutzmann, Lesh, McKernan, Weir), 'In The Midnight Hour' (Cropper, Pickett)
November 10, 1967: Shrine Auditorium, Los Angeles, California
'Viola Lee Blues' (Noah Lewis), 'It Hurts Me Too' (Elmore James), 'Beat It On Down the
Line' (Jesse Fuller), 'Morning Dew' (Dobson, Rose), 'Good Morning Little Schoolgirl'

(Williamson) 'That's It for The Other One' (Constanten, Garcia, Kreutzmann, Lesh, McKernan, Weir) I) 'Cryptical Envelopment', II) 'The Other One', III) 'Cryptical Envelopment', 'New Potato Caboose' (Lesh, Petersen), 'Alligator' (Lesh, McKernan, Hunter), 'Caution (Do Not Stop On Tracks)' (Garcia, Kreutzmann, Lesh, McKernan, Weir)
October 20, 1968: Greek Theatre, Berkeley, California
'Good Morning Little Schoolgirl' (Williamson), 'Turn On Your Lovelight' (Scott, Malone), 'Dark Star' (Garcia, Mickey Hart, Kreutzmann, Lesh, McKernan, Weir, Hunter), 'St. Stephen' (Garcia, Lesh, Hunter), 'The Eleven' (Lesh, Hunter), 'Caution (Do Not Stop On Tracks)' (Garcia, Kreutzmann, Lesh, McKernan, Weir), 'Feedback' (Garcia, Hart, Kreutzmann, Lesh, McKernan, Weir)

February 22, 1969: Dream Bowl, Vallejo, California
'Dupree's Diamond Blues' (Garcia, Hunter), 'Mountains Of The Moon' (Garcia, Hunter), 'Dark Star' (Garcia, Hart, Kreutzmann, Lesh, McKernan, Weir, Hunter), 'Cryptical Envelopment' (Garcia), 'The Other One' (Weir, Kreutzmann), 'Cryptical Envelopment' (Garcia), 'Death Don't Have No Mercy' (Rev. Gary Davis), 'Doin' That Rag' (Garcia, Hunter), 'St. Stephen' (Garcia, Lesh, Hunter), 'The Eleven' (Lesh, Hunter), Turn On Your Lovelight' (Scott, Malone)

April 15, 1970: Winterland, San Francisco, California
'Cold Rain And Snow' (trad.), 'China Cat Sunflower' (Garcia, Hunter), ' I Know You Rider' (trad.), Technical Difficulties: 'Mama Tried' false start, Mama Tried' (Merle Haggard), 'It's A Man's, Man's, Man's World' (Brown, Newsome), 'Candyman' (Garcia, Hunter), 'Hard To Handle' (Redding, Isbell, Jones), 'Cumberland Blues' (Garcia, Lesh, Hunter), 'Cryptical Envelopment' (Garcia), 'Drums' (Hart, Kreutzmann), 'Jam' (Garcia, Hart, Kreutzmann, Lesh, McKernan, Weir), 'The Other One', (Weir, Kreutzmann), 'Cryptical Envelopment', (Garcia), 'Dire Wolf' (Garcia, Hunter), 'Dancing In The Street' (Stevenson, Gaye, Hunter), 'Turn On Your Lovelight' (Scott, Malone), 'Not Fade Away' (Hardin, Petty), 'Turn On Your Lovelight' (Scott, Malone)

March 18, 1971: Fox Theatre, St. Louis, Missouri
'Casey Jones' (Garcia, Hunter), 'Me And My Uncle' (John Phillips), 'Big Boss Man' (Smith, Dixon), 'Bertha' (Garcia, Hunter), 'Me And Bobby McGee' (Kristofferson, Foster), 'Loser' (Garcia, Hunter), 'China Cat Sunflower' (Garcia, Hunter), 'I Know You Rider' (trad.), 'Ain't It Crazy (The Rub)' (Sam Hopkins), 'Playing In The Band' (Weir, Hart, Hunter), 'Cumberland Blues' (Garcia, Lesh, Hunter), 'Truckin'' (Garcia, Lesh, Weir, Hunter) 'Drums' (Kreutzmann), 'The Other One' (Weir, Kreutzmann), 'Wharf Rat' (Garcia, Hunter), 'Sugar Magnolia' (Weir, Hunter), 'Greatest Story Ever Told' (Weir, Hart, Hunter), 'Johnny B. Goode' (Chuck Berry), 'Not Fade Away' (Hardin, Petty), 'Goin' Down The Road Feeling Bad' (trad.), 'Caution (Do Not Stop On Tracks)' (Garcia, Kreutzmann, Lesh, McKernan, Weir), 'Feedback' (Garcia, Kreutzmann, Lesh, McKernan, Weir), 'Uncle John's Band' (Garcia, Hunter)

September 24, 1972: Palace Theatre, Waterbury, Connecticut
'Big Railroad Blues' (Noah Lewis), 'Mexicali Blues' (Weir, Barlow), 'Loser' (Garcia, Hunter), 'Black-Throated Wind' (Weir, Barlow), 'Cumberland Blues' (Garcia, Lesh, Hunter), 'Sugaree' (Garcia, Hunter), 'El Paso' (Marty Robbins), 'Tennessee Jed' (Garcia, Hunter), 'Beat It On Down The Line' (Jesse Fuller), 'Bird Song' (Garcia, Hunter), 'Big River' (Johnny Cash), 'Brown-Eyed Women' (Garcia, Hunter), 'Playing In The Band' (Weir, Hart, Hunter), 'Greatest Story Ever Told' (Weir, Hart, Hunter), 'Bertha' (Garcia, Hunter), 'Promised Land' (Chuck Berry), 'Friend Of The Devil' (Garcia, Dawson, Hunter), 'Jack Straw' (Weir, Hunter), 'Tomorrow Is Forever' (Dolly Parton), 'Me And My Uncle' (John Phillips), 'Dark Star' (Garcia, Hart, Kreutzmann, Lesh, McKernan, Weir, Hunter), 'Drums' (Kreutzmann), 'Dark Star' (Garcia, Hart, Kreutzmann, Lesh, McKernan, Weir, Hunter), 'China Cat Sunflower' (Garcia,

316

Hunter), 'I Know You Rider (trad.), 'Sugar Magnolia' (Weir, Hunter), 'One More Saturday Night' (Bob Weir)

November 14, 1973: San Diego Sports Arena, San Diego, California
'Big Railroad Blues' (Noah Lewis), 'Jack Straw' (Weir, Hunter), Sugaree (Garcia, Hunter), 'Mexicali Blues' (Weir, Barlow), 'Here Comes Sunshine' (Garcia, Hunter), 'Black-Throated Wind' (Weir, Barlow), 'Cumberland Blues' (Garcia, Lesh, Hunter), 'Row Jimmy' (Garcia, Hunter), 'The Race Is On' (Don Rollins), 'Brown-Eyed Women' (Garcia, Hunter), 'Beat It On Down The Line' (Jesse Fuller), 'Tennessee Jed' (Garcia, Hunter), 'El Paso' (Marty Robbins), 'China Cat Sunflower' (Garcia, Hunter), 'I Know You Rider (trad.), 'Around And Around' (Chuck Berry), 'Me And My Uncle' (John Phillips), 'Goin' Down the Road Feeling Bad' (trad.), 'One More Saturday Night' (Weir), 'Truckin'' (Garcia, Lesh, Weir, Hunter), 'The Other One' (Weir, Kreutzmann), 'Big River' (Johnny Cash), 'The Other One' (Weir, Kreutzmann), 'Eyes Of The World' (Garcia, Hunter), 'The Other One' (Weir, Kreutzmann), 'Wharf Rat' (Garcia, Hunter)

September 18, 1974: Parc Des Expositions, Dijon, France
'Uncle John's Band' (Garcia, Hunter), 'Jack Straw' (Weir, Hunter), 'Friend Of The Devil' (Garcia, Dawson, Hunter), 'Black-Throated Wind' (Weir, Barlow), 'Scarlet Begonias' (Garcia, Hunter), 'Mexicali Blues' (Weir, Barlow), 'Row Jimmy' (Garcia, Hunter), 'Beat It On Down the Line' (Jesse Fuller), 'Deal' (Garcia, Hunter), 'The Race Is On' (Don Rollins), 'To Lay Me Down' (Garcia, Hunter), 'Playing In The Band' (Weir, Hart, Hunter) Interlude: 'Seastones' (performed by Ned Lagin and Phil Lesh), 'Loose Lucy' (Garcia, Hunter), 'Big River' (Johnny Cash), 'Peggy-O' (trad.), 'Me And My Uncle' (John Phillips), 'Eyes Of The World' (Garcia, Hunter), 'China Doll' (Garcia, Hunter), 'He's Gone' (Garcia, Hunter), 'Truckin'' (Garcia, Lesh, Weir, Hunter), Drums (Kreutzmann), 'Caution Jam' (Garcia, Keith Godchaux, Kreutzmann, Lesh, Weir), 'Ship Of Fools' (Garcia, Hunter), 'Johnny B. Goode' (Chuck Berry), 'U.S. Blues' (Garcia, Hunter)

September 28, 1975: Golden Gate Park, San Francisco, California
'Help On The Way' (Garcia, Hunter), 'Slipknot!' (Garcia, Godchaux, Kreutzmann, Lesh, Weir), 'The Music Never Stopped' (Weir, Barlow), 'They Love Each Other' (Garcia, Hunter), 'Beat It On Down the Line' (Jesse Fuller), 'Franklin's Tower' (Garcia, Kreutzmann, Hunter), 'Big River' (Johnny Cash), 'It Must Have Been the Roses' (Hunter), 'Truckin'' (Garcia, Lesh, Weir, Hunter), 'The Eleven Jam' (Garcia, Godchaux, Hart, Kreutzmann, Lesh, Weir), 'Drums' (Hart, Kreutzmann), 'Stronger Than Dirt/Milkin' the Turkey' (Hart, Kreutzmann, Lesh), 'Not Fade Away' (Hardin, Petty), 'Goin' Down The Road Feeling Bad' (trad.), 'One More Saturday Night' (Weir)

October 3, 1976: Cobo Arena, Detroit, Michigan
'Bertha' (Garcia, Hunter), 'Mama Tried' (Merle Haggard), 'Sugaree' (Garcia, Hunter), New 'Minglewood Blues' (trad.), 'Ramble On Rose' (Garcia, Hunter), 'Looks Like Rain' (Weir, Barlow), 'Loser' (Garcia, Hunter), 'El Paso' (Marty Robbins), 'Scarlet Begonias' (Garcia, Hunter), 'The Music Never Stopped' (Weir, Barlow), 'Samson And Delilah' (trad.), 'It Must Have Been The Roses' (Hunter), 'Playing In The Band' (Weir, Hart, Hunter), 'Drums '(Hart, Kreutzmann), 'The Wheel' (Garcia, Kreutzmann, Hunter), 'Good Lovin'' (Clark, Resnick), 'Comes A Time' (Garcia, Hunter), 'Dancing In The Street' (Stevenson, Gaye, Hunter), 'Not Fade Away' (Hardin, Petty), 'Dancing In The Street' (Stevenson, Gaye, Hunter), 'Around And Around' (Chuck Berry)

April 25, 1977: Capitol Theatre, Passaic, New Jersey
'New Minglewood Blues' (trad.), 'Deal' (Garcia, Hunter), 'Mama Tried' (Merle Haggard), 'They Love Each Other' (Garcia, Hunter), 'Looks Like Rain' (Weir, Barlow), 'Peggy-O' (trad.), 'Lazy Lightnin'' (Weir, Barlow), 'Supplication' (Weir, Barlow), 'Ship Of Fools' (Garcia,

Hunter), 'Estimated Prophet' (Weir, Barlow), 'Brown-Eyed Women' (Garcia, Hunter), 'The Music Never Stopped' (Weir, Barlow), 'Scarlet Begonias' (Garcia, Hunter), 'Fire On The Mountain' (Hart, Hunter), 'Samson And Delilah' (trad.), 'Terrapin Station' (Garcia, Hunter), 'Playing In The Band' (Weir, Hart, Hunter), 'Drums' (Hart, Kreutzmann), 'Wharf Rat' (Garcia, Hunter), 'Playing In The Band' (Weir, Hart, Hunter), 'U.S. Blues' (Garcia, Hunter)

May 14, 1978: Providence Civic Center, Providence, Rhode Island
'Mississippi Half Step Uptown Toodeloo' (Garcia, Hunter), 'Cassidy' (Weir, Barlow), 'They Love Each Other' (Garcia, Hunter), 'Looks Like Rain' (Weir, Barlow), 'It Must Have Been The Roses' (Hunter), 'Me And My Uncle' (John Phillips), 'Big River' (Johnny Cash), 'Brown-Eyed Women' (Garcia, Hunter), 'Let It Grow' (Weir, Barlow), 'Samson And Delilah' (trad.), 'Ship Of Fools' (Garcia, Hunter), 'Estimated Prophet' (Weir, Barlow), 'Eyes Of The World' (Garcia, Hunter), 'Drums' (Hart, Kreutzmann), 'Not Fade Away' (Hardin, Petty), 'Goin' Down The Road Feeling Bad' (trad.), 'Around and Around' (Chuck Berry), 'U.S. Blues' (Garcia, Hunter)

October 27, 1979: Cape Cod Coliseum, South Yarmouth, Massachusetts
'Jack Straw' (Garcia, Hunter), 'Candyman' (Garcia, Hunter), 'Me And My Uncle' (John Phillips), 'Big River' (Johnny Cash), 'Brown-Eyed Women' (Garcia, Hunter), 'Easy To Love You' (Mydland, Barlow), 'New Minglewood Blues' (trad.), 'Stagger Lee' (Garcia, Hunter), 'Lost Sailor' (Weir, Barlow), 'Saint Of Circumstance' (Weir, Barlow), 'Deal' (Garcia, Hunter), 'Dancing In The Street' (Stevenson, Gaye, Hunter), 'Franklin's Tower' (Garcia, Kreutzmann, Hunter), 'He's Gone' (Garcia Hunter), 'Caution Jam' (Garcia, Hart, Kreutzmann, Lesh, Mydland, Weir), 'The Other One' (Weir, Kreutzmann), 'Drums' (Hart, Kreutzmann), 'Not Fade Away' (Hardin, Petty), 'Black Peter' (Garcia, Hunter), 'Around And Around' (Chuck Berry), 'One More Saturday Night' (Bob Weir)

November 28, 1980: Lakeland Civic Center, Lakeland, Florida
'Jack Straw '(Weir, Hunter), 'Peggy-O' (trad.), 'Little Red Rooster' (Willie Dixon),'Tennessee Jed' (Garcia, Hunter), 'Passenger' (Lesh, Monk), 'Deep Elem Blues' (trad.), 'Looks Like Rain' (Weir, Barlow), 'Deal' (Garcia, Hunter), 'Feel Like A Stranger' (Weir, Barlow), 'To Lay Me Down' (Garcia, Hunter), 'Let It Grow' (Weir, Barlow), 'Terrapin Station' (Garcia, Hunter), 'Drums' (Hart, Kreutzmann), 'Space' (Garcia, Hart, Kreutzmann, Lesh, Mydland, Weir), 'Not Fade Away' (Hardin, Petty), 'Black Peter' (Garcia, Hunter), 'Sugar Magnolia' (Weir, Hunter), 'U.S. Blues' (Garcia, Hunter)

May 16, 1981: Barton Hall, Cornell University, Ithaca, New York
'Feel Like A Stranger' (Weir, Barlow), 'Friend Of The Devil' (Garcia, Dawson, Hunter), 'Me And My Uncle' (John Phillips), 'Big River' (Johnny Cash), 'Althea' (Garcia, Hunter), 'C.C. Rider' (trad.), 'Brown-Eyed Women' (Garcia, Hunter), 'Passenger' (Lesh, Monk), 'High Time' (Garcia, Hunter), 'Let It Grow' (Weir, Barlow), 'Don't Ease Me In' (trad.), 'Shakedown Street' (Garcia, Hunter), 'Bertha' (Garcia, Hunter), 'Lost Sailor' (Weir, Barlow), 'Saint Of Circumstance' (Weir, Barlow), 'Spanish Jam' (Garcia, Hart, Kreutzmann, Lesh, Mydland, Weir), 'Drums' (Hart, Kreutzmann), 'Jam' (Garcia, Hart, Kreutzmann, Lesh, Mydland, Weir), 'Truckin'' (Garcia, Lesh, Weir, Hunter), 'Nobody's Jam' (Garcia, Hart, Kreutzmann, Lesh, Mydland, Weir), 'Stella Blue' (Garcia, Hunter), 'Goin' Down The Road Feeling Bad' (trad.), 'One More Saturday Night' (Weir), 'Uncle John's Band' (Garcia, Hunter)

July 31, 1982: Manor Downs, Austin, Texas
'Alabama Getaway' (Garcia, Hunter), 'Promised Land' (Chuck Berry), Candyman (Garcia, Hunter), 'El Paso' (Marty Robbins), 'Bird Song' (Garcia, Hunter), 'Little Red Rooster' (Willie Dixon), 'Ramble On Rose' (Garcia, Hunter), 'It's All Over Now' (Womack, Womack), 'Brown-Eyed Women' (Garcia, Hunter), 'The Music Never Stopped' (Weir, Barlow), 'Deal' (Garcia, Hunter), 'Scarlet Begonias' (Garcia, Hunter), 'Fire On The Mountain' (Hart, Hunter), 'Estimated Prophet' (Weir, Barlow), 'Eyes Of The World' (Garcia, Hunter), 'Drums' (Hart,

Kreutzmann), 'Space' (Garcia, Lesh, Mydland, Weir), 'Uncle John's Band' (Garcia, Hunter), 'Truckin'' (Garcia, Lesh, Weir, Hunter), 'Morning Dew' (Dobson, Rose), 'One More Saturday Night' (Bob Weir), 'Don't Ease Me In' (trad.)

October 21, 1983: The Centrum, Worcester, Massachusetts
'The Music Never Stopped' (Weir, Barlow), 'Loser' (Garcia, Hunter), 'C.C. Rider' (trad.), 'Cumberland Blues' (Garcia, Lesh, Hunter), 'Cassidy' (Weir, Barlow), 'Ramble On Rose' (Garcia, Hunter), 'My Brother Esau' (Weir, Barlow), 'Big Railroad Blues' (Noah Lewis), 'Promised Land' (Chuck Berry), 'Scarlet Begonias' (Garcia, Hunter), 'Fire On The Mountain' (Hart, Hunter), 'Uncle John's Band' (Garcia, Hunter), 'Playing In The Band' (Weir, Hart, Hunter), 'Drums' (Hart, Kreutzmann), 'Space' (Garcia, Lesh, Mydland, Weir), 'Truckin'' (Garcia, Lesh, Weir, Hunter), 'Wharf Rat' (Garcia, Hunter), 'I Need A Miracle' (Weir, Barlow), 'Touch Of Grey' (Garcia, Hunter), 'Johnny B. Goode' (Chuck Berry)

October 12, 1984: Augusta Civic Center, Augusta, Maine
'Feel Like A Stranger' (Weir, Barlow), 'It Must Have Been The Roses' (Hunter), 'On The Road Again' (trad.), 'Jack-A-Roe' (trad.), 'It's All Over Now' (Womack, Womack), 'Cumberland Blues' (Garcia, Lesh, Hunter), 'The Music Never Stopped' (Weir, Barlow), 'Cold Rain And Snow' (trad.), 'Lost Sailor' (Weir, Barlow), 'Saint Of Circumstance' (Weir, Barlow), 'Don't Need Love' (Brent Mydland), 'Uncle John's Band' (Garcia, Hunter), 'Drums' (Hart, Kreutzmann), 'Space' (Garcia, Lesh, Mydland, Weir), 'Playing In The Band' (Weir, Hart, Hunter), 'Uncle John's Band' (Garcia, Hunter), 'Morning Dew' (Dobson, Rose), 'Good Lovin'' (Clark, Resnick)

June 24, 1985: Riverbend Music Center, Cincinnati, Ohio
'Alabama Getaway' (Garcia, Hunter), 'Greatest Story Ever Told' (Weir, Hunter), 'They Love Each Other' (Garcia, Hunter), 'New Minglewood Blues' (trad.), 'Tennessee Jed' (Garcia, Hunter), 'My Brother Esau' (Weir, Barlow), 'Loser' (Garcia, Hunter), 'Let It Grow' (Weir, Barlow), 'Iko Iko' (Crawford, Hawkins, Hawkins, Johnson), 'Samson And Delilah' (trad.), 'He's Gone' (Garcia, Hunter), 'Smokestack Lightnin'' (Chester Burnette), 'Cryptical Envelopment' (Garcia), 'Drums' (Hart, Kreutzmann), 'Space' (Garcia, Lesh, Mydland, Weir), 'Comes A Time' (Garcia, Hunter), 'The Other One' (Weir, Kreutzmann), 'Cryptical Envelopment' (Garcia), 'Wharf Rat' (Garcia, Hunter), 'Around And Around' (Chuck Berry), 'Good Lovin'' (Clark, Resnick), 'U.S. Blues' (Garcia, Hunter)

May 3, 1986: Cal Expo Amphitheatre, Sacramento, California
'Cold Rain And Snow' (trad.), 'The Race Is On' (Don Rollins), 'They Love Each Other' (Garcia, Hunter), 'C.C. Rider' (trad.), High Time' (Garcia, Hunter), 'Beat It On Down The Line' (Jesse Fuller), 'Promised Land' (Chuck Berry), 'Deal' (Garcia, Hunter), 'Scarlet Begonias' (Garcia, Hunter), 'Fire On The Mountain (Hart, Hunter), 'Man Smart, Woman Smarter' (Norman Span), 'Goin' Down The Road Feeling Bad' (trad.), 'Drums' (Hart, Kreutzmann), 'Space' (Garcia, Lesh, Mydland, Weir), 'The Other One' (Weir, Kreutzmann), 'Comes A Time' (Garcia, Hunter), 'Sugar Magnolia' (Weir, Hunter)

September 18, 1987: Madison Square Garden, New York
'Hell In A Bucket' (Weir, Barlow, Mydland), 'Sugaree' (Garcia, Hunter), 'Walkin' Blues' (Robert Johnson), 'Candyman' (Garcia, Hunter), 'When I Paint My Masterpiece' (Bob Dylan), 'Bird Song' (Garcia, Hunter), 'Shakedown Street' (Garcia, Hunter), 'Man Smart, Woman Smarter' (Norman Span), 'Terrapin Station' (Garcia, Hunter), 'Drums' (Hart, Kreutzmann), 'Space' (Garcia, Lesh, Hart, Hunter), 'Goin' Down The Road Feeling Bad' (trad.), 'All Along The Watchtower' (Bob Dylan), 'Morning Dew' (Dobson, Rose), 'Good Lovin'' (Clark, Resnick), 'La Bamba' (Ritchie Valens), 'Good Lovin'' (Clark, Resnick), 'Knockin' On Heaven's Door' (Bob Dylan)

July 3, 1988: Oxford Plains Speedway, Oxford, Maine
'Hell In A Bucket' (Weir, Barlow), 'Sugaree' (Garcia, Hunter), 'Walkin' Blues' (Robert

Johnson), 'Tennessee Jed' (Garcia, Hunter), 'Queen Jane Approximately' (Dylan), 'Bird Song' (Garcia, Hunter), 'Touch Of Grey' (Garcia, Hunter), 'Hey Pocky Way' (Modeliste, Neville, Nocentelli, Porter Jr.), 'Looks Like Rain' (Weir, Barlow), Estimated Prophet, (Weir, Barlow), Eyes Of The World' (Garcia, Hunter), 'I Will Take You Home' (Mydland, Barlow), 'Drums' (Hart, Kreutzmann), 'Space' (Garcia, Lesh, Mydland, Weir), 'Goin' Down The Road Feeling Bad' (trad.), 'I Need A Miracle' (Weir, Barlow), 'Dear Mr. Fantasy' (Capaldi, Winwood, Wood), 'Hey Jude' (Lennon, McCartney), 'Not Fade Away' (Hardin, Petty)

October 26, 1989: Miami Arena, Miami, Florida
'Foolish Heart' (Garcia, Hunter), 'Little Red Rooster' (Willie Dixon), 'Stagger Lee' (Garcia, Hunter), 'Me And My Uncle' (John Phillips), 'Big River' (Johnny Cash), 'Brown-Eyed Women' (Garcia, Hunter), 'Victim Or The Crime' (Weir, Graham), 'Don't Ease Me In' (trad.), 'Estimated Prophet' (Weir, Barlow), 'Blow Away' (Mydland, Barlow), 'Dark Star' (Garcia, Hart, Kreutzmann, Lesh, McKernan, Weir, Hunter), 'Drums' (Hart, Kreutzmann), 'Space' (Garcia, Lesh, Mydland, Weir), 'The Wheel' (Garcia, Kreutzmann, Hunter), 'All Along The Watchtower' (Bob Dylan), 'Stella Blue' (Garcia, Hunter), 'Not Fade Away' (Hardin, Petty), 'And We Bid You Goodnight' (trad.)

October 27, 1990: Le Zénith, Paris, France
'Hell In A Bucket' (Weir, Barlow), 'Sugaree' (Garcia, Hunter), 'New Minglewood Blues' (trad.), 'Jack-A-Roe' (trad.), 'Black-Throated Wind' (Weir, Barlow), 'Ramble On Rose' (Garcia, Hunter), 'When I Paint My Masterpiece' (Bob Dylan), 'Bird Song' (Garcia, Hunter), 'Promised Land' (Chuck Berry), 'China Cat Sunflower' (Garcia, Hunter), 'I Know You Rider' (trad.), 'Saint Of Circumstance' (Weir, Barlow), 'Crazy Fingers' (Garcia, Hunter), 'Playing In The Band' (Weir, Hart, Hunter), 'Drums' (Hart, Kreutzmann), 'Space' (Garcia, Lesh, Weir), 'Playing In The Band' (Weir, Hart, Hunter), 'Stella Blue' (Garcia, Hunter), Throwing Stones' (Weir, Barlow), 'Not Fade Away' (Hardin, Petty), 'One More Saturday Night' (Weir)

September 10, 1991: Madison Square Garden, New York
'Shakedown Street' (Garcia, Hunter), 'C.C. Rider' (trad.), 'It Takes A Lot To Laugh, It Takes A Train to Cry' (Bob Dylan), 'Black-Throated Wind' (Weir, Barlow), 'High Time' (Garcia, Hunter), 'Cassidy' (Weir, Barlow), 'Deal' (Garcia, Hunter), 'Help On The Way' (Garcia, Hunter), 'Slipknot!' (Garcia, Godchaux, Kreutzmann, Lesh, Weir), 'Franklin's Tower' (Garcia, Hunter), 'Estimated Prophet' (Weir, Barlow), 'Dark Star' (Garcia, Hart, Kreutzmann, Lesh, McKernan, Weir, Hunter), 'Drums' (Hart, Kreutzmann), 'Space' Garcia, Lesh, Weir, Welnick), 'Dark Star' (Garcia, Hart, Kreutzmann, Lesh, McKernan, Weir, Hunter), 'I Need A Miracle' (Weir, Barlow), 'Standing On The Moon' (Garcia, Hunter), 'Turn On Your Lovelight' (Scott, Malone), 'It's All Over Now, Baby Blue' (Bob Dylan)

March 20, 1992: Copps Coliseum, Hamilton, Ontario
'Hell In A Bucket' (Weir, Barlow), 'Althea' (Garcia, Hunter), 'The Same Thing' (Willie Dixon), 'Brown-Eyed Women' (Garcia, Hunter), 'Mexicali Blues' (Weir, Barlow), 'Maggie's Farm' (Bob Dylan), 'Bird Song' (Garcia, Hunter), 'Promised Land' (Chuck Berry), 'Shakedown Street' (Garcia, Hunter), 'Man Smart, Woman Smarter' (Norman Span), 'Dark Star' (Garcia, Hart, Kreutzmann, Lesh, McKernan, Weir, Hunter), 'Drums' (Hart, Kreutzmann), 'Space' (Garcia, Lesh, Weir, Welnick), 'The Other One' (Weir, Kreutzmann), 'Standing On The Moon' (Garcia, Hunter), 'Turn On Your Lovelight' (Scott, Malone), 'U.S. Blues' (Garcia, Hunter)

March 27, 1993: Knickerbocker Arena, Albany, New York
'Hell In A Bucket' (Weir, Barlow), 'Bertha' (Garcia, Hunter), 'The Same Thing' (Willie Dixon), 'Peggy-O' (trad.), 'Queen Jane Approximately' (Bob Dylan), 'Broken Arrow' (Robbie Robertson), 'Loose Lucy' (Garcia, Hunter), 'Cassidy' (Weir, Barlow), 'Casey Jones' (Garcia, Hunter), 'Eyes Of The World' (Garcia, Hunter), 'Estimated Prophet' (Weir, Barlow), 'Comes A Time' (Garcia, Hunter), 'Corrina' (Weir, Hart, Hunter), 'Drums' (Hart, Kreutzmann),

'Space' (Garcia, Lesh, Weir, Welnick), 'The Wheel' (Garcia, Kreutzmann, Hunter), 'All Along The Watchtower' (Bob Dylan), 'Days Between' (Garcia, Hunter), 'One More Saturday Night' (Weir), 'I Fought the Law' (Sonny Curtis)

October 1, 1994: Boston Garden, Boston, Massachusetts
'Help On The Way' (Garcia, Hunter), 'Slipknot!' (Garcia, Godchaux, Kreutzmann, Lesh, Weir), 'Franklin's Tower' (Garcia, Hunter), 'Walkin' Blues' (Robert Johnson), 'Althea' (Garcia, Hunter), 'Me And My Uncle' (John Phillips), 'Big River' (Johnny Cash), 'Just Like Tom Thumb's Blues' (Bob Dylan), 'So Many Roads' (Garcia, Hunter), 'Promised Land' (Chuck Berry), 'Scarlet Begonias' (Garcia, Hunter), 'Fire On The Mountain' (Hart, Hunter), 'Way To Go Home' (Welnick, Hunter), 'Saint Of Circumstance' (Weir, Barlow), 'Terrapin Station' (Garcia, Hunter), 'Drums' (Hart, Kreutzmann), 'Space' (Garcia, Lesh, Weir, Welnick), 'The Last Time '(Jagger, Richards), 'Stella Blue' (Garcia, Hunter), 'One More Saturday Night' (Weir), 'Liberty' (Garcia, Hunter)

February 21, 1995: Delta Center, Salt Lake City, Utah
'Salt Lake City' (Weir, Barlow), 'Friend Of The Devil' (Garcia, Hunter), 'Wang Dang Doodle' (Willie Dixon), 'Tennessee Jed' (Garcia, Hunter), 'Broken Arrow' (Robertson), 'Black-Throated Wind' (Weir, Barlow), 'So Many Roads' (Garcia, Hunter), 'The Music Never Stopped' (Weir, Barlow), 'Foolish Heart' (Garcia, Hunter), 'Samba In The Rain' (Welnick, Hunter), 'Truckin'' (Garcia, Lesh, Weir, Hunter), 'I Just Want To Make Love To You' (Willie Dixon), 'That Would Be Something' (Paul McCartney), 'Drums' (Hart, Kreutzmann), 'Space' (Garcia, Lesh, Weir, Welnick), 'Visions Of Johanna' (Bob Dylan), 'Sugar Magnolia' (Weir, Hunter), 'Liberty' (Garcia, Hunter)

Giants Stadium 1987, 1989, 1991 (2019)
Personnel:
Jerry Garcia: guitar, vocals
Mickey Hart: drums
Bruce Hornsby: keyboards, vocals (1991)
Bill Kreutzmann: drums
Phil Lesh: bass, vocals
Brent Mydland: keyboards, vocals (1987, 1989)
Bob Weir: guitar, vocals
Vince Welnick: keyboards, vocals (1991)
Recorded live at Giants Stadium in East Rutherford, New Jersey on July 12, 1987, July 9 and 10, 1989, and June 16 and 17, 1991. Compilation produced for release by David Lemieux. Release date: September 2019

July 12, 1987
'Hell In A Bucket' (Weir, Mydland, Barlow), 'West L.A. Fadeaway' (Garcia, Hunter), 'Greatest Story Ever Told' (Weir, Hart, Hunter), 'Loser' (Garcia, Hunter), 'Tons Of Steel' (Mydland), 'Ramble On Rose' (Garcia, Hunter), 'When I Paint My Masterpiece' (Bob Dylan), 'When Push Comes To Shove' (Garcia, Hunter), 'Promised Land' (Chuck Berry), 'Bertha' (Garcia, Hunter), 'Morning Dew' (Dobson, Rose), 'Playing In The Band' (Weir, Hart, Hunter), 'Drums' (Hart, Kreutzmann), 'Space' (Garcia, Lesh, Weir), 'The Other One' (Weir, Kreutzmann). 'Stella Blue' (Garcia, Hunter), 'Throwing Stones' (Weir, Barlow), 'Not Fade Away' (Holly, Petty)

July 9, 1989
'Shakedown Street' (Garcia, Hunter), 'Jack Straw' (Weir, Hunter), 'West L.A. Fadeaway' (Garcia, Hunter), 'Victim Or The Crime' (Weir, Gerrit Graham), 'Brown-Eyed Women' (Garcia, Hunter), 'Queen Jane Approximately' (Bob Dylan), 'Bird Song' (Garcia, Hunter), 'China Cat Sunflower' (Garcia, Hunter), 'I Know You Rider' (trad.), 'Samson And Delilah'

(trad.), 'Built To Last' (Garcia, Hunter), 'Truckin'' (Garcia, Lesh, Weir, Hunter), 'Drums' (Hart, Kreutzmann), 'Space' (Garcia, Lesh, Weir), 'Gimme Some Lovin'' (Winwood, Davis, Winwood), 'Goin' Down The Road Feeling Bad' (trad.), 'Throwing Stones' (Weir, Barlow), 'Not Fade Away' (Holly, Petty), 'Brokedown Palace' (Garcia, Hunter)

July 10, 1989
'Feel Like A Stranger' (Weir, Barlow), 'Franklin's Tower' (Garcia, Kreutzmann, Hunter), 'Walkin' Blues' (Robert Johnson), 'Jack-A-Roe' (trad.), 'When I Paint My Masterpiece' (Bob Dylan), 'Tennessee Jed' (Garcia, Hunter), 'The Music Never Stopped' (Weir, Barlow), 'Don't Ease Me In' (trad.), 'Foolish Heart' (Garcia, Hunter), 'Just A Little Light' (Mydland, Barlow), 'Playing In The Band' (Weir, Hart, Hunter), 'Uncle John's Band' (Garcia, Hunter), 'Drums' (Hart, Kreutzmann), 'Space' (Garcia, Lesh, Weir), 'Iko Iko' (James Crawford), 'All Along The Watchtower' (Bob Dylan), 'Morning Dew' (Dobson, Rose), 'Sugar Magnolia' (Weir, Hunter), 'Knockin' On Heaven's Door' (Bob Dylan)

June 16, 1991
'Picasso Moon' (Weir, Barlow, Bralove), 'Bertha' (Garcia, Hunter), 'Little Red Rooster' (Willie Dixon), 'Candyman' (Garcia, Hunter), 'Stuck Inside Of Mobile With The Memphis Blues Again' (Bob Dylan), 'Stagger Lee' (Garcia, Hunter), 'Let It Grow' (Weir, Barlow), 'Jack Straw' (Weir, Hunter), 'Crazy Fingers' (Garcia, Hunter), 'China Cat Sunflower' (Garcia, Hunter), 'I Know You Rider' (trad.), 'Drums' (Hart, Kreutzmann), 'Space' (Garcia, Lesh, Weir), 'I Need A Miracle' (Weir, Barlow), 'Black Peter' (Garcia, Hunter), 'Throwing Stones' (Weir, Barlow), 'Not Fade Away' (Holly, Petty), 'Box Of Rain' (Lesh, Hunter)

June 17, 1991
'Eyes Of The World' (Garcia, Hunter), 'Walkin' Blues' (Robert Johnson), 'Brown-Eyed Women' (Garcia, Hunter), 'Dark Star' (Garcia, Hart, Kreutzmann, Lesh, McKernan, Weir, Hunter), 'When I Paint My Masterpiece' (Bob Dylan), 'Loose Lucy' (Garcia, Hunter), 'Cassidy' (Weir, Barlow), 'Might As Well' (Garcia, Hunter), 'Saint Of Circumstance' (Weir, Barlow), 'Ship Of Fools' (Garcia, Hunter), Dark Star' (Garcia, Hart, Kreutzmann, Lesh, McKernan, Weir, Hunter), 'Truckin'' (Garcia, Lesh, Weir, Hunter), 'New Speedway Boogie' (Garcia, Hunter), 'Dark Star' (Garcia, Hart, Kreutzmann, Lesh, McKernan, Weir, Hunter), 'Uncle John's Band' (Garcia, Hunter), 'Dark Star' (Garcia, Hart, Kreutzmann, Lesh, McKernan, Weir, Hunter), 'Drums' (Hart, Kreutzmann), 'Space' (Garcia, Lesh, Weir), 'China Doll' (Garcia, Hunter), 'Playing In The Band' (Weir, Hart, Hunter), 'Sugar Magnolia' (Weir, Hunter), 'The Weight' (Robbie Robertson)

Listen to the River: St. Louis '71 '72 '73 (2021)
Personnel:
Jerry Garcia: guitar, vocals
Donna Jean Godchaux: vocals
Keith Godchaux: keyboards
Bill Kreutzmann: drums,
Phil Lesh: bass guitar, vocals
Ron 'Pigpen' McKernan: keyboards, harmonica, vocals (1971)
Bob Weir: rhythm guitar, vocals
Recorded live at the Fox Theatre and the Kiel Auditorium, St Louis, Missouri, December 9, 1971 – October 30, 1973. Produced for release by David Lemieux
Release date: October 2021

Fox Theatre, December 9, 1971
'Truckin'' (Garcia, Lesh, Weir, Hunter), 'Brown-Eyed Women' (Garcia, Hunter), 'Mr. Charlie' (McKernan, Hunter), 'Jack Straw' (Weir, Hunter), 'Sugaree' (Garcia, Hunter), 'Beat It On

Down The Line' (Jesse Fuller), 'It Hurts Me Too' (James, Sehorn), 'Tennessee Jed' (Garcia, Hunter), 'El Paso' (Marty Robbins), 'Run Rudolph Run' (Marks, Brodie), 'Black Peter' (Garcia, Hunter), 'Playing In The Band' (Weir, Mickey Hart, Hunter), 'Casey Jones' (Garcia, Hunter), 'One More Saturday Night' (Weir), 'Ramble On Rose' (Garcia, Hunter), 'Mexicali Blues' (Weir, Barlow), 'Big Boss Man' (Smith, Dixon), 'Sugar Magnolia' (Weir, Hunter), 'Not Fade Away' (Petty, Hardin), 'Goin' Down The Road Feeling Bad' (trad.), 'Not Fade Away' (Petty, Hardin)

Fox Theatre December 10, 1971
'Bertha' (Garcia, Hunter), 'Me And My Uncle' (John Phillips), 'Mr. Charlie' (McKernan, Hunter), 'Loser' (Garcia, Hunter), 'Beat It On Down The Line' (Jesse Fuller), 'Sugaree' (Garcia, Hunter), 'Jack Straw' (Weir, Hunter), 'Next Time You See Me' (Harvey, Forest), 'Tennessee Jed' (Garcia, Hunter), 'El Paso' (Marty Robbins), 'Big Railroad Blues' (Noah Lewis), 'Casey Jones' (Garcia, Hunter), 'Good Lovin'' (Clark, Resnick), 'Brokedown Palace' (Garcia, Hunter), 'Playing In The Band' (Weir, Hart, Hunter), 'Run Rudolph Run' (Marks, Brodie), 'Deal' (Garcia, Hunter), 'Sugar Magnolia' (Weir, Hunter), 'Comes A Time' (Garcia, Hunter), 'Truckin'' (Garcia, Lesh, Weir, Hunter), 'Drums' (Bill Kreutzmann), 'The Other One' (Weir, Kreutzmann), 'Sittin' On Top Of The World' (Carter, Jacobs), 'The Other One' (Weir, Kreutzmann), 'Not Fade Away' (Petty, Hardin), 'Goin' Down The Road Feeling Bad' (trad.), 'Not Fade Away' (Petty, Hardin), 'One More Saturday Night' (Weir)

Fox Theatre October 17, 1972
'Promised Land' (Chuck Berry), 'Bird Song' (Garcia, Hunter), 'El Paso' (Marty Robbins), 'Sugaree' (Garcia, Hunter), 'Me And My Uncle' (John Phillips), 'Tennessee Jed' (Garcia, Hunter), 'Big River' (Johnny Cash), 'China Cat Sunflower' (Garcia, Hunter), 'I Know You Rider' (trad.), 'Black-Throated Wind' (Weir, Barlow), 'Deal' (Garcia, Hunter), 'Cumberland Blues' (Garcia, Lesh, Hunter), 'Playing In The Band' (Weir, Hart, Hunter), 'Casey Jones' (Garcia, Hunter), 'Greatest Story Ever Told' (Weir, Hart, Hunter), 'Don't Ease Me In' (trad.), 'Mexicali Blues' (Weir, Barlow), 'Black Peter' (Garcia, Hunter), 'Me And Bobby McGee' (Kristofferson, Foster), 'Bertha' (Garcia, Hunter), 'Jack Straw' (Weir, Hunter), 'Friend Of The Devil' (Garcia, Dawson, Hunter), 'Beat It On Down the Line' (Jesse Fuller), 'Ramble On Rose' (Garcia, Hunter), 'Mississippi Half-Step Uptown Toodeloo' (Garcia, Hunter), 'Sugar Magnolia' (Weir, Hunter), 'Not Fade Away' (Petty, Hardin), 'Goin' Down The Road Feeling Bad' (trad.), 'Not Fade Away' (Petty, Hardin), 'Uncle John's Band' (Garcia, Hunter), 'Johnny B. Goode' (Chuck Berry)

Fox Theatre October 18, 1972
'Bertha' (Garcia, Hunter), 'Me And My Uncle' (John Phillips), 'Don't Ease Me In' (trad.), 'Mexicali Blues' (Weir, Barlow), 'Brown-Eyed Women' (Garcia, Hunter), 'Beat It On Down The Line' (Jesse Fuller), 'Bird Song' (Garcia, Hunter), 'Big River' (Johnny Cash), 'Loser' (Garcia, Hunter), 'Jack Straw' (Weir, Hunter), 'Big Railroad Blues' (Noah Lewis), 'El Paso' (Marty Robbins), 'China Cat Sunflower' (Garcia, Hunter), 'I Know You Rider' (trad.), 'Playing In The Band' (Weir, Hart, Hunter), 'Drums' (Kreutzmann), 'Dark Star' (Garcia, Hart, Kreutzmann, Lesh, McKernan, Weir, Hunter), 'Morning Dew' (Dobson, Rose), 'Playing In The Band' (Weir, Hart, Hunter), 'Deal' (Garcia, Hunter), 'Promised Land' (Chuck Berry), 'Brokedown Palace' (Garcia, Hunter), 'One More Saturday Night' (Weir), 'Casey Jones' (Garcia, Hunter)

Fox Theatre October 19, 1972
'Promised Land' (Chuck Berry), 'Tennessee Jed' (Garcia, Hunter), 'Jack Straw' (Weir, Hunter), 'Don't Ease Me In' (trad.), 'Black-Throated Wind' (Weir, Barlow), 'Sugaree' (Garcia, Hunter), 'Mexicali Blues' (Weir, Barlow), 'Bertha' (Garcia, Hunter), 'El Paso' (Marty Robbins), 'China Cat Sunflower' (Garcia, Hunter), 'I Know You Rider' (trad.), 'Beat It On

Down The Line' (Jesse Fuller), 'Dire Wolf' (Garcia, Hunter), 'Around And Around' (Chuck Berry), 'Casey Jones' (Garcia, Hunter), 'Big River' (Johnny Cash), 'Friend Of The Devil' (Garcia, Dawson, Hunter), 'Me And My Uncle' (John Phillips), 'Bird Song' (Garcia, Hunter), 'Truckin'' (Garcia, Lesh, Weir, Hunter), 'Drums' (Kreutzmann), 'The Other One' (Weir, Kreutzmann), 'He's Gone' (Garcia, Hunter), 'The Other One' (Weir, Kreutzmann), 'Greatest Story Ever Told' (Weir, Hart, Hunter), 'Comes A Time' (Garcia, Hunter), 'Not Fade Away' (Petty, Hardin), 'Goin' Down The Road Feeling Bad' (trad.), 'Not Fade Away' (Petty, Hardin)

Kiel Auditorium October 29, 1973
'Cold Rain And Snow' (trad.), 'Beat It On Down The Line' (Jesse Fuller), 'Brown-Eyed Women' (Garcia, Hunter), 'Mexicali Blues' (Weir, Barlow), 'Don't Ease Me In' (trad.), 'Black-Throated Wind' (Weir, Barlow), 'Tennessee Jed' (Garcia, Hunter), 'The Race Is On' (Don Rollins), 'Row Jimmy' (Garcia, Hunter), 'El Paso' (Marty Robbins), 'Eyes Of The World' (Garcia, Hunter), 'China Doll' (Garcia, Hunter), 'Around And Around' (Chuck Berry), 'Promised Land' (Chuck Berry), 'Bertha' (Garcia, Hunter), 'Greatest Story Ever Told' (Weir, Hart, Hunter), 'Loser' (Garcia, Hunter), 'Big River' (Johnny Cash), 'Brokedown Palace' (Garcia, Hunter), 'Truckin'' (Garcia, Lesh, Weir, Hunter), 'Drums' (Kreutzmann), 'The Other One' (Weir, Kreutzmann), 'Wharf Rat' (Garcia, Hunter), 'Sugar Magnolia' (Weir, Hunter), 'Casey Jones' (Garcia, Hunter),

Kiel Auditorium, October 30, 1973
'Here Comes Sunshine' (Garcia, Hunter), 'Me And My Uncle' (John Phillips), 'Ramble On Rose' (Garcia, Hunter), 'Looks Like Rain' (Weir, Barlow), 'Deal' (Garcia, Hunter), 'Mexicali Blues' (Weir, Barlow), 'They Love Each Other' (Garcia, Hunter), 'El Paso' (Marty Robbins), 'Row Jimmy' (Garcia, Hunter), 'Jack Straw' (Weir, Hunter), 'China Cat Sunflower' (Garcia, Hunter), 'I Know You Rider' (trad.), 'Playing In The Band' (Weir, Hart, Hunter), 'Mississippi Half-Step Uptown Toodeloo' (Garcia, Hunter), 'Big River' (Johnny Cash), 'Goin' Down The Road Feeling Bad' (trad.), 'Johnny B. Goode' (Chuck Berry), 'One More Saturday Night' (Weir), 'Dark Star' (Garcia, Hart, Kreutzmann, Lesh, McKernan, Weir, Hunter), 'Stella Blue' (Garcia, Hunter) 'Eyes Of The World' (Garcia, Hunter) 'Weather Report Suite': l) 'Prelude' (Weir), ll) 'Part 1' (Weir, Eric Andersen), lll) 'Part 2 – Let It Grow' (Weir, Barlow)

Appendix Four – Compilation albums

Skeletons From The Closet: The Best Of The Grateful Dead (1974)
Personnel:
Jerry Garcia: lead guitar, vocals, pedal steel on 'Sugar Magnolia'
Bill Kreutzmann: drums, percussion except 'Rosemary'
Phil Lesh: bass guitar, vocals, backup vocals on 'Mexicali Blues'
Ron 'Pigpen' McKernan: organ, harmonica, vocals, lead vocals and conga on 'Turn On Your Love Light'
Bob Weir: rhythm guitar, vocals, lead vocals on 'Truckin'', 'Sugar Magnolia', 'Mexicali Blues'
Mickey Hart: drums, percussion on 'Truckin'', 'Sugar Magnolia', 'St Stephen', 'Uncle John's Band', 'Casey Jones', 'Turn On Your Love Light', 'Friend Of The Devil'
Tom Constanten: keyboards on 'Rosemary', 'St Stephen', 'Turn On Your Love Light'
Keith Godchaux: piano on 'Mexicali Blues', 'One More Saturday Night'
Donna Jean Godchaux: backing vocals on 'One More Saturday Night'
Additional Performers:
John 'Marmaduke' Dawson, Debbie, Peter Grant, Mouse David Nelson, Wendy on 'Rosemary' and 'St Stephen'
David Grisman: mandolin on 'Friend Of The Devil'
Howard Wales: organ on 'Truckin''
Snooky Flowers: horns on 'Mexicali Blues'
Luis Gasca: horns on 'Mexicali Blues'
The Space Rangers: horns on 'Mexicali Blues'
Produced by Stephen Barncard, Betty Cantor, David Hassinger, The Grateful Dead and Bob Matthews
Release date: February 1974
Running time: 44:53
'The Golden Road (To Unlimited Devotion)' (Garcia, Lesh, Weir, Kreutzmann, McKernan), 'Truckin'' (Garcia, Lesh, Weir, Hunter), 'Rosemary' (Garcia, Hunter), 'Sugar Magnolia' (Weir, Hunter), 'St. Stephen' (Garcia, Lesh, Hunter), 'Uncle John's Band' (Garcia, Hunter), 'Casey Jones' (Garcia, Hunter) 'Mexicali Blues' (Weir, Barlow) 'Turn On Your Love Light' (Malone, Scott), 'One More Saturday Night' (Bob Weir) 'Friend Of The Devil' (Garcia, Dawson, Hunter)

What A Long Strange Trip It's Been (1977)
Personnel:
Tom Constanten: keyboards
Jerry Garcia: guitar, vocals
Donna Jean Godchaux: vocals
Keith Godchaux: piano, keyboards
Mickey Hart: drums
Bill Kreutzmann: drums
Phil Lesh: bass guitar, vocals
Ron 'Pigpen' McKernan: organ, vocals
Bob Weir: guitar, vocals
Production and engineering by Betty Cantor and Bob Matthews. Production by David Hassinger and Owsley Stanley. Executive production by Paul Wexler.
Release date: August 1977
Running time: 85:38

'New, New Minglewood Blues' (McGannahan Skjellyfetti), 'Cosmic Charlie' (Garcia, Hunter), 'Truckin'' (Garcia, Lesh, Weir, Hunter), 'Black Peter' (Garcia, Hunter), 'Born Cross-Eyed' (The Grateful Dead), 'Ripple' (Garcia, Hunter), 'Doin' That Rag' (Garcia, Hunter), 'Dark Star' (Garcia, Hunter), 'High Time' (Garcia, Hunter), 'New Speedway Boogie' (Garcia, Hunter), 'St. Stephen' (Garcia, Lesh, Hunter), 'Jack Straw' (Weir, Hunter), 'Me And My Uncle' (John Phillips), 'Tennessee Jed' (Garcia, Hunter), 'Cumberland Blues' (Garcia, Lesh, Hunter), 'Playing In The Band' (Weir, Hart, Hunter) 'Brown-Eyed Women' (Garcia, Hunter), 'Ramble On Rose' (Garcia, Hunter)

The Arista Years (1996)
Personnel:
Jerry Garcia: guitar, vocals
Donna Jean Godchaux: vocals
Keith Godchaux: keyboards, vocals
Mickey Hart: drums
Bill Kreutzmann: drums
Phil Lesh: bass
Breny Mydland: keyboards, vocals
Bob Weir: guitar, vocals
Additional Performers:
Jordan Amarantha: percussion
Branford Marsalis: saxophone (soprano, tenor)
Matthew Kelly: harmonica, harp
Tom Scott: saxophone, lyricon
Production: Jerry Garcia, Lowell George. Programming, associate producer: Bob Bralove. Producers, engineers: Betty Cantor-Jackson, John Cutler, Dan Healy, Gary Lyons, Keith Olsen. Engineers: Guy Charbonneau, David DeVore, Tom Flye, Justin Kreutzmann, Bob Matthews, Peter Miller, Jeffrey Norman, David Roberts, Jeff Sterling, Pete Thea, Chris Wiske 'Estimated Prophet' (Weir, Barlow), 'Passenger' (Lesh, Monk), 'Samson And Delilah' (Weir), 'Terrapin Station: Medley' (Garcia, Hunter), 'Good Lovin'' (Resnick, Clark), 'Shakedown Street' (Garcia, Hunter), 'Fire On The Mountain' (Hart, Hunter), 'I Need A Miracle' (Weir, Barlow) 'Alabama Getaway' (Garcia, Hunter), 'Far From Me' (Mydland), 'Saint Of Circumstance' (Weir, Barlow) 'Dire Wolf' (Garcia, Hunter), 'Cassidy' (Weir, Barlow), 'Feel Like A Stranger' (Weir, Barlow), 'Franklin's Tower' (Garcia, Kreutzmann, Hunter) 'Touch Of Grey' (Garcia, Hunter), 'Hell In A Bucket' (Weir, Barlow, Mydland), 'West L.A. Fadeaway' (Garcia, Hunter), 'Throwing Stones' (Weir, Barlow), 'Black Muddy River' (Garcia, Hunter), 'Foolish Heart' (Garcia, Hunter), 'Built To Last' (Garcia, Hunter), 'Just A Little Light' (Mydland, Barlow), 'Picasso Moon' (Weir, Barlow, Bralove) 'Standing On The Moon' (Garcia, Hunter), 'Eyes Of The World' (Garcia, Hunter)

The Very Best Of Grateful Dead (2003)
Personnel:
Tom Constanten: keyboards
Jerry Garcia: guitar, pedal steel vocals
Donna Godchaux: vocals
Keith Godchaux: keyboards
Mickey Hart: drums
Bill Kreutzmann: drums, percussion
Phil Lesh: bass guitar

Ron McKernan: organ on 'The Golden Road (To Unlimited Devotion)' and 'One More Saturday Night'
Bob Weir: guitar, vocals
Produced by James Austin and David Lemieux.
Release date: March 1967
Running time: 77:05
'Truckin'' (Garcia, Lesh, Weir, Hunter), 'Touch Of Grey' (Garcia, Hunter), 'Sugar Magnolia' (Weir, Hunter), 'Casey Jones' (Garcia, Hunter), 'Uncle John's Band' (Garcia, Hunter), 'Friend Of The Devil' (Garcia, Dawson, Hunter), 'Franklin's Tower' (Garcia, Hunter), 'Estimated Prophet' (Weir, Barlow), 'Eyes Of The World' (Garcia, Hunter), 'Box Of Rain' (Lesh, Hunter), 'U.S. Blues' (Garcia, Hunter), 'The Golden Road (To Unlimited Devotion)' (Garcia, Kreutzmann, Lesh, McKernan, Weir), 'One More Saturday Night' (Weir), 'Fire On The Mountain' (Hart, Hunter), 'The Music Never Stopped' (Weir, Barlow), 'Hell In A Bucket' (Weir, Mydland, Barlow), 'Ripple' (Garcia, Hunter)

Flashback With The Grateful Dead (2011)
Personnel:
Tom Constanten: keyboards on 'China Cat Sunflower'
Jerry Garcia: guitar, vocals
Donna Jean Godchaux: vocals on 'Unbroken Chain', 'U.S. Blues', 'The Music Never Stopped', 'Shakedown Street'
Keith Godchaux: keyboards on 'Unbroken Chain', 'U.S. Blues', 'The Music Never Stopped' 'Shakedown Street',
Mickey Hart: drums
Bill Kreutzmann: drums on 'Truckin'', 'China Cat Sunflower', 'The Music Never Stopped', 'Shakedown Street', 'Alabama Getaway', 'Throwing Stones', 'Standing On The Moon', 'Touch Of Grey'
Phil Lesh: bass, vocals
Ron 'Pigpen' McKernan: keyboards on 'Truckin'', 'China Cat Sunflower'
Brent Mydland: keyboards, vocals on 'Alabama Getaway', 'Throwing Stones', 'Standing On The Moon', 'Touch Of Grey'
Bob Weir: guitar, vocals
Additional Musicians:
Howard Wales: organ on 'Truckin''
Mastered by David Glasser
Release date: April 2011
Running time: 51:52
'Truckin'' (Garcia, Lesh, Weir, Hunter), 'China Cat Sunflower' (Garcia, Hunter), 'Unbroken Chain' (Lesh, Petersen) 'U.S. Blues' (Garcia, Hunter), 'The Music Never Stopped' (Weir, Barlow) 'Shakedown Street' (Garcia, Hunter), 'Alabama Getaway' (Garcia, Hunter), 'Throwing Stones' (Weir, Barlow), 'Standing On The Moon' (Garcia, Hunter), 'Touch Of Grey' (Garcia, Hunter)

The Best Of The Grateful Dead (2015)
Personnel:
Tom Constanten: keyboards
Jerry Garcia: guitar, vocals
Donna Jean Godchaux: vocals
Keith Godchaux: keyboards

327

Mickey Hart: drums, percussion
Bill Kreutzmann: drums, percussion
Phil Lesh: bass, vocals
Ron 'Pigpen' McKernan: organ, harmonica, percussion, vocals
Bob Weir: guitar, vocals
Producer (Compilation) David Lemieux.
Release date: March 2015
'The Golden Road (To Unlimited Devotion)' (Garcia, Kreutzmann, Lesh, McKernan, Weir), 'Cream Puff War' (Garcia), 'Born Cross-Eyed' (Weir), 'Dark Star' (Single Version) (Garcia, Hart, Kreutzmann, Lesh, McKernan, Weir, Hunter), 'St. Stephen' (Garcia, Lesh, Hunter), 'China Cat Sunflower' (Garcia, Hunter), 'Uncle John's Band' (Garcia, Hunter), 'Easy Wind' (Hunter), 'Casey Jones' (Garcia, Hunter), 'Truckin'' (Garcia, Lesh, Weir, Hunter), 'Box Of Rain' (Lesh, Hunter), 'Sugar Magnolia' (Weir, Hunter), 'Friend Of The Devil' (Garcia, Dawson, Hunter), 'Ripple' (Garcia, Hunter), 'Eyes Of The World' (Garcia, Hunter), 'Unbroken Chain' (Lesh, Petersen), 'Scarlet Begonias' (Garcia, Hunter), 'The Music Never Stopped' (Weir, Barlow), 'Estimated Prophet' (Weir, Barlow), 'Terrapin Station' (Garcia, Hart, Kreutzmann, Hunter), 'Shakedown Street' (Garcia, Hunter), 'I Need A Miracle' (Weir, Barlow), 'Fire On The Mountain' (Hart, Hunter), 'Feel Like A Stranger' (Weir, Barlow), 'Far From Me' (Mydland), 'Touch Of Grey' (Garcia, Hunter), 'Hell In A Bucket' (Weir, Barlow, Mydland), 'Throwing Stones' (Weir, Barlow), 'Black Muddy River' (Garcia, Hunter), 'Blow Away' (Mydland, Barlow), 'Foolish Heart' (Garcia, Hunter), 'Standing On The Moon' (Garcia, Hunter)

Ramble On Rose (2015)

Personnel:
Jerry Garcia: guitar, vocals
Donna Jean Godchaux: vocals
Keith Godchaux: keyboards
Bill Kreutzmann: drums
Phil Lesh: bass, vocals
Ron 'Pigpen' McKernan: organ, harmonica, vocals
Bob Weir: guitar, vocals
Compiled by John Mulvey, Jon Dale, Nigel Williamson
Given away free with issue 220 of Uncut magazine, Jul 2015
'Mr Charlie' (McKernan, Hunter), 'Brown-Eyed Woman' (Garcia, Hunter), [From *Dick's Picks Vol. 35*], 'Looks Like Rain' (Weir, Barlow) [From *Dick's Picks Vol. 28*], 'He's Gone' (Garcia, Hunter) [*From Europe '72: Olympia Theatre, Paris France 5/3/1972*], 'Loser' (Garcia, Hunter) [From *Dick's Picks Vol. 36*], 'Comes A Time' [From *Hundred Year Hall*], 'Ramble On Rose' (Garcia, Hunter) [From *Dick's Picks Vol. 36*], 'Chinatown Shuffle' (Ron McKernan) [From *So Many Roads (1965-1995)*], 'Black-Throated Wind' (Weir, Barlow) [From *Dick's Picks Vol.11*], 'To Lay Me Down' (Garcia, Hunter) [From *So Many Roads (1965-1995)*]

Long Strange Trip Soundtrack (2017)

Personnel
Tom Constanten: keyboards
Jerry Garcia: guitar, vocals
Donna Jean Godchaux: vocals
Keith Godchaux: keyboards

Mickey Hart: drums, percussion
Bill Kreutzmann: drums, percussion
Phil Lesh: bass, vocals
Brent Mydland: keyboards, vocals
Ron 'Pigpen' McKernan: organ, harmonica, percussion, vocals
Bob Weir: guitar, vocals
Vince Welnick: keyboards, vocals
Compilation produced by David Lemieux and Amir Bar-Lev
Release date: May 2017
Running time: 3:52:59
'Death Don't Have No Mercy' (Rev. Gary Davis) [*Live/Dead*, Live: Fillmore West, San Francisco, February 27 1969], 'St. Stephen' (Garcia, Lesh, Hunter) [*Live/Dead*, Live: Fillmore West, San Francisco, February 27 1969], 'Uncle John's Band' (Garcia, Hunter) [*Workingman's Dead*], 'Dark Star' (Garcia, Hart, Kreutzmann, Lesh, McKernan, Weir, Hunter) [Live, Fillmore East, New York, February 14 1970], 'Easy Wind' (Hunter) [*Workingman's Dead*], 'Candyman' (Garcia, Hunter) [*American Beauty*], 'China Cat Sunflower' ((Garcia, Hunter), [Live, Chateau d'Herouville, Herouville, France, June 21 1971], 'I Know You Rider' (trad.) [Live, Chateau d'Herouville, Herouville, France June 21 1971], 'Morning Dew' (Dobson, Rose) [*Europe '72*], 'He's Gone' (Garcia, Hunter) [Sunshine Daydream], 'The Music Never Stopped' (Weir, Barlow) [*One From The Vault*], 'Scarlet Begonias' (Garcia, Hunter) [Cornell 5/8/77], 'Fire On The Mountain' (Hart, Hunter) [Cornell 5/8/77], 'Althea' (Garcia, Hunter) [*Go To Nassau*], 'Touch Of Grey' (Garcia, Hunter) [*In The Dark*], 'Dear Mr. Fantasy' (Capaldi, Winwood, Wood) [Live, Sullivan Stadium, Foxboro, Massachusetts, July 2/1989], 'Hey Jude' (Lennon, McCartney) [Live, Sullivan Stadium, Foxboro, Massachusetts, July 2/1989], 'Ripple' (Garcia, Hunter) [*American Beauty*], 'Brokedown Palace' (Garcia, Hunter) [*American Beauty*], 'Playing In The Band' (Weir, Hunter) [*Europe '72: The Complete Recordings*], 'Eyes Of The World' (Garcia, Hunter) [*Dick's Picks, Vol. 31*], 'St. Stephen' (Garcia, Lesh, Hunter) [*Cornell 5/8/77*], 'Not Fade Away' (Holly, Petty) [*Cornell 5/8/77*], 'St. Stephen' (Garcia, Hunter) [*Cornell 5/8/77*], 'Dark Hollow' (Bill Browning) [*Reckoning*], 'Stella Blue' (Garcia, Hunter) [Live, Zoo Amphitheater, Oklahoma City, Oklahoma July 5 1981], 'Days Between' (Garcia, Hunter) [Live, Madison Square Garden, New York, October 18 1994]

Smiling On A Cloudy Day (2017)

Personnel:
Tom Constanten: keyboards, piano
Jerry Garcia: lead guitar, vocals, pedal steel, piano
Mickey Hart: drums, percussion
Bill Kreutzmann: drums, percussion
Phil Lesh: bass, vocals, guitar, piano
Ron 'Pigpen' McKernan: organ, harmonica, vocals, keyboards, acoustic guitar, congas, percussion
Bob Weir: guitar, vocals
Compilation producer: David Lemieux
Release date: July 2017
Running time: 40:22
'The Golden Road (To Unlimited Devotion)' (Garcia, Weir, McKernan, Lesh, Kreutzmann), 'Cream Puff War' (Jerry Garcia), 'Morning Dew' (Dobson, Rose), 'That's It For The Other One – Cryptical Envelopment' (Garcia, Weir) – 'Quadlibet For Tender Feet' (Weir,

Garcia, McKernan, Lesh, Kreutzmann) – 'The Faster We Go, The Rounder We Get' (Weir, Kreutzmann) – 'We Leave The Castle' (Constanten), 'Born Cross-Eyed' (Weir), Dark Star (Single Version) (Garcia, Hunter), 'St. Stephen' (Garcia, Lesh, Hunter), 'China Cat Sunflower' (Garcia, Hunter), 'Doin' That Rag' (Garcia, Hunter), 'Cosmic Charlie' (Garcia, Hunter)

The Best Of The Grateful Dead Live (2018)

Personnel:
Jerry Garcia: guitar, vocals
Bob Weir: guitar, vocals
Phil Lesh: bass, vocals
Bill Kreutzmann: drums, percussion
Mickey Hart: drums, percussion on 'St. Stephen', 'The Music Never Stopped', 'Estimated Prophet', 'Friend Of The Devil', 'Feel Like A Stranger', 'Fire On The Mountain', 'Bird Song', 'Ripple', 'Eyes Of The World', 'Touch Of Grey', 'Blow Away', 'So Many Roads'
Ron 'Pigpen' McKernan: organ, harmonica, percussion, vocals on 'St. Stephen', 'Bertha', 'Wharf Rat', Sugar Magnolia', 'Jack Straw', 'Truckin'', 'Morning Dew', 'Brown-Eyed Women'
Tom Constanten: keyboards on 'St. Stephen'
Keith Godchaux: keyboards on 'Sugar Magnolia', 'Jack Straw', 'Truckin'', 'Morning Dew', 'Brown-Eyed Women', 'The Music Never Stopped', 'Estimated Prophet'
Donna Jean Godchaux: vocals on 'Sugar Magnolia', 'Jack Straw', 'Truckin'', 'Morning Dew', 'Brown-Eyed Women', 'The Music Never Stopped', 'Estimated Prophet'
Brent Mydland: keyboards, vocals on 'Friend Of The Devil', 'Feel Like A Stranger', 'Fire On The Mountain', 'Bird Song', 'Ripple', 'Eyes Of The World', 'Touch Of Grey', 'Blow Away'
Vince Welnick: keyboards, vocals on 'So Many Roads'
Additional personnel:
Merl Saunders: organ on Bertha, Wharf rat
Branford Marsalis: saxophone on 'Eyes Of The World'
Compilation produced for release by David Lemieux
Release date: March 2018
Running time: 2:33:37
'St. Stephen' (Garcia, Lesh, Hunter) [From *Live/Dead*], 'Bertha' (Garcia, Hunter) [From *Grateful Dead*], 'Wharf Rat' (Garcia, Hunter) [From *Grateful Dead*], 'Sugar Magnolia' (Garcia, Hunter) [From *Europe '72*], 'Jack Straw' (Weir, Hunter) [From *Europe '72*], 'Truckin'' (Garcia, Lesh, Weir, Hunter) [From *Europe '72*], 'Morning Dew' (Dobson, Rose) [From *Europe '72*], 'Brown-Eyed Women' (Garcia, Hunter) [From *Europe '72*], 'The Music Never Stopped' (Weir, Barlow) [From *One From The Vault*], 'Estimated Prophet' (Weir, Barlow) [From *Cornell 5/8/77*], 'Friend Of The Devil' ((Garcia, Dawson, Hunter) [From *Dead Set*], 'Feel Like A Stranger' (Weir, Barlow) [From *Dead Set*], 'Fire On The Mountain' (Hart, Hunter) [From *Dead Set*], 'Bird Song' (Garcia, Hunter) [From *Reckoning*], 'Ripple' (Garcia, Hunter) [From *Reckoning*], 'Eyes Of The World' (Garcia, Hunter) [From *Without A Net*], 'Touch of Grey' (Garcia, Hunter) [From *Truckin' Up To Buffalo*], 'Blow Away' (Mydland, Hunter) [From *Crimson, White And Indigo*], 'So Many Roads' (Garcia, Hunter) [From *So Many Roads (1965-1995)*]

Sage And Spirit (2019)

Personnel:
Jerry Garcia: guitar, vocals
Bob Weir: guitar, vocals

Phil Lesh: guitar, vocals
Bill Kreutzmann: drums
Mickey Hart: drums
Ron 'Pigpen' McKernan: organ on 'Brown Eyed Women' and percussion on 'Jack Straw'
Keith Godchaux: keyboards
Brent Mydland: keyboards, vocals
Donna Jean Godchaux : vocals
Compilation produced for release by David Lemieux
Release date: April 2019
Running time: 49:33
'Sugar Magnolia' [From *American Beauty*], 'Eyes Of Tthe World' (Garcia, Hunter) [From *Wake Of The Flood*], 'Lost Sailor' [From *Go To Heaven*], 'Saint Of Circumstance' [From *Go To Heaven*], 'High Time' (Garcia, Hunter) [From *Workingman's Dead*], 'Sage And Spirit' (Weir) [From *Blues For Allah*], 'Jack Straw' (Weir, Hunter) [From *Europe '72*]], 'Unbroken Chain' (Lesh, Petersen) [From *From The Mars Hotel*] 'Brown-Eyed Women' (Garcia, Hunter) [From *Europe '72*], 'If I Had the World to Give' (Garcia, Hunter) [From *Shakedown Street*]
Fire On The Mountain Soundtrack (2020)
Compiled by David Lemieux
Release date: December 2020
Running time: 46:13
'Brown-Eyed Women' (Garcia, Hunter) [From *Europe '72*], 'New Speedway Boogie' (Garcia, Hunter) [From *Workingman's Dead*], 'Playing In The Band' (Garcia, Hunter) [From *Europe '72 Vol. 2*], 'Fire On The Mountain' (Weir, Hunter) [From *Cornell 5/8/77*,] 'Ripple' (Garcia, Hunter) [From *American Beauty*]

Appendix Five – Significant solo albums by year of release

Garcia (1972) (Jerry Garcia)
Personnel:
Jerry Garcia: acoustic guitar, electric guitar, pedal steel guitar, bass, piano, organ. vocals
Bill Kreutzmann: drums
Recorded in July 1971. Produced by Bob Matthews, Betty Cantor and Bill Kreutzmann.
Release date: January 1972
Running time: 40:00
'Deal' (Garcia, Hunter), 'Bird Song' (Garcia, Hunter), 'Sugaree' (Garcia, Hunter),
'Loser' (Garcia, Hunter), 'Late for Supper' (Garcia, Kreutzmann), 'Spidergawd' (Garcia,
Kreutzmann), 'Eep Hour' (Garcia, Kreutzmann), 'To Lay Me Down' (Garcia, Hunter), 'An
Odd Little Place' (Garcia, Kreutzmann), 'The Wheel' (Hunter, Garcia, Kreutzmann)
2004 reissue bonus tracks: 'Sugaree (Alternate Take)' (Garcia, Hunter), 'Loser (Alternate
Take)' (Garcia, Hunter), 'Late For Supper/Spidergawd/Eep Hour (Alternate Takes)' (Garcia,
Kreutzmann), 'The Wheel (Alternate Take #1)' (Garcia, Hunter), 'The Wheel (Alternate
Take #2)' (Garcia, Hunter), 'Study for EEP Hour' (Garcia, Kreutzmann), 'Dealin' From The
Bottom (Studio Jam)' (Garcia, Kreutzmann), 'Study For The Wheel' (Garcia, Kreutzmann)

Ace (1972) (Bob Weir)
Personnel:
Jerry Garcia: lead guitar, pedal steel guitar on 'Looks Like Rain', backing vocals on 'Greatest
Story Ever Told'
Keith Godchaux: piano, organ
Bill Kreutzmann: drums, percussion
Phil Lesh: bass guitar, production; backup vocals on 'Mexicali Blues'
Bob Weir: lead vocals, electric and acoustic guitars
Additonal personnel:
Ed Bogas: string arrangement on 'Looks Like Rain'
Snooky Flowers, Luis Gasca and The Space Rangers: horns on 'Black-Throated Wind',
'Mexicali Blues' and 'One More Saturday Night'
Donna Jean Godchaux: backing vocals on 'Greatest Story Ever Told', 'Walk In The Sunshine',
'Playing In The Band' and 'Cassidy'
Dave Torbert: bass guitar on 'Greatest Story Ever Told'
Recorded in January – March 1972. Produced by 'everyone involved'
Release date: May 1972
Running time: 37:45
'Greatest Story Ever Told' (Weir, Hart, Hunter), 'Black-Throated Wind' (Weir, Barlow), 'Walk
In The Sunshine' (Weir, Barlow), 'Playing In The Band' (Weir, Hart, Hunter), 'Looks Like
Rain' (Weir, Barlow), 'Mexicali Blues' (Weir, Barlow), 'One More Saturday Night' (Weir),
'Cassidy' (Weir, Barlow)

Rolling Thunder (1972) (Mickey Hart)
Personnel:
Sam Andrew: guitar
Bill Champlin: organ

John Cipollina: guitar
Greg Errico: drums
David Freiberg: Vocals, bass, piano
Jerry Garcia: guitar, vocals
Carmelo Garcia: timbales
Terry Haggerty: guitar
Mickey Hart: drums
Zakir Hussain: tabla
Paul Kanter: vocals
Phil Lesh: vocals
Barry Melton: acoustic guitar, vocals
Steven Schuster: flute
Grace Slick: piano, vocals
Stephen Stills: bass
Robbie Stokes: guitar
Tower Of Power: horn section
Bob Weir: guitar, vocals
Recorded 1972 at Mickey's Barn, Marin County, California. Engineering by Dan Healy, Rick Davis, John Wollman, David Freiberg, Mickey Hart .
Release date: September 1972
Running time 39.06
'Rolling Thunder/Shoshone Invocation' (Rolling Thunder), 'The Main Ten (Playing In The Band)', (Hart, Weir, Hunter), 'Fletcher Carnaby' (Hart, Hunter), 'The Chase (Progress)' (Hart), 'Blind John' (Stetson, Monk), 'Young Man' (Hart, Monk), 'Deep, Wide, And Frequent' (Hart), 'Pump Song' (Weir, Hart, Hunter), 'Granma's Cookies' (Hart), 'Hangin' On' (Stetson, Monk; arr. Hart)

Compliments (1974) (Jerry Garcia)
Personnel:
Arthur Adams: guitar
Larry Carlton: guitar
Jerry Garcia: guitar, vocals, classical guitar
John Kahn: bass, horn arrangement, string arrangement
Michael Omartian, piano, tack piano, Fender Rhodes
Merl Saunders: organ
Ron Tutt: drums
Produced by John Kahn.
Release date: June 1974
Running time: 35:18
'Let It Rock' (Chuck Berry), 'When The Hunter Gets Captured By The Game' (Smokey Robinson), 'That's What Love Will Make You Do' (Thigpen, Banks, Marion), 'Russian Lullaby' (Irving Berlin), 'Turn On The Bright Lights' (Albert Washington), 'He Ain't Give You None' (Van Morrison), 'What Goes Around' (Mac Rebbenack), 'Let's Spend The Night Together' (Jagger, Richards), 'Mississippi Moon' (Peter Rowan), 'Midnight Town' (Hunter, Kahn)
2004 reissue bonus tracks: 'That's A Touch I Like' (Jesse Winchester), '(I'm A) Road Runner' (Holland, Dozier, Holland), 'It's Too Late (She's Gone)' (Chuck Willis), 'I'll Forget You' (copyright control), 'Tragedy' (Burch, Nelson), 'Think' (Malone, McKracklin), 'I Know It's A Sin' (Jimmy Reed), 'Lonesome Town' (Thomas Baker Knight), 'Cardiac Arrest (Studio Jam)' (Garcia, Kahn, Omartian, Saunders, Tutt), 'Back Home In Indiana' (Hanley, McDonald)

Old And In The Way (1975) (Jerry Garcia/Old and In The Way)
Personnel:
Vassar Clements: fiddle
Jerry Garcia: banjo, vocals
David Grisman: mandolin, vocals
John Kahn: acoustic bass
Peter Rowan: guitar, vocals
Recorded live on October 8, 1973, at the Boarding House in San Francisco. Produced by David Grisman
Release date: February 1975
Running time: 42:48
'Pig In A Pen' (trad.), 'Midnight Moonlight' (Peter Rowan), 'Old And In The Way' (David Grisman), 'Knockin' On Your Door' (trad.), 'The Hobo Song' (Jack Bonus), 'Panama Red' (Peter Rowan), 'Wild Horses' (Jagger, Richards), 'Kissimmee Kid' (Vassar Clements), 'White Dove' (Carter Stanley), 'Land Of The Navajo' (Peter Rowan)

Seastones (1975) (Ned Lagin and Phil Lesh)
Personnel:
Ned Lagin: piano, clavichord, organ, prepared piano, percussion, synthesizers, computers
Phil Lesh: electric bass
Jerry Garcia: electric guitar, voice
David Crosby: electric twelve-string guitar, voice
Grace Slick: voice
David Freiberg: voice
Mickey Hart: percussion
Spencer Dryden: percussion
Recorded in February 1975 at Mickey Hart's Rolling Thunder, Bob Weir's studio, Massachusetts Institute of Technology, Brandeis University. Produced by Ned Lagin
Release date: April 1975
Running time: 44:40
'I' (Ned Lagin), 'II (vocals)' (Ned Lagin), 'IIIA' (Ned Lagin), 'IIIB' (Ned Lagin), 'IV A (vocals)' (Ned Lagin), 'IV B (vocals)' (Ned Lagin), 'V A' (Ned Lagin), 'V B' (Ned Lagin), 'V I (vocals)' (Ned Lagin),'V II' (Ned Lagin)

Diga (1976) (Diga Rhythm Band/Mickey Hart)
Personnel:
Mickey Hart: traps, gongs, timbales, timpani
Zakir Hussain: tabla, folk drums, tar
Jordan Amarantha: congas, bongos
Peter Carmichael: tabla
Aushim Chaudhuri: tabla
Vince Delgado: dumbek, tabla, talking drum
Tor Dietrichson: tabla
Jim Loveless: marimbas
Joy Shulman: tabla
Ray Spiegel: vibes
Arshad Syed: duggi tarang, nal
Additional personnel
Jerry Garcia: guitar on 'Happiness Is Drumming', 'Razooli'

Jim McPherson: vocals on 'Razooli'
Kathy MacDonald: vocals on 'Razooli'
David Freiberg: vocals on 'Razooli'
Recorded in 1976 at Mickey's Barn, Marin County, California. Produced by Mickey Hart .
Release date: 1976
Razooli' (Ray Spiegel), 'Happiness Is Drumming' (Hart), 'Tal Mala' (Ustad Alla Rahka, Diga
Rhythm Band), 'Sweet Sixteen' (Diga Rhythm Band), 'Magnificent Sevens' (Diga Rhythm
Band)

Reflections (1976) (Jerry Garcia)
Personnel:
Jerry Garcia – lead guitar, acoustic guitar, organ, synthesizer, percussion, chimes, vocals
The Grateful Dead on 'Might As Well', 'They Love Eack Other' 'It Must Have Been The
Roses', 'Comes A Time' and 'Orpheus'
Bob Weir: second guitar, backing vocals
Phil Lesh: bass
Bill Kreutzmann: drums
Keith Godchaux: Fender Rhodes, acoustic piano, tack piano
Donna Jean Godchaux: backing vocals on 'Might as Well' and 'It Must Have Been the Roses'
Mickey Hart: drums, percussion
John Kahn: organ on 'They Love Each Other'
Jerry Garcia Band on 'Mission In The Rain', 'I'll Take A Melody', 'Tore Up Over You', 'Catfish
John', 'Mystery Train', 'All By Myself', 'Oh Babe, It Ain't No Lie', 'You Win Again'
Nicky Hopkins: piano
Larry Knechtel: Fender Rhodes, piano
John Kahn: bass, organ, synthesizer, vibraphone, clavinet
Ron Tutt: drums
Donna Jean Godchaux, Bob Weir: backing vocals on 'I'll Take a Melody' and 'Catfish John'
Mickey Hart: percussion on 'I'll Take a Melody', 'Tore up over You' and 'Catfish John'
Produced by Jerry Garcia.
Release date: February 1976
'Might As Well' (Garcia, Hunter), Mission In The Rain' (Garcia, Hunter), 'They Love Each
Other' (Garcia, Hunter), 'I'll Take a Melody' (Allen Toussaint), 'It Must Have Been the
Roses' (Hunter), 'Tore Up Over You' (Hank Ballard), 'Catfish John' (McDill, Reynolds),
'Comes a Time' (Garcia, Hunter)
2004 reissue bonus tracks: 'Mystery Train (Studio Jam)' (Parker, Phillips) 'All By Myself
(Studio Jam)' (Bartholomew, Domino), 'Oh Babe, It Ain't No Lie' (Elizabeth Cotten), 'You
Win Again' (Hank Williams), 'Orpheus' (Grateful Dead)

Kingfish (1976) (Bob Weir)
Personnel:
Chris Herold: drums, percussion
Robby Hoddinott: lead guitar, slide guitar
Matthew Kelly: guitar, harmonica, vocals
Dave Torbert: bass, vocals
Bob Weir: guitar, vocals, lead vocals on 'Lazy Lightnin'', 'Supplication', 'Home To Dixie', 'Big
Iron' and 'Bye And Bye'
Additonal personnel:
Steve Evans: bass

Barry Flast: piano, vocals
Pablo Green: percussion on 'Hypnotize'
Anna Rizzo: vocals
Jim Sanchez: drums
J.D. Sharp: string synthesizer on tracks 1, 9, and 10
Recorded in 1975. Produced by Dan Healy and Bob Weir
Release date: March 1976
Running time: 40:07
'Lazy Lightnin'' (Barlow, Weir), 'Supplication' (Barlow, Weir), 'Wild Northland' (Hovey, Torbert), 'Asia Minor' (Carter, Gilbert, Hovey, Quigley), 'Home To Dixie' (Barlow, Cutler, Kelly, Weir), 'Jump For Joy' (Carter, Gilbert), 'Good-Bye Yer Honor' (Hovey, Kelly, Torbert), 'Big Iron' (Marty Robbins), 'This Time' (Kelly, Torbert), 'Hypnotize' (Kelly, Torbert), 'Bye And Bye' (trad.)

Heaven Help The Fool (1978) Bob Weir
Personnel:
Bob Weir: rhythm guitar, vocals
Mike Baird: drums on tracks 1, 3-6, 8
Bill Champlin: backing vocals on tracks 1, 3-8, keyboards on tracks 2 and 7, organ on tracks 3 and 8
David Foster: keyboards on tracks 1-8
Lynette Gloud: background vocals on tracks 5-8
Tom Kelly: background vocals on tracks 1-6 and 8
Dee Murray: bass guitar on track 2
Nigel Olsson: drums on tracks 2 and 7
David Paich: keyboards on tracks 1, 3-6 and 8
Mike Porcaro: bass guitar on tracks 1 and 3-8
Peggy Sandvig: keyboards on track 4
Tom Scott: saxophones on tracks 1, 3 and 5
Carmen Twilley: background vocals on tracks 5-8
Waddy Wachtel: lead guitar on tracks 2-3 and 7
Recorded in summer 1977. Produced by Keith Olsen
Release date: January 1978
Running time: 34:43
'Bombs Away' (Barlow, Weir), 'Easy To Slip' (George, Kibbee), 'Salt Lake City' (Barlow, Weir), 'Shade Of Grey' (Barlow, Weir), 'Heaven Help The Fool' (Barlow, Weir), 'This Time Forever' (Barlow, Weir), 'I'll Be Doggone' (Moore, Robinson, Tarplin), 'Wrong Way Feelin'' (Barlow, Weir)

Cats Under The Stars (1978) (The Jerry Garcia Band/Jerry Garcia)
Personnel:
Jerry Garcia: guitar, vocals
Donna Jean Godchaux: vocals
Keith Godchaux: keyboards, background vocals
John Kahn: basses, keyboards, guitar, orchestration
Ron Tutt: drums, percussion
Maria Muldaur: background vocals on tracks 2, 8 and 10
Additional personnel:
Merl Saunders: organ

Stephen Schuster: flute, clarinet, saxophone
Brian Godchaux: violin
Candy Godchaux – violin
Produced by Jerry Garcia.
Release date: April 1978
Running time: 35:09
'Rubin And Cherise' (Garcia, Hunter), 'Love In The Afternoon' (Hunter, Kahn), 'Palm Sunday' (Garcia, Hunter), 'Cats Under The Stars' (Garcia, Hunter), 'Rhapsody In Red' (Hunter, Garcia, Kahn), 'Rain' (Donna Godchaux), 'Down Home' (Kahn), 'Gomorrah' (Garcia, Hunter)
2004 reissue bonus tracks: 'Magnificent Sanctuary Band' (Dorsey Burnette), 'I'll Be With Thee' (Dorothy Love Coates), The Way You Do the Things You Do' (Robinson, Rogers), 'Mighty High' (Crawford, Downing), Don't Let Go' (Jesse Stone), 'Down Home' (Rehearsal Version) (John Kahn), 'Palm Sunday' (Alternate Take) (Garcia, Hunter)

The Apocalypse Now Sessions (1980) (The Rhythm Devils/Mickey Hart and Bill Kreutzmann)
Personnel:
Mickey Hart, Bill Kreutzmann, Airto Moreira, Michael Hinton, Jim Loveless, Greg Errico, Jordan Amarantha, Flora Purim, Phil Lesh
Recorded at Club Front, San Rafael, California. Produced by Mickey Hart.
Release date: May 1980
All songs composed by The Rhythm Devils
'Compound', 'Trenches', 'Street Gang', 'The Beast', 'Steps', 'Tar', 'Lance', 'Cave', 'Hell's Bells', 'Kurtz', 'Napalm for Breakfast'

Bobby And The Midnites (1981) (Bob Weir)
Personnel:
Billy Cobham: drums, vocals
Bobby Cochran: guitar, vocals
Alphonso Johnson: bass guitar, vocals
Matt Kelly: harmonica, vocals
Brent Mydland: keyboards, Hammond B3, vocals
Bob Weir: guitar, vocals
Produced by Gary Lyons
Release date: October 1981
Running time: 38:47
'Haze' (Mydland, Mohawk, Weir, Cochran, Kelly), 'Too Many Losers' (Cochran, Weir), 'Far Away' (Weir, Cochran, Kelly), 'Book of Rules' (Johnson, Llewellyn), 'Me, Without You' (Barlow, Johnson), 'Josephine' (Weir), '(I Want to) Fly Away' (Barlow, Weir), 'Carry Me' (Weir), 'Festival' (Weir)

Run for the Roses (1982) (Jerry Garcia)
Personnel:
Jerry Garcia: guitar, vocals
John Kahn: bass, fretless bass, synthesizer, piano, clavinet, guitar
Michael Neuman: trumpet
Michael O'Martian – piano, clavinet

Merl Saunders: organ
Melvin Seals: organ
Liz Stires: vocals
Julie Stafford: vocals
Ron Tutt: drums, percussion
James Warren: piano, clavinet
Recorded September – December 1981. Produced by Jerry Garcia and John Kahn
Release date: November 1982
'Run For The Roses' (Garcia, Hunter), 'I Saw Her Standing There' (Lennon, McCartney),
'Without Love' (Clyde McPhatter), 'Midnight Getaway' (Garcia, Kahn, Hunter), 'Leave The
Little Girl Alone' (Kahn, Hunter), 'Valerie' (Garcia, Hunter), 'Knockin' On Heaven's Door'
(Bob Dylan)
2004 reissue bonus tracks: 'Fennario' (trad.) (aka Peggy-O), 'Alabama Getaway' (Garcia,
Hunter), 'Tangled Up In Blue' (Bob Dylan), 'Simple Twist Of Fate' (Bob Dylan), 'Dear
Prudence' (Lennon, McCartney), 'Valerie' (alternative mix) (Garcia, Hunter)

Where The Beat Meets The Street (1984) (Bobby and the Midnites/ Bob Weir)
Personnel:
Jeff Baxter: guitar, synthesizer
Paulette Brown: vocals
Billy Cobham: drums, vocals
Bobby Cochran: guitar, vocals
Steve Cropper: guitar
Paulinho Da Costa: percussion
Chuck Domenico: bass guitar
Jim Ehinger: keyboards
Kenny Gradney: bass, vocals
Alphonso Johnson: bass guitar, vocals
Sherlie Matthews: vocals
Brian Setzer: guitar
Bob Weir: guitar, vocals
Produced by Jeff Baxter
Release date: August 1984
'(I Want to Live in) America' (Barlow, Graham, Cochran, Weir), 'Where The Beat Meets
The Street' (Chinn, Glen), 'She's Gonna Win Your Heart' (Burnette, Williams), 'Ain't That
Peculiar' (Moore, Robinson, Rogers, Tarplin), 'Lifeguard' (Beckett, Lambert), 'Rock In The
80's' (Cochran), 'Lifeline' (Frederiksen, Haselden, Medica, Roddy), 'Falling' (Barlow, Baxter,
Gradney, Weir), 'Thunder And Lightning' (Cochran, Weir), 'Gloria Monday' (Barlow, Baxter,
Weir)

Almost Acoustic (1988) (Jerry Garcia Acoustic Band)
Personnel:
Jerry Garcia: guitar, vocals
John Kahn: acoustic bass,
David Kemper: snare drum
Kenny Kosek – fiddle
David Nelson: guitar, vocals
Sandy Rothman: mandolin, Dobro, vocals

Recorded live November 27-December 6, 1987. Produced by Sandy Rothman.
Release date: December 1988
Running time: 70:11
'Swing Low, Sweet Chariot' (trad.), 'Deep Elem Blues' (trad.), 'Blue Yodel #9 (Standing On
The Corner)' (Jimmie Rodgers), 'Spike Driver's Blues' (Mississippi John Hurt), 'I've Been All
Around This World' (trad.), 'Here To Get My Baby Out Of Jail' (Davis, Taylor), 'I'm Troubled'
(trad.), 'Oh, The Wind And Rain' (trad.), 'The Girl at the Crossroads Bar' (Bill Bryson), 'Oh,
Babe, It Ain't No Lie' (Elizabeth Cotten), 'Casey Jones' (Mississippi John Hurt), 'Diamond
Joe' (Tex Logan), 'Gone Home' (Bill Carlisle), 'Ripple' (Garcia, Hunter)

Jerry Garcia / David Grisman (1991) (Jerry Garcia)
Personnel:
Jerry Garcia: guitar, vocals
David Grisman: mandolin
Jim Kerwin: bass
Joe Craven: percussion, fiddle
Recorded in spring 1991. Produced by Jerry Garcia and David Grisman
Release date: August 1991
'The Thrill Is Gone' (Hawkins, Darnell), 'Grateful Dawg' (Garcia, Grisman), 'Two Soldiers'
(trad.), 'Friend Of The Devil' (Garcia, Hunter, Dawson), 'Russian Lullaby' (Irving Berlin),
'Dawg's Waltz' (David Grisman), 'Walkin' Boss' (trad.), 'Rockin' Chair' (Hoagy Carmichael),
'Arabia' (Grisman; middle part based on 'Hasta Siempre' (Carlos Puebla)

Jerry Garcia Band (1991)
Personnel:
Jerry Garcia: guitar, vocals
Gloria Jones: background vocals
John Kahn: bass guitar
David Kemper: drums
Jackie LaBranch: background vocals
Melvin Seals: organ, keyboards
Recorded live in spring/summer 1990. Produced by Jerry Garcia, John Kahn and John Cutler.
Release date: August 1991
'The Way You Do The Things You Do' (Robinson, Rogers), 'Waiting For A Miracle' (Bruce
Cockburn), 'Simple Twist Of Fate' (Bob Dylan), 'Get Out Of My Life' (Allen Toussaint), 'My
Sisters And Brothers' (Charles Johnson), 'I Shall Be Released' (Bob Dylan), 'Dear Prudence'
(Lennon, McCartney), 'Deal' (Garcia, Hunter), 'Stop That Train' (Peter Tosh), 'Senor (Tales
Of Yankee Power)' (Bob Dylan), 'Evangeline' (Hidalgo, Perez), 'The Night They Drove
Old Dixie Down' (Robbie Robertson), 'Don't Let Go' (Jesse Stone), 'That Lucky Old Sun'
(Gillespie, Smith), 'Tangled Up In Blue' (Bob Dylan)

Not for Kids Only (1993) (Jerry Garcia and David Grisman)
Personnel:
David Grisman: mandolin, mandocello, tenor banjo, vocals
Jerry Garcia: guitar, vocals, artwork
Hal Blaine: percussion, tambourine
Joe Craven: violin, percussion, foot stomping
Matt Eakle: piccolo, penny whistle
Larry Granger: violoncello

Larry Hanks: Jew's-Harp
Heather Katz: violin
Jim Kerwin: bass
Daniel Kobialka: violin
Pamela Lanford: English horn, oboe
Jim Miller: slap bass
Rick Montgomery: guitar
Kevin Porter: trombone
John Rosenberg: piano
Jim Rothermel: clarinet
Willow Scarlett: harmonica
Nanci Severance: viola
Jody Stecher: violin, vocals
Peter Welker: trumpet
Recorded 1993. Produced by David Grisman.
Release date: October 1993
'Jenny Jenkins' (trad.), 'Freight Train' (Elizabeth Cotten), 'A Horse Named Bill' (trad.), 'Three
Men Went A-Hunting' (trad.), 'When First Unto This Country' (trad.), 'Arkansas Traveller'
(trad.), 'Hopalong Peter' (trad.), 'Teddy Bears' Picnic' (trad.), 'There Ain't No Bugs On Me'
(trad.), 'The Miller's Will' (trad.), 'Hot Corn, Cold Corn' (trad.), 'A Shenandoah Lullaby' ('Oh
Shenandoah' and an instrumental version of Brahms' Lullaby) (trad.)

Live (1998) (Weir/Wasserman)
Personnel:
Bob Weir: acoustic guitar, vocals
Rob Wasserman: electric upright bass
Recorded live in autumn 1988, 'Eternity' recorded in summer 1992. Produced by Rob
Wasserman.
Release date: January 1998
Running time: 77:08
'Festival' (Weir), 'Walking Blues' (Robert Johnson), 'The Winners' (Weir, Kipling), 'K.C.
Moan' (trad.), 'Victim Or The Crime' (Weir, Graham), 'Looks Like Rain' (Weir, Barlow), 'Easy
To Slip' (Kibbee, George), 'Fever' (Davenport, Cooley), 'Eternity' (Weir, Wasserman, Willie
Dixon), 'This Time Forever' (Weir, Barlow), 'Shade Of Grey' (Weir, Barlow), 'Heaven Help
The Fool' (Weir, Barlow), 'Blue Sky Bop' (Wasserman), 'Throwing Stones' (Weir, Barlow)

Mother McCree's Uptown Jug Champions (1999) (Jerry Garcia, Pigpen, Bob Weir)
Personnel:
Jerry Garcia: guitar, kazoo, banjo, vocals
Ron 'Pigpen' McKernan: harmonica, vocals
Bob Weir: guitar, washtub bass, foot crusher, jug, kazoo, vocals
Dave Parker: washboard, kazoo, tin cup, vocals
Tom Stone: banjo, mandolin, guitar, vocals
Mike Garbett: washtub bass, guitar, kazoo
Recorded live at The Tangent in July 1964. Produced by Michael Wanger
Release date: 1999
Running time: 49:05
Overseas Stomp' (Will Shade), 'Ain't It Crazy' (Sam 'Lightnin'' Hopkins), Boo break, 'Yes She

Do, No She Don't' (DeRose, Trent), 'Memphis' (Chuck Berry), 'Boodle Am Shake' (Palmer, Williams), 'Big Fat Woman' (Huddie Ledbetter), 'Borneo' (Walter Donaldson), 'My Gal' (trad.), 'Shake That Thing' (Papa Charlie Jackson), 'Beat It On Down the Line' (Jesse Fuller), 'Cocaine Habit Blues' (trad.), 'Beedle Um Bum' (Booker T. Bradshaw), 'On the Road Again' (trad.), 'The Monkey And The Engineer' (Jesse Fuller), 'In The Jailhouse Now' (Jimmie Rodgers), 'Crazy Words, Crazy Tune' (Yellen, Ager), Band Interview

Weir Here (2004)

Personnel: As per source recordings. Unreleased RatDog rehearsal features:
Bob Weir: lead guitar, vocals
Jay Lane: drums, vocals
Jeff Chimenti: keyboards
Mark Karan: guitar
Kenny Brooks: Saxophone
Robin Sylvester: bass
Mastering by Joe Gastwirt at Joe's Mastering Joint
Release date: March 2004
Running time: 155:24
'Cassidy' (Barlow, Weir),' Mexicali Blues' (Barlow, Weir), 'Looks Like Rain' (Barlow, Weir), 'Playing In The Band' (Hart, Hunter, Weir), 'One More Saturday Night' (Bob Weir) [From *Ace* by Bob Weir], 'Lazy Lightnin'' (Barlow, Weir), 'Supplication' (Barlow, Weir) [From *Kingfish* by Kingfish], 'Feel Like A Stranger' (Barlow, Weir) [From *Go To Heaven* by The Grateful Dead], 'Easy To Slip' (George, Kibbee), 'Wrong Way Feelin'' (Barlow, Weir), 'Shade Of Grey' (Barlow, Weir) [From *Heaven Help The Fool* by Bob Weir], 'I Want To (Fly Away)' (Barlow, Weir) [From *Bobby And The Midnites* by Bobby And The Midnites], 'Easy Answers' (Bralove, Hunter, Wasserman, Weir, Welnick) [From *Trios* by Rob Wasserman], 'Two Djinn' (Chimenti, Karan, Lane, McGinn, Wasserman, Weir, Graham), 'Ashes And Glass' (Chimenti, D. Ellis, Karan, Lane, McGinn, Wasserman, Weir, Pessis) [From *Evening Moods* by RatDog], 'Wabash Cannonball' (trad.) [From *House Party* by Dan Zanes and Friends], Truckin' (Garcia, Hunter, Lesh, Weir) [From *Ladies And Gentlemen...The Grateful Dead*], 'Estimated Prophet' (Barlow, Weir) [Live, Copps Coliseum, Hamilton Ontario March 21, 1990], 'Hell In A Bucket' (Barlow, Weir, Mydland) [Live, Meadowlands Arena, East Rutherford, New Jersey, October 12, 1989], 'Me And Bobby McGee' (Kristofferson, Foster) [Live, Rheinhalle, Dusseldorf, West Germany, April 24, 1972], 'New Minglewood Blues' (trad.) [Live, Meadowlands, East Rutherford, New Jersey, October 14 1989], 'Man Smart, Woman Smarter' (Norman Span) [Live, Rich Stadium, Orchard Park, New York, July 4 1989], 'Jack Straw' (Hunter, Weir) [Live, Lyceum Theatre, London, May 26 1972], 'Sugar Magnolia' (Hunter, Weir) [From *Ladies And Gentlemen...The Grateful Dead*], 'Throwing Stones' (Barlow, Weir) [From *View From The Vault IV*], 'The Music Never Stopped' (Barlow, Weir) [From *Fallout From The Phil Zone*], 'Masters Of War' (Bob Dylan) [Unreleased RatDog rehearsal March 19 2003]

Garcia Plays Dylan (2005)

Personnel:
Jerry Garcia: guitar, vocals
Jerry Garcia And Merl Saunders
Merl Saunders: organ
John Kahn: electric bass
Bill Vitt: drums
Jerry Garcia Band

Nicky Hopkins: piano
John Kahn: bass
Ron Tutt: drums
Keith Godchaux: piano
Donna Godchaux: vocals
Buzz Buchanan: drums
Gloria Jones: vocals
David Kemper: drums
Jackie LaBranch: vocals
Ozzie Ahlers: keyboards
Johnny de Fonseca: drums
Legion of Mary
Merl Saunders: organ
John Kahn: bass
Ron Tutt: drums
Martin Fierro: saxophone
Grateful Dead
Bob Weir: guitar, vocals
Phil Lesh: bass, vocals
Brent Mydland: keyboards, vocals
Mickey Hart: drums
Bill Kreutzmann: drums
Vince Welnick: keyboards
Recorded live at various venues 1973-1995.
Compilation produced for release by Blair Jackson and Peter McQuaid
Release date: October 2005
Running time: 2:27:39
'It Takes A Lot to Laugh, It Takes A Train To Cry' (Bob Dylan) [Jerry Garcia and Merl
Saunders], 'Tough Mama' (Bob Dylan) [Jerry Garcia Band], 'Positively 4th Street' (Bob
Dylan) [Jerry Garcia Band], 'The Wicked Messenger' (Bob Dylan) [Legion Of Mary],
'Knockin' On Heaven's Door' (Bob Dylan) [Jerry Garcia Band], 'Simple Twist Of Fate' (Bob
Dylan) [Jerry Garcia Band], 'I Shall Be Released' (Bob Dylan) [Jerry Garcia Band], 'When I
Paint My Masterpiece' (Bob Dylan) [Jerry Garcia Band], 'She Belongs To Me' (Bob Dylan)
[Grateful Dead], 'Forever Young' (Bob Dylan) [Jerry Garcia Band], 'Tangled Up In Blue'
(Bob Dylan) [Jerry Garcia Band], 'Senor' (Tales of Yankee Power) (Bob Dylan) [Jerry Garcia
Band], 'Visions Of Johanna' (Bob Dylan) [Grateful Dead], 'Quinn The Eskimo' (The Mighty
Quinn) (Bob Dylan) [Grateful Dead], 'It's All Over Now, Baby Blue' (Bob Dylan) [Grateful
Dead], Bonus tracks: 'It Takes A Lot To Laugh, It Takes A Train to Cry' (acoustic) (Bob Dylan)
[Garcia/Kahn], 'Tears Of Rage' (Dylan, Manuel) [Jerry Garcia Band], 'Going, Going, Gone'
(Bob Dylan) [Legion Of Mary]

Before The Dead (2018) (Jerry Garcia)
Personnel:
Bob and Jerry
Jerry Garcia: guitar, vocals
Robert Hunter: vocals
Jerry Garcia, Marshall Leicester, and Robert Hunter
Jerry Garcia: guitar, vocals
Robert Hunter: bass, mandolin

Marshall Leicester: banjo, guitar, vocals
Jerry Garcia and unknown musician
Jerry Garcia: guitar, vocals
Unknown musician: bass
Sleepy Hollow Hog Stompers
Jerry Garcia: banjo, guitar, vocals
Dick Arnold: fiddle, vocals
Marshall Leicester: banjo, guitar, vocals
Hart Valley Drifters
Jerry Garcia: banjo, guitar, vocals
Ken Frankel: banjo, fiddle, guitar
Robert Hunter: bass, vocals
Norm Van Maastricht: dobro
David Nelson: guitar, vocals
The Wildwood Boys
Jerry Garcia: banjo, guitar, vocals
Robert Hunter: mandolin, vocals
David Nelson: guitar, vocals
Norm Van Maastricht: bass, guitar, vocals
Jerry and Sara
Jerry Garcia: banjo, guitar, mandolin, vocals
Sara Ruppenthal Garcia: guitar, vocals
Black Mountain Boys (autumn 1963 and January 10, 1964)
Jerry Garcia: banjo, guitar, vocals
Robert Hunter: bass, vocals
David Nelson: mandolin, vocals
Eric Thompson: guitar, vocals
Black Mountain Boys (March 6, 1964)
Jerry Garcia: banjo, guitar, vocals
Geoff Levin: bass
David Nelson: mandolin, vocals
Sandy Rothman: guitar, vocals
Black Mountain Boys (spring 1964)
Jerry Garcia: banjo, vocals
David Nelson: mandolin, vocals
Sandy Rothman: guitar, vocals
Asphalt Jungle Mountain Boys
Jerry Garcia: banjo, vocals
Jody Stecher: mandolin, vocals
Eric Thompson: guitar
Herb Pedersen: vocals on 'These Men Of God'
Butch Waller: vocals on 'These Men Of God'
Recorded 1961 – 1964. Produced by Dennis McNally and Brian Miksis
Release date: May 2018
Running time: 221:59
[Bob and Jerry, recorded on May 26, 1961]: 'Santy Anno' (trad.), 'I Got A Home In That Rock' (trad.), 'Oh, Mary Don't You Weep' (trad.), 'All My Trials' (trad.), 'I Was Born Ten Thousand Years Ago' (Verner, Clyde), 'Blow The Candles Out' (trad.), 'Rake And A Rambling Boy' (trad.), 'Trouble in Mind' (Richard M. Jones) [Jerry Gacia, Marshall Leicester and

Robert Hunter, recorded in July 1961]: 'Brown's Ferry Blues' (Delmore, Delmore), 'Jesse James' (trad.), [Jerry Garcia and unknown musician recorded in 1961]: 'Down in the Willow Garden' (trad.), 'Long Lonesome Road' (trad.), 'Railroad Bill' (trad.), 'The Wagoner's Lad' (trad.), 'Katie Cruel' (trad.) [Sleepy Hollow Hog Stompers recorded on June 11, 1962]: 'Cannonball Blues' (A. P. Carter), 'Little Birdie (trad.), 'Sally Goodin' (trad.), 'Hold That Woodpile Down' (Harrigan, Hart), 'Legend Of The Johnson Boys' (trad.), 'Shady Grove' (trad.), 'Sweet Sunny South' (trad.), 'Man Of Constant Sorrow' (trad.) [Hart Valley Drifters recorded in autumn 1962]: Band introductions, 'Roving Gambler' (trad.), 'Ground Speed' (Earl Scruggs), 'Pig In A Pen' (Fiddlin' Arthur Smith), 'Standing In The Need Of A Prayer' (trad.), 'Flint Hill Special' (Earl Scruggs), 'Nine Pound Hammer' (trad.), 'Handsome Molly' (Grayson, Whitter), 'Clinch Mountain Backstep' (Stanley, Rakes), 'Think Of What You've Done' (Carter Stanley), 'Cripple Creek' (trad.), 'All The Good Times Have Past And Gone' (trad.), 'Billy Grimes, The Rover' (trad.), 'Paddy On The Turnpike' (trad.), 'Run Mountain' (J. E. Mainer), 'Sugar Baby' (Dock Boggs), 'Sitting On Top Of The World' (Vinson, Carter) [The Wildwood Boys recorded on February 23, 1963]: 'Roll In My Sweet Baby's Arms' (Carter, Young), 'Jerry's Breakdown' (Garcia), 'Standing In The Need Of Prayer' (trad.), 'Mule Skinner Blues' (Rodgers, Vaughn), 'Saturday Night Shuffle' (Merle Travis), 'Pike County Breakdown' (Rupert Jones), 'My Little Sparrow' (trad.), 'We Shall Not Be Moved' (trad.) [Jerry and Sara recorded on May 4, 1963]: 'Deep Elem Blues' (Shelton, Shelton), 'Will the Weaver' (trad.), 'I Truly Understand' (trad.), 'Long Black Veil' (Dill, Wilkin), 'The Man That Wrote That Home Sweet Home Never Was a Married Man' (trad.), 'Foggy Mountain Top' (A. P. Carter) [Black Mountain Boys recorded in autumn 1963]: 'Barefoot Nellie' (Reno, Davis), 'She's More To Be Pitied' (Carter Stanley), 'Noah's Breakdown' (Noah Crase), 'Who Will Sing for Me?' (Thomas J. Farris) [Black Mountain Boys recorded on January 10, 1964]: 'Salt Creek' (Keith, Monroe), 'Jody's Hornpipe' (Bill Monroe), 'Rosa Lee McFall' (Charlie Monroe), 'John Hardy' (trad.) [Black Mountain Boys recorded on March 6, 1964]: 'Katie Kline' (trad.), 'Walkin' The Dog' (Grimsley, Grimsley), 'Paddy On Tthe Turnpike' (trad.), 'Love And Wealth' (Louvin, Louvin), 'Sourwood Mountain' (trad.), 'If I Lose' (Ralph Stanley), 'Homestead On The Farm' (A. P. Carter), 'Stony Creek' (McReynolds, McReynolds), 'Salty Dog Blues' (Morris, Morris), 'Love Please Come Home' (Leon Jackson), 'Make Me A Pallet On The Floor' (trad.), 'Darlin' Allalee' (trad.), 'In The Pines' (Bryant, Davis, McMichen), 'Raw Hide' (Bill Monroe), 'Black Mountain Rag' (trad.), 'True Life Blues' (Bill Monroe), Medley: 'Devil's Dream'/'Sailor's Hornpipe' (trad.) [Black Mountain Boys recorded in spring 1964]: 'Drink Up And Go Home' (Freddie Hart) [Asphalt Jungle Mountain Boys recorded in summer 1964]: 'These Men Of God' (Ellis, Williams, Williams), 'Roll On Buddy' (trad.), 'Goodbye Old Pal' (Bill Monroe), 'Back Up And Push' (trad.)

On Track series

Tori Amos – Lisa Torem 978-1-78952-142-9

Asia – Peter Braidis 978-1-78952-099-6

Barclay James Harvest – Keith and Monica Domone 978-1-78952-067-5

The Beatles – Andrew Wild 978-1-78952-009-5

The Beatles Solo 1969-1980 – Andrew Wild 978-1-78952-030-9

Blue Oyster Cult – Jacob Holm-Lupo 978-1-78952-007-1

Marc Bolan and T.Rex – Peter Gallagher 978-1-78952-124-5

Kate Bush – Bill Thomas 978-1-78952-097-2

Camel – Hamish Kuzminski 978-1-78952-040-8

Caravan – Andy Boot 978-1-78952-127-6

Cardiacs – Eric Benac 978-1-78952-131-3

Eric Clapton Solo – Andrew Wild 978-1-78952-141-2

The Clash – Nick Assirati 978-1-78952-077-4

Crosby, Stills and Nash – Andrew Wild 978-1-78952-039-2

The Damned – Morgan Brown 978-1-78952-136-8

Deep Purple and Rainbow 1968-79 – Steve Pilkington 978-1-78952-002-6

Dire Straits – Andrew Wild 978-1-78952-044-6

The Doors – Tony Thompson 978-1-78952-137-5

Dream Theater – Jordan Blum 978-1-78952-050-7

Elvis Costello and The Attractions – Georg Purvis 978-1-78952-129-0

Emerson Lake and Palmer – Mike Goode 978-1-78952-000-2

Fairport Convention – Kevan Furbank 978-1-78952-051-4

Peter Gabriel – Graeme Scarfe 978-1-78952-138-2

Genesis – Stuart MacFarlane 978-1-78952-005-7

Gentle Giant – Gary Steel 978-1-78952-058-3

Gong – Kevan Furbank 978-1-78952-082-8

Hawkwind – Duncan Harris 978-1-78952-052-1

Roy Harper – Opher Goodwin 978-1-78952-130-6

Iron Maiden – Steve Pilkington 978-1-78952-061-3

Jefferson Airplane – Richard Butterworth 978-1-78952-143-6

Jethro Tull – Jordan Blum 978-1-78952-016-3

Elton John in the 1970s – Peter Kearns 978-1-78952-034-7

The Incredible String Band – Tim Moon 978-1-78952-107-8

Iron Maiden – Steve Pilkington 978-1-78952-061-3

Judas Priest – John Tucker 978-1-78952-018-7

Kansas – Kevin Cummings 978-1-78952-057-6
Led Zeppelin – Steve Pilkington 978-1-78952-151-1
Level 42 – Matt Philips 978-1-78952-102-3
Aimee Mann – Jez Rowden 978-1-78952-036-1
Joni Mitchell – Peter Kearns 978-1-78952-081-1
The Moody Blues – Geoffrey Feakes 978-1-78952-042-2
Mike Oldfield – Ryan Yard 978-1-78952-060-6
Tom Petty – Richard James 978-1-78952-128-3
Porcupine Tree – Nick Holmes 978-1-78952-144-3
Queen – Andrew Wild 978-1-78952-003-3
Radiohead – William Allen 978-1-78952-149-8
Renaissance – David Detmer 978-1-78952-062-0
The Rolling Stones 1963-80 – Steve Pilkington 978-1-78952-017-0
The Smiths and Morrissey – Tommy Gunnarsson 978-1-78952-140-5
Steely Dan – Jez Rowden 978-1-78952-043-9
Steve Hackett – Geoffrey Feakes 978-1-78952-098-9
Thin Lizzy – Graeme Stroud 978-1-78952-064-4
Toto – Jacob Holm-Lupo 978-1-78952-019-4
U2 – Eoghan Lyng 978-1-78952-078-1
UFO – Richard James 978-1-78952-073-6
The Who – Geoffrey Feakes 978-1-78952-076-7
Roy Wood and the Move – James R Turner 978-1-78952-008-8
Van Der Graaf Generator – Dan Coffey 978-1-78952-031-6
Yes – Stephen Lambe 978-1-78952-001-9
Frank Zappa 1966 to 1979 – Eric Benac 978-1-78952-033-0
10CC – Peter Kearns 978-1-78952-054-5

Decades Series
The Bee Gees in the 1960s – Andrew Mon Hughes et al 978-1-78952-148-1
Alice Cooper in the 1970s – Chris Sutton 978-1-78952-104-7
Curved Air in the 1970s – Laura Shenton 978-1-78952-069-9
Fleetwood Mac in the 1970s – Andrew Wild 978-1-78952-105-4
Focus in the 1970s – Stephen Lambe 978-1-78952-079-8
Genesis in the 1970s – Bill Thomas 978178952-146-7
Marillion in the 1980s – Nathaniel Webb 978-1-78952-065-1
Pink Floyd In The 1970s – Georg Purvis 978-1-78952-072-9

The Sweet in the 1970s – Darren Johnson 978-1-78952-139-9
Uriah Heep in the 1970s – Steve Pilkington 978-1-78952-103-0
Yes in the 1980s – Stephen Lambe with David Watkinson 978-1-78952-125-2

On Screen series

Carry On... – Stephen Lambe 978-1-78952-004-0
David Cronenberg – Patrick Chapman 978-1-78952-071-2
Doctor Who: The David Tennant Years – Jamie Hailstone 978-1-78952-066-8
Monty Python – Steve Pilkington 978-1-78952-047-7
Seinfeld Seasons 1 to 5 – Stephen Lambe 978-1-78952-012-5

Other Books

Babysitting A Band On The Rocks – G.D. Praetorius 978-1-78952-106-1
Derek Taylor: For Your Radioactive Children – Andrew Darlington 978-1-78952-038-5
Iggy and The Stooges On Stage 1967-1974 – Per Nilsen 978-1-78952-101-6
Jon Anderson and the Warriors – the road to Yes – David Watkinson 978-1-78952-059-0
Nu Metal: A Definitive Guide – Matt Karpe 978-1-78952-063-7
Tommy Bolin: In and Out of Deep Purple – Laura Shenton 978-1-78952-070-5
Maximum Darkness – Deke Leonard 978-1-78952-048-4
Maybe I Should've Stayed In Bed – Deke Leonard 978-1-78952-053-8
Psychedelic Rock in 1967 – Kevan Furbank 978-1-78952-155-9
The Twang Dynasty – Deke Leonard 978-1-78952-049-1

and many more to come!

Bob Dylan in the 1980s
Decades

Don Klees
128 pages
44 colour photographs
978-1-78952-157-3
£14.99
USD 21.95

This most famous of folk / rock musicians in the decade that cemented his legend.

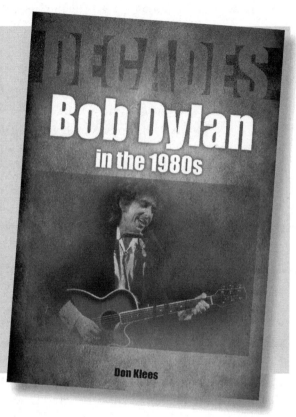

No period of Bob Dylan's six-decade career confounds fans more than the 1980s. The singer began the decade with Saved, the second in a trio of explicitly religious records, and a tour in which he declined to play his older songs because of concern they were anti-God. Indeed many fans found his post-conversion messages strident and judgmental making Saved his worst selling album in years and setting a pattern for the next several years.

Despite being a prolific time, in which the singer released seven studio albums, the decade was defined by inconsistency. Throughout the 1980s, some of his most profound work alternated with lackluster compositions and indifferent performances - sometimes on the same album. However, even as Dylan struggled artistically, all of his albums contained reminders of why he continued to be celebrated.

By the end of the decade, his perseverance - both on stage and in the studio - and a spontaneous collaboration with some of his peers, coalesced into his best received releases since the 1970s. Rather than closing a book, the combination of Oh Mercy and the first Traveling Wilburys record pointed to new chapters and the following decade began a remarkable run of success that few popular artists have managed at any stage of their careers.

1967: A year in Psychedelic Rock
The Bands and the Sounds of the Summer of Love

Kevan Furbank
160 pages
40 colour photographs
978-1-78952-155-9
£14.99
USD 21.95

The year of the Summer of Love when psychedelic rock had its greatest success.

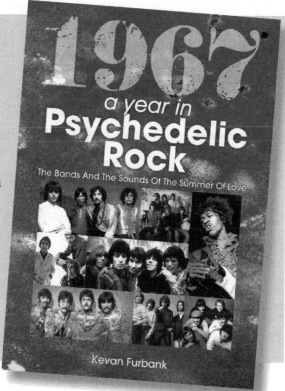

It was the year the Sixties really started swinging - the Summer of Love, when the Rolling Stones said 'We Love You' and The Beatles pointed out that 'All You Need Is Love'. At the centre of the year's tumultuous social and cultural change was the mind-expanding music called psychedelic rock, a multi-coloured mixture of amazing sounds, when imagination and experimentation ran riot and the old musical boundaries were torn down in a haze of hallucinogenic abandon.

Kevan Furbank looks at the roots of psychedelic rock and examines the contributions made by some of the biggest bands of the year, including The Beatles, The Doors, Jimi Hendrix, the Rolling Stones, Love, Pink Floyd and The Beach Boys.

He examines the hits and misses, the successes and failures, the bands that were born to be psychedelic and those that had psychedelia thrust upon them – sometimes with disastrous results. And he shows how the genre planted the seeds for other forms of popular music to take root and flourish. If you love music and want to know why 1967 was such a watershed year, then you will want this book. It is eye-popping, mind-opening and horizon-expanding – and a splendid time is guaranteed for all.

1970: A Year in Rock

The Year Rock Became Mainstream

John Van der Kiste
144 pages
40 colour photographs
978-1-78952-147-4
£14.99
USD 21.95

This pivotal year in rock music dissected and 25 key albums discussed.

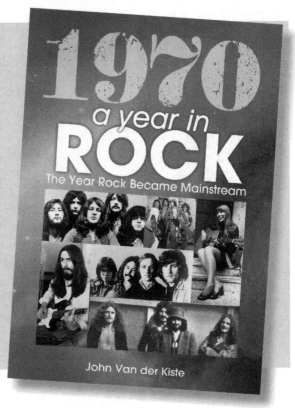

1970 was a year of change in pop and rock music, with divisions between both becoming ever more blurred. More ambitiously-constructed epics, heavy rock numbers and contemporary folk songs competed with mainstream and easy listening fare on Top of the Pops and in the Top 30 singles, while progressive and jazz-rock took their bow in the album charts. Some acts disbanded, notably The Beatles, all of whom relished their freedom and launched solo careers, and Simon & Garfunkel, or else parted company and partially regrouped under new names.

Festivals came into their own, particularly in Britain where the first Glastonbury event was launched, as did live albums, notably from The Rolling Stones and The Who, partly to combat the market in bootleg recordings; several singer-songwriters found major acceptance; the death of Jimi Hendrix was widely mourned; and the likes of Marc Bolan, Elton John, Rod Stewart (as a soloist, and as front man of The Faces), Lindisfarne and Hot Chocolate achieved their initial successes. By the end of the year, many a critic and music fan could look back on a 12-month period in which their landscape had altered almost beyond recognition.

This is the story of that year and the key albums that helped define it.

Jefferson Airplane – *on track*
Every album, every song

Richard Butterworth
160 pages
40 colour photographs
978-1-78952-143-6
£14.99
USD 21.95

**Every album produced
by this legendary
psychedelic band
and symbol of the
Summer of Love.**

Jefferson Airplane were not the sole exemplars of 1960s Californian acid rock; the Grateful Dead could equally claim the mantle of house band to the Summer of Love. Airplane's instrumentation was conventional, comprising mainly vocal harmonies, guitars, bass and drums. The band drew upon the folk traditions of The Weavers, the legendary bluesmen Gary Davis and B.B. King, improvisational masters from Miles Davis to Cream, even literary visionaries such as James Joyce and Isaac Asimov.

Yet fusing together these influences in the creative furnace of San Francisco between 1966 and 1970, Jefferson Airplane's classic lineup – one ex-model, two ex-folkies, one ex-jazzer and two ex-D.C. guitarslingers – crafted music that was at once powerful, innovative and beautiful. Birthed in the dizzy hippie heartland of Haight-Ashbury, no other group were so wedded to their environment, winning international acclaim with two anthemic hit singles even as they impishly prodded the morés of middle Amerika. A musical and social force of nature, Airplane mirrored the psychedelic dream, burning higher, fiercer and brighter than any of their contemporaries.

Combining a concise history of this magnificent band and their milieu with comprehensive and entertaining reviews of all their recordings, this is the most accessible book on the band yet written.

Would you like to write for Sonicbond Publishing?

We are mainly a music publisher, but we also occasionally publish in other genres including film and television. At Sonicbond Publishing we are always on the look-out for authors, particularly for our two main series, On Track and Decades.

Mixing fact with in depth analysis, the On Track series examines the entire recorded work of a particular musical artist or group. All genres are considered from easy listening and jazz to 60s soul to 90s pop, via rock and metal.

The Decades series singles out a particular decade in an artist or group's history and focuses on that decade in more detail than may be allowed in the On Track series.

While professional writing experience would, of course, be an advantage, the most important qualification is to have real enthusiasm and knowledge of your subject. First-time authors are welcomed, but the ability to write well in English is essential.

Sonicbond Publishing has distribution throughout Europe and North America, and all our books are also published in E-book form. Authors will be paid a royalty based on sales of their book. Further details about our books are available from www.sonicbondpublishing.com. To contact us, complete the contact form there or email info@sonicbondpublishing.co.uk